P9-CQH-336

Cultures and Organizations

SOFTWARE OF THE MIND

Intercultural Cooperation and Its Importance for Survival

Geert Hofstede
Gert Jan Hofstede
Michael Minkov

New York   Chicago   San Francisco   Lisbon   London   Madrid   Mexico City
Milan   New Delhi   San Juan   Seoul   Singapore   Sydney   Toronto

Library of Congress Cataloging-in-Publication Data

Hofstede, Geert H.
    Cultures and organizations : software of the mind : intercultural cooperation and its importance for survival / by Geert Hofstede, Gert Jan Hofstede, and Michael Minkov. — 3rd ed.
       p.   cm.
    Includes bibliographical references and index.
    ISBN-13: 978-0-07-166418-9
    ISBN-10: 0-07-166418-1
    1. Intercultural communication.   2. Organization—Research.   3. International cooperation.   4. National characteristics.   5. Ethnopsychology.   6. Cultural pluralism.   I. Hofstede, Gert Jan .   II. Minkov, Michael.   III. Title.

    HM1211.H574   2010
    306—dc22   2010010437

4 5 6 7 8 9 10 11 12 13 14 15 16 17 18   DOC/DOC   1 9 8 7 6 5 4 3 2 1

ISBN   978-0-07-166418-9
MHID   0-07-166418-1

McGraw-Hill books are available at special quantity discounts to use as premiums and sales promotions or for use in corporate training programs. To contact a representative, please e-mail us at bulksales@mcgraw-hill.com.

Contents

124842

PART II

Dimensions of National Cultures

PART III

Cultures in Organizations

PART IV

Implications

Preface

In the late 1960s Geert accidentally became interested in national cultural differences—and got access to rich data for studying them. His research resulted in the publication in 1980 of a book called *Culture's Consequences*. It was written for a scholarly readership; it had to be, because it cast doubts on the universal validity of established theories in psychology, organization sociology, and management theory: so it should show the theoretical reasoning, base data, and statistical treatments used to arrive at the conclusions. A 1984 paperback edition of the book left out the base data and the statistics but was otherwise identical to the 1980 hardcover version.

Culture's Consequences appeared at a time when the interest in cultural differences, both between nations and between organizations, was sharply rising, and there was a dearth of empirically supported information on the subject. The book provided such information, but maybe too much of it at once. Many readers evidently got only parts of the message. For example,

Geert lost count of the number of people who claimed that Geert had studied the values of IBM (or "Hermes") *managers.* The data used actually were from IBM *employees,* and that, as the book itself showed, makes quite a difference.

In 1991, after having taught the subject to many different audiences and tested his text on various helpful readers, Geert published a book for an intelligent lay readership—the first edition of *Cultures and Organizations: Software of the Mind.* The theme of cultural differences is, of course, not only—and even not primarily—of interest to social scientists or international business students. It pertains to anyone who meets people from outside his or her own narrow circle, and in the modern world this is virtually everybody. The new book addressed itself to any interested reader. It avoided social scientific jargon where possible and explained it where necessary; a Glossary was added for this purpose. Slightly updated paperback editions appeared in 1994 and 1997.

In the meantime the worlds of politics, of business, and of ideas kept changing fast. In 2001 Geert published a rewritten and updated version of *Culture's Consequences* that included a discussion of the many replications by other researchers that had appeared since 1980. Anybody whose purpose is research or academic scrutiny is referred to this source.

In 2005 Geert issued a rewritten and updated version of *Cultures and Organizations: Software of the Mind.* Gert Jan Hofstede joined him as a coauthor. After having majored in biology and taught information systems at Wageningen agricultural university, Gert Jan had started to use his father's work in his own teaching and research. In 2002 he had already published his own book, *Exploring Culture: Exercises, Stories and Synthetic Cultures,* which included contributions from Paul B. Pedersen and from Geert. Gert Jan contributed experience with the role of culture in international networks, hands-on experience in teaching the subject through simulation games, and insight into the biological origins of culture.

Ever since his first cross-cultural research studies, Geert has continued exploring alternative sources of data, to validate and supplement his original, accidental IBM employee data set. In the past three decades the volume of available cross-cultural data on self-scored values has increased enormously. Geert used to say that if he had to start his research again, he would use a choice from these new databases. About ten years ago, Geert got into e-mail contact with a researcher in Sofia, Bulgaria, who seemed to be engaged in exactly that: scanning available databases and looking for structure in their combined results. The name of this researcher was Michael Minkov, and we learned to call him Misho. In 2007 Misho published his analyses in a book, *What Makes Us Different and Similar: A New Interpretation of the World Values Survey and Other Cross-Cultural Data*, bringing the kind of progress in insight we had been hoping for. In addition, Misho, as an East European, brought insider knowledge about a group of nations missing in Geert's original database and of great importance in the future of the continent.

For this new, 2010, third edition of *Cultures and Organizations: Software of the Mind*, Misho has joined Gert Jan and Geert as a third coauthor. The division of labor in our team is that Gert Jan has substantially contributed to Chapter 1 and entirely written Chapter 12. Misho has contributed to Chapters 2, 4, and especially 7 and has entirely written Chapter 8. In addition, each of us has commented on the work of his colleagues. Geert takes responsibility for the final text.

On a trip around the world several years ago, Geert bought three world maps. All three are of the flat kind, projecting the surface of the globe on a plane. The first shows Europe and Africa in the middle, the Americas to the west, and Asia to the east. The terms *the West* and *the East* were products of a Euro-centered worldview. The second map, bought in Hawaii, shows the Pacific Ocean in the center, Asia and Africa on the left (and Europe, tiny, in the far upper left-hand corner), and the Americas to the right. From Hawaii, the East lies west and the West lies east! The third map, bought in New Zealand, was like the second but upside down: south on top and north at the bottom. Now Europe is in the far lower right-hand corner. Which of these maps is right? All three, of course; Earth is round, and any place on the surface is as much the center as any other. All peoples have considered their country the center of the world; the Chinese call China the "Middle Kingdom" (*zhongguo*), and the ancient Scandinavians called their country by a similar name (*midgardr*). We believe that even today most citizens, politicians, and academics in any country feel in their hearts that their country is the middle one, and they act correspondingly.

These feelings are so powerful that it is almost always possible, when reading a book, to determine the nationality of the author from the content alone. The same, of course, applies to our own work—Geert and Gert Jan are from Holland, and even when we write in English, the Dutch software of our minds will remain evident to the careful reader. Misho's East European mind-set can also be detected. This makes reading the book by others than our compatriots a cross-cultural experience in itself, maybe even a culture shock. That is OK. Studying culture without experiencing culture shock is like practicing swimming without water. In *Asterix*, the famous French cartoon, the oldest villager expresses his dislike of visiting foreigners as follows: "I don't have anything against foreigners. Some of my best friends are foreigners. But *these* foreigners are not from here!"

In the booming market for cross-cultural training, there are courses and books that show only the sunny side: cultural synergy, no cultural conflict. Maybe that is the message some business-minded people like to hear, but it is false. Studying culture without culture shock is like listening only to the foreigners who are from here.

Geert in 1991 dedicated the first edition of this book to his first grandchildren, the generation to whom the future belongs. For the second edition Gert Jan's eldest daughter, Liesbeth, acted as our documentation assistant, typing among other things the Bibliography. This time her sister Katy Hofstede was our indispensable help, especially in preparing the tables and figures.

From our academic contacts we thank in particular Marieke de Mooij, who was our guide in the worlds of marketing, advertising, and consumer behavior, where culture plays a decisive role. References to her work are found at many places in the book. For Chapter 12, which was an entirely new venture, Gert Jan was inspired by David Sloan Wilson, and he benefited very much from comments by his proofreaders Duur Aanen, Josephie Brefeld, Arie Oskam, Inge van Stokkom, Arjan de Visser and Wim Wiersinga.

The first edition appeared in seventeen languages (English with translations into Bulgarian, Chinese, Czech, Danish, Dutch, Finnish, French, German, Japanese, Korean, Norwegian, Polish, Portuguese, Romanian, Spanish, and Swedish). The second edition has appeared so far in Chinese, Czech, Danish, Dutch, German, Hungarian, Polish, and Swedish. We hope that this new edition will again reach many readers through their native language.

THE CONCEPT
OF CULTURE

The Rules of the Social Game

11th juror: (*rising*) "I beg pardon, in discussing . . ."

10th juror: (*interrupting and mimicking*) "I beg pardon. What are you so goddam polite about?"

11th juror: (*looking straight at the 10th juror*) "For the same reason you're not. It's the way I was brought up."

    –Reginald Rose, *Twelve Angry Men*

T*welve Angry Men* is an American theater piece that became a famous motion picture, starring Henry Fonda. The play was published in 1955. The scene consists of the jury room of a New York court of law. Twelve jury members who never met before have to decide unanimously on the guilt or innocence of a boy from a slum area, accused of murder. The quote cited is from the second and final act when emotions have reached the boiling point. It is a confrontation between the tenth juror, a garage owner, and the eleventh juror, a European-born, probably Austrian, watchmaker. The tenth juror is irritated by what he sees as the excessively polite manners of the other man. But the watchmaker cannot behave otherwise. Even after many years in his new home country, he still behaves the way he was raised. He carries within himself an indelible pattern of behavior.

Different Minds but Common Problems

The world is full of confrontations between people, groups, and nations who think, feel, and act differently. At the same time these people, groups, and nations, just as with our twelve angry men, are exposed to common problems that demand cooperation for their solution. Ecological, economical, political, military, hygienic, and meteorological developments do not stop at national or regional borders. Coping with the threats of nuclear warfare, global warming, organized crime, poverty, terrorism, ocean pollution, extinction of animals, AIDS, or a worldwide recession demands cooperation of opinion leaders from many countries. They in their turn need the support of broad groups of followers in order to implement the decisions taken.

Understanding the differences in the ways these leaders and their followers think, feel, and act is a condition for bringing about worldwide solutions that work. Questions of economic, technological, medical, or biological cooperation have too often been considered as merely technical. One of the reasons why so many solutions do not work or cannot be implemented is that differences in thinking among the partners have been ignored.

The objective of this book is to help in dealing with the differences in thinking, feeling, and acting of people around the globe. It will show that although the variety in people's minds is enormous, there is a structure in this variety that can serve as a basis for mutual understanding.

Culture as Mental Programming

Every person carries within him- or herself patterns of thinking, feeling, and potential acting that were learned throughout the person's lifetime. Much of it was acquired in early childhood, because at that time a person is most susceptible to learning and assimilating. As soon as certain patterns of thinking, feeling, and acting have established themselves within a person's mind, he or she must unlearn these patterns before being able to learn something different, and unlearning is more difficult than learning for the first time.

Using the analogy of the way computers are programmed, this book will call such patterns of thinking, feeling, and acting *mental programs*, or, as per the book's subtitle, *software of the mind*. This does not mean, of course, that people are programmed the way computers are. A person's behavior is only partially predetermined by his or her mental programs: he or she has a basic ability to deviate from them and to react in ways that are new, creative, destructive, or unexpected. The software of the mind that this book is about only indicates what reactions are likely and understandable, given one's past.

The sources of one's mental programs lie within the social environments in which one grew up and collected one's life experiences. The programming starts within the family; it continues within the neighborhood, at school, in youth groups, at the workplace, and in the living community. The European watchmaker from the quote at the beginning of this chapter came from a country and a social class in which polite behavior is still at a premium today. Most people in that environment would have reacted as he did. The American garage owner, who worked himself up from the slums, acquired quite different mental programs. Mental programs vary as much as the social environments in which they were acquired.

A customary term for such mental software is *culture*. This word has several meanings, all derived from its Latin source, which refers to the tilling of the soil. In most Western languages *culture* commonly means "civilization" or "refinement of the mind" and in particular the results of such refinement, such as education, art, and literature. This is culture in the narrow sense. Culture as mental software, however, corresponds to a much broader use of the word that is common among sociologists and, especially, anthropologists:[1] this is the meaning that will be used throughout this book.

Social (or cultural) anthropology is the science of human societies— in particular (although not only) traditional or "primitive" ones. In social anthropology, *culture* is a catchword for all those patterns of thinking, feeling, and acting referred to in the previous paragraphs. Not only activities supposed to refine the mind are included, but also the ordinary and menial things in life: greeting, eating, showing or not showing feelings, keeping a certain physical distance from others, making love, and maintaining body hygiene.

Culture is always a collective phenomenon, because it is at least partly shared with people who live or lived within the same social environment, which is where it was learned. Culture consists of the unwritten rules of the social game. It is *the collective programming of the mind that distinguishes the members of one group or category of people from others.*[2]

Culture is learned, not innate. It derives from one's social environment rather than from one's genes.[3] Culture should be distinguished from human nature on one side and from an individual's personality on the other (see Figure 1.1), although exactly where the borders lie between nature and culture, and between culture and personality, is a matter of discussion among social scientists.[4]

Human nature is what all human beings, from the Russian professor to the Australian aborigine, have in common: it represents the universal level in one's mental software. It is inherited within our genes; within the computer analogy it is the "operating system" that determines our physical and basic psychological functioning. The human ability to feel fear, anger, love, joy, sadness, and shame; the need to associate with others and to play and exercise oneself; and the facility to observe the environment and to talk about it with other humans all belong to this level of mental program-

FIGURE 1.1 Three Levels of Uniqueness in Mental Programming

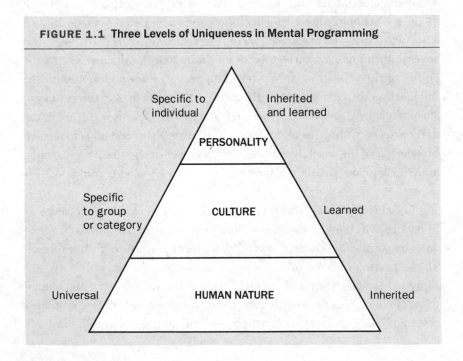

ming. However, what one does with these feelings, how one expresses fear, joy, observations, and so on, is modified by culture.

The *personality* of an individual, on the other hand, is his or her unique personal set of mental programs that needn't be shared with any other human being. It is based on traits that are partly inherited within the individual's unique set of genes and partly learned. *Learned* means modified by the influence of collective programming (culture) *as well as* by unique personal experiences.

Cultural traits have often been attributed to heredity, because philosophers and other scholars in the past did not know how to otherwise explain the remarkable stability of differences in culture patterns among human groups. They underestimated the impact of learning from previous generations and of teaching to a future generation what one has learned oneself. The role of heredity is exaggerated in pseudotheories of *race*, which have been responsible, among other things, for the holocaust organized by the Nazis during World War II. Ethnic strife is often justified by unfounded arguments of cultural superiority and inferiority.

In the United States there have been periodic scientific discussions on whether certain ethnic groups, in particular blacks, could be genetically less intelligent than others, in particular whites.[5] The arguments used for genetic differences, by the way, make Asians in the United States on average *more* intelligent than whites. However, it is extremely difficult, if not impossible, to find tests of intelligence that are culture free. Such tests should reflect only innate abilities and be insensitive to differences in the social environment. In the United States a larger share of blacks than of whites has grown up in socially disadvantaged circumstances, which is a cultural influence no test known to us can circumvent. The same logic applies to differences in intelligence between ethnic groups in other countries.

Symbols, Heroes, Rituals, and Values

Cultural differences manifest themselves in several ways. From the many terms used to describe manifestations of culture, the following four together cover the total concept rather neatly: symbols, heroes, rituals, and values. In Figure 1.2 these have been pictured as the skins of an onion, indicating that symbols represent the most superficial and values the deepest manifestations of culture, with heroes and rituals in between.

FIGURE 1.2 The "Onion": Manifestations of Culture at Different Levels of Depth

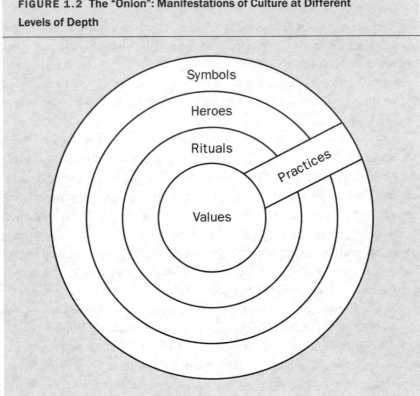

Symbols are words, gestures, pictures, or objects that carry a particular meaning that is recognized as such only by those who share the culture. The words in a language or jargon belong to this category, as do dress, hairstyles, flags, and status symbols. New symbols are easily developed and old ones disappear; symbols from one cultural group are regularly copied by others. This is why symbols have been put into the outer, most superficial layer of Figure 1.2.

Heroes are persons, alive or dead, real or imaginary, who possess characteristics that are highly prized in a culture and thus serve as models for behavior. Even Barbie, Batman, or, as a contrast, Snoopy in the United States, Asterix in France, or Ollie B. Bommel (Mr. Bumble) in the Netherlands have served as cultural heroes. In this age of television, outward appearances have become more important in the choice of heroes than they were before.

Rituals are collective activities that are technically superfluous to reach desired ends but that, within a culture, are considered socially essential. They are therefore carried out for their own sake. Examples include ways of greeting and paying respect to others, as well as social and religious ceremonies. Business and political meetings organized for seemingly rational reasons often serve mainly ritual purposes, such as reinforcing group cohesion or allowing the leaders to assert themselves. Rituals include *discourse*, the way language is used in text and talk, in daily interaction, and in communicating beliefs.[6]

In Figure 1.2 symbols, heroes, and rituals have been subsumed under the term *practices*. As such they are visible to an outside observer; their cultural meaning, however, is invisible and lies precisely and only in the way these practices are interpreted by the insiders.

The core of culture according to Figure 1.2 is formed by *values*. Values are broad tendencies to prefer certain states of affairs over others. Values are feelings with an added arrow indicating a plus and a minus side. They deal with pairings such as the following:

- Evil versus good
- Dirty versus clean
- Dangerous versus safe
- Forbidden versus permitted
- Decent versus indecent
- Moral versus immoral
- Ugly versus beautiful
- Unnatural versus natural
- Abnormal versus normal
- Paradoxical versus logical
- Irrational versus rational

Figure 1.3 pictures when and where we acquire our values and practices. Our values are acquired early in our lives. Compared with most other creatures, humans at birth are very incompletely equipped for survival. Fortunately, our human physiology provides us with a receptive period of some ten to twelve years, a span in which we can quickly and largely unconsciously absorb necessary information from our environment. This includes symbols (such as language), heroes (such as our parents), and rituals (such as toilet training), and, most important, it includes our basic

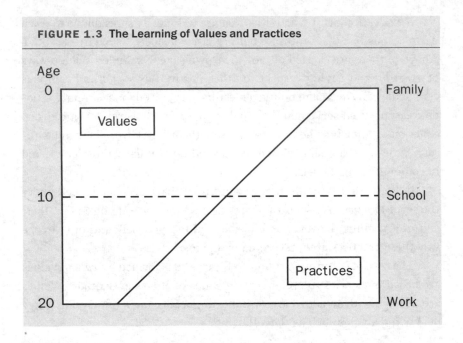

FIGURE 1.3 The Learning of Values and Practices

values. At the end of this period, we gradually switch to a different, conscious way of learning, focusing primarily on new practices.

Culture Reproduces Itself

Remember being a small child? How did you acquire your values? The first years are likely gone from your memory, but they are influential. Did you move about on your mother's hip or on her back all day? Did you sleep with her, or with your siblings, or were you kept in your own cot or pram? Did both your parents handle you, or only your mother, or other persons? Was there noise or silence around you? Did you see tacit people, laughing ones, playing ones, working ones, tender or violent ones? What happened when you cried?

Then, memories begin. Who were your models, and what was your aim in life? Quite probably, your parents or elder siblings were your heroes, and you tried to imitate them. You learned which things were dirty and bad and how to be clean and good. For instance, you learned rules about what is clean and dirty in regard to bodily functions such as spitting, eating with your left hand, blowing your nose, defecating, or belching in public, along with gestures such as touching various parts of your body or exposing them while sitting or standing. You learned how bad it was to break rules.

You learned how much initiative you were supposed to take and how close you were supposed to be to people, and you learned whether you were a boy or a girl, who else was also a boy or a girl, and what that implied.

Then when you were a child of perhaps six to twelve, schoolteachers and classmates, sports and TV idols, and national or religious heroes entered your world as new models. You imitated now one, then another. Parents, teachers, and others rewarded or punished you for your behavior. You learned whether it was good or bad to ask questions, to speak up, to fight, to cry, to work hard, to lie, to be impolite. You learned when to be proud and when to be ashamed. You also exercised politics, especially with your age-mates: How does one make friends? Is it possible to rise in the hierarchy? How? Who owes what to whom?

In your teenage years, your attention shifted to others your age. You were intensely concerned with your gender identity and with forming relationships with peers. Depending on the society in which you lived, you spent your time mainly with your own sex or with mixed sexes. You may have intensely admired some of your peers.

Later you may have chosen a partner, probably using criteria similar to that of other young people in your country. You may have had children— and then the cycle starts again.

There is a powerful stabilizing force in this cycle that biologists call *homeostasis*. Parents tend to reproduce the education that they received, whether they want to or not. And there is only a modest role for technology. The most salient learning in your tender years is all about the body and about relationships with people. Not coincidentally, these are also sources of intense taboos.

Because they were acquired so early in our lives, many values remain unconscious to those who hold them. Therefore, they cannot be discussed, nor can they be directly observed by outsiders. They can only be inferred from the way people act under various circumstances. If one asks people why they act as they do, they may say they just "know" or "feel" how to do the right thing. Their heart or their conscience tells them.

No Group Can Escape Culture

There normally is continuity in culture. But if you were caught in a gale at sea and found yourself stranded on an uninhabited island with twenty-nine unknown others, what would you do?[7] If you and your fellow passengers were from different parts of the world, you would lack a common language and shared habits. Your first task would be to develop an embryonic common language and some shared rules for behavior, cooperation, and leadership. Role divisions would emerge between young and old, men and women. Conflicts would arise and somehow be handled. Whose responsibility would it be whether two people mate? Who would take care of the sick, the dead, and the children born on the island?

The point of this example is to show that no group can escape culture. Creating shared rules, even if they are never written down, is a precondition for group survival. This pioneer group of thirty people united at random will have to create a new culture. The particulars of that culture will largely depend on chance, inheriting from existing values, particularly those of the most prominent group members. However, once the culture is set, and supposing children are born into the group, that culture will reproduce itself.

Values and the Moral Circle

From 1940 to 1945, during World War II, Germany occupied the Netherlands. In April 1945, German troops withdrew in disorder, confiscating many bicycles from the Dutch population. In April 2009, the Parish Council of the Saint-Catharina church in the Dutch town of Nijkerk received a letter from a former German soldier who, on his flight to Germany from the advancing Canadians, had taken a bike that was parked in front of the church. The letter's author wished to make amends and asked the Parish Council to trace the owner or his heirs, in order to refund the injured party for the damage.[8]

It is perplexing that human beings possess magnificent skills of reflection, empathy, and communication but are nonetheless capable of waging intergroup conflicts on massive scales over just about anything. Why is intergroup conflict still with us if it is so obviously destructive? Apparently, we do not use the same moral rules for members of our group as we do for others. But who is "our group"? This turns out to be a key question for any group, and from childhood on we learn who are members of our group and who are not, as well as what that means. People draw a mental line around those whom they consider to be their group. Only members of the *moral circle* thus delineated have full rights and full obligations.[9]

The German soldier in our story has probably spent long years revisiting his war experiences. In his old age he has redefined himself as belonging to the same moral circle as the churchgoer whose bicycle he took sixty-four years before, and he has come to see his confiscation of the bike as a theft for which he wants to make amends.

Our mental programs are adapted to life in a moral circle. We take pride in the achievements of our children; we are happy when our favorite sports team wins; many of us sing patriotic or religious songs with feeling and pledge allegiance to our national flag. We are ashamed of the failures of members of our group, and we feel guilty about our crimes. There are differences among groups in the fine tuning of these emotions: in some societies a woman can get killed by male family members based on rumors that she slept with the wrong man, and in others a man can be punished by law for having paid sex. Nevertheless, moral, group-related emotions are universal. We have these emotions even about frivolous things such as sports, song festivals, and TV quiz shows. The moral circle affects not only our symbols, heroes, and rituals but also our values.

There may be dissent in societies regarding who within the group is good and who is bad. Politics serves to sort out the difference. In societies that are politically pluralistic, right-wing parties typically protect the strong members, left-wing parties protect the weak members, green parties protect the environment, and populist parties brand parts of the population as bad guys. Leaders such as former U.S. president George W. Bush try to promote internal group cohesion by creating enemies: they make the moral circle smaller, in the same way that populists and dictators often do. The perception of a threat makes people close ranks behind their current leader. Leaders such as U.S. president Barack Obama strive to enlarge the moral circle by creating friends, in the same way that diplomats and negotiators do. In doing so, however, they risk achieving fission in their own moral circle. President Anwar el-Sadat, of Egypt (1918–81), and Prime Minister Yitzhak Rabin, of Israel (1922–95), were both assassinated by one of their own people after reconciling with the traditional enemy.

The moral circle, in many guises and on scales from a single marriage to humanity as a whole, is the key determinant of our social lives, and it both creates and carries our culture.

Boundaries of the Moral Circle: Religion and Philosophy

Philosophy, spirituality, and religion are ways of sorting out the difference between good and bad. For 2,500 years, philosophers in the East and West have taught the Golden Rule: "Do to others as you would wish them to do to you"—which reads like an affirmation of the moral circle.[10] Religious prescriptions such as "Love thy neighbor as thyself" serve the same purpose. Religious sects tend to draw their moral circle around members of their own community. Moral rights and duties, as well as rewards in the afterlife, are granted only to members of the faith. Religion, in essence and whatever the specific beliefs of a particular one, plays an important role in creating and delineating moral circles.

Nations and religions can come into competition if they both attempt to delineate a society-level moral circle in the same country. This has frequently happened during our history, and it is still happening today. The violence of these conflicts testifies to the importance of belonging to a moral circle. It also shows how great a prerogative it is to be the one who defines its boundaries. Through visits and speeches, new leaders typically take action to redefine the boundaries of the moral circle that they lead.

Some societies and religions have a tendency to expand the moral circle and to consider all humans as belonging to a single moral community. Hence the Universal Declaration of Human Rights,[11] and hence calls for development aid. Indeed, animals can be drawn into the moral circle: people form associations or even political parties to protect animal rights, and pet animals are solemnly buried. However, in such a vast moral circle, rights and duties are necessarily diluted. Historically, religions that were tolerant of religious diversity have lost out against those that were more closed on themselves. Most empires have disintegrated from the inside.

Rules for dealing with bad people and with would-be newcomers also differ across societies, of which we shall see examples in subsequent chapters. We humans are continually negotiating the boundaries of our moral circles, and we do it in ways that differ across cultures. Culture is about how to be a good member of the moral circle, depending on one's personal or ascribed properties, about what to do if people are bad, and about whom to consider for admission.

Beyond Race and Family

Gert Jan once took a night train from Vienna to Amsterdam. An elderly Austrian lady shared his compartment and offered him some delicious homegrown apricots. Then a good-looking young black man entered. The lady seemed terrified to find herself within touching distance of a black man, and Gert Jan set to work trying to reestablish a pleasant atmosphere. The young man turned out to be a classical ballet dancer from the Dutch

National Ballet, with Surinamese origins, who had performed in Vienna. But the lady continued to be out of her wits with fear—xenophobia, in a literal sense. She could not get beyond the idea that when the dancer and Gert Jan talked music, they must mean African tam-tam. Luckily, the dancer was well traveled and did not take offense. The three arrived in Amsterdam safely after some polite chitchatting in English.

Humans whose ancestors came from different parts of the world look different. Some of our genetic differences are visible from the outside, even though our genetic variation as a species is small—smaller, for instance, than that of chimpanzees. Biologists call the human genome well mixed. We certainly are one single species, and it is becoming morally preferable to say that we are one human race.[12] Still, biologically speaking, there are races in our species that can be identified through visual and genetic means. However, genetic differences are not the main basis for group boundaries. There is continuity in our genomes, but there is discontinuity in our group affiliations. Millions of migrants live in other continents than their ancestors. It takes an expert observer to guess both ethnic origin and adoptive nationality just by looking at somebody. And yet recognizing group identity matters a lot. Religion, language, and other symbolic group boundaries are important to humans, and we spend much of our time establishing, negotiating, and changing them. People can unite or fight over just about any symbolic matter, from good-old family feuds to territorial fights, defense of honor in response to an insult, or the meaning of a book.

The historical expansion of human societies to millions of individuals has changed the nature of relatedness. Today, many people feel related to people with whom they share a symbolic group membership, not necessarily a genetic one. We fight and die for our country, sometimes even for our soccer team. We form ecstatic crowds of millions that feel united in admiration of a pop star, a gripping politician, or a charismatic preacher. We are active on computer-mediated social networks with people all across the world, and these relationships can be meaningful even with people whom we have never met face-to-face. We have laws that allocate rights and duties to people regardless of family ties, except in special cases such as birth and inheritance. Family loyalty is still important and will no doubt continue to be so, but it is part of a larger societal framework. We live in societies that are so large that blood ties cannot be the only, or even the most important, way to determine moral rights and duties. That said, there is no doubt that blood is still thicker than water, and this is more so in some societies than in others, as we shall see in Chapter 4.

We and They

Social scientists use the terms *in-group* and *out-group*. In-group refers to what we intuitively feel to be "we," while out-group refers to "they." Humans really function in this simple way: we have a persistent need to classify others in either group. The definition of in-group is quite variable in some societies, but it is always noticeable. We use it for family versus in-laws ("the cold side of the family"), for our team versus the opponents, for people looking like us versus another race. In one experiment, U.S. researchers tested affective reactions of African-American and European-American participants to pictures of members of their own and of the opposite ethnic group.[13] Both African-American and European-American participants showed more emotional and physiological reactions when viewing pictures of people of their own race than when viewing people of the other race. They were more emotionally involved with in-group members. While the experiment supported in-group empathy, it did not find a general out-group antipathy.

Gender also plays a role in we-they dynamics, as we might expect in a species in which gender roles have historically been very different regarding crossing group boundaries. Women have usually come into other groups as young adults, to live as loyal members of the new group. Men have frequently come to new groups to dominate or to fight them. Both males and females can easily learn to overcome fear of an unfamiliar-looking female, but they tend to remain scared of faces of out-group males.[14] Of course, this depends on which faces are thought of as out-group, and that in turn depends on exposure in infancy.

In we-versus-they experiments, physiological measurements can be used alongside questionnaires to measure fear. People's bodies can tell stories that their minds feel as taboo. These results confirm that family in a very wide sense is linked to human social biology and that ethnic characteristics are important as a quick aid in determining who belongs. People are we-versus-they creatures. In infancy they can learn to consider anyone, or any kind of face, as "we," but after a few months their recognition is fixed. Later in life it becomes hard for people to change intuitive we-they responses to racial characteristics. Physiological reactions to a we-they situation can be based on any distinction among groups—even that among students from different university departments.[15]

Ideologies as Group Markers

If you could make three statements about yourself, what would you say? Would you mention individual characteristics such as the color of your eyes, your favorite sports or food, or the like? More likely, you would mention group membership attributes such as gender, profession, nationality, religion, which sports team you favor, and which role you fulfill in society. Even if you mention only personal attributes, they are probably attributes that are esteemed among people who matter to you. Much of people's social activity is spent explicitly maintaining symbolic group ties. Most people most of the time are busy being good members of the groups to which they belong. They show it in their clothes, their movements, their way of speaking, their possessions, and their jobs. They spend time with these groups in rituals that strengthen them: talking, laughing, playing, touching, singing, fighting playfully, eating, drinking, and so forth. These activities all aim at reinforcing the moral circle. On a conscious level, however, few would look at their daily lives that way. Instead, people describe what they do in terms of its ritual justification. They go to work, they make strategic plans, they do team building, they attend church services, they serve their country, they celebrate a special occasion.

So, most people see differences where an anthropologist or a biologist sees similarities. These differences are important because we are continually defining and redefining who belongs to what group and in what role. Creating groups and changing membership is one of people's core activities in life. Every society has different rules about how bad it is to leave one group and to join another. It is not surprising that many groups have strong prohibitions against leaving, sometimes backed up by severe penalties. It is never easy to be of a minority religion, for instance, whatever the country one lives in. The degree to which groups penalize deviant symbolic identities and behaviors differs enormously across societies, as shall be discussed in subsequent chapters.

Layers of Culture

In the course of our lives, each of us has to find his or her place in many moral circles. Every group or category of people carries a set of common mental programs that constitutes its culture. As almost everyone belongs to a number of different groups and categories at the same time, we unavoidably carry several layers of mental programming within ourselves, corresponding to different levels of culture. In particular:

- A national level according to one's country (or countries, for people who migrated during their lifetimes)
- A regional and/or ethnic and/or religious and/or linguistic affiliation level
- A gender level, according to whether one was born as a girl or as a boy
- A generation level, separating grandparents from parents from children
- A social class level, associated with educational opportunities and with a person's occupation or profession
- For those who are employed, organizational, departmental, and/or corporate levels according to the way employees have been socialized by their work organization

The mental programs from these various levels are not necessarily in harmony. In modern society they are often partly conflicting: for example, religious values may conflict with generation values; gender values may conflict with organizational practices. Conflicting mental programs within people make it difficult to anticipate their behavior in a new situation.

Culture Change: Changing Practices, Stable Values

If you could step into a time machine and travel back sixty years to the time of your parents or grandparents, you would find the world much changed. There would be no computers, and television sets would rarely be seen. The cities would appear small and provincial, with only the occasional car and no big retail chain outlets. Travel back another sixty years and cars would disappear from the streets as well, as would telephones, washing machines, and vacuum cleaners from our houses and airplanes from the air.

Our world is changing. Technology invented by people surrounds us. The World Wide Web has made our world appear smaller, so that the notion of a "global village" seems appropriate. Business companies operate worldwide. They innovate rapidly; many do not know today what products they will manufacture and sell next year or what new job types they will need in five years. Mergers and stock market fluctuations shake the business landscape.

So, on the surface, change is all-powerful. But how deep are these changes? Can human societies be likened to ships that are rocked about aimlessly on turbulent seas of change? Or to shores, covered and then bared again by new waves washing in, altered ever so slowly with each successive tide?

A book by a Frenchman about his visit to the United States contains the following text:

> *The American ministers of the Gospel do not attempt to draw or to fix all the thoughts of man upon the life to come; they are willing to surrender a portion of his heart to the cares of the present. . . . If they take no part themselves in productive labor, they are at least interested in its progress, and they applaud its results.*

The author, we might think, refers to U.S. TV evangelists. In fact, he was a French visitor, Alexis de Tocqueville, and his book appeared in 1835.[16]

Recorded comments by visitors from one country to another are a rich source of information on how national culture differences were perceived in the past, and they often look strikingly modern, even if they date from centuries ago.

There are many things in societies that technology and its products do not change. If young Turks drink Coca-Cola, this does not necessarily affect their attitudes toward authority. In some respects, young Turks differ from old Turks, just as young Americans differ from old Americans. In the "onion" model of Figure 1.2, such differences mostly involve the relatively superficial spheres of symbols and heroes, of fashion and consumption. In the sphere of values—that is, fundamental feelings about life and about other people—young Turks differ from young Americans just as much as old Turks differ from old Americans. There is no evidence that the values of present-day generations from different countries are converging.

Culture change can be fast for the outer layers of the onion diagram, labeled *practices*. Practices are the visible part of cultures. New practices can be learned throughout one's lifetime; people older than seventy happily learn to surf the Web on their first personal computer, acquiring new symbols, meeting new heroes, and communicating through new rituals. Culture change is slow for the onion's core, labeled *values*. As already argued, these were learned when we were children, from parents who acquired them when *they* were children. This makes for considerable stability in the basic values of a society, in spite of sweeping changes in practices.

These basic values affect primarily the gender, the national, and maybe the regional layer of culture. Never believe politicians, religious leaders, or business chiefs who claim they will reform national values. National value systems should be considered given facts, as hard as a country's geographical position or its weather. Layers of culture acquired later in life tend to be more changeable. This is the case, in particular, for organizational cultures, which the organization's members joined as adults. It doesn't mean that changing organizational cultures is easy—as will be shown in Chapter 10—but at least it is feasible.

There is no doubt that dazzling technological changes are taking place that affect all but the poorest or remotest of people, but people put these new technologies to familiar uses. Many of them are used to do much the same things as our grandparents did: to make money, to impress other people, to make life easier, to coerce others, or to seduce potential partners. All these activities are part of the social game. We are attentive to how other people use technology, what clothes they wear, what jokes they make, what food they eat, and how they spend their vacations. And we have a fine antenna that tells us what choices to make ourselves if we wish to belong to a particular social circle.

The social game itself is not deeply changed by the changes in today's society. The unwritten rules for success, failure, belonging, and other key attributes of our lives remain similar. We need to fit in, to behave in ways that are acceptable to the groups to which we belong. Most changes concern the toys we use in playing the game.

More about cultural change, including its origins and dynamics, will be found in Chapter 12.

National Culture Differences

The invention of *nations*, political units into which the entire world is divided and to one of which every human being is supposed to belong—as manifested by his or her passport—is a recent phenomenon in human history. Earlier, there were states, but not everybody belonged to one of these or identified with one. The nation system was introduced worldwide only in the mid-twentieth century. It followed the colonial system that had developed during the preceding three centuries. In this colonial period the technologically advanced countries of Western Europe divided among themselves virtually all territories of the globe that were not held by another strong political power. The borders between the former colonial nations still reflect the colonial legacy. In Africa in particular, most national borders correspond to the logic of the colonial powers rather than to the cultural dividing lines of the local populations.

Nations, therefore, should not be equated to *societies*. Societies are historically, organically developed forms of social organization. Strictly speaking, the concept of a common culture applies to societies, not to nations. Nevertheless, many nations do form historically developed wholes even if they consist of clearly different groups and even if they contain less integrated minorities.

Within nations that have existed for some time there are strong forces toward further integration: (usually) one dominant national language, common mass media, a national education system, a national army, a national political system, national representation in sports events with a strong symbolic and emotional appeal, a national market for certain skills, products, and services. Today's nations do not attain the degree of internal homogeneity of the isolated, usually nonliterate societies studied by field anthropologists, but they are the source of a considerable amount of common mental programming of their citizens.[17]

On the other hand, there remains a tendency for ethnic, linguistic, and religious groups to fight for recognition of their own identity, if not for national independence; this tendency has been increasing rather than decreasing since the 1960s. Examples are the Ulster Roman Catholics; the Belgian Flemish; the Basques in Spain and France; the Kurds in Iran, Iraq, Syria, and Turkey; the ethnic groups of former Yugoslavia; the Hutu and Tutsi tribes in Rwanda; and the Chechens in Russia.

In research on cultural differences, nationality—the passport one holds—should therefore be used with care. Yet it is often the only feasible criterion for classification. Rightly or wrongly, collective properties are ascribed to the citizens of certain countries: people refer to "typically American," "typically German," and "typically Japanese" behavior. Using nationality as a criterion is a matter of expediency, because it is immensely easier to obtain data for nations than for organic homogeneous societies. Nations as political bodies supply all kinds of statistics about their populations. Survey data (that is, the answers people give on paper-and-pencil questionnaires related to their culture) are also mostly collected through national networks. Where it *is* possible to separate results by regional, ethnic, or linguistic group, this is useful.

A strong reason for collecting data at the level of nations is that one of the purposes of cross-cultural research is to promote cooperation among nations. As argued at the beginning of this chapter, the (more than two hundred) nations that exist today populate one single world, and we either survive or perish together. So, it makes practical sense to focus on cultural factors separating or uniting nations.

National Identities, Values, and Institutions

Countries and regions differ in more than their cultures. Figure 1.4 distinguishes three kinds of differences between countries: identity, values, and institutions, all three rooted in history. Identity answers the question "To which group do I belong?" It is often rooted in language and/or religious affiliation, and it is visible and felt both by the holders of the identity and by the environment that does not share it. Identity, however, is not a core part of national cultures; in the terminology of Figure 1.2, identity differences are rooted in practices (shared symbols, heroes, and rituals), not necessarily in values.

Identities can shift over a person's lifetime, as happens among many successful migrants. A common experience for second-generation immigrants is to identify with their country of origin while they live in the

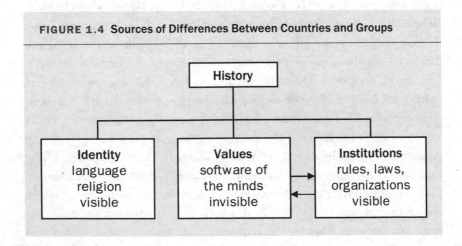

FIGURE 1.4 Sources of Differences Between Countries and Groups

adoptive country of their parents but, in contrast, to feel that they belong to their new country when they visit their parents' country of origin. This is because they are likely to live by a mix of cultural (hidden) rules from both societies while emotionally needing a primary group with which to identify. To no surprise, they often seek comfort with one another.

Identity is explicit: it can be expressed in words, such as "a woman," "a bicultural individual," "an American citizen." In fact, the same person could report being any of these three things, depending on the setting in which you asked. The degree to which identities can be multiple depends on culture. It relates to the individualism-collectivism distinction, which we will meet in Chapter 4. Individualistic environments such as modern cities, academia, and modern business allow people to have several identities and to easily change their identity portfolios. In collectivistic societies, in which most of the world's population still lives, one conceives as oneself much more as belonging to a community, whether this be ethnic, regional, or national, and one's sense of identity derives mainly from that group affiliation.

Values are implicit: they belong to the invisible software of our minds. Talking about our own values is difficult, because it implies questioning our motives, emotions, and taboos. Our own culture is to us like the air we breathe, while another culture is like water—and it takes special skills to be able to survive in both elements. Intercultural encounters are about that, and Chapter 11 will be devoted to them.

In popular parlance and in the press, identity and culture are often confused. Some sources refer to *cultural identity* to describe what we would call group identity. Groups within or across countries that fight each other on the basis of their different identities may very well share basic cultural values; this was or is the case in many parts of the Balkans, for the Catholics and Protestants in Northern Ireland, and for the Flemish and French speakers in Belgium. On the other hand, persons with different cultural backgrounds may form a single group with a single identity, as in intercultural teams—in business, in academia, or in professional soccer.

Countries also obviously differ in their historically grown institutions, which comprise the rules, laws, and organizations dealing with family life, schools, health care, business, government, sports, media, art, and sciences. Some people, including quite a few sociologists and economists, believe these are the true reasons for differences in thinking, feeling, and acting among countries. If we can explain such differences by institutions that are clearly visible, do we really need to speculate about cultures as invisible mental programs?

The answer to this question was given more than two centuries ago by a French nobleman, Charles-Louis de Montesquieu (1689–1755), in *De l'esprit des lois* (*The Spirit of the Laws*).

Montesquieu argued that there is such a thing as "the general spirit of a nation" (what we now would call its culture), and that "the legislator should follow the spirit of the nation . . . for we do nothing better than what we do freely and by following our natural genius."[18] Thus, institutions follow mental programs, and in the way they function they adapt to local culture. Similar laws work out differently in different countries, as the European Union has experienced on many occasions. In their turn, institutions that have grown within a culture perpetuate the mental programming on which they were founded. Institutions cannot be understood without considering culture, and understanding culture presumes insight into institutions. Reducing explanations to either one or the other is sterile.

A country's values are strongly related to the structure and functioning of its institutions and much less to differences in identity; therefore, in Figure 1.4 the horizontal arrows appear only between the "values" and the "institutions" blocks.

An important consequence of this fact is that we cannot change the way people in a country think, feel, and act by simply importing foreign institutions. After the demise of communism in the former Soviet Union and other parts of Eastern Europe, some economists thought that all that the former communist countries needed was capitalist institutions, U.S. style, in order to find the road to wealth. Things did not work out that way. Each country has to struggle through its own type of reforms, adapted to the software of its people's minds. Globalization by multinational corporations and supranational institutions such as the World Bank meets fierce local resistance because economic systems are not culture free.

What About National *Management* Cultures?

The business and business school literature often refers to national "management" or "leadership" cultures. Management and leadership, however, cannot be isolated from other parts of society. U.S. anthropologist Marvin Harris has warned that "one point anthropologists have always made is that aspects of social life which do not seem to be related to one another, actually are related."[19]

Managers and leaders, as well as the people they work with, are part of national societies. If we want to understand their behavior, we have to understand their societies. For example, we need to know what types of personalities are common in their country; how families function and what this means for the way children are brought up; how the school system works, and who goes to what type of school; how the government and the political system affect the lives of the citizens; and what historical events their generation has experienced. We may also need to know something about their behavior as consumers and their beliefs about health and sickness, crime and punishment, and religious matters. We may learn a lot from their countries' literature, arts, and sciences. The following chapters will at times pay attention to all of these fields, and most of them will prove relevant for understanding a country's management as well. In culture there is no shortcut to the business world.

Cultural Relativism

In daily conversations, in political discourse, and in the media that feed them, alien cultures are often pictured in moral terms, as better or worse. Yet there are no scientific standards for considering the ways of thinking, feeling, and acting of one group as intrinsically superior or inferior to those of another.

Studying differences in culture among groups and societies presupposes a neutral vantage point, a position of cultural relativism. A great French anthropologist, Claude Lévi-Strauss (1908–2009), has expressed it as follows:

> *Cultural relativism affirms that one culture has no absolute criteria for judging the activities of another culture as "low" or "noble." However, every culture can and should apply such judgment to its own activities, because its members are actors as well as observers.*[20] //

Cultural relativism does not imply a lack of norms for oneself, nor for one's society. It does call for suspending judgment when dealing with groups or societies different from one's own. One should think twice before applying the norms of one person, group, or society to another. Information about the nature of the cultural differences between societies, their roots, and their consequences should precede judgment and action.

Even after having been informed, the foreign observer is still likely to deplore certain ways of the other society. If professionally involved in the other society, for example as an expatriate manager or development cooperation expert, he or she may very well want to induce changes. In colonial days foreigners often wielded absolute power in other societies, and they could impose their rules on it. In these postcolonial days, in contrast, foreigners who want to change something in another society will have to negotiate their interventions. Negotiation again is more likely to succeed when the parties concerned understand the reasons for the differences in viewpoints.

Culture as a Phoenix

During a person's life, new body cells continually replace old ones. The twenty-year-old does not retain a single cell of the newborn. In a restricted physical sense, therefore, one could say we exist only as a sequence of cell assemblies. Yet we exist as ourselves. This is because all these cells share the same genes.

At the level of societies, an analogous phenomenon occurs. Our societies have a remarkable capacity for conserving their distinctive culture through generations of successive members and despite varied and numerous forces of change. While change sweeps the surface, the deeper layers remain stable, and the culture rises from its ashes like a phoenix.

But what do these deeper layers consist of? Although our genes give us the capacity to create and maintain culture, the evidence that is available so far suggests that culture is influenced far more by our experiences than by our genes. Culture is the unwritten book with rules of the social game that is passed on to newcomers by its members, nesting itself in their minds. In the following chapters we will describe the main themes that these unwritten rules cover. They deal with the basic issues of human social life.

Studying Cultural Differences

At the start a new candidate for paradigm may have few supporters, and on occasions the supporters' motives may be suspect. Nevertheless, if they are competent, they will improve it, explore its possibilities, and show what it would be like to belong to the community guided by it. And if that goes on, if the paradigm is one destined to win its fight, the number and strength of the persuasive arguments in its favor will increase. More scientists will then be converted, and the exploration of the new paradigm will go on. Gradually the number of experiments, instruments, articles, and books based upon the paradigm will multiply. Still more men, convinced of the new view's fruitfulness, will adopt the new mode of practicing normal science, until at last a few elderly holdouts remain. And even they, we cannot say, are wrong.

—Thomas S. Kuhn, *The Structure of Scientific Revolutions*

Thomas Kuhn (1922–96) was an American philosopher and historian of science. The citation here is from his well-known book in which he describes, with examples from various sciences, how scientific innovation is brought about. In a given period certain assumptions called *paradigms* dominate a scientific field and constrain the thinking of the scientists in that field. Kuhn called the work done within these paradigms *normal science*. Every now and then, normal science runs into limits: it is unable to explain new facts or unable to meet new challenges. Then, a paradigm change is initiated. As gradually more and more people move to the new paradigm, this then becomes a new type of normal science.

In this chapter we will describe the research process on which this book was based. It is based on a paradigm introduced by Geert in the 1980 edition of his book *Culture's Consequences*, the *dimensions* approach, which since has acquired normal science status.

Measuring Values

As values, more than practices, are the stable element in culture, comparative research on culture starts from the measurement of values. Inferring values from people's actions only is cumbersome and ambiguous. Various paper-and-pencil questionnaires have been developed that ask for people's preferences among alternatives. The answers should not be taken too literally: in reality people will not always act as they have scored on the questionnaire. Still, questionnaires provide useful information, because they show differences in answers between groups or categories of respondents. For example, suppose a question asks for one's preference for time off from work versus more pay. An individual employee who states that he or she prefers time off may in fact opt for the money if presented with the actual choice, but if in group A more people claim to prefer time off than in group B, this does indicate a cultural difference between these groups in the relative value of free time versus money.

In interpreting people's statements about their values, it is important to distinguish between the *desirable* and the *desired*: how people think the world ought to be versus what people want for themselves. Questions about the desirable refer to people in general and are worded in terms of right/wrong, should/should not, agree/disagree, important/unimportant, or something similar. In the abstract, everybody is in favor of virtue and opposed to sin, and answers about the desirable express people's views about what represents virtue and what corresponds to sin. The desired, on the contrary, is worded in terms of "you" or "me" and what we want for ourselves, including our less virtuous desires. The desirable bears only a faint resemblance to actual behavior, but even statements about the desired, although closer to actual behavior, do not necessarily correspond to the way people really behave when they have to choose.

The desirable differs from the desired in the nature of the *norms* involved. Norms are standards for behavior that exist within a group or category of people.[1] In the case of the desirable, the norm is absolute, pertaining to what is ethically right. In the case of the desired, the norm is statistical: it indicates the choices made by the majority. The desirable relates more to ideology, the desired to practical matters.

Interpretations of value studies that neglect the difference between the desirable and the desired may lead to paradoxical results. A case in which the two produced diametrically opposed answers was found in the IBM studies, to be described later on in this chapter. Employees in different countries were asked for their agreement or disagreement with the statement "Employees in industry should participate more in the decisions made by management." This is a statement about the desirable. In another question people were asked whether they personally preferred a manager who "usually consults with subordinates before reaching a decision." This is a statement about the desired. A comparison of the answers to these two questions revealed that in countries in which the consulting manager was less popular, people agreed more with the general statement that employees should participate in decisions, and vice versa; the ideology was the mirror image of the day-to-day relationship with the boss.[2]

Dimensions of National Cultures

In the first half of the twentieth century, social anthropology developed the conviction that all societies, modern or traditional, face the same basic problems; only the answers differ. American anthropologists, in particular Ruth Benedict (1887–1948) and Margaret Mead (1901–78), played an important role in popularizing this message for a wide audience.

The logical next step was that social scientists attempted to identify *what* problems were common to all societies, through conceptual reasoning and reflection on field experiences as well as through statistical studies. In 1954 two Americans, the sociologist Alex Inkeles and the psychologist Daniel Levinson, published a broad survey of the English-language literature on national culture. They suggested that the following issues qualify as common basic problems worldwide, with consequences for the functioning of societies, of groups within those societies, and of individuals within those groups:

- Relation to authority
- Conception of self—in particular:
  - The relationship between individual and society
  - The individual's concept of masculinity and femininity
- Ways of dealing with conflicts, including the control of aggression and the expression of feelings[3]

Twenty years later Geert was given the opportunity to study a large body of survey data about the values of people in more than fifty countries around the world. These people worked in the local subsidiaries of one large multinational corporation: International Business Machines (IBM). At first it may seem surprising that employees of a multinational corporation—a very special kind of people—could serve for identifying differences in *national* value systems. However, from one country to another they represented almost perfectly matched samples: they were similar in all respects except nationality, which made the effect of nationality differences in their answers stand out unusually clearly.

A statistical analysis[4] of the country averages of the answers to questions about the values of similar IBM employees in different countries revealed common problems, but with solutions differing from country to country, in the following areas:

- Social inequality, including the relationship with authority
- The relationship between the individual and the group
- Concepts of masculinity and femininity: the social and emotional implications of having been born as a boy or a girl
- Ways of dealing with uncertainty and ambiguity, which turned out to be related to the control of aggression and the expression of emotions

These empirical results covered amazingly well the areas predicted by Inkeles and Levinson twenty years before. The discovery of their prediction provided strong support for the theoretical importance of the empirical findings. Problems that are basic to all human societies should be reflected in different studies, regardless of their methods. The Inkeles and Levinson study had strikingly predicted what Geert found twenty years later.

The four basic problem areas defined by Inkeles and Levinson and empirically found in the IBM data represent *dimensions of cultures*. A dimension is an aspect of a culture that can be measured relative to other cultures. The four dimensions found will be described in Chapters 3 through 6. They have been named *power distance* (from small to large), *collectivism versus individualism, femininity versus masculinity*, and *uncertainty avoidance* (from weak to strong). Each of these terms existed already in some part of the social sciences, and they seemed to apply reasonably well to the basic problem area each dimension stands for. Together they form a four-dimensional model of differences among national cultures. Each country in the model is characterized by a score on each of the four dimensions.

A dimension groups together a number of phenomena in a society that were empirically found to occur in combination, regardless of whether there seems to be a logical necessity for their going together. The logic of societies is not the same as the logic of individuals looking at them. The grouping of the different aspects of a dimension is always based on statistical relationships—that is, on *trends* for these phenomena to occur in combination, not on iron links. Some aspects in some societies may go against a general trend found across most other societies. Because they are found with the help of statistical methods, dimensions can be detected only on the basis of comparative information from a number of countries—say, at least ten. In the case of the IBM research, Geert was fortunate to obtain comparable data about culturally determined values from (initially) forty countries, which made the dimensions within their differences stand out clearly.

The scores for each country on one dimension can be pictured as points along a line. For two dimensions at a time, they become points in a diagram. For three dimensions, they could, with some imagination, be seen as points in space. For four or more dimensions, they become difficult to imagine. This is a disadvantage of dimensional models. Another way of picturing differences among countries (or other social systems) is through *typologies*. A typology describes a set of ideal types, each of them easy to imagine. A common typology of countries in the second half of the twentieth century was dividing them into a first, second, and third world (a capitalist, communist, and former colonial bloc).

Whereas typologies are easier to grasp than dimensions, they are problematic in empirical research. Real cases seldom fully correspond to one single ideal type. Most cases are hybrids, and arbitrary rules have to be made for classifying them as belonging to one type or another. With a dimensional model, on the contrary, cases can always be scored unambiguously. On the basis of their dimension scores, cases can *afterward* empirically be sorted into clusters with similar scores. These clusters then form an empirical typology. More than fifty countries in the IBM study could, on the basis of their scores on the four dimensions, be sorted into twelve such clusters.[5]

In practice, typologies and dimensional models are complementary. Dimensional models are preferable for research, and typologies are useful for teaching purposes. This book will use a kind of typology approach for explaining each of the dimensions. For every separate dimension, it describes the two opposite extremes as pure types. Later on, some dimensions are plotted two by two, every plot creating four types. The country scores on the dimensions will show that most real cases are somewhere in between the extremes.

Using Correlations

Dimensions are based on *correlations*. Two measures (called *variables*) are said to be correlated if they vary together. For example, if we were to measure the height and weight of a hundred people randomly picked from the street, we would find the height and weight measures to be correlated: taller people would also usually be heavier, and shorter ones would also tend to be lighter. Because some people are tall and skinny and some are short and fat, the correlation would not be perfect.

The *coefficient of correlation*[6] expresses the strength of the relationship. If the correlation is perfect, so that one measure follows entirely from the other, the coefficient takes the value 1.00. If the correlation is nonexistent—the two measures are completely unrelated—the coefficient is 0.00. The coefficient can become negative if the two measures are each other's opposite—for example, a person's height and the number of times he or she would meet someone who is still taller. The lowest possible value is −1.00; in this case the two measures are again perfectly correlated, only the one is positive when the other is negative, and vice versa. In the example of the height and weight of people, one could expect a coefficient of about 0.80 if the sample included only adults—and even higher if both children and adults were included in the sample, because children are extremely small and light compared with adults.

A correlation coefficient is said to be (statistically) significant if it is sufficiently different from zero (to the positive or to the negative side) to rule out the possibility that the similarity between the two measures is due to pure chance. The *significance level*, usually 0.05, 0.01, or 0.001, is the remaining risk that the similarity is still accidental. If the significance level is 0.05, the odds against an association by chance are 19 to one; if it is 0.001, the odds are 999 to one.[7]

If the correlation coefficient between two variables is 1.00 or −1.00, we can obviously completely predict one if we know the other. If their correlation coefficient is ±0.90, we can predict 81 percent of the differences (called the *variance*) in one if we know the other; if it is ±0.80, we can predict 64 percent of the variance, and so on. The predictive power decreases with the square of the correlation coefficient. If we have a lot of data, a correlation coefficient of 0.40 may still be significant, although the first variable predicts only 0.40 × 0.40 = 16 percent of the variance in the second. The reason we are interested in such relatively weak correlations is that often, phenomena in the social world are the result of many factors working at the same time: they are multicausal. Correlation analysis helps us to isolate possible causes.

In the case of three or more measures, we can choose one as our *dependent* variable and calculate the combined effect of the remaining, *independent* variables on this dependent variable. For example, we could measure not only the height but also the shoulder width of our hundred randomly picked test persons, and these two "independent" variables together would correlate with our "dependent" weight measure even more strongly than height alone. A statistical technique called *regression* allows us to measure the contribution of each of the independent variables separately. In our analysis we often use *stepwise regression*, a method to sort the independent variables step-by-step in order of their contribution to the dependent variable. This contribution is usually expressed as a percent of the variance in the independent variable. In a stepwise regression of the body measures of our imaginary hundred persons, we might find, for example, that height contributed 64 percent to the variance in weight, and height plus shoulder width contributed 83 percent.

For readability reasons, correlation coefficients and regression results in this book are given in the endnotes; the text refers to the conclusions drawn from them and sometimes to percentages of variance explained. Readers interested in additional statistical proof are referred to Geert's book *Culture's Consequences*, 2001.

Replications of the IBM Research

In the 1970s, while IBM survey data continued to come in, Geert administered some of the same questions to an international population of non-IBM managers. These people, who came from different companies in fifteen countries, attended courses at a business school in Switzerland where Geert was a visiting lecturer.[8] At that time, he did not yet have a clear concept of dimensions in the data, but the replication showed that on a key question about power (later part of the *power distance* dimension), the countries ranked almost exactly the same as in IBM. Other questions indicated country differences in what we now call individualism versus collectivism, again very similar to those in IBM. This was Geert's first indication that the country differences found inside IBM existed elsewhere as well.

In later years many people administered the IBM questionnaire—or parts of it, or its later, improved versions, called Values Survey Modules (VSMs)—to other groups of respondents.[9] The usefulness of replications increases with the number of countries included. The more countries, the easier it becomes to use statistical tests for verifying the degree of similarity in the results. As of this writing, along with many smaller studies, we count six major replication studies, each covering fourteen or more countries from the IBM database. Those six are listed in Table 2.1.

Four of the six replications in Table 2.1 confirm only three out of the four dimensions—and each time the one missing is different. For example, data obtained from consumers did not replicate the power distance dimension. We assume this is because the respondents included people in different jobs with different relationships to power or people without paid jobs at all, such as students and housewives.

Most of the smaller studies compared two or three countries at a time. It would seem too idealistic to expect confirmation of the IBM results in all these cases, but a review of nineteen small replications by the Danish researcher Mikael Søndergaard found that together they did statistically confirm all four dimensions.[10] The strongest confirmation was for individualism. Most small replications start from the United States, which in the IBM studies was the highest scorer on individualism, and any comparison with the United States is likely to show a clear individualism difference.

The success of the replications does not necessarily mean that the countries' cultures did not change since the IBM research, but if they changed, they changed together, so that their relative position remained intact.

TABLE 2.1 Six Major Replications of the IBM Research

Author	Year Publ	Sample	No. of Ctrs	DIMENSIONS REPLICATED			
				Power	Indiv	Mascu	Uncer
Hoppe	1990	Elites[1]	18	x	x	x	x
Shane	1995	Employees[2]	28	x	x		x
Merritt	1998	Pilots[3]	19	x	x	x	x
de Mooij	2001	Consumers[4]	15		x	x	x
Mouritzen	2002	Municipal[5]	14	x		x	x
van Nimwegen	2002	Bank empl[6]	19	x	x	x	

1 Members of government, parliamentarians, labor and employers' leaders, academics, and artists. These people were surveyed in 1984 via the Salzburg Seminar in American Studies. On the basis of the formulas in the VSM 82, their answers confirmed power distance, uncertainty avoidance, and individualism (Hoppe, 1990); using the VSM 94 they also confirmed masculinity (Hoppe, 1998).

2 Employees of six international corporations (but not IBM) from between 28 and 32 countries: Shane (1995); Shane & Venkataraman (1996). This study confirmed power distance, uncertainty avoidance, and individualism. It did not include questions about masculinity, which was judged politically incorrect(!).

3 Commercial airline pilots from 19 countries: Helmreich & Merritt (1998). Using the VSM 82 this study confirmed power distance and individualism; including other IBM questions judged more relevant to the pilot's situation, it confirmed all four dimensions (Merritt, 2000).

4 Consumers from 15 European countries: de Mooij (2004); *Culture's Consequences* (2001), pp. 187, 262, 336. Using the VSM 94 this study confirmed uncertainty avoidance, individualism, and masculinity. It did not confirm power distance, probably because the consumers were not selected on the basis of the jobs they did (or whether they had a paid job at all).

5 Top municipal civil servants from 14 countries: Søndergaard (2002); Mouritzen & Svara (2002). Using the VSM 94 they confirmed power distance, uncertainty avoidance, and masculinity and related the first two to the forms of local government in the countries.

6 Employees of an international bank in 19 countries: van Nimwegen (2002). This study confirmed power distance and individualism and also, but with a somewhat lesser fit, masculinity and long-term orientation, but not uncertainty avoidance.

Table 2.2 lists in alphabetical order all countries and regions for which dimension scores are presented in this book. Chapters 3 through 6, based on the IBM research and its replications, give scores for seventy-six countries and regions; Chapters 7 and 8, based on World Values Survey data, list scores for ninety-three cases each.

TABLE 2.2 107 Countries or Regions for Which Dimension Scores Are Listed

(Names in **bold** were part of the original IBM dataset.)

Africa Eastern region[1] (Ethiopia, Kenya, Tanzania, Zambia)
Africa Western region[1] (Ghana, Nigeria, Sierra Leone)
Albania[2]
Algeria[2]
Andorra[5]
Arab-speaking countries[1] (Egypt, Iraq, Kuwait, Lebanon, Libya, Saudi Arabia, Emirates)
Argentina
Armenia[3]
Australia
Austria
Azerbaijan[2]
Bangladesh
Belarus[2]
Belgium Flanders[6] (Dutch speaking)
Belgium Wallonia[6] (French speaking)
Bosnia[2]
Brazil
Bulgaria
Burkina Faso[2]
Canada Québec[1] (French speaking)
Canada total
Chile
China
Colombia
Costa Rica[1]
Croatia
Cyprus[5]

Czech Republic
Denmark
Dominican Republic[2]
Ecuador[1]
Egypt
El Salvador
Estonia
Finland
France
Georgia[2]
Germany
Germany East[2]
Ghana[2]
Great Britain
Greece
Guatemala[1]
Hong Kong (China)
Hungary
Iceland[2]
India
Indonesia
Iran
Iraq[2]
Ireland
Israel[4]
Italy
Jamaica[1]
Japan
Jordan[2]
Korea South
Kyrgyz Republic[2]
Latvia
Lithuania
Luxembourg
Macedonia FYR[2]
Malaysia
Mali[2]
Malta
Mexico
Moldova[2]
Montenegro[2]

Morocco
Netherlands
New Zealand
Nigeria[2]
Norway
Pakistan
Panama[1]
Peru
Philippines
Poland
Portugal
Puerto Rico (U.S.A.)[2]
Romania
Russia
Rwanda[2]
Saudi Arabia[2]
Serbia
Singapore
Slovakia
Slovenia
South Africa[7]
Spain
Suriname[1]
Sweden
Switzerland[6] (French speaking)
Switzerland[6] (German speaking)
Taiwan
Tanzania[2]
Thailand
Trinidad and Tobago
Turkey
Uganda[2]
Ukraine[2]
United States
Uruguay
Venezuela
Vietnam
Zambia[2]
Zimbabwe[2]

---

1 First four dimensions only; 2 Last two dimensions only; 3 LTO only; 4 IVR missing; 5 IVR only; 6 LTO and IVR total country; 7 IBM: whites only

Extending the IBM Model:
The Chinese Value Survey

In late 1980, just after *Culture's Consequences* had been published, Geert met Michael Harris Bond, from the Chinese University of Hong Kong. Bond and a number of his colleagues from the Asia-Pacific region had just finished a comparison of the values of female and male psychology students from each of ten national or ethnic groups in their region.[11] They had used an adapted version of the Rokeach Value Survey (RVS), developed by U.S. psychologist Milton Rokeach on the basis of an inventory of values in U.S. society around 1970. When Bond analyzed the RVS data in the same way that Geert had analyzed the IBM data, he also found four meaningful dimensions. Across the six countries that were part of both studies, each RVS dimension was significantly correlated with one of the IBM dimensions.[12]

The discovery of similar dimensions in completely different material represented strong support for the basic nature of what was found. With another questionnaire, using other respondents (students instead of IBM employees), at another point in time (data collected around 1979 instead of 1970) and in a restricted group of countries, four similar dimensions emerged. Both Michael and Geert were not just pleased but also puzzled. The survey results themselves demonstrated that people's ways of thinking are culturally constrained. As the researchers were human, they were also children of their cultures; both the IBM questionnaire and the RVS were products of Western minds. In both cases, respondents in non-Western countries had answered Western questions. To what extent had this circumstance been responsible for the correlation between the results of the two studies? To what extent had irrelevant questions been asked and relevant questions been omitted?

Michael Bond, a Canadian having lived and worked in the Far East since 1971, found a creative solution to the Western bias problem. He asked a number of his Chinese colleagues from Hong Kong and Taiwan to help him compose a list of basic values for Chinese people. The new questionnaire was called the Chinese Value Survey (CVS). It was administered in translation to one hundred students, fifty men and fifty women, in each of twenty-three countries around the world. A statistical analysis of the CVS results yielded again four dimensions. Across twenty overlapping countries, three dimensions of the CVS replicated dimensions earlier found in the IBM surveys, but the fourth CVS dimension was not correlated with the fourth IBM dimension: uncertainty avoidance had no equivalent in the CVS. The fourth CVS dimension instead combined values opposing an orientation on the future to an orientation on the past and present.[13] Geert labeled it *long-term versus short-term orientation* (LTO) and adopted it as a fifth universal dimension. Twenty years later Misho Minkov unraveled from the World Values Survey a dimension that was correlated with LTO and helped us to redefine it and extend it to many more countries. The full story will be told in Chapter 7.

Validation of the Country Culture Scores Against Other Measures

The next step was showing the practical implications of the dimension scores for the countries concerned. This was done quantitatively by correlating the dimension scores with other measures that could be logically expected to reflect the same culture differences. These quantitative checks were supplemented with qualitative, descriptive information about the countries. This entire process is called *validation*.

Examples, which will be elaborated upon in Chapters 3 through 8, are that power distance was correlated with the use of violence in domestic politics and with income inequality in a country. Individualism was correlated with national wealth (GNI per capita) and with mobility between social classes from one generation to the next. Masculinity was correlated negatively with the share of the gross national income that governments of wealthy countries spent on development assistance to the third world. Uncertainty avoidance was associated with Roman Catholicism and with the legal obligation of citizens in developed countries to carry identity cards. Long-term orientation was correlated with national savings rates.

Relationships between measurable phenomena in the world can be complex. The dimensions of national cultures described in the following chapters are meant to improve our understanding by reducing this complexity, but they cannot eliminate it. For each dimension, we describe with which phenomena it is most strongly correlated. Sometimes we need two, or rarely three, dimensions for our explanation, but our goal is to keep it as simple as our data permit.

Altogether, the 2001 edition of *Culture's Consequences* lists more than four hundred significant correlations of the IBM dimension scores with other measures; in one out of six cases, we need two dimensions, and in one out of fifty, we need three.[14] A striking fact of the various validations is that correlations do not tend to become weaker over time. The IBM national dimension scores (or at least their relative positions) have remained as valid in the year 2010 as they were around 1970, indicating that they describe relatively enduring aspects of these countries' societies.

Culture Scores and Personality Scores: No Reason for Stereotyping

American social anthropologists in the first half of the twentieth century saw a close relationship between cultures and the personalities of the people in them. What we now call *national culture* was then called *national character* or *modal personality*; American pioneer anthropologist Ruth Benedict saw human cultures as "personality writ large."[15]

A criticism of this viewpoint was that it led to the *stereotyping* of individuals. Stereotypes are literally printing plates; figuratively they are conventional notions that are usually associated uncritically with a person on the basis of his or her background. The accusation of stereotyping individuals has sometimes also been raised against the national culture dimensions paradigm.

The relationship between national culture and personality received new attention at the end of the twentieth century, due to the availability of better data. On the culture side, these came from our values research; on the personality side, from developments in personality testing. In a personality test an individual answers a number of questions about him- or herself. In the mid-twentieth century there used to be a confusing variety of competing personality tests, but in the 1990s a consensus was growing that a useful common denominator of most personality tests in most countries is a set of five dimensions of personality variation (the so-called Big Five):

O: Openness to experience versus rigidity

C: Conscientiousness versus undependability

E: Extraversion versus introversion

A: Agreeableness versus ill-temperedness

N: Neuroticism versus emotional stability

U.S. psychologists Paul T. Costa and Robert R. McCrae developed a self-scored personality test based on the Big Five, the Revised NEO Personality Inventory (NEO-PI-R). By the end of the century, it had been translated from American English into a number of other languages and used on samples of the same kind of people in many countries.

In a joint article, McCrae and Hofstede explored the relationship between personality dimension scores and national culture dimension scores. Mean scores on the five NEO-PI-R dimensions for comparative samples from thirty-three countries correlated significantly with all four IBM culture dimensions.[16] We will meet some of these correlations in the following chapters. Our joint study showed that culture and personality are not independent. Refer again to Figure 1.1: while there is a wide range of different personalities within every country, the way these individuals describe themselves in personality tests is partly influenced by the national culture of the country.

The association between personality and culture, however, is statistical, not absolute. It does not justify the use of national culture scores as stereotypes for individuals from these nations. The range of personalities within each country is far too wide for that. National culture scores are not about individuals, but about national societies.

Other Classifications of National Cultures

The basic innovation of *Culture's Consequences*, when it appeared in 1980, was classifying national cultures along a number of dimensions. As we argued at the beginning of this chapter, this represented a new paradigm in the study of culture—that is, a radically new approach. A paradigm is not a theory, but one step before a theory: a way of thinking that leads to developing theories. New paradigms invariably lead to controversy, as they reverse cherished truths but also open new perspectives. Since *Culture's Consequences*, several other theories of national cultures have used the same paradigm, each suggesting its own way of classifying them.

An elaborate and widely known application of the dimensions paradigm was by the Israeli psychologist Shalom H. Schwartz. From a survey of the literature, he selected a list of fifty-six value items. A major inspiration for his list was the work of the American psychologist Milton Rokeach (1973), who compared different groups in the American population on eighteen "terminal values" (nouns describing desirable end states, such as *equality*) and eighteen "instrumental values" (adjectives describing ways to get there, such as *honest*). Respondents were asked to score the extent to which each item is important as "a guiding principle in your life," on a nine-point scale from $-1 =$ "opposed to values" and $0 =$ "not important" to $7 =$ "supreme importance." In terms of the distinction cited in the section on measuring values earlier in this chapter, Schwartz's value items are closer to the *desirable* than to the *desired*.[17]

Through a network of colleagues, Schwartz collected scores from samples of college students and elementary school teachers in more than sixty countries.[18] He initially compared individuals and, through a statistical procedure (*smallest space analysis*), divided his values into ten dimensions. As with Geert before him, Schwartz went through a learning experience when he moved his analysis to the country level: contrary to his initial expectations, he found that at this level he needed a different set of dimensions. His seven country-level dimensions were labeled *conservatism, hierarchy, mastery, affective autonomy, intellectual autonomy, egalitarian commitment*, and *harmony*. There are significant correlations between Schwartz's country scores and our scores, but mainly with individualism/collectivism; one reason may be that Schwartz's country scores do not control for national wealth (see Chapter 4).[19]

Another large-scale application of the dimensions paradigm is the GLOBE (Global Leadership and Organizational Behavior Effectiveness) project, conceived by U.S. management scholar Robert J. House in 1991. At first House focused on leadership, but soon the study branched out into other aspects of national and organizational cultures. In the period 1994–97 some 170 voluntary collaborators collected data from about seventeen thousand managers in nearly one thousand local (nonmultinational) organizations belonging to one of three industries—food processing, financial services, and telecommunication services—in some sixty societies throughout the world. In the preface to the book describing the project,[20] House writes, "We have a very adequate data set to replicate Hofstede's (1980) landmark study and extend that study to test hypotheses relevant to relationships among societal-level variables, organizational practices, and leader attributes and behavior."

For conceptual reasons GLOBE expanded the five Hofstede dimensions to nine. It maintained the labels *power distance* and *uncertainty avoidance*. It split collectivism into *institutional collectivism* and *in-group collectivism*, and masculinity-femininity into *assertiveness* and *gender egalitarianism*. Long-term orientation became *future orientation*. It added two more dimensions, also inspired by our masculinity-femininity distinction: *humane orientation* and *performance orientation*. The nine dimensions were covered by seventy-eight survey questions, half of them asking respondents to describe their culture ("as it is") and the other half asking them to judge it ("as it should be"). GLOBE thus produced $9 \times 2 = 18$ culture scores for each country: nine "as is" dimensions and nine "as should be" dimensions. Also, GLOBE used two versions of the questionnaire: half of the respondents were asked about the culture "in this society" and the other half about the culture "in this organization."

In an evaluation of the GLOBE project,[21] Geert criticized GLOBE for having formulated the questions in researchers' jargon, not reflective of the problems on the responding (mainly first-line) managers' minds. GLOBE asked for the respondents' descriptions and evaluations of their fellow citizens' traits and behaviors, as well as for generalized descriptions and evaluations of their country's cultures. This method yields meaningful results only when the issue is simple, such as family relations. For more abstract issues, it is difficult to know what the answers mean.[22] An example is the following GLOBE item: "In this society, most people lead highly structured lives with few unexpected events." How are managers supposed to answer such a question, which even expert social scientists would find difficult?

GLOBE's "as is" questions are supposed to be descriptive, but many of them just produce national (character) stereotypes.[23] GLOBE's "as should be" questions, in terms of the distinction made earlier in this chapter, deal with the desirable. Unlike in the Hofstede research, none of the GLOBE questions deals with the personally desired.

Across countries, some GLOBE dimensions were strongly correlated among each other; "as is" and "as should be" dimensions often correlated negatively. In a reanalysis, Geert found that the eighteen dimensions on the basis of their country scores sorted themselves into five clusters. The strongest, grouping seven GLOBE dimensions, was highly significantly correlated with national wealth, and next with the Hofstede power distance, individualism, and uncertainty avoidance dimensions, in this order. Three more clusters were each significantly correlated with only one Hofstede dimension: respectively, uncertainty avoidance, individualism, and long-term orientation dimensions. The GLOBE questionnaire contained very few items covering masculinity in the Hofstede sense, but whatever there was belonged to the fifth cluster. In spite of the very different approach taken, the massive body of GLOBE data still reflected the structure of the original Hofstede model.

A complication in the comparison of GLOBE's conclusions with ours is that the GLOBE report often uses the same terms we used but with quite different meanings. This is evident in the names of the dimensions; owing to the entirely different way of formulating the questions, GLOBE dimensions with the names "power distance" and "uncertainty avoidance" cannot even be expected to measure the same things as the Hofstede dimensions. We will show this in Chapters 3 through 7. Further, GLOBE uses the terms *practices* for answers about culture "as it is" and *values* for answers about culture "as it should be." In Figure 1.2, as previously discussed, we used "practices" for symbols, heroes, and rituals visible to the outside observer, and we used "values" for what a respondent prefers for him- or herself, often unconsciously. Finally, GLOBE assumed that questions starting with "In this society" would reflect national culture and that the same questions starting with "In this organization" would yield organizational culture. GLOBE reports that in practice both types of answers were virtually the same, so the two sets of data were later combined. Geert and colleagues, in a large research project focusing solely on organizational cultures, to be introduced at the end of this chapter and extensively described in Chapter 10, found that organizational and national culture are very different phenomena and cannot even be measured with the same questions.

An author sometimes cited as having researched dimensions of national culture is the Dutch management consultant Fons Trompenaars. He distinguishes seven dimensions: *universalism versus particularism, individualism versus collectivism, affectivity versus neutrality, specificity versus diffuseness, achievement versus ascription, time orientation,* and *relation to nature.*[24] However, these are not based on empirical research but rather are borrowed from conceptual distinctions made by American sociologists in the 1950s and 1960s,[25] not specifically for describing countries. Trompenaars collected a database of survey items, also found in American mid-twentieth-century sociology literature,[26] among his audiences and business contacts in a number of countries; on the Web he claimed it contained data from fifty-five thousand "managers." Unfortunately, Trompenaars has no peer-reviewed academic publications, and he nowhere specifies what exactly his database contains; it is unclear what it contributes to his conceptual distinctions. The only peer-reviewed statistical analysis of Trompenaars's data so far was done in the 1990s by British psychologists Peter Smith and Shaun Dugan. In the scores of some nine thousand respondents (managers and nonmanagers) from forty-three countries, they found two independent dimensions, one correlated with our individualism-collectivism dimension and the other primarily with our power distance dimension and secondarily again with individualism-collectivism.[27] Trompenaars's questionnaire did not cover other aspects of national cultures.

A Second Expansion of the Hofstede Dimensional Model: Minkov's Exploration of the World Values Survey

In the early 1980s departments of divinity at six European universities, concerned with a loss of Christian faith, jointly surveyed the values of their countries' populations through public-opinion survey methods. In the following years their "European Values Survey" expanded and changed focus: led by U.S. sociologist Ronald Inglehart, it grew into a periodic World Values Survey (WVS). Subsequent data-collection rounds took place in ten-year intervals; as of this writing, a fourth round is in process. The survey now covers more than one hundred countries worldwide with a questionnaire including more than 360 forced-choice items. Areas covered are ecology, economy, education, emotions, family, gender and sexuality, government and politics, happiness, health, leisure and friends, morality, religion, society and nation, and work. The entire WVS data bank, including previous rounds and down to the individual respondent scores, is freely accessible on the Web.[28]

Along with the WVS, many other rich value data sources have become accessible to anyone who has the courage to search the Web, including the European Social Survey and the Economic and Social Survey of Asia and the Pacific. When Geert started his values research in the 1970s, the IBM employee survey data comprised the largest cross-national collection of comparative value statements anywhere in the world. If he had to start again now, he would do it from the World Values Survey.

WVS coordinator Ronald Inglehart, in an initial analysis of his database, announced two main factors, which he called *well-being versus survival* and *secular-rational versus traditional authority*. As the following chapters will show, both correlate with our dimension scores. However, it was evident from the start that the enormous data mine of the WVS hid more treasures.

The challenge was taken up by Misho Minkov. In a courageous expedition into the WVS jungle—and adding recent data from other relevant sources—he extracted three dimensions, which he labeled *exclusionism versus universalism, indulgence versus restraint,* and *monumentalism versus flexhumility.*[29]

As a result, Misho has joined our authors' team, and we have integrated our research results.[30] From the three Minkov dimensions, exclusionism versus universalism was strongly correlated with collectivism versus individualism, and references to it will be included in Chapter 4. Monumentalism versus flexhumility correlated significantly with short- versus long-term orientation. This led to another search of the WVS database, which has produced a new measurement of the LTO dimension, enriching our understanding of its implications and drastically increasing the number of countries for which reliable scores are available. All of this will be described in Chapter 7. Indulgence versus restraint (IVR) has been added as an entirely new, sixth dimension in Chapter 8.

Cultural Differences According to Region, Ethnicity, Religion, Gender, Generation, and Class

Regional, ethnic, and religious cultures account for differences within countries; ethnic and religious groups often transcend political country borders. Such groups form minorities at the crossroads between the dominant culture of the nation and their own traditional group culture. Some assimilate into the mainstream, although this process may take a generation or more; others continue to stick to their own ways. The United States, as the world's most prominent example of a people composed of immigrants, shows examples of both assimilation (the melting pot) and retention of group identities over generations (for example, the Pennsylvania Dutch). Discrimination according to ethnic origin delays assimilation and represents a problem in many countries. Regional, ethnic, and religious cultures, in so far as they are learned from birth onward, can be described in the same terms as national cultures: basically the same dimensions that were found to differentiate among national cultures apply to these differences within countries.

Gender differences are not usually described in terms of cultures. It can be revealing to do so. If we recognize that within each society there is a men's culture that differs from a women's culture, this recognition helps to explain why it is so difficult to change traditional gender roles. Women are not considered suitable for jobs traditionally filled by men, not because they are technically unable to perform these jobs, but because women do not carry the symbols, do not correspond to the hero images, do not participate in the rituals, or are not supposed to foster the values dominant in the men's culture, and vice versa. Feelings and fears about behaviors by the opposite sex can be of the same order of intensity as reactions of people exposed to foreign cultures. The subject of gender cultures will return in Chapter 5.

Generation differences in symbols, heroes, rituals, and values are evident to most people. They are often overestimated. Complaints about youths' having lost respect for the values of their elders have been found on Egyptian papyrus scrolls dating from 2000 B.C. and in the writings of Hesiod, a Greek author from the end of the eighth century B.C. Many differences in practices and values between generations are normal attributes of age that repeat themselves for each successive pair of generations. Historical events, however, do affect some generations in a special way. The Chinese who were of student age during the 1966–76 Cultural Revolution stand witness to this. Chinese young people who in this period would normally have become students were sent to the countryside as laborers and missed their education. The Chinese speak of "the lost generation." The development of technology may also lead to a difference between generations. An example is the spread of television, which showed people life in other parts of the world previously outside their perspective.

Social classes carry different class cultures. Social class is associated with educational opportunities and with a person's occupation or profession. Education and occupation are in themselves powerful sources of cultural learning. There is no standard definition of social class that applies across all countries, and people in different countries distinguish different types and numbers of classes. The criteria for allocating a person to a class are often cultural: symbols play an important role, such as manners, accents in speaking the national language, and the use and nonuse of certain words. The confrontation between the two jurors in *Twelve Angry Men* (Chapter 1) clearly contains a class component.

Gender, generation, and class cultures can only partly be classified by the dimensions found for national cultures. This is because they are categories of people within social systems, not integrated social systems such as countries or ethnic groups. Gender, generation, and class cultures should be described in their own terms, based on special studies of such cultures.

Organizational Cultures

Organizational, or corporate, cultures have been a fashionable topic in the management literature since the early 1980s. At that time, authors began to popularize the claim that the "excellence" of an organization is contained in the common ways by which its members have learned to think, feel, and act. *Corporate culture* is a soft, holistic concept with, however, presumed hard consequences.

Organization sociologists have stressed the role of the soft factor in organizations for more than half a century. Using the label *culture* for the shared mental software of the people in an organization is a convenient way of repopularizing these sociological views. However, organizational cultures are a phenomenon by themselves, different in many respects from national cultures. An organization is a social system of a different nature from that of a nation, if only because the organization's members usually did not grow up in it. On the contrary, they had a certain influence in their decision to join it, are involved in it only during working hours, and will one day leave it.

Research results regarding national cultures and their dimensions proved to be only partly useful for the understanding of organizational cultures. The part of this book that deals with organizational culture differences (Chapter 10) is based not on the IBM studies but rather on a special research project carried out in the 1980s within twenty organizational units in Denmark and the Netherlands.

Reading Mental Programs: Suggestions for Researchers

The manner in which animals learn has been much studied in recent years, with a great deal of patient observation and experiment. Certain results have been obtained as regards the kinds of problems that have been investigated, but on general principles there is still much controversy. One may say broadly that all the animals that have been carefully observed have behaved so as to confirm the philosophy in which the observer believed before his observations began. Nay, more, they have all displayed the national characteristics of the observer. Animals studied by Americans rush about frantically, with an incredible display of hustle and pep, and at last achieve the desired result by chance. Animals observed by Germans sit still and think, and at last evolve the solution out of their inner consciousness. To the plain man, such as the present writer, this situation is discouraging. I observe, however, that the type of problem which a man naturally sets to an animal depends upon his own philosophy, and this probably accounts for the differences in the results. The animal responds to one type of problem in one way and to another in another; therefore the results obtained by different investigators, though different, are not incompatible. But it remains necessary to remember that no one investigator is to be trusted to give a survey of the whole field.

—Bertrand Russell, *Outline of Philosophy*, 1927[31]

This quote from an eminent British philosopher, written three generations ago, is a warning that results of scientific research depend on the researcher in ways that may not even be conscious to him or her. The same theme returns in a different way in the work of Thomas Kuhn, whom we quoted at the beginning of this chapter. Scientists are caught in the paradigms of their contemporaries.

Intercultural comparative studies often belong to a new normal science in the Kuhn sense. A common approach is for a master's or doctoral student to take an instrument (mostly a paper-and-pencil questionnaire) developed in one country, usually in the United States by a U.S. scholar who tested it on U.S. respondents, and to have it administered to respondents in one or more other countries. Unfortunately, such instruments cover only issues considered relevant in the society in which they were developed, and they exclude questions unrecognized by the designer because they do not occur in his or her society. Such questions are precisely the ones most interesting from a cultural point of view. The hidden ethnocentrism in this type of research leads to trivial results.

Prospective cross-cultural researchers who feel inspired by this book and who want to use parts of its approach in their own project are referred to the 2001 edition of Geert's scholarly volume *Culture's Consequences*, especially its Chapter 10. This will caution them against many pitfalls that continue to await novice and even experienced researchers.

One strong piece of advice we offer is to think twice before collecting one's own culture scores. Research is about interpreting data, not necessarily about collecting them. A search of the literature and the Internet will show that for almost any application, relevant and professionally collected databases lie waiting to be consulted, interpreted, compared, and applied. Misho's use of the World Values Survey is an example. A single researcher's attempts to measure culture are usually a waste of time, a source of confusion, and at best a reinvention of the wheel. This also applies to using the Values Survey Module[32] that evolved from the IBM research, unless one has access to at least ten countries. It is far better to familiarize yourself with the literature, select from the available databases, and apply them critically to your specific topic.

DIMENSIONS OF NATIONAL CULTURES

More Equal than Others

I n a peaceful revolution—the last revolution in Swedish history—the nobles of Sweden in 1809 deposed King Gustav IV, whom they considered incompetent, and surprisingly invited Jean Baptiste Bernadotte, a French general who served under their enemy Napoleon, to become king of Sweden. Bernadotte accepted and became King Charles XIV John; his descendants have occupied the Swedish throne to this day. When the new king was installed, he addressed the Swedish parliament in their language. His broken Swedish amused the Swedes, and they roared with laughter. The Frenchman who had become king was so upset that he never tried to speak Swedish again.

In this incident Bernadotte was a victim of culture shock: never in his French upbringing and military career had he experienced subordinates who laughed at the mistakes of their superior. Historians tell us he had more problems adapting to the egalitarian Swedish and Norwegian mentality (he later became king of Norway as well) and to his subordinates' constitutional rights. He was a good learner, however (except for language), and he ruled the country as a highly respected constitutional monarch until 1844.

Inequality in Society

One of the aspects in which Sweden differs from France is the way society handles *inequality*. There is inequality in any society. Even in the simplest hunter-gatherer band, some people are bigger, stronger, or smarter than others. Further, some people have more power than others: they are more able to determine the behavior of others than vice versa. Some people acquire more wealth than others. Some people are given more status and respect than others.

Physical and intellectual capacities, power, wealth, and status may or may not go together. Successful athletes, artists, and scientists usually enjoy status, but only in some societies do they enjoy wealth as well, and rarely do they have political power. Politicians in some countries can enjoy status and power without wealth; businesspeople can have wealth and power without status. Such inconsistencies among the various areas of inequality are often felt to be problematic. In some societies people try to resolve them by making the areas more consistent. Athletes turn professional to become wealthy; politicians exploit their power and/or move on to attractive business positions in order to do the same; successful businesspeople enter public office in order to acquire status. This trend obviously increases the overall inequalities in these societies.

In other societies the dominant feeling is that it is a good thing, rather than a problem, if a person's rank in one area does not match his or her rank in another. A high rank in one area should partly be offset by a low rank in another. This process increases the size of the middle class in between those who are on top in all respects and those who lack any kind of opportunity. The laws in many countries have been conceived to serve this ideal of equality by treating everybody as equal regardless of status, wealth, or power, but there are few societies in which reality matches the ideal. The praise of poverty in the Christian Bible can be seen as a manifestation of a desire for equality; the same is true for Karl Marx's plea for a "dictatorship of the proletariat."

Measuring the Degree of Inequality in Society: The Power Distance Index

Not only Sweden and France but other nations as well can be distinguished by the way they tend to deal with inequalities. The research among IBM employees in similar positions but in different countries has allowed us to assign to each of these countries a score indicating its level of *power distance*. Power distance is one of the *dimensions* of national cultures introduced in Chapter 2. It reflects the range of answers found in the various countries to the basic question of how to handle the fact that people are unequal. It derives its name from research by a Dutch experimental social psychologist, Mauk Mulder, into the emotional distance that separates subordinates from their bosses.[1]

Scores on power distance for fifty countries and three multicountry regions have been calculated from the answers by IBM employees in the same kind of positions on the same survey questions. All questions were of the precoded-answer type so that answers could be represented by a score number. usually 1, 2, 3, 4, or 5. Standard samples composed of respondents from the same mix of jobs were taken from each country. A mean score was computed for each sample (say, 2.53 as the mean score for country X and 3.43 for country Y), or the percentage of people choosing particular answers was computed (say, 45 percent of the sample choosing answer 1 or 2 in country X and 33 percent in country Y) From that data, a table was composed presenting mean scores or percentages for each question and for all countries.

A statistical procedure (*factor analysis*) was used to sort the survey questions into groups, called *factors* or *clusters*, for which the mean scores or percentages varied together.[2] This meant that if a country scored high on one of the questions from the cluster, it also could be expected to score high on the others; likewise, it could be expected to score not high but *low* for questions carrying the opposite meaning. If, on the other hand, a country scored low on one question from the cluster, it also would most likely score low on the others and score *high* on questions formulated the other way around. If a country scored average on one question from the cluster, it probably would score average on all of them.

One of the clusters found was composed of questions that all seemed to have something to do with power and (in)equality. From the questions in this cluster, we selected the three that were most strongly related.[3] From the mean scores of the standard sample of IBM employees in a country on these three questions, a *power distance index* (PDI) for the country was calculated. The formula developed for this purpose uses simple mathematics (adding or subtracting the three scores after multiplying each by a fixed number, and finally adding another fixed number). The purpose of the formula was (1) to ensure that each of the three questions would carry equal weight in arriving at the final index and (2) to get index values ranging from about 0 for a small-power-distance country to about 100 for a large-power-distance country. Two countries that were added later score above 100.

The three survey items used for composing the power distance index were as follows:

1. Answers by nonmanagerial employees to the question "How frequently, in your experience, does the following problem occur: employees being afraid to express disagreement with their managers?" (mean score on a 1–5 scale from "very frequently" to "very seldom")

2. Subordinates' *perception* of the boss's actual decision-making style (percentage choosing the description of either an autocratic style or a paternalistic style, out of four possible styles plus a "none of these" alternative)[4]

3. Subordinates' *preference* for their boss's decision-making style (percentage preferring an autocratic or a paternalistic style, or, on the contrary, a style based on majority vote, but *not* a consultative style)

Country PDI scores are shown in Table 3.1. For fifty-seven of the countries or regions (see Table 2.2) the scores were calculated directly from the IBM data set. The remaining cases were calculated from replications or based on informed estimates.[5] Because of the way the scores were calculated, they represent *relative*, not absolute, positions of countries: they are measures of differences only. The scores that were based on answers by IBM employees paradoxically contain no information about the corporate culture of IBM: they show only to what extent people from the subsidiary in country X answered the same questions differently from similar people in country Y. The conclusion that the score differences reflect different national cultures is confirmed by the fact that we found the same differences in populations outside IBM (the validation process as described in Chapter 2).

TABLE 3.1 Power Distance Index (PDI) Values for 76 Countries and Regions Based on Three Items in the IBM Database Plus Extensions

RANK	AMERICA C/S	EUROPE S/SE	EUROPE N/NW ANGLO WORLD	EUROPE C/E EX-SOVIET	MUSLIM WORLD M.E & AFRICA	ASIA EAST ASIA SE	INDEX
1–2						Malaysia	104
1–2				Slovakia			104
3–4	Guatemala						95
3–4	Panama						95
5						Philippines	94
6				Russia			93
7				Romania			90
8				Serbia			86
9	Suriname						85
10–11	Mexico						81
10–11	Venezuela						81
12–14					Arab ctrs		80
12–14						Bangladesh	80
12–14						China	80
15–16	Ecuador						78
15–16						Indonesia	78
17–18					Africa W		77
17–18						India	77
19						Singapore	74
20				Croatia			73
21				Slovenia			71
22–25				Bulgaria			70
22–25					Morocco		70
22–25			Switzerland Fr				70

continued

TABLE 3.1 Power Distance Index (PDI) Values for 76 Countries and Regions Based on Three Items in the IBM Database Plus Extensions, *continued*

RANK	AMERICA C/S	EUROPE S/SE	EUROPE N/NW ANGLO WORLD	EUROPE C/E EX-SOVIET	MUSLIM WORLD M.E & AFRICA	ASIA EAST ASIA SE	INDEX
22–25						Vietnam	70
26	Brazil						69
27–29		France					68
27–29						Hong Kong	68
27–29				Poland			68
30–31			Belgium Fr				67
30–31	Colombia						66
32–33	El Salvador						66
32–33		Turkey					66
34–36	Peru						64
34–36					Africa E		64
34–36						Thailand	64
37–38	Chile						63
37–38		Portugal					63
39–40			Belgium Nl				61
39–40	Uruguay						61
41–42		Greece					60
41–42						S Korea	60
43–44					Iran		58
43–44						Taiwan	58
45–46				Czech Rep.			57
45–46		Spain					57
47		Malta					56
48					Pakistan		55
49–50			Canada Quebec				54

Rank	Country	Value
49–50	Japan	54
51	Italy	50
52–53	Argentina	49
52–53	Trinidad	49
54	S Africa (wte)	47
55	Jamaica	46
56	Hungary	45
57	Latvia	44
58	Lithuania	42
59–61	Estonia	40
59–61	Luxembourg	40
59–61	United States	40
62	Canada total	39
63	Netherlands	38
64	Australia	38
65–67	Costa Rica	35
65–67	Germany	35
65–67	Great Britain	35
68	Finland	33
69–70	Norway	31
69–70	Sweden	31
71	Ireland	28
72	Switzerland Ge	26
73	New Zealand	22
74	Denmark	18
75	Austria	13
76	Israel	11

For the multilingual countries Belgium and Switzerland, Table 3.1 gives the scores by the two largest language areas. For Canada there is an IBM score for the whole country and a replication-based score for the French-speaking part. The IBM sample for what was once Yugoslavia has been split into Croatia, Serbia, and Slovenia. The other countries in Table 3.1 all have a single score. This does not mean that they are necessarily culturally homogeneous; it means only that the available data did not allow a splitting up into subcultures.

Table 3.1 shows high power distance values for most Asian countries (such as Malaysia and the Philippines), for Eastern European countries (such as Slovakia and Russia), for Latin countries (Latin America, such as Panama and Mexico, and to a somewhat lesser extent Latin Europe, such as France and Wallonia, the French-speaking part of Belgium), for Arabic-speaking countries, and for African countries. The table shows low values for German-speaking countries, such as Austria, the German-speaking part of Switzerland, and Germany; for Israel; for the Nordic countries (Denmark, Finland, Norway, and Sweden) and the Baltic States (Estonia, Latvia, and Lithuania); for the United States; for Great Britain and the white parts of its former empire (New Zealand, Ireland, Australia, Canada); and for the Netherlands (but not for Flanders, the Dutch-speaking part of Belgium, which scored quite similar to Wallonia). Sweden scored 31 and France 68. If such a difference existed already two hundred years ago—for which, as will be argued, there is a good case—this explains Bernadotte's culture shock.

Power Distance Defined

Looking at the three questions used to compose the PDI, you may notice something surprising: questions 1 (employees afraid) and 2 (boss autocratic or paternalistic) indicate the way the respondents perceive their daily work environment. Question 3, however, indicates what the respondents express as their *preference*: how they would like their work environment to be.

The fact that the three questions are part of the same cluster shows that from one country to another there is a close relationship between the reality one perceives and the reality one desires.[6] In countries in which employees are not seen as very afraid and bosses as not often autocratic or paternalistic, employees express a preference for a *consultative* style of decision making: a boss who, as the questionnaire expressed, "usually consults with subordinates before reaching a decision."

In countries on the opposite side of the power distance scale, where employees are seen as frequently afraid of disagreeing with their bosses and where bosses are seen as autocratic or paternalistic, employees in similar jobs are less likely to prefer a consultative boss. Instead, many among them express a preference for a boss who decides autocratically or paternalistically; however, some switch to the other extreme—that is, preferring a boss who governs by majority vote, which means that he or she does not actually make the decision at all. In the real-world practices of most organizations, majority vote is difficult to handle, and few people actually perceived their bosses as using this style (bosses who pretend to do so are often accused of manipulation).

In summary, PDI scores inform us about *dependence* relationships in a country. In small-power-distance countries, there is limited dependence of subordinates on bosses, and there is a preference for consultation (that is, *interdependence* among boss and subordinate). The emotional distance between them is relatively small: subordinates will rather easily approach and contradict their bosses. In large-power-distance countries, there is considerable dependence of subordinates on bosses. Subordinates respond by either *preferring* such dependence (in the form of an autocratic or paternalistic boss) or rejecting it entirely, which in psychology is known as *counterdependence*—that is, dependence but with a negative sign. Large-power-distance countries thus show a pattern of polarization between dependence and counterdependence. In these cases the emotional distance between subordinates and their bosses is large: subordinates are unlikely to approach and contradict their bosses directly.

Power distance can therefore be defined as *the extent to which the less powerful members of institutions and organizations within a country expect and accept that power is distributed unequally. Institutions* are the basic elements of society, such as the family, the school, and the community; *organizations* are the places where people work.

Power distance is thus described based on the value system of the *less* powerful members. The way power is distributed is usually explained from the behavior of the *more* powerful members, the leaders rather than those led. The popular management literature on leadership often forgets that leadership can exist only as a complement to "subordinateship." Authority survives only where it is matched by obedience. Bernadotte's problem was not a lack of leadership on his side; rather, the Swedes had a different conception of the deference due to a ruler from that of the French—and Bernadotte was a Frenchman.

Comparative research projects studying leadership values from one country to another show that the differences observed exist in the minds of both the leaders *and* those led, but often the statements obtained from those who are led are a better reflection of the differences than those obtained from the leaders. This is because we are all better observers of the leadership behavior of our bosses than we are of ourselves. Besides the questions on perceived and preferred leadership style of the boss—questions 2 and 3 in the PDI—the IBM surveys also asked managers to rate their *own* style. It appeared that self-ratings by managers resembled closely the styles these managers preferred in their own bosses—but not at all the styles their subordinates perceived them to have. In fact, the subordinates saw their managers in just about the same way as the managers saw *their* bosses. The moral for managers is: if you want to know how your subordinates see you, don't try to look in the mirror—that just produces wishful thinking. Turn around 180 degrees and face your own boss.[7]

Power Distance in Replication Studies

In Chapter 2, Table 2.1, six studies were listed, published between 1990 and 2002, that used the IBM questions or later versions of them with other cross-national populations. Five of these, covering between fourteen and twenty-eight countries from the IBM set, produced PDI scores highly significantly correlated with the original IBM scores.[8] The sixth got its data from consumers who were not selected on the basis of their relationships to power, who were in very different jobs, or, as in the case of students and housewives, who did not have paid jobs at all. We investigated whether the new scores would justify correcting some of the original IBM scores, and we concluded that the new scores were not consistent enough for this purpose.[9] None of the new populations covered as many countries or represented such well-matched samples as the original IBM set. Also, correlations of the original IBM scores with other data, such as consumer purchases, have not become weaker over time.[10] One should remember that the scores measured *differences between* country cultures, not cultures in an absolute sense. The cultures may have shifted, but as long as they shifted together under the influence of the same global forces, the scores remain valid.

Bond's Chinese Value Survey study among students in twenty-three countries, described in Chapter 2, produced a *moral discipline* dimension on which the countries positioned themselves largely in the same way as they had done in the IBM studies on power distance (in statistical terms, moral discipline was significantly correlated with PDI).[11] Students in countries scoring high on power distance answered that the following were particularly important:

- Having few desires
- Moderation, following the middle way
- Keeping oneself disinterested and pure

In unequal societies, ordinary people such as students felt they should not have aspirations beyond their rank.

Students in countries scoring low on power distance, on the other hand, answered that the following were particularly important:

- Adaptability
- Prudence (carefulness)

In more egalitarian societies, where problems cannot be resolved by someone's show of power, students stressed the importance of being flexible in order to get somewhere.

The GLOBE study, also described in Chapter 2, included items intended to measure a *power distance* dimension. As we argued, GLOBE's questions were formulated very differently from ours. Rather than the respondents' daily terminology, they used researchers' jargon, making it often difficult for the respondents to guess what the answers meant. From GLOBE's eighteen dimensions (nine asking respondents to describe their culture "as it is" and nine "as it should be"), no fewer than nine were significantly correlated with our PDI. The strongest correlation of PDI was with the GLOBE dimension *in-group collectivism* "as is." There was only a weakly significant correlation between PDI and GLOBE's *power distance* "as is," and there was none at all between PDI and GLOBE's *power distance* "should be."[12] In fact, GLOBE's *power distance* "as is" and "should be" both correlated more strongly with our uncertainty avoidance index (Chapter 6).[13] GLOBE's *power distance* presents no alternative for our PDI.

Power Distance Differences Within Countries: Social Class, Education Level, and Occupation

Inequality within a society is visible in the existence of different social classes: upper, middle, and lower, or however one wants to divide them—this varies by country. Classes differ in their access to and their opportunities for benefiting from the advantages of society, one of them being education. A higher education automatically makes one at least middle class. Education, in turn, is one of the main determinants of the occupations to which one can aspire, so that in practice in most societies, social class, education level, and occupation are closely linked. In Chapter 1 all three have been listed as sources of our mental software: there are class, education, and occupation levels in our culture, but they are mutually dependent.

The data used for the computation of the PDI in IBM were from employees in various occupations and, therefore, from different education levels and social classes. However, the mix of occupations studied was kept constant for all countries. Comparisons of countries or regions should always be based on people in the same set of occupations. One should not compare Spanish engineers with Swedish secretaries. The mix of occupations to be compared across all the subsidiaries was taken from the sales and service offices: these were the only activities that could be found in all countries. IBM's product development laboratories were located in only ten of the larger subsidiaries, and its manufacturing plants in thirteen.

The IBM sales and service people had all completed secondary or higher education and could be considered largely middle class. The same applies to the people in the replication studies. The PDI scores in Table 3.1, therefore, are really expressing differences among middle-class persons in these countries. Middle-class values affect the institutions of a country, such as governments and education systems, more than do lower-class values. This is because the people who control the institutions usually belong to the middle class. Even representatives of lower-class groups, such as union leaders, tend to be better educated or self-educated, and by this fact alone they have adopted some middle-class values. Lower-class parents often have middle-class ambitions for their children.

For three large countries (France, Germany, and Great Britain) in which the IBM subsidiaries contained the fullest possible range of industrial activities, PDI scores were computed for all the different occupations in the corporation, including those demanding only a lower level of education and therefore usually taken by lower- or "working"-class persons.[14] Altogether, thirty-eight different occupations within these three countries could be compared.

The three questions used for calculating the PDI across countries were also correlated across occupations; it was therefore possible to compute occupational PDI values as well.[15]

The result of the comparison across thirty-eight occupations is summarized in Table 3.2. It demonstrates that the occupations with the lowest status and education level (unskilled and semiskilled workers) showed the highest PDI values, and those with the highest status and education level (managers of professional workers, such as engineers and scientists) produced the lowest PDI values. Between the extremes in terms of occupation, the range of PDI scores was about 100 score points—which is of the same order of magnitude as across seventy-six countries and regions (see Table 3.1; but the country differences were based on samples of people with equal jobs and equal levels of education!).

TABLE 3.2 PDI Values for Six Categories of Occupations (Based on IBM Data from Great Britain, France, and Germany)

		PDI RANGE		
CATEGORY OF OCCUPATIONS	NUMBER OF OCCUPATIONS IN THIS CATEGORY	FROM	TO	MEAN
Unskilled and semiskilled workers	3	85	97	90
Clerical workers and nonprofessional salespeople	8	57	84	71
Skilled workers and technicians	6	33	90	65
Managers of the previous categories	8	22	62	42
Professional workers	8	−22[1]	36	22
Managers of professional workers	5	−19[1]	21	8
Total	38	−22[1]	97	47

1 Negative values exceed the 0 to 100 range established for countries.

The next question is whether the differences in power distance between occupations were equally strong within all countries. In order to test this, a comparison was done of four occupations of widely different status, from each of eleven country subsidiaries of widely different power distance levels. It turned out that the occupation differences were largest in the countries with the lowest PDI scores and were relatively small in the countries with high PDI scores.[16] In other words, if the country as a whole scored larger power distance in Table 3.1, this applied to all employees, those in high-status occupations as well as those in low-status occupations. If the country scored smaller power distance, this applied most to the employees of middle or higher status: the lower-status, lower-educated employees produced power distance scores nearly as high as their colleagues in the large-PDI countries. The values of high-status employees with regard to inequality seem to depend strongly on nationality; those of low-status employees much less.[17]

The fact that less-educated, low-status employees in various Western countries hold more "authoritarian" values than their higher-status compatriots had already been described by sociologists. These authoritarian values not only are manifested at work but also are found in their home situations. A study in the United States and Italy in the 1960s showed that working-class parents demanded more obedience from their children than middle-class parents but that the difference was larger in the United States than in Italy.[18]

Measures Associated with Power Distance: The Structure in This and Following Chapters

In the next part of this chapter, the differences in power distance scores for countries will be associated with differences in family, school, workplace, state, and ideas prevailing within the countries. Chapters 4 through 8, which deal with the other dimensions, will also be mostly structured in this way. Most of the associations described are based on the results of statistical analyses, in which the country scores have been correlated with the results of other quantitative studies, in the way described in Chapter 2. In addition, use has been made of qualitative information about families, schools, workplaces, and so on, in various countries. In this book the statistical proof will be omitted; interested readers are referred to *Culture's Consequences.*

Power Distance Difference Among Countries: Roots in the Family

Most people in the world are born into a family. All people started acquiring their mental software immediately after birth, from the elders in whose presence they grew up, modeling themselves after the examples set by these elders.

In the large-power-distance situation, children are expected to be obedient toward their parents. Sometimes there is even an order of authority among the children themselves, with younger children being expected to yield to older children. Independent behavior on the part of a child is not encouraged. *Respect* for parents and other elders is considered a basic virtue; children see others showing such respect and soon acquire it themselves. There is often considerable warmth and care in the way parents and older children treat younger ones, especially those who are very young. They are looked after and are not expected to experiment for themselves. Respect for parents and older relatives lasts through adulthood: parental authority continues to play a role in a person's life as long as the parents are alive. Parents and grandparents are treated with formal deference even after their children have actually taken control of their own lives. There is a pattern of dependence on seniors that pervades all human contacts, and the mental software that people carry contains a strong need for such dependence. When parents reach old age or if they become otherwise infirm, children are expected to support them financially and practically; grandparents often live with their children's families.

In the small-power-distance situation, children are more or less treated as equals as soon as they are able to act, and this may already be visible in the way a baby is handled in its bath.[19] The goal of parental education is to let children take control of their own affairs as soon as they can. Active experimentation by the child is encouraged; being allowed to contradict their parents, children learn to say "no" very early. Behavior toward others is not dependent on the other's age or status; formal respect and deference are seldom shown. Family relations in such societies often strike people from other societies as lacking intensity. When children grow up, they start relating to their parents as friends, or at least as equals, and a grown-up person is not apt to ask his or her parents' permission or even advice regarding an important decision. In the ideal family, adult members are mutually independent. A need for *independence* is supposed to be a major component of the mental software of adults. Parents should make their own provisions for when they become old or infirm; they cannot count on their children to support them, nor can they expect to live with them.

The pictures in the two preceding paragraphs have deliberately been polarized. Reality in a given situation will most likely be in between the opposite ends of the power distance continuum: countries score somewhere along the continuum. We saw that the social class and education levels of the parents, especially in the small-power-distance countries, play an important role. Families develop their own family cultures that may be at variance with the norms of their society, and the personalities of individual parents and children can lead to nontypical behavior. Nevertheless, the two pictures indicate the ends of the line along which solutions to the human inequality dilemma in the family vary.

The Eurobarometer, a periodic survey of representative samples of the population in member countries and candidate member countries of the European Union, collected data in 2008 on the sharing of full-time and part-time work between parents in a family. In countries with larger power distances, more often both parents worked full-time; in countries with smaller power distances, more often only one of the parents worked full-time, while the other worked as well but part-time. Except in the poorest countries, these differences were independent of the countries' national wealth. They imply a closer contact between parent and children in smaller-power-distance cultures.[20]

As the family is the source of our very first social mental programming, its impact is extremely strong, and programs set at this stage are difficult to change. Psychiatrists and psychoanalysts are aware of this importance of one's family history but not always of its cultural context. Psychiatry tries to help individuals whose behavior deviates from societal norms. This book describes how the norms themselves vary from one society to another. Different norms mean that psychiatric help to a person from another society or even from a different sector of the same society is a risky affair. It demands that the helper be aware of his or her own cultural differences with and biases toward the client.[21]

Power Distance at School

In most societies today, children go to school for at least some years. In the more affluent societies, the school period may cover more than twenty years of a young person's life. In school the child further develops his or her mental programming. Teachers and classmates inculcate additional values, being part of a culture that honors these values. It is an unanswered question as to what extent an education system can contribute to changing a society. Can a school create values that were not yet there, or will it unwittingly only be able to reinforce what already exists in a given society? In a comparison of schools across societies, the same patterns of differences that were found within families resurge. The role pair parent-child is replaced by the role pair teacher-student, but basic values and behaviors are carried forward from one sphere into the other. And of course, most schoolchildren continue to spend most of their time within their families.

In the large-power-distance situation, the parent-child inequality is perpetuated by a teacher-student inequality that caters to the need for dependence well established in the student's mind. Teachers are treated with respect or even fear (and older teachers even more so than younger ones); students may have to stand when they enter. The educational process is teacher centered; teachers outline the intellectual paths to be followed. In the classroom there is supposed to be a strict order, with the teacher initiating all communication. Students in class speak up only when invited to; teachers are never publicly contradicted or criticized and are treated with deference even outside school. When a child misbehaves, teachers involve the parents and expect them to help set the child straight. The educational process is highly personalized: especially in more advanced subjects at universities, what is transferred is seen not as an impersonal "truth," but as the personal wisdom of the teacher. The teacher is a *guru*, a term derived from the Sanskrit word for "weighty" or "honorable," and in India and Indonesia this is, in fact, what a teacher is called. The French term is a *maître à penser*, a "teacher for thinking." In such a system the quality of one's learning is highly dependent on the excellence of one's teachers.

In the small-power-distance situation, teachers are supposed to treat the students as basic equals and expect to be treated as equals by the students. Younger teachers are more equal and are therefore usually more liked than older ones. The educational process is student centered, with a premium on student initiative; students are expected to find their own intellectual paths. Students make uninvited interventions in class; they are supposed to ask questions when they do not understand something. They argue with teachers, express disagreement and criticisms in front of the teachers, and show no particular respect to teachers outside school. When a child misbehaves, parents often side with the child against the teacher. The educational process is rather impersonal; what is transferred are "truths" or "facts" that exist independently of this particular teacher. Effective learning in such a system depends very much on whether the supposed two-way communication between students and teacher is, indeed, established. The entire system is based on the students' well-developed need for independence; the quality of learning is to a considerable extent determined by the excellence of the students.

Earlier in this chapter it was shown that power distance scores are lower for occupations needing a higher education, at least in countries that as a whole score relatively low on power distance. This means that in these countries, students will become more independent from teachers as they proceed in their studies: their need for dependence decreases. In large-power-distance countries, however, students remain dependent on teachers even after reaching high education levels.

Small-power-distance countries spend a relatively larger part of their education budget on secondary schools for everybody, contributing to the development of middle strata in society. Large-power-distance countries spend relatively more on university-level education and less on secondary schools, maintaining a polarization between the elites and the uneducated.

Corporal punishment at school, at least for children of prepuberty age, is more acceptable in a large-power-distance culture than in its opposite. It accentuates and symbolizes the inequality between teacher and student and is often considered good for the development of the child's character. In a small-power-distance society, it will readily be classified as child abuse and may be a reason for parents to complain to the police. There are exceptions, which relate to the dimension of masculinity (versus femininity) to be described in Chapter 5: in some masculine, small-power-distance cultures, such as Great Britain, corporal punishment at school is not considered objectionable by everybody.

As in the case of the family as discussed in the previous section, reality is somewhere in between these extremes. An important conditioning factor is the ability of the students: less gifted children and children with disabilities in small-power-distance situations will not develop the culturally expected sense of independence and will be handled more in the large-power-distance way. Able children from working-class families in small-power-distance societies are at a disadvantage in educational institutions such as universities that assume a small-power-distance norm: as shown in the previous section, working-class families often have a large-power-distance subculture.

Power Distance and Health Care

Comparative studies of the functioning of health-care systems in European Union member countries have shown that, not surprisingly, the level of power distance in a society is also reflected in the relationship between doctors and patients. In countries with larger-power-distance cultures, consultations take less time, and there is less room for unexpected information exchanges.[22]

These differences also affect the use of medication. In countries with large-power-distance cultures, doctors more frequently prescribe antibiotics, which are seen as a quick general solution; in these countries antibiotics are also more frequently used in self-medication.[23] These findings are important in view of the danger of germs' becoming resistant to antibiotics if these treatments are used too frequently.

Another study compared blood transfusion practice across twenty-five European countries. Blood transfusion tends to be a within-nation process; there is little international trade in blood products. Countries with smaller-power-distance cultures have more blood donors, more blood collections, and more blood supplied to hospitals; in the latter two cases also, the average education level of the population plays a role. The differences are considerable: among the countries studied, the number of donors per thousand inhabitants in 2004 ranged from two to fifty-one. In all cases blood donation was an unpaid, voluntary act. Its negative correlation with PDI shows that such an act was much more likely in cultures in which people depend less on the authority of more powerful persons and are better educated. National wealth had no influence whatsoever.[24]

Table 3.3 summarizes the key differences between small- and large-power-distance societies discussed so far.

TABLE 3.3 Key Differences Between Small- and
Large-Power-Distance Societies
I: General Norm, Family, School, and Health Care

SMALL POWER DISTANCE	LARGE POWER DISTANCE
Inequalities among people should be minimized.	Inequalities among people are expected and desired.
Social relationships should be handled with care.	Status should be balanced with restraint.
Less powerful people and more powerful people should be interdependent.	Less powerful people should be dependent.
Less powerful people are emotionally comfortable with interdependence.	Less powerful people are emotionally polarized between dependence and counterdependence.
Parents treat children as equals.	Parents teach children obedience.
Children treat parents and older relatives as equals.	Respect for parents and older relatives is a basic and lifelong virtue.
Children play no role in old-age security of parents.	Children are a source of old-age security to parents.
Students treat teachers as equals.	Students give teachers respect, even outside class.
Teachers expect initiatives from students in class.	Teachers should take all initiatives in class.
Teachers are experts who transfer impersonal truths.	Teachers are gurus who transfer personal wisdom.
Quality of learning depends on two-way communication and excellence of students.	Quality of learning depends on excellence of the teacher.
Less educated persons hold more authoritarian values than more educated persons.	More educated and less educated persons show equally authoritarian values.
Educational policy focuses on secondary schools.	Educational policy focuses on universities.
Patients treat doctors as equals and actively supply information.	Patients treat doctors as superiors; consultations are shorter and controlled by the doctor.

Power Distance in the Workplace

Most people start their working lives as young adults, after having gone through learning experiences in the family and at school. The role pairs parent-child, teacher-student, and doctor-patient are now complemented by the role pair boss-subordinate, and it should not surprise anybody when attitudes toward parents, especially fathers, and toward teachers, which are part of our mental programming, are transferred toward bosses.

In the large-power-distance situation, superiors and subordinates consider each other as existentially unequal; the hierarchical system is based on this existential inequality. Organizations centralize power as much as possible in a few hands. Subordinates expect to be told what to do. There is a large number of supervisory personnel, structured into tall hierarchies of people reporting to each other. Salary systems show wide gaps between top and bottom in the organization. Workers are relatively uneducated, and manual work has a much lower status than office work. Superiors are entitled to privileges (literally "private laws"), and contacts between superiors and subordinates are supposed to be initiated by the superiors only. The ideal boss in the subordinates' eyes, the one they feel most comfortable with and whom they respect most, is a benevolent autocrat or "good father." After some experiences with "bad fathers," they may ideologically reject the boss's authority completely, while complying in practice.

Relationships between subordinates and superiors in a large-power-distance organization are frequently loaded with emotions. Philippe d'Iribarne headed up a French public research center on international management. Through extensive interviews his research team compared manufacturing plants of the same French multinational in France (PDI 68), the United States (PDI 40), and the Netherlands (PDI 38). In his book on this project, d'Iribarne comments:

> *The often strongly emotional character of hierarchical relationships in France is intriguing. There is an extreme diversity of feelings towards superiors: they may be either adored or despised with equal intensity. This situation is not at all universal: we found it neither in the Netherlands nor in the United States.*[25]

This quote confirms the polarization in France between dependence and counterdependence versus authority figures, which we found to be characteristic of large-power-distance countries in general.

Visible signs of status in large-power-distance countries contribute to the authority of bosses; a subordinate may well feel proud if he can tell his neighbor that *his* boss drives a bigger car than the neighbor's boss. Older superiors are generally more respected than younger ones. Being a victim of power abuse by one's boss is just bad luck; there is no assumption that there should be ways of redress in such a situation. If it gets too bad, people may join forces for a violent revolt. Packaged leadership methods invented in the United States, such as management by objectives (MBO),[26] will not work, because they presuppose some form of negotiation between subordinate and superior, with which neither party will feel comfortable.

In the small-power-distance situation, subordinates and superiors consider each other as existentially equal; the hierarchical system is just an inequality of roles, established for convenience, and roles may be changed, so that someone who today is my subordinate may tomorrow be my boss. Organizations are fairly decentralized, with flat hierarchical pyramids and limited numbers of supervisory personnel. Salary ranges between top and bottom jobs are relatively small; workers are highly qualified, and high-skill manual work has a higher status than low-skill office work. According privileges to higher-ups is basically undesirable, and everyone should use the same parking lot, restrooms, and cafeteria. Superiors should be accessible to subordinates, and the ideal boss is a resourceful (and therefore respected) democrat. Subordinates expect to be consulted before a decision is made that affects their work, but they accept that the boss is the one who finally decides.

Status symbols are suspect, and subordinates will most likely comment negatively to their neighbors if their boss spends company money on an expensive car. Younger bosses are generally more appreciated than older ones. Organizations are supposed to have structured ways of dealing with employee complaints about alleged power abuse. Some packaged leadership methods, such as MBO, may work if given sufficient management attention.

Peter Smith, of the University of Sussex in the UK, through a network of colleagues, in the 1990s collected statements from more than seven thousand department managers in forty-seven countries on how they handled each of eight common work "events" (for example: "when some of the equipment or machinery in your department seems to need replacement"). For each event, eight possible sources of guidance were listed, for which the managers had to indicate to what extent they relied on each of these (for example: "formal rules and procedures"). For each of the forty-seven countries, Smith computed a *verticality index*, combining reliance on one's superior and on formal rules, *not* on one's own experience and *not* on one's subordinates. Verticality index scores were strongly correlated with PDI: in large-power-distance countries, the managers in the sample reported relying more on their superiors and on formal rules and less on their own experience and on their subordinates.[27]

There is no research evidence of a systematic difference in effectiveness between organizations in large-power-distance versus small-power-distance countries. They may be good at different tasks: small-power-distance cultures at tasks demanding subordinate initiative, large-power-distance cultures at tasks demanding discipline. The important thing is for management to utilize the strengths of the local culture.

This section has again described the extremes, and most work situations will be in between and contain some elements of both large and small power distance. Management theories have rarely recognized that these different models exist and that their occurrence is culturally determined. Chapter 9 will return to this issue and show how different theories of management and organization reflect the different nationalities of their authors.

Table 3.4 summarizes key differences in the workplace between small- and large-power-distance societies.

Power Distance and the State

The previous sections have looked at the implications of power distance differences among countries for the role pairs of parent-child, teacher-student, doctor-patient, and boss-subordinate; one that is obviously equally affected is authority-citizen. It must be immediately evident to anyone who follows any world news at all that in some countries power differences between authorities and citizens are not handled the same way they are in other countries. What is not so evident, but is essential for understanding,

TABLE 3.4 Key Differences Between Small- and Large-Power-Distance Societies
II: The Workplace

SMALL POWER DISTANCE	LARGE POWER DISTANCE
Hierarchy in organizations means an inequality of roles, established for convenience.	Hierarchy in organizations reflects existential inequality between higher and lower levels.
Decentralization is popular.	Centralization is popular.
There are fewer supervisory personnel.	There are more supervisory personnel.
There is a narrow salary range between the top and the bottom of the organization.	There is a wide salary range between the top and the bottom of the organization.
Managers rely on their own experience and on subordinates.	Managers rely on superiors and on formal rules.
Subordinates expect to be consulted.	Subordinates expect to be told what to do.
The ideal boss is a resourceful democrat.	The ideal boss is a benevolent autocrat, or "good father."
Subordinate-superior relations are pragmatic.	Subordinate-superior relations are emotional.
Privileges and status symbols are frowned upon.	Privileges and status symbols are normal and popular.
Manual work has the same status as office work.	White-collar jobs are valued more than blue-collar jobs.

is that ways of handling power in a country tend to be rooted in the beliefs of large sectors of the population as to the proper ways for authorities to behave.

In an analysis of data from forty-three societies, collected through the World Values Survey (see Chapter 2), U.S. political scientist Ronald Inglehart found that he could order countries on a "secular-rational versus traditional authority" dimension. Correlation analysis showed that this dimension corresponds closely to what we call power distance.[28] In a society in which power distances are large, authority tends to be traditional, sometimes even rooted in religion. Power is seen as a basic fact of society that precedes the choice between good and evil. Its legitimacy is irrelevant. Might prevails over right. This is a strong statement that may rarely be presented in this form but is reflected in the behavior of those in power *and* of ordinary people. There is an unspoken consensus that there should be an order of inequality in this world, in which everybody has his or her place. Such an order satisfies people's need for dependence, and it gives a sense of security both to those in power and to those lower down.

At the beginning of this chapter, reference was made to the tendency in some societies to achieve consistency in people's positions with regard to power, wealth, and status. A desire for status consistency is typical for large-power-distance cultures. In such cultures the people who hold power are entitled to privileges and are expected to use their power to increase their wealth. Their status is enhanced by symbolic behavior that makes them look as powerful as possible. The main sources of power are one's family and friends, charisma, and/or the ability to use force; the latter explains the frequency of military dictatorships in countries on this side of the power distance scale. Scandals involving persons in power are expected, and so is the fact that these scandals will be covered up. If something goes wrong, the blame goes to people lower down the hierarchy. If it gets too bad, the way to change the system is by replacing those in power through a revolution. Most such revolutions fail even if they succeed, because the newly powerful people, after some time, repeat the behaviors of their predecessors, in which they are supported by the prevailing values regarding inequality.

In large-power-distance countries, people read relatively few newspapers (but they express confidence in those they read), and they rarely discuss politics: political disagreements soon deteriorate into violence. The system often admits only one political party; where more parties are allowed, the same party usually always wins. The political spectrum, if it is allowed to be visible, is characterized by strong right and left wings with a weak center, a political reflection of the polarization between dependence and counterdependence described earlier. Incomes in these countries are very unequally distributed, with a few very rich people and many very poor people. Moreover, taxation protects the wealthy, so that incomes after taxes can be even more unequal than before taxes. Labor unions tend to be government controlled; where they are not, they are ideologically based and involved in politics.

Authority in small-power-distance societies was qualified by Inglehart as secular-rational: being based on practical considerations rather than on tradition. In these societies the feeling dominates that politics and religion should be separated. The use of power should be subject to laws and to the judgment between good and evil. Inequality is considered basically undesirable; although unavoidable, it should be minimized by political means. The law should guarantee that everybody, regardless of status, has equal rights. Power, wealth, and status need not go together—it is even considered a good thing if they do not. Status symbols for powerful people are suspect, and leaders may enhance their informal status by renouncing formal symbols (for example, taking the streetcar to work). Most countries in this category are relatively wealthy, with a large middle class. The main sources of power are one's formal position, one's assumed expertise, and one's ability to give rewards. Scandals usually mean the end of a political career. Revolutions are unpopular; the system is changed in evolutionary ways, without necessarily deposing those in power. Newspapers are read a lot, although confidence in them is not high. Political issues are often discussed, and violence in domestic politics is rare. Countries with small-power-distance value systems usually have pluralist governments that can shift peacefully from one party or coalition to another on the basis of election results. The political spectrum in such countries shows a powerful center and weaker right and left wings. Incomes are less unequally distributed than in large-power-distance countries. Taxation serves to redistribute income, making incomes after taxes less unequal than before. Labor unions are independent and less oriented to ideology and politics than to pragmatic issues on behalf of their members.

The reader will easily recognize elements of both extremes in the history and the current practices of many countries. The European Union is based on the principles of pluralist democracy, but many member states cope with a dictatorial past. The level of power distance in their cultures helps to explain their current struggles with democracy. The Eurobarometer surveys mentioned earlier reveal, for example, that where PDI is higher, fewer people trust the police, fewer young people join a political party, and fewer people have ever participated in debates with policy makers.[29] Even in the most democratic system, journalists and whistle-blowers exposing scandals have a difficult time. In less democratic systems they risk their lives.

Institutions from small-power-distance countries are sometimes copied in large-power-distance countries, because political ideas travel. Political leaders who studied in other countries may try to emulate these countries' political systems. Governments of smaller-power-distance countries often eagerly try to export their institutional arrangements in the context of development cooperation. However, just going through the moves of an election will not change the political mores of a country if these mores are deeply rooted in the mental software of a large part of the population. In particular, underfed and uneducated masses make poor democrats, and the ways of government that are customary in more well-off countries are unlikely to function in poor ones. Actions by foreign governments intended to lead other countries toward democratic ways and respect for human rights are clearly inspired by the mental programming of the foreign helpers, and they are usually more effective in dealing with the opinions of the foreign electorate than with the problems in the countries supposed to be helped. In Chapter 11 we will come back to this dilemma and possible ways out of it.

Power Distance and Ideas

Parents, teachers, managers, and rulers are all children of their cultures; in a way, they are the followers of their followers, and their behavior can be understood only if one also understands the mental software of their offspring, students, subordinates, and subjects. Moreover, not only the doers in this world but also the thinkers are children of a culture. The authors of management books and the founders of political ideologies generate their ideas from the background of what they learned when they were growing up. Thus, differences among countries along value dimensions such as power distance help not only in understanding differences in thinking, feeling, and behaving by the leaders and those led but also in appreciating the theories produced or adopted in these countries to explain or prescribe thoughts, feelings, and behavior.

In world history, philosophers and founders of religions have dealt explicitly with questions of power and inequality. In China around 500 B.C., Kong Ze, whose name the Jesuit missionaries two thousand years later latinized as Confucius (from the older name Kong-Fu Ze), maintained that the stability of society was based on unequal relationships between people. He distinguished the *wu lun*, the five basic relationships: ruler-subject, father-son, older brother–younger brother, husband–wife, and senior friend–junior friend. These relationships contain mutual and complementary obligations: for example, the junior partner owes the senior respect and obedience, while the senior partner owes the junior protection and consideration. Confucius's ideas have survived as guidelines for proper behavior for Chinese people to this day. In the People's Republic of China, Mao Zedong tried to wipe out Confucianism, but in the meantime his own rule contained strong Confucian elements.[30] Countries in the IBM study with a Chinese majority or that have undergone Chinese cultural influences are, in the order in which they appear in Table 3.1, China, Singapore, Hong Kong, South Korea, Taiwan, and Japan; they occupy the upper-medium and medium PDI zones. People in these countries accept and appreciate inequality but feel that the use of power should be moderated by a sense of obligation.

In ancient Greece around 350 B.C., Plato recognized a basic need for equality among people, but at the same time, he defended a society in which an elite class, the guardians, would exercise leadership. He tried to resolve the conflict between these diverging tendencies by playing on two meanings of the word *equality*, a quantitative one and a qualitative one, but to us, his arguments resemble the famous quote from George Orwell's *Animal Farm*: "All animals are equal, but some animals are more equal than others." Present-day Greece in Table 3.1 is found about halfway on power distance (rank 41–42, score 60).

The Christian New Testament, composed in the first centuries A.D., preaches the virtue of poverty.[31] Pursuing this virtue will lead to equality in society, but its practice has been reserved to members of religious orders. It has not been popular with Christian leaders—neither of states, nor of businesses, nor of the Church itself. The Roman Catholic Church has maintained the hierarchical order of the Roman Empire; the same holds for the Eastern Orthodox churches, whereas Protestant denominations to various degrees are nonhierarchical. Traditionally Protestant nations tend to score lower on PDI than Catholic or Orthodox nations.

The Italian Niccolò Machiavelli (1469–1527) is one of world literature's greatest authorities on the use of political power. He distinguished
two models: the model of the fox and the model of the lion. The prudent
ruler, Machiavelli writes, uses both models, each at the proper time: the
cunning of the fox will avoid the snares, and the strength of the lion will
scare the wolves.[32] Relating Machiavelli's thoughts to national power distance differences, one finds small-power-distance countries to be accustomed to the fox model and large-power-distance countries to the lion
model. Italy, in the twentieth-century IBM research data, scores in the
middle zone on power distance (rank 51, score 50). It is likely that, were
one to study Italy by region, the North will be more foxy and the South
more lionlike. What Machiavelli did not write but what the association
between political systems and citizens' mental software suggests is that
which animal the ruler should impersonate depends strongly on what animals the followers are.

Karl Marx (1818–83) also dealt with power, but he wanted to give it
to people who were powerless; he never really dealt with the question of
whether the revolution he preached would actually create a new powerless
class. In fact, he seemed to assume that the exercise of power can be transferred from persons to a system, a philosophy in which we can recognize
the mental software of the small-power-distance societies to which Marx's
mother country, Germany, today belongs. It was a tragedy for the modern
world that Marx's ideas have been mainly exported to countries at the
large-power-distance side of the continuum, in which, as was argued earlier in this chapter, the assumption that power should yield to law is absent.
This absence of a check to power has enabled government systems claiming Marx's inheritance to survive even where these systems would make
Marx himself turn in his grave. In Marx's concept of the "dictatorship
of the proletariat," the *dictatorship* has appealed to rulers in some large-
power-distance countries, but the *proletariat* has been forgotten. In fact, the
concept is naive: in view of what we know of the human tendency toward
inequality, a dictatorship by a proletariat is a logical contradiction.

The exportation of ideas to people in other countries without regard
for the values context in which these ideas were developed—and the importation of such ideas by gullible believers in those other countries—is not
limited to politics; it can also be observed in the domains of education
and, in particular, management and organization. The economic success of

the United States in the decades before and after World War II has made people in other countries believe that U.S. ideas about management must be superior and therefore should be copied. They forgot to ask about the kind of society in which these ideas were developed and applied—*if* they were really applied as the books claimed. Since the late 1960s the same has happened with Japanese ideas.

The United States in Table 3.1 scores on the low side, but not extremely low, on power distance (rank 57–59 out of 74). U.S. leadership theories tend to be based on subordinates with medium-level dependence needs: not too high, not too low. A key idea is *participative management*—that is, a situation in which subordinates are involved by managers in decisions at the discretion and initiative of these managers. Comparing U.S. theories of leadership with "industrial democracy" experiments in countries such as Sweden and Denmark (which scored extremely low on PDI), one finds that in these Scandinavian countries initiatives to participate are often taken by the subordinates, something U.S. managers find difficult to digest, because it represents an infringement on their "management prerogatives." Management prerogatives, however, are less sacred in Scandinavia. On the other hand, U.S. theories of participative management are also unlikely to apply in countries higher on the power distance scale. Subordinates accustomed to larger Power Distances may feel embarrassed when the boss steps out of his or her role by asking their opinion, or they may even lose respect for such an ignorant superior.[33]

Table 3.5 summarizes key differences between small- and large-power-distance societies from the last two sections; together with Tables 3.3 and 3.4, it provides an overview of the essence of power distance differences across all spheres of life discussed in this chapter.

Origins of Power Distance Differences

European countries in which the native language is Romance (French, Italian, Portuguese, Romanian, Spanish) scored medium to high on the power distance scale (in Table 3.1. from 50 for Italy to 90 for Romania). European countries in which the native language is Germanic (Danish, Dutch, English, German, Norwegian, Swedish) scored low (from 11 in Austria to 40 in Luxembourg). There seems to be a relationship between language area and present-day mental software regarding power distance. The fact that a country belongs to a language area is rooted in history: Romance

**TABLE 3.5 Key Differences Between Small- and
Large-Power-Distance Societies
III: The State and Ideas**

SMALL POWER DISTANCE	LARGE POWER DISTANCE
The use of power should be legitimate and follow criteria of good and evil.	Might prevails over right: whoever holds the power is right and good.
Skills, wealth, power, and status need not go together.	Skills, wealth, power, and status should go together.
Mostly wealthier countries with a large middle class.	Mostly poorer countries with a small middle class.
All should have equal rights.	The powerful should have privileges.
Power is based on formal position, expertise, and ability to give rewards.	Power is based on tradition or family, charisma, and the ability to use force.
The way to change a political system is by changing the rules (evolution).	The way to change a political system is by changing the people at the top (revolution).
There is more dialogue and less violence in domestic politics.	There is less dialogue and more violence in domestic politics.
Pluralist governments based on the outcome of majority votes.	Autocratic or oligarchic governments based on co-optation.
The political spectrum shows a strong center and weak right and left wings.	The political spectrum, if allowed to exist, has a weak center and strong right and left wings.
There are small income differentials in society, further reduced by the tax system.	There are large income differentials in society, further increased by the tax system.
Scandals end political careers of those involved.	Scandals involving power holders are usually covered up.
Participative theories of management: Christian New Testament, Marx.	Power-based practice of management: Confucius, Plato, Machiavelli.

languages all derive from Low Latin and were adopted in countries once part of the Roman Empire, or, in the case of Latin America, in countries colonized by Spain and Portugal, which themselves were former colonies of Rome. Germanic languages are spoken in countries that remained "barbaric" in Roman days, in areas once under Roman rule but reconquered by barbarians (such as England), and in former colonies of these entities. Thus, some roots of the mental program called power distance go back at least to Roman times—two thousand years ago. Countries with a Chinese (Confucian) cultural inheritance also cluster on the medium to high side of the power distance scale—and they carry a culture at least four thousand years old.

None of us was present when culture patterns started to diverge between peoples: the attribution of causes for these differences is a matter of educated speculation on the basis of historical and prehistorical sources. Both the Roman and the Chinese Empires were ruled from a single power center, which presupposes a population prepared to take orders from the center. The Germanic part of Europe, on the other hand, was divided into small tribal groups under local lords who were not inclined to accept directives from anybody else. It seems a reasonable assumption that early statehood experiences helped to develop in these peoples the common mental programs necessary for the survival of their political and social systems.

The question remains, of course, as to why these early statehood experiences deviated. One way of supporting the guesswork for causes is to look for quantitative data about countries that might be correlated with the power distance scores. A number of such quantitative variables were available. Stepwise regression, described in Chapter 2, allowed us to select from these variables the ones that successively contributed most to explaining the differences in PDI scores in Table 3.1. The result is that a country's PDI score can be fairly accurately predicted from the following:

- The country's geographic latitude (higher latitudes associated with lower PDI)
- Its population size (larger size associated with higher PDI)
- Its wealth (richer countries associated with lower PDI)[34]

Geographic latitude (the distance from the equator of a country's capital city) alone allows us to predict 43 percent of the differences (the variance) in PDI values among the fifty countries in the original IBM set. Latitude and population size together predicted 51 percent of the variance; and latitude, population size, plus national wealth (per capita gross national income in 1970, the middle year of the survey period), predicted 58 percent.

If one knew nothing about these countries other than those three hard to fairly hard areas of data, one would be able to compile a list of predicted PDI scores resembling Table 3.1 pretty closely. On average, the predicted values deviate 11 scale points from those found in the IBM surveys.

Statistical relationships do not indicate the direction of causality: they do not tell which is cause and which is effect or whether the related elements may both be the effects of a common third cause. However, in the unique case of a country's geographic position, it is difficult to consider this factor as anything other than a cause, unless we assume that in prehistoric times peoples migrated to climates that fit their concepts of power distance, which is rather far-fetched.

The logic of the relationship, supported by various research studies,[35] could be about as follows: First of all, the societies involved have all developed to the level of sedentary agriculture and urban industry. The more primitive hunter-gatherer societies, for which a different logic may apply, are not included. At lower latitudes (that is, more tropical climates), agricultural societies generally meet a more abundant nature. Survival and population growth in these climates demand a relatively limited intervention of humans with nature: everything grows. In this situation the major threat to a society is the competition of other human groups for the same territory and resources. The better chances for survival exist for the societies that have organized themselves hierarchically and in dependence on one central authority that keeps order and balance.

At higher latitudes (that is, moderate and colder climates), nature is less abundant. There is more of a need for people's intervention with nature in order to carve out an existence. These conditions support the creation of industry next to agriculture. Nature, rather than other humans, is the first enemy to be resisted. Societies in which people have learned to fend for themselves without being too dependent on more powerful others have a better chance of survival under these circumstances than societies that educate their children toward obedience.

The combination of climate and affluence is the subject of a highly interesting study by Dutch social psychologist Evert van de Vliert, to which we will refer again in Chapter 12. Van de Vliert studied the effect of climate on culture, opposing *survival* (high PDI) cultures to *self-expression* (low PDI) cultures. He proves that demanding cold or hot climates have led to survival cultures, except in affluent societies that have the means to cope with heat and cold, where we find self-expression cultures. In temperate climates, the role of affluence is less pronounced.[36]

National wealth in itself stands for a lot of other factors, each of which could be both an effect and a cause of smaller power distances. Here we are dealing with phenomena for which causality is almost always *spiral*, such as the causality of the chicken and the egg. Factors associated with more national wealth *and* less dependence on powerful others are as follows:

- Less traditional agriculture
- More modern technology
- More urban living
- More social mobility
- A better educational system
- A larger middle class

More former colonies than former colonizing nations show large power distances, but having been either a colony or a colonizer at some time during the past two centuries is also strongly related to current wealth. The data do not allow establishing a one-way causal path among the three factors of poverty, colonization, and large power differences. Assumptions about causality in this respect usually depend on what one likes to prove.

Size of population, the second predictor of power distance, fosters dependence on authority because people in a populous country will have to accept a political power that is more distant and less accessible than people from a small nation. On the other hand, a case can be made for a reversal of causality here because less dependently minded peoples will fight harder to avoid being integrated into a larger nation.

The Future of Power Distance Differences

So far, the picture of differences among countries with regard to power distance has been static. The previous section claimed that some of the differences have historical roots of four thousand years or more. So much for the past, but what about the future? We live in an era of unprecedented intensification of international communication: shouldn't this achievement eradicate the differences and help us to grow toward a world standard? And if so, will this be one of large, small, or medium power distances?

Impressionistically at least, it seems that dependence on the power of others in a large part of our world has been reduced over the past few generations. Many of us feel less dependent than we assume our parents and grandparents to have been. Moreover, independence is a politically attractive topic. Liberation and emancipation movements abound. Educational opportunities have been improved in many countries, and we have seen that power distance scores within countries decrease with increased education level. This does not mean, however, that the *differences* among countries described in this chapter should necessarily have changed. Countries can all have moved to lower power distance levels without changes in their mutual ranking as shown in Table 3.1.

One may try to develop a prediction about longer-term changes in power distance by looking at the underlying forces identified in the previous section. Of the factors shown to be most closely associated with power distance (latitude, size, and wealth), the first is immutable. As to the second, size of population, one could argue that in a globalizing world small and even large countries will be less and less able to make decisions at their own level and all will be more and more dependent on decisions made internationally. This development should lead to a global *increase* in power distances.

The third factor, wealth, increases for some countries but not for others. Increases in wealth may reduce power distances, but only if and where they benefit an entire population. Since the last decade of the twentieth century, income distribution in some wealthy countries, led by the United States, has become more and more uneven: wealth increases have benefited disproportionally those who were very wealthy already. This has the opposite effect: it increases inequality in society, not only in economic terms but also in legal terms, as the superrich can lobby with legislators and pay lawyers who earn a multiple of the salaries of judges. This kind of wealth increase, therefore, also *increases* power distances. In countries in which the economy stagnates or deteriorates (that is, mainly in countries that are already poor), no reduction or even a further increase in power distance is to be expected anyway.

Nobody, as far as we know, has offered evidence of a convergence of countries toward smaller differences in power distance.[37] We believe that the picture of national variety presented in this chapter, with its very old historical roots, is likely to survive at least for some centuries. A worldwide homogenization of mental programs about power and dependence, independence, and interdependence under the influence of a presumed cultural melting-pot process is still very far away, if it will ever happen.

In December 1988 the following news item appeared in the press:

> *Stockholm, December 23. The Swedish King Carl Gustav this week experienced considerable delay while shopping for Christmas presents for his children, when he wanted to pay by check but could not show his check card. The salesperson refused to accept the check without identification. Only when helpful bystanders dug in their pockets for one-crown pieces showing the face of the king to prove his identity did the salesperson decide to accept the check, not, however, without testing the check thoroughly for authenticity and noting name and address of the holder.*[38]

This Bernadotte (a direct descendant of the French general) still met with the same equality norm as his ancestor. How much time will have to pass before the citizens of the United States, Russia, or Zimbabwe will treat their presidents in this way? Or before Swedes start to venerate their king in the same way as the Thai do theirs?

I, We, and They

A medium-size Swedish high-technology corporation was approached with a profitable opportunity by a compatriot, a businessman with good contacts in Saudi Arabia. The corporation sent one of its engineers—let us call him Johannesson—to Riyadh, where he was introduced to a small Saudi engineering firm run by two brothers in their mid-thirties, both with British university degrees. The request was to assist in a development project on behalf of the Saudi government. However, after six visits over a period of two years, nothing seemed to happen. Johannesson's meetings with the brothers were always held in the presence of the Swedish businessman who had established the first contact. This annoyed him and his superiors, because they were not at all sure that this businessman did not have contacts with their competitors as well—but the Saudis wanted the intermediary to be there. Discussions often dwelt on issues having little to do with the business—for instance, Shakespeare, of whom both brothers were fans.

Just when Johannesson's superiors started to seriously doubt the wisdom of the corporation's investment in these expensive trips, a fax arrived from Riyadh inviting Johannesson for an urgent visit. A contract worth several million dollars was ready to be signed. Back he went. From one day to the next, the Saudis' attitude had changed: the businessman-intermediary's presence was no longer necessary, and Johannesson for the first time saw the Saudis smile and even make jokes.

So far, so good—but the story goes on. Acquiring the remarkable order contributed to Johannesson's being promoted to a management position in a different division. Thus, he was no longer in charge of the Saudi account. A successor was nominated, another engineer with considerable international experience, whom Johannesson personally introduced to the Saudi brothers. A few weeks later another fax arrived from Riyadh; in this one the Saudis threatened to cancel the contract over a detail in the delivery conditions. Johannesson's help was requested. When he arrived in Riyadh, it appeared that the conflict was over a minor issue and could easily be resolved—but only, the Saudis felt, with Johannesson as the corporation's representative. So, the corporation twisted its structure to allow Johannesson to handle the Saudi account even though his main responsibilities were now in a completely different field.

The Individual and the Collective in Society

The Swedes and the Saudis in this true story have different concepts of the role of personal relationships in business. For the Swedes, business is done with a company; for the Saudis, it's done with a person whom one has learned to know and trust. When one does not know another person well enough, it is best that contacts take place in the presence of an intermediary or go-between, someone who knows and is trusted by both parties. At the root of the difference between these cultures is a fundamental issue in human societies: the role of the individual versus the role of the group.

The vast majority of people in our world live in societies in which the interest of the group prevails over the interest of the individual. We will call these societies *collectivist*, using a word that to some readers may have political connotations, but the word is not meant here in any political sense. It does not refer to the power of the state over the individual; it refers to the *power of the group*. The first group in our lives is always the family into which we are born. Family structures, however, differ among societies. In most collectivist societies, the "family" within which the child grows up consists of a number of people living closely together: not just the parents and other children but also, for example, grandparents, uncles, aunts, servants, or other housemates. This is known in cultural anthropology as the *extended family*. When children grow up, they learn to think of themselves as part of a "we" group, a relationship that is not voluntary but is instead given by nature. The "we" group is distinct from other people in society who belong to "they" groups, of which there are many. The "we" group (or *in-group*) is the major source of one's identity and the only secure protection one has against the hardships of life. Therefore, one owes lifelong loyalty to one's in-group, and breaking this loyalty is one of the worst things a person can do. Between the person and the in-group, a mutual dependence relationship develops that is both practical and psychological.

A minority of people in our world live in societies in which the interests of the individual prevail over the interests of the group, societies that we will call *individualist*. In these, most children are born into families consisting of two parents and, possibly, other children; in some societies there is an increasing share of one-parent families. Other relatives live elsewhere and are rarely seen. This type is the *nuclear family* (from the Latin *nucleus*, meaning "core"). Children from such families, as they grow up, soon learn to think of themselves as "I." This "I," their personal identity, is distinct from other people's "I"s, and these others are classified not according to their group membership but instead according to individual characteristics. Playmates, for example, are chosen on the basis of personal preferences. The purpose of education is to enable children to stand on their own feet. Children are expected to leave the parental home as soon as this has been achieved. Not infrequently, children, after having left home, reduce relationships with their parents to a minimum or break them off altogether. Neither practically nor psychologically is the healthy person in this type of society supposed to be dependent on a group.

Measuring the Degree of Individualism in Society

Extreme collectivism and extreme individualism can be considered the opposite poles of a second global dimension of national cultures, after power distance (which was described in Chapter 3). All countries in the IBM studies could be given an individualism index score that was low for collectivist societies and high for individualist societies.

The new dimension is defined as follows: *Individualism* pertains to *societies in which the ties between individuals are loose: everyone is expected to look after him- or herself and his or her immediate family. Collectivism* as its opposite pertains to *societies in which people from birth onward are integrated into strong, cohesive in-groups, which throughout people's lifetime continue to protect them in exchange for unquestioning loyalty.*

Degrees of individualism obviously vary within countries as well as among them, so it is again important to base the country scores on comparable samples from one country to another. The IBM samples offered this comparability.

The survey questions on which the individualism index is based belong to a set of fourteen *work goals.* People were asked: "Try to think of those factors that would be important to you in an ideal job; disregard the extent to which they are contained in your present job. How important is it to you to . . . " followed by fourteen items, each to be scored on a scale from 1 (of utmost importance to me) to 5 (of very little or no importance). When the answer patterns for the respondents from forty countries on the fourteen items were analyzed, they reflected two underlying dimensions. One was *individualism versus collectivism.* The other came to be labeled *masculinity versus femininity* (see Chapter 5).

The dimension to be identified with individualism versus collectivism was most strongly associated with the relative importance attached to the following work goal items:

For the individualist pole
1. **Personal time:** have a job that leaves you sufficient time for your personal or family life
2. **Freedom:** have considerable freedom to adopt your own approach to the job
3. **Challenge:** have challenging work to do—work from which you can get a personal sense of accomplishment

For the opposite, collectivist pole

4. **Training:** have training opportunities (to improve your skills or learn new skills)
5. **Physical conditions:** have good physical working conditions (good ventilation and lighting, adequate work space, etc.)
6. **Use of skills:** fully use your skills and abilities on the job

If the IBM employees in a country scored work goal 1 as relatively important, they generally also scored 2 and 3 as important but scored 4, 5, and 6 as unimportant. Such a country was considered individualist. If work goal 1 was scored as relatively unimportant, the same generally held for 2 and 3, but 4, 5, and 6 would be scored as relatively more important. Such a country was considered collectivist.

Obviously, these items from the IBM questionnaire do not totally cover the distinction between individualism and collectivism in a society. They only represent the issues in the IBM research that relate to this distinction. The correlations of the IBM individualism country scores with non-IBM data about other characteristics of societies confirm (validate) the claim that this dimension from the IBM data does indeed measure individualism.

It is not difficult to identify the importance of personal time, freedom, and (personal) challenge with individualism: they all stress the employee's independence from the organization. The work goals at the opposite pole— training, physical conditions, and skills being used on the job—refer to things the organization does for the employee and in this way stress the employee's dependence on the organization, which fits with collectivism. Another link in the relationship is that, as will be shown, individualist countries tend to be rich, while collectivist countries tend to be poor. In rich countries, training, physical conditions, and the use of skills may be taken for granted, which makes them relatively unimportant as work goals. In poor countries, these things cannot at all be taken for granted: they are essential in distinguishing a good job from a bad one, which makes them quite important among one's work goals.

The actual calculation of the individualism index is not, as in the case of power distance, based on simply adding or subtracting question scores after multiplying them by a fixed number. The statistical procedure used to identify the individualism dimension and, in Chapter 5, the masculinity dimension (a *factor analysis* of the country scores for the fourteen work goals) produced a *factor score* for each dimension for each country. These factor scores are a more accurate measure of that country's position on the dimension than could be obtained by adding or subtracting question scores. The factor scores for the individualism dimension were multiplied by 25, and a constant number of 50 points was added. This process puts the scores in a range from close to 0 for the most collectivist country to close to 100 for the most individualist one. This manner of calculation was used for the countries represented in the IBM database. For the various follow-up studies, approximation formulas were used in which the individualism index value could be directly computed by simple mathematics from the mean scores of four of the work goals.[1]

The individualism index (IDV) scores are shown in Table 4.1. As in the case of the power distance index in Chapter 3, the scores represent *relative* positions of countries. Table 4.1 confirms that nearly all wealthy countries score high on IDV while nearly all poor countries score low. There is a strong relationship between a country's national wealth and the degree of individualism in its culture; we will come back to this subject later in the chapter.

Sweden scored 71 on IDV, and the group of Arab-speaking countries to which Saudi Arabia belongs scored an average of 38, which demonstrates the cultural roots of Johannesson's dilemma. Of course, the Arab countries differ among themselves, and the Saudis within this region seem to be even more collectivist than some other Arabs, such as the Lebanese and the Egyptians. In the IBM sample, the latter were more strongly represented than the Saudis. Sweden's rank among seventy-six countries and regions is 13–14, and the Arab countries rank 41–42, so there are still a lot of countries scoring more collectivist than the Arab average. As stated earlier, collectivism is the rule in our world, and individualism the exception.

Individualism and Collectivism in the World Values Survey: Universalism Versus Exclusionism

Inglehart's overall analysis of the huge database of the World Values Survey (WVS), described in Chapter 2, produced two statistical factors. One of these, *secular-rational versus traditional authority*, was associated with small versus large power distance, and we encountered it in the previous chapter. The other, *well-being versus survival*, was correlated with IDV, with femininity (see Chapter 5), and with small power distance, in that order.[2]

TABLE 4.1 Individualism Index (IDV) Values for 76 Countries and Regions Based on Factor Scores from 14 Items in the IBM Database Plus Extensions

RANK	AMERICA C/S	EUROPE S/SE	EUROPE N/NW ANGLO WORLD	EUROPE C/E EX-SOVIET	MUSLIM WORLD M.E & AFRICA	ASIA EAST ASIA SE	INDEX
1			United States				91
2			Australia				90
3			Great Britain				89
4–6			Canada total				80
4–6				Hungary			80
4–6			Netherlands				80
7			New Zealand				79
8			Belgium Nl				78
9		Italy					76
10			Denmark				74
11			Canada Quebec				73
12			Belgium Fr				72
13–14		France					71
13–14			Sweden				71
15–16			Ireland				70
15–16				Latvia			70
17–18			Norway				69
17–18			Switzerland Ge				69
19			Germany				67
20					S Africa (wte)		65
21			Switzerland Fr				64
22			Finland				63
23–26				Estonia			60
23–26				Lithuania			60

continued

TABLE 4.1 Individualism Index (IDV) Values for 76 Countries and Regions Based on Factor Scores from 14 Items in the IBM Database Plus Extensions, continued

RANK	AMERICA C/S	EUROPE S/SE	EUROPE N/NW ANGLO WORLD	EUROPE C/E EX-SOVIET	MUSLIM WORLD M.E & AFRICA	ASIA EAST ASIA SE	INDEX
23–26			Luxembourg				60
23–26				Poland			60
27		Malta					59
28				Czech Rep.			58
29			Austria				55
30					Israel		54
31				Slovakia			52
32		Spain					51
33						India	48
34	Suriname						47
35–37	Argentina						46
35–37					Morocco		46
35–37						Japan	46
38					Iran		41
39–40	Jamaica						39
39–40				Russia			39
41–42	Brazil						38
41–42					Arab ctrs		38
43		Turkey					37
44	Uruguay						36
45		Greece					35
46				Croatia			33
47					Philippines		32
48–50				Bulgaria			30
48–50	Mexico						30

48–50			Romania			30
51–53		Portugal				27
51–53			Slovenia			27
51–53				Africa E		27
54					Malaysia	26
55–56					Hong Kong	25
55–56			Serbia			25
57	Chile					23
58–63					Bangladesh	20
58–63					China	20
58–63					Singapore	20
58–63					Thailand	20
58–63					Vietnam	20
58–63				Africa W		20
64	El Salvador					19
65					S Korea	18
66					Taiwan	17
67–68	Peru					16
67–68	Trinidad					16
69	Costa Rica					15
70–71					Indonesia	14
70–71				Pakistan		14
72	Colombia					13
73	Venezuela					12
74	Panama					11
75	Ecuador					8
76	Guatemala					6

In his 2007 book, Misho analyzed the WVS database in more detail, including its latest additions.[3] He found Inglehart's second dimension conceptually diffuse. In a factor analysis, it split into two components. One reflected, among other things, differences in happiness; it will be described in Chapter 8 as part of the dimension *indulgence versus restraint*. The other component consisted of items dealing with in-group and out-group relationships:

At the positive pole
- Rejection of people of another race as neighbors

plus a number of conservative views on family and gender issues:

- Strong agreement that men make better leaders than women
- Strong agreement that children must always love their parents, even if the parents have deficiencies
- Agreement that a child needs two parents to be happy
- Agreement that a woman needs to have children to be fulfilled

At the negative pole
- Tolerance and respect for everybody

Misho concluded that the positive pole of this dimension reflects strong in-group cohesion and exclusion of members of other groups, whereas the negative pole indicates acceptance of others regardless of the group(s) to which they belong. He labeled it *exclusionism versus universalism*.

Exclusionism can be defined as the cultural tendency to treat people on the basis of their group affiliation and to reserve favors, services, privileges, and sacrifices for friends, relatives, and other groups with which one identifies, while excluding outsiders from the circle of those who deserve such privileged treatment. While exclusionist cultures strive to achieve harmony and good relationships within one's in-group, they may be indifferent, inconsiderate, rude, and sometimes even hostile toward members of out-groups.

Universalism is the opposite cultural tendency: treating people primarily on the basis of who they are as individuals and disregarding their group affiliations.

Geert had earlier related collectivism to the distinction between in-groups and out-groups, and Misho's WVS dimension of exclusionism versus universalism turned out to be strongly negatively correlated with IDV. For forty-one countries that were part of Geert's original IBM set, IDV predicted 59 percent of universalism in the WVS, thirty-five years later, a strong validation of the IBM database.[4]

The distinction of in-group versus out-group, previously described in Chapter 1, is a central aspect of cultural collectivism. The correlation between exclusionism and IDV is strong but not perfect. A comparison of the rankings of forty-one countries from the IBM database on individualism and on exclusionism finds six countries that score considerably more universalist than could be predicted on the basis of their IDV scores: Colombia, Venezuela, Peru, Slovenia, Finland, and Sweden. Their cultures according to their WVS data are more open to out-group members than expected. Five other countries score much more exclusionist than their IDV scores predict: India, Italy, Turkey, Iran, and the Philippines. Their cultures are more hostile to out-group members than expected.

Universalism implies respect for other cultures. The Eurobarometer in 2008 asked representative samples of the population in twenty-six countries to choose "the most important values for you personally" (three out of a list of twelve). One of these values was "respect for other cultures." Differences among countries in percentages of respondents choosing this answer related primarily to IDV.[5]

Individualism and Collectivism in Other Cross-National Studies

Table 2.1 listed six major replications of the IBM research, published between 1990 and 2002. Five of these, covering between fifteen and twenty-eight countries from the IBM set, produced IDV scores significantly correlated with the original IBM scores.[6] As in the case of PDI (Chapter 3), the various replications did not sufficiently agree to justify changing the score of any of the countries. The original IBM set still served as the best common denominator for the various studies.

Bond's Chinese Value Survey study among students in twenty-three countries, described in Chapter 2, produced an *integration* dimension, on which the countries positioned themselves largely in the same way as they had done on individualism-collectivism in the IBM studies. The CVS integration dimension resembles the WVS exclusionism dimension.[7] Students from countries scoring individualist answered that the following values were particularly important:

- Tolerance of others
- Harmony with others
- Noncompetitiveness
- A close, intimate friend
- Trustworthiness
- Contentedness with one's position in life
- Solidarity with others
- Being conservative

This was the largest cluster of CVS values associated with any single IBM dimension pole. In the individualist society, relationships with others are not obvious and prearranged; they are voluntary and have to be carefully fostered. The values at the individualist pole of the integration dimension describe conditions for the ideal voluntary relationship.

Students in collectivist societies, instead, answered that the following values were particularly important:

- Filial piety (obedience to parents, respect for parents, honoring of ancestors, financial support of parents)
- Chastity in women
- Patriotism

In the collectivist society, there is no need to make specific friendships: who one's friends are is predetermined by one's family or group membership. The family relationship is maintained by filial piety and by chastity in women and is associated with patriotism. In some versions of the IBM questionnaire, a work goal "serve your country" was included. This too was found to be strongly associated with collectivism.

Chapter 2 mentioned three other cross-national values databases: those of Schwartz, GLOBE, and Trompenaars. All three produced dimensions or categories strongly correlated with IDV. Schwartz identified seven categories of values, from which no fewer than five were significantly correlated with IDV.[8] When Schwartz's seven categories were simplified into three clusters, two of these were found to be highly significantly correlated with IDV: *autonomy versus embeddedness,* and *egalitarianism versus mastery.*[9]

The GLOBE study defined and tried to measure two categories of collectivism: *institutional collectivism* and *in-group collectivism*—both "as is" and "should be." Ten out of GLOBE's eighteen dimensions were significantly correlated with IDV, but the dominant correlation was with in-group collectivism "as is." GLOBE's questions in this case dealt with relatively simple aspects of human behavior, which explains why its measure came closer to ours than in the case of the other dimensions. IDV explained 58 percent of the country differences on in-group collectivism "as is."[10] In Chapter 3 we saw that in-group collectivism "as is" was also the strongest correlated GLOBE dimension for PDI, but the correlation with IDV was slightly stronger.

From GLOBE's other three measures of collectivism, only institutional collectivism "should be" was weakly negatively correlated with IDV but more strongly with our uncertainty avoidance index (UAI, Chapter 6). Institutional collectivism "as is" was exclusively correlated with our UAI. In-group collectivism "should be" was correlated with our long-term orientation index (Chapter 7).[11]

Peter Smith's analysis of the Trompenaars database produced two major dimensions. Both were correlated with IDV; the second one was also, and even more, correlated with PDI.[12] However, the correlation with PDI was influenced by the fact that there were no Eastern European, high-PDI countries in the IBM sample. In fact, the second dimension opposed most Eastern European countries to East Asian countries, and the questionnaire items involved focused mainly on teamwork, which received positive associations in China and negative associations in most Eastern European countries.

Subsequently, an ingenious study by Smith compared not the results of the various international studies but rather the degree of *acquiescence* in their answers. Acquiescence occurs in all paper-and-pencil surveys: it is the tendency among respondents to give positive answers regardless of the content of the questions. Smith compared six studies that each covered thirty-four or more countries, including studies by Geert, Schwartz, and GLOBE. For sections of the questionnaires dealing with values, all six studies demonstrated similar acquiescence patterns. Smith showed that the common tendency to give positive answers in the six studies was stronger in countries that, according to our measures, were collectivist and had large power distances. Smith's study has supplied us with a nonobtrusive measure of the degree to which respondents in a culture want to maintain formal harmony and respect toward the researchers.[13]

Are Individualism and Collectivism One or Two Dimensions?

A frequently asked question is whether it is correct to treat individualism and collectivism as opposite poles of the same dimension. Shouldn't they be seen as two separate dimensions? The answer is that it depends on whether we compare entire societies (which is what our book is about) or individuals within societies. This is known as the *level of analysis* issue.

Societies are composed of a wide variety of individual members, holding a variety of personal values. Tests have shown that a person can score either high on both individualist and collectivist values, high on one kind and low on the other, or low on both. So, when we compare the values of individuals, individualism and collectivism should be treated as two separate dimensions.[14]

When we study societies, we compare two types of data: average value scores of the individuals within each society and characteristics of the societies as wholes, including their institutions. Research by us and by others has shown that in societies in which people on average hold more individualist values, they also on average hold less collectivist values. Individual persons may differ from this pattern, but those who differ are fewer than those who conform to it. The institutions of such societies reflect the fact that they evolved or were designed primarily for catering to individualists. In societies in which people on average hold more collectivist values, they also on average hold less individualist values. The institutions of such societies assume that people are primarily collectivist. Therefore, at the society (or country) level, individualism and collectivism appear as opposite poles of one dimension. The position of a country on this dimension shows the society's solution for a universal dilemma: the desirable strength of the relationships of an adult person with the group(s) with which he or she identifies.

Collectivism Versus Power Distance

Many countries that score high on the power distance index (Table 3.1) score low on the individualism index (Table 4.1), and vice versa. In other words, the two dimensions tend to be negatively correlated: large-power-distance countries are also likely to be more collectivist, and small-power-distance countries to be more individualist. The relationship between the two indexes is plotted in Figure 4.1.

In the plot of Figure 4.1, the countries are grouped around a diagonal from lower left to upper right, reflecting the correlation between power distance and collectivism.[15] In cultures in which people are dependent on

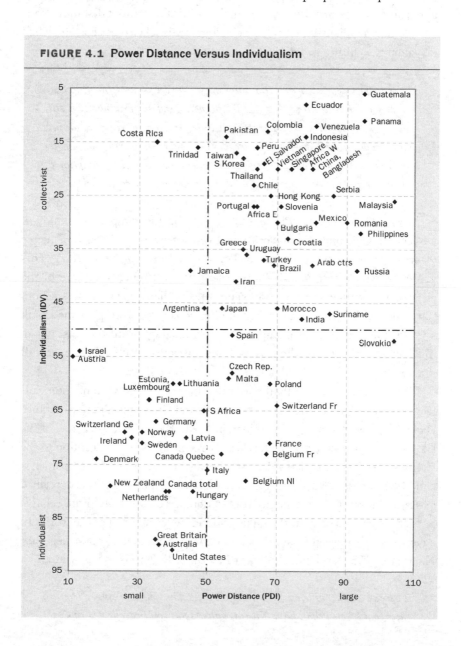

FIGURE 4.1 Power Distance Versus Individualism

in-groups, these people are *usually* also dependent on power figures. Most extended families have patriarchal structures, with the head of the family exercising strong moral authority. In cultures in which people are relatively independent from in-groups, they are *usually* also less dependent on powerful others.

However, there are exceptions. The Latin European countries, and in particular France and Belgium, combined medium power distances with strong individualism. The French sociologist Michel Crozier has described his country's culture as follows:

> *Face-to-face dependence relationships are . . . perceived as difficult to bear in the French cultural setting. Yet the prevailing view of authority is still that of . . . absolutism. . . . The two attitudes are contradictory. However, they can be reconciled within a bureaucratic system since impersonal rules and centralization make it possible to reconcile an absolutist conception of authority and the elimination of most direct dependence relationships.*[16]

Crozier's compatriot Philippe d'Iribarne, in his comparative study of a French, a U.S., and a Dutch organization, describes the French principle of organizing as "the rationale of honor" (*la logique de l'honneur*). This principle, which he finds already present in the French kingdom of the eighteenth century, prior to Napoleon, means that everybody has a rank (large power distance) but that the implications of belonging to one's rank are less imposed by one's group than determined by tradition. It is "not so much what one owes to others as what one owes to oneself."[17] We could call it a *stratified* form of individualism.

The reverse pattern, small power distance combined with medium collectivism, was found in Austria and Israel, and fairly small power distance is combined with strong collectivism in Costa Rica. Costa Rica, one of the six Central American republics, is widely recognized as an exception to the Latin American rule of dependence on powerful leaders, which in Spanish is called *personalismo*. Costa Rica does not have a formal army. It is described as Latin America's "most firmly rooted democracy," in spite of its relative poverty as compared with the industrial market economies of the world. In a comparison between Costa Rica and its larger but much poorer neighbor Nicaragua, U.S. development expert Lawrence E. Harrison has written:

> *There is ample evidence that Costa Ricans have felt a stronger bond to their countrymen than have Nicaraguans. That bond is reflected in Costa*

Rica's long-standing emphasis on public education and public health; in its more vigorous cooperative movement; in a judicial system notable by Latin American standards for its impartiality and adherence to fundamental concepts of due process; and above all in the resilience of its politics, its capacity to find peaceful solutions, its appreciation of the need for compromise.[18]

Cases such as France and Costa Rica justify treating power distance and collectivism as two separate dimensions, in spite of the fact that for most countries they go together. One reason for the correlation between them is that both are associated with a third factor: national wealth. If national wealth is held constant (that is, if rich countries are compared with rich ones only and poor with poor ones only), the relationship considerably weakens.[19]

Comparisons between the results of the IBM study and other studies support the distinction between power distance and collectivism. Studies dealing with inequality show results that are more correlated with power distance than with individualism-collectivism, and studies dealing with the integration of individuals into groups show results more correlated with collectivism than with power distance.[20]

Individualism and Collectivism According to Occupation

One more argument in favor of distinguishing power distance from collectivism is that while, as Chapter 3 showed, power distance indexes could be computed not only for countries but also for occupations, individualism indexes can be calculated only for countries, not for occupations. In a comparison of how people in different *occupations* answered the fourteen work goal questions from which the IDV was computed, their answers could not be classified in terms of individualist or collectivist. In distinguishing occupations, for example, the importance of challenge and the importance of use of skills go together, while in distinguishing countries they are opposites. Across occupations, when personal time is rated more important, challenge tends to be less important, while across countries the two reinforce each other.[21]

A pair of terms that can be used to distinguish occupations is *intrinsic* versus *extrinsic*. These words refer to what motivates people in a job, the work itself (intrinsically motivating jobs) or the conditions and material rewards provided (extrinsically motivating jobs). This distinction was popularized in the late 1950s through the research on work motivation by the American psychologist Frederick Herzberg and his team, who argued that the intrinsic factors are the real "motivators," while the extrinsic ones represent the psychological "hygiene" of the job.[22] People in occupations demanding more education tend to score intrinsic elements as more important, while people in lower-status, lower- education occupations prefer extrinsic elements. The intrinsic-extrinsic distinction, while useful for distinguishing occupation cultures, in its turn is not suitable for comparing countries.

Individualism and Collectivism in the Family

In the beginning of this chapter, individualism was associated with a nuclear family structure and collectivism with an extended family structure, the latter leading to the distinction between in-group and out-groups. The relationship between the individual and the group, as with other basic elements of human culture, is first learned in the family setting. The fact that Japan scores halfway in Table 4.1 (with a rank of 35–37 and an IDV of 46) can at least partly be understood from the fact that in the traditional Japanese family only the oldest son continued to live with the parents, thus creating a lineal structure somewhere in between nuclear and extended.

The child who grows up among a number of elders, peers, and juniors learns naturally to conceive of him- or herself as part of a "we," much more so than does the child in a nuclear family. A child of an extended family is seldom alone, whether during the day or at night. An African student who went to Belgium to attend university told us that this was the first time in her life she had ever been alone in a room for any sizable length of time. Conversely, northern European students returning from internships in Peru or Malaysia complained that they were never left alone by their hosts.

In a situation of intense and continuous social contact, the maintenance of harmony with one's social environment becomes a key virtue that extends to other spheres beyond the family. In most collectivist cultures, direct confrontation of another person is considered rude and undesirable. The word *no* is seldom used, because saying "no" *is* a confrontation; "you may be right" and "we will think about it" are examples of polite ways of turning down a request. In the same vein, the word *yes* should not necessarily be inferred as an approval, since it is used to maintain the line of communication: "yes, I heard you" is the meaning it has in Japan.

In individualist cultures, on the other hand, speaking one's mind is a virtue. Telling the truth about how one feels is characteristic of a sincere and honest person. Confrontation can be salutary; a clash of opinions is believed to lead to a higher truth. The effect of communications on other people should be taken into account, but it does not, as a rule, justify changing the facts. Adult individuals should be able to take direct feedback constructively. In the family, children are instructed that one should always tell the truth, even if it hurts. Coping with conflict is a normal part of living together as a family.

A former Dutch missionary in Indonesia (a country with an IDV of 14 and a rank of 70–71) told about his parishioners' unexpected exegesis of the following parable from the Bible: "A man had two sons. He went to the first and said, 'Son, go and work in the vineyard today'; he replied, 'I will go, sir,' but he did not go. The man went to the second and said the same to him. He replied, 'I will not,' but afterwards he changed his mind and did go. Which of the two did the will of the father?"[23] The biblical answer is that the last did, but the missionary's Indonesian parishioners chose the first, for this son observed the formal harmony and did not contradict his father. Whether he actually went was of secondary importance. In one of Gert Jan's classes, a Greek student inquired, "Were others present?" If so, the first son would, in the student's opinion, have something going for him, for not shaming his father in public. Greece has a culture of intermediate collectivism.

In the collectivist family, children learn to take their bearings from others when it comes to opinions. Personal opinions do not exist: opinions are predetermined by the group. If a new issue comes up on which there is no established group opinion, some kind of family conference is necessary before an opinion can be given. A child who repeatedly voices opinions deviating from what is collectively felt is considered to have a bad character. In the individualist family, on the contrary, children are expected and encouraged to develop opinions of their own, and a child who always only reflects the opinions of others is considered to have a weak character. The behavior corresponding with a desirable character depends on the cultural environment.

The loyalty to the group that is an essential element of the collectivist family also means that resources are shared. If one member of an extended family of twenty persons has a paid job and the others do not, the earning member is supposed to share his or her income in order to help feed the entire family. On the basis of this principle, a family may collectively cover the expenses for sending one member to get a higher education, expecting that when this member subsequently gets a well-paid job, the income will also be shared.

In individualist cultures, parents will be proud if children at an early age take small jobs in order to earn pocket money of their own, which they alone can decide how to spend. In the Netherlands, as in many other individualist Western European countries, the government contributes substantially to the living expenses of students. In the 1980s the system was changed from an allowance to the parents to an allowance directly to the students themselves, which stressed their independence. Boys and girls are treated as independent economic actors from age eighteen onward. In the United States it is normal for students to pay for their own studies by getting temporary jobs and personal loans; without government support they, too, are less dependent on their parents and not at all on more distant relatives.

In individualist cultures, most children expect, and are expected, to move out of their parents' home and live on their own when they start pursuing higher education. In collectivist cultures, this is less the case. Eurobarometer survey data across nineteen relatively wealthy European Union countries show that whether young people use the argument "can't afford to move out" is a matter of collectivism, not of national wealth! Economic arguments are often rationalizations of cultural values.[24]

Obligations to the family in a collectivist society are not only financial but also ritual. Family celebrations and observances such as baptisms, marriages, and, especially, funerals are extremely important and should not be missed. Expatriate managers from individualist societies are often surprised by the family reasons given by employees from a collectivist host society who apply for a special leave; the expatriates think they are being fooled, but most likely the reasons are authentic.

In an individualist culture, when people meet, they feel a need to communicate orally. Silence is considered abnormal. Social conversations can be depressingly banal, but they are compulsory. In a collectivist culture, the fact of being together is emotionally sufficient; there is no compulsion to talk unless there is information to be transferred. Raden Mas Hadjiwibowo, an Indonesian businessman from a Javanese noble family, recalled the family visits from his youth in the 1930s as follows:

Visits among Javanese family members needed no previous appointment. Actually that could easily be done, for although the telephone had not come into common use yet, one could always send a servant with a letter asking for an appointment. But it was not done; it never occurred to one that a visit would not suit the other party. It was always convenient. Unexpected visitors did not exist. The door was (and still is) always open.

The visitors were welcomed with joyful courtesy and would be asked to take a seat. The host and hostess hurriedly withdrew to change into more suitable attire than their workaday clothes. Without asking, a servant brought in coffee or tea. Cookies were offered, while in the meantime the host and hostess had joined the party.

There we sat, but nobody spoke. We were not embarrassed by this silence; nobody felt nervous about it. Every now and then, thoughts and news were exchanged. But this was not really necessary. We enjoyed being together, seeing each other again. After the first exchange of news, any other communication was utterly redundant. If one did not have anything to say, there was no need to recite platitudes. After an hour or so, the guests would ask permission to leave. With mutual feelings of satisfaction, we parted. In smaller towns on the island of Java life is still like this.[25]

Eurobarometer survey data for nineteen wealthier European countries show striking differences in the extent to which people claim to "visit a restaurant or bar daily": in the more collectivist cultures, this form of socialization is much more normal.[26] In individualist cultures, people prefer to meet at home, if at all: "My home is my castle" is a saying from individualist Britain.

U.S. anthropologist and popular author Edward T. Hall (1914–2009) distinguished cultures on the basis of their way of communicating along a dimension from high-context to low-context.[27] A high-context communication is one in which little has to be said or written because most of the information is either in the physical environment or supposed to be known by the persons involved, while very little is in the coded, explicit part of the message. This type of communication is frequent in collectivist cultures; Hadjiwibowo's family visit is a prime example. A low-context communication is one in which the mass of information is vested in the explicit code, which is typical for individualist cultures. Lots of things that in collectivist cultures are self-evident must be said explicitly in individualist cultures. American business contracts are much longer than Japanese business contracts.

Along with harmony, another important concept in connection with the collectivist family is *shame*. Individualist societies have been described as *guilt* cultures: persons who infringe on the rules of society will often feel guilty, ridden by an individually developed conscience that functions as a private inner pilot. Collectivist societies, on the contrary, are shame cultures: persons belonging to a group from which a member has infringed on the rules of society will feel ashamed, based on a sense of collective obligation. Shame is social in nature, whereas guilt is individual; whether shame is felt depends on whether the infringement has become known by others. This becoming known is more of a source of shame than the infringement itself. Such is not the case for guilt, which is felt whether or not the misdeed is known by others.

One more concept bred in the collectivist family is *face*. "Losing face," in the sense of being humiliated, is an expression that penetrated the English language from the Chinese; the English had no equivalent for it. David Yau-Fai Ho, a Hong Kong social scientist, defined it as follows: "Face is lost when the individual, either through his action or that of people closely related to him, fails to meet essential requirements placed upon him by virtue of the social position he occupies."[28] The Chinese also speak of "giving someone face," in the sense of honor or prestige. Basically, *face* describes the proper relationship with one's social environment, which is as essential to a person (and that person's family) as the front part of his or her head. The importance of face is the consequence of living in a society that is very conscious of social contexts. The languages of other collectivist cultures have words with more or less similar meanings. In Greece, for example, there is a word *philotimo*; Harry Triandis, a Greek American psychologist, has written:

> *A person is philotimos to the extent in which he conforms to the norms and values of his in-group. These include a variety of sacrifices that are appropriate for members of one's family, friends, and others who are "concerned with one's welfare"; for example, for a man to delay marriage until his sisters have married and have been provided with a proper dowry is part of the normative expectations of traditional rural Greeks as well as rural Indians (and many of the people in between).*[29]

In the individualist society, the counterpart characteristic is self-respect, but this again is defined from the point of view of the individual, whereas face and *philotimo* are defined from the point of view of the social environment.

Collectivist societies usually have ways of creating family-like ties with persons who are not biological relatives but who are socially integrated into one's in-group. In Latin America, for example, this can be done via the institution of *compadres* and *comadres* who are treated as relatives even if they are not. The institution of *godfathers* and *godmothers*, which was traditionally strong in the Catholic and Orthodox countries of Europe, is another example. In Japan younger sons in past times became apprentices to crafts masters through a form of adoption. Similar customs existed in medieval central Europe.

Because people in collectivist societies have to respect the opinions of their relatives, selection of marriage partners is a crucial event, not only for the partners but also for both their families. The American David Buss coordinated a survey study of criteria for selecting a potential marriage partner.[30] His respondents comprised almost ten thousand young women and men, with an average age of twenty-three, from thirty-seven countries. Universally desired characteristics of both brides and grooms were mutual love, kindness, emotional stability, intelligence, and health. Other characteristics varied between brides and grooms and across countries. Country differences were primarily related to individualism. In collectivist countries, bridegrooms preferred brides to be younger, and they put more stress on their being wealthy, industrious, and chaste. Brides in collectivist countries wanted their grooms to be older and wealthier, but the groom's industriousness to them played a smaller role, and the groom's chastity none at all.

The bridegrooms' desire for chastity in their brides, however, depended even more on the countries' poverty than on their collectivism. Increasing affluence provides women with more educational opportunities (in any society, when education first becomes available, parents give priority to boys, who are not needed around the house). Girls start to move around more freely and get more opportunities for meeting boys. People have more living space and privacy. Medical care and dissemination of information improve, including know-how about contraception. Young people get more opportunities for sexual exploration, and sexual norms adapt to this situation.

The stress on the brides' industriousness, wealth, and chastity in collectivist societies is a consequence of the fact that marriage is a contract between families, not individuals. The bride and groom may have little say in the choice of a partner. This does not mean that such marriages are less happy. Research in India has shown more marital satisfaction in arranged than in love marriages and more in Indian love marriages than in American marriages. While cultural individualism fosters the valuing of romantic love, it can make developing intimacy problematic.[31] In a survey about the role of love in marriage, answered by female and male undergraduate students in eleven countries, one question was: "If a man (woman) had all the other qualities you desired, would you marry this person if you were not in love with him (her)?" The answers varied with the degree of individualism in the eleven societies, from 4 percent "yes" and 86 percent "no" in the United States to 50 percent "yes" and 39 percent "no" in Pakistan.[32] In collectivist societies, other considerations than love weigh heavily in marriage.

In 2005 a New York–based market research company studied the ideals of beauty and body image among fifteen- to seventeen-year-old girls, through telephone interviews in cities in ten countries around the world: Brazil, Canada, China, Germany, Great Britain, Italy, Japan, Mexico, Saudi Arabia, and the United States. One question asked who had the most powerful influence on their beauty ideals. In collectivist cultures, the respondents most often referred to girlfriends—their in-group; in individualist cultures, they most often referred to boys (in general).[33]

Table 4.2 summarizes the key differences between collectivist and individualist societies described so far.

Language, Personality, and Behavior in Individualist and Collectivist Cultures

A Japanese-Australian couple, Yoshi and Emiko Kashima, he a psychologist, she a linguist, studied the relationship between culture and language. Among other features of languages, they studied *pronoun drop*, the practice of omitting the first-person singular pronoun ("I") from a sentence (for example, "I love you" in Spanish: *te quiero* rather than *yo te quiero*). They included thirty-nine languages used in seventy-one countries and looked for correlations with a number of other variables. The strongest correlation they found was with IDV.[34] Languages spoken in individualist cultures tend to require speakers to use the "I" pronoun when referring to themselves; languages spoken in collectivist cultures allow or prescribe dropping this pronoun. The

TABLE 4.2 Key Differences Between Collectivist and
Individualist Societies
I: General Norm and Family

COLLECTIVIST	INDIVIDUALIST
People are born into extended families or other in-groups that continue protecting them in exchange for loyalty.	Everyone grows up to look after him- or herself and his or her immediate (nuclear) family only.
Children learn to think in terms of "we."	Children learn to think in terms of "I."
Value standards differ for in-groups and out-groups: exclusionism.	The same value standards are supposed to apply to everyone: universalism.
Harmony should always be maintained and direct confrontations avoided.	Speaking one's mind is a characteristic of an honest person.
Friendships are predetermined.	Friendships are voluntary and should be fostered.
Resources should be shared with relatives.	Individual ownership of resources, even for children.
Adult children live with parents.	Adult children leave the parental home.
High-context communication prevails.	Low-context communication prevails.
Frequent socialization in public places.	My home is my castle.
Trespasses lead to shame and loss of face for self and group.	Trespasses lead to guilt and loss of self-respect.
Brides should be young, industrious, and chaste; bridegrooms should be older.	Criteria for marriage partners are not predetermined.
The most powerful influence on girls' beauty ideals is girlfriends.	The most powerful influence on girls' beauty ideals is boys in general.

English language, spoken in the most individualist countries in Table 4.1, is the only one we know of that writes "I" with a capital letter.

Languages change over time, but only slowly. The first-person singular pronoun was used in Western European languages in medieval poetry. An Arab saying dating from the same period is "The satanic 'I' be damned!"[35]

The link between culture scores and language features illustrates the very old roots of cultural differences. It is naive to expect present-day differences to disappear over anybody's lifetime.

The Chinese-American anthropologist Francis Hsu has argued that the Chinese language has no equivalent for *personality* in the Western sense. Personality in the West is a separate entity, distinct from society and culture: it is an attribute of the individual. The closest translation into Chinese is *ren*, but this word includes not only the individual but also the intimate societal and cultural environment that makes his or her existence meaningful.[36]

The same point was made by two U.S. psychologists, Hazel Rose Markus and Shinobu Kitayama, the latter of Japanese descent. They argued that many Asian cultures have conceptions of individuality that insist on the fundamental relatedness of individuals to each other, while in America individuals seek to maintain their independence from others by focusing on the self and by discovering and expressing their unique inner attributes. The way people experience the self differs with the culture.[37] In our interpretation, individualist cultures encourage an independent self, while collectivist cultures encourage an interdependent self.

U.S. psychologist Solomon E. Asch (1907–96) designed a rather nasty experiment to test to what extent U.S. individuals would stick to their own judgment against a majority. The subject believed he or she was a member of a group of people who had to judge which of two lines was longer. Unknown to the subject, all other group members were confederates of the experimenter and deliberately gave a false answer. In this situation a sizable percentage of the subjects conformed to the group opinion against their own conviction. Since the 1950s, this experiment has been replicated in a number of countries. The percentage of subjects conforming to the false judgment was negatively correlated with the countries' IDV score.[38]

In Chapter 2 we referred to the relationship between personality and national culture, established by correlating across thirty-three countries the mean "Big Five" personality dimension scores with our culture dimension scores. There were significant correlations between country mean Big Five scores and all four IBM culture dimensions, but the strongest correlation was between extraversion and IDV.[39] Extraversion (as opposed to introversion) combines the following set of self-scored personality facets that tend to go together: warmth, gregariousness, assertiveness, activity, excitement seeking, and positive emotions. What the correlations show is that on average, people in more individualist cultures rate themselves higher on these facets than people in more collectivist cultures. It may seem surprising that people in cultures that encourage an independent self tend to score themselves higher on gregariousness, but it is precisely when relationships between people are *not* prescribed by the culture that the conscious decision to get together becomes more important.

U.S. psychologist David Matsumoto analyzed a large number of studies of the recognition of emotions in facial expressions. Students classified the emotions from photos of faces into happiness, surprise, sadness, fear, disgust, and anger. For fifteen countries from the IBM set, percentages of observers correctly perceiving happiness were correlated positively with IDV, and those correctly perceiving sadness were correlated negatively. Our interpretation is that individualist cultures encourage the showing of happiness but discourage the sharing of sadness; collectivist cultures do the opposite.[40]

U.S. professor Robert Levine asked his international students to collect data on the pace of life in their hometowns. One measure collected was walking speed, defined as the stopwatch time it took seventy healthy adults (of both genders, fifty-fifty) to cover a distance of sixty feet in one of two uncrowded locations in each city, when walking. Of thirty-one countries covered, twenty-three overlapped with the IBM set. Walking speed turned out to be strongly correlated with IDV. People in individualist cultures tended to walk faster.[41] We interpret this result as a physical expression of their self-concept: people in more individualist cultures are more active in trying to get somewhere.

Powerful information about differences in behavior across countries can be obtained from consumer surveys. Dutch marketing professor and consultant Marieke de Mooij, comparing fifteen European countries, found many meaningful correlations between consumer behavior data and IDV.[42] Persons in high-IDV countries were more likely than those in low-IDV countries to live in detached houses versus apartments or flats. They were more likely to have a private garden and to own a caravan (mobile home) for leisure. They more frequently had dogs as pets and especially cats, as measured by household consumption of pet food. (Cats are more individualistic animals than dogs!) They were more likely to possess home and life insurance. They more often engaged in do-it-yourself activities: painting walls and woodwork, wallpapering, home carpentry, electrical upgrades and repairs, and plumbing projects. In all these cases IDV explained the country differences better than national wealth. They all suggest a lifestyle in which the person tries to be self-supporting and not dependent on others.

In matters of information, persons in high-IDV countries read more books, and they were more likely to own a personal computer and a telephone with voice mail. High-IDV country residents more often rated TV advertising useful for information about new products. They relied more on media and less on their social networks.

There is no indication that inhabitants of countries with individualist cultures are healthier or unhealthier than those from countries with collectivist ones, but the fact that people in high-IDV cultures are more focused on the self is visible in a greater concern for their own health than is found in low-IDV cultures. If we limit our analysis to the higher- income countries, where full medical provisions can be assumed to be available, people in countries with a more individualist culture spend a larger share of their private income on their health. Governments of the same countries also spend a larger share of public budgets on health care.[43]

Individualist and collectivist cultures deal differently with disability. A survey among Australian health-care workers showed different reactions to becoming disabled among the Anglo, Arabic-speaking, Chinese, German-speaking, Greek, and Italian immigrant communities. In the individualist communities (Anglo and German), people with disabilities tended to remain cheerful and optimistic, to resent dependency and being helped, and to plan for a future life as normal as possible. In the collectivist communities (Greek, Chinese, Arabic), there would be more expression of grief, shame, and pessimism; family members would be asked for advice and assistance, and they would make the main decisions about the person's future. The Italians tended to be in the middle; northern Italy is more individualist, but a large share of Italian immigrants in Australia are from the collectivist southern region. Another study described the answers of the same panel of health-care workers to questions about the way the different groups dealt with *children* with disabilities. Again in the individualist communities, the dominant philosophy was to treat these children as much as possible like other children, letting them participate in all activities when this was feasible. In the collectivist communities, the disability would be seen as a shame on the family and a stigma on its members—especially if the child was a son—and the child would more often be kept out of sight.[44]

Table 4.3 summarizes the key differences between collectivist and individualist societies from this section.

TABLE 4.3 Key Differences Between Collectivist and
Individualist Societies
II: Language, Personality, and Behavior

COLLECTIVIST	INDIVIDUALIST
Use of the word "I" is avoided.	Use of the word "I" is encouraged
Interdependent self	Independent self
On personality tests, people score more introvert.	On personality tests, people score more extravert.
Showing sadness is encouraged, and happiness discouraged.	Showing happiness is encouraged, and sadness discouraged.
Slower walking speed	Faster walking speed
Consumption patterns show dependence on others.	Consumption patterns show self-supporting lifestyles.
Social network is primary source of information.	Media is primary source of information.
A smaller share of both private and public income is spent on health care.	A larger share of both private and public income is spent on health care.
People with disabilities are a shame on the family and should be kept out of sight.	People with disabilities should participate as much as possible in normal life.

Individualism and Collectivism at School

The relationship between the individual and the group that has been established in a child's consciousness during his or her early years in the family is further developed and reinforced at school. This is clearly visible in classroom behavior. In the context of development assistance, it often happens that teachers from a more individualist culture move to a more collectivist environment. A typical complaint from such teachers is that students do not speak up, not even when the teacher puts a question to the class. For the student who conceives of him- or herself as part of a group, it is illogical to speak up without being sanctioned by the group to do so. If the teacher wants students to speak up, the teacher should address a particular student personally.

Students in a collectivist culture will also hesitate to speak up in larger groups without a teacher present, especially if these groups are partly composed of relative strangers: out-group members. This hesitation decreases in smaller groups. In a large, collectivist or culturally heterogeneous class, creating small subgroups is a way to increase student participation. For example, students can be asked to turn around in their seats and discuss a question for five minutes in groups of three or four. Each group is asked to appoint a spokesperson. In this way, individual answers become group answers, and those who speak up do so in the name of their group. Often in subsequent exercises the students will spontaneously rotate the spokesperson role.

In the collectivist society, in-group–out-group distinctions springing from the family sphere will continue at school, so that students from different ethnic or clan backgrounds often form subgroups in class. In an individualist society, the assignment of joint tasks leads more easily to the formation of new groups than in the collectivist society. In the latter, students from the same ethnic or family background as the teacher or other school officials will expect preferential treatment on this basis. In an individualist society, this practice would be considered nepotism and intensely immoral, but in a collectivist environment, it is immoral *not* to treat one's in-group members better than others.

In the collectivist classroom, the virtues of harmony and maintaining face reign supreme. Confrontations and conflicts should be avoided or at least should be formulated so as not to hurt anyone; students should not lose face if this can be avoided. Shaming (that is, invoking the group's honor) is an effective way of correcting offenders: they will be set straight by their in-group members. At all times, the teacher is dealing with the student as part of an in-group, never as an isolated individual.

In the individualist classroom, of course, students expect to be treated as individuals and impartially, regardless of their background. Group formation among students is much more ad hoc, operating according to the task or to particular friendships and skills. Confrontations and open discussion of conflicts are often considered salutary, and face-consciousness is weak or nonexistent.

The purpose of education is perceived differently between the individualist and the collectivist societies. In the former it aims at preparing the individual for a place in a society of other individuals. This means learning to cope with new, unknown, unforeseen situations. There is a basically positive attitude toward what is new. The purpose of learning is less to know how to do than to know *how to learn.* The assumption is that learning in life never ends; even after school and college it will continue (for example, through postgraduate courses).

In the collectivist society, there is a stress on adaptation to the skills and virtues necessary to be an acceptable group member. This leads to a premium on the products of tradition. Learning is more often seen as a onetime process, reserved for young people, who have to learn *how to do* things in order to participate in society. It is an extended rite of passage.

The role of diplomas or certificates as a result of successful completion of a study is also different between the two poles of the individualism-collectivism dimension. In the individualist society, the diploma improves not only the holder's economic worth but also his or her self-respect: it provides a sense of achievement. In the collectivist society, a diploma is an honor to the holder (and his or her in-group) and entitles the holder to associate with members of higher-status groups—for example, to get a more attractive marriage partner. It is to a certain extent "a ticket to a ride." The social acceptance that comes with the diploma is more important than the individual self-respect that comes with mastering a subject, so that in collectivist societies, the temptation is stronger to obtain diplomas in some irregular way, such as on the black market.

Individualism and Collectivism in the Workplace

Sons in collectivist societies are more likely than sons in individualist societies to follow in the occupation of their fathers.[45] We noticed that Geert and Gert Jan's operating as a father-and-son author team tends to be admired in collectivist cultures but is sometimes scorned in individualist ones. In more individualist societies, sons of fathers in manual occupations will more frequently move to nonmanual occupations, and vice versa. In more collectivist societies, occupational mobility is lower.

Employed persons in an individualist culture are expected to act according to their own interests, and work should be organized in such a way that this self-interest and the employer's interest coincide. Workers are supposed to act as "economic persons," or as people with a combination of economic and psychological needs, but anyway as individuals with their own needs. In a collectivist culture, an employer never hires just an individual, but rather a person who belongs to an in-group. The employee will act according to the interest of this in-group, which may not always coincide with his or her individual interest: self-effacement in the interest of the in-group belongs to the normal expectations in such a society. Often earnings have to be shared with relatives.

The hiring process in a collectivist society always takes the in-group into account. Usually, preference is given to hiring relatives, first of all of the employer, but also of other persons already employed by the company. Hiring persons from a family one already knows reduces risks. Also, relatives will be concerned about the reputation of the family and help to correct misbehavior of a family member. In the individualist society, family relationships at work are often considered undesirable, as they may lead to nepotism and to a conflict of interest. Some companies have a rule that if one employee marries another, one of them has to leave.

The workplace itself in a collectivist society may become an in-group in the emotional sense of the word. This is more the case in some countries than in others, but the feeling that it should be this way is nearly always present. The relationship between employer and employee is seen in moral terms. It resembles a family relationship with mutual obligations of protection in exchange for loyalty. Poor performance of an employee in this relationship is no reason for dismissal: one does not dismiss one's child. Performance and skills, however, do determine what tasks one assigns to an employee. This pattern of relationships is best known from Japanese organizations. In Japan it applies in a strict sense only to the group of permanent employees, which may be less than half of the total workforce. Japan scores halfway on the IDV scale. In individualist societies, the relationship between employer and employee is primarily conceived of as a business transaction, a calculative relationship between buyers and sellers in a labor market. Poor performance on the part of the employee and a better pay offer from another employer are both legitimate and socially accepted reasons for terminating a work relationship.

Christopher Earley, a management researcher from the United States, has illustrated the difference in work ethos between an individualist and a collectivist society very neatly with a laboratory experiment. In the experiment forty-eight management trainees from southern China and forty-eight matched management trainees from the United States were given an "in-basket task." The task consisted of forty separate items requiring between two and five minutes each, such as writing memos, evaluating plans, and rating job candidates' application forms. Half of the participants in each country were given a group goal of two hundred items to be completed in an hour by ten people; participants in the other half were each given an individual goal of twenty items. Also, half of the participants in each country, both from the group goal subset and from the individual goal subset, were asked to mark each item completed with their names, while the other half turned them in anonymously.

The Chinese collectivist participants performed best when operating with a group goal and anonymously. They performed worst when operating individually and with their names marked on the items produced. The American individualist participants performed best when operating individually and with their names marked but abysmally low when operating as a group and anonymously. All participants were also given a values test to determine their personal individualism or collectivism: a minority of the Chinese scored individualist, and these performed according to the U.S. pattern; a minority of the Americans scored collectivist, and these performed like the Chinese.[46]

In practice there is a wide range of types of employer-employee relationships *within* collectivist and individualist societies. There are employers in collectivist countries who do not respect the societal norm to treat their employees as in-group members, but then the employees in turn do not repay the employers in terms of loyalty. Labor unions in such cases may replace the work organization as an emotional in-group, and there can be violent union-management conflicts, as in parts of India. There are employers in individualist societies who have established strong group cohesion with their employees, with the same protection-versus-loyalty balance that is the norm in the collectivist society. Organization cultures can deviate to some extent from majority norms and derive a competitive advantage from their originality. Chapter 10 will go into these issues more deeply.

Management in an individualist society is management of individuals. Subordinates can usually be moved around individually; if incentives or bonuses are given, these should be linked to an individual's performance. Management in a collectivist society is management of groups. The extent to which people actually feel emotionally integrated into a work group may differ from one situation to another. Ethnic and other in-group differences within the work group play a role in the integration process, and managers within a collectivist culture will be extremely attentive to such factors. It often makes good sense to put persons from the same ethnic background into one crew, although individualistically programmed managers usually consider this practice dangerous and want to do the opposite. If the work group functions as an emotional in-group, incentives and bonuses should be given to the group, not to individuals.

Within countries with a dominant individualist middle-class culture, regional rural subcultures have sometimes retained strongly collectivist elements. The same applies to the migrant-worker minorities that form majorities among the workforce in some industries in some individualist countries. In such cases a culture conflict is likely between managers and regional or minority workers. This conflict expresses itself, among other ways, in the management's extreme hesitation to use group incentives in cases in which such incentives would suit the culture of the workforce.

Management techniques and training packages have almost exclusively been developed in individualist countries, and they are based on cultural assumptions that may not hold in collectivist cultures. A standard element in the training of first-line managers is how to conduct *appraisal interviews*, periodic discussions in which the subordinate's performance is reviewed. These sessions can form a part of management by objectives,[47] but even where MBO does not exist, conducting performance appraisals and ably communicating bad news are considered key skills for a successful manager. In a collectivist society, discussing a person's performance openly with him or her is likely to clash head-on with the society's harmony norm and may be felt by the subordinate as an unacceptable loss of face. Such societies have more subtle, indirect ways of supplying feedback—for example, by the withdrawal of a normal favor or verbally via an intermediary. We know of a case in which an older relative of a poorly performing employee, also in the service of the employer, played this intermediary role. He communicated the bad news to his nephew, avoiding the loss of face that a formal appraisal interview would have provoked.

For the same reason, training methods based on honest and direct sharing of feelings about other people, which have periodically been fashionable in the United States with labels such as *sensitivity training*, *encounter groups*, or *transactional analysis*, are unfit for use in collectivist cultures.

The distinction between in-groups and out-groups that is so essential in the collectivist culture pattern has far-reaching consequences for business relationships, beyond those between employers and employees. It is the reason behind the cultural embarrassment of Mr. Johannesson and his Swedish superiors in Saudi Arabia, related at the beginning of this chapter. In individualist societies, the norm is that one should treat everybody alike. In sociological jargon this is known as *universalism*. Preferential treatment of one customer over others is considered bad business practice and unethical. In collectivist societies, the reverse is true. As the distinction between "our group" and "other groups" is at the very root of people's consciousness, treating one's friends better than others is natural and ethical and is a sound business practice. Sociologists call this way of acting *particularism*; it is similar to what Misho's analysis of the World Values Survey calls *exclusionism*.

A consequence of particularist thinking is that in a collectivist society, a relationship of trust should be established with another person before any business can be done. Through this relationship the other is adopted into one's in-group and is from that moment onward entitled to preferential treatment. In Johannesson's case this process of adoption took two years. During this period the presence of the Swedish businessman as an intermediary was essential. After the adoption had taken place, it became superfluous. However, the relationship was with Johannesson personally and not with his company. To the collectivist mind, only natural persons are worthy of trust, and via these persons their friends and colleagues become worthy, but not impersonal legal entities such as a company. In summary, in the collectivist society, *the personal relationship prevails over the task* and should be established first, whereas in the individualist society, *the task is supposed to prevail over any personal relationships.* The naive Western businessperson who tries to force quick business in a collectivist culture condemns him- or herself to the role of out-group member and to negative discrimination.

Individualism, Collectivism, and the Internet

Surveys and observations about the use of modern information and communication technologies (ICT) show significant differences among countries. Most of these tools originated in a highly individualist society: the United States. ICT tools link individuals, so these tools are more easily, frequently, and eagerly used in individualist societies than in collectivist societies. In the latter, people have more direct ways to relate to their social environment. Along with societal individualism, two other cultural dimensions, masculinity and uncertainty avoidance, play a role in the use of ICT; we will deal with these influences in Chapters 5 and 6.

Eurobarometer surveys have shown that people in more individualist European countries were more likely to have access to the Internet and to use e-mail. They more often used the computer for shopping, banking, and supplying information to public authorities.[48]

Asked about the effects of the introduction of the Internet, respondents in the *less* individualist European countries stressed that people who do not use the Internet have more time for themselves, their family, and their friends.[49]

Table 4.4 lists the key differences between collectivist and individualist societies related to school, the workplace, and ICT.

TABLE 4.4 Key Differences Between Collectivist and Individualist Societies III: School, Workplace, and ICT

COLLECTIVIST	INDIVIDUALIST
Students speak up in class only when sanctioned by the group.	Students are expected to individually speak up in class.
The purpose of education is learning how to do.	The purpose of education is learning how to learn.
Diplomas provide entry to higher-status groups.	Diplomas increase economic worth and/or self-respect.
Occupational mobility is lower.	Occupational mobility is higher.
Employees are members of in-groups who will pursue the in-group's interest.	Employees are "economic persons" who will pursue the employer's interest if it coincides with their self-interest.
Hiring and promotion decisions take employee's in-group into account.	Hiring and promotion decisions are supposed to be based on skills and rules only.
The employer-employee relationship is basically moral, like a family link.	The employer-employee relationship is a contract between parties in a labor market.
Management is management of groups.	Management is management of individuals.
Direct appraisal of subordinates spoils harmony.	Management training teaches the honest sharing of feelings.
In-group customers get better treatment (*particularism*).	Every customer should get the same treatment (*universalism*).
Relationship prevails over task.	Task prevails over relationship.
The Internet and e-mail are less attractive and less frequently used.	The Internet and e-mail hold strong appeal and are frequently used to link individuals.

Individualism, Collectivism, and the State

Alfred Kraemer, an American author in the field of intercultural communication, cited the following comment in a Russian literary journal by a poet, Vladimir Korotich, who had completed a two-month lecture tour at American universities:

> *Attempts to please an American audience are doomed in advance, because out of twenty listeners five may hold one point of view, seven another, and eight may have none at all.*[50]

What strikes the Western reader about this comment is not the described attitudes of American students but the fact that Korotich expected otherwise. He was obviously accustomed to audiences in which people would not express a confronting view, a characteristic of a collectivist culture. Table 4.1 shows Russia to score considerably more collectivist than Western countries.

Naive observers of the world political scene often see only the different political systems and are not aware of the different mind-sets of the populations that led to and maintain these different systems. If the commonly held value system is that collective interests should prevail over individual interests, this leads to a different kind of state from the kind that results if the dominant feeling is that individual interest should prevail over collective ones.

In American parlance the term *collectivist* is sometimes used to describe communist political systems. Countries in Table 4.1 that had or still have either communist or state capitalist governments are found on the medium to low IDV—that is, the collectivist side. The weaker the individualism in the citizens' mental software, the greater the likelihood of a dominating role of the state in the economic system.

Since the 1990s increasing individualism has been one of the forces leading to deregulation and reduction of public expenditures in Western countries. Even public monopolies such as energy provision and public transportation have sometimes been privatized at the expense of their performance and reliability, for ideological rather than pragmatic reasons—which shows the power of cultural values.

The capitalist invention of the joint-stock company—an enterprise owned by dispersed shareholders who can trade their shares on a stock

exchange—was made in individualist Britain and for its functioning supposes an individualist mind-set among its actors.[51] In practice it is regularly threatened by particularist interests, and in a curious paradox, its
supposedly free market needs strong regulation by government.

On the other hand, the economic life in collectivist societies, if not
dominated by government, is in any case based on collective interests.
Family enterprises abound; in the People's Republic of China, after the
economic liberalization of the 1980s, villages, the army, and municipal
police corps units started their own enterprises.

Individualist countries tend to be wealthier and to have smaller power
distances than collectivist ones. This is a statistical relationship that does
not hold for all countries, but because of this relationship it is sometimes
difficult to separate the effects of wealth, individualism, and smaller power
distance on government. For example, political scientists have developed
an index of press freedom for a large number of countries. This index is
significantly correlated with high IDV and low PDI, but it is most strongly
correlated with national wealth. Greater press freedom in wealthier countries is a matter not only of individualism and equality but also of resources
such as more newspapers and TV channels and of interest groups with the
means to disseminate their opinions.[52]

The right to privacy is a central theme in many individualist societies
that does not find the same sympathy in collectivist societies, where it is
seen as normal and right that one's in-group can at any time invade one's
private life.

The difference between a universalist and a particularist treatment of
customers, illustrated by the Johannesson case, applies to the functioning
of the state as a whole. In the individualist society, laws and rights are supposed to be the same for all members and to be applied indiscriminately to
everybody (whether this standard is always met is another question). In the
collectivist society, laws and rights may differ from one category of people
to another—if not in theory, then in the way laws are administered—and
this is not seen as wrong.

If differences in the political systems found in countries are rooted
in their citizens' mental software, the possibility of influencing these systems by propaganda, money, or arms from another country is limited. If
the minds are not receptive to the message, propaganda and money are

mostly wasted. Even the most powerful foreign state cannot brainwash entire populations out of their deeply held values.

A main issue in international politics is national governments' respect for human rights. The Universal Declaration of Human Rights was adopted by the United Nations in 1948. Charles Humana, a former researcher for Amnesty International, calculated human rights ratings for a large number of countries on the basis of forty questions derived from UN criteria. Across fifty-two countries from the IBM set, Humana's human rights ratings correlated primarily with gross national income (GNI) per capita, which explained 50 percent of the differences; adding culture scores did not improve the explanation. The picture changed when we looked separately at the twenty-five wealthier countries: now the single explaining variable, accounting for 53 percent of the differences in human rights ratings, became IDV. For the remaining twenty-seven poorer countries, GNI per capita remained the single explaining variable, but it now accounted for only 14 percent of the differences.[53] Our conclusion from these relationships is that respect for human rights as formulated by the United Nations is a luxury that wealthy countries can afford more easily than poor ones; to what extent these wealthy countries do conform to UN criteria, however, depends on the degree of individualism in the culture. The Universal Declaration of Human Rights and other UN covenants were inspired by the values of the dominant powers at the time of their adoption, and these were individualistic.

Individualism, Collectivism, and Ideas

Individualist societies not only practice individualism but also consider it superior to other forms of mental software. Most Americans feel that individualism is good and that it is at the root of their country's greatness. On the other hand, the late chairman Mao Zedong of China identified individualism as evil. He found individualism and liberalism responsible for selfishness and aversion to discipline; they led people to placing personal interests above those of the group or simply to devoting too much attention to their own things. In Table 4.1 the places with a predominantly Chinese population all score very low on IDV (Hong Kong 25, mainland China 20, Singapore 20, Taiwan 17).

In the European Values Survey, which preceded the World Values Survey, representative samples of the population in nine European countries in 1981 were asked to choose between the following statements:

> *A: I find that both freedom and equality are important. But if I were to make up my mind for one or the other, I would consider personal freedom more important—that is, everyone can live in freedom and develop without hindrance.*

> *B: Certainly both freedom and equality are important. But if I were to make up my mind for one of the two, I would consider equality more important—that is, that nobody is underprivileged and that social class differences are not so strong.*[54]

This is, of course, an ideological choice. In most of the nine European countries, respondents on average preferred freedom over equality. The French sociologist Jean Stoetzel (1910–87), who published a brilliant analysis of the data, has computed a ratio for each country: preference for freedom divided by preference for equality. This ratio runs from about 1 in Spain (equal preference) to about 3 in Great Britain (freedom three times as popular as equality). The values of the freedom/equality ratio for the nine countries were significantly correlated with IDV: the more individualist a country, the stronger its citizens' preference for freedom over equality.[55] Freedom is an individualist ideal, equality a collectivist ideal.

The choice between individualism and collectivism at the society level has considerable implications for economic theories. Economics as a discipline was founded in Britain in the eighteenth century; among the founding fathers, Adam Smith (1723–90) stands out. Smith assumed that the pursuit of self-interest by individuals through an "invisible hand" would increase the wealth of nations. This is an individualist idea from a country that even today ranks high on individualism. Economics has remained an individualist science, and most of its leading contributors have come from strongly individualist nations such as Britain and the United States. However, because of the individualist assumptions on which economic theories are based, these theories as developed in the West are unlikely to apply in societies in which group interests prevail. This point has profound consequences for development assistance to poor countries and for economic globalization. There is a dire need for alternative economic theories that take into account cultural differences on this dimension.

The degree of individualism or collectivism of a society affects the conceptions of human nature produced in that society. In the United States the ideas of Abraham Maslow (1908–70) about human motivation have been and are still influential, in particular for the training of management students and practitioners. Maslow's famous "hierarchy of human needs" states that human needs can be ordered in a hierarchy from lower to higher, as follows: physiological, safety, belongingness, esteem, and self-actualization.[56] In order for a higher need to appear, it is necessary that the lower needs have been satisfied up to a certain extent. A starving person, one whose physiological needs are not at all satisfied, will not be motivated by anything other than the quest for food, and so forth. The top of Maslow's hierarchy, often pictured as a pyramid, is occupied by the motive of *self-actualization*: realizing to the fullest possible extent the creative potential present within the individual. This means doing one's own thing. It goes without saying that this can be the supreme motivation only in an individualist society. In a collectivist culture, what will be actualized is the interest and honor of the in-group, which may very well ask for self-effacement from many of the in-group members. The interpreter for a group of young Americans visiting China in the late 1970s found the idea of "doing your own thing" untranslatable into Chinese. Harmony and consensus are more attractive ultimate goals for such societies than individual self-actualization.

Since *Culture's Consequences* first appeared in 1980, the individualism-collectivism dimension has gained much popularity among psychologists, especially those from the economically emerging Asian nations. The dimension implies that traditional psychology is as little a universal science as traditional economics: it is a product of Western thinking, caught in individualist assumptions. When these assumptions are replaced by more collectivist assumptions, another psychology emerges, and it differs from the former in important respects. For example, as we discussed earlier in this chapter, individualist psychology is universalist, opposing the "ego" to any "other." In collectivist psychology, the ego is inseparable from its social context. People in collectivist societies make exclusionist distinctions: the in-group, which includes the ego, is opposed to all out-groups.

This means that the results of psychological experiments in a collectivist society depend on whether participants belong to the same in-group.

Table 4.5 is a continuation of Tables 4.2, 4.3, and 4.4: it summarizes the key differences between collectivist and individualist societies from the last two sections.

TABLE 4.5 Key Differences Between Collectivist and Individualist Societies IV: Politics and Ideas

COLLECTIVIST	INDIVIDUALIST
Opinions are predetermined by group membership.	Everyone is expected to have a private opinion.
Collective interests prevail over individual interests.	Individual interests prevail over collective interests.
State has dominant role in the economic system.	State has restrained role in the economic system.
Low per capita GNI	High per capita GNI
Companies are owned by families or collectives.	Joint-stock companies are owned by individual investors.
Private life is invaded by group(s).	Everyone has a right to privacy.
Laws and rights differ by group.	Laws and rights are supposed to be the same for all.
Lower Human Rights rating	Higher Human Rights rating
Ideologies of equality prevail over ideologies of individual freedom.	Ideologies of individual freedom prevail over ideologies of equality.
Imported economic theories are unable to deal with collective and particularist interests.	Native economic theories are based on pursuit of individual self-interests.
Harmony and consensus in society are ultimate goals.	Self-actualization by every individual is an ultimate goal.
Patriotism is the ideal.	Autonomy is the ideal.
Outcome of psychological experiments depends on in-group–out-group distinction	Outcome of psychological experiments depends on ego-other distinction.

Origins of Individualism-Collectivism Differences

The origins of differences on the individualism-collectivism dimension, just as with those on power distance, are a matter of conjecture. Nevertheless, statistical relationships with geographic, economic, and historic variables can support the guesswork.

It is a common assumption among archaeologists that the development of human societies started with groups of hunter-gatherer nomads; that subsequently people settled down into a sedentary existence as farmers; and that farming communities grew into larger settlements that became towns, cities, and finally modern megalopolises. Cultural anthropologists have compared present-day hunter-gatherer tribes, agricultural societies, and urbanized societies. They have found that from the most primitive to the most modern society, family complexity first increased and then decreased. Hunter-gatherers tend to live in nuclear families or small bands. Sedentary agricultural societies mostly show complex extended families or village community in-groups. When farmers migrate to cities, the sizes of extended families become reduced, and the typical urban family is again nuclear. In most countries today, one finds only agricultural and urban subcultures. For these two types, modernization corresponds to individualization.

Information about one hunter-gatherer society comes from an Australian researcher, Ray Simonsen, who administered the VSM94 (the 1994 improved version of the IBM questionnaire) to aboriginal entrepreneurs in Darwin, Northern Territory, and to a comparable group of white Australians. Aboriginal society is still largely based on hunting and gathering. While unlike the white Australians, the aborigines scored high on power distance, low on masculinity, and high on uncertainty avoidance, on individualism they scored as high as their white compatriots.[57]

In Figure 4.1 we find societies with a large traditional rural sector mostly at the collectivist side and modern industrial societies at the individualist side. There are some exceptions, especially in East Asia, where Japan, South Korea, Taiwan, Hong Kong, and Singapore have retained considerable collectivism in spite of industrialization.

As in the case of PDI in Chapter 3, we used stepwise regression to determine what quantitative information about our countries best explained the differences in IDV scores. We found that a country's IDV score can be fairly accurately predicted from two factors:

- The country's wealth (richer countries associated with higher IDV)
- Its geographical latitude (countries closer to the equator associated with lower IDV)

Wealth (GNI per capita at the time of the IBM surveys) explained no less than 71 percent of the differences in IDV scores for the original fifty IBM countries. This finding is amazing in light of the fact that the two measures came from entirely different sources and that both were rather imprecise—subject to measuring error.

A correlation does not show which of two related phenomena is cause and which is effect, or whether both could be caused by a third factor. If individualism were the cause of wealth, one should find that IDV scores relate not only to national wealth per se but also to ensuing *economic growth*. The latter is measured by the World Bank as the average annual percentage increase in GNI per capita during a longer period. If individualism leads to wealth, IDV should be positively correlated with economic growth in the period following the collection of the IDV data. However, the relationship between IDV scores (collected around 1970) and subsequent economic growth was, if anything, negative: the more individualist countries showed *less*, not more, economic growth than the less individualist ones.

We can draw the same conclusion by looking at the correlations of 1970 IDV with country wealth in later years. Wealth differences in 1970 explained 72 percent of IDV differences; wealth in 1980 explained 62 percent; in 1990, 55 percent; and in 2000, 52 percent.[58] If causality went from IDV to subsequent GNI, the correlation should have become stronger over time. The correlation between wealth differences in different periods is much stronger.[59]

The reverse causality, national wealth causing individualism, is therefore more plausible.[60] When a country's wealth increases, its citizens get access to resources that allow them to do their own thing. The storyteller in the village market is replaced by TV sets, first one per village, but soon more. In wealthy Western family homes, every family member may have his or her own TV set. The caravan through the desert is replaced by a number of buses, and these by a larger number of automobiles, until each adult family member drives a different car. The village hut in which the entire family lives and sleeps together is replaced by a house with a number of private rooms. Collective life is replaced by individual life. However, the negative relationship between individualism and economic growth for the wealthier countries suggests that this development can lead to its own undoing. The 2008 economic crisis started in very wealthy countries.

Besides national wealth, the only other measure statistically related to IDV was geographic latitude: the distance from the equator of a country's capital city. It explained an additional 7 percent of the IDV differences. In Chapter 3 latitude was the *first* predictor of power distance scores. As we argued there, in countries with moderate and cold climates, people's survival depends more on their ability to fend for themselves. This circumstance favors educating children toward independence from more powerful others (lower PDI). It also seems to favor a degree of individualism.

The size of the population of a country, which contributed significantly to predicting power distance, did not relate to collectivism. The *growth* of the population (average percent per year over a ten-year period) did relate to collectivism, but its first correlation was with country wealth—in poor countries families tend to have more children. There are a number of reasons for this, the most prominent of which are poor education of women and the expectation that children will support their parents in old age. Children in larger families obviously are more likely to acquire collectivist rather than individualist values.

Historical factors, apart from economic ones, can also account for part of the country differences on this dimension, although not as clearly as in the case of the influence of the Roman Empire on power distance. The influence of the teachings of Confucius in the East Asian countries, to which part of Chapter 7 will be devoted, supports the maintenance of a collectivist value system. On the other hand, in parts of Western Europe, in particular in England, Scotland, and the Netherlands, individualist values could be recognized centuries ago, when the average citizen in these countries was still quite poor and the economies were overwhelmingly rural. India is another example of a country with a rather individualistic culture despite poverty.

The Future of Individualism and Collectivism

The deep roots of national cultures make it likely that individualism-collectivism differences, such as power distance differences, will survive for a long time into the future. That said, if there is to be any convergence between national cultures, it should be on this dimension. The strong relationship between national wealth and individualism is undeniable, with the arrow of causality directed, as shown earlier, from wealth to individualism. Countries having achieved fast economic development have experienced a shift toward individualism. For example, care for elderly members by the family is becoming less self-evident.

Nevertheless, even at equal levels of per capita income, countries also preserve individualist and collectivist values from their history. East Asian societies such as Japan and Korea do conserve distinctive collectivist elements in their family, school, and work spheres. Among Western countries such as Britain, Sweden, and Germany, in spite of a noticeable convergence toward individualism under the influence of common economic development, relationships between the individual and the group continue to differ. The cultures shift, but they shift together, so that their relative positions remain intact, and there is no reason why differences between them should disappear.

As far as the poor countries of the world are concerned, they cannot be expected to become more individualist as long as they remain poor. Also, if differences in wealth between rich and poor countries continue to increase (as in many instances they do), gaps on the individualism-collectivism dimension can only increase further.

Differences in values associated with the individualism-collectivism dimension will continue to exist and to play a big role in international affairs. Individualism versus collectivism as a dimension of national cultures is responsible for many misunderstandings in intercultural encounters. In Chapter 11 it will be shown that many problems of such encounters can be explained from differences on this dimension.

He, She, and (S)he

As a young Dutch engineer, Geert once applied for a junior management job with an American engineering company that had recently settled in Flanders, the Dutch-speaking part of Belgium. He felt well qualified, with a degree from the leading technical university of the country, good grades, a record of active participation in student associations, and three years' experience as an engineer with a well-known (although somewhat sleepy) Dutch company. He had written a short letter to the company indicating his interest and providing some salient personal data. He was invited for an interview, and after a long train ride he sat facing the American plant manager. Geert behaved politely and modestly, as he knew an applicant should, and waited for the other man to ask the usual questions that would enable him to find out how qualified Geert was. To his surprise, the plant manager touched on very few of the areas that Geert thought should be discussed. Instead, he asked about some highly detailed facts pertaining to Geert's experience in tool design, using English words that Geert did not know, and the relevance of the questioning escaped him. Those were things he could learn within a week once he worked there. After half an hour of painful misunderstandings, the interviewer said, "Sorry—we need a first-class man." And Geert was out on the street.

Assertiveness Versus Modesty

Years later Geert was the interviewer, and he met with both Dutch and American applicants. Then he understood what had gone wrong in that earlier case. American applicants, to Dutch eyes, oversell themselves. Their curricula vitae are worded in superlatives, mentioning every degree, grade, award, and membership to demonstrate their outstanding qualities. During the interview they try to behave assertively, promising things they are very unlikely to realize—such as learning the local language in a few months.

Dutch applicants, in American eyes, undersell themselves. They write modest and usually short CVs, counting on the interviewer to find out how good they really are by asking. They expect an interest in their social and extracurricular activities during their studies. They are careful not to be seen as braggarts and not to make promises they are not absolutely sure they can fulfill.

American interviewers know how to interpret American CVs and interviews, and they tend to discount the information provided. Dutch interviewers, accustomed to Dutch applicants, tend to upgrade the information. The scenario for cross-cultural misunderstanding is clear. To an uninitiated American interviewer, an uninitiated Dutch applicant comes across as a sucker. To an uninitiated Dutch interviewer, an uninitiated American applicant comes across as a braggart.

Dutch and American societies are reasonably similar on the dimensions of power distance and individualism as described in the two previous chapters, but they differ considerably on a third dimension, which opposes, among other things, the desirability of assertive behavior against the desirability of modest behavior. We will label it *masculinity versus femininity*.

Genders and Gender Roles

All human societies consist of men and women, usually in approximately equal numbers. They are biologically distinct, and their respective roles in biological procreation are absolute. Other physical differences between women and men, not directly related to the bearing and begetting of children, are not absolute but *statistical*. Men are *on average* taller and stronger, but many women are taller and stronger than quite a few men. Women have *on average* greater finger dexterity and, for example, faster metabolism, which enables them to recover faster from fatigue, but some men excel in these respects.

The absolute and statistical biological differences between men and women are the same the world over, but the social roles of men and women in society are only partly determined by the biological constraints. Every society recognizes many behaviors, not immediately related to procreation, as more suitable to females or more suitable to males, but which behaviors belong to either gender differs from one society to another. Anthropologists having studied nonliterate, relatively isolated societies stress the wide variety of social sex roles that seem to be possible.[1] For the biological distinction, this chapter will use the terms *male* and *female*; for the social, culturally determined roles, the terms are *masculine* and *feminine*. The latter terms are *relative*, not absolute: a man can behave in a "feminine" way and a woman in a "masculine" way; this means only that they deviate from certain conventions in their society.

Which behaviors are considered feminine or masculine differs not only among traditional societies but also among modern societies. This is most evident in the distribution of men and women over certain professions. Women dominate as doctors in Russia, as dentists in Belgium, and as shopkeepers in parts of West Africa. Men dominate as typists in Pakistan and form a sizable share of nurses in the Netherlands. Female managers are virtually nonexistent in Japan but frequent in the Philippines and Thailand.

In spite of the variety found, there is a common trend among most societies, both traditional and modern, as to the distribution of social sex roles. From now on, this chapter will use the more politically correct term *gender roles*. Men are supposed to be more concerned with achievements outside the home—hunting and fighting in traditional societies, the same but translated into economic terms in modern societies. Men, in short, are supposed to be assertive, competitive, and tough. Women are supposed to be more concerned with taking care of the home, of the children, and of people in general—to take the tender roles. It is not difficult to see how this role pattern is likely to have developed: women first bore the children and then usually breast-fed them, so at least during this period they had to stay close to the children. Men were freer to move around, to the extent that they were not needed to protect women and children against attacks by other men and by animals.

Male achievement reinforces masculine assertiveness and competition; female care reinforces feminine nurturance and a concern for relationships and for the living environment.[2] Men, taller and stronger and free to get out, tend to dominate in social life outside the home; inside the home a variety of role distributions between the genders is possible. The role pattern demonstrated by the father and mother (and possibly other family members) has a profound impact on the mental software of the small child who is programmed with it for life. Therefore, it is not surprising that one of the dimensions of national value systems is related to gender role models offered by parents.

The gender role socialization that started in the family continues in peer groups and in schools. A society's gender role pattern is daily reflected in its media, including TV programs, motion pictures, children's books, newspapers, and women's journals. Gender role–confirming behavior is a criterion for mental health.[3] Gender roles are part and parcel of every society.

Masculinity-Femininity as a Dimension of Societal Culture

Chapter 4 referred to a set of fourteen work goals in the IBM questionnaire: "Try to think of those factors that would be important to you in an ideal job; disregard the extent to which they are contained in your present job." The analysis of the answers to the fourteen work goal items produced two underlying dimensions. One was *individualism versus collectivism*: the importance of personal time, freedom, and challenge stood for individualism, while the importance of training, physical conditions, and use of skills stood for collectivism.

The second dimension came to be labeled *masculinity versus femininity*. It was associated most strongly with the importance attached to the following work goal items:

For the masculine pole
1. **Earnings:** have an opportunity for high earnings
2. **Recognition:** get the recognition you deserve when you do a good job
3. **Advancement:** have an opportunity for advancement to higher-level jobs
4. **Challenge:** have challenging work to do—work from which you can get a personal sense of accomplishment

For the opposite, feminine pole
5. **Manager:** have a good working relationship with your direct superior
6. **Cooperation:** work with people who cooperate well with one another
7. **Living area:** live in an area desirable to you and your family
8. **Employment security:** have the security that you will be able to work for your company as long as you want to

Note that the work goal *challenge* was also associated with the individualism dimension (Chapter 4). The other seven goals are associated only with masculinity or femininity.

The decisive reason for labeling the second work goals dimension *masculinity versus femininity* is that *this dimension is the only one on which the men and the women among the IBM employees scored consistently differently* (except, as will be shown, in countries at the extreme feminine pole). Neither power distance nor individualism nor uncertainty avoidance showed a systematic difference in answers between men and women. Only the present dimension produced such a gender difference, with men attaching greater importance to, in particular, work goals 1 and 3 and women to goals 5 and 6. The importance of earnings and advancement corresponds to the masculine, assertive, and competitive social role. The importance of relations with the manager and with colleagues corresponds to the caring and social-environment-oriented feminine role.

As in the case of the individualism versus collectivism dimension, the eight items from the IBM questionnaire do not cover all there is to the distinction between a masculine and a feminine culture in society. They just represent the aspects of this dimension that were represented by questions in the IBM research. Again the correlations of the IBM country scores with non-IBM data about other characteristics of societies allow for a full grasp of what the dimension encompasses.

The differences in mental programming among societies related to this new dimension are social but are even more emotional. Social roles can be imposed by external factors, but what people feel while playing them comes from the inside. This state of affairs leads us to the following definition:

A society is called masculine *when emotional gender roles are clearly distinct: men are supposed to be assertive, tough, and focused on material success, whereas women are supposed to be more modest, tender, and concerned with the quality of life.*

A society is called feminine *when emotional gender roles overlap: both men and women are supposed to be modest, tender, and concerned with the quality of life.*

For the countries in the IBM database, masculinity index (MAS) values were calculated in a way similar to individualism index values (Chapter 4). MAS was based on the country's *factor score* in a *factor analysis* of the fourteen work goals. Scores were put into a range from about 0 for the most feminine country to about 100 for the most masculine country through multiplying the factor scores by 20 and adding 50. For follow-up studies, an approximation formula was used in which MAS was directly computed from the mean scores of four work goals.

Country MAS scores are shown in Table 5.1. As with the scores for power distance and individualism, the masculinity scores represent *relative*, not absolute, positions of countries. Unlike with individualism, masculinity is unrelated to a country's degree of economic development: we find rich and poor masculine and rich and poor feminine countries.

The most feminine-scoring countries (ranks 76 through 72) were Sweden, Norway, Latvia, the Netherlands, and Denmark; Finland came close with a rank of 68. The lower third of Table 5.1 further contains some Latin countries: Costa Rica, Chile, Portugal, Guatemala, Uruguay, El Salvador, Peru, Spain, and France; and some Eastern European countries: Slovenia, Lithuania, Estonia, Russia, Croatia, Bulgaria, Romania, and Serbia. From Asia it contains Thailand, South Korea, Vietnam, and Iran. Other femi-

TABLE 5.1 Masculinity Index (MAS) Values for 76 Countries and Regions Based on Factor Scores from 14 Items in the IBM Database Plus Extensions

RANK	AMERICA C/S	EUROPE S/SE	EUROPE N/NW ANGLO WORLD	EUROPE C/E EX-SOVIET	MUSLIM WORLD M.E & AFRICA	ASIA EAST ASIA SE	INDEX
1				Slovakia			110
2						Japan	95
3				Hungary			88
4			Austria				79
5	Venezuela						73
6			Switzerland Ge				72
7		Italy					70
8	Mexico						69
9–10			Ireland				68
9–10	Jamaica						68
11–13						China	66
11–13			Germany				66
11–13			Great Britain				66
14–16	Colombia						64
14–16						Philippines	64
14–16				Poland			64
17–18					S Africa (wte)		63
17–18	Ecuador						63
19			United States				62
20			Australia				61
21			Belgium Fr				60
22–24			New Zealand				58
22–24			Switzerland Fr				58
22–24	Trinidad						58

continued

TABLE 5.1 Masculinity Index (MAS) Values for 76 Countries and Regions Based on Factor Scores from 14 Items in the IBM Database Plus Extensions, *continued*

RANK	AMERICA C/S	EUROPE S/SE	EUROPE N/NW ANGLO WORLD	EUROPE C/E EX-SOVIET	MUSLIM WORLD M.E & AFRICA	ASIA EAST ASIA SE	INDEX
25–27		Greece		Czech Rep.			57
25–27							57
25–27						Hong Kong	57
28–29	Argentina					India	56
28–29						Bangladesh	56
30					Arab ctrs		55
31–32			Canada total		Morocco		53
31–32			Luxembourg				53
33							52
34–36						Malaysia	50
34–36					Pakistan		50
34–36							50
37	Brazil						49
38						Singapore	48
39–40		Malta			Israel		47
39–40							47
41–42						Indonesia	46
41–42			Canada Quebec		Africa W		46
43–45						Taiwan	45
43–45		Turkey					45
43–45							45
46	Panama		Belgium Nl				44
47–50		France					43
47–50					Iran		43
47–50							43

Rank	Latin America	W. Europe	N. Europe	E. Europe	Africa	Asia	Score
47–50				Serbia			43
51–53	Peru						42
51–53		Spain					42
51–53				Romania			42
54					Africa E		41
55–58	El Salvador						40
55–58				Bulgaria			40
55–58				Croatia			40
55–58						Vietnam	40
59						S Korea	39
60	Uruguay						38
61–62	Guatemala						37
61–62	Suriname						37
63				Russia			36
64						Thailand	34
65		Portugal					31
66				Estonia			30
67	Chile						28
68			Finland				26
69	Costa Rica						21
70–71				Lithuania			19
70–71				Slovenia			19
72			Denmark				16
73			Netherlands				14
74				Latvia			9
75			Norwa/				8
76			Sweden				5

nine-scoring cultures were the former Dutch colony of Suriname in South America, the Flemish (Dutch-speaking Belgians), and countries from the East African region.

The top third of Table 5.1 includes all Anglo countries: Ireland, Jamaica, Great Britain, South Africa, the United States, Australia, New Zealand, and Trinidad. Also from Europe are Slovakia (with a rank of 1), Hungary, Austria, German-speaking Switzerland, Italy, Germany, Poland, and the French-speaking Belgians and Swiss. In Asia are Japan (rank 2), China, and the Philippines. From Latin America are the larger countries around the Caribbean—Venezuela, Mexico, and Colombia—and Ecuador.

The United States scored 62 on MAS (rank 19) and the Netherlands 14 (rank 73), so these two countries figuring in the story at the beginning of this chapter were markedly far apart.

Masculinity and Femininity in Other Cross-National Studies

Masculinity-femininity has been the most controversial of the five dimensions of national cultures. This is a matter not only of labeling (users are free to adapt the labels to their taste—for instance, performance-oriented versus cooperation-oriented) but also of recognizing that national cultures do differ dramatically on the value issues related to this dimension. At the same time, ever since Geert's first publication on the subject in the 1970s, the number and scope of validations of the dimension have continued to grow. Several of these validations have been bundled in a 1998 book, *Masculinity and Femininity: The Taboo Dimension of National Cultures.*[4] Of note is that the dimension is politically incorrect mainly in masculine cultures such as the United States and the UK, but not in feminine cultures such as Sweden and the Netherlands. Taboos are strong manifestations of cultural values.

One reason the masculinity-femininity dimension is not recognized is that it is entirely unrelated to national wealth. For the other three IBM dimensions, wealthy countries are more often found on one of the poles (small power distance, individualist, and somewhat weaker uncertainty avoidance), and poor countries on the other. The association with wealth serves as an implicit justification that one pole must be better than the other. For masculinity-femininity, though, this does not work. There are just as many poor as there are wealthy masculine, or feminine, countries. So, wealth is no clue on which to base one's values, and this fact unsettles people. In several research projects, the influence of MAS became evident only after the influence of wealth had been controlled for.

From the six major replications of the IBM surveys described earlier in Table 2.1, five found a dimension similar to masculinity-femininity. The sixth, Shane's study among employees of six other international companies, excluded the questions related to MAS because the dimension was considered offensive. What is not asked cannot be found. In Søndergaard's review of nineteen smaller replications, also mentioned in Chapter 2, fourteen confirmed the MAS differences. This in itself is a statistically significant result.[5]

Schwartz's value study among elementary school teachers produced a country-level *mastery* dimension that correlated significantly with MAS.[6] Mastery combines the values *ambitious, capable, choosing own goals, daring, independent,* and *successful,* all on the positive pole. These values clearly confirm a masculine ethos.[7]

Robert House, when designing the GLOBE study, meant to replicate the Hofstede study, but he did not go as far as using the taboo terms *masculinity* and *femininity.* Instead, GLOBE included four other dimensions with potential conceptual links to Geert's masculinity versus femininity dimension: *assertiveness, gender egalitarianism, humane orientation,* and *performance orientation.* Across forty-eight common countries, the only GLOBE dimension significantly correlated with MAS was *assertiveness* "as is," but we came closer to our MAS dimension with a combination of *assertiveness* "as is" and *assertiveness* "should be."[8] GLOBE did tap the assertiveness aspect of our MAS dimension, although in a diluted form.

From the other potentially associated GLOBE dimensions, *gender egalitarianism,* both "as is" and "should be," correlated not with MAS but with our IDV. In Chapter 4 some aspects of gender equality in society (men make better leaders; women should be chaste, but men don't need to be) were shown to relate to collectivism. Gender equality has a lot to do with women's education level, which relates strongly to national wealth and therefore indirectly to individualism. The relationships of women's and men's roles to the MAS dimension, as this chapter will show, are more on the emotional level.

Performance orientation "as is" correlated negatively with our *uncertainty avoidance* (UAI, see Chapter 6), and *performance orientation* "should be" correlated negatively with *long-term orientation* (LTO, see Chapter 7). *Humane orientation* "as is" and "should be" produced no significant correlations. We doubt whether this GLOBE dimension makes any sense at all.[9]

Masculinity Versus Individualism

In the literature the distinction between country-level masculinity and femininity is easily confused with the distinction between individualism and collectivism. Authors from the United States tend to classify feminine goals as collectivist, whereas a student from Korea in her master's thesis classified masculine goals as collectivist.

In reality the individualism-collectivism and masculinity-femininity dimensions are independent, as is evident in Figure 5.1, in which the two dimensions are crossed. All combinations occur with about equal frequency. The difference between them is that individualism-collectivism is about "I" versus "we," independence from in-groups versus dependence on in-groups. Masculinity-femininity is about a stress on ego versus a stress on relationship with others, regardless of group ties. Relationships in collectivist cultures are basically predetermined by group ties: "groupiness" is collectivist, not feminine. The biblical story of the Good Samaritan who helps a Jew in need—someone from another ethnic group—is an illustration of feminine and not of collectivist values.

As we mentioned in Chapter 4, Inglehart's overall analysis of the World Values Survey found a key dimension, well-being versus survival, that was associated with the combination of high IDV and low MAS.[10] This means that the highest stress on well-being occurred in individualist, feminine societies (such as Denmark), while the highest stress on survival was found in collectivist, masculine societies (such as Mexico). We will meet this dimension from Inglehart again in Chapter 8, relating it to Misho's new dimension *indulgence versus restraint.*

Are Masculinity and Femininity One or Two Dimensions?

As in the case of individualism and collectivism, the objection is sometimes made that masculinity and femininity should be seen as two separate dimensions. Again the answer to the question of whether we're talking

FIGURE 5.1 Masculinity Versus Individualism

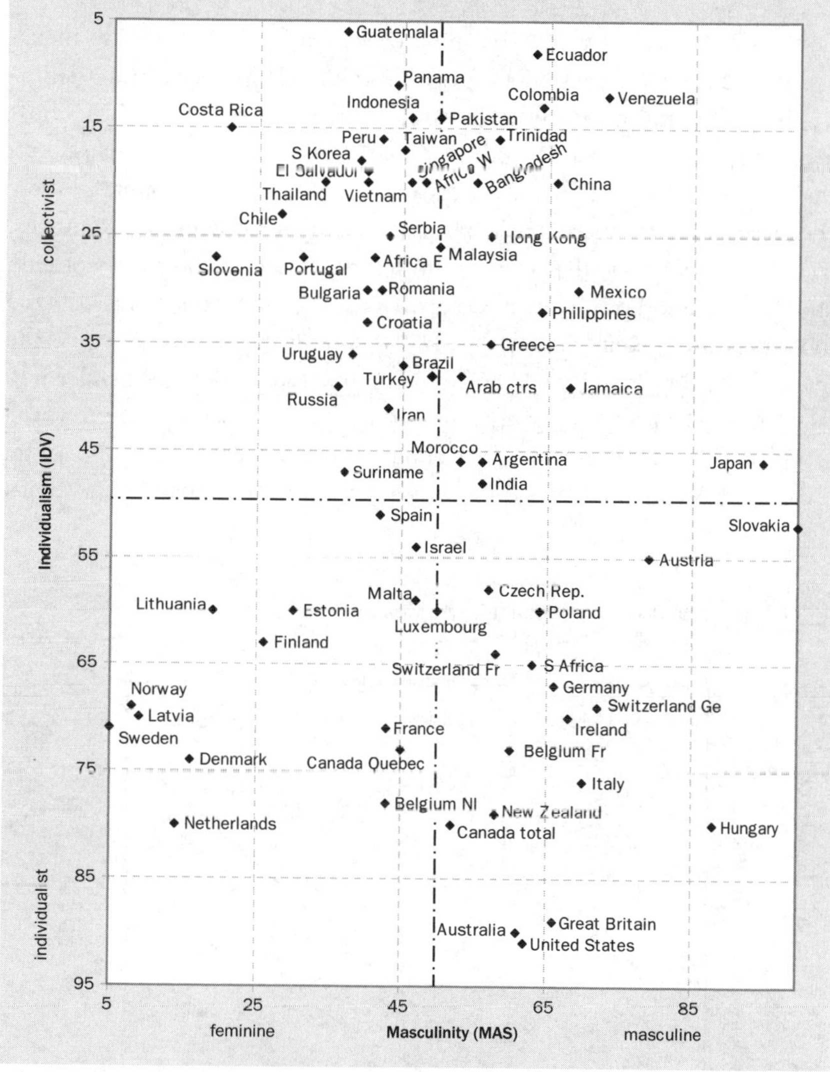

about one dimension or two is that it depends on our level of analysis. It depends on whether we try to compare the cultures of entire societies (which is what this book is about) or to compare individuals within societies. An individual can be both masculine and feminine at the same time,[11] but a country culture is either predominantly one or predominantly the other. If in a country more people hold masculine values, fewer people hold feminine values.

Country Masculinity Scores by Gender and Gender Scores by Age

Country MAS scores were also computed separately for men and women.[12] Figure 5.2 shows in simplified form the relationship between masculinity by gender and masculinity by country. It reveals that from the most feminine (tender) countries to the most masculine (tough) countries, both the values of men and of women became tougher, but the country difference was larger for men than for women. In the most feminine countries, Sweden and Norway, there was no difference between the scores of men and women, and both expressed equally tender, nurturing values. In the most masculine countries in the IBM database, Japan and Austria, the men scored very tough and the women fairly tough, but the gender gap was largest. From the most feminine to the most masculine country, the range of MAS scores for men was about 50 percent wider than the range for women. Women's values differ less among countries than men's values

FIGURE 5.2 Country Masculinity Scores by Gender

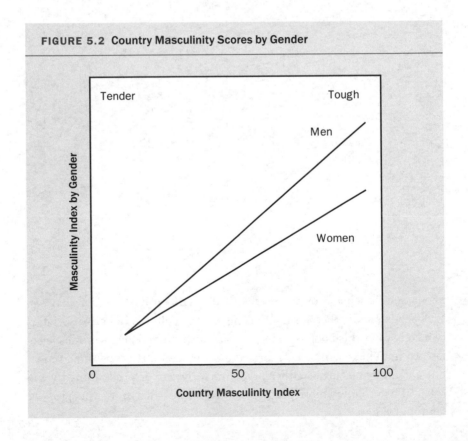

do, and a country's femininity is more clearly reflected in the values of its men than in those of its women. Women across countries can be expected to agree more easily on issues in which ego values are at stake. A U.S. best-seller was called *Men Are from Mars, Women Are from Venus,* but in feminine cultures both sexes are from Venus.[13]

Richard Lynn, from Northern Ireland, collected data about attitudes toward competitiveness and money from male and female university students in forty-two countries. Overall, men scored higher on com-petitiveness than women. In a reanalysis, Evert van de Vliert, from the Netherlands, showed that the ratio between men's and women's scores was significantly correlated with MAS. It was lowest in Norway, where the women rated their competitiveness higher than the men, and was highest in Germany.[14]

Figure 5.3 shows schematically the age effects on masculinity values.[15] When people grow older, they tend to become more social and less ego oriented (lower MAS). At the same time, the gap between women's and

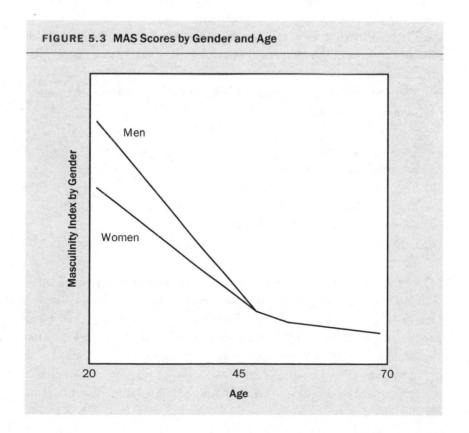

FIGURE 5.3 MAS Scores by Gender and Age

men's MAS values becomes smaller, and at around age forty-five it has closed completely. This is the age at which a woman's role as a potential child-bearer has generally ended; there is no more biological reason for her values to differ from a man's (except that men can still beget).

This development fits the observation that young men and women foster more technical interests (which could be considered masculine), and older men and women foster more social interests. In terms of values (but not necessarily in terms of energy and vitality), older persons are more suitable as people managers and younger persons as technical managers.

Masculinity and Femininity According to Occupation

In the IBM research, occupations could (on the basis of the values of those who were engaged in them) be ordered along a tough-tender dimension. It did make sense to call some occupations more masculine and others more feminine. It was no surprise that the masculine occupations were mostly filled by men, and the feminine occupations mostly by women. However, the differences in values were not caused by the gender of the occupants. Men in feminine occupations held more feminine values than women in masculine occupations.

The ordering of occupations in IBM from most masculine to most feminine was as follows:

1. Sales representatives
2. Engineers and scientists
3. Technicians and skilled craftspeople
4. Managers of all categories
5. Semiskilled and unskilled workers
6. Office workers

Sales representatives were paid on commission, in a strongly competitive climate. Scientists, engineers, technicians, and skilled workers focused mostly on technical performance. Managers dealt with both technical *and* human problems, in roles with both assertive *and* nurturing elements. Unskilled and semiskilled workers had no strong achievements to boast of but usually worked in cooperative teams. Office workers also were less oriented toward achievements and more toward human contacts with insiders and outsiders.

Masculinity and Femininity in the Family

As only a small part of gender role differentiation is biologically deter-mined, the stability of gender role patterns is almost entirely a matter of socialization. *Socialization* means that both girls and boys learn their place in society, and once they have learned it, the majority of them want it that way. In male-dominated societies, most women want the male dominance.

The family is the place where most people received their first social-ization. The family contains two unequal but complementary role pairs· parent-child and husband-wife. The effects of different degrees of inequal-ity in the parent-child relationship were related to the dimension of power distance in Chapter 3. The prevailing role distribution between husband and wife is reflected in a society's position on the masculinity-femininity scale.

Figure 5.4 crosses PDI against MAS. In the right half of the diagram (where PDI values are high), inequality between parents and children is a societal norm. Children are supposed to be controlled by obedience. In the left half, children are controlled by the examples set by parents. In the lower half of the diagram (where MAS scores are high), inequality between fathers' and mothers' roles (father tough, mother less tough) is a societal norm. Men are supposed to deal with facts, women with feelings. In the upper half, both men and women are allowed to deal with the facts and with the soft things in life.

Thus, the lower right-hand quadrant (unequal and tough) stands for a norm of a dominant, tough father and a submissive mother who, although also fairly tough, is at the same time the refuge for consolation and tender feelings. This quadrant includes the Latin American countries in which men are supposed to be macho. The complement of *machismo* for men is *marianismo* (being like the Virgin Mary) or *hembrismo* (from *hembra*, a female animal) for women: a combination of near-saintliness, submissive-ness, and sexual frigidity.[16]

The upper right-hand quadrant (unequal and tender) represents a societal norm of two dominant parents, sharing the same concern for the quality of life and for relationships, both providing at times authority *and* tenderness.

In the countries in the lower left-hand quadrant (equal and tough), the norm is for nondominant parents to set an example in which the father is tough and deals with facts and the mother is somewhat less tough and deals with feelings. The resulting role model is that boys should assert them-

FIGURE 5.4 Power Distance Versus Masculinity

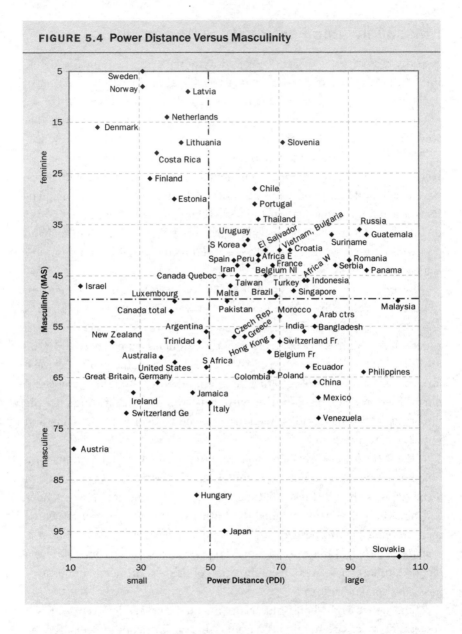

selves and girls should please and be pleased. Boys don't cry and should fight back when attacked; girls may cry and don't fight.

Finally, in the upper left-hand quadrant (equal and tender), the norm is for mothers and fathers not to dominate and for them both to be concerned with relationships, with the quality of life, with facts, *and* with feelings, setting an example of a relative equality of gender roles in the family context.

In Chapter 4 we referred to a 2005 market research study regarding ideals of beauty and body image among fifteen- to seventeen-year-old girls from ten countries around the world. As the source of the most powerful influence on their beauty ideals, girls in feminine cultures more often mentioned their father and their mother. In the case of the mother's influence, (higher) power distance also played a role. In masculine cultures, girls most often referred to the media and to celebrities.[17]

In Chapter 3 we referred to Eurobarometer data about full-time and part-time work between sets of parents. Whether the second parent worked full-time or part-time related to power distance. The same database also registered the frequency of cases in which one parent worked full-time and the other looked after the children full-time. This percentage related positively to MAS. In more masculine cultures, the strict role division between a father who earns the family income and a mother who handles the household is relatively more common.[18]

Studies of schoolchildren in the United States asked boys and girls why they chose the games they played. Boys chose games allowing them to compete and excel; girls chose games for the fun of being together and for not being left out. Repeating these studies in the Netherlands, Dutch researcher Jacques van Rossum found no significant differences in playing goals between boys and girls; thinking he made an error, he tried again, but with the same negative result. Child socialization in the feminine Dutch culture differs less between the sexes.[19]

The family context in Figure 5.4 depends also on individualism-collectivism. Individualist societies include one-parent families in which role models are incomplete or in which outsiders perform the missing functions. Collectivist societies maintain extended family links, and the center of authority could very well be the grandfather as long as he is still alive, with the father as a model of obedience.

Chapter 4 mentioned as well a massive study by David Buss and his associates regarding the selection of marriage partners in thirty-seven countries. Preferences were strongly related to individualism and collectivism, but further analysis showed that certain differences between the preferences of brides and grooms were related to MAS. Masculine cultures tended to show a double morality in which the chastity and the industriousness of the partner were considered important only by the men. In feminine cultures, they were seen as equally important or unimportant by brides and grooms alike.[20]

In 1993 a Japanese market research agency, Wacoal, asked young working women in eight Asian capital cities for their preferred characteristics of husbands and of steady boyfriends. In the masculine cultures, husbands should be healthy, wealthy, and understanding, while boyfriends should exhibit personality, affection, intelligence, and a sense of humor. In the more feminine cultures, there was hardly any difference between the preferred characteristics of husbands and of boyfriends. If we see the boyfriend as the symbol of love and the husband as the symbol of family life, this means that in the masculine countries, love and family life were more often seen as separate, whereas in the feminine countries, they were expected to coincide. In the feminine countries, the husband was the boyfriend. A unique aspect of this analysis was that the comparison with the IBM data was made exclusively across Asian countries, showing that the masculinity-femininity dimension could also be validated without including European countries.[21]

U.S. anthropologist Margaret Mead once observed that in the United States boys become less attractive sex partners by career failure, girls by career success.[22] In Japan a woman's marriage chances diminish if she has a career of her own.

Table 5.2 summarizes the key issues described so far on which masculine and feminine societies tend to differ.

Masculinity and Femininity in Gender Roles and Sex

The Wacoal survey also asked young working women in eight Asian cities whether they thought certain characteristics applied to men, to women, or to both. Answers differed between masculine and feminine countries. In the more masculine countries, sense of responsibility, decisiveness, liveliness, and ambitiousness were considered characteristics for men only, while caring and gentleness were seen as for women only. In the more feminine cultures, all these terms were considered as applying to both genders.[23]

Whereas gender roles in the family strongly affect the values about appropriate behavior for boys and for girls, they do not have immediate implications for the distribution of gender roles in the wider society. As argued earlier in this chapter, men, being on average taller and stronger

TABLE 5.2 Key Differences Between Feminine and Masculine Societies I: General Norm and Family

FEMININE	MASCULINE
Relationships and quality of life are important.	Challenge, earnings, recognition, and advancement are important.
Both men and women should be modest.	Men should be assertive, ambitious, and tough.
Both men and women can be tender and focus on relationships.	Women are supposed to be tender and to take care of relationships.
In the family, both fathers and mothers deal with facts and feelings.	In the family, fathers deal with facts, and mothers deal with feelings.
Girls' beauty ideals are most influenced by the father and mother.	Girls' beauty ideals are most influenced by the media and by celebrities.
Parents share earning and caring roles.	The standard pattern is that the father earns, and the mother cares.
Both boys and girls are allowed to cry, but neither should fight.	Girls cry, but boys don't; boys should fight back, and girls shouldn't fight at all.
Boys and girls play for the same reasons.	Boys play to compete; girls play to be together.
The same standards apply for bridegrooms and brides.	Brides need to be chaste and industrious; grooms don't.
Husbands should be like boyfriends.	Husbands should be healthy, wealthy, and understanding; boyfriends should be fun.

and free to get out, have traditionally dominated in social life outside the home in virtually all societies. Only exceptional and usually upper-class women had the means to delegate their child-rearing activities to others and to step into a public role. If women entered dominant positions in society at all, this was mostly after the age of forty-five, when their mother status changed into grandmother status. Unmarried women were, and still are, rare in traditional societies and often discriminated against.

The much greater liberty of choice among social roles that women in modern industrialized societies enjoy, beyond those of wife, mother, and housekeeper, is a recent phenomenon. Its impact on the distribution of gender roles *outside* the home follows more slowly. Therefore, a country's position on the masculinity-femininity scale need not be closely related to women's activities outside the family sphere. Economic possibilities and necessities play a bigger role in this respect than values.

A masculine gender role model is pictured in the following description of a popular U.S. movie:

> *Lucas, a 14-year-old boy, is unlike other kids. He's slight, inquisitive, and something of a loner, more interested in science and symphonies than in football and parties. But when he meets Maggie, a lovely 16-year-old girl who has just moved to town, things change. They become friends—but for Lucas it is more than friendship.*
>
> *During the summer they seem to have the same idea: football players and cheerleaders are superficial; but when school begins, Maggie shows an increasing interest in this side of school life, leaving Lucas out in the cold. He watches from the sidelines as Maggie becomes a cheerleader and starts dating Cappie Roew, the captain of the football team.*
>
> *Suddenly, Lucas wants to "belong," and in his attempt to win back Maggie, risks life and limb in the game of football. . . .*[24]

Mainstream movies are modern myths—they create hero models according to the dominant culture of the society in which they are made. Both Lucas and Maggie in this movie go through a rite of passage toward their rightful roles in a society in which men fight while playing football and girls stand adoringly and adorably by on the sidelines as cheerleaders.

Femininity should not be confused with feminism. *Feminism* is an ideology, either organized or not, that wants to change the role of women in society. The masculinity-femininity dimension is relevant to this ideology because across countries we find a more masculine and a more feminine form of feminism. The masculine form claims that women should have the same possibilities that men have. In terms of Figure 5.2, it wants to move the female line up toward the male line; this could also be achieved by moving the entire society toward the right. The feminine form wants to change society, men included. It calls for not only women's liberation but men's lib as well. In Figure 5.2 this could be achieved by moving the male line downward toward the female line or by moving the entire society toward the left.

Obviously, a country's position on the masculinity-femininity scale also affects its norms about sexual behavior.[25] Feelings about sex and ways in which sex is practiced and experienced are culturally influenced. Although individuals and groups within countries differ, too, women and men are affected by the written and unwritten norms of their country's culture.

The basic difference in sexual norms between masculine and feminine cultures follows the pattern of Figure 5.2. Masculine countries tend to maintain different standards for men and for women: men are the subjects, women the objects. In the section on family, we already found this double moral standard in masculine cultures with regard to the chastity of brides: women should be chaste, but men need not. It can also be noticed in norms about nudity in photos and movies: the taboo on showing naked men is much stronger than on showing naked women. Feminine cultures tend to maintain a single standard—equally strict or equally loose—for both sexes, and no immediate link is felt between nudity and sexuality.

Sex is more of a taboo subject in masculine than in feminine cultures. This is evident in information campaigns for the prevention of AIDS, which in feminine countries tend to be straightforward, whereas in masculine countries they are restricted by what can be said and what cannot. Paradoxically, the taboo also makes the subject more attractive, and there is more implicit erotic symbolism in TV programs and advertising in masculine than in feminine countries.

Double standards breed a stress on sexual performance: "scoring" for men, and a feeling of being exploited for women. In single-standard feminine countries, the focus for both is primarily on the relationship between two persons.

In the 1980s Geert was involved in a large survey study on organizational cultures in Denmark and the Netherlands.[26] The questionnaire contained among other items a list of possible reasons for dismissal. In a feedback session in Denmark, Geert asked respondents why nobody in their company had considered "a married man having sexual relationships with a subordinate" as a valid reason for the man's dismissal. A woman stood up and said, "Either she likes it, and then there is no problem, or she doesn't like it, and then she will tell him to go to hell." There are two pertinent assumptions in this answer: (most) Danish subordinates will not hesitate to speak up to their bosses (small power distance), and (most) male Danish bosses will "go to hell" if told so by a female subordinate (femininity).

In a study of "sexual harassment" in four countries in the 1990s, Brazilian students of both sexes differed from their colleagues in Australia, the United States, and Germany. They saw sexual harassment less as an abuse of power, less as related to gender discrimination, and more as a relatively harmless pastime.[27] Brazil in the IBM research scored lower on MAS than the three other countries (49, versus 61, 62, and 66, respectively).

Attitudes toward homosexuality are also affected by the degree of masculinity in the culture. In a comparison among Australia, Finland, Ireland, and Sweden, it was found that young homosexuals had more problems accepting their sexual orientation in Ireland and Australia, less in Finland, and least in Sweden. This is the order of the countries on MAS. Homosexuality tends to be felt as a threat to masculine norms and rejected in masculine cultures; this attitude is accompanied by an overestimation of its frequency. In feminine cultures, homosexuality is more often considered a fact of life.[28]

Culture is heavy with values, and values imply judgment. The issues in this section are strongly value-laden. They are about moral and immoral, decent and indecent behavior. The comparisons offered should remind us that morality is in the eye of the beholder, not in the act itself. There is no one best way, neither in social nor in sexual relationships; any solution is the best according to the norms that come with it.

Table 5.3 follows on Table 5.2 and summarizes the key issues from the past two sections on which masculine and feminine societies were shown to differ.

Masculinity and Femininity in Education

A Dutch management consultant taught part of a course for Indonesian middle managers from a public organization that operated all over the archipelago. In the discussion following one of his presentations, a Javanese participant made a particularly lucid comment, and the teacher praised him openly. The Javanese responded, "You embarrass me. Among us, parents never praise their children to their face."[29]

This anecdote illustrates two things. First, it demonstrates how strong, at least in Indonesia, is the transfer of behavior models from the family to the school situation, the teacher being identified with the father. Second, it expresses the virtue of modesty in the Javanese culture to an extent that even surprised the Dutchman. Indonesia is a multiethnic country, one for which national culture scores may be misleading. Indonesians

TABLE 5.3 **Key Differences Between Feminine and Masculine Societies II: Gender and Sex**

FEMININE	MASCULINE
Being responsible, decisive, ambitious, caring, and gentle is for women and men alike.	Being responsible, decisive, and ambitious is for men; being caring and gentle is for women.
Girls don't cheer for boys.	Women's ambition is channeled toward men's success.
Women's liberation means that men and women take equal shares both at home and at work.	Women's liberation means that women are admitted to positions so far occupied by men.
Single standard: both sexes are subjects.	Double standards: men are subjects, women objects.
Same norms for showing male or female nudity	Stronger taboo on showing male than female nudity
Explicit discussion of sex, less implicit symbolism	Taboo on explicit discussion of sex, but implicit erotic symbolism
Sex is a way for two persons to relate.	Performance for a man can be exploitation for a woman.
Sexual harassment is a minor issue.	Sexual harassment is a big issue.
Homosexuality is considered a fact of life.	Homosexuality is considered a threat to society.

agree that especially on the tough-tender dimension, ethnic groups within the country vary considerably, with the Javanese taking an extreme position toward the tender side. The Dutch consultant said that even some of the other Indonesians were surprised by the Javanese's feelings. A Batak from the island of Sumatra said that he now understood why his Javanese boss never praised him when he himself felt that praise should have been due. In feminine cultures, teachers will rather praise weaker students, in order to encourage them, than openly praise good students. Awards for excellence—whether for students or for teachers—are not popular; in fact, *excellence* is a masculine term.[30]

For a number of years Geert taught U.S. students in a semester-long program of European studies at a Dutch university. To some of the Americans, he gave the assignment to interview Dutch students about their goals in life. The Americans were struck by the fact that the Dutch seemed much less concerned with grades than they expected. Passing was considered enough; excelling was not an openly pronounced goal. Gert Jan's experiences with students from all over the world are similar. Students from masculine countries may ask to take an exam again after passing with a mediocre grade—Dutch students almost never do so. Such experiences in teaching at home and abroad and discussions with teachers from different countries have led us to conclude that in the more feminine cultures, the *average* student is considered the norm, while in more masculine countries, the *best* students are the norm. Parents in these masculine countries expect their children to try to match the best. The "best boy in class" in the Netherlands is a somewhat ridiculous figure.[31]

This difference is noticeable in classroom behavior. In masculine cultures, students try to make themselves visible in class and compete openly with each other (unless collectivist norms put a limit to this; see Chapter 4).

In feminine countries, assertive behavior and attempts at excelling are easily ridiculed. Excellence is something one keeps to oneself; it easily leads to jealousy. Gert Jan remembers being told by a classmate when he was fourteen, "We know you are smart—but you don't have to show it all the time." When he moved to Lausanne, in Switzerland, the following year, he was admired, not rebuked, for being clever.

In the feminine Scandinavian countries, people call their own attitude in this regard the Law of Jante (*Janteloven*). The Law of Jante, a nickname chosen for a small Danish town, was codified in the 1930s by the Danish-born Norwegian author Aksel Sandemose, and in an English translation it runs as follows:

You should not believe that
you are anything
you are just as much as us
you are wiser than us
you are better than us
you know more than we do
you are more than we are
or that you are good at anything

You should not laugh at us

You should not think
that anybody likes you
or that you can teach us anything.[32]

Failing in school is a disaster in a masculine culture. In strongly masculine countries such as Japan and Germany, the newspapers carry reports each year about students who killed themselves after failing an examination. In a 1973 insider story, a Harvard Business School graduate reported four suicides—one teacher, three students—during his time at this elite American institution.[33] Failure in school in a feminine culture is a relatively minor incident. When young people in these cultures take their lives, it tends to be for reasons unrelated to performance.

Competitive sports play an important role in the curriculum in countries such as Britain and the United States. To a prominent U.S. sports coach the dictum is attributed, "Winning isn't everything, it's the only thing,"[34] which doesn't encourage friendly encounters in sports. In most other European countries, sports are extracurricular and not a part of the school's main activities.

In an imaginative research project, ten- to fifteen-year-old children from five countries were shown a picture of one person sitting on the ground, with another standing over him saying, "Go ahead and fight back if you can!" They were asked to choose one of eight responses from a card. Aggressive answers were: "You've hit me. Now I'm going to teach you a lesson," "I'll tell the teacher," "We are not friends anymore," and "You'll get caught by the police!" Appeasing answers were: "We don't have to fight," "Let's talk it over," "Let's not fight. Let's be friends," "I'm sorry. I was wrong," and "What if somebody gets hurt by fighting?"[35] An aggressive answer was chosen by 38 percent of the children in Japan, 26 percent in Britain, 22 percent in Korea, 18 percent in France, and 17 percent in Thailand. This outcome almost exactly followed the countries' MAS scores.[36] It clearly shows the different socializing of children with regard to aggression. Another study, this time among university students in six countries, contained a question asking whether children in their country were allowed to express aggression. The percentages of "yes" answers varied from 61 in the United States to 5 in Thailand and again correlated significantly with MAS.[37]

The IBM research found Thailand to be the most feminine Asian country. A book about Thai culture by a British-Thai couple notes: "The Thai learns how to *avoid* aggression rather than how to *defend* himself against it. If children fight, even in defense, they are usually punished. The only way to stay out of trouble is to flee the scene."[38]

Following the story at the beginning of this chapter about Geert's job interview, we commented that U.S. applicants tend to oversell and Dutch applicants to undersell themselves. There is confirming evidence for this observation from two studies in a school or learning context.

In the first study, some eight hundred U.S. and eight hundred Dutch youngsters, aged eleven to eighteen, completed questionnaires about their personal competencies and problems. The Americans reported many more problems *and* competencies than the Dutch. Some items on which Americans scored higher were "argues a lot," "can do things better than most kids," "stores up unneeded things," and "acts without thinking." The only item on which the Dutch scored higher was "takes life easy." Reports by parents and teachers showed no difference in problem behavior by these children, but U.S. parents rated their children's competencies higher than Dutch parents did.[39] Young people in U.S. society have been socialized to boost their egos: they take both their problems and their competencies seriously.[40] Young people in the Netherlands are socialized rather to efface the ego. An earlier comparison between the U.S. and (masculine) Germany had not found such differences.

The second study compared levels of literacy across seven countries. In 1994 representative samples comprising between two thousand and more than four thousand younger and older adults (aged sixteen to sixty-five) all took the same tests to measure their literacy based on three skills: reading, writing, and using numbers. From those with the best results (literacy levels 4 and 5 out of 5), 79 percent of the Americans rated their own skills "excellent," but only 31 percent of the Dutch did so[41]—this in spite of the fact that the tests had shown both groups to be equally good.

Criteria for evaluating both teachers and students differ between masculine and feminine cultures. On the masculine side, teachers' brilliance and academic reputation and students' academic performance are the dominant factors. On the feminine side, teachers' friendliness and social skills and students' social adaptation play a bigger role.

Interviews with teachers suggest that in masculine countries, job choices by students are strongly guided by perceived career opportunities, while in feminine countries, students' intrinsic interest in the subject plays a bigger role.

In feminine countries, men and women more often follow the same academic curricula, at least if the country is wealthy. In poor countries, boys almost always get priority in educational opportunities.[42]

Different job choices by women and men can be partly explained by differences in perceptual abilities. Psychologists studying human perception distinguish between *field-independent* and *field-dependent* persons.[43] Field-independent persons are able to judge whether a line, projected on a wall, is horizontal even if it is put within a frame that is slanted or if they themselves sit on a chair that is slanted. Field-dependent persons are influenced by the position of the frame or the chair. Field-independent persons rely on internal frames of reference; field-dependent persons take their clues from the environment. Therefore, field-independent people tend to have better analytical skills, and field-dependent people tend to have better social and linguistic skills. Men are more often field-independent, women field-dependent. Masculine cultures tend to score more field-independent, and feminine cultures more field-dependent,[44] and there is less difference in perceptual abilities between the genders in feminine than in masculine countries.

Segregation in job choice also determines whether teachers themselves are women or men. In masculine societies, women mainly teach younger children, while men teach at universities. In feminine societies, roles are more mixed and men also teach younger children. Paradoxically, therefore, children in masculine societies are exposed longer to female teachers. The status of these teachers, however, is often low so that they will be antiheroines rather than models for behavior.

Masculinity and Femininity in Shopping

Dutch marketing expert Marieke de Mooij studied data on consumer behavior across sixteen affluent European countries.[45] She found several significant differences related to the masculinity-femininity dimension. One was the division of buying roles between the genders. In feminine culture countries, a larger share of the family's food shopping is done by the husband. Other differences relate to the family car. In buying a new car, the husband in a feminine country will involve his partner. In a masculine country, this tends to be the man's sovereign decision, in which the car's engine power plays an important role. In feminine cultures, car owners often don't even know their car's engine power. The car has often been described as a sex symbol; to many people it certainly is a status symbol. Masculine cultures have relatively more two-car families than feminine cultures; in the latter, husband and wife more often share one family car.

Status purchases in general are more frequent in masculine cultures. People in masculine cultures buy more expensive watches and more real jewelry; they more often consider foreign goods as more attractive than local products. They more often fly business class on pleasure trips.

Feminine cultures spend more on products for the home. More people in these cultures take their "home" (their caravan, RV, or trailer) with them on vacation. They spend more on do-it-yourself carpentry, on making their own dresses, and, for smokers, on rolling their own cigarettes. Coffee is a symbol of togetherness; people in feminine cultures own more electric coffeemakers, guaranteeing that coffee in the home is always ready.

People in feminine cultures buy more fiction books, and people in masculine cultures more nonfiction. U.S. author Deborah Tannen has pointed to differences between male and female discourse: more "report talk" (transferring information) for men, more "rapport talk" (using the conversation to exchange feelings and establish a relationship) for women.[46] De Mooij's data show that at the culture level, too, masculine readers are more concerned with data and facts; readers from feminine cultures are more interested in the story behind the facts.

In Chapter 4 we saw that survey data related the frequency of Internet use to IDV; the Net is basically an individualistic tool. However, the use of the Internet for private (nonwork) purposes correlates even more with low MAS. Both the Internet and e-mail can be used for "rapport" purposes and for "report" purposes; the former usage is more frequent in less masculine societies.[47]

Table 5.4 is a continuation of Tables 5.2 and 5.3, summarizing the key issues from the past two sections.

Masculinity and Femininity in the Workplace

The Dutch manufacturing plant of a major U.S. corporation had lost three Dutch general managers in a period of ten years. To the divisional vice president in the United States, all these men had come across as "softies." They hesitated to implement unpopular measures with their personnel, claiming the resistance of their works council—a body elected by the employees and required by Dutch law that the vice president did not like anyway. After the third general manager had left, the vice president stepped in personally and nominated the plant controller as his successor—ignoring strong warnings by the human resources manager. To the vice president, this controller was the only "real man" in the plant management team. He had always supported the need for drastic action, disregarding its

TABLE 5.4 Key Differences Between Feminine and Masculine Societies III: Education and Consumer Behavior

FEMININE	MASCULINE
Average student is the norm; praise for weak students.	Best student is the norm; praise for excellent students.
Jealousy of those who try to excel.	Competition in class; trying to excel.
Failing in school is a minor incident.	Failing in school is a disaster.
Competitive sports are extracurricular.	Competitive sports are part of the curriculum.
Children are socialized to be nonaggressive.	Aggression by children is accepted.
Students underrate their own performance: ego-effacement.	Students overrate their own performance: ego-boosting.
Friendliness in teachers is appreciated.	Brilliance in teachers is admired.
Job choice is based on intrinsic interest.	Job choice is based on career opportunities.
Men and women partly study the same subjects.	Men and women study different subjects.
Women and men teach young children.	Women teach young children.
Women and men shop for food and cars.	Women shop for food, men for cars.
Couples share one car.	Couples need two cars.
More products for the home are sold.	More status products are sold.
More fiction is read (rapport talk).	More nonfiction is read (report talk).
The Internet is used for rapport building.	The Internet is used for fact gathering.

popularity or unpopularity. In his reports he had indicated the weak spots. He should be able to maintain the prerogatives of management, without being sidetracked by this works council nonsense.

The new plant general manager proved the biggest disaster ever. Within six months he was on sick leave and the organization was in a state of chaos. Nobody in the plant was surprised. Everyone had known the controller as a congenial but weak personality, who had compensated for his insecurity by using powerful language toward the American bosses. The assertiveness that impressed the American vice president was recognized within the Dutch environment as bragging. As a general manager he received no cooperation from anyone, tried to do everything himself, and suffered a nervous breakdown in short order. Thus, the plant lost both a good controller and another general manager. Both the plant and the controller were victims of a culturally induced error of judgment.

Historically, management is an Anglo-Saxon concept, developed in masculine British and American cultures. The English—and international—word *management* comes from the Latin *manus*, or "hand"; the modern Italian word *maneggiare* means "handling." In French, however, the Latin root is used in two derivations: *manège* (a place where horses are drilled) and *ménage* (household); the former is the masculine side of management, the latter the feminine side. Classic American studies of leadership distinguished two dimensions: initiating structure versus consideration, or concern for work versus concern for people.[48] Both are equally necessary for the success of an enterprise, but the optimal balance between the two differs for masculine and feminine cultures.

A Dutchman who had worked with a prestigious consulting firm in the United States for several years joined the top management team of a manufacturing company in the Netherlands. After a few months he commented on the different function of meetings in his present job compared with his previous one. In the Dutch situation, meetings were occasions when problems were discussed and common solutions were sought; they served for making consensus decisions.[49] In the U.S. situation as he had known it, meetings were opportunities for participants to assert themselves, to show how good they were. Decisions were made by individuals elsewhere.

The masculinity-femininity dimension affects ways of handling industrial conflicts. In the United States as well as in other masculine cultures such as Britain and Ireland, there is a feeling that conflicts should be resolved by a good fight: "Let the best man win." The industrial relations scene in these countries is marked by such fights. If possible, management tries to avoid having to deal with labor unions at all, and labor union behavior justifies management's aversion. In the United States, the relationships between labor unions and enterprises are governed by extensive contracts serving as peace treaties between both parties.[50]

In feminine cultures such as the Netherlands, Sweden, and Denmark, there is a preference for resolving conflicts by compromise and negotiation.

In France, which scored moderately feminine in the IBM studies, there is occasionally a lot of verbal insult, both between employers and labor and between bosses and subordinates, but behind this seeming conflict there is a typically French "sense of moderation," which enables parties to continue working together while agreeing to disagree.[51]

Organizations in masculine societies stress results and try to reward achievement on the basis of equity—that is, to everyone according to performance. Organizations in feminine societies are more likely to reward people on the basis of equality (as opposed to equity)— that is, to everyone according to need.

The idea that small is beautiful is a feminine value. The IBM survey itself as well as public opinion survey data from six European countries showed that a preference for working in larger organizations was strongly correlated with MAS.[52]

The place that work is supposed to take in a person's life differs between masculine and feminine cultures. A successful early twentieth-century U.S. inventor and businessman, Charles F. Kettering, is reputed to have said:

> *I often tell my people that I don't want any fellow who has a job working for me; what I want is a fellow whom a job has. I want the job to get the fellow and not the fellow to get the job. And I want that job to get hold of this young man so hard that no matter where he is the job has got him for keeps. I want that job to have him in its clutches when he goes to bed at night, and in the morning I want that same job to be sitting on the foot of his bed telling him it's time to get up and go to work. And when a job gets a fellow that way, he's sure to amount to something.*[53]

Kettering refers to a "young man" and not to a "young woman"—his is a masculine ideal. It would certainly not be popular in more feminine cultures; there, such a young man would be considered a workaholic. In a masculine society, the ethos tends more toward "live in order to work," whereas in a feminine society, the work ethos would rather be "work in order to live."

A public opinion survey in the European Union contained the question "If the economic situation were to improve so that the standard of living could be raised, which of the following two measures would you consider to be better: Increasing the salaries (for the same number of hours worked) or reducing the number of hours worked (for the same salary)?" Preferences varied from 62 percent in favor of salary in Ireland to 64 percent in favor of fewer hours worked in the Netherlands. The differences (percent preferring salary minus percent preferring fewer hours) were significantly correlated with MAS more than with national wealth. Although respondents in the poorer countries stressed the need for increasing salaries more, values (MAS) played a stronger role.[54]

Boys in a masculine society are socialized toward assertiveness, ambition, and competition. When they grow up, they are expected to aspire to career advancement. Girls in a masculine society are polarized between some who want a career and most who don't. The family within a feminine society socializes children toward modesty and solidarity, and in these societies both men and women may or may not be ambitious and may or may not want a career.

The feminine side of management opens possibilities in any culture for women managers, who may be better able to combine manège and ménage than men. U.S. researcher Anne Statham interviewed matched groups of female and male U.S. managers and their secretaries, and she concluded that the women predominantly saw job and people orientation as interdependent, while to the men they were each other's opposites.[55]

Worldwide there is no relationship between the masculinity or femininity of a society's culture and the distribution of employment over men and women. An immediate relationship between a country's position on this dimension and the roles of men and women exists only within the home. Outside the home, men have historically dominated, and only in the wealthier countries—and this only recently in history—have women in any numbers been sufficiently freed from other constraints to be able to enter the worlds of work and politics as men's equals. Lower-class women have entered work organizations before, but only in low-status, low-paid jobs—not out of a need for self-fulfillment, but rather out of a need for material survival of the family. Statistics therefore show no relationship between a country's share of women working outside the home per se and its degree of femininity. Feminine wealthier countries do have more working women in higher-level technical and professional jobs.[56]

Many jobs in business demand few skills and cause a qualitative underemployment of people. A need for "humanization of work" has been felt in industrialized masculine as well as feminine countries, but what is considered a humanized job depends on one's model of what it means to be human. In masculine cultures, a humanized job should give more opportunities for recognition, advancement, and challenge. This is the principle of job enrichment as once defended, among others, by U.S. psychologist Frederick Herzberg.[57] An example is making workers on simple production tasks also responsible for the setting up and preventive maintenance of their machines, tasks that had previously been reserved for more highly trained specialists. Job enrichment represents a "masculinization" of unskilled and semiskilled work that, as shown earlier in this chapter, has a relatively "feminine" occupation culture.

In feminine cultures, a humanized job should give more opportunities for mutual help and social contacts. Classic experiments were conducted in the 1970s by the Swedish car and truck manufacturers Saab and Volvo featuring assembly by autonomous work groups. These groups represent a reinforcement of the social side of the job: its "femininization." In 1974 six U.S. Detroit automobile workers, four men and two women, were invited to work for three weeks in a group assembly system in the Saab-Scania plant in Södertälje, Sweden. The experiment was covered by a U.S. journalist who reported on the Americans' impressions. All four men and one of the women said they continued to prefer the U.S. work system. "Lynette Stewart chose Detroit. In the Cadillac plant where she works, she is on her own and can make her own challenge, while at Saab-Scania she has to consider people in front and behind her."[58] Of course, this was precisely what made the group assembly system attractive to the Swedes.

Based on their cultural characteristics, masculine and feminine countries excel in different types of industries. Industrially developed masculine cultures have a competitive advantage in manufacturing, especially in large volume: doing things efficiently, well, and fast. They are good at the production of big and heavy equipment and in bulk chemistry. Feminine cultures have a relative advantage in service industries such as consulting and transportation, in manufacturing according to customer specification, and in handling live matter such as in high-yield agriculture and biochemistry. There is an international division of labor in which countries are relatively more successful in activities that fit their population's cultural preferences than in activities that go against these preferences. Japan has a history of producing high-quality consumer electronics; Denmark and the Netherlands have a history of excellence in services, in agricultural exports, and in biochemical products such as enzymes and penicillin.

Table 5.5 is a continuation of Tables 5.2, 5.3, and 5.4, summarizing the key issues from the past section on which masculine and feminine societies differ.

TABLE 5.5 Key Differences Between Feminine and Masculine Societies
IV: The Workplace

FEMININE	MASCULINE
Management as ménage: intuition and consensus	Management as manège: decisive and aggressive
Resolution of conflicts by compromise and negotiation	Resolution of conflicts by letting the strongest win
Rewards are based on equality.	Rewards are based on equity.
Preference for smaller organizations	Preference for larger organizations
People work in order to live.	People live in order to work.
More leisure time is preferred over more money.	More money is preferred over more leisure time.
Careers are optional for both genders.	Careers are compulsory for men, optional for women.
There is a higher share of working women in professional jobs.	There is a lower share of working women in professional jobs.
Humanization of work by contact and cooperation	Humanization of work by job content enrichment
Competitive agriculture and service industries	Competitive manufacturing and bulk chemistry

Masculinity, Femininity, and the State

National value patterns are present not only in the minds of ordinary citizens but, of course, also in those of political leaders, who also grew up as children of their societies. As a matter of fact, people are usually elected or co-opted to political leadership *because* they are supposed to stand for certain values dear to citizens.

Politicians translate values dominant in countries into political priorities. The latter are most clearly visible in the composition of national government budgets. The masculinity-femininity dimension affects priorities in the following areas:

- Solidarity with the weak versus reward for the strong
- Aid to poor countries versus investing in armaments
- Protection of the environment versus economic growth

Masculine culture countries strive for a performance society; feminine countries for a welfare society. They get what they pay for: in 1994–95, across ten developed industrial countries for which data were available, the share of the population living in poverty varied from 4.3 percent in feminine Norway to 17.6 percent in masculine Australia. In the period 1992–2002, across eighteen developed countries, the share of the population earning less than half the median income varied from 5.4 percent in Finland to 17.0 percent in the United States. The share of functional illiterates (people who completed school but in actual fact cannot read or write) across thirteen developed countries varied from 7.5 percent in Sweden to 22.6 percent in Ireland.[59] In all three cases the percentages were strongly correlated with MAS.[60]

In criticisms by politicians and journalists from masculine countries such as the United States and Great Britain versus feminine countries such as Sweden and the Netherlands, strong and very different value positions appear. There is a common belief in, for example, the United States that economic problems in Sweden and the Netherlands are due to high taxes, while there is a belief in feminine European countries that economic problems in the United States are due to too much tax relief for the rich. Tax systems, however, do not just happen: they are created by politicians as a consequence of preexisting value judgments. Most Swedes feel that society should provide a minimum quality of life for everyone. It is normal that the financial means to that end are collected from those in society who have them. Even conservative politicians in northwestern Europe do not basically disagree with this view, only with the extent to which it can be realized.

The northwestern European welfare state is not a recent invention. The French philosopher Denis Diderot, who visited the Netherlands in 1773–74, described both the high taxes and the absence of poverty as a consequence of welfare payments, good medical care for all, and high standards of public education: "The poor in hospitals are well cared for: They are each put in a separate bed."[61]

The performance versus welfare antithesis is reflected in views about the causes of poverty. A survey in the European Union countries included the following question: "Why, in your opinion, are there people who live in need? Here are four opinions; which is the closest to yours? (1) Because they have been unlucky; (2) Because of laziness and lack of willpower; (3) Because there is much injustice in our society; (4) It is an inevitable part of modern progress." Across twelve European Union member states, the percentages attributing poverty to having been unlucky varied from 14 percent in Germany to 33 percent in the Netherlands; they were significantly negatively correlated with MAS.[62] The percentages attributing poverty to laziness varied from 10 percent in the Netherlands to 25 percent in Greece and Luxembourg; these results were positively correlated with MAS. In masculine countries, more people believe that the fate of the poor is their own fault; that if they would work harder, they would not be poor; and that the rich certainly should not pay to support them.

Attitudes toward the poor are replicated in attitudes toward lawbreakers. A public opinion poll in nine European countries in 1981 asked to what extent a number of debatable acts were justifiable: joyriding, using soft drugs, accepting bribes, prostitution, divorce, and suicide. The answers were summarized in an index of permissiveness, which across countries was strongly correlated with femininity. Mother is less strict than father.[63]

The masculinity-femininity dimension is also related to opinions about the right way of handling immigrants. In general, two opposing views are found. One defends *assimilation* (immigrants should give up their old culture), the other *integration* (immigrants should adapt only those aspects of their culture and religion that conflict with their new country's laws). In a public opinion survey covering fourteen European Union countries in 1997, the public preference for integration over assimilation was strongly negatively correlated with MAS; there was a weaker additional correlation with gross national income per capita.[64] Respondents in more masculine and poorer countries required assimilation; those in feminine and wealthier countries favored integration. In Chapter 4 we associated "respect for other cultures" with universalism, citing 2008 Eurobarometer data. Europeans in twenty-six countries were asked to choose "the most important values for you personally" (three out of a list of twelve). One of these values was "respect for other cultures." Differences among countries in percentages of respondents choosing this answer related both to IDV and to low MAS.[65]

In wealthy countries, the value choice between reward for the strong and solidarity with the weak is also reflected in the share of the national budget spent on development assistance to poor countries. The percentage of their GNI that governments of rich countries have allocated to helping poor ones varies widely. In 2005 the United States spent 0.22 percent of its GNI, while Denmark, Luxembourg, the Netherlands, Norway, and Sweden each spent more than 0.7 percent.[66] The proportions spent are unrelated to the wealth of the donor countries. What does correlate with a high aid quote is a feminine national value system.[67]

The Internet Journal *Foreign Policy* has computed for twenty-one rich countries a Commitment to Development Index (CDI) by measuring not only flows of aid money but also positive and negative impacts of other policies: trade flows, migration, investment, peacekeeping, and environmental policies. Again the CDI was significantly (negatively) correlated only with MAS. The correlation was weaker than for money flows, as policies on behalf of welfare in the home country sometimes conflict with policies on help abroad.[68]

Countries that spend little money on helping the poor in the world probably spend more on armaments. However, reliable data on defense spending are difficult to come by, as both the suppliers and the purchasers of arms have a vested interest in secrecy. The only conclusion we could draw from the available figures was that among donor countries, the less wealthy spent a larger share of their budgets on supplying arms than the wealthier ones.[69] Guns had priority over butter.

Masculine countries tend to (try to) resolve international conflicts by fighting; feminine countries by compromise and negotiation (as in the case of work organizations). A striking example is the difference between the handling of the Åland crisis and of the Falkland crisis.

The Åland islands are a small archipelago halfway between Sweden and Finland; as part of Finland they belonged to the tsarist Russian Empire. When Finland declared itself independent from Russia in 1917, the thirty thousand inhabitants of the islands in majority wanted to join Sweden, which had ruled them before 1809. The Finns then arrested the leaders of the pro-Swedish movement. After emotional negotiations in which the newly created League of Nations participated, all parties in 1921 agreed with a solution in which the islands remained Finnish but with a large amount of regional autonomy.

The Falkland Islands are also a small archipelago disputed by two nations: Great Britain, which has occupied the islands since 1833, and nearby Argentina, which has claimed rights on them since 1767 and tried to get the United Nations to support its claim. The Falklands are about eight times as large as the Ålands but with less than one-fifteenth of the Ålands' population: about 1,800 poor sheep farmers. The Argentinean military occupied the islands in April 1982, whereupon the British sent an expeditionary force that chased the occupants, at the cost of (officially) 725 Argentinean and 225 British lives and enormous financial expense. The economy of the islands, dependent on trade relations with Argentina, was severely jeopardized.

What explains the difference in approach and in results between these two remarkably similar international disputes? Finland and Sweden are both feminine cultures; Argentina and Great Britain are both masculine. The masculine symbolism in the Falkland crisis was evident in the language used on either side. Unfortunately, the sacrifices resolved very little. The Falklands remain a disputed territory needing constant British subsidies and military presence; the Ålands have become a prosperous part of Finland, attracting many Swedish tourists.

In 1972 an international team of scientists nicknamed the Club of Rome published a report titled *Limits to Growth*, which was the first public recognition that continued economic growth and conservation of our living environment are fundamentally conflicting objectives. Their report has been attacked on details, and for a time the issues it raised seemed less urgent. Its basic thesis, however, has never been refuted, and at least in our view, it is irrefutable. Nothing can grow forever, and ignoring this basic fact is the principal weakness of present-day economics. Governments have to make painful choices, and apart from local geographic and ecological constraints, these choices will be made according to the values dominant in a country. Governments in masculine cultures are more likely to give priority to growth and sacrifice the living environment for this purpose. Governments in feminine cultures are more likely to reverse priorities.[70] As environmental problems cross borders and oceans, international diplomacy is needed for solutions. A worldwide approach was laid down in the Kyoto Protocol, the result of a United Nations convention in 1997. Then U.S. president George W. Bush, following his election in 2001, showed his masculine priorities by withdrawing from it. Former U.S. vice president Al Gore in 2006 put the environment back on the U.S. public agenda with his film *An Inconvenient Truth*, and U.S. president Barack Obama in 2008 committed himself to a new leading role for the United States in this field—which, however, will be an uphill struggle within U.S. politics.

The 1990–93 World Values Survey asked representative samples of the populations to place their political views on a scale from "left" to "right."

Voters from masculine countries placed themselves mostly in the center; voters from feminine countries were slightly more to the left. Few people placed themselves on the right.[71]

Masculinity or femininity in democratic politics is not just a matter of policy priorities; it is also reflected in the informal rules of the political game. In masculine cultures such as Britain, Germany, and the United States, the style of political discourse is strongly adversarial. This is not a recent phenomenon. In 1876 the Dutch-language newspaper *De Standaard* reported that "the American political parties eschewed no means to sling mud at their adversaries, in a way which foreigners find disgusting."[72] This statement is still valid today. In feminine cultures such as the Nordic countries and the Netherlands, governments are nearly always coalitions between different parties that treat each other relatively gently.

In democratic countries, cultural masculinity and femininity influence the likelihood that elected delegates and members of government will be women. In 2006, among twenty-four established parliamentary democracies, percentages of women in parliament were below 20 in Britain, France, Greece, Ireland, Israel, Italy, Japan, and the United States; they were over 30 in Austria, Belgium, Denmark, Finland, Germany, Iceland, the Netherlands, New Zealand, Norway, Spain, and Sweden. Female ministers in 2005 were fewer than 20 percent in France, Greece, Israel, Italy, Japan, Luxembourg, Portugal, Switzerland, and the United States; they were more than 30 percent in Austria, Denmark, Finland, Germany, the Netherlands, Norway, Spain, and Sweden.[73] This is mainly a masculine-feminine split, although the low percentages for France and Portugal and the high percentages for Austria and Germany suggest that power distance also plays a role. However, women do advance more easily in politics than in work organizations. The election process reacts faster to changes in society than co-optation processes in business. Capable women in business organizations still have to wait for aged gentlemen to retire or die. Possibly politics as a public good attracts more women than does business as private achievement.

Masculinity, Femininity, and Religion

The issues related to the masculinity-femininity dimension are central to any religion. Masculine cultures worship a tough God or gods who justify tough behavior toward fellow humans; feminine cultures worship a tender God or gods who demand caring behavior toward fellow humans.

Christianity has always maintained a struggle between tough, masculine elements and tender, feminine elements. In the Christian Bible as a whole, the Old Testament reflects tougher values (an eye for an eye, a tooth for a tooth), while the New Testament reflects more tender values (turn the other cheek). God in the Old Testament is majestic. Jesus in the New Testament helps the weak and suffers. Catholicism has produced some very masculine, tough currents (Templars, Jesuits) but also some feminine, tender ones (Franciscans); outside Catholicism we also find groups with strongly masculine values (such as the Mormons) and groups with very feminine values (such as the Quakers and the Salvation Army). On average, countries with a Catholic tradition tend to maintain more masculine values and those with Protestant traditions more feminine values.[74]

Outside the Christian world there are also tough and tender religions. Buddhism in masculine Japan is very different from Buddhism in feminine Thailand. Some young men in Japan follow Zen Buddhist training aimed at self-development by meditation under a tough master. In the 1970s more than half of all young men in Thailand spent some time as a Buddhist monk, serving and begging.[75] In Islam, Sunni is a more masculine version of the faith than Shia, which stresses the importance of suffering. In the IBM studies, Iran, which is predominantly Shiite, scored more feminine than the predominantly Sunnite Arabic-speaking countries.

In the 1990s Dutch sociologist Johan Verweij devoted his Ph.D. research to explaining differences in secularization (loss of religion) in Western Christianity. From the 1990–93 World Values Survey, he obtained data for various aspects of religiosity across sixteen Christian countries.[76] Existing theories sought the reason for secularization in the modernization of society, but these theories did not account for the situation in the United States, a modern country relatively untouched by secularization. To Verweij's surprise, he found that the best available predictor of a country's degree of secularization was the degree of femininity of its culture—this in spite of the fact that women tend to be more religious than men. In masculine Christian countries, people rated their religiosity higher and attached more importance in their lives to God, Christian rites, orthodoxy, and Christian worldviews. Countries with feminine values had secularized faster than those with masculine ones; this applied across the board, including in the United States.

The Christian Gospel offers a choice of values for different positions on the masculinity-femininity scale. The New Testament carefully balances the importance of the relationships with God and with one's fellow humans. In one story Jesus is approached by a Pharisee with the question, "What is the greatest command in the Law?"

Jesus replied: "You must love the Lord your God with your whole heart, with your whole soul, and with your whole mind. This is the greatest and chief command. There is a second like it: you must love your neighbor as yourself. The whole Law and the prophets hang upon these two commands."[77]

The comparison between Christian religiosity in more masculine and more feminine countries implies that the balance between these two commands is difficult to find. There are cultural necessities that lead Christians in some countries to stress the first and lead Christians in other countries to stress the second.

One could argue that it is obvious that among Christian countries the tough, masculine societies endorse more strongly the importance of God—and other values derived from it. The Christian God is the Father: He is masculine. The importance of God as rated by the respondents to the European Values Survey and the masculinity index from the IBM studies were both correlated with the claimed observance of the Ten Commandments, but they most strongly correlated with the purely religious commandments (no other God, not abusing God's name, and honoring the Sabbath). Masculinity was less correlated with the claimed observance of the sexual commandments (no adultery, do not desire thy neighbor's wife) and least with the claimed observance of the moral commandments (honoring parents, no killing, no stealing, no false witnesses, do not desire thy neighbor's belongings). What was predominantly stressed in masculine cultures was the emotional and symbolic meaning of God's name.[78] The name of God the Father appeals strongly to the population of a masculine society—including the women who were socialized to inequality of gender values. In a feminine society, the stress is more on the importance of relationships with fellow humans than with God.

Secularization in feminine countries does not imply a loss of civil morality. A comparison of 1981–82 with 1990 European/World Values

Survey data for Ireland, the Netherlands, and Switzerland found no evidence for a relationship between the two.[79] Simplistic recipes that immoral behavior should be countered by a return to religion are thus proved false. On the contrary, it turns out that femininity, which as we saw correlates with secularization, relates positively to civil morality. In 1996 the results were published of an experiment by *Reader's Digest* magazine. Some two hundred wallets, each containing about $50 worth of cash, as well as family snapshots and contact numbers of the putative owners, were "accidentally" dropped in public places in big and small cities in the United States and in fourteen European countries. From ten wallets dropped, all ten were returned in Oslo, Norway; and in Odense, Denmark; but only two in Lausanne, Switzerland (one of them found by an Albanian!); in Ravenna, Italy; and in Weimar, Germany. The number returned was significantly correlated with the countries' femininity, with an additional influence of small power distance.[80]

A similar result was produced by another experiment, this one carried out by international students of U.S. psychology professor Robert Levine. These students in their twenty-three home cities "accidentally" dropped a pen in full view of a solitary pedestrian walking in the opposite direction. The score was the percentage of times the pedestrian warned the experimenter or picked up the pen and returned it to him or her. Percentages of helping pedestrians in twenty-three countries were significantly correlated with the countries' femininity score.[81]

All religions specify different religious roles for men and for women. In Christianity many Protestant churches now practice equality between men and women in their leadership and clergy, while the Roman Catholic Church strongly maintains the male prerogative to the priesthood. At the same time, in all Christian churches women are more religious than men. "God is apparently not an equal opportunity employer: He has a bias to the women."[82] The European Values Study showed that this difference applied in particular for women without paid jobs. Where the role of the woman changed from a housekeeper to a wage earner, her attitude toward religion moved closer to the attitude of men.[83]

It should be no surprise that the same dimension, masculinity versus femininity, relates to both sexual and religious behavior. Religion is a way for humankind to influence the supernatural—to provide certainties beyond the unpredictable risks of human existence. Birth, marital fertility, and death figure foremost among these unpredictables. All religions accentuate and celebrate the events of procreation: births, weddings, and deaths.

Fertility rites are known from virtually all human civilizations since pre-history; they survive to the present day, such as in wedding ceremonies and in sanctuaries devoted to prayers for pregnancy. In Judaism and most of Islam, circumcision of the male organ is a condition for being admitted to the religious community. In Hinduism, the architecture of temples models the lingam and yoni (phallus and vulva). Chinese philosophy and religious practices give strong importance to the complementarity of yang and yin, the male and female element.

Most or all religions contain dos and don'ts about love and sex. Human sexuality has the two facets of procreation and recreation, of reproduction and pleasure. Different religions, and currents within religions, have taken different positions toward the pleasure side of sex; the general trend is for religions in masculine cultures to stress procreation and for those in more feminine cultures to also value pleasure. Masculine Roman Catholicism has rejected sex for pleasure, institutionalizing celibacy for priests, the cult of the Virgin Mary, and marriage as a sacrament with the purpose of procreation, while prohibiting divorce, contraception, and abortion. When the less masculine Protestant Christian churches split from Rome, they did away with celibacy, did not consider marriage a sacrament, and accepted divorce. Orthodox Islam accepts sexual pleasure for men but considers sexual pleasure in women a danger. Currents in Hinduism have taken a positive attitude toward sexual pleasure, as manifested by the *Kamasutra* love guide and the erotic temples of Khajuraho and Konarak in India. In feminine Buddhist Thailand, the profession of prostitute carries less of a stigma than in the West. In very feminine Sweden, female prostitution is forbidden, but the client is punished, not the woman.

In the domain of scientific theories about sex, it is remarkable that the work of Sigmund Freud (1856–1939) originated in Austria, a country with one of the highest MAS scores in the IBM list (79). Freud, the founder of psychoanalysis, argues for the fundamental importance of sexuality in the development of the human personality; he attributed many psycho-pathological problems to the repression of sexuality. Freud attributed *penis envy* (jealousy about not having one) to all women. We wonder whether an author from a less masculine society would have imagined this. Every author or scientist is a child of his or her society; Freud's work comes directly out of the masculine Austrian context in which he was raised.

Table 5.6 complements Tables 5.2, 5.3, 5.4, and 5.5 by summarizing the key differences between feminine and masculine societies from the last two sections.

TABLE 5.6 Key Differences Between Feminine and Masculine Societies V: Politics and Religion

FEMININE	MASCULINE
Welfare society ideal; help for the needy	Performance society ideal; support for the strong
Permissive society	Corrective society
Immigrants should integrate.	Immigrants should assimilate.
Government aid for poor countries	Poor countries should help themselves.
The environment should be preserved: small is beautiful.	The economy should continue growing: big is beautiful.
International conflicts should be resolved by negotiation and compromise.	International conflicts should be resolved by a show of strength or by fighting.
More voters place themselves left of center.	More voters place themselves in the political center.
Politics are based on coalitions with polite political manners.	The political game is adversarial, with frequent mudslinging.
Many women are in elected political positions.	Few women are in elected political positions.
Tender religions	Tough religions
In Christianity, more secularization; stress on loving one's neighbor	In Christianity, less secularization: stress on believing in God
Dominant religions give equal roles to both sexes.	Dominant religions stress the male prerogative.
Religions are positive or neutral about sexual pleasure.	Religions approve sex for procreation rather than recreation.

Origins of Masculinity-Femininity Differences

In human thinking the issue of the equality or inequality between the sexes is as old as religion, ethics, and philosophy themselves. Genesis, the first book of the Judaeo-Christian Old Testament (which was codified in the fifth century B.C.), contains two conflicting versions of the creation of the sexes. The first, Genesis 1:27–28, states:

So God created man in his own image, in the image of God created he him;
male and female created he them. And God blessed them, and God said to
them, Be fruitful, and multiply, and replenish the earth, and subdue it.

This text suggests equal partnership between the sexes. The second version, Genesis 2:8ff. (which Old Testament experts suppose to have been derived from a different source document), contains the story of the garden in Eden, in which God first put "the man" alone. Then, in Genesis 2:18, it states:

And the Lord God said, It is not good that the man should be alone: I will
make him a help meet for him."[84]

Then follows the story of woman made from Adam's rib. This text gives clear priority to the male partner and defines the woman as "a help meet" (that is, appropriate) for him; it justifies a society in which there is male dominance.

In ancient Greece, Plato (in the fourth century B.C.) describes the sexes as equal in principle and (apart from their role in procreation) only statistically different. In *The Republic* he offers a design for an ideal state governed by an elite composed of men as well as women. Of course, in actual fact the Greek state was male dominated. So was the Roman state, but at least one Roman writer, C. Musonius Rufus (in the first century A.D.), defended the equality of the sexes and in particular the study of philosophy by women and men alike.

The German sociologist Norbert Elias argued that the balance of power between the genders varies with the development of a society. During the Roman Republic and early Empire (400 B.C. to 100 A.D.), the influence and rights of patrician women improved gradually along with the development of the city-state into a world empire and of the senatorial class from peasant warriors into aristocrats. With the disintegration of the Roman Empire in the third century A.D., the status of women deteriorated. In an earlier book Elias had described how around the eleventh century A.D. in Europe, and particularly in France, the gradual reestablishment of an orderly society and reduction of fighting gave the noble women a social and civilizing role. In the history of European civilization, the French nobility and court have been major models, being followed at a distance by other countries and classes. The present differences on the masculinity-femininity dimension between France, Spain, and Portugal on one side and Britain, Germany, and Italy on the other can be interpreted as different outcomes of this process.

Anthropologist Margaret Mead found in New Guinea very different gender role distributions among adjacent tribal groups. She showed that history and tradition allow the survival of considerable variety in gender roles. We did not find strong correlations with outside factors that could explain why some countries have dominant masculine cultures and others dominant feminine culture. Feminine cultures are somewhat more likely in colder climates, suggesting that in this case an equal partnership between men and women improves chances of survival and population growth.

The concentration of feminine cultures in northwestern Europe (Denmark, Finland, the Netherlands, Norway, Sweden) points to common historical factors. The elites in these countries consisted to a large extent of traders and seafarers. In trading and sailing, maintaining good interpersonal relationships and caring for the ships and the merchandise are essential virtues. The Viking period in the Scandinavian countries (A.D. 800–1000) also meant that the women had to manage the villages while the men were away on their long trips; however, Vikings did not settle in the Netherlands for any length of time. The Hanseatic League (A.D. 1200–1500) covered all northwestern European countries, including the free cities of Hamburg, Bremen, and Lübeck in northern Germany and the Baltic states. The Hansa was a free association of trading towns in which women played an important role:

> *Although the wife did not share her husband's legal status, they usually formed a business team. Even in merchant circles, the family was the smallest functional cell of society, where the women and the children had a role to play. This meant that women had a certain degree of emancipation, and their independence and business skills increased. Indeed, some women managed to win the "battle for the trousers" even while their husbands were still alive.*[85]

Erasmus of Rotterdam in his *Colloquia* of 1524 compared the service in French and German inns—both of which he knew from experience. He referred to the charming behavior of French innkeepers' wives and daughters, the quality of the food, and French *savoir vivre*. He opposed this to German strictness, inflexibility, and lack of manners. He actually used the word *masculine* to distinguish the German style from the French. At the same time, he recognized that the Germans maintained greater equality among customers.[86]

Comparing Britain and the Netherlands, the English statesman Sir Francis Walsingham wrote in a political pamphlet in 1585 that England and the Low Countries "have been by common language resembled and termed as man and wife." Half a century later some Englishmen connected Dutch commercial success with the fact that the Dutch "generally breed their youth *of both sexes* more in the study of Geometry and Numbers than the English do." And elsewhere it was remarked that Dutch merchants *and their wives* were more conversant in trade than the English.[87] Although women in seventeenth-century Netherlands were excluded from public office, "within these limits they managed to assert themselves, both individually and collectively, in public life." And in paintings from this period, "fathers are occasionally shown participating in the work of caring for small children." Also, "Military glory . . . was liable to be regarded with more circumspection than enthusiasm in the Netherlands. . . . Even though professional soldiers . . . played a crucial role in the defense of the [Dutch] Republic in the seventeenth century, they went conspicuously without honor in the patriotic culture of the time."[88] Military heroes belong to the history of masculine countries such as Britain and the United States.

It is noteworthy that symbolic personalities representing Western countries in the nineteenth and twentieth centuries were gendered according to their cultures' masculinity or femininity: John Bull for Britain and Uncle Sam for the United States but Marianne[89] for France and the Dutch maiden (called *Frau Antje* in Germany) for the Netherlands.

Latin American countries varied considerably on the masculinity-femininity scale. Small Central American countries as well as Peru and Chile scored feminine; Mexico, Venezuela, Colombia, and Ecuador strongly masculine. One speculative explanation is that these differences reflect the inheritance of the different Indian civilizations dominant prior to the Spanish conquest. Most of Mexico inherited the tough Aztec culture, but the southern Mexican peninsula of Yucatan and the adjacent Central American republics inherited the less militant Maya culture. Peru and Northern Chile inherited the Inca culture, resembling the Maya.

All these historical examples show that differences among countries on the masculinity-femininity dimension were noticed and described centuries ago: the way in which a country deals with gender roles is deeply rooted.

The Future of Differences in Masculinity and Femininity

At the time of the IBM surveys, 1960–70, MAS and fertility (the number of children per family) were negatively related for the wealthier countries but positively for the poorer countries. Masculine cultures meant larger families in poor countries and smaller families in wealthy countries.[90] Anthropological studies of traditional cultures had also concluded that populations increased most in societies in which females were subservient to males.[91] In the ensuing decades, birthrates in most countries, except the very poorest, dropped considerably. Fertility is still related to national poverty,[92] but the relationship to masculinity is no longer significant.[93] Instead, we found a relationship with *indulgence versus restraint*, which will be discussed in Chapter 8.

Lower fertility in the wealthier part of the world means an aging population. Figure 5.3 showed that masculinity scores decreased with age, so an older population will shift toward more feminine values. When birthrates fall, this trend also implies that women will be both available for and needed in the workforce (as there will be fewer young men). This too predicts for the wealthier countries a shift toward more feminine cultures.

Technology imposes changes on the work people do. In the wealthier countries, the information revolution is moving on, eliminating old jobs and creating new ones. Jobs that can be structured will increasingly be automated. What remains are activities that by their very nature cannot be automated. These are, in the first place, the jobs that deal with the setting of human and social goals, with defining the purpose of life for individuals and societies. This category includes all political and organizational top-leadership functions. In the second place, they are the creative jobs, those concerned with inventing new things and subjecting them to criteria of usefulness, beauty, and ethics. A third and sizable category of jobs that cannot be automated comprises those that deal with unforeseeable events: safety, security, defense, maintenance. Finally, there is a large category of jobs whose essence is human contact: supervision, entertainment, keeping people company, listening to them, helping them materially and spiritually, motivating them to learn. In these jobs computers can be introduced as resources, but they can never take over the job itself. For all these non-automatable jobs, feminine values are as necessary in performing them as masculine ones, regardless of whether the job incumbents themselves are women or men. For the last category, in which human contact is the core of the task, feminine values are even superior. Tasks related with achievement can more easily be automated than nurturing tasks. In balance, technological developments are also likely to support a shift from masculine to feminine values in industrial societies.

For the poorer part of the world, as long as a country remains poor, it is unlikely to shift toward more feminine values. Masculinity-femininity differences play a role in what is becoming a dramatic problem for mainly Asian countries, the prevention or suppression of female births. Asia around 2000 counted some 100 million fewer females than would have been the result of normal birthrates. This fact is attributable to the desire of parents to have sons rather than daughters, the availability of ultrasound scanning of the sex of a fetus followed by selective abortion, and the old practice of killing baby girls. The female/male ratio in the population is higher in feminine cultures such as Thailand and Indonesia than in masculine cultures such as India and China. A surplus of men over women may further increase the masculinity of the societies in question. In the book *Bare Branches*, political scientists Valerie Hudson and Andrea den Boer show that a surplus of young men in society is associated with more violence and with authoritarian political systems.[94] The direction of causality between male surpluses and cultural masculinity could go both ways, and they may reinforce each other.

Conservation of the global environment demands a worldwide nurturing mentality. The vicious circle from poverty to masculinity and back is bad for global survival. This is another good reason to strive for a fair distribution of resources over the world's population.

What Is Different Is Dangerous

In the 1960s Arndt Sorge did his military service in the West German army. Near his hometown, where he spent his free weekends, there were barracks of the British "Army on the Rhine." Sorge was keen on watching British motion pictures with the original sound track, which were shown in the British barracks, and he walked up to the sentry to ask whether he, as a German soldier, could attend. The sentry referred him to the sergeant of the guard, who called the second in command on the telephone and then tore a page out of a notebook, on which he wrote, "Mr Arndt Sorge has permission to attend film shows," and signed it, adding that permission was granted by the second in command.

Sorge used his privilege not only on that occasion but also several other times, and the notebook page always opened the gate for him, in conjunction with his German army identity card. After he was demobilized, he asked the British sentry whether he, now as a civilian, could continue to come. The sentry looked at the notebook page, said, "This is for you personally," and let him in.

Arndt Sorge became an organization sociologist, and he remembers this experience as an example of how differently the British seemed to handle such an unplanned request in comparison with what he was accustomed to in the German army. The Germans would have taken more time and would have needed the permission of more authorities; they would have asked for more information about the applicant and issued a more formal document. Finally, the document would have been issued to him as a member of the armed forces, and there would have been no possibility of his using it after his demobilization.[1]

The Avoidance of Uncertainty

Germany and Britain have a lot in common. Both are Western European countries, both speak a Germanic language, their populations are of roughly equal size, and the British royal family is of German descent. Yet it does not take a very experienced traveler to notice the considerable cultural difference between the two countries.

Peter Lawrence is a British sociologist who wrote about Germany:

> *What strikes a foreigner traveling in Germany is the importance attached to the idea of punctuality, whether or not the standard is realized. Punctuality, not the weather, is the standard topic of conversation for strangers in railway compartments. Long distance trains in Germany have a pamphlet laid out in each compartment called a Zugbegleiter (literally, "train accompanier") which lists all the stops with arrival and departure times and all the possible connections en route. It is almost a national sport in Germany, as a train pulls into a station, for hands to reach out for the Zugbegleiter so that the train's progress may be checked against the digital watch. When trains are late and it happens, the loudspeaker announcements relay this fact in a tone which falls between the stoic and the tragic. The worst category of lateness which figures in these announcements is unbestimmte Verspätung (indeterminable lateness: we don't know how late it is going to be!) and this is pronounced as a funeral oration.[2]*

Sorge's surprise at the easygoing approach of the British sentry and Lawrence's at the punctual German travelers suggest that the two countries differ in their tolerance of the ambiguous and the unpredictable. In the IBM research, Britain and Germany score exactly alike on the two dimensions of power distance (both 35) and masculinity (both 66). On individualism, though, the British score considerably higher (89 versus 67). The largest difference between the two countries, however, is on a fourth dimension, labeled *uncertainty avoidance.*

The term *uncertainty avoidance* has been borrowed from American organization sociology, in particular from the work of James G. March.[3] March and his colleagues recognized it in American organizations. Ways of handling uncertainty, of course, are part and parcel of any human institution in any country. All human beings have to face the fact that we do not know what will happen tomorrow: the future is uncertain, but we have to live with it anyway.

Extreme ambiguity creates intolerable anxiety. Every human society has developed ways to alleviate this anxiety. These ways belong to the domains of technology, law, and religion. Technology, from the most primitive to the most advanced, helps people to avoid uncertainties caused by nature. Laws and rules try to prevent uncertainties in the behavior of other people. Religion is a way of relating to the transcendental forces that are assumed to control people's personal future. Religion helps followers to accept the uncertainties against which one cannot defend oneself, and some religions offer the ultimate certainty of a life after death or of victory over one's opponents.

Anthropologists studying traditional societies have spent a good deal of their attention on technology, law, and religion. They have illustrated the enormous variety of ways in which human societies deal with uncertainty. Modern societies do not differ essentially from traditional ones in this respect. In spite of the availability of the same information virtually anywhere around the globe, technologies, laws, and religions continue to vary. Moreover, there are no signs of spontaneous convergence.

The essence of uncertainty is that it is a subjective experience, a feeling. A lion tamer may feel reasonably comfortable when surrounded by his animals, a situation that would make most of us almost die from fear. You may feel reasonably comfortable when driving on a crowded freeway at fifty-five miles per hour or more, a situation that, statistically, is probably riskier than the lion tamer's.

Feelings of uncertainty may also be partly shared with other members of one's society. As with the values discussed in the past three chapters, feelings of uncertainty are acquired and learned. Those feelings and the ways of coping with them belong to the cultural heritage of societies. They are transferred and reinforced through basic institutions such as the family, the school, and the state. The collectively held values of the members of a particular society reflect them. Their roots are nonrational. They lead to collective patterns of behavior in one society that may seem aberrant and incomprehensible to members of other societies.

Measuring the (In)tolerance of Ambiguity in Society: The Uncertainty Avoidance Index

Following on power distance, individualism-collectivism, and masculinity-femininity, uncertainty avoidance (from strong to weak) is the fourth dimension found in the IBM research project. Each country and region in this project could be assigned an uncertainty avoidance index (UAI) score.

Differences among countries on uncertainty avoidance were originally discovered as a by-product of power distance. It all started with a question about job stress: "How often do you feel nervous or tense at work?"—with answers ranging from (1) I always feel this way to (5) I never feel this way. Geert had been struck by the regularity of answer patterns on this question from country to country. For example, British employees always scored less nervous than German employees, be they managers, engineers, secretaries, or unskilled factory workers. However, across all countries in the IBM database, differences in stress were unrelated to power distance.

Close scrutiny of all questions producing stable country differences revealed that the country mean scores on the following three items were strongly correlated:

1. Job stress, as just described (mean score on a 1 to 5 scale).
2. Agreement with the statement "Company rules should not be broken—even when the employee thinks it is in the company's best interest" (mean score on a 1 to 5 scale). This question was labeled *rule orientation*.
3. The percentage of employees expressing their intent to stay with the company for a long-term career. The question was "How long do you think you will continue working for IBM?"—and the answers ran as follows: (1) Two years at the most; (2) From two to five years; (3) More than five years (but I probably will leave before I retire); and (4) Until I retire. The percentage in a country answering 3 or 4 was correlated with the mean answers on questions 1 and 2.

At first the combination of these three questions did not make sense. Why should someone who feels under stress also want rules to be respected and want his or her career to be long-term? But this is a false interpretation. The data do not suggest that "someone" shares these three attitudes. When we looked at the answers of individual "someones," the answers to the three questions were not correlated. It was the *differences in mean answers by country* for the three questions that were correlated. So, if in a country more people felt under stress at work, in the same country more people wanted rules to be respected, and more people wanted to have a long-term career. The distinction is that the individuals who held each of these feelings did not need to be the same persons.

As we argued in Chapter 2, the culture of a country—or of another category of people—is not a combination of properties of the "average citizen," nor a "modal personality." It is, among other things, a set of likely reactions of citizens with a common mental programming. One person may react in one way (such as feeling more nervous), and another in another way (such as wanting rules to be respected). Such reactions need not be found within the same *individuals*, but only statistically more often in the same *society*.

The interpretation of the association among questions 1 through 3 *at the society level* does make sense. We assume that all three are expressions of the level of anxiety that exists in a particular society in the face of an uncertain future. This level of anxiety forms part of the shared mental programming of people in that society—in the family, at school, and in adult life. Because of this anxiety level, a relatively larger share of individuals will feel nervous or tense at work (question 1). The idea of breaking a company rule—for whatever good reason—is rejected by more people (question 2), because it introduces ambiguity: what if all employees would just start doing as they pleased? Finally, changing employers is less popular in such a country (question 3), for it means venturing into the unknown.

Uncertainty avoidance can therefore be defined as *the extent to which the members of a culture feel threatened by ambiguous or unknown situations.* This feeling is, among other manifestations, expressed through nervous stress and in a need for predictability: a need for written and unwritten rules.

The UAI values for seventy-six countries and regions are listed in Table 6.1. In a way similar to the computation of the power distance index (Chapter 3), the index value for each country was computed from the mean scores of questions 1 and 2 and the percentage score for question 3. The formula used is based on simple mathematics: adding or subtracting the three scores after multiplying each by a fixed number, and finally adding

TABLE 6.1 Uncertainty Avoidance Index (UAI) Values for 76 Countries and Regions Based on Three Items in the IBM Database Plus Extensions

RANK	AMERICA C/S	EUROPE S/SE	EUROPE N/NW ANGLO WORLD	EUROPE C/E EX-SOVIET	MUSLIM WORLD M.E & AFRICA	ASIA EAST ASIA SE	INDEX
1		Greece					112
2		Portugal					104
3	Guatemala						101
4	Uruguay						100
5			Belgium Nl				97
6		Malta					96
7				Russia			95
8	El Salvador						94
9–10			Belgium Fr				93
9–10				Poland			93
11–13						Japan	92
11–13				Serbia			92
11–13	Suriname						92
14				Romania			90
15				Slovenia			88
16	Peru						87
17–22	Argentina						86
17–22	Chile						86
17–22	Costa Rica						86
17–22		France					86
17–22	Panama						86
17–22				Bulgaria			86
23–25		Spain					85
23–25						S Korea	85
23–25		Turkey					85

Rank						Score
26–27	Mexico					82
26–27			Hungary			82
28	Colombia					81
29–30				Israel		80
29–30			Croatia			80
31–32	Brazil					76
31–32	Venezuela					76
33	Italy					75
34			Czech Rep.			74
35–38		Austria				70
35–38		Luxembourg				70
35–38				Pakistan		70
35–38		Switzerland Fr				70
39					Taiwan	69
40–41				Arab ctrs		68
40–41				Morocco		68
42	Ecuador					67
43–44		Germany				65
43–44			Lithuania			65
45					Thailand	64
46			Latvia			63
47–49		Canada Quebec				60
47–49			Estonia			60
47–49					Bangladesh	60
50–51		Finland				59
50–51				Iran		59
52		Switzerland Ge				56
53	Trinidad					55
54				Africa W		54
55		Netherlands				53
56				Africa E		52

continued

TABLE 6.1 Uncertainty Avoidance Index (UAI) Values for 76 Countries and Regions Based on Three Items in the IBM Database Plus Extensions, *continued*

RANK	AMERICA C/S	EUROPE S/SE	EUROPE N/NW ANGLO WORLD	EUROPE C/E EX-SOVIET	MUSLIM WORLD M.E & AFRICA	ASIA EAST ASIA SE	INDEX
57–58			Australia				51
57–58				Slovakia			51
59			Norway				50
60–61			New Zealand				49
60–61					S Africa (wte)		49
62–62			Canada total				48
62–63						Indonesia	48
64			United States				46
65						Philippines	44
66						India	40
67						Malaysia	36
68–69			Great Britain				35
68–69			Ireland				35
70–71						China	30
70–71						Vietnam	30
72–73			Sweden				29
72–73						Hong Kong	29
74			Denmark				23
75	Jamaica						13
76						Singapore	8

another fixed number. The formula was developed such that (1) each of the three questions would contribute equally to the final index and (2) index values would range from around 0 for the country with the weakest uncertainty avoidance to around 100 for the strongest. The latter objective was not completely attained, because after the formula had been developed, some more countries were added that produced scores greater than 100.

Table 6.1 shows a new grouping of countries, unlike the ones found for any of the previous three dimensions. Even within regions we find large differences, which suggests different causes from those for power distance and individualism. High scores occur for Latin American, Latin European, and Mediterranean countries (from 112 for Greece to 67 for Ecuador). Also high are the scores of Japan and South Korea (92 and 85). Medium high are the scores of the German-speaking countries Austria, Germany, and Switzerland (70, 65, and 58). Medium to low are the scores of all Asian countries other than Japan and Korea (from 69 for Taiwan to 8 for Singapore), for the African countries, and for the Anglo and Nordic countries plus the Netherlands (from 59 for Finland to 23 for Denmark). West Germany scored 65 (rank 43–44) and Great Britain 35 (rank 68–69). This confirms a culture gap between these otherwise similar countries with regard to the avoidance of uncertainty, as illustrated in the story with which this chapter opened.

Uncertainty Avoidance and Anxiety

Anxiety is a term taken from psychology and psychiatry that expresses a diffuse "state of being uneasy or worried about what may happen."[4] It should not be confused with *fear*, which has an object. We are afraid of something, but anxiety has no object. The idea that levels of anxiety may differ among countries goes back to the French sociologist Emile Durkheim (1858–1917), who as early as 1897 published a study on the phenomenon of suicide. It showed that suicide rates in different countries and regions were surprisingly stable from year to year. He used this stability as proof that a highly individual act such as taking one's life could nevertheless be influenced by social forces that differed among countries and remained largely the same over time.

High suicide rates are one, but only one, possible outcome of anxiety in a society. In the 1970s the results were published of a large study of anxiety-related phenomena in eighteen developed countries by the Irish psychologist Richard Lynn. Lynn used data from official health and related statistics and showed that a number of indicators were correlated across countries: the suicide death rate, alcoholism (measured by the death rate due to liver cirrhosis), the accident death rate, and the rate of prisoners per ten thousand population. These together formed a factor that he labeled *anxiety* or *neuroticism*. Some other indicators were negatively related with the anxiety factor: the consumption of caffeine (in coffee and tea), the average daily intake of calories of food, the death rate due to coronary heart disease, and the occurrence of chronic psychosis (measured through the number of patients per one thousand population). Lynn calculated scores for the strength of the anxiety factor of each of his eighteen countries, based on data from 1960. He found Austria, Japan, and France to score highest, and New Zealand, Great Britain, and the Republic of Ireland lowest. There is a strong correlation between Lynn's country anxiety scores and the UAI scores found in the IBM studies and listed in Table 6.1.[5] Because the two studies use completely different sources of data, the agreement between their results is supportive of the solidity of their conclusions: anxiety levels differ from one country to another. Some cultures are more anxious than others.

Anxious cultures tend to be expressive cultures. They are the places where people talk with their hands and where it is socially acceptable to raise one's voice, to show one's emotions, and to pound the table. Japan may seem to be an exception in this respect; as with other Asians, the Japanese generally behave unemotionally in Western eyes. In Japan, however, and to some extent also in Korea and Taiwan, there is the outlet of getting drunk among colleagues after working hours. During these parties men release their pent-up aggression, even toward superiors, but the next day business continues as usual. Such drinking bouts represent one of the major institutionalized places and times for anxiety release.

In weak uncertainty-avoidance countries, anxiety levels are relatively low. According to Lynn's study, more people in these countries die from coronary heart disease. This statistic can be explained by the lower expressiveness of these cultures. Aggression and emotions are not supposed to be shown: people who behave emotionally or noisily meet with social disapproval. This means that stress cannot be released in activity; it has to be internalized. If this happens again and again, it may cause cardiovascular damage.

Lynn explains the larger number of chronic psychosis patients in low anxiety countries by a lack of mental stimuli in such societies, a certain gloom or dullness. Coffee and tea are stimulating drugs, and these societies show a high consumption of such caffeine carriers. Alcohol has the opposite effect; that is, it releases stress. Weak uncertainty-avoidance societies tend to have low average alcohol consumption figures as manifested by their frequency of liver sclerosis deaths. Many people in the Scandinavian countries show a particular pattern of periodic excessive drinking—in which case the alcohol does act as a stimulus, but for a short period only—followed by longer periods of abstention; the *average* alcohol consumption in the Scandinavian countries is low compared with the rest of Europe.[6]

A comparison across thirty-three countries of UAI with national norms for the Big Five personality test showed that in more uncertainty-avoiding cultures, respondents scored themselves higher on neuroticism and lower on agreeableness. Neuroticism scores increased further if the culture was also masculine.[7] Neuroticism (the opposite of emotional stability) combines the following set of self-scored personality facets: anxiety, angry hostility, depression, self-consciousness, impulsiveness, and vulnerability. Agreeableness combines trust, straightforwardness, altruism, compliance, modesty, and tender-mindedness.

These correlations explain why people from strong uncertainty-avoidance cultures may come across to others as busy, fidgety, emotional, aggressive, or suspicious and why people from weak uncertainty avoidance countries to others may give the impression of being dull, quiet, easygoing, indolent, controlled, or lazy. These impressions are in the eye of the beholder: they show the difference with the level of emotionality in the observer's own culture.

Uncertainty Avoidance Is Not the Same as Risk Avoidance

Uncertainty avoidance should not be confused with risk avoidance. Uncertainty is to risk as anxiety is to fear. Fear and risk are both focused on something specific: an object in the case of fear, and an event in the case of risk. Risk is often expressed as a percentage of probability that a particular event will happen. Anxiety and uncertainty are both diffuse feelings. Anxiety, it was argued earlier, has no object. Uncertainty has no probability attached to it. It is a situation in which anything can happen and we have no idea what. As soon as uncertainty is expressed as risk, it ceases to be a source of anxiety. It may become a source of fear, but it may also be accepted as routine, like the risks of driving a car or practicing a sport.

Rather than leading to reducing risk, uncertainty avoidance leads to a reduction of *ambiguity*. Uncertainty-avoiding cultures shun ambiguous situations. People in such cultures look for structure in their organizations, institutions, and relationships that makes events clearly interpretable and predictable. Paradoxically, they are often prepared to engage in risky behavior in order to reduce ambiguities, such as starting a fight with a potential opponent rather than sitting back and waiting.

The analysis of the IBM data shows a correlation between the strength of uncertainty avoidance in a (developed) country and the maximum speeds allowed in freeway traffic in that country. The relationship is positive: stronger uncertainty avoidance means faster driving. Faster driving, other things being equal, means more fatal accidents, thus more risk. However, this is a *familiar* risk, which uncertainty-avoiding cultures do not mind running. Their emotionality provides them with a sense of stress, of urgency, which in turn leads to wanting to drive faster. The higher speed limits in stronger uncertainty-avoidance countries show, in fact, a priority of saving time over saving lives.[8]

In countries with weaker uncertainty avoidance, there is less of a prevailing sense of urgency, and therefore, there is more public acceptance of a lower speed limit. Not only familiar risks but also unfamiliar risks are accepted, such as those involved in a change of jobs or in engaging in activities for which there are no rules.

Uncertainty Avoidance in Replication Studies: Project GLOBE

The GLOBE study, introduced in Chapter 2, included items intended to measure a dimension called *uncertainty avoidance*, once "as it is" and once "as it should be." As we argued, GLOBE's questions were formulated so differently from ours that they could hardly be expected to measure the same thing. Our analysis of GLOBE's "uncertainty avoidance" confirms this argument, and it produces a number of surprises.

First of all, across forty-eight overlapping countries, our UAI correlates strongly *negatively* with GLOBE's uncertainty avoidance "as is" and weakly positively with GLOBE's uncertainty avoidance "should be." There is a strikingly strong negative correlation between GLOBE's uncertainty avoidance "as is" and "should be" scores.[9]

In countries where we measured a strong uncertainty avoidance (high UAI, validated against societal stress, neuroticism, need for rules, and other factors to follow in this chapter), GLOBE measured *weak* uncertainty avoidance "as is." Examples of GLOBE's questions used are "In this society, orderliness and consistency are stressed, even at the expense of experimentation and innovation" (disagree) and "In this society, societal requirements and instructions are spelled out in detail so citizens know what they are expected to do" (disagree). Basically, where we measured strong uncertainty avoidance, GLOBE respondents say there is no order and there are no detailed instructions in their society.[10]

GLOBE's uncertainty avoidance "should be" was primarily correlated not with our UAI but with our PDI. In Chapter 3 we noted that GLOBE's power distance "as is" and "should be" both correlated better with our UAI than with our PDI. It seems the meanings of our power and uncertainty dimensions and those of GLOBE have been at least partly reversed.[11]

Examples of GLOBE questions associated with uncertainty avoidance "should be" are "I believe that orderliness and consistency should be stressed, even at the expense of experimentation and innovation" (agree) and "I believe that societal requirements and instructions should be spelled out in detail so citizens know what they are expected to do" (agree). These statements are primarily found in countries that in our studies score a large power distance.[12]

GLOBE's uncertainty avoidance measures therefore present no alternative for our UAI. In Chapter 3 we saw that GLOBE's power distance measures presented no alternative for our PDI. GLOBE's use of the terms *power distance* and *uncertainty avoidance* just confuses the concepts.

Uncertainty Avoidance According to Occupation, Gender, and Age

It is easy to imagine occupations that are more uncertainty avoiding versus less so (such as bank clerk versus journalist). Nevertheless, the analysis of the IBM data across the thirty-eight available occupations did not permit the use of the UAI for characterizing occupations. The reason is that the three questions used to compute the index for countries (stress, rule orientation, and intent to stay) had different meanings for different occupations, so that across occupations, the three were not correlated. Anybody who wants to measure the amount of uncertainty avoidance in occupations will have to use other questions.

The same holds for gender differences. Women and men *in the same countries and occupations* showed exactly the same stress levels and rule orientation. Only their intent to stay differed (men on average wanting to stay longer), but this result does not express their greater avoidance of uncertainty: it just shows that the IBM population contained a percentage of younger women who planned to stop working for some time when they had small children.

The only aspect of the IBM population other than nationality that did show a close relationship with the uncertainty avoidance index was average age. In countries in which IBM employees were older, we found higher stress, more rule orientation, and a stronger intent to stay. There is a circular logic in the relationship between UAI and age: in countries with stronger uncertainty avoidance, people not only intended to but did change employers less frequently; therefore, IBM employees in these countries on average had been with the company longer and were older.[13]

Uncertainty Avoidance in the Family

An American grandparent couple spent two weeks in a small Italian town babysitting for their grandchildren, whose American parents, temporarily located in Italy, were away on a trip. The children loved to play in the public piazza, amid lots of Italian children with their mothers or nannies. The American children were allowed to run around; they would fall down but get up again, and the grandparents felt there was little real danger. The Italians reacted quite differently. They would not let their children out of their sight for a moment, and when one fell down, an adult would immediately pick the child up, brush off the dirt, and console the child.[14]

Among the first things a child learns are the distinctions between clean and dirty, and between safe and dangerous. What is considered clean and safe, or dirty and dangerous, varies widely from one society to the next, and even among families within a society. What a child has to learn is to classify clean things from dirty things and safe things from dangerous things. In strongly uncertainty-avoiding cultures, classifications with regard to what is dirty and dangerous are tight and absolute. The Italian mothers and nannies (UAI 75) saw dirt and danger in the piazza where the American grandparents (UAI 46) saw none.

British-American anthropologist Mary Douglas has argued that dirt— that which pollutes—is a relative concept, depending entirely on cultural interpretation. Dirt is basically matter out of place. What are dangerous and polluting are things that do not fit our usual frameworks of thinking, our normal classifications.[15]

Dirt and danger are not limited to matter. Feelings of dirty and dangerous can also be held about people. Racism is bred in families. Children learn that persons from a particular category are dirty and dangerous. They learn to avoid children from social, ethnical, religious, or political out-groups as playmates.

Ideas too can be considered dirty and dangerous. Children in their families learn that some ideas are good and others taboo. In some cultures the distinction between good and evil ideas is sharp. There is a concern about Truth with a capital *T*. Ideas that differ from this Truth are dangerous and polluting. Little room is left for doubt or relativism.

The stronger systems of rules and norms in strongly uncertainty-avoiding societies make children more often feel guilty and sinful. In fact, the education process in high-UAI societies develops in its children stronger *superegos* (the concept was developed by Sigmund Freud in high-UAI Austria). Children in these societies are more likely to learn that the world is a hostile place and are more likely to be protected from experiencing unknown situations.

Weak uncertainty-avoidance cultures also have their classifications as to dirt and danger, but these classifications are less precise and more likely to give the benefit of the doubt to unknown situations, people, and ideas. In these societies rules are more flexible, superegos are weaker, the world is pictured as basically benevolent, and experiencing novel situations is encouraged.

The less-flexible system of rules and norms for children in stronger uncertainty-avoiding cultures is also reflected in language. Data about the structure of languages presented by Kashima and Kashima, whose work we met in Chapter 4, show that languages in uncertainty-avoiding cultures more often have different modes of address for different persons, like *tu* and *vous* in French. Children learning such languages face more choices according to tight cultural rules. Languages in lower UAI cultures tend to have fewer such rules.[16]

The strong uncertainty-avoidance sentiment can be summarized by the credo of xenophobia: "What is different is dangerous." The weak uncertainty-avoidance sentiment, on the contrary, is: "What is different is curious."

Family life in high-UAI societies is inherently more stressful than where UAI is low. Feelings are more intense, and both parents and children express their positive sentiments as well as their negative sentiments more emotionally. Data from the World Values Survey showed that in balance, satisfaction with home life was negatively correlated with UAI, at least in the more affluent countries. When poorer countries were included, satisfaction with home life related more to individualism and femininity.[17]

Eurobarometer data from 2008 showed that differences in percentages of EU citizens scoring "very satisfied with the life I lead" were explained by national wealth (GNI per capita) when all twenty-six countries in the study were included. When the analysis was limited to the nineteen more affluent countries, the differences were explained by (low) UAI, low MAS, *plus* high GNI per capita. Percentages scoring "very satisfied with my family life" showed a similar pattern: across all EU countries they related to national wealth, but for the affluent countries they also related to low UAI.[18]

In the same Eurobarometer study, EU citizens were asked about difficulties faced by families in daily life. Percentages marking "the cost of raising children" were, not surprisingly, related to GNI per capita. However, in the affluent countries they were also related to high UAI.[19]

Table 6.2 summarizes the key differences between weak and strong uncertainty-avoidance societies described so far. Obviously, the descriptions refer to the extreme poles of the dimension, and most real countries are somewhere in between, with considerable variation *within* each country.

Uncertainty Avoidance, Health, and (Un)happiness

Self-ratings of health across countries tend to correlate negatively with UAI. Where medical statistics show no evidence of objective health differences, people in uncertainty-tolerant countries still feel healthier. One is as healthy as one feels.[20]

Health-care practices vary considerable among countries, as any traveler who has consulted a doctor abroad can testify. Theories and practices of medicine are tightly interwoven with cultural traditions, in which uncertainty avoidance plays an important role. Lynn Payer, a medical journalist,

TABLE 6.2 Key Differences Between Weak and Strong Uncertainty-Avoidance Societies
I: General Norm and Family

WEAK UNCERTAINTY AVOIDANCE	STRONG UNCERTAINTY AVOIDANCE
Uncertainty is a normal feature of life, and each day is accepted as it comes.	The uncertainty inherent in life is a continuous threat that must be fought.
Low stress and low anxiety	High stress and high anxiety
Aggression and emotions should not be shown.	Aggression and emotions may at proper times and places be vented.
In personality tests, higher scores on agreeableness	In personality tests, higher scores on neuroticism
Comfortable in ambiguous situations and with unfamiliar risks	Acceptance of familiar risks; fear of ambiguous situations and of unfamiliar risks
Lenient rules for children on what is dirty and taboo	Tight rules for children on what is dirty and taboo
Weak superegos developed	Strong superegos developed
Similar modes of address for different others	Different modes of address for different others
What is different is curious.	What is different is dangerous.
Family life is relaxed.	Family life is stressful.
If country is affluent: satisfaction with family life.	If country is affluent: worried about cost of raising children.

described her personal experiences as a patient in Britain, France, Germany, and the United States. One of her examples is that low blood pressure is seen as a reason for living longer (and maybe getting a lower life insurance premium) in Britain and the United States, but it is treated as a disorder in (higher UAI) Germany, where several drugs are on the market to cure it.[21] A comparative study of doctor-patient interactions in ten European countries showed that doctors in uncertainty-tolerant countries on average had more eye contact with the patient and paid more attention to rapport building.[22]

Doctors in uncertainty-tolerant countries more often send the patient away with a comforting talk, without any prescription. In uncertainty-avoiding cultures, meanwhile, doctors usually prescribe several drugs, and patients expect them to do so. It is said that in France when a village is slowly depopulating, the local pharmacy survives longer than the local pub. This is certainly not the case in (lower UAI) Ireland.

A country's uncertainty-avoidance norm is also reflected in the way health-care resources are spent. The United Nations Development Programme (UNDP) lists the number of doctors and the number of nurses per 100,000 inhabitants. Dividing the latter number (nurses) by the former number (doctors) provides an index of nurses per doctor that is independent of the absolute size of the health budget—that is, of the country's wealth. There is a significant negative correlation between nurses per doctor and UAI, meaning that uncertainty-avoiding countries tend to spend more money on doctors, while uncertainty-accepting countries spend more on nurses. In high-UAI cultures, thus, more tasks are performed by the doctors themselves, who are seen as the indispensable experts.[23]

Lower self-ratings on health in uncertainty-avoiding cultures are reflected in higher self-ratings on unhappiness. Dutch sociologist Ruut Veenhoven compiled data about happiness (subjective well-being) in nations for a period of more than fifty years. For all countries together and for the period before 1990, average happiness scores were primarily correlated with wealth (richer countries happier). For the affluent countries and for all countries since 1990, we found UAI to produce the strongest correlation with average happiness.[24] However, average happiness may not be the most meaningful yardstick. Veenhoven's database includes a measure for the distribution (*dispersion*) of happiness scores within each country. These dispersion scores are positively correlated with UAI.[25] Very happy people could be found in both high- and low-UAI countries, but very unhappy people existed especially in high-UAI countries. This means that UAI tends to correlate with unhappiness, rather than with happiness. Uncertainty avoidance tends to explain why some nations have higher percentages of unhappy people.[26] Our new cultural dimension of *indulgence versus restraint* (Chapter 8) will explain why some nations have higher percentages of *very happy* people.

An ingenious indirect measurement of unhappiness was supplied by Peter Smith's comparison of national levels of "acquiescence" in large international surveys, mentioned in Chapter 4. *Acquiescence* is the tendency to give positive answers to any question, regardless of its content. For questions dealing with values, this tendency was correlated with collectivism and large power distance. For questions dealing with descriptions of the actual situation, the tendency to give positive answers all across was correlated with weak uncertainty avoidance. In high-UAI countries people showed a negative tendency in describing their work and life situation.[27]

Uncertainty Avoidance at School

The International Teachers Program (ITP) around 1980 was a summer refresher course for teachers in management subjects. In a class of fifty there might be twenty or more different nationalities. Such a class offered excellent opportunities to watch the different learning habits of the students (who were teachers themselves at other times) and the different expectations they had of the behavior of those who taught them.

One dilemma Geert experienced when teaching in the ITP was choosing the proper amount of structure to be put into the various activities. Most Germans, for example, favored structured learning situations with precise objectives, detailed assignments, and strict timetables. They liked situations in which there was one correct answer that they could find. They expected to be rewarded for accuracy. These preferences are typical for stronger uncertainty-avoidance countries. Most British participants, on the other hand, despised too much structure. They liked open-ended learning situations with vague objectives, broad assignments, and no timetables at all. The suggestion that there could be only one correct answer was taboo with them. They expected to be rewarded for originality. Their reactions are typical for countries with weak uncertainty avoidance.

Students from strong uncertainty-avoidance countries expect their teachers to be the experts who have all the answers. Teachers who use cryptic academic language are respected; some of the eminent gurus from these countries write such difficult prose that one needs commentaries by more ordinary creatures explaining what the guru really meant. It has been remarked that "German students are brought up in the belief that anything which is easy enough for them to understand is dubious and probably unscientific."[28] French academic books not infrequently contain phrases of half a page long.[29] Students in these countries will not, as a rule, confess to intellectual disagreement with their teachers. A Ph.D. candidate who finds him- or herself in conflict with a thesis adviser on an important issue has the choice of changing his or her mind or finding another adviser. Intellectual disagreement in academic matters is felt as personal disloyalty.

Students from weak uncertainty-avoidance countries accept a teacher who says, "I don't know." Their respect goes to teachers who use plain language and to books explaining difficult issues in ordinary terms. Intellectual disagreement in academic matters in these cultures can be seen as a stimulating exercise, and we know of thesis advisers whose evaluation of a Ph.D. candidate is positively related to the candidate's amount of well-argued disagreement with the professor's position.

In similar situations students in low-UAI countries were more likely to attribute their achievements to their own ability, and students in high-UAI countries to circumstances or luck. In two different studies, each covering students from five countries, the relative tendency to attribute achievement to ability was significantly negatively correlated with UAI.[30]

The examples used so far stem from university and postgraduate teaching and learning situations, but the behavior and expectations of both students and teachers in these examples were clearly developed during earlier school experiences. One more difference related to uncertainty avoidance, which operates specifically at the elementary- and secondary-school level, is the expected role of parents versus teachers. In cultures with strong uncertainty avoidance, parents are sometimes brought in by teachers as an audience, but they are rarely consulted. Parents are laypersons, and teachers are experts who know. In countries with weak uncertainty avoidance, teachers often try to get parents involved in their children's learning process: they actively seek parents' ideas.

Uncertainty Avoidance in Shopping

The previous chapter referred to the studies of Dutch marketing expert Marieke de Mooij. She found many significant links between the IBM indexes and consumer behavior differences among sixteen affluent European countries.[31] Next to masculinity-femininity, uncertainty avoidance played the most important role.

In shopping for food and beverages, higher UAI stands for valuing purity and basic products. Uncertainty-avoiding cultures used mineral water rather than tap water, even where the tap water was of good quality. They ate more fresh fruits and used more pure sugar. Uncertainty-accepting cultures valued convenience over purity: they consumed more ready-made products, such as ice cream, frozen foods, confectionery, and savory snacks.

Uncertainty-avoiding cultures believed more in cleanliness: they used more laundry detergent. On the other hand, uncertainty-accepting cultures valued looks more than cleanliness: they used more beauty products, such as lipstick, mascara, body lotion, deodorant, hair conditioner, facial moisturizing cream, face cleaner, and other cosmetics.

People in uncertainty-avoiding cultures bought new cars rather than used ones. People in uncertainty-accepting cultures would more often perform jobs in the home themselves—for example, painting and wallpapering; in high-UAI countries people preferred playing it safe and leaving such jobs to experts.

People in uncertainty-accepting cultures were found to read more books and newspapers. They more often claimed that ethical considerations influenced their buying decisions.[32]

Customers in higher-UAI cultures tended to be hesitant toward new products and information. They were slower in introducing electronic communication tools (mobile telephones,[33] e-mail, the Internet).[34] Customers in lower UAI cultures more often used the Internet to compare service providers.[35]

Advertising campaigns, in print and on TV, for uncertainty avoiding cultures frequently feature experts, such as doctors in white coats, who recommend the product. Ads in uncertainty-accepting cultures more frequently use humor. Ads from sellers in other EU countries are more frequently read in low-UAI cultures.[36]

In financial matters people from high-UAI countries take fewer risks: they tend to invest less in stocks and more in precious metals and gems. They are also slower in paying their bills, which may be a problem in trade with uncertainty-accepting countries.[37]

Table 6.3 continues the summary of key differences between weak and strong uncertainty-avoidance societies started in Table 6.2. Again the

TABLE 6.3 Key Differences Between Weak and Strong Uncertainty-Avoidance Societies

II: Health, Education, and Shopping

WEAK UNCERTAINTY AVOIDANCE	STRONG UNCERTAINTY AVOIDANCE
Fewer people feel unhappy.	More people feel unhappy.
People have fewer worries about health and money.	People have more worries about health and money.
People have more heart attacks.	People have fewer heart attacks.
There are many nurses but few doctors.	There are many doctors but few nurses.
Students are comfortable with open-ended learning situations and concerned with good discussions.	Students are comfortable in structured learning situations and concerned with the right answers.
Teachers may say, "I don't know."	Teachers are supposed to have all the answers.
Results are attributed to a person's own ability.	Results are attributed to circumstances or luck.
Teachers involve parents.	Teachers inform parents.
In shopping, the search is for convenience.	In shopping, the search is for purity and cleanliness.
Used cars, do-it-yourself home repairs	New cars, home repairs by experts
People more often claim ethical considerations in buying.	People read fewer books and newspapers.
There is fast acceptance of new features such as mobile phones, e-mail, and the Internet.	There is a hesitancy toward new products and technologies.
Risky investments	Conservative investments
Appeal of humor in advertising.	Appeal of expertise in advertising

descriptions refer to extremes, and most real countries are somewhere in between, with considerable variation *within* each country.

Uncertainty Avoidance in the Workplace

In the summer of 2009, the international press reported on a wave of suicides among employees of France Telecom, which, with more than a hundred thousand employees, is the largest French telecommunications company. On September 28, 2009, the twenty-fourth employee in a period of just over eighteen months killed himself, by jumping off a bridge on a Monday morning. The suicide explosion was blamed on a drastic restructuring of the former government monopoly after its privatization; employees, previously considered civil servants, were relocated, and tasks were changed by management decree with little concern for employees' personal feelings. In Table 6.1 France is a high-UAI country (score 86, rank 17–22). The stress of the restructuring became too high for the victims' tolerance level.

Along with stress, another component of the UAI was the percentage of IBM employees expressing their intent to stay with the company for a long-term career. This was not only an IBM phenomenon: in higher-UAI countries, other factors being equal, more employees and managers look for long-term employment. At the same time, more people in these countries (at least in Europe) find it difficult to achieve the right work-life balance.[38]

Laws, rules, and regulations were mentioned in the beginning of this chapter as ways in which a society tries to prevent uncertainties in the behavior of people. Uncertainty-avoiding societies have more formal laws and informal rules controlling the rights and duties of employers and employees. They also have more internal regulations controlling the work process, although in this case the power distance level plays a role too. Where power distances are large, the exercise of discretionary power by superiors replaces to some extent the need for internal rules.

The need for rules in a society with a strong uncertainty-avoidance culture is emotional. People—employers and employees but also civil servants and members of governments—have been programmed since early childhood to feel comfortable in structured environments. Matters that can be structured should not be left to chance.

The emotional need for laws and regulations in a strong uncertainty-avoidance society can lead to rules or rule-oriented behaviors that are purely ritual, inconsistent, or even dysfunctional. Critics from countries with weaker uncertainty avoidance often do not realize that ineffective rules can also satisfy people's emotional need for formal structure. What happens in reality is less important. Philippe d'Iribarne, in his comparative study of a French, a U.S., and a Dutch manufacturing plant, remarked that some procedures in the French plant were formally followed but only after having been divested of any practical meaning. He compared this situation to what has been written about the French ancien régime (the eighteenth-century, pre–Napoleon monarchy): "une règle rigide, une pratique molle" ("a strict rule, but a lenient practice").[39]

Countries with weak uncertainty avoidance can show the opposite, an emotional horror of formal rules. People think that rules should be established only in case of absolute necessity, such as to determine whether traffic should keep left or right. They believe that many problems can be solved without formal rules. Germans, coming from a fairly uncertainty-avoiding culture, are impressed by the public discipline shown by the British in forming neat queues at bus stops and in shops. There is no law in Britain governing queuing behavior; it is based on a public habit continuously reinforced by social control. The paradox here is that although rules in countries with weak uncertainty avoidance are less sacred, they are often better followed.

British queuing behavior is facilitated by the unemotional and patient nature of most British subjects. As argued earlier in this chapter, weak uncertainty avoidance also stands for low anxiety. At the workplace the anxiety component of uncertainty avoidance leads to noticeable differences between strong and weak uncertainty-avoidance societies. In strong uncertainty-avoidance societies, people like to work hard or at least to be always busy. Life is hurried, and time is money. In weak uncertainty-avoidance societies, people are able to work hard if there is a need for it, but they are not driven by an inner urge toward constant activity. They like to relax. Time is a framework in which to orient oneself but not something one is constantly watching.

In the 1970s, during courses at INSEAD business school in Fontainebleau, France, professor André Laurent surveyed managers from ten industrialized countries about their beliefs regarding organization. Items for which the country mean scores correlated with UAI were as follows:

- Most organizations would be better off if conflict could be eliminated forever.
- It is important for a manager to have at hand precise answers to most of the questions that subordinates may raise about their work.
- If you want a competent person to do a job properly, it is often best to provide precise instructions on how to do it.

- When the respective roles of the members of a department become complex, detailed job descriptions are a useful way of clarifying.
- An organizational structure in which certain subordinates have two direct bosses should be avoided at all costs.[40]

All of these items show a dislike of ambiguity and a need for precision and formalization in organizations in high-UAI countries. In low-UAI countries ambiguity and chaos are sometimes praised as conditions for creativity.

Uncertainty-avoiding cultures also have a strong belief in expertise on the work floor; their organizations contain more specialists. Uncertainty-accepting cultures have an equally strong belief in common sense and in generalists; a well-known example is the British tradition of considering the study of classic literature at a good university a valid entry ticket for a business management career.

A French study of top-management control in British, French, and German companies by Jacques Horovitz concluded that in Britain top managers occupied themselves more with strategic problems and less with daily operations; in France and Germany the reverse was the case.[41] In the IBM studies, France and Germany scored considerably higher on UAI than Britain (86 and 65, respectively, versus 35). Strategic problems, being by definition unstructured, demand a greater tolerance for ambiguity than do operational problems. During the period in which Horovitz did his study, the French and German economies did better than the British, so weak uncertainty avoidance leading to more strategic planning does not necessarily increase business effectiveness. Strategic planning in these countries is rather a matter of faith. The economic success of companies and countries depends on many more factors.

U.S. researcher Scott Shane found that across thirty-three countries, the number of new trademarks granted to nationals was negatively correlated with UAI. He concluded that uncertainty-avoiding cultures were slower in innovating.[42] Shane and his colleagues also surveyed employees of four multinational companies in thirty countries about their roles in innovation processes. In stronger uncertainty-avoidance countries, employees more often felt constrained by existing rules and regulations.[43]

A different story, however, is told by d'Iribarne. In the early 1990s two European car manufacturers, Renault of France and Volvo of Sweden, created a joint venture. In the IBM studies, France scored high on UAI,

Sweden very low. A mixed team of engineers and technicians from both nations worked on the design of a new model. After a few years the venture was dissolved. French and Swedish social scientists interviewed the actors to find out what went wrong and possibly learn from the experience. D'Iribarne described what they found:

> In the joint team, the French rather than the Swedes produced the more innovative designs. French team members did not hesitate to try out new ideas and to defend these aggressively. The Swedes, on the other hand, were constantly seeking consensus. The need for consensus limited what ideas they could present, even what ideas they could conceive of. To the Swedes the expression of ideas was subject to the need for agreement between people; to the French, it was only subject to the search for technical truth. The French were primarily concerned with the quality of decisions; the Swedes with the legitimacy of the decision process. In the negotiations within the team, the French usually won. They had the support of their superiors who were involved all along, while the Swedish superiors had delegated the responsibility to the team members and were nowhere to be seen. The danger of this asymmetric structure was discovered too late. A mutual distrust had developed at top management level that led to the termination of the venture.[44]

This case suggests that stronger uncertainty avoidance does not necessarily constrain creativity, not does weaker uncertainty avoidance guarantee its free flow. Comparing the conclusions by Shane and by d'Iribarne, we are also warned that the results of social research are not independent of the nationality of the researcher.

The IBM surveys had found that a preference for larger over smaller companies to work for was positively correlated not only with MAS but also with UAI. In the organizational literature large companies are often supposed to be less innovative than small ones, unless they reward *intrapreneurs* who dare to break rules. This term is a pun on the word *entrepreneurs*, the independent self-starters who, according to the Austrian-American economist Joseph Schumpeter (1883–1950), are the main source of innovation in a society.

Schumpeter's ideas played a role in a research project in which Geert took part, together with a number of Dutch colleagues. The project looked for economic and cultural factors affecting levels of self-employment in twenty-one industrialized countries. Comparing self-employment levels with the countries' UAI scores produced a surprise. While one would expect that in strong uncertainty-avoidance cultures, fewer people would risk self-employment, the opposite turned out to be the case: self-employment rates were consistently *positively* correlated with UAI. A further search revealed that, in particular, one aspect associated with strong uncertainty avoidance accounted for the correlation: low subjective well-being in a society. Self-employment was therefore more often chosen in countries in which people were dissatisfied with their lives, versus countries with a higher tolerance for the unknown.[45]

If Schumpeter was right that entrepreneurs innovate more than non-entrepreneurs, we thus found a reason for expecting more, not less, innovation in high-UAI countries. Innovation, however, has more than one face. It may be true that weak uncertainty-avoidance cultures are better at basic innovations, but they seem to be at a disadvantage in developing these innovations into new products or services. Implementation of new processes demands a considerable sense of detail and punctuality. The latter are more likely to be found in strong uncertainty-avoidance countries. Britain has produced more Nobel Prize winners than Japan, but Japan has put more new products on the world market. There is a strong case here for synergy between innovating cultures and implementing cultures—the first supplying ideas, the second developing them.

Uncertainty Avoidance, Masculinity, and Motivation

The motivation of employees is a classic concern of management and probably even more of management trainers and of the authors of management books. Differences in uncertainty avoidance imply differences in motivation patterns, but the picture becomes clearer when we simultaneously consider the masculinity-femininity dimension described in Chapter 5. Figure 6.1 therefore presents a two-dimensional plot of country scores on uncertainty avoidance (vertically) and masculinity (horizontally).

The usefulness of combining UAI and MAS for studying motivation patterns was suggested by a comparison of the IBM survey results with the work of Harvard University psychologist David McClelland (1917–98), who in 1961 issued a now-classic book, *The Achieving Society*. In this book he attempted to trace different dominant motivation patterns in different

FIGURE 6.1 Masculinity Versus Uncertainty Avoidance

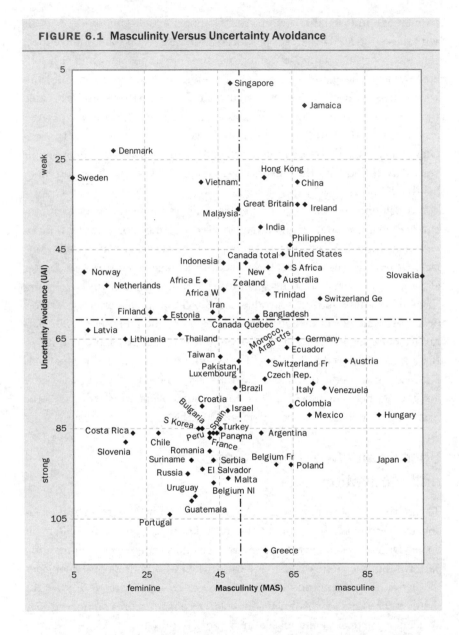

countries. He distinguished three types of motives: achievement, affiliation (associating with other people), and power. The strength of each motive for each country was measured through a content analysis of the stories appearing in children's readers. McClelland argued that the stories read by second- to fourth-grade schoolchildren, their first readings, are to modern nations what folktales are to traditional societies. Folktales have been widely used by field anthropologists to infer motives of nonliterate peoples; McClelland wanted to do the same for modern nations.

McClelland's research team analyzed children's stories from a large number of countries dating from 1925 and from 1950. For each country and either period, twenty-one stories were studied. Each story and each country was scored on need for achievement, need for affiliation, and need for power. McClelland's own hypothesis was that the need for achievement in children's stories would predict a country's rate of economic development at the time when these children grew up. On this account later events did not prove him right. A comparison of McClelland's country scores with the IBM dimension scores, however, revealed that the need for achievement as measured from 1925 children's books (the more traditional ones) was strongly correlated with *weak* uncertainty avoidance and even more strongly with the combination of weak uncertainty avoidance and strong masculinity.[46]

This means that McClelland's 1925 ranking of countries on their need for achievement follows a diagonal line through Figure 6.1, from upper right (strong need for achievement) to lower left (weak need for achievement). Low UAI means willingness to run unfamiliar risks, and high MAS reflects the importance of visible results. Both are components of entrepreneurial activity in the American tradition. It should be no surprise that the United States and the other Anglo countries in Figure 6.1 are to be found in the upper right-hand quadrant, where UAI is low, MAS is high, and need for achievement is strong. In choosing the achievement motive, the American McClelland has promoted a typical Anglo value complex to a *universal* recipe for economic success. A French, Swedish, or Japanese researcher would have been unlikely to conceive of a worldwide achievement motive. Even the word *achievement* is difficult to translate in most languages other than English.[47]

Leaving McClelland's work aside, the combination of cultural uncertainty avoidance and masculinity-femininity in Figure 6.1 highlights different motivation patterns for different clusters of countries. A point of departure is the "hierarchy of human needs" formulated by Abraham Maslow and referred to in Chapter 4. Maslow ordered needs from lower to higher: physiological, safety and security, belongingness, esteem, and self-actualization. Chapter 4 took issue with the individualistic assumptions in putting *self*-actualization on top. In view of the cultural variety in the world with regard to uncertainty avoidance and masculinity, some other provisos should also be made.

Safety or security is likely to prevail over other needs where uncertainty avoidance is strong. Belongingness (human relationships) will prevail over esteem in a feminine culture, but esteem prevails over belonging in a masculine culture. Thus, the supreme motivators—other things such as type of work being equal—in Figure 6.1 will be achievement (of self or group) and esteem in the upper right-hand corner (United States, etc.); achievement and belongingness in the upper left-hand corner (Sweden, etc.); security and esteem in the lower right-hand corner (Japan, Germany, etc.); and security and belongingness in the lower left-hand corner (France, etc.).

In this classification Maslow's five categories have been maintained, but they have been reshuffled according to a country's prevailing culture pattern. An additional question is whether other needs should be added that were missing in Maslow's model because they were not recognized in his mid-twentieth-century U.S. middle-class cultural environment. Candidate needs identified in the previous chapters include respect, harmony, face, and duty.

Table 6.4 summarizes the key differences between weak and strong uncertainty-avoidance societies related to work, organization, and motivation. Again most real situations will be somewhere in between.

Uncertainty Avoidance, the Citizen, and the State

In countries with strong uncertainty avoidance, there tend to be more—and more precise—laws than in those with weak uncertainty avoidance. Germany, for example, has laws for the event that all other laws become unenforceable (*Notstandsgesetze*), while Britain does not even have a written constitution. Labor-management relations in Germany have been codified in detail, while attempts to pass an Industrial Relations Act in Britain have never succeeded.

In countries with weak uncertainty avoidance, a feeling prevails that if laws do not work, they should be withdrawn or changed. In countries with strong uncertainty avoidance, laws can fulfill a need for security even if they are not followed—very similar to religious commandments.

Establishing laws is one thing; applying them is another. Legal experts from the World Bank, in cooperation with law firms in more than a hundred countries, have amassed information on the practical duration in each

TABLE 6.4 Key Differences Between Weak and Strong Uncertainty-Avoidance Societies

III: Work, Organization, and Motivation

WEAK UNCERTAINTY AVOIDANCE	STRONG UNCERTAINTY AVOIDANCE
More changes of employer, shorter service	Fewer changes of employer, longer service, more difficult work-life balance
There should be no more rules than strictly necessary.	There is an emotional need for rules, even if they will not work.
Work hard only when needed.	There is an emotional need to be busy and an inner urge to work hard.
Time is a framework for orientation.	Time is money.
Tolerance for ambiguity and chaos	Need for precision and formalization
Belief in generalists and common sense	Belief in experts and technical solutions
Top managers are concerned with strategy.	Top managers are concerned with daily operations.
More new trademarks	Fewer new trademarks
Focus on decision process	Focus on decision content
Intrapreneurs are relatively free from rules.	Intrapreneurs are constrained by existing rules.
There are fewer self-employed people.	There are more self-employed people.
Better at invention, worse at implementation	Worse at invention, better at implementation
Motivation by achievement and esteem or belonging	Motivation by security and esteem or belonging

country of two relatively simple civil procedures: collecting a bounced check (one refused by the bank) and evicting a tenant for nonpayment of rent. The figures varied between forty days and three years, and across sixty-seven countries for which culture indexes were available, the duration of either procedure was highly significantly correlated with UAI, and not with any of the other indexes or with national wealth.[48] More uncertainty-avoiding cultures are well provided with laws, but for the citizen to make them work in these two simple cases takes more time—possibly so much that citizens may not even try.

The effect of uncertainty avoidance on a society's legislation depends also on its degree of individualism or collectivism. In Figure 6.2 these two dimensions have been plotted against each other. Whereas in strongly uncertainty-avoiding, individualist countries, rules will tend to be explicit and written into laws (low-context communication; see Chapter 4), in

FIGURE 6.2 Uncertainty Avoidance Versus Individualism

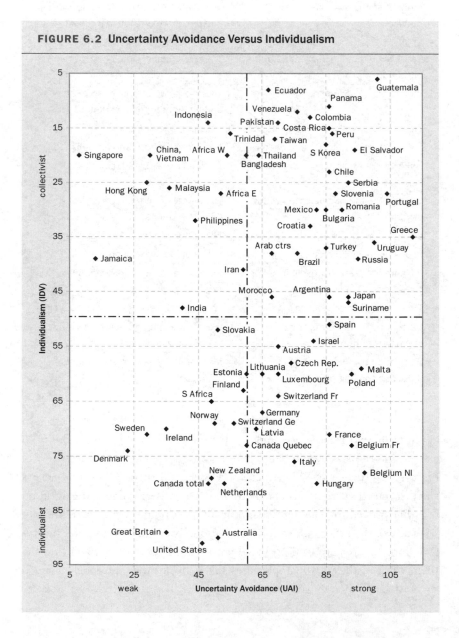

strongly uncertainty-avoiding, collectivist countries, rules are often implicit and rooted in tradition (high-context communication). The latter is clearly the case in Japan, and it represents a bone of contention in the negotiations between Western countries and Japan about the opening of Japanese markets for Western products. The Japanese rightly argue that there are no formal rules preventing the foreign products from being brought in, but the Western would-be importers run up against the many implicit rules of the Japanese distribution system, which they do not understand.

The implications of uncertainty avoidance for the relationship between authorities and citizens differ from those of power distance, as described in Chapter 3. In high-PDI countries authorities have more unchecked power, status, and material rewards than in low-PDI countries. In high-UAI countries authorities are deemed to have more expertise than in low-UAI countries. The inequality in this latter case is not in the *power* but in the *competence* of authorities versus other citizens.

The term *citizen competence* was coined in a classic study by U.S. political scientists Gabriel Almond and Sidney Verba: they found that the competence attributed to ordinary citizens versus authorities varied strongly among five countries in their research.[49] In *Culture's Consequences* it is shown that Almond and Verba's citizen competence measure correlates strongly negatively with uncertainty avoidance: perceived competence is higher in countries that scored lower on uncertainty avoidance.

In another study, citizens from strong uncertainty-avoidance countries were less optimistic about their possibilities to influence decisions made by authorities than were citizens of weak uncertainty avoidance societies. Few citizens in high-UAI countries were prepared to protest against decisions by the authorities, and if they did protest, their means of doing so were relatively conventional, such as through petitions and demonstrations. With regard to more extreme protest actions such as boycotts and sit-ins, most citizens in high-UAI countries thought these actions should be firmly repressed by the government.[50]

Citizens from weak uncertainty-avoidance countries believed that they could participate in political decisions at the lowest, local level. More than in strong uncertainty-avoidance countries, they were prepared to protest against government decisions, and they sympathized with strong and unconventional protest actions if the milder actions did not help. They did not think the government should repress such protests.[51] Eurobarometer data from 2007 showed that young Europeans from nineteen prosperous countries were more likely to have signed a petition if their country's UAI was lower. As for having taken part in a public demonstration, however, the trend was, if anything, the other way around.[52]

Citizens in strong uncertainty-avoidance countries not only were more dependent on the expertise of the government but also seemed to feel that this was how things should be. The authorities and the citizens shared the same norms about their mutual roles. The authorities tended to think in legal terms: in high-UAI countries higher civil servants more frequently had law degrees than in low-UAI countries (a 1977 article reported 65 percent with law degrees in Germany versus 3 percent in Britain).[53] Civil servants in high-UAI countries tended to have negative feelings about politicians and the political process; in low-UAI countries their feelings were more positive.

Citizens of strong uncertainty-avoidance countries were less interested in politics and less inclined to trust their country's politicians and civil servants. While we observed that these countries tend to have more laws and bylaws, this situation did not imply a greater trust in the legal system.[54] Citizens of weak uncertainty-avoidance countries participated more often in voluntary associations and activities for the benefit of their society.

An American family living in a suburb of Brussels worried about the increasing noise level caused by their proximity to the airport. They circulated a petition to the authorities to demand measures for noise reduction. Only the foreign families in the neighborhood were prepared to sign. The Belgians (from a high-UAI culture) either denied the problem ("What noise?") or declined to sign, claiming the authorities would pay no attention anyway.[55]

Chapter 5 described the "dropped pen" experiment by U.S. psychology professor Robert Levine and his international students. This experiment was part of a project studying helping behavior across cultures. The same project included an experiment on "helping a blind person across the street." Students played the role of a blind person at a busy pedestrian traffic light. "Helping" meant that within sixty seconds after the light turned green, someone informed the "blind person" that it was green or helped him or her across. Percentages of helping pedestrians in twenty-three countries were significantly positively correlated with the countries' UAI score. In more uncertainty-avoiding cultures, members of the public could not stand by and see a blind person wait while the light was green.[56]

In this case uncertainty avoidance had a *positive* effect on citizens' taking responsibility—but the other party was not the government.

In most higher-UAI countries in Europe, citizens are obliged to carry identity cards in order to be able to show proof of who they are whenever requested to do so by an authority figure. No such obligation exists in most lower-UAI countries, and the burden of proof of identifying the citizen is on the authorities.[57]

In high-UAI countries there is more conservatism, even within parties that call themselves progressive, and a stronger need for law and order. The public in low-UAI countries tends to be more liberally minded. In these countries a positive attitude toward young people prevails, whereas in high-UAI countries youngsters are more often considered as suspect.[58] The reverse can also be true; quite a few French chansonniers wrote texts that depict adults in a negative light, including Georges Brassens, Pierre Chastellain, Catherine Leforestier, and Henri Tachan.[59] High-UAI countries are more likely to harbor extremist minorities within their political landscape than low-UAI countries, and they are also more likely to ban political groups whose ideas are considered dangerous. Banned groups may continue an underground existence or may even resort to terrorism. These countries have more native terrorists.

Uncertainty Avoidance and Corruption

A phenomenon that affects the functioning of the state, and sometimes also of private organizations, is corruption. Official and unofficial side payments occur in many situations throughout the world. What is called corruption is partly a matter of definition. We speak of corruption when people use the power of their positions to illegally enrich themselves, or when citizens buy the collaboration of authorities for their private purposes. But what about the large sums spent in some countries on lobbying, which, although formally legal, rests on similar motives? What about the excessive levels of self-compensation and golden handshakes at executive levels in some companies and industries? In Japan, China, and many other cultures, the giving of gifts is an important ritual, and the borderline between gift giving and bribing is diffuse. To a purist, even tipping can be considered a form of bribing.

Since 1995 Transparency International (a nongovernmental organization located in Berlin) has issued an online yearly Corruption Perception Index (CPI) for a large number of countries, which combines information from up to thirteen sources in business, the press, and the foreign services. The index ranges from 10 for a perfectly "clean" country to 1 for an extremely corrupt country. Our analysis of the 2008 CPI scores showed that worldwide, they depended very strongly on national wealth—or rather on national poverty. The wealthier half of the seventy-three countries for which we had all the necessary data was also the cleaner half, and vice versa; only four of the poorer countries were rated cleaner than average, and only five of the wealthier countries were rated more corrupt than average.[60]

Under conditions of poverty, acquiring money in unofficial ways is not simply a matter of greed; it may be a matter of survival. Officials, police officers, and teachers in poor countries are often so poorly paid that without side payments they cannot feed their families, and the habit of collecting such payments pervades the entire system.

Among wealthier countries, differences in wealth no longer explain differences in CPI. Instead, among the thirty wealthiest countries in our data set, more than half of the differences in the 2008 CPI scores could be explained by UAI.[61] To Lord Acton, a nineteenth-century British politician turned Cambridge professor, we owe a famous aphorism: "Power tends to corrupt and absolute power corrupts absolutely." This observation is probably still true, but more often, power is not absolute, but relative. In those cases the less competent the citizens feel toward persons in authority, the easier the latter get away with illegal practices.

Corruption, of course, presumes corruptors. Along with the CPI, Transparency International periodically publishes a Bribe Payers Index (BPI). Across twenty-two exporting countries, BPI 2008 scores were not correlated with UAI but were inversely correlated with the exporting country's national wealth—exporters from poorer countries such as China and India pay more bribes. The exporting country's power distance also played a sizable role—exporters from countries with a higher PDI pay more bribes.[62]

Table 6.5 summarizes imortant differences between weak and strong uncertainty-avoidance societies related to politics and the state.

**TABLE 6.5 Key Differences Between Weak and Strong
Uncertainty-Avoidance Societies
IV: The Citizen and the State**

WEAK UNCERTAINTY AVOIDANCE	STRONG UNCERTAINTY AVOIDANCE
Few and general laws or unwritten rules	Many and precise laws or unwritten rules
If laws cannot be respected, they should be changed.	Laws are necessary, even if they cannot be respected.
Fast result in case of appeal to justice	Slow result in case of appeal to justice
Citizens are competent toward authorities.	Citizens are incompetent toward authorities.
Citizen protest is acceptable.	Citizen protest should be repressed.
Civil servants do not have law degrees.	Civil servants have law degrees.
Civil servants are positive toward the political process.	Civil servants are negative toward the political process.
Citizens are interested in politics.	Citizens are not interested in politics.
Citizens trust politicians, civil servants, and the legal system.	Citizens are negative toward politicians, civil servants, and the legal system.
There is high participation in voluntary associations and movements.	There is low participation in voluntary associations and movements.
The burden of proof for identifying a citizen is on the authorities.	Citizens should be able to identify themselves at all times.
Outside observers perceive less corruption.	Outside observers perceive more corruption.
Liberalism	Conservatism, law and order
Positive attitudes toward young people	Negative attitudes toward young people
Tolerance, even of extreme ideas	Extremism and repression of extremism

Uncertainty Avoidance, Xenophobia, and Nationalism

In 1983 a sixteen-year-old high school student from Rotterdam, whom we will call Anneke, participated in a youth exchange program between Holland and Austria. She stayed with the family of a high school teacher in a middle-sized Austrian town. There were Dr. Riedl and his wife; their daughter, Hilde (of Anneke's age); and two younger boys.

Anneke went to school with Hilde. Her German improved rapidly. On Sundays she went to Mass with the Riedls, who were pious Roman Catholics. Anneke was a Protestant, but she did not mind; she liked the experience and the singing. She had taken her violin along to Austria, and after school she played pieces for violin and piano with Hilde.

One day when Anneke had been with the Riedls for about two months, the dinner conversation somehow turned to the subject of Jewish people. The Riedls seemed to be tremendously prejudiced on the subject. Anneke became upset. She asked Mrs. Riedl whether she knew any Jewish people. "Of course not!" was the answer.

Anneke felt the blood go to her face. "Well, you know one now," she said. "I am Jewish. At least, my mother is from a Jewish family, and according to Jewish tradition anybody born from a Jewish mother is also Jewish."

The dinner ended in silence. The next morning Dr. Riedl took Anneke aside and told her that she could no longer eat with the Riedls. They would serve her separately. Nor could she go to church with them. They should have been told that she was a Jew. Anneke returned to Holland a few days later.[63]

Among European Union members, Austria and other central European countries in the IBM studies and their replications scored relatively high on uncertainty avoidance. In this part of Europe, ethnic prejudice, including anti-Semitism, has been rampant for centuries. Until the 1930s there was a large Jewish community in Vienna. Many of the leading Austrian scholars were Jewish, among them Sigmund Freud. In 1936, Nazi Germany invaded Austria. Large numbers of Jewish Austrians fled, many to the United States. Those who did not perished in the Nazi holocaust. Since 1945 there have been few Jews in Austria.[64] Our true story shows that prejudice can survive, perhaps even thrive unchecked, long after its object has disappeared.

The Riedl parents in our story were programmed with the feeling that what is different is dangerous, and they transferred this feeling to their children. We don't know how the Riedl children experienced the incident or whether they became as prejudiced as their parents. Feelings of danger may be directed toward minorities (or even minorities from the past), toward immigrants and refugees, and toward citizens of other countries. Data from a European Commission report entitled *Racism and Xenophobia in Europe* (1997) showed that the opinion that immigrants should be sent back was strongly correlated with uncertainty avoidance. In IBM it had already been found that foreign managers were less well accepted in high-UAI countries.[65]

Feelings toward other nations vary not only with uncertainty avoidance but also with masculinity. The combination was illustrated in Figure 6.1. The Axis powers from World War II (Germany, Italy, and Japan) were all located in the lower right-hand quadrant: strong uncertainty avoidance plus masculinity. Under the conditions prior to the war, ethnocentric, xenophobic, and aggressive tendencies could get the upper hand in these countries more easily than in countries with different culture patterns. Fascism and racism find their most fertile ground in cultures with strong uncertainty avoidance plus pronouncedly masculine values. The paradox is that these same values in the postwar period contributed to these countries' fast economic recovery. A culture's weaknesses may in different circumstances become its strengths.

The combination of uncertainty avoidance and individualism, illustrated in Figure 6.2, suggests the different ways in which societies deal with intergroup conflict. The presence within the borders of a country of different ethnic, linguistic, or religious groups is a historical fact; some countries are more homogeneous than others. How a population and a government deal with such conflict, however, is a cultural phenomenon. In countries in the upper right-hand corner, strong uncertainty avoidance ("what is different is dangerous") is combined with collectivist exclusionism (strong identification with in-groups). Such countries often attempt to eliminate intergroup conflict by denying it and trying either to assimilate or to repress minorities. The chances of violent intergroup strife within these countries are considerable, as the minorities often hold the same strong uncertainty avoiding, collectivist values. Countries with severe intergroup conflicts within the upper right-hand quadrant of Figure 6.2 are Serbia, Arab countries, and Turkey. Indonesia and African countries are close to this quadrant.

Countries in the upper left-hand corner of Figure 6.2, such as Malaysia and Singapore, may contain different groups with strong group identities but are more likely to find a modus vivendi in which groups tolerate and complement each other. Countries in the lower right-hand corner often harbor considerable antagonism toward minorities and ethnic, religious, or linguistic opponent groups (Belgium!), but the universalism of the individualist state tries to guarantee that everybody's rights are respected; extremism versus others is restricted to the political margin. Finally, in countries in the lower left-hand corner, such as the United States, a majority will at least in theory support integration of minorities and equal rights for all. An event such as the terrorist attacks on September 11, 2001, puts this tolerance to a rough test, as Arab-Americans and Arab-looking Americans have experienced.

Strong uncertainty avoidance leading to intolerance of deviants and minorities has at times been costly to countries. The expulsion of the Jews from Spain and Portugal by the Catholic kings after the Reconquista of the Iberian Peninsula from the Moors (1492) has deprived these countries of some of their most enterprising citizens and is believed to have contributed to the decadence of the empire in the following centuries. One group of Iberian Jews settled in the Netherlands and played an important role in the seventeenth-century Dutch colonial expansion. Others went to Costa Rica, which even today is a favorable exception to Latin American *personalismo* and stagnation (see Chapter 4). In more recent history the exodus of top scientists, many of them Jewish, from Hitler's Germany enabled the Americans to develop the atomic bomb.

Uncertainty Avoidance, Religion, and Ideas

Earlier in this chapter religion was mentioned as one of the ways in which humankind avoids anxiety. Religious beliefs and rituals help us to accept the uncertainties against which we cannot defend ourselves. Some religions offer the ultimate certainty of a life after death.

The grouping of countries according to UAI score in Table 6.1 is somewhat associated with their dominant religion. Most Orthodox and Roman Catholic Christian countries score high; exceptions are the Philippines and Ireland. Muslim countries tend to score in the middle; Protestant Christian countries below average; and Buddhist and Hindu countries medium to very low, with Japan as an exception.

A problem in classifying countries by religion is that the major religions of the world are all internally heterogeneous. Polish, Peruvian, Italian, and Dutch Roman Catholicism are very different. Indonesian, Iranian, Saudi, and Balkan Islam mean quite different things to their believers and to their countries. Thai, Singaporean, and Japanese Buddhism have quite dissimilar affective and practical consequences.

It is evident, as was suggested in Chapter 1, that religious conversion does not cause a total change in cultural values. The value complexes described by the dimensions of power distance, individualism or collectivism, masculinity or femininity, and uncertainty avoidance seem to have survived religious conversions. These value complexes may even have influenced to what extent a population has been receptive to certain religions and how the accepted religion has evolved in that country. Indonesian (Javanese) mysticism has survived Hindu, Buddhist, Muslim, and Christian conversions. In the Christian countries, the Reformation has separated almost exactly those European countries once under the Roman Empire from the rest. All former Roman countries (the ones now speaking Romance languages) refuted the Reformation and remained Roman Catholic; most others became Protestant or mixed. Poland and Ireland were never part of the Roman Empire, but in their case Roman Catholicism provided an identity against non-Catholic oppressors.

In establishing a relationship between uncertainty avoidance and religious belief, it makes sense to distinguish between Western and Eastern religions. The Western religions—Judaism, Christianity, and Islam—are based on divine revelation, and all three originated from what is now called the Middle East. What distinguishes the Western from the Eastern religions is their concern with Truth with a capital *T*. The Western revelation religions share the assumption that there is an absolute Truth that excludes all other truths and that human beings can possess. The difference between strong and weak uncertainty-avoidance societies adhering to these religions lies in the amount of certainty one needs about having this Truth. In strong uncertainty-avoidance cultures, the belief is more frequent that "There is only one Truth and we have it. All others are wrong." Possessing this Truth is the only road to salvation and the main purpose in a person's life. The consequence of the others' being wrong may be trying to convert them, avoiding them, or killing them.

Weak uncertainty-avoidance cultures from the West still believe in Truth, but they have less of a need to believe that they alone possess it. "There is only one Truth and we are looking for it. Others are looking for it as well and we accept as a fact of life that they look in different directions."

One certainty of these cultures is that God wants nobody to be prosecuted for holding a given belief.

For centuries the Roman Catholic church maintained an Inquisition, which sent many people with deviant ideas to their deaths and banned or burned books; some books are banned by the Roman Catholic church even today. In Iran, Ayatollah Ruhollah Khomeini, shortly before his death in 1989, banned the book *The Satanic Verses* by Salman Rushdie and invited all believers to kill the author and his publishers. It is somewhat amazing that many people in Christian countries were so shocked by this action, in view of their own countries' histories of religious intolerance. With some exceptions, and Khomeini's action is one of them, Islam in history has been more tolerant of other religions than has Roman Catholic Christianity. The medieval Crusades, which cost hundreds of thousands of lives, were a product of Christian, not of Muslim, intolerance. In the Muslim Turkish Empire, People of the Book (that is, Jews and Christians) were tolerated and could exercise their religions, as long as they paid a special tax. On the other hand, even Protestant Christians, generally considered to be more broad-minded, have made victims of religious intolerance, such as Michael Servetus, who was burned to death by John Calvin's followers in Geneva in 1553. Protestant nations have also in past centuries burned supposed witches. In the early twenty-first century, fundamentalist Christian preachers denounced J. K. Rowling's Harry Potter series as a work of the devil.

Confession of sins fits the strong uncertainty-avoidance culture pattern. If a rule cannot be kept, confession is a way to preserve the rule and put the blame on the individual. The Roman Catholic practice of confession is relatively mild and discreet; militant communism in the Soviet Union in the days of Stalin made it a public show. In weak uncertainty-avoidance cultures, there will be more of a tendency to change a rule if it is evident that it cannot be respected.

Eastern religions are less concerned about Truth. The assumption that there is one Truth that a person can possess is absent in their thinking. There is more to this view than uncertainty acceptance, and we will discuss it further in Chapter 7.

Across all countries with a Christian majority, there is a strong correlation between the percentage of Catholics in the population (as opposed to Protestants) and the country's UAI. A second correlation is with masculinity, implying that where Catholicism prevails, masculine values tend to prevail as well—for instance, in refusing to admit women to leadership positions (see Chapter 5).[66] The correlation with uncertainty avoidance is easy to interpret, as the Catholic Church supplies its believers with a certainty that most protestant groups lack (apart from some of the smaller sects). The Catholic Church appeals to cultures with a need for such certainty. Within the Protestant nations the dominant cultures have equipped people with a lesser need for certainty. Those who do need it find a spiritual home in sects and fundamentalist groups

Both within Islam and within Judaism there is also a clearly visible conflict between more and less uncertainty-avoiding factions, the first dogmatic, intolerant, fanatical, and fundamentalist ("There is only one Truth and we have it"), the second pragmatic, tolerant, liberal, and open to the modern world. In recent years the fanatic wings in all three revelation religions have been active and vocal. In history fanaticism has always led to its own undoing, so there is some hope that the excesses will not last.

What holds for religions applies also to political ideologies that can become secular neoreligions. Marxism in many places has been an example. When East Germany was still solidly communist, the facade of the University of Leipzig was decorated with an enormous banner reading *"Der Marxismus ist allmächtig, weil er wahr ist!"* ("Marxism is all-powerful because it is true!")[67] In strong uncertainty-avoidance cultures, we find intolerant political ideologies; in weak uncertainty-avoidance cultures, we find tolerant ones. The respect for what are commonly called human rights assumes a tolerance for people with different political ideas. Violation of human rights in some countries is rooted in the strong uncertainty avoidance within their cultures. In other countries it is rather an outcome of a power struggle (and related to power distance) or of collectivist intergroup strife.

In the area of philosophy and science,[68] grand theories are more likely to be conceived within strong uncertainty-avoidance cultures than in weak uncertainty avoidance ones. The quest for Truth is an essential motivator for a philosopher. In Europe, Germany and France have produced more great philosophers than Britain and Sweden (for example, Descartes, Kant, Hegel, Marx, Nietzsche, and Sartre). Weak uncertainty-avoidance cultures have produced great empiricists, people developing conclusions from observation and experiments rather than from pure reflection (such as Newton, Linnaeus, and Darwin).

In serving as peer reviewers of manuscripts submitted to scientific journals, we notice that papers by Germans and French writers often present broad conclusions unsupported by data. Manuscripts by British and American writers present extensive data analysis but shy away from bold conclusions. The Germans and French tend to reason by deduction, British and Americans by induction.[69]

Scientific disputes sometimes hide cultural assumptions. A famous example is the discussion between the German physicist Albert Einstein (1879–1955) and his Danish colleague Niels Bohr (1885–1962) on whether certain processes inside the atom are governed by laws or random. "I cannot imagine God playing dice," Einstein is supposed to have said. Bohr could; recent research has proved him right, not Einstein. Denmark scores very low on uncertainty avoidance (rank 74, score 23).

A society's level of uncertainty avoidance has practical consequences regarding the ability of people who hold different convictions to be personal friends. Stories of scientists who separated their ties of friendship after a scientific disagreement tend to come from high-UAI countries. The conflict between psychiatrists Sigmund Freud (Austria) and Carl Gustav Jung (Switzerland) is one example. In weak uncertainty-avoidance countries, different scientific opinions do not necessarily bar friendships.

Before and during World War II many German and Austrian scientists of Jewish descent or who were otherwise anti-Nazi fled their countries, mostly to Britain and the United States. Examples are Albert Einstein, Sigmund Freud, Karl Popper, Kurt Lewin, and Theodor Adorno. This "brain injection" has been highly beneficial to the host countries. The younger among the refugees have made substantial contributions to their scientific fields in the new country. They brought synergy between the Middle European taste for theory (rooted in strong uncertainty avoidance) and the Anglo-American sense of empiricism fostered by weak uncertainty avoidance.

Some of the refugees experienced scientific culture shock. Former Frankfurt sociologist Herbert Marcuse, when preaching his critique of modern society in California, met with what he labeled *repressive tolerance*. This is a nonsensical term, because repression and tolerance are mutually exclusive. However, the term reflects Marcuse's embarrassment at trying to provoke—and expecting—heated debate in the German style, but instead meeting with intellectual tolerance American style.

Marieke de Mooij has pointed out that cultural values can be recognized in both the subjects and the style of literary fiction produced in a country. As examples of world literature from high-UAI countries, she mentions Franz Kafka's *The Castle* from Czechia and Goethe's *Faust* from Germany. In the former the main character is haunted by impersonal rules; in the latter the hero sells his soul for knowledge of Truth. Low-UAI Britain has produced literature in which the most unreal things happen: Lewis Carroll's *Alice in Wonderland*, J. R. R. Tolkien's *Lord of the Rings*, and J. K. Rowling's Harry Potter series.[70]

Table 6.6 completes the summary of key differences between weak and strong uncertainty-avoidance societies started in Table 6.2, adding issues covered in the past two sections.

TABLE 6.6 Key Differences Between Weak and Strong
Uncertainty-Avoidance Societies
V: Tolerance, Religion, and Ideas

WEAK UNCERTAINTY AVOIDANCE	STRONG UNCERTAINTY AVOIDANCE
More ethnic tolerance	More ethnic prejudice
Positive or neutral toward foreigners	Xenophobia
Refugees should be admitted.	Immigrants should be sent back.
Defensive nationalism	Aggressive nationalism
Lower risk of violent intergroup conflict	High risk of violent intergroup conflict
One religion's truth should not be imposed on others.	In religion, there is only one Truth, and we have it.
If commandments cannot be respected, they should be changed.	If commandments cannot be respected, we are sinners and should repent.
Human rights: nobody should be persecuted for his or her beliefs.	More religious, political, and ideological intolerance and fundamentalisms
In philosophy and science, there is a tendency toward relativism and empiricism.	In philosophy and science, there is a tendency toward grand theories.
Scientific opponents can be personal friends.	Scientific opponents cannot be personal friends.
Literature dealing with fantasy worlds	Literature dealing with rules and Truth

Origins of Uncertainty-Avoidance Differences

Possible origins of power distance differences were explored in Chapter 3. The grouping of countries suggested that the roots of the differences could go back as far as the Roman Empire two thousand years ago. In East Asia it assumed roots in the even older Chinese Empire. Both empires left a legacy of large power distances.

On uncertainty avoidance we again find the countries with a Romance language together. These heirs of the Roman Empire all score on the strong uncertainty-avoidance side. The Chinese-speaking countries Taiwan, Hong Kong, and Singapore score low on uncertainty avoidance, as do countries with important minorities of Chinese origin: Thailand, Indonesia, the Philippines, and Malaysia.

The Roman and Chinese Empires were both powerful centralized states, supporting a culture pattern in their populations prepared to take orders from the center. The two empires differed, however, in an important respect. The Roman Empire had developed a unique system of codified laws that in principle applied to all people with citizen status regardless of origin. The Chinese Empire never knew this concept of law. The main continuous principle of Chinese administration has been described as "government of man," in contrast to the Roman idea of "government by law." Chinese judges were supposed to be guided by broad general principles, like those attributed to Confucius (see Chapter 7).

The contrast between the two intellectual traditions explains the fact that IBM employees from countries with a Roman inheritance scored higher on uncertainty avoidance than their colleagues from countries with a Chinese inheritance. It is another powerful illustration of the deep historical roots of national culture differences. Their long history should make us modest about expectations of fundamental changes in these value differences within our lifetime.

Power distance differences in Chapter 3 were found to be statistically related to geographic latitude, population size, and national wealth. No such broad relationships could be found for uncertainty avoidance. The relationship between UAI and economic growth varies depending on the region and the period. It was negative in Europe for the period 1925–50, because the strong uncertainty-avoidance countries were more actively belligerent in World War II, and their economies suffered badly. After

1950 the relationship reversed as they were catching up. All in all, the statistical analysis does not allow us to identify any *general* sources of weak or strong uncertainty avoidance, other than history.[71]

The Future of Uncertainty-Avoidance Differences

UAI scores based on the IBM studies are not available over time, and we know of no studies that have measured equivalent scores longitudinally for any population. Interesting historical information about the development of anxiety over time was supplied by Richard Lynn, whose national anxiety scores were shown earlier in this chapter to correlate with UAI. Lynn was able to follow national anxiety levels for eighteen countries from 1935 to 1970.[72] The five countries with the highest anxiety scores in 1935 were Austria, Finland, Germany, Italy, and Japan (the World War II Axis powers and two countries that got involved in the war on their side). From 1935 to 1950 all countries that had been defeated or occupied during World War II (1939–45) increased in anxiety level, while six out of the nine countries not defeated or occupied decreased. The overall average was highest in 1950, shortly after the war, and then sank to an overall low in 1965, to increase again after that.

Lynn's data suggest that national anxiety levels fluctuate and that high anxiety levels are associated with wars. It seems a reasonable assumption that a similar wave of anxiety earlier accompanied World War I and the various wars before it. The process could be as follows: When anxiety levels in a country increase, uncertainty avoidance increases. This is noticeable in intolerance, xenophobia, religious and political fanaticism, and all the other manifestations of uncertainty avoidance presented in this chapter. Leadership passes into the hands of fanatics, and these may drive the country toward war. War, of course, pulls in other countries that did not show the same fanaticism but that will develop increasing anxiety because of the war threat.

In countries experiencing war within their territory, anxiety mounts further. After the war the stress is released, first for the countries not directly touched and some years later for the others, which start reconstructing. Anxiety decreases and tolerance increases, but after a number of years the trend is reversed, and a new wave of anxiety sets in that could be the prelude to a new conflict. Economic processes play a role; increasing prosperity supports individualism and reduces the explosive combination of strong uncertainty avoidance with the collectivism of the poor (Figure 6.2).

Breaking this vicious spiral demands international concerted action. The formation of the European Union among partners that less than sixty years before were deadly enemies is an example. The ultimate recourse is the United Nations, and it has no substitute in legitimizing actions on behalf of world peace.

Yesterday, Now, or Later?

The Dream of the Red Chamber is a famous Chinese novel that was published around 1760. In it the author, Cao Xueqin, describes the rise and fall of two branches of an aristocratic family who live in adjacent plots in Beijing. In between their properties they have laid out a magnificent common garden with several pavilions, for the young, mostly female, members of both families. The maintenance of such a big garden poses many problems, until one of the young women, Tan Chun, is put in charge. She announces a new business plan:

> I think we ought to pick out a few experienced trustworthy old women from among the ones who work in the Garden—women who know something about gardening already—and put the upkeep of the Garden into their hands. We needn't ask them to pay us rent; all we need ask them for is an annual share of the produce. There would be four advantages in this arrangement. In the first place, if we have people whose sole occupation is to look after trees and flowers and so on, the condition of the Garden will

improve gradually year after year and there will be no more of those long periods of neglect followed by bursts of feverish activity when things have been allowed to get out of hand. Secondly there won't be the spoiling and wastage we get at present. Thirdly the women themselves will gain a little extra to add to their incomes, which will compensate them for the hard work they put in throughout the year. And fourthly, there's no reason why we shouldn't use the money we should otherwise have spent on nurserymen, rockery specialists, horticultural cleaners and so on for other purposes.[1]

As the story goes on, Tan Chun's privatization is successfully carried through. Cao has described a society in which entrepreneurial spirit could be taken for granted, among old women as much as among others. It was in the software of their minds.

National Values and the Teachings of Confucius

In Chapter 2 we described why and how Michael Bond asked his Chinese colleagues to develop what became the Chinese Value Survey (CVS). In 1985 his international connections administered it to students in twenty-three countries around the world.[2] His analysis of the CVS database produced four dimensions, of which three, across twenty common countries, were each significantly correlated with one of Geert's IBM dimensions. The fourth CVS dimension was not correlated with the fourth IBM dimension: uncertainty avoidance had no equivalent in the CVS. Instead, the fourth CVS dimension contrasted values unrelated to anything in the IBM database. However, to our excitement, this dimension correlated strongly with recent economic growth; as it turned out later, it also predicted future economic growth.[3] From the IBM dimensions, IDV and to some extent PDI correlated with national wealth, but none correlated with growth—that is, increase of wealth. Nor did we know of any other noneconomic index that correlated with growth. This discovery was sufficient reason to add the new dimension as a fifth to our model.

The fourth CVS dimension combined on the one side these values:

1. Persistence (perseverance)
2. Thrift
3. Ordering relationships by status and observing this order
4. Having a sense of shame

And on the opposite side:

5. Reciprocation of greetings, favors, and gifts
6. Respect for tradition
7. Protecting one's "face"
8. Personal steadiness and stability

Students of Chinese culture recognized in these values elements of the teachings of Confucius, to whom we referred in Chapters 3 and 4.

Confucius (or K'ung-tzu, as he is called in Chinese) was an intellectual of humble origins in China around 500 B.C. He sought, rather unsuccessfully, to serve various local rulers in the divided China of his day. He did succeed, however, in gaining a reputation for wit and wisdom, and in his later life he was surrounded by a host of disciples who recorded his ideas. Confucius thus held a position rather similar to that of Socrates in ancient Greece, who was his virtual contemporary (Confucius was born about eighty years before Socrates).

The teachings of Confucius are lessons in practical ethics without a religious content. Confucianism is not a religion but a set of pragmatic rules for daily life derived from Chinese history. The following are the key principles of Confucian teaching:

1. *The stability of society is based on unequal status relationships between people.* This part of Confucius's teaching was described in Chapter 3. He distinguished five basic relationships (the *wu lun*): ruler-subject, father-son, older brother–younger brother, husband-wife, and senior friend–junior friend. These relationships are based on mutual and complementary obligations: for example, the junior partner owes the senior partner respect and obedience, and the senior owes the junior protection and consideration. Value 3, "ordering relationships by status and observing this order," fits this principle.
2. *The family is the prototype of all social organizations.* A person is not primarily an individual; rather, he or she is a member of a family. In Chapter 4 we already stressed the importance in the (collectivist) family of *shame* (rather than *guilt*). Value 4, "having a sense of shame," is essential in the Confucian family-based society.
3. *Virtuous behavior toward others consists of not treating others as one would not like to be treated oneself.* In Western philosophy this precept is

known as the Golden Rule, but without the double *not*. Confucius prescribes a basic human benevolence toward others, but it does not go as far as the Christian injunction to love one's enemies. Geert heard the Confucian comment that if one should love one's enemies, what would remain for one's friends?

4. *Virtue with regard to one's tasks in life consists of trying to acquire skills and education, working hard, not spending more than necessary, being patient, and persevering.* Conspicuous consumption is taboo, as is losing one's temper. Everything should be done with moderation, a rule that was also formulated by Socrates. Value 1, "persistence," and value 2, "thrift," closely fit this principle. So from the eight values found related to the fourth CVS dimension, the first four, all on one side, directly resonate with Confucius's principles. Values five to eight include the importance of "reciprocation of greetings, favors, and gifts" and "protecting one's face," behaviors well recognizable in a Chinese environment but not specifically Confucian. The concepts "respect for tradition" and "personal steadiness and stability" are not even specifically Chinese.

The fourth CVS dimension is not "Confucianism" *per se.* Some very Confucian values were not related to the dimension—for example, "filial piety," which in the CVS was associated with collectivism. And a non-Confucian country like India also scored quite high on the dimension.

At this point let us stop a moment and recall how this group of eight values (four on each side) was created:

- The Chinese scholars who designed the CVS questionnaire chose to include them. Considering these values relevant was a matter of Chinese judgment. Some other values embraced in the Western-conceived IBM dimensions, in particular those related to uncertainty avoidance, were not included in the CVS. This does not mean that they did not make sense in China: for example, uncertainty avoidance accounts for striking differences between Chinese and Japanese culture.
- The scores on each of these eight values, produced by students from twenty-three countries and averaged by country, ranked the countries in a similar way (which means these values formed a cross-national *dimension* together). Combining the eight values into a

common dimension was the result of an empirical statistical analysis at the country level; it was not a matter of either Western or Chinese judgment.[4]

The reason the dimension had not been found in the IBM research was that the relevant questions had not been asked. The Western designers of the IBM questionnaire had not considered them relevant. However, because the dimension correlated with economic growth, Geert considered it an essential addition for a global instrument. As persistence and thrift reflect an orientation toward the future, whereas personal stability and tradition can be seen as a static orientation toward the present and the past, starting with his 1991 book Geert labeled this fifth dimension *long-term versus short-term orientation* (LTO).[5]

The fifth dimension was defined as follows: *long-term orientation* stands for *the fostering of virtues oriented toward future rewards—in particular, perseverance and thrift.* Its opposite pole, *short-term orientation,* stands for *the fostering of virtues related to the past and present—in particular, respect for tradition, preservation of "face," and fulfilling social obligations.*

Table 7.1 lists index scores on the new dimension for the twenty-three countries that participated in the CVS. The top positions are occupied by China[6] and other East Asian countries. (Japan, Hong Kong, Taiwan, South Korea, and Singapore were known in the last decades of the twentieth century as the "Five Dragons" because of their fast economic growth.) Continental European countries occupied a middle range. Great Britain and its Anglo partners Australia, New Zealand, the United States, and Canada scored on the short-term side. The African countries Zimbabwe and Nigeria scored very short-term, as did the Philippines and Pakistan.

A problem with the new dimension was that scores were available for only twenty-three countries, fewer than half the more than fifty in the IBM database. The 2005 edition of this book listed LTO scores for sixteen additional countries based on replications and extrapolations; still too few, and of doubtful quality.[7] Misho Minkov's analysis of the World Values Survey offered us an opportunity to extend our database fourfold at one stroke. This meant redefining long-term orientation in some respects.

Before we present the new scores and their implications we will first review some major conclusions from the CVS-based scores for twenty-three countries.

TABLE 7.1 Long-Term Orientation Index Scores for 23 Countries Based on the Chinese Value Survey (LTO-CVS)

RANK	COUNTRY/REGION	SCORE
1	China	118
2	Hong Kong	96
3	Taiwan	87
4	Japan	80
5	Korea (South)	75
6	Brazil	65
7	India	61
8	Thailand	56
9	Singapore	48
10	Netherlands	44
11	Bangladesh	40
12	Sweden	33
13	Poland	32
14	Australia	31
15	Germany	31
16	New Zealand	30
17	United States	29
18	Great Britain	25
19	Zimbabwe	25
20	Canada	23
21	Philippines	19
22	Nigeria	16
23	Pakistan	00

Implications of LTO-CVS Differences for Family Life

In all human societies, children have to learn an amount of self-restraint and deferment of gratification in order to be accepted as civilized persons. The German sociologist Norbert Elias (1897–1990) described self-control and developing a longer-term view on life as essential steps in the civilization process.[8] Within societies, deferment of gratification increases with social class: children of lower classes seek more immediate reward in spending their time and their money than middle-class children.[9] Among societies in the CVS, deferment of gratification varies with LTO.

Marriage in high-LTO countries is a pragmatic, goal-oriented arrangement. Questions in the 1990–93 WVS about "things that make a marriage successful" showed that for families in high-LTO countries, living with in-laws was considered normal, and differences in tastes and interests between spouses did not matter. In another study students in high LTO countries agreed most with the statement "If love has completely disappeared from a marriage, it is best for the couple to make a clean break and start new lives." At the same time, actual divorce rates in these high-LTO countries were lower.[10]

Chapter 5 cited a survey by the Japanese market research company Wacoal, asking young working women in eight Asian cities about traits preferred in husbands versus steady boyfriends. The trait that differentiated most between high- and low-LTO countries was affection. In high-LTO cultures affection was associated with the husband, in low-LTO countries with the boyfriend. In the section of the Wacoal study dealing with gender stereotypes, the trait that differentiated most between high- and low-LTO countries was humility. In the high-LTO cultures humility was considered a general human virtue; in low-LTO countries humility was seen as feminine. As a Chinese student in one of Geert's classes wrote, "Without a sense of humility we become worse than an animal." He saw humility as the consequence of "having a sense of shame."[11] We will come back to this topic.

Another study, this one covering nineteen countries, surveyed students' views about aging. The age at which a person was described as "old" (an overall mean of sixty for men and sixty-two for women) correlated positively with national wealth and (across ten overlapping countries) negatively with LTO. In poorer countries, but also in high-LTO cultures, old age was seen as starting earlier. Then again, the same survey showed that students in the high-LTO countries expected to be more satisfied with their lives when they were old.[12]

In the 1990–93 WVS section about "things that make a marriage successful," mentioned earlier, another question that correlated with LTO was whether children of preschool age suffer when the mother does not stay at home. Respondents in high-LTO countries thought the children would suffer.

A study in Australia asked mothers from two ethnic categories what was on their minds when choosing presents for their children. White Australian mothers mentioned making the children feel good and gaining their love. First-generation Chinese-Vietnamese immigrant mothers mentioned contributing to their children's education and financial situation; these mothers did not mention any benefits to themselves. The first group went for short-term benefits, the second for long-term benefits.[13]

In summary, family life in the high-LTO culture is a pragmatic arrangement but is supposed to be based on real affection and with attention paid to small children. The children learn thrift, not to expect immediate gratification of their desires, tenacity in the pursuit of their goals, and humility. Self-assertion is not encouraged.[14]

Children growing up in a *low*-LTO culture experience two sets of norms. One is toward respecting "musts": traditions, face-saving, being seen as a stable individual, respecting the social codes of marriage even if love has gone, and reciprocation of greetings, favors, and gifts as a social ritual. The other is toward immediate need gratification, spending, and sensitivity to social trends in consumption ("keeping up with the Joneses"). There is a potential tension between these two sets of norms that leads to a wide variety of individual behaviors.

Table 7.2 summarizes the differences between societies with a short- versus long-term orientation based on CVS data discussed so far.

Implications of LTO-CVS Differences for Business

U. T. Qing went to Singapore in 1921 when he was twenty and started peddling embroidered textiles, mainly to expatriate clients. In 1932 he opened his own shop. After World War II a son and a nephew joined him in the business, which kept expanding and grew into a major upscale department store.

The structure at the store was familial and the culture, simple. The founder was autocratic and respected by his obedient and docile followers. The Qings led in decision-making and supervision while workers complemented with their obedience, and harmony prevailed. All shared values of thrift, a habitual respect for hierarchy, perseverance, and focused on one objective of profit maximization. The old-timers said they "didn't think very much" which meant that their thoughts were not distracted by ambitions. They merely did their jobs to the utmost of their ability in the hope that their performance was accepted.[15]

TABLE 7.2 Key Differences Between Short- and Long-Term Orientation Societies Based on CVS Data: General Norm and Family

SHORT-TERM ORIENTATION	LONG-TERM ORIENTATION
Social pressure toward spending	Thrift, being sparing with resources
Efforts should produce quick results.	Perseverance, sustained efforts toward slow results
Concern with social and status obligations	Willingness to subordinate oneself for a purpose
Concern with "face"	Having a sense of shame
Respect for traditions	Respect for circumstances
Concern with personal stability	Concern with personal adaptiveness
Marriage is a moral arrangement.	Marriage is a pragmatic arrangement.
Living with in-laws is a source of trouble.	Living with in-laws is normal.
Young women associate affection with a boyfriend.	Young women associate affection with a husband.
Humility is for women only.	Humility is for both men and women.
Old age is an unhappy period, but it starts late.	Old age is a happy period, and it starts early.
Preschool children can be cared for by others.	Mothers should have time for their preschool children.
Children get gifts for fun and love.	Children get gifts for education and development.

In the overseas Chinese environment, family and work are not separated. Family enterprises are normal. The values at the LTO pole support entrepreneurial activity. *Persistence* (perseverance), or tenacity in the pursuit of whatever goals one has set, is an essential asset for a beginning entrepreneur. *Ordering relationships by status and observing this order* reflects the Confucian stress on unequal relationship pairs. A sense of a harmonious and stable hierarchy and complementarities of roles makes the entrepreneurial role easier to play. *Thrift* leads to savings and to the availability of capital for reinvestment by oneself or one's relatives. The value of *having a sense of shame* supports interrelatedness through sensitivity to social contacts and a stress on keeping one's commitments. These were the values at the positive pole of LTO-CVS.

The values at the negative pole of LTO-CVS are not mentioned in the Qing story. No reference is made to *protecting one's face*; even if there is in fact a lot of face-saving going on in East Asia, the LTO-CVS scores show that at the conscious level, the student respondents wanted to de-emphasize it. No reference is made to *respect for tradition*; part of the secret of the Dragons' economic success is the ease with which these countries have accepted Western technological innovations.

Adaptiveness was described by one of Confucius's disciples as follows:

> *The superior man goes through his life without any one preconceived action or any taboo. He merely decides for the moment what is the right thing to do.*"[16]

Sixty senior business leaders from the five Dragons plus Thailand and an equivalent group in the United States were asked to rank seventeen possible work values. The top seven values selected by the Asians were hard work, respect for learning, honesty, openness to new ideas, accountability, self-discipline, and self-reliance. The Americans selected freedom of expression, personal freedom, self-reliance, individual rights, hard work, personal achievement, and thinking for oneself.[17] This finding confirms both the LTO differences (hard work, learning, openness, accountability, self-discipline) and the IDV differences (freedoms, rights, thinking for oneself) between East Asia and the United States. In successive rounds of the WVS, the relative importance in one's life of leisure time compared with family, work, friends, religion, and politics was consistently negatively correlated with LTO-CVS.[18]

Investing in building up strong market positions, at the expense of immediate results, is supposed to be a characteristic of Asian, high-LTO companies. Managers (often family members) are allowed time and resources to make their own contribution. In cultures that are short-term oriented, the "bottom line" (the results of the past month, quarter, or year) is a major concern; control systems are focusing on it, and managers are constantly judged by it. This state of affairs is supported by arguments assumed to be rational, but this rationality rests on cultural—that is, prerational—choices. The cost of short-term decisions in terms of "pecuniary considerations, myopic decisions, work process control, hasty adoption and quick abandonment of novel ideas"[19] is evident; managers are rewarded or victimized by today's bottom line even where that is clearly the outcome of decisions made by their predecessors or pre-predecessors years ago, yet the force of a cultural belief system perpetuates the system.

Supported by a network of associates, Geert studied the goals that part-time M.B.A. students in seventeen countries ascribed to the country's business leaders. The combination of the importance of "profits 10 years from now" and the *un*importance of "this year's profits" was significantly correlated with LTO.[20]

East Asian entrepreneurship is not based only on the values of the entrepreneurs. Both the story at the beginning of this section and the way the CVS scores were found (by surveying student samples) suggest that the decisive values are held broadly within entire societies, among entrepreneurs and future entrepreneurs, among their employees and their families, and among other members of the society.

Gordon Redding, in a book based on interviews with overseas Chinese businessmen, divided the reasons for respondents' efficiency and failure into four parts: vertical cooperation, horizontal cooperation, control, and adaptiveness. About *vertical cooperation* he wrote:

> *The atmosphere is not . . . one in which workers and owner/managers naturally divide into two camps psychologically. They tend to be similar socially, in terms of their values, their behavior, their needs, and their aspirations. . . . One of the outcomes of this vertical cooperativeness is willing compliance. This tendency is also reinforced by early conditioning of people during childhood and education, and the respect for authority figures, deeply ingrained in the Confucian tradition, tends to be maintained throughout life. . . . An extension of this willingness to comply is willingness to engage diligently in routine and possibly dull tasks, something one might term perseverance. This nebulous but nonetheless important component of Overseas Chinese work behavior, a kind of micro form of the work ethic, pervades their factories and offices. . . . The huge diligence required to master the Chinese language has played a part here, as has also the strict order of a Confucian household.*[21]

We recognize the LTO components of ordering relationships by status and maintaining this order and of perseverance; the latter functions not only in the sustained efforts of the entrepreneur in building a business but also in those of his or her workers in carrying out their daily tasks.

An international public opinion survey of human values and satisfactions asked respondents to choose between two opinions:

1. There is too much emphasis upon the principle of equality. People should be given the opportunity to choose their own economic and social life according to their individual abilities.
2. Too much liberalism has been producing increasingly wide differences in people's economic and social life. People should live more equally.

The percentages of respondents choosing opinion 2 varied from 30 in France to 71 in Japan and were correlated significantly with LTO-CVS.[22] *Long-term orientation* stands for a society in which wide differences in economic and social conditions are considered undesirable. *Short-term orientation* stands for meritocracy, differentiation according to abilities.

Horizontal coordination refers to networks. The key concept of *guanxi* (pronounced "gwon shee") in Asian business is by now known worldwide. It refers to personal connections; it links the family sphere to the business sphere. In high-LTO societies, having one's personal network of acquaintances is essential for success. This is an evident consequence of collectivism (relationships before task), but it also demands a long-term view. One's capital of *guanxi* lasts a lifetime, and one would not want to damage it for short-term, bottom-line reasons.[23]

One consequence of adaptiveness in business *plus* the importance of networks is that high-LTO exporting countries on average score higher on the Bribe Payers Index (BPI) than low-LTO countries (see the section on corruption in Chapter 6). Companies in high-LTO countries will more easily use side payments and services to their customers and prospects abroad, which Transparency International classifies as bribing.[24]

Implications of LTO-CVS Differences for Ways of Thinking

Dr. Rajendra Pradhan was a Nepalese anthropologist who in 1987–88 conducted a ten-month field research project in the Dutch village of Schoonrewoerd. He thus reversed the familiar pattern of Western anthropologists doing field research in Eastern villages. Schoonrewoerd was a typical Dutch village in the rural heart of the province of South Holland, with 1,500 inhabitants and two churches from different Calvinist Protestant denominations. Dr. Pradhan became a regular churchgoer in both, and he established his contacts with the local population predominantly through the congregations. He was often invited to people's homes for coffee after church, and the topic, usually, was religion. He used to explain that his parents respected Hindu rituals but that he stopped doing this, because it would take him too much time. His Dutch hosts always wanted to know what he *believed*—an exotic question to which he did not have a direct answer. "Everybody over here talks about believing, believing, believing," he said, bewildered. "Where I come from, what counts is the ritual, in which only the priest and the head of the family participate. The others watch and make their offerings. Over here so much is *mandatory*. Hindus will never ask, 'Do you believe in God?' Of course one should believe, but the important thing is what one does."[25]

The Chinese Value Survey research revealed an important difference between Eastern and Western thinking. The CVS questionnaire, designed by Eastern minds, did not detect the uncertainty avoidance dimension. The IBM and Rokeach Value Survey questionnaires, both designed by Western minds, did not detect long- versus short-term orientation. The other three dimensions deal with basic human relationships that were recognized by the questionnaire designers both in the East and in the West.

Uncertainty avoidance was described in Chapter 6. It deals ultimately with a society's search for Truth. Uncertainty-avoiding cultures foster a belief in an absolute Truth, and uncertainty-accepting cultures take a more relativistic stance. In Western thinking this is an important choice, reflected in key values. In Eastern thinking the question of Truth is less relevant.

Long- versus short-term orientation can be interpreted as dealing with a society's search for Virtue. It is no accident that this dimension relates to the teachings of Confucius. As mentioned earlier in this chapter, Confucius was a teacher of practical ethics without a religious content. He dealt with Virtue but left the question of Truth open. In Eastern thinking the search for Virtue is key. In Western thinking Virtue is secondary to Truth.

The 1990–93 WVS asked respondents to choose between two statements:

1. There are absolutely clear guidelines about what is good and evil. These always apply to everyone, whatever the circumstances.
2. There can never be absolutely clear guidelines about what is good and evil. What is good and evil depends entirely upon the circumstances at the time.

The agreement with statement 1 varied from 60 percent in Nigeria and 50 percent in the United States to 19 percent in Sweden and 15 percent in Japan. On average, poorer countries believed more in absolute guidelines. When the influence of wealth was eliminated, answers were correlated with LTO-CVS. Respondents in high-LTO countries believed less in universal guidelines about what is good and evil and more in considering the circumstances.[26]

These differences are partly reflected in rates of imprisonment—the share of the population that is locked up in a penitentiary institution. In 2002 this share ranged from 690 per 100,000 inhabitants in the United States, to 140 in Britain, 85 in Germany, 65 in Sweden, and 45 in Japan.[27] Worldwide, rates of imprisonment relate primarily to national poverty (they are higher in poorer countries), but this variable cannot explain the huge differences between equally wealthy countries. We believe that these differences are affected by what these societies consider the purpose of punishment. The short-term solution is to protect society by locking criminals away. The long-term solution is to reform criminals and recycle them into productive citizens. If good and evil are clearly separated, evil people should be locked away. If good and evil reside within every person, those who committed evil should learn to be good.

Eastern religions (Hinduism, Buddhism, Shintoism, and Taoism) are separated from Western religions (Judaism, Christianity, and Islam) by a deep philosophical dividing line. The three Western religions belong to the same thought family; historically, they grew from the same roots. As argued in Chapter 6, all three are based on the existence of a Truth that is accessible to the true believers. All three have a Book. In the East neither Confucianism, which is a nonreligious ethic, nor any major religion is based on the assumption that there is a Truth that a human community can embrace. They offer various ways in which a person can improve him- or herself; however, these consist not of believing, but of ritual, meditation, or ways of living. Some of these may lead to a higher spiritual state and, eventually, to unification with God or gods. This difference in thinking explains why Dr. Pradhan was so puzzled by the question about what he believed. It is an irrelevant question in the East. What one *does* is important. U.S. mythologist Joseph Campbell, comparing Western and Eastern religious myths, concluded that Judaism, Christianity, and Islam separate matter and spirit, while Eastern religions and philosophers have kept them integrated.[28] This difference in thinking also explains why a questionnaire invented by Western minds produced a fourth dimension dealing with Truth; a questionnaire invented by Eastern minds found a fourth dimension dealing with Virtue.

Data from the public opinion survey of human values and satisfactions mentioned earlier showed that people in high-LTO countries were more satisfied than people in low-LTO countries with their personal contributions in the areas of "Being attentive to daily human relations, deepening human bonds in family, neighborhood and friends or acquaintances" and "Making efforts to correct social inequality and injustice, bringing about fair and equal life for everybody."[29] Respondents in cultures with a short-term orientation felt less satisfied with their contributions to these good causes. In a culture that believes in absolute criteria for good and evil, it is difficult to be satisfied with one's own efforts at doing good. In cultures with a long-term orientation, a strong concern for Virtue allows a pragmatic integration of morals and practice. Virtue is not based on absolute standards for good and evil; what is virtuous depends on the circumstances, and when behaving virtuously, one doesn't feel a strong need to do more for correcting social injustice.

The Western concern with Truth is supported by an axiom in Western logic that a statement excludes its opposite: if A is true, B (which is the opposite of A) must be false. Eastern logic does not have such an axiom. If A is true, its opposite B may also be true, and together they produce a wisdom superior to either A or B. Human truth in this philosophical approach is always partial. People in East and Southeast Asian countries see no problem in adopting elements from different religions or adhering to more than one religion at the same time. In countries with such a philosophical background, a practical nonreligious ethical system like Confucianism can become a cornerstone of society. In the West ethical rules tend to be derived from religion: Virtue from Truth.

According to Danish sinologist Verner Worm, the Chinese give priority to common sense over rationality. Rationality is abstract, analytical, and idealistic, with a tendency to logical extremes, whereas the spirit of common sense is more human and in closer contact with reality.[30]

Western psychology assumes that people seek cognitive consistency, meaning that they avoid mutually conflicting bits of information. This seems to be less the case in East and Southeast Asian countries.[31] In comparison with North Americans, the Chinese viewed disagreement as less harmful to personal relationships than injury or disappointment. A different opinion did not hurt their egos.[32]

Korean psychologist Uichol Kim believes the Western way of practicing psychology does not fit in East Asia:

> Psychology . . . is deeply enmeshed with Euro-American cultural values that champion rational, liberal and individualistic ideals. . . . This belief affects how conferences are organized, research collaborations are developed, research is funded, and publications are accepted. In East Asia, human relationships that can be characterized as being "virtue-based" rather than "rights-based" occupy the center stage. Individuals are considered to be linked in a web of inter-relatedness and ideas are exchanged through established social networks.[33]

In science and technology, Western Truth stimulated analytical, Eastern Virtue, synthetic thinking. A Chinese student told Geert:

> The biggest difference between the Chinese and the Western society is that the Western society worships the hero and the Chinese worship the saint. If one is good in doing one thing, one can be a hero. To be a saint, you have to be good in everything.

During the Industrial Revolution in the West, the search for Truth led to the discovery of laws of nature that could then be exploited for the sake of human progress. Chinese scholars, despite their high level of civilization, never discovered Newton's laws. They were simply not looking for laws. The Chinese script betrays this lack of interest in generalizing. It needs three thousand or more different characters, one for each syllable, while by splitting the syllables into separate letters, Western languages need only about thirty signs. Western analytical thinking focused on elements, while Eastern synthetic thinking focused on wholes. A Japanese Nobel Prize winner in physics is quoted as having said that "the Japanese mentality is unfit for abstract thinking."[34]

By the middle of the twentieth century, the Western concern for Truth gradually ceased to be an asset and turned instead into a liability. Science may benefit from analytical thinking, but management and government are based on the art of synthesis. With the results of Western, analytically derived technologies freely available, Eastern cultures could start putting these technologies into practice using their own superior synthetic abilities. What is true or who is right is less important than what works and how the efforts of individuals with different thinking patterns can be coordinated toward a common goal. Japanese management, especially with Japanese employees, is famous for this pragmatic synthesis.

Table 7.3 summarizes the differences between societies having a short- versus long-term orientation based on CVS data from the past two sections.

TABLE 7.3 Key Differences Between Short- and Long-Term Orientation Societies Based on CVS Data: Business and Ways of Thinking

SHORT-TERM ORIENTATION	LONG-TERM ORIENTATION
Main work values include freedom, rights, achievement, and thinking for oneself.	Main work values Include learning, honesty, adaptiveness, accountability, and self-discipline.
Leisure time is important.	Leisure time is not important.
Focus is on the "bottom line."	Focus is on market position.
Importance of this year's profits	Importance of profits ten years from now
Managers and workers are psychologically in two camps.	Owner-managers and workers share the same aspirations.
Meritocracy, reward by abilities	Wide social and economic differences are undesirable.
Personal loyalties vary with business needs	Investment In lifelong personal networks, *guanxi*
Concern with possessing the Truth.	Concern with respecting the demands of Virtue.
There are universal guidelines about what is good and evil.	What is good and evil depends on the circumstances.
Dissatisfaction with one's own contributions to daily human relations and to correcting injustice	Satisfaction with one's own contributions to daily human relations and to correcting injustice
Matter and spirit are separated.	Matter and spirit are integrated.
If A is true, its opposite B must be false.	If A is true, its opposite B can also be true.
Priority is given to abstract rationality.	Priority is given to common sense.
There is a need for cognitive consistency.	Disagreement does not hurt.
Analytical thinking	Synthetic thinking

Long-Term Orientation Scores Based on World Values Survey Data

In 2007 Misho Minkov published his analysis of World Values Survey (WVS) data, introducing three new dimensions. The first, *exclusionism versus universalism*, was correlated with our collectivism, and we discussed it in Chapter 4. The second, *indulgence versus restraint*, will be the subject of Chapter 8. The third was called *monumentalism versus flexhumility*,[35] and it correlated strongly (and negatively) with LTO-CVS.[36] Monumentalism predicted 42 percent of the country differences in LTO-CVS, which suggested that the two measures share common underlying values.[37]

Misho's monumentalism versus flexhumility dimension had been inspired by the work of Canadian psychologist Steve Heine, who saw a link between self-enhancement (a tendency to seek positive information about oneself) and self-stability or self-consistency (a tendency to believe that one should have unchangeable values, beliefs, and behaviors that do not depend on shifting circumstances).[38] Although Heine referred to individuals, Misho guessed that Heine's theory might also apply at the national cultural level. WVS data proved him right.

WVS measurements of pride (a self-enhancing feeling) and religiousness (which tends to imply unchangeable values and beliefs) did correlate at the national level. Nations with higher percentages of people who state that they are very proud to be citizens of their country, or that one of their main goals in life has been to make their parents proud, also tend to have higher percentages of very religious people. Pride and religiousness together formed a strong cultural dimension. The dimension contrasts societies in which the human self is like a proud and stable monolithic monument versus societies whose cultures promote humility, flexibility, and adaptability to changing circumstances.

In the Chinese Value Survey, *saving face* can be seen as a form of self-enhancement, and *personal steadiness and stability* is the same thing as self-consistency; both goals appear at the short-term pole of the LTO-CVS dimension. This explains the negative correlation between LTO and monumentalism. On monumentalism too, East Asian countries formed a compact cluster at one pole (flexhumility). African and Islamic countries were found closer to the opposite pole (monumentalism), and so was the United States.

This demonstrated that conceptually and statistically similar dimensions could be arrived at starting from very different databases and theoretical perspectives—Chinese or North American. LTO-CVS and monumentalism overlapped only partly, because monumentalism does not predict thrift or persistence, and LTO-CVS is not about religious-ness. The correlation between the two indexes encouraged a search for WVS items that would replicate the meaning of *both* poles of the LTO-CVS dimension.

Misho scoured the WVS database up to the year 2008 for items that fulfill the following conditions:

- They are conceptually similar to the LTO-CVS items.
- They correlate significantly with LTO-CVS.

The WVS items that best satisfied these conditions were the following:[39]

1. **Thrift as a desirable trait for children:** "Here is a list of qualities that children can be encouraged to learn at home. Which, if any, do you consider to be especially important? Please choose up to five." The list included independence, hard work, feeling of responsibility, imagination, tolerance and respect for other people, thrift (saving money and things), determination (perseverance), religious faith, unselfishness, and obedience. Measured was the percentage choosing "thrift."

2. **National pride:** "How proud are you to be (name of your nation-ality)? very proud, quite proud, not very proud, not at all proud." Measured was the percentage choosing "very proud," which scored negatively.[40] This item measures an aspect of self-enhancement.

3. **Importance of service to others:** "For each of the following, indi-cate how important it is in your life—very important, rather impor-tant, not very important, or not at all important: family, friends, leisure time, politics, work, religion, service to others." Measured was the percentage choosing "very important" for service to others.

"Service to others" resembles the LTO-CVS item "reciprocation of greetings, favors, and gifts." Scoring "service to others" as very important in one's life can be seen as another form of self-enhancement (like pride): a concern for maintaining a positive self-image. The three items were mutu-ally correlated, and across the available countries each of the three was significantly correlated with LTO-CVS.[41] From the three items, we could calculate new, WVS-based LTO scores for eighty-four countries.[42] New data later allowed us to expand this number to ninety-three countries.[43]

Across the countries represented in both studies, these scores share 52 percent of their variance with the original LTO-CVS scores.[44] Conceptually, the new LTO scores follow the old ones also in correlating with (other WVS) items that measure the importance of tradition as well as perseverance as a desirable trait for children.[45] The new LTO scores for ninety-three countries are presented in Table 7.4.

We deliberately maintained the label *long-term orientation* for the new index. We will call it LTO-WVS because it is similar to LTO-CVS but is not identical. The new index was inspired by the old one, but it had to be based on a very different questionnaire, with different respondents in a different time period. Experience with replication of concepts in surveys shows that 50 percent common variance in such a case is about the best attainable.

The differences between LTO-CVS and LTO-WVS are that the first originated from a survey designed by Chinese scholars, and it produced its highest score for mainland China. In the first part of this chapter we interpreted the implications of the LTO dimension with its Chinese origins in mind. Its scores are available for only twenty-three countries, and attempts at expansion using the same questions produced disappointing results.

LTO-WVS tries to replicate the essence of long-term orientation from a massive and permanently updated survey database that originated in Europe and expanded worldwide under American leadership—a product of Western minds. It lacks the Chinese flavor of the earlier study. However, it allows us to expand the basic distinctions from the CVS to many more countries.

As LTO-WVS is partly based on national pride, it is strongly correlated with Misho's monumentalism.[46] At the same time, it is statistically entirely independent from the four IBM dimensions.[47] Unlike LTO-CVS, which was independent of national wealth, LTO-WVS is weakly positively correlated with national wealth.[48] The relationship with economic growth depends on the period and on the countries included, and we will come back to this point later in the chapter.

From the twenty-three countries of the LTO-CVS scale, six have noticeably shifted on the LTO-WVS scale: Pakistan, Germany, and Great Britain moved up; Australia, Brazil, and Hong Kong moved down. Pakistan joins India and Bangladesh; Germany and Great Britain join a Western European cluster. Australia moves closer to the United States, Brazil

TABLE 7.4 Long-Term Orientation (LTO) Index Values for 93 Countries and Regions Based on Factor Scores from Three Items in the World Values Survey

SCORES ARE BASED ON THE MOST RECENT WVS DATA FROM THE PERIOD 1995–2004; NINE COUNTRIES MARKED WITH AN ASTERISK (*) WERE ADDED USING 2005–08 DATA.

RANK	AMERICA C/S	EUROPE S/SE	EUROPE N/NW ANGLO WORLD	EUROPE C/E EX-SOVIET	MUSLIM WORLD M.E & AFRICA	ASIA EAST ASIA SE	INDEX
1						S Korea	100
2						Taiwan	93
3						Japan	88
4						China	87
5				Ukraine			86
6			Germany				83
7–9				Estonia			82
7–9			Belgium				82
7–9				Lithuania			82
10–11				Russia			81
10–11				Belarus			81
12			Germany E				78
13				Slovakia			77
14				Montenegro			75
15			Switzerland				74
16						Singapore	72
17				Moldova			71
18–19				Czech Rep.			70
18–19				Bosnia			70
20–21				Bulgaria			69
20–21				Latvia			69
22			Netherlands				67

continued

TABLE 7.4 Long-Term Orientation (LTO) Index Values for 93 Countries and Regions Based on Factor Scores from Three Items in the World Values Survey, *continued*

SCORES ARE BASED ON THE MOST RECENT WVS DATA FROM THE PERIOD 1995–2004; NINE COUNTRIES MARKED WITH AN ASTERISK (*) WERE ADDED USING 2005–08 DATA.

RANK	AMERICA C/S	EUROPE S/SE	EUROPE N/NW ANGLO WORLD	EUROPE C/E EX-SOVIET	MUSLIM WORLD M.E & AFRICA	ASIA EAST ASIA SE	INDEX
23				Kyrgyzstan			66
24			Luxembourg				64
25		France					63
26–27						Indonesia	62
26–27				Macedonia			62
28–32				Albania			61
28–32		Italy					61
28–32				Armenia			61
28–32						Hong Kong*	61
28–32				Azerbaijan			61
33			Austria				60
34–35				Croatia			58
34–35				Hungary			58
36						Vietnam	57
37			Sweden				53
38–39				Serbia			52
38–39				Romania			52
40–41			Great Britain				51
40–41						India	51
42						Pakistan	50
43				Slovenia			49
44		Spain					48
45–46						Bangladesh	47

Rank						Value
45–46	Malta					47
47	Turkey					46
48	Greece					45
49	Brazil					44
50					Malaysia*	41
51–54		Finland				38
51–54			Georgia			38
51–54			Poland			38
51–54				Israel		38
55–56		Canada				36
55–56				Saudi Arabia		36
57–58		Denmark				35
57–58		Norway				35
59–60				Tanzania		34
59–60				S Africa		34
61		New Zealand				33
62					Thailand*	32
63	Chile					31
64				Zambia*		30
65–66	Portugal					28
65–66		Iceland				28
67–68				Burkina Faso*		27
67–68					Philippines	27
69–71		United States				26
69–71	Uruguay					26
69–71				Algeria		26
72–73	Peru					25
72–73				Iraq		25
74–76		Ireland				24
74–76	Mexico					24
74–76				Uganda		24

continued

TABLE 7.4 Long-Term Orientation (LTO) Index Values for 93 Countries and Regions Based on Factor Scores from Three Items in the World Values Survey, *continued*

SCORES ARE BASED ON THE MOST RECENT WVS DATA FROM THE PERIOD 1995–2004; NINE COUNTRIES MARKED WITH AN ASTERISK (*) WERE ADDED USING 2005–08 DATA.

RANK	AMERICA C/S	EUROPE S/SE	EUROPE N/NW ANGLO WORLD	EUROPE C/E EX-SOVIET	MUSLIM WORLD M.E & AFRICA	ASIA EAST ASIA SE	INDEX
77			Australia				21
78–80	Argentina						20
78–80					Mali*		20
78–80	El Salvador						20
81					Rwanda*		18
82–83					Jordan		16
82–83	Venezuela						16
84					Zimbabwe		15
85–86					Morocco		14
85–86					Iran		14
87–90	Colombia						13
87–90	Dominican Rep.						13
87–90					Nigeria		13
87–90	Trinidad*						13
91					Egypt		7
92					Ghana*		4
93	Puerto Rico						0

joins other Latin American countries, and Hong Kong scores lower than Singapore. For the remaining countries, the shifts between the CVS and WVS rankings are minor.[49]

The four highest-scoring countries in Table 7.4 are still East Asian, and with three exceptions (Malaysia, Thailand, and the Philippines), all other South and Southeast Asian countries are found in the top half of the table. The top half further holds all countries from Eastern Europe, including the entire former Soviet Union, with the exception of Poland and Georgia. Finally, it includes most other European countries, except Greece, Finland, Denmark, Norway, Portugal, and Iceland.

The lower half of the table contains four Anglo countries overseas: Canada, New Zealand, the United States, and Australia. It contains all countries from the Middle East and Africa, as well as all countries from Middle and South America.

Long-Term Orientation and the GLOBE Dimensions

In Chapter 2 we introduced the GLOBE study, which claimed to replicate and improve Geert's model across some sixty countries. For each of the topics discussed in Chapters 3 through 6, we compared GLOBE's findings with ours. The GLOBE dimension inspired by our LTO was called *future orientation*.

Our old LTO measure, LTO-CVS, across twenty-one common countries correlated significantly with four of the eighteen GLOBE measures, but in the end only one (strong negative) relationship remained: with *performance orientation* "should be"; this explained 51 percent of the variance in LTO-CVS.[50] Performance orientation "should be" also correlated with Misho's monumentalism: it implies that "we should be a great performing nation!"—a self-enhancing feeling, typical of cultures with a short-term orientation. Long-term orientation correlates with flexhumility, so the negative relationship makes sense.

Across forty-nine common countries, our new LTO-WVS measure correlated significantly with six of the eighteen GLOBE measures. The strongest correlations were (again negatively) with *performance orientation* "should be" and (also negatively) with *group collectivism* "should be."[51] Group collectivism "should be" means family pride; in the first half of this chapter we saw that families in high-LTO cultures are pragmatic rather than proud about family matters.

GLOBE's *future orientation* "as is," meant to express long-term orienta-tion, did not correlate with either of our measures of LTO but did with a combination of low UAI and low PDI.[52] It is about planning for the future, and GLOBE respondents in relatively relaxed, egalitarian societies claimed to do more of this.

GLOBE's *future orientation* "should be" correlated with a combination of high PDI and *low* LTO-WVS.[53] It stands for "the accepted norm should be to plan for the future" and "people should worry about current cri-ses." Respondents in cultures that are more authoritarian and with more of a short-term orientation were more likely to agree with such "should" statements.

GLOBE's attempts to replicate long-term orientation as "future ori-entation" has therefore completely failed; the only significant correlation between the two is negative.

Long- and Short-Term Orientation, Family Relations, and School Results

In Chapters 4 and 5 we referred to a 2005 market research study on ideals of beauty and body image held by fifteen- to seventeen-year-old girls from ten countries around the world. The same study also conducted telephone interviews with larger samples of women between the ages of eighteen and sixty-four in the same ten countries. Women in cultures with a short-term orientation more often mentioned their mothers as having positively influenced their feelings about themselves and beauty and said that the mother's ideas of beauty had shaped their own.[54] We recognize the mother's contribution to the daughter's self-enhancement as part of the short-term orientation of a culture.

TIMSS (Trends in International Mathematics and Science Study) is an international comparative test of mathematics and science performance administered every four years in now more than fifty countries among all continents. Its latest round, at the time of this writing, was in 2007. Par-ticipants are fourth-grade students (age about ten) and/or eighth-grade students (age about fourteen). Consistently, the East Asian students (those from Singapore, South Korea, Taiwan, Hong Kong, and Japan) outperform all other students, especially in mathematics. The lowest-achieving nations are found in Africa, the Middle East, and Latin America.

Using TIMSS data from 1999, Geert had found that performance in mathematics correlated significantly with LTO-CVS; performance in science did not, although science and math scores were mutually strongly correlated. There was something in high-LTO cultures that contributed to mathematical skills. Wealthier countries did slightly better than poorer countries, but the math performance was more correlated with LTO-CVS than with national wealth.[55]

Misho had explained both mathematics and science performance differences from his *monumentalism* dimension and Heine's theory. Cultures encouraging self-enhancement will reduce children's interest in self-improvement activities, such as education. In monumentalist cultures people seek positive information about themselves and dismiss negative information. It takes a flexhumble culture to encourage admitting that one needs self-improvement.[56]

Older studies had shown that in the United States, Asian students more than Western students tended to attribute success to effort, and to attribute failure to lack of it, which is in line with Misho's interpretation.[57]

We analyzed the 2007 TIMSS scores, correlating them with LTO-CVS, LTO-WVS, and national wealth. Again, LTO-CVS correlated only with math performance, not with science performance, although the two were very strongly mutually correlated.[58] LTO-WVS correlated highly significantly with both math and science performance, although the math correlations were always slightly stronger.[59]

These results suggest that for the 2007 TIMMS scores, both Geert's interpretation and Misho's interpretation are still correct. Higher scores on LTO-WVS come with higher scores on both math and science, and this effect remains when we eliminate the effect of national wealth, at least for the eighth-grade students. For the fourth-grade students, the better school results can be entirely attributed to national wealth.[60]

At the same time, the correlations with LTO-CVS remain significant only for math performance, not for science performance. In these correlations there are relatively many East Asian countries. In the correlations with LTO-WVS, East Asian countries represent a smaller share; these correlations are significant for both math and science performance, but always somewhat more for math. We conclude that East Asian students have a double advantage: they not only work harder but also have a cultural talent for understanding mathematics. This advantage exists already for fourth-grade students (ten-year-olds), while the hard work effect only starts to affect the eighth-graders (fourteen-year-olds).

A traditional assumption has been that East Asian students focus on rote learning instead of comprehension, but the superior performance in basic mathematics of students in high-LTO-CVS cultures refutes this assumption. What Western minds interpret as rote learning may in fact be a way toward understanding. Teaching and learning are culturally conditioned, and apparently similar behaviors may have different deep meanings.[61]

Basic mathematics poses well-defined problems in which goals are explicitly stated—that is, "formal" rather than "open" problems.[62] Students from high-LTO cultures prove to be well equipped for solving such problems. Professor Gordon Redding, who spent many years at Hong Kong University, wrote:

> *The Chinese student, if he has been initially educated in his own culture, and in his own language, will have begun to use a set of cognitive processes which give him a "fix" on the world of a very distinctive kind. . . . It is possible to see some rationale for the noticeable tendency of Chinese to excel in certain subjects, particularly the applied sciences, where "the individual and the concrete" is paramount, and for their tendency not to move naturally into the abstract realms of philosophy and sociology.*
>
> *It is a common question why an active tradition of scientific investigation failed to develop in China in the way it did in the West. The most appealing explanations for it center upon differences in cognitive structures of a fundamental kind.*[63]

A talent for the concrete implies a talent for solving practical problems. What works is more important in high-LTO cultures than why it works. China's Chairman Deng Xiaoping is credited for the dictum "What does the color of the cat matter as long as it catches mice?"

Long- and Short-Term Orientation and Economic Growth

After World War II (1939–45) the victorious powers claimed a new world order led by the United Nations, with universal human rights. The first issue on the world's agenda in the 1950s and '60s was political independence. The colonial era ended, and many former colonies of rich countries became new states. Around 1970 priorities shifted to economic development. Three international organizations already founded in 1944—the World Bank, the International Monetary Fund (IMF), and the World Trade Organization (WTO)—made a commitment to end poverty.

Poverty, however, did not disappear. From 1970 to 2000 some countries were extremely successful in moving from "rags to riches." The absolute winners were the five Dragons: Taiwan, South Korea, Singapore, Hong Kong, and Japan—this in spite of a serious economic crisis in their region in 1997. In U.S. dollars, Taiwan's 2000 GNI per capita was thirty-six times as high as its 1970 GNI per capita. Japan's nominal GNI per capita increased by a factor of eighteen. On the other hand, the GNIs per capita of the countries of sub-Saharan Africa and Latin America rose insignificantly or not at all.

The economic success of the Dragons had not been predicted by economists. (Even after it happened, some failed for a time to recognize it.) A forecast for the region by prominent World Bank economists in the *American Economic Review* in 1966[64] did not even include Hong Kong and Singapore, because they were considered insignificant; it underrated the performances of Taiwan and South Korea and overrated those of India and Sri Lanka. Fifteen years later Singapore, with a population of 2.5 million, exported more than India with its 700 million.

After the Dragons' economic miracle had become undeniable, economics had no explanation for it. According to economic criteria, Colombia, for example, should have outperformed South Korea, while the reverse was true.[65] The American futurologist Herman Kahn (1922–83)[66] formulated a neo-Confucian hypothesis. He suggested that the economic success of the countries of East Asia could be attributed to Confucian values, common cultural roots going back far into history.

Kahn's hypothesis remained unproved until the Chinese Value Survey appeared. Economic growth in the last three decades of the twentieth century was highly significantly correlated with LTO-CVS; this was Geert's initial reason for adopting long-term orientation as a fifth dimension.

The Chinese Value Survey was conducted in 1985 and covered twenty-three countries around the world; the LTO index derived from it not only correlated with the economic growth of these countries in the preceding twenty years (1965–85) but also turned out to even better predict their growth in the next ten years (1985–95).[67]

As of this writing, fifteen more years have passed, and our LTO-CVS has been succeeded by a new scale, LTO-WVS, extending our database from twenty-three countries to ninety-three. Does our new LTO scale still explain economic growth, across so many more countries in a changed world?

For the period 1970–95, included in our correlations with LTO-CVS, we find that LTO-WVS still correlates with an increase in GNI per capita.[68] This is no longer the case for the period 1995–2005. Across all countries for which we have data, the correlation between LTO-WVS and increase in GNI per capita from 1995 to 2005 is about zero.[69]

However, the post-1995 data refer neither to the same set of countries nor to the same world economy. Our new list of countries includes nineteen names that did not yet exist as independent economies in 1970. The former Yugoslavia disintegrated in 1991 into Croatia, Slovenia, Macedonia, Bosnia, and a loose alliance of Serbia and Montenegro. The Soviet Union also ceased to exist in 1991 and was replaced by the Russian Federation ("Russia") plus many new republics, of which Estonia, Lithuania, Latvia, Belarus, Ukraine, Moldova, Armenia, Georgia, Azerbaijan, and Kyrgyzstan figure on our list. Czechoslovakia in 1993 split into a Czech and a Slovak republic. The transition was accompanied by economic liberation and the opportunity to develop a market economy, which the new countries each seized in their own way. With the demise of the Soviet Union, the Soviet influence in Eastern Europe also disappeared, and countries formerly under an imposed communist economic system could now choose their own economic ways. This applied to East Germany, which already in 1990 had reunified with West Germany, and to Poland, Hungary, Romania, and Bulgaria, which later joined the European Union. By 1995 all these new economies were supplying more or less reliable data on GNI per capita, and by 2005 one could compare their rates of growth over the past ten years.

Cultural theories that addressed the East Asian economic miracle were often criticized for failing to explain why East Asia did not achieve strong economic growth much earlier. After all, its Confucian values are extremely old. Why were they dormant for 2,500 years, triggering a miracle only in the second half of the twentieth century? The answer to this conundrum was known to German sociologist Max Weber eighty years ago. He observed that the so-called Protestant work ethic (basically another name for the set of values related to economic growth that we discuss in this chapter) could yield results only in a specific historical period. In our case two conditions had to be satisfied:

1. Availability of Western technology and of educational resources to use it
2. Integration of local markets into a world market of supply and demand for goods and services

A third condition, however, turns out to be initial poverty. LTO explains why some societies succeeded better than others in moving from rags to riches, but not from riches to more riches. The successful East Asian Dragons, for example, were hit by a regional economic crisis in 1997, which abruptly cut their economic ascent.

These considerations inspired us to take another look at the relationship between LTO-WVS and increase in GNI per capita from 1995 to 2005. We split the eighty-four countries for which we had both LTO-WVS and GNI growth data into fifty-four poor and thirty wealthy cases, on the base of their 1995 GNI per capita.[70]

In Figure 7.1 the ratio of GNI per capita in 2005 over GNI per capita in 1995 is plotted against LTO-WVS for eighty-four countries. For fifty-four poor countries, the correlation is significantly positive; for thirty wealthy countries, it is significantly negative.[71]

FIGURE 7.1 LTO-WVS Versus GNI per Capita Ratio 2005/1995 for 54 Poor and 30 Wealthy Nations

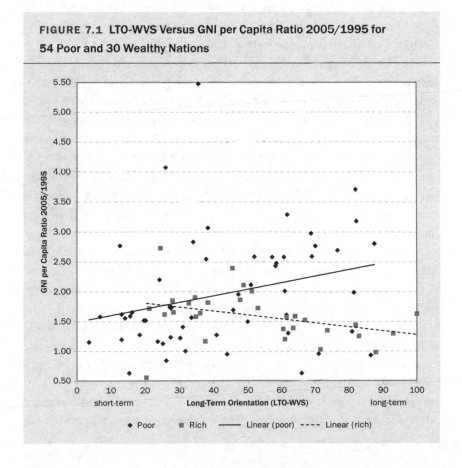

The correlation between LTO and economic growth for poor countries, even after 1995, confirms Herman Kahn's neo-Confucian hypothesis. It also indicates *which* of the various Confucian values were associated with economic growth. Very important was thrift. In a separate study, Misho Minkov and Vesselin Blagoev added to this conclusion a low importance of leisure. They cite prominent twentieth-century U.S. development economists who saw nothing miraculous in the East Asian economic performance and attribute it to old-fashioned hard work, thrift, and better education.[72] Of course, the question remains as to why East Asian countries did follow this road and others did not.

It also is noteworthy that it took an East Asian instrument, the Chinese Value Survey, to isolate a dimension that proved the role of culture in the development of East Asia and to provide an explanation of the economic success of the Dragons. In the meantime, we moved one step further: we discovered that similar conclusions can be drawn from data that had been hidden in the World Values Survey, basically a Western instrument. The logic of the growth of the Dragons now extends to the growth of several Eastern European economies between 1995 and 2005.

In 1993 a U.S. political scientist, Russell Read, proved the relationship between long-term orientation and various measures of saving. The strongest link he found was with the marginal propensity to save (MPS)—the change in real per capita saving—from 1970 to 1990, in percentages of the total changes in private consumption plus saving. MPS ranged from a low of 3 percent in the United States to a high of 64 percent in Singapore.[73]

In her analysis of consumer behavior, de Mooij found that people in high-LTO countries invested more in real estate, which is a long-term commitment, while people in low-LTO countries invested more in mutual funds.[74]

In 2008 a new economic crisis hit the world, spreading from the United States by the interdependence of globalized financial markets. Lack of thrift—overspending in economies that are short-term oriented—seems to lie at the heart of this new disaster.

The value item "thrift" (as with "persistence") was missing in the Rokeach Value Survey, which is supposed to have been based on a complete inventory of American values around 1970. Spending, not thrift, seems to have been a U.S. value at least since the second part of the twentieth century, both at the individual level and at the government level. When asked why Americans did not save more, Herbert Stein, former chairman of the

Council of Economic Advisers of two Republican U.S. presidents, said: "Economists have been unable to answer this question. Our savings quote . . . has always been lower than elsewhere. . . . It is most likely a reflection of the American lifestyle, although this is no explanation."[75]

Economic Growth and Politics

Along with the economic conditions for growth discussed in the previous section, growth also depends on the political context. The growth of the Dragons started only after 1955, when for the first time in history a truly global market developed. The need for a supportive political context was met in all five Dragon countries, but in very different ways, with the role of government varying from active support to laissez-faire. Labor unions were weak and company oriented in all five countries, and a relatively egalitarian income distribution meant that support for revolutionary social changes was weak. The Confucian sense of moderation affected political life as well, in spite of occasional outbreaks of unrest and violence.

The influence of the political context was evident in the country that was the cradle of Confucianism, mainland China. Overseas Chinese were at the core of the economic miracles in Hong Kong, Singapore, and Taiwan and contributed to the emerging economies of Indonesia, Malaysia, Thailand, and the Philippines. They seem to have been able to use their entrepreneurial skills better than their relatives who stayed in the mother country.

In 1970 the Chinese currency was not convertible, which led to an overestimate of 1970 GNI per capita and an underestimated 2000/1970 ratio. China's economic growth also suffered from political events: the disasters of the Great Leap Forward (1958–59) and the Great Proletarian Cultural Revolution (1966–76) and the backlash after the dramatic suppression of student demonstrations at the Square of the Gate of Heavenly Peace (Tiananmen Square) in Beijing in 1989. On the other hand, tight political control, by enforcing a one-child family policy, prevented a population explosion that would have diluted per capita growth. From 1975 to 2007 the Chinese population grew by 42 percent from 930 million to 1.32 billion, an average of 1.3 percent a year. The forecast for the period extending to 2015 is 0.7 percent a year. With a less effective population control, the population of India in the same period grew by 81 percent from 620 million to 1.12 billion, an average of 1.9 percent a year. Without any planned population control at all, the population of Nigeria grew by 169 percent from 55 million to 148 million, an average of 2.9 percent a year.[76]

China's rulers have to cope with the domestic political consequences of the country's economic opening toward the rest of the world. Turning around a nation of 1.3 billion people without falling into despotism, anarchy, or fatal destruction of the environment is immensely more difficult than modernizing an island with 5 million inhabitants as with Singapore. In a 1988 article that analyzed the implications of the Chinese Value Survey, at a time when China was still exceedingly poor, Geert interpreted China's top score on what he later called LTO as a likelihood that "the People's Republic will follow the success of the Five Dragons—albeit at some distance—and eventually become the sixth—and most powerful— dragon of them all." History has proved this prophecy correct.[77]

The opposite example in the 1980s was the Soviet Union and its sphere of political influence, which stifled initiative in places where—according to their LTO-WVS scores—the mental software for development was present. The fast economic growth in a number of Eastern European countries since the end of the Soviet era has demonstrated this.

The development of East Asia was strongly guided by a desire to learn from others. Japan has actively studied European (in particular, Dutch) science and technology since the seventeenth century. Western fads and fashions are popular in East Asia even where governments don't like them. Likewise, Eastern European countries in spite of communism have always taken the West as a model.

This desire to learn from others is not necessarily present in countries scoring low on the LTO-WVS index. National pride is a component of short-term orientation, and too much national pride is a recipe for economic disaster. In the United States it contributed to the decision to start the Iraq war with a cost of a trillion dollars. It supports a lack of interest in and understanding of other countries, and it played a major role in the 2008 financial crisis.[78]

In Chapter 9 we will compare business goals and corporate governance across major economic powers and will show that the dominant concern of U.S. business leaders for short-term growth and greed without continuity and responsibility was already visible in an international comparison in the 1990s.

Fundamentalisms as Short-Term Orientation

As argued earlier in this chapter, Judaism, Christianity, and Islam are three Western religions belonging to the same thought family and having historically grown from the same roots. All three derive Virtue from Truth. All three have modern wings, focusing on the present, and fundamentalist wings, focusing on wisdom from the past. Religious fundamentalisms represent the extreme short-term pole of the long-term versus short-term dimension. Decisions are based not on what works today but on an interpretation of what was written in the old holy books. Fundamentalisms are unable to cope with the problems of the modern world. British philosopher Bertrand Russell (1872–1970) wrote:

> *All fanatical creeds do harm. This is obvious when they have to compete with other fanaticisms, since in that case they promote hatred and strife. But it is true even when only one fanatical creed is in the field. It cannot allow free inquiry, since this might shake its hold. It must oppose intellectual progress. If, as is usually the case, it involves a priesthood, it gives great power to a caste professionally devoted to maintenance of the intellectual status quo, and to a pretence of certainty where in fact there is no certainty.*[79]

Politically influential fundamentalisms that represent a threat to world peace and prosperity exist within all three Western religions. The opposing modern wings are weakest in Islam. There was a period in history, from about the ninth to the fourteenth century A.D., when the Muslim world was not only militarily but also scientifically advanced, while Christian Europe was backward. With the Renaissance and the Reformation, Christian countries embarked on the road to modernization, while the world of Islam withdrew into traditionalism.

U.S. Islamologist Bernard Lewis has described the Muslim scholars after the fourteenth century as having a "feeling of timelessness, that nothing really changes," and a lack of interest into what happened in the rest of the world. Knowledge was seen as a "corpus of eternal verities which could be acquired, accumulated, transmitted, interpreted and applied but not modified or transformed." Innovation was bad and similar to heresy.

While in Europe printing had been invented around 1450, the first printing press in Turkey was installed in 1729, and it was closed down in 1742
by conservative Muslims. Lewis writes:

> *The contrast has sometimes been drawn between the very different responses*
> *of the Islamic world and of Japan to the challenge of the West. Their situa-*
> *tions were very different. . . . Muslim perceptions of Europe were influenced,*
> *indeed dominated, by an element which had little or no effect on the Jap-*
> *anese—namely religion. Like the rest of the world, Europe was perceived*
> *by Muslims first and foremost in religious terms, i.e., not as Western or*
> *European or white but as Christian—and in the Middle East, unlike the*
> *Far East, Christianity was familiar and discounted. What lesson of value*
> *could be learned from the followers of a flawed and superseded religion?*[80]

Today modern technology has penetrated into the Muslim world. There
are both traditional and modern forms of Islam, but the first are still strong
and aggressive. Confronted with backwardness and poverty, some groups
react by calling for reinstating the sharia, laws from the Prophet Muham-
mad's day. Muslim countries that temporarily collected enormous riches
from their oil resources have hardly adapted better to the modern world
than those that remained poor. The oil benefits seem to have been a liability
rather than an asset. None of the five Dragons had any natural resources
worth mentioning besides the mental software of their populations.

In the second half of the twentieth century, many Muslims migrated
to Western countries. Europe in the beginning of the twenty-first century
counted some 13 million Muslim citizens. Many have integrated and moved
into the working and middle classes, occupying positions of responsibility
in Western societies. Others have failed to integrate, mostly remaining
underclass, and populate new ghettos. The latter group is most tempted
by fundamentalist forms of Islam that compensate their marginal position
in the host society by preaching pride in possessing the right doctrine.

A manifestation of national pride—rather than religiosity—in some
Muslim cultures with a short-term orientation is the migrants' hesitation
at changing nationality, leading to dual citizenship. The government of
Morocco, as one example, actively encourages this practice; Moroccans
cannot understand why a child of their great country would ever want to
renounce his or her citizenship.

Short-Term Orientation in Africa

Around 1970 Geert was a manager of personnel research in IBM's Europe, Africa, and Middle East area. One of his responsibilities was the development of tests for employee selection. One day he received a call from the regional manager for Africa, an American to whom all English-speaking African countries, except South Africa, reported. The regional manager had a problem with IBM's Programming Aptitude Test, at that time the instrument used to select persons able to learn computer programming. In Africa, the manager said, nobody could pass the test, so they had no way of selecting candidates, neither for IBM itself nor on behalf of its customers.

It so happened that the U.S. designer of the original Programming Aptitude Test, Dr. Walter McNamara, had just retired, and he agreed to make a three-month study trip through a number of African countries and to try to resolve the problem. Upon his return, McNamara reported these conclusions:

- It wasn't true that nobody passed. Some African candidates did pass, but the percentages were lower than elsewhere.
- The original test existed in two versions, one for college graduates and one for high school graduates. IBM offices in Africa had been supplied with only the college-level test, while the majority of candidates came straight from high school and should have been given the other version.
- Most candidates had no experience with forced-choice tests and should first be instructed on how they worked.
- The tests used American English; some words were unknown in the local English varieties.
- The time limits used applied to native speakers; for those with English as a second (or third or fourth) language, a wider limit existed, but the administrators of the test were not aware of this option.

McNamara had run a trial with an adapted version of the test among graduates of a number of high schools in Zambia, and the results obtained were almost equivalent to those in the United States. Thanking McNamara for his excellent work, Geert had the new version printed as "Programming Aptitude Test for Countries with English as a Second Language."

He proudly presented it at a conference of country managers from IBM's African region.

Geert's announcement met with less enthusiasm than he had expected. During the ensuing break the country manager of IBM-Ghana, one of the first Africans to have reached this level, stood next to Geert in the men's room and told him in his deep voice, "I want the American test for my people."

This true story tells us that the problem of selecting personnel in the African subsidiaries of IBM was not a lack of skills: given the same care to the process as is usual in other countries, enough capable candidates could be selected. However, to the African country manager, this was a matter not of solving a problem but of satisfying his national pride, which he felt to be hurt by the fact that his compatriots would not get the same test as the Americans.[81]

Africa, and particularly sub-Saharan Africa, is a development economist's headache. In 2009 thirty-two of the forty poorest countries in the world were African.[82] African countries are plagued by a population explosion, with growth rates of 3 percent annually, leading to a doubling of the population within twenty-five years. They are also plagued by AIDS and other epidemics (which may be nature's answer to the population explosion); by extremely bloody wars and massacres (man's answer); and by ineffective governments perceived as corrupt and as enemies by their own people. In many of the fifty African states, with a few favorable exceptions, basic government tasks such as health care have deteriorated or disappeared.

The extreme case is Somalia, which Siad Barre, president since 1969, fled in 1991, leaving the country in chaos in the hands of competing warlords. Foreign interventions by Americans and Ethiopians were unsuccessful.[83] In the 2000s the Somalis hit the world news as highly proficient pirates hunting commercial vessels for ransom, and there was no government that could be held responsible.

It was evident that Western logic often did not apply in Africa. The example of Bond's Chinese Value Survey led Geert to suggest a similar exercise for Africa: asking Africans to develop a values questionnaire, administer this instrument in both African and non-African countries, and see whether any new dimension emerged that explained why Western recipes for development don't seem to work in Africa.

The project was undertaken at Geert's former institute, the Institute for Research on Intercultural Cooperation (IRIC),[84] by his successor, Niels

Noorderhaven, with Bassirou Tidjani from Senegal. African scientists in Africa and African students abroad were asked to suggest value survey items. Through a "Delphi" approach, the first results were anonymously fed back to the contributors, and their comments were incorporated. The questionnaire, in an English or a French version, was then administered to samples of male and female students in the African countries Cameroon, Ghana, Senegal, South Africa, Tanzania, and Zimbabwe and outside Africa in Belgium, Germany, Great Britain, Guyana, Hong Kong, Malaysia, the Netherlands, and the United States; it yielded a total of 1,100 respondents in fourteen countries.[85]

Unlike the case with the Chinese Value Survey, the African Value Survey did not reveal a new, African-inspired value dimension. It produced six factors. Four of these were significantly correlated each with one of the IBM dimensions. One other was trivial, caused by differences between the two language versions.[86] The remaining factor (the second strongest in Noorderhaven and Tidjani's analysis), traditional wisdom, was significantly correlated with LTO-CVS and opposed the African countries (and some of the European countries) to the Asian countries in the study.[87] Distinctive items on the short-term pole of this dimension were "Wisdom is more important than knowledge" and "Wisdom comes from experience and time, not from education." These statements fiercely oppose Confucian values.

This result of the African Value Survey, just as with the story at the beginning of this section, confirms the low scores for African countries on both LTO-CVS and LTO-WVS. In Table 7.4 the scores for three northern African and ten middle and southern African countries are all on the short-term side. Putting pride over practical results and expecting wisdom without knowledge and education does not encourage working and studying today for reaping benefits tomorrow.

In African countries, cause-effect relationships that are obvious to outsiders are sometimes denied. An example was the refusal of then-president Thabo Mbeki of South Africa to recognize the link between HIV contagion and AIDS. A widespread belief in witchcraft supports blaming others and occult forces for evils that, according to outsiders, Africans have brought on themselves.

The values scores do not imply that all Africans are short-term thinkers, nor that all East Asians are long-term thinkers. They do mean that these ways of thinking are sufficiently general to affect common behavior patterns and the structure and functioning or malfunctioning of national institutions. Through these processes, thinking affects economic development.

Nearly all African countries have become dependent on foreign aid and on loans from the International Monetary Fund. According to Joseph Stiglitz, former chief economist of the World Bank and 2001 Nobel Prize winner in economics, Africa's economic problems have been compounded by the conditions for loans dictated by the IMF. Even more than the World Bank, the IMF has been dominated by short-term-oriented market fundamentalism. This posture has led to a stress on budget discipline at the expense of education, health, and infrastructure and to forced liberalization of imports while keeping Western markets closed for African exports, ruining fledgling local enterprises.[88] Table 7.4 classifies the U.S. mind-set, which dominates among the IMF advisers, in the same short-term orientation bracket as that of the country's African clients.

Very short-term values were also found in a study of Australian aborigines, as mentioned in Chapter 4. This, too, is a group whose economic development is problematic.[89] Also in their case, conditions created by short-term-oriented white policies often compound their problem.

Table 7.5 summarizes key differences between societies on the dimension of short- versus long-term orientation based on WVS data.

The Future of Long- and Short-Term Orientation

The second time Duke Ching called Confucius to an audience, he again asked him, "What is the secret of good government?" Confucius replied, "Good government consists in being sparing with resources." [90]

The future is by definition a long-term problem. Our grandchildren and their grandchildren will have to live with the long-term consequences of our present actions.

The question Duke Ching put before Confucius 2,500 years ago is still as topical as ever: What is good government? In 1999–2000 social scientists from East Asia (China, Japan, and South Korea) and from Nordic Europe (Denmark, Finland, and Sweden) in a joint project surveyed representative samples of the populations of their countries about the same issue. The survey showed differences in opinions about how the relationship between rulers and citizens should be, reflecting the countries' differ-

TABLE 7.5 Key Differences Between Short- and Long-Term Orientation Societies Based on WVS Data

SHORT-TERM ORIENTATION	LONG-TERM ORIENTATION
Service to others is an important goal.	Children should learn to save money and things.
Proud of my country	Learn from other countries
Tradition is important.	Children should learn to persevere.
Monumentalist (Minkov)	Flexhumble (Minkov)
Family pride	Family pragmatism
Mothers positively influence daughters' feelings about themselves and beauty.	Daughters' ideas of beauty are independent of mothers' ideas.
Students attribute success and failure to luck.	Students attribute success to effort and failure to lack of it.
Weaker mathematics and science results of fourteen-year-olds due to less effort	Better mathematics and science results of fourteen-year-olds due to harder work
No special skills for mathematics	In East Asia, better at mathematics
Talent for theoretical, abstract sciences	Talent for applied, concrete sciences
Slow or no economic growth of poor countries	Fast economic growth of poor countries
Small savings quote, little money for investment	Large savings quote, funds available for investment
Investment in mutual funds	Investment in real estate
Appeal of fundamentalisms	Appeal of pragmatism
Appeal of folk wisdom and witchcraft	Appeal of knowledge and education

ent positions on the power distance and uncertainty avoidance dimensions. On the role of government as such, the survey showed remarkable consensus. A majority in all six countries supported "a strong government to handle today's complex economic problems" and did not believe that "the free market can handle these problems without governmental involvement." Next to its role in the economy, the government tasks about which there was the strongest consensus were fighting environmental pollution and maintaining harmonious social relations.[91]

The report on the Asian-Nordic study takes issue with the ongoing process of *globalization,* perceived by the Asians as "Westernization" and by the Nordic Europeans as "Americanization." It signals a values discrepancy between all six countries and what the authors see as the values behind this kind of globalization.[92]

In our interpretation, the main value-based objections of these Asians and Northern Europeans were directed against the short-term focus of this kind of globalization. In Table 7.4 the countries participating in this research project all scored more long-term than the United States. Their respondents saw good government as future directed, while the ongoing U.S.- and IMF-led globalization stressed quick fixes. In fact, according to economist Joseph Stiglitz, it was based on a market fundamentalism that as much as other fundamentalisms was predicated on maintaining or returning to past positions rather than guided by a view of a common future for humankind as a whole.

Responsible thinking about the long term cannot avoid the conclusion that in a finite world, any growth has its limits. The human population cannot continue growing forever, nor can the economy of a state, unless its growth comes at the expense of other states. Few politicians have been prepared to face this reality. The most evident area where this applies is the environment. Climate changes through global warming, water shortages, and radioactive waste deposits are examples of environmental costs of unbridled growth, with which good government should take issue.

Religious, political, and economic fundamentalisms are aggressive enemies of long-term thinking. They are based on the past and tend to escape their share of responsibility for the future, putting it in the hands of God or the market. For example, in many parts of the world an immediate threat to peace, health, and justice is human overpopulation. Adequate methods of family planning exist, but religious and economic fundamentalists in a remarkable consensus try to resist making it widely accessible.

The economic importance of East Asia in this twenty-first century is likely to increase. One precious gift the wise men and women from the East can carry to the others would be a shift toward global long-term thinking.

Light or Dark?

In its special Christmas edition, at a time when people in the traditionally Christian world are supposed to be merry and happy, the
well-known British magazine *The Economist* once published the following story:[1]

*Once a week, on Sundays, Hong Kong becomes a different city. Thousands
of Filipina women throng into the central business district, around Statue
Square, to picnic, dance, sing, gossip, and laugh. . . . They hug. They chat-
ter. They smile. Humanity could stage no greater display of happiness.
This stands in stark contrast to the other six days of the week. Then it is
the Chinese, famously cranky and often rude, and expatriate businessmen,
permanently stressed, who control the center. On these days, the Filipinas
are mostly holed up in the 154,000 households across the territory where
they work as "domestic helpers" or amahs in Cantonese. There they suffer not only the loneliness of separation from their own families, but often
virtual slavery under their Chinese or expatriate masters. Hence a mystery:
those who should be Hong Kong's most miserable are, by all appearances,
its happiest. . . .*

Happiness, or subjective well-being (SWB), as academics prefer to call it, is a universally cherished goal. Some philosophical schools, such as classic Buddhism, condemn the pursuit of happiness and consider it a reproachable waste of time in which an enlightened person should not engage. However, such elitist doctrines cannot have been easily embraced by the masses. Throughout the world and regardless of their religion, most people would like to attain a state of bliss here and now and, in contrast to classic Buddhist pundits, are not deterred by the certainty of its transience.

Unfortunately, some nations as a whole do much better than others in the universal chase of happiness. Even more disturbing for the stragglers is that research on cross-cultural differences in SWB evidences a high level of stability in the country rankings. There are fluctuations, to be sure, but no major shifts have been observed since the first national rankings were reported decades ago, based on large-scale measurements of happiness. Moreover, some studies have demonstrated a high similarity between the SWB rank order of twenty nations and the SWB rank order of groups of Americans with ancestors from those nations. This means that even when people of different ethnic origins share the same environment, they do not become equally happy, and some old differences remain for some time.[2]

The Nature of Subjective Well-Being

There is a vast academic literature on SWB. Usually, two main aspects are distinguished: a cognitive evaluation of one's life and a description of one's feelings.[3] Life satisfaction and emotional affect are not necessarily one and the same phenomenon. Some people may perceive that their lives are going well without necessarily being in an elevated mood, and vice versa.

The World Values Survey addresses both aspects of SWB by asking people how satisfied they are with their lives and how happy they feel. Nations that score high on the first of these two questions usually score high on the second as well, but the correlation is not very strong. National differences in life satisfaction can be explained convincingly by means of differences in national wealth, but this variable has relatively little to do with the happiness item in the WVS. The countries with the highest percentages of very happy respondents are typically poor or not particularly wealthy. They are located in western Africa (Nigeria, Ghana) and in northern Latin America (Mexico, El Salvador, Colombia, Venezuela). What are we to make of this?

Disbelief is not an uncommon reaction to such findings. Not only some laypersons but also a few scholars consider the practice of measuring happiness dubious. It seems to them that this is simply something too elusive, vague, and changeable to be measured. Such views, however, are a minority in mainstream social science. Leading experts on the matter, including U.S. psychologist Ed Diener and Dutch sociologist Ruut Veenhoven, have demonstrated beyond any doubt that measuring happiness is meaningful.[4] Also, Misho has pointed out that nations with higher percentages of people who state that they are very happy have a lower incidence of deaths from cardiovascular diseases.[5] A strong correlation between the two remains even after taking into account a major factor: national differences in wealth (and hence in the quality of health care that people receive). People's reports of their personal happiness are not empty words removed from reality.

There is no shortage of theories that explain the observed national differences in happiness.[6] Many of them are based on relatively small country samples and are consequently unreliable as a general explanation. No one denies the evident fact that the determinants of happiness are numerous and that some of them may be more prominent in one society than in another. Nevertheless, that does not mean that universal trends are impossible to find.

Subjective Well-Being and the World Values Survey

In Chapters 4 and 5 we cited the dimension *well-being versus survival* in Inglehart's overall analysis of the WVS. It was associated with the combination of high individualism (IDV) and low masculinity (MAS). Although a search of the cultural determinants of happiness was not in the focus of Inglehart's interests, his dimension includes at the survival side a measure of unhappiness.[7] Other items that defined this dimension had to do with giving priority to economic and physical security over quality of life, being politically passive, rejecting homosexuality, and being very careful about trusting people. Further, the dimension was strongly correlated with a belief that men make better political leaders and that women need children to be fulfilled, an emphasis on technology, a rejection of out-group members (such as foreigners), a perception of low life control, and many more characteristics.

Inglehart's well-being versus survival dimension is statistically correct. Also, despite the mind-boggling diversity of items that define it, it is after all conceptually defendable, since everything with which it is associated seems to stem, one way or another, from national differences in wealth versus poverty. It functions well as a catchall dimension that explains the differences between rich and poor nations and indicates what cultural and social changes one might expect after a particular country has achieved economic development. However, this telescopic view leaves many salient details unexplained. In particular, it says nothing about the important question of why some poor nations have such high percentages of very happy people.[8]

Indulgence Versus Restraint as a Societal Dimension

Intrigued by Inglehart's analysis of the WVS, Misho performed his own. He discovered that Inglehart's well-being versus survival dimension can be split into two, not only conceptually but also statistically. Items that have to do with relationships between groups of people or between individuals and groups (such as agreement that men make better leaders or that a woman needs children) form the dimension that Misho called *universalism versus exclusionism*, discussed in Chapter 4 as a variant of individualism versus collectivism. Items primarily related to happiness form a separate group and a different dimension.[9] Across more than ninety countries, two WVS items in particular predicted happiness better than any other survey variables reported so far.

Misho considered these as the core of a new dimension. This is how they—and the happiness item—were formulated in the WVS:

1. **Happiness:** "Taking all things together, would you say you are very happy, quite happy, not very happy, or not at all happy." Measured was the percentage choosing "very happy."
2. **Life control:** "Some people feel they have completely free choice over their lives, while other people feel that what they do has no real effect on what happens to them. Please use this scale where 1 means 'none at all' and 10 means 'a great deal' to indicate how much freedom of choice and control you feel you have over the way your life turns out." Measured were the average national scores reported by the WVS.[10]
3. **Importance of leisure:** "For each of the following, indicate how important it is in your life: very important, rather important, not very

important, or not at all important: family, friends, leisure time, politics, work, religion, service to others." Measured was the percentage choosing "very important" for leisure time.[11]

The correlates and predictors of happiness at the national level are therefore, first, a perception of life control, a feeling that one has the liberty to live one's life more or less as one pleases, without social restrictions that curb one's freedom of choice; and second, importance of leisure as a personal value. Happiness, life control, and importance of leisure are mutually correlated, and these associations remained stable over subsequent survey waves. They thus defined a strong common dimension.

Apart from the three key items, the dimension was also positively associated with a high importance of having friends and negatively with choosing thrift as a valuable trait for children.

It follows that one of the two poles of this dimension is characterized by a perception that one can act as one pleases, spend money, and indulge in leisurely and fun-related activities with friends or alone. All this predicts relatively high happiness. At the opposite pole we find a perception that one's actions are restrained by various social norms and prohibitions and a feeling that enjoyment of leisurely activities, spending, and other similar types of indulgence are somewhat wrong. Because of these properties of the dimension, Misho has called it *indulgence versus restraint* (IVR).[12]

National scores for the dimension are listed in Table 8.1.[13]

The definition that we propose for this dimension is as follows: *Indulgence* stands for *a tendency to allow relatively free gratification of basic and natural human desires related to enjoying life and having fun*. Its opposite pole, *restraint*, reflects *a conviction that such gratification needs to be curbed and regulated by strict social norms*. As a cultural dimension, indulgence versus restraint rests on clearly defined research items that measure very specific phenomena. Note that the gratification of desires on the *indulgence* side refers to enjoying life and having fun, not to gratifying human desires in general.

This is a truly new dimension that has not been reported so far in the academic literature; it deserves more study. It somewhat resembles a distinction in U.S. anthropology between loose and tight societies. In loose societies norms are expressed with a wide range of alternative channels, and deviant behavior is easily tolerated; tight societies maintain strong values of group organization, formality, permanence, durability, and soli-

TABLE 8.1 Indulgence Versus Restraint (IVR) Index Scores for 93 Countries and Regions Based on Factor Scores from Three Items in the World Values Survey

RANK	AMERICA C/S	EUROPE S/SE	EUROPE N/NW ANGLO WORLD	EUROPE C/E EX-SOVIET	MUSLIM WORLD M.E & AFRICA	ASIA EAST ASIA SE	INDEX
1	Venezuela						100
2	Mexico						97
3	Puerto Rico						90
4	El Salvador						89
5					Nigeria		84
6	Colombia						83
7	Trinidad						80
8			Sweden				78
9			New Zealand				75
10					Ghana		72
11			Australia				71
12–13		Cyprus					70
12–13			Denmark				70
14			Great Britain				69
15–17			Canada				68
15–17			Netherlands				68
15–17			United States				68
18			Iceland				67
19–20			Switzerland				66
19–20		Malta					66
21–22		Andorra					65
21–22			Ireland				65
23–24					S Africa		63
23–24			Austria				63
25	Argentina						62

Rank	Brazil group	Finland group	Uganda group	Malaysia group	Score
26	Brazil				59
27–29		Finland			57
27–29				Malaysia	57
27–29					57
30		Belgium			56
31		Luxembourg			55
32		Norway			54
33	Dominican Rep.				53
34–35	Uruguay				52
34–35			Uganda		52
34–35			Saudi Arabia		52
36	Greece				50
37–38				Taiwan	49
37–38	Turkey				49
39–40	France				48
39–40		Slovenia			48
41–43				Singapore	46
41–43			Ethiopia		46
41–43	Peru				46
44				Thailand	45
45–46	Spain				44
45–46		Bosnia			44
47–48			Jordan		43
47–48			Mali		43
49–51				Philippines	42
49–51				Japan	42
49–51			Zambia		42
52–53	Germany				40
52–53			Iran		40
54		Kyrgyzstan			39
55–56			Tanzania		38
55–56				Indonesia	38

continued

TABLE 8.1 Indulgence Versus Restraint (IVR) Index Scores for 93 Countries and Regions Based on Factor Scores from Three Items in the World Values Survey, *continued*

RANK	AMERICA C/S	EUROPE S/SE	EUROPE N/NW ANGLO WORLD	EUROPE C/E EX-SOVIET	MUSLIM WORLD M.E & AFRICA	ASIA EAST ASIA SE	INDEX
57					Rwanda		37
58–59						Vietnam	35
58–59				Macedonia			35
60			Germany E				34
61–62		Portugal					33
61–62				Croatia			33
63–64					Algeria		32
63–64				Georgia			32
65				Hungary			31
66		Italy					30
67–69						S Korea	29
67–69				Czech Rep.			29
67–69				Poland			29
70–72				Slovakia			28
70–72				Serbia			28
70–72					Zimbabwe		28
73						India	26
74						China	25
75					Morocco		24
76				Azerbaijan			22
77–80				Russia			20
77–80				Montenegro			20
77–80				Romania			20
77–80						Bangladesh	20
81				Moldova			19

82	Burkina Faso	18
83–84	Hong Kong	17
83–84	Iraq	17
85–87	Estonia	16
85–87	Bulgaria	16
85–87	Lithuania	16
88–89	Belarus	15
88–89	Albania	15
90	Ukraine	14
91	Latvia	13
92	Egypt	4
93	Pakistan	0

darity.[14] In Geert's earlier publications, this distinction was conceptually associated with *uncertainty avoidance*, but he did not find objective ways of measuring it.[15]

The indulgence versus restraint dimension solves the paradox of the poor Filipinas who are happier than the rich citizens of Hong Kong. The Philippines in Table 8.1 can be seen to rank higher on *indulgence* than Hong Kong, but still a lot lower than societies in northern Latin America or some western African nations.

The correlations of IVR with the IBM dimensions described in this book are as follows: IVR shows a weak negative correlation with *power distance* (PDI), indicating a slight tendency for more hierarchical societies to be less indulgent. It is not correlated with the other IBM dimensions, nor with long-term orientation as measured with the Chinese Values Survey (LTO-CVS).[16]

The relationship of IVR with LTO-WVS is shown in Figure 8.1, which crosses the two dimensions among ninety common countries. The overall correlation is significantly negative.[17] This is to be expected, in view of the lack of support in indulgent societies for thrift as a desirable trait in children. However, the common variance of LTO-WVS and IVR is just 20 percent, much less than, for example, the 35 percent shared variance of two other established dimensions, PDI and IDV.

The quadrants of the diagram show a clear regional pattern. The relatively rare combination of high indulgence plus long-term orientation groups nine European Union member countries plus Switzerland, Taiwan, and Singapore. The most common pattern—high indulgence plus short-term orientation—groups twelve Latin American countries, four African countries, four Anglo countries, five northern European countries, four southern European countries, and two Southeast Asian countries. The next most common pattern—restraint plus long-term orientation—groups nine East and South Asian countries, nineteen Eastern European countries, and a few others. The rarer combination of restraint plus short-term orientation is found in five Muslim countries, six black African countries, and a few others.

Statistically, there is a positive relationship between indulgence and national wealth, significant but weak.[18] National wealth explains about 10 percent of country differences in indulgence. Restraint is somewhat more likely under poverty, which makes sense.

FIGURE 8.1 Indulgence Versus Long-Term Orientation (LTO-WVS)

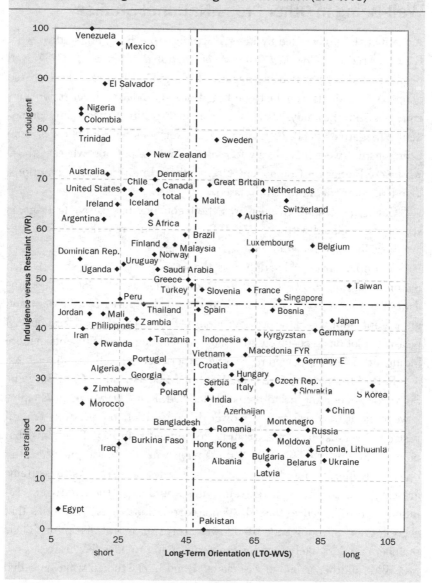

Indulgence Versus Restraint and Subjective Well-Being in Other Cross-National Studies

A team of researchers led by Peter Kuppens, from Belgium, studied what they referred to as *recalled frequency of emotional experience* (or how well people remember positive and negative feelings).[19] Their sample consisted of 9,300 individuals from forty-eight nations. Two nation-level dimensions emerged from the study, labeled Component 1 (positive affect) and Component 2 (negative affect). Participants from societies with higher scores on Component 1 were more likely to recall positive emotions, whereas those who were higher on Component 2 remembered more negative emotions. The two components were unrelated.

Component 1, which measures the frequency of positive feelings, is strongly correlated with our IVR.[20] People from more indulgent societies are more likely to remember positive emotions.

A similar large-scale study was reported by U.S. researchers Ulrich Schimmack, Shigeiro Oishi, and Ed Diener. They asked 6,780 college students from forty countries how often they had experienced pleasant and unpleasant emotions in the previous month. The reported mean frequency of pleasant emotions is positively correlated with indulgence.[21] Students in more indulgent societies reported more often experiencing positive emotions.

IVR did not relate to LTO-CVS, but Michael Bond's Chinese Value Survey reported another dimension, labeled *moral discipline*; in Chapter 3 we found it to correlate with power distance. Its two poles were "moral restraint" versus "lack of a strongly disciplined stance."[22] The items that defined the positive pole of this dimension were "moderation," "keeping oneself disinterested and pure," and "having few desires." As these items are easy to associate with restraint, one would expect a negative correlation with indulgence. Indeed, such a correlation exists.[23] Societies that score higher on indulgence have lower scores on moral discipline. Their members are less likely to value moderation and to have few desires.

With another group of associates, Bond later studied what he called *social axioms* in the general beliefs of 7,672 students from forty-one societies.[24] The researchers obtained two cultural dimensions, one of which they labeled *societal cynicism*. It implies agreement with statements such as "To care about societal affairs only brings trouble to yourself," "Kindhearted people usually suffer losses," "Old people are usually stubborn and biased," and "People will stop working after they secure a comfortable life." It also reflects a view that powerful people are arrogant exploiters of less powerful individuals. According to the available data, societal cynicism is strongest in Eastern Europe, East Asia (Korea, Taiwan), Pakistan, and Thailand. It is weakest in Norway, the United States, and Canada. Societal cynicism is significantly and negatively correlated with IVR.[25] This suggests that members of less indulgent and more restrained societies tend to have a more cynical outlook. Societal restriction not only makes people less happy but also seems to foster various forms of negativism. Cynicism is only one of them. Other forms will be discussed in the following sections.

Finally, indulgence is correlated with national norms for two of the five personality dimensions in the Big Five model of personality traits, described in Chapter 2 and referred to in several other chapters: positively with *extraversion* and negatively with *neuroticism*.[26] Since extraversion is associated with positive affect, whereas neuroticism reflects a tendency to experience negative feelings, this finding is consistent with the nature of the indulgence versus restraint dimension. Indulgent societies are likely to host more extroverted individuals and fewer persons manifesting neuroticism.

Indulgence Versus Restraint, Subjective Health, Optimism, and Birthrates

Societies with higher scores on indulgence have higher percentages of respondents who in the WVS described their personal health as "very good." This correlation is especially high across the wealthy countries.[27]

The Pew Research Center, a public opinion survey agency located in the United States, collects data from some fifty countries, using mostly nationally representative samples. One of the questions in its cross-national surveys asks respondents how optimistic they are about the future. The percentages of respondents who expressed high optimism are significantly correlated with the indulgence scores.[28] More indulgent societies have more optimistic people, and vice versa.

Happiness, subjective health, and optimism about the future all play a role in the number of children born in a society.

Evidence of a relationship among wealth, cultural femininity, and number of children was reported in Chapter 5. Education level has an influence as well: less educated populations tend to have more children. Across twenty-eight wealthy countries (those that had a GNI per capita of more than 10,000 U.S. dollars in 1999), indulgence versus restraint is the main significant predictor of birthrates, explaining more than education level or national wealth.[29] Populations that do not feel very happy and healthy are not very excited about having children, especially if they reflect the education level that is typical of an economically developed country.

We mentioned already that higher indulgence is associated with lower death rates from cardiovascular diseases even after controlling for national differences in wealth.[30] This association proves that the higher subjective well-being that indulgence represents is actually not so subjective. More restrained societies have some tangible health problems that are not the product of people's imaginations. Cardiovascular disease is a complex phenomenon with multiple causes at the individual level, but it seems that unhappiness can be one of them.

National governments of low-fertility countries are usually concerned about raising birthrates, but they have few tools to achieve this goal. Apart from lowering education levels, which is hardly a choice, their only option is to increase the level of happiness in the country, which would enhance subjective health and optimism. Unfortunately, there is no known method for boosting the percentage of happy people in a given nation. It may seem that economic development should have such an effect. However, this process may take a long time. Between 1998 and 2008 almost all countries in the European part of the former Soviet Union, as well as Bulgaria and Romania, doubled their GNI per capita. Still, the dismally low happiness levels that characterized them at the outset of the period remained virtually unchanged a decade later. And the demographic crisis that is devastating all of them continued.

Table 8.2 summarizes the differences between indulgent and restrained societies discussed so far.

Indulgence Versus Restraint, Importance of Friends, and Consumer Attitudes

In Chapter 4 we saw that having a "close, intimate friend" is a value that is more likely to be selected by respondents in individualist societies. But what about the importance of friends in general? If indulgence stands for a

TABLE 8.2 **Key Differences Between Indulgent and Restrained Societies I: General Norm, Personal Feelings, and Health**

INDULGENT	RESTRAINED
Higher percentages of very happy people	Lower percentages of very happy people
A perception of personal life control	A perception of helplessness: what happens to me is not my own doing.
Higher importance of leisure	Lower importance of leisure
Higher importance of having friends	Lower importance of having friends
Thrift is not very important.	Thrift is important.
Loose society	Tight society
More likely to remember positive emotions	Less likely to remember positive emotions
Less moral discipline	Moral discipline
Positive attitude	Cynicism
More extroverted personalities	More neurotic personalities
Higher percentages of people who feel healthy	Lower percentages of people who feel healthy
Higher optimism	More pessimism
In countries with well-educated populations, higher birthrates	In countries with well-educated populations, lower birthrates
Lower death rates from cardiovascular diseases	Higher death rates from cardiovascular diseases

propensity to enjoy life, friends should have a higher importance in indulgent societies, since one of the functions of friends is to provide fun and entertainment.

The WVS provides an opportunity to test this hypothesis. One item asks respondents how important friends are in their lives. The percentages of respondents who answered "very important" are positively correlated with IVR. This is consistent with the finding that indulgent cultures are characterized by greater extraversion—a personal-level measurement of sociability and fun-orientation.

The Pew Research Center in its 2002–03 surveys asked respondents whether foreign movies and music are a good thing. The percentages of respondents who chose the "very good" option are positively correlated with indulgence. More indulgent societies have higher percentages of people who fully approve of some imports of entertainment, such as music and films. These percentages range from 68 (highest approval) in Nigeria to 11 (lowest approval) in Pakistan. They are completely uncorrelated with WVS measures of religiousness or patriotism, so the observed differences in acceptance of foreign music and films cannot be explained in those terms.

Dutch marketing expert Marieke de Mooij correlated IVR scores with recent Eurobarometer and other consumer-related data. Among the twenty-seven European Union countries covered by the Eurobarometer, IVR separates most Western member states (more indulgent) from most Eastern ones (more restrained). De Mooij found a number of significant correlations. In more indulgent societies people report more satisfaction with their family life; they more often consider unequal sharing of house-hold tasks between partners a problem.[31] They are more frequently (at least once a week) actively involved in sports.[32] They more often exchange e-mails with family, friends, and colleagues, and they report more Internet and e-mail contacts with foreigners.[33] They also consume less fish and more soft drinks and beer.[34]

The World Health Organization provides obesity data on men and women for most countries in the world. There is not much sense in com-paring obesity rates across countries in which many people may suffer from undernourishment, so those countries are excluded from this analysis. Across twenty-six wealthy countries for which data are available, and after controlling for GNI at purchasing power parity, indulgence is positively correlated with obesity.[35] Although many influences play a part, it appears that when affordability is not an issue, more indulgent societies will be more inclined toward unrestrained consumption of so-called junk foods that can result in obesity.

We also correlated IVR with the national culture dimensions in the GLOBE project. Across forty-nine common countries, IVR was signifi-cantly correlated with five of GLOBE's eighteen measures. The strongest correlation of indulgence was with *gender egalitarianism* "should be" (there was no correlation with *gender egalitarianism* "as is").[36] Strictly prescribed gender role differences belong to restrained societies. Next, indulgence correlated negatively with *in-group collectivism* "as is" and positively with *in-group collectivism* "should be."[37] Restrained societies report more in-group collectivism and are less happy with it. The remaining correlations are with *performance orientation* "should be" (positive) and with *assertiveness* "should be" (negative).[38] The indulgent society wants performance without assertive behavior.

Indulgence Versus Restraint and Sexual Relationships

U.S. psychologist David Schmitt founded the International Sexuality Description Project and coordinated a number of interesting cross-kcultural studies under its umbrella. One of them focused on what he called *sociosexuality.* According to Schmitt, this is a single strategic dimension of human mating:[39]

> *Those who are relatively low on this dimension are said to possess a restricted sociosexual orientation—they tend toward monogamy, prolonged court-ship, and heavy emotional investment in long-term relationships. Those residing at the high end of sociosexuality are considered more unrestricted in mating orientation, they tend toward promiscuity, are quick to have sex, and experience lower levels of romantic relationship closeness.*

The findings of Schmitt and his team show that self-reported female socio-sexuality is strongly positively correlated with individualism/universalism (and strongly negatively with collectivism/exclusionism). This could mean that women in Western countries are more liberated sexually, but a parallel interpretation, which does not preclude the first one, is that women in collectivist countries are more inhibited when discussing their sexuality. It is interesting that the reported *male* sociosexuality differences do not correlate significantly with individualism and exclusionism. Men, all over the world, are probably less reluctant to talk about sex, and in many cultures they are actually inclined to boast about their exploits—be they real or imaginary.

This means that conclusions about national differences in sociosexuality on the basis of self-reports should be guarded. However, across wealthy countries, in which sex is less likely to be a taboo subject, respondents can be expected to be somewhat sincere about it, at least in anonymous surveys. Results from paper-and-pencil studies are therefore probably more reliable. All told, differences in individualism (and hence in the degree to which respondents are inclined to be outspoken) and in masculinity, with its taboos, may still contribute to differences in self-reported sociosexuality. Nevertheless, across twenty-one wealthy countries, national sociosexuality scores for men as well as for women correlated positively with indulgence.[40] This correlation suggests another facet of the indulgence versus restraint dimension: members of more indulgent societies, especially wealthy ones, are more likely to report greater sociosexuality. It is presumable that these reports reflect real behavior, although this point merits more research.

One item in the WVS asks respondents (only European samples) what they think of casual sex. The national percentages of those choosing position 10 (always acceptable) correlate positively with indulgence.[41] In this case the question is formulated as a norm; the respondents do not necessarily talk about themselves but rather refer to the behavior that they wish to prescribe to others. Therefore, the results are more reliable. More indulgent societies have higher percentages of people who have nothing against lax norms concerning casual sex.

Indulgence Versus Restraint in the Workplace

Russian management professor and cross-cultural expert Sergey Myasoedov is known across Eastern European business schools for his colorful narratives that illustrate cultural conflicts between American expatriate managers and local employees or customers. He noticed that American front-desk personnel are required to smile at the customers. This practice seems normal in a generally indulgent and happy culture such as that of the United States. But when a company—in the present case, McDonald's—tries to mimic its American practices in a highly restrained society, there may be unexpected consequences:

> *When they came to Russia, they brought their very strong corporate culture. They decided to train the Russian sales boys and girls. They wanted to get them to smile in the McDonald's way that makes one display all thirty-two teeth. Yet, sometime later, the McDonald's experts found out that Russian customers were shocked by those broad smiles. They stared in amazement at the sales personnel: "Why are you grinning at me?" They did their research and found that a broad smile at a stranger does not work in Russia. The Russians never smile like that when they run across a stranger. When somebody does that to a Russian, the likely reaction is "What is wrong with this person?"[42]*

These differences also translate into norms for the public image of political leaders. In the United States, maintaining a poker face would be a virtual death sentence for a political candidate or a holder of a high-ranking political office. American public figures are expected to exude joy and optimism even if they are privately worried about the way their political careers are going. Over in Russia, a stern face is a sign of seriousness, and it only seems to bolster the high rating that Vladimir Putin has always enjoyed.

Geert postulates that indulgence also explains the norm of smiling in photographs ("say cheese"). His Eastern European friends lack this habit.[43]

Indulgence Versus Restraint and the State

One item in the WVS waves from 1995 to 2004 asks respondents to choose the most important of four national goals: maintaining order in the nation, giving people more say, fighting rising prices, and protecting freedom of speech.[44] The percentages of respondents choosing "maintaining order in the nation" as a first goal correlate negatively with indulgence;[45] hence, they correlate positively with restraint as a cultural trait. People in more restrained societies are more likely to see the maintenance of order (whatever they understand by that) as an important national goal superseding other goals.

In the WVS there is an even stronger correlation between indulgence and choosing freedom of speech as the most important national goal.[46] This is a key finding for Western politicians and journalists, many of whom have trouble understanding the fact that people in quite a few nations do not prioritize their national goals in the way the Americans or Dutch do. Freedom of speech may be a prominent goal in an indulgent Western society, but in a restrained one it may be downplayed, especially if people have to make more compelling choices. Percentages of respondents who chose freedom of speech as the first national goal range from 36.6 in the Netherlands to 1.5—the lowest in the world—in Russia. Russians, as well as other Eastern Europeans, give low priority to a number of human rights that citizens of rich Western countries consider very important. This finding explains why such a high percentage of Russians do not mind being governed by autocrats: in a restrained society with large power distance, authoritarian rule can be well accepted. It also explains why many citizens of Russia who have lived abroad and are familiar with life in the West are far from being impressed with the freedoms that they have witnessed. Commenting on the strong-arm tactics of the Kremlin, they insist it is a good thing to have a strong government; otherwise, there would be chaos, and that is the last thing the country needs.

The same conclusion emerges from 2008 Eurobarometer data. Across twenty-six European countries, the percentage of respondents choosing "freedom of speech" as a goal to be pursued for the future is strongly correlated with indulgence. The same holds for the percentage who select "democracy" as most important in connection with their idea of happiness.[47]

In the preceding chapters the occurrences of freedom of expression and of democratic government in a country have been shown to be related to people's values in the fields of power distance, individualism, and uncertainty avoidance. The correlations with IVR show another influence on how people in a country feel about the related political ideals.

Not only does the indulgence index predict attitudes toward national governance in paper-and-pencil studies, but also it is de facto negatively correlated with the number of police officers per 100,000 people across forty-one countries for which data are available.[48] Societies that are more restrained are more serious about their restrictiveness—they have more police officers per capita.

Table 8.3 completes the key differences between indulgent and restrained societies described in this chapter.

Origins of Societal Differences in Indulgence Versus Restraint

As in the case of most other cultural dimensions, it is hard to explain with certainty what historical processes have created the differences in indulgence versus restraint that we observe today. One possible explanation was offered by Misho in an article for the anthropological Sage journal *Cross-Cultural Research* as well as in his previous publications.[49] He argues that indulgent societies do not have a millennia-old history of Eurasian intensive agriculture stretching all the way to the present.

Traditionally, intensive agriculture was never practiced in sub-Saharan Africa. Some forms of such agriculture existed in some places in the Americas, but just as in Africa, no draught animals were available there, which was a severe impediment to its development. As for the Scandinavian and English-speaking countries, the cultural legacy of traditional intensive agriculture has long since been overcome. Highly intensive agriculture of the Eurasian type brought innumerable calamities upon those who practiced it: strenuous work, alternating periods of food abundance

TABLE 8.3 **Key Differences Between Indulgent and Restrained Societies II: Private Life, Consumer Behavior, Sex, and Politics**

INDULGENT	RESTRAINED
Higher approval of foreign music and films	Lower approval of foreign music and films
More satisfying family life	Less satisfied with family life
Household tasks should be shared between partners.	Unequal sharing of household tasks is no problem.
People are actively involved in sports.	People are rarely involved in sports.
E-mail and the Internet are used for private contacts.	Less use of e-mail and the Internet for private contacts
More e-mail and Internet contacts with foreigners	Fewer e-mail and Internet contacts with foreigners
Less consumption of fish	More consumption of fish
More consumption of soft drinks and beer	Less consumption of soft drinks and beer
In wealthy countries, higher percentages of obese people	In wealthy countries, lower percentages of obese people
Loosely prescribed gender roles	Strictly prescribed gender roles
In wealthy countries, less strict sexual norms	In wealthy countries, stricter sexual norms
Smiling as a norm	Smiling as suspect
Freedom of speech is viewed as relatively important.	Freedom of speech is not a primary concern.
Maintaining order in the nation is not given a high priority.	Maintaining order in the nation is considered a high priority.
Lower numbers of police officers per 100,000 population	Higher numbers of police officers per 100,000 population

and starvation, oppressive states and exploitation, devastating epidemics, and never-ending wars for territory. It is not unreasonable then that the Eurasian societies of intensive agriculturalists have generated philosophies such as Buddhism, according to which all life is suffering and the pursuit of happiness is a waste of time, or the three great Middle Eastern religions—Judaism, Christianity, and Islam—which teach that real bliss is achievable only in the hereafter.

Societies of hunter-gatherers and horticulturalists were not burdened by the evils of intensive agriculture to the same extent, which may partly explain their stronger sense of freedom and happiness. As U.S. experts in SWB Ed Diener and William Tov indicate, research among Inuit and Masai populations revealed that these people are about as happy as the richest Americans.[50] Further, intensive agriculture requires a restrained discipline, planning and saving for the future, indifference to leisure, and tight social management, conditions that are neither necessary nor possible to the same degree in a society of hunter-gatherers or horticulturalists.

Highly advanced modern societies with service-based economies seem to be reverting to the more indulgent culture of the distant past, before the advent of intensive agriculture.

CULTURES IN ORGANIZATIONS

Pyramids, Machines, Markets, and Families: Organizing Across Nations

S omewhere in Western Europe a middle-sized textile printing company struggled for survival. Cloth, usually imported from Asian
countries, was printed in multicolored patterns according to the desires
of customers, firms producing fashion clothing for the local market. The
company was run by a general manager, to whom three functional managers reported: one for design and sales, one for manufacturing, and one
for finance and personnel. The total workforce numbered about 250.

The working climate in the firm was often disturbed by conflicts
between the sales manager and the manufacturing manager. The manufacturing manager had an interest, as manufacturing managers have
the world over, in maintaining a smooth production process with minimal product changes. He preferred grouping customer orders into large
batches. Changing colors and/or designs involved cleaning the machines,
which cut into productive time and also wasted costly dyestuffs. The worst
was changing from a dark color set into a light one, because every bit of
dark-colored dye left would show on the cloth and spoil the product quality.
Therefore, the manufacturing planners tried to start on a clean machine

with the lightest shades and gradually move toward darker ones, postponing the need for an overall cleaning round as long as possible.

The design and sales manager tried to satisfy his customers in a highly competitive market. These fashion clothing firms were notorious for short-term planning changes. As their supplier, the printing company often got requests for rush orders. Even when these orders were small and unlikely to be profitable, the sales manager hated to say no; the customer might go to a competitor, and then the printing firm would miss out on that big order that the sales manager was sure would come afterward. The rush orders, however, usually upset the manufacturing manager's schedules and forced him to print short runs of dark color sets on a beautifully clean machine, thus forcing the production operators to start cleaning all over again.

There were frequent disagreements between the two managers over whether a certain rush order should or should not be taken into production. The conflict was not limited to the department heads: production personnel publicly expressed doubts about the competence of the salespeople, and vice versa. In the cafeteria the production workers and salespeople would not sit together, although they had known each other for years.

Implicit Models of Organizations

This story describes a banal problem of a kind that occurs regularly in all types of organizations. As with most other organization problems, it has both structural and human aspects. The people involved react according to their mental software. Part of this mental software consists of people's ideas about what an organization should be like.

From the dimensions of national culture described in Chapters 3 through 6, power distance and uncertainty avoidance in particular affect our thinking about organizations. Organizing always requires answering two questions: (1) who has the power to decide what? and (2) what rules or procedures will be followed to attain the desired ends? The answer to the first question is influenced by cultural norms of power distance; the answer to the second question, by cultural norms about uncertainty avoidance. The remaining two dimensions, individualism and masculinity, affect our thinking about people in organizations, rather than about organizations themselves.

Power distance (PDI) and uncertainty avoidance (UAI) have been plotted against each other in Figure 9.1, and if the preceding analysis is correct, the position of a country in this diagram should tell us something about the country's way of solving organizational problems.

There is empirical evidence for the relationship between a country's position within the PDI-UAI matrix and models of organizations implicit in the minds of people from those countries that affect the way problems are tackled. In the 1970s Owen James Stevens, an American professor at INSEAD business school in Fontainebleau, France, used as an examination assignment for his organizational behavior course a case study very

FIGURE 9.1 Power Distance Versus Uncertainty Avoidance

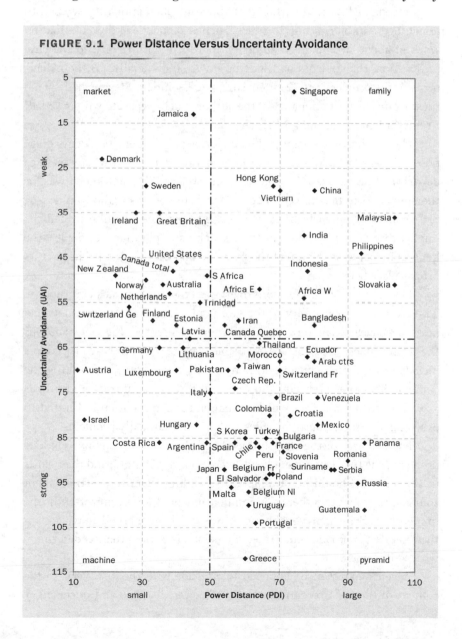

similar to the one presented at the beginning of this chapter. This case, too, dealt with a conflict between two department heads within a company. Among the INSEAD M.B.A. (master of business administration) students taking the exam, the three largest national contingents were the French, the Germans, and the British. In Figure 9.1 we find their countries in the lower right, lower left, and upper left quadrants, respectively.

Stevens had noticed earlier that the students' nationality seemed to affect their way of handling this case. He had kept a file of the examination work of about two hundred students, in which, with regard to the case in question, the students had written down, individually, (1) their diagnosis of the problem and (2) their suggested solution. Stevens had sorted these exams by the nationality of the author, and he separately reviewed all French, all German, and all British answers.

The results were striking. The majority of the French students diagnosed the case as negligence by the general manager to whom the two department heads reported. The solution preferred by the French was for the opponents to take the conflict to their common boss, who would issue orders for settling such dilemmas in the future. Stevens interpreted the implicit organization model of the French as a "pyramid of people": the general manager at the top of the pyramid and each successive level at its proper place below.

The majority of the Germans diagnosed the case as a lack of structure. The scope of responsibility of the two conflicting department heads had never been clearly laid down. The solution preferred by the Germans was the establishment of procedures. Possible ways to develop these procedures included calling in a consultant, nominating a task force, and asking the common boss. The Germans, Stevens felt, saw an organization ideally as a "well-oiled machine" in which management intervention is limited to exceptional cases because the rules should settle all daily problems.

The majority of the British diagnosed the case as a human relations problem. The two department heads were poor negotiators, and their skills in this respect should be developed by sending them to a management course, preferably together. The implicit model of an organization in the minds of the British, Stevens thought, was a "village market" in which neither hierarchy nor rules but rather the demands of the situation determine what will happen.

Stevens's experience happened to coincide with the discovery, in the context of the IBM research project, of power distance and uncertainty avoidance as dimensions of country cultures. These two dimensions resembled those found a few years earlier through a piece of academic research commonly known as the Aston Studies. From 1961 through 1973 the University of Aston, in Birmingham, England, hosted an Industrial Administration Research Unit. Among the researchers involved were Derek Pugh, David Hickson, and John Child.[1] The Aston Studies represented a large-scale attempt to assess quantitatively—that is, to measure—key aspects of the structure of different organizations. At first the research was limited to the United Kingdom, but later on it was replicated in a number of other countries. The principal conclusion from the Aston Studies was that the two major dimensions along which structures of organizations differ are concentration of authority and structuring of activities. It did not take much imagination to associate the first with power distance and the second with uncertainty avoidance.

The Aston researchers had tried to measure the "hard" aspects of organization structure: *objectively* assessable characteristics. Power-distance and uncertainty-avoidance indexes measure soft, *subjective* characteristics of the people within a country. A link between the two would mean that organizations are structured in order to meet the subjective cultural needs of their members. Stevens's implicit models of organization in fact provided the proof. French INSEAD M.B.A. students with their "pyramid of people" model, coming from a country with large power distance *and* strong uncertainty avoidance, advocated measures to concentrate the authority *and* structure the activities. Germans with their "well-oiled machine" model, coming from a country with strong uncertainty avoidance but small power distance, wanted to structure the activities *without* concentrating the authority. British INSEAD M.B.A. students with a "village market" model, and with a national culture characterized by small power distance and weak uncertainty avoidance, advocated neither concentrating authority nor structuring activities. And all of them were dealing with the same case study. People with international business experience have confirmed many times over that, other things being equal, French organizations *do* concentrate authority more, German ones *do* need more structure, and people in British ones *do* believe more in resolving problems ad hoc.

Stevens's three implicit models leave one quadrant in Figure 9.1 unexplained. The upper right-hand corner contains no European countries, only Asian and African ones, and, just in the corner, the French-speaking part of Canada. People from these countries at that time were rare at INSEAD, so that there were insufficient data from this group. A discussion of Stevens's models with Indian and Indonesian colleagues led to the suggestion that the equivalent implicit model of an organization in these countries is the (extended) "family," in which the owner-manager is the almighty (grand)father. It corresponds to large power distance but weak uncertainty avoidance, a situation in which people would resolve the conflict we pictured by permanent referral to the boss: concentration of authority without structuring of activities. Anant Negandhi and S. Benjamin Prasad, two Americans originally from India, quoted a senior Indian executive with a Ph.D. from a prestigious American university:

> *What is most important for me and my department is not what I do or achieve for the company, but whether the Master's favor is bestowed on me. . . . This I have achieved by saying "yes" to everything the Master says or does. . . . To contradict him is to look for another job. . . . I left my freedom of thought in Boston.*[2]

More recently, psychologist Jan Pieter van Oudenhoven, of Holland, collected spontaneous descriptions of local organizations from more than seven hundred business administration students in ten countries.[3] The students were asked to describe a company they knew well in a number of freely chosen adjectives. The seven hundred stories were content analyzed, and the adjectives used were combined into opposing pairs. One pair was bureaucratic versus nonbureaucratic, and the frequency of "bureaucratic" correlated with the countries' power distance and uncertainty avoidance. Another pair was teamwork versus individual work, and the frequency of "individual work" correlated with individualism. A third was friendly versus hostile work ambiance, and the frequency of "hostile work ambiance" correlated with masculinity.[4] So, the way these students described organizations in their respective countries reflected aspects of their national culture.

A network of political scientists coordinated by Poul Erik Mouritzen, of Denmark, and James Svara, of the United States, studied local government administration in more than four thousand municipalities covering fourteen Western democracies. Among other things, they collected scores on national cultures, through survey answers by the top civil servant in each municipal administration. Their study is one of the larger replications of the IBM survey (see Table 2.1). They distinguished four ways in which local government was organized, dividing roles between elected political leaders and appointed civil servants:

1. The *strong-mayor form*, in which an elected mayor controls the majority of the city council and is in charge of all executive functions. The top civil servant serves at the mayor's will. This form was found in France, Italy, Portugal, and Spain, as well as in major cities in the United States.
2. The *council-manager form*, in which all executive functions are in the hands of the top civil servant, who is appointed by an elected council that has responsibility for setting policies but not for their execution. This form was found in Australia, Finland, Ireland, and Norway and in the smaller municipalities in the United States.
3. The *committee-leader form*, in which the executive functions are shared by standing committees composed of elected politicians, the political leader (with or without the title of mayor), and the top civil servant. This form was found in Denmark, Sweden, and the United Kingdom.
4. The *collective form*, in which all executive functions are in the hands of an executive committee of elected politicians presided over by an appointed mayor, to whom the top civil servant reports. This form was found in Belgium and the Netherlands.[5]

The researchers relate these forms to the national cultural dimensions of power distance and uncertainty avoidance, as measured by the top civil servant's answers on the culture survey. These measures were significantly correlated with, but not identical with, those found in the IBM studies. On this basis and within this group of fourteen countries, the strong-mayor form was found where uncertainty avoidance was relatively strong. The council-manager form was found where uncertainty avoidance was relatively weak and power distance medium. The committee-leader form was found where uncertainty avoidance was relatively weak and power distance small.[6]

Management Professors Are Human

Not only organizations are culture bound; theories about organizations are equally culture bound. The professors who wrote the theories are children of a culture; they grew up in families, went to schools, worked for employers. Their experiences represent the material on which their thinking and writing have been based. Scholars are as human and as culturally biased as other mortals.

For each of the four corners of Figure 9.1, we selected a classical author who described organizations in terms of the model belonging to his corner of the diagram: the pyramid, the machine, the market, or the family. The four are approximate contemporaries; all were born in the mid-nineteenth century.

Henri Fayol (1841–1925) was a French engineer whose management career culminated in the position of *président-directeur-général* of a mining company. After his retirement he formulated his experiences in a groundbreaking text on organization: *Administration industrielle et générale* (1916). On the issue of the exercise of authority, Fayol wrote:

> *We distinguish in a manager his statutory authority which is in the office, and his personal authority which consists of his intelligence, his knowledge, his experience, his moral value, his leadership, his service record, etc. For a good manager, personal authority is the indispensable complement to statutory authority.*[7]

In Fayol's conception the authority is both in the person *and* in the rules (the statute). We recognize the model of the organization as a pyramid of people with both personal power *and* formal rules as principles of coordination.

Max Weber (1864–1920) was a German academic with university training in law and some years' experience as a civil servant. He became a professor of economics and a founder of German sociology. Weber quotes a seventeenth-century Puritan Protestant Christian textbook about "the sinfulness of the belief in authority, which is only permissible in the form of an impersonal authority."[8] In his own design for an organization, Weber describes the *bureaucracy*. The word was originally a joke, a classic Greek ending grafted on a modern French stem. Nowadays it has a distinctly negative connotation, but to Weber it represented the ideal type for any large organization. About the authority in a bureaucracy, Weber wrote:

> *The authority to give the commands required for the discharge of (the assigned) duties should be exercised in a stable way. It is strictly delimited by rules concerning the coercive means . . . which may be placed at the disposal of officials.*[9]

In Weber's conception the real authority is in the rules. The power of the "officials" is strictly delimited by these rules. We recognize the model of the organization as a well-oiled machine that runs according to the rules.

Frederick Winslow Taylor (1857–1915) was an American engineer who, contrary to Fayol, had started his career in industry as a worker. He attained his academic qualifications through evening studies. From chief engineer in a steel company, he became one of the first management consultants. Taylor was not really concerned with the issue of authority at all; his focus was on efficiency. He proposed splitting the task of the first-line boss into eight specialisms, each exercised by a different person. Thus, each worker would have eight bosses, each with a different responsibility. This part of Taylor's ideas was never completely implemented, although we find elements of it in the modern *matrix organization,* in which an employee has two (or even three) bosses, usually one concerned with productivity and one with technical expertise.

Taylor's book *Shop Management* (1903) appeared in a French translation in 1913, and Fayol read it and devoted six full pages of his own 1916 book to Taylor's ideas. Fayol shows himself generally impressed but shocked by Taylor's "denial of the principle of the Unity of Command" in the case of the eight-boss system. "For my part," Fayol writes, "I do not believe that a department could operate in flagrant violation of the Unity of Command principle. Still, Taylor has been a successful manager of large organizations. How can we explain this contradiction?"[10] Fayol's rhetorical question had been answered by his compatriot Blaise Pascal two and a half centuries before: there are truths in one country that are falsehoods in another.

In a 1981 article André Laurent, another of Fayol's compatriots, demonstrated that French managers in a survey reacted very strongly against a suggestion that one employee could report to two different bosses, while Swedish and U.S. managers, among others, in the same survey showed fewer misgivings in this respect.[11] Matrix organization has never become as popular in France as it has in the United States. It is amusing to read Laurent's suggestion that in order to make matrix organizations acceptable in France, they should be translated into hierarchical terms—that is, one real boss plus one or more staff experts. Exactly the same solution was put forward by Fayol in his 1916 discussion of the Taylor system; in fact, Fayol writes that he supposes this is how the Taylor system really worked in Taylor's companies.

Whereas Taylor dealt only implicitly with the exercise of authority in organizations, another American pioneer of organization theory, Mary Parker Follett (1868–1933), did address the issue squarely. She wrote:

> *How can we avoid the two extremes: too great bossism in giving orders, and practically no orders given? . . . My solution is to depersonalize the giving of orders, to unite all concerned in a study of the situation, to discover the law of the situation and to obey that. . . . One person should not give orders to another person, but both should agree to take their orders from the situation.*[12]

In the conception of Taylor and Follett, the authority is neither in the person nor in the rules but rather, as Follett puts it, in the situation. We recognize the model of the organization as a market, in which market conditions dictate what will happen.

Sun Yat-sen (1867–1925), from China, was a scholar from the fourth corner of the power distance–uncertainty avoidance diagram. He received a Western education in Hawaii and Hong Kong and became a political revolutionary. As China started industrialization much later than the West, there is no indigenous theorist of industrial organization contemporary with Fayol, Weber, and Taylor. However, Sun was concerned with organization, albeit political. He wanted to replace the ailing government of the Manchu emperors by a modern Chinese state. He eventually became, for a short period, nominally the first president of the Chinese Republic. Sun's design for a Chinese form of government represents an integration of Western and traditional Chinese elements. From the West, he introduced Montesquieu's *trias politica*: the executive, legislative, and judicial branches. Unlike in the West, though, all three are placed under the authority of the president. Two more branches are added, both derived from Chinese tradition—the examination branch (determining access to the civil service) and the control branch, supposed to audit the government—bringing the total up to five.[13]

This remarkable mix of two systems is formally the basis of the present government structure of Taiwan, which has inherited Sun's ideas through the Kuomintang party. It stresses the authority of the president (large power distance): the legislative and judicial powers, which in the West are meant to guarantee government by law, are made dependent on the ruler and paralleled by the examination and control powers, which are based on government of man (weak uncertainty avoidance). It is the family model, with the ruler as the country's father and with whatever structure there is based on personal relationships.

Paradoxically, in the other China (which expelled the Kuomintang), the People's Republic, the 1966–76 Cultural Revolution experiment can also be interpreted as an attempt to maintain the authority of the ruler (in this case Chairman Mao Zedong, 1893–1976) while rejecting the authority of the rules, which were felt to suffocate the modernization of the minds. The Cultural Revolution is now publicly recognized as a disaster. What passed for modernization may in fact have been a revival of centuries-old unconscious fears.

In the previous paragraphs the models of organization in different cultures have been related to the theories of the founding fathers (including one founding mother) of organization theory. The different models can also be recognized in more recent theories.

In the United States in the 1970s and '80s, it became fashionable to look at organizations from the point of view of transaction costs. Economist Oliver Williamson opposed hierarchies to markets.[14] The reasoning is that human social life consists of economic transactions between individuals. These individuals will form hierarchical organizations when the cost of the economic transactions (such as getting information or finding out whom to trust) is lower in a hierarchy than if all transactions took place on a free market. What is interesting about this theory from a cultural point of view is that *the "market" is the point of departure or base model,* and the organization is explained from market failure. A culture that produces such a theory is likely to prefer organizations that internally resemble markets to organizations that internally resemble more structured models, such as pyramids. The ideal principle of control in organizations in the "market" philosophy is *competition* between individuals.

Williamson's colleague William Ouchi, an American of Japanese descent, has suggested two alternatives to markets: "bureaucracies" and "clans"; they come close to what earlier in this chapter we called the "machine" model and the "family" model, respectively.[15] If we take Williamson's and Ouchi's ideas together, we find all four organizational models described. The market, however, takes a special position as the theory's starting point, and this can be explained by the nationality of the authors.

In the work of both German and French organization theorists, markets play a modest role. German books tend to focus on formal systems—on the running of the machine.[16] The ideal principle of control in organizations is a system of *formal rules* on which everybody can rely. French books usually stress the exercise of power and sometimes the defenses of the individual against being crushed by the pyramid.[17] The principle of control is *hierarchical authority*; there is a system of rules, but contrary to the German case, the personal authority of the superiors prevails over the rules.

In China, in the days of Mao and the Cultural Revolution, it was neither markets nor rules nor hierarchy but *indoctrination* that was the attempted principle of control in organizations, in line with a national tradition that for centuries used comparative examinations as a test of adequate indoctrination.

Models of organizations in people's minds vary also *within* countries. In any given country, banks will function more like pyramids, post offices like machines, advertising agencies like markets, and orchestras like (autocratically led) families. We expect such differences, but when we cross national borders, we run into differences in organizational models that were not expected. More about this subject will follow in Chapter 11.

Culture and Organizational Structure: Elaborating on Mintzberg

Henry Mintzberg, from Canada, is one of today's leading authorities on organizational structure, at least in the English-speaking world. His chief merit has been to summarize the academic state of the art into a small number of concepts that are highly practical and easy to understand.

To Mintzberg, all good things in organizations come in fives.[18] Organizations in general contain up to five distinct parts:

1. The operating core (the people who do the work)
2. The strategic apex (the top management)
3. The middle line (the hierarchy in between)
4. The technostructure (people in staff roles supplying ideas)
5. The support staff (people in staff roles supplying services)

Organizations in general use one or more of five mechanisms for coordinating activities:

1. Mutual adjustment (of people through informal communication)
2. Direct supervision (by a hierarchical superior)
3. Standardization of work processes (specifying the contents of work)

4. Standardization of outputs (specifying the desired results)
5. Standardization of skills (specifying the training required to perform the work)

Most organizations show one of five typical configurations:

1. **The simple structure.** Key part: the strategic apex. Coordinating mechanism: direct supervision.
2. **The machine bureaucracy.** Key part: the technostructure. Coordinating mechanism: standardization of work processes.
3. **The professional bureaucracy.** Key part: the operating core. Coordinating mechanism: standardization of skills.
4. **The divisionalized form.** Key part: the middle line. Coordinating mechanism: standardization of outputs.
5. **The adhocracy.** Key part: the support staff (sometimes with the operating core). Coordinating mechanism: mutual adjustment.

Mintzberg recognized the role of values in the choice of coordinating mechanisms. For example, about formalization of behavior within organizations (a part of the standardization of work processes), he wrote:

> *Organizations formalize behavior to reduce its variability, ultimately to predict and control it . . . to coordinate activities . . . to ensure the machine-like consistency that leads to efficient production . . . to ensure fairness to clients. . . . Organizations formalize behavior for other reasons as well, of more questionable validity. Formalization may, for example, reflect an arbitrary desire for order. . . . The highly formalized structure is above all the neat one; it warms the heart of people who like to see things orderly.*[19]

Mintzberg's reference to "questionable validity" obviously represents his own values choice. He did not go as far as recognizing the link between values and nationality. The IBM research has demonstrated to what extent values about the desirability of centralization (reflected in power distance) and formalization (reflected in uncertainty avoidance) affect the implicit models of organizations in people's minds and to what extent these models differ from one country to another. This suggests that it should be possible to link Mintzberg's typology of organizational configurations to national culture profiles based on the IBM data. The link means that, other factors being equal, people from a particular national background will prefer a particular configuration because it fits their implicit model and that otherwise similar organizations in different countries will resemble different Mintzberg configuration types because of different cultural preferences.

The link between Mintzberg's five configurations and the quadrants of the power distance–uncertainty avoidance diagram is easy to make; it is presented in Figure 9.2.

Mintzberg uses the term *machine* in a different sense from that used by Stevens and by us: in his machine bureaucracy Mintzberg stresses the role of the technostructure (that is, the higher-educated specialists) but not the role of the highly trained workers who belong to his operating core. Therefore, Mintzberg's machine bureaucracy corresponds not with Stevens's machine but rather with his pyramid. In order to avoid confusion, in Figure 9.2 we have renamed it "full bureaucracy." This is the term used

FIGURE 9.2 Mintzberg's Five Preferred Configurations of Organizations

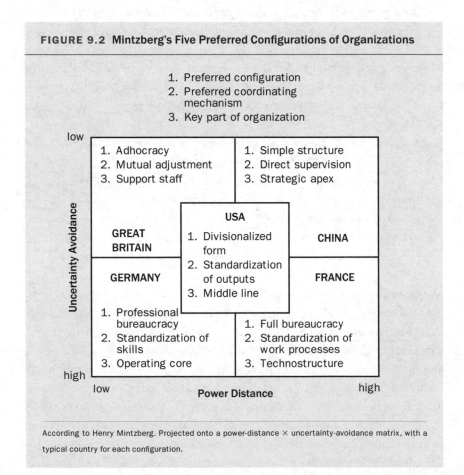

According to Henry Mintzberg. Projected onto a power-distance × uncertainty-avoidance matrix, with a typical country for each configuration.

for a very similar configuration in the Aston Studies, referenced earlier in this chapter.

The adhocracy corresponds with the "village market" implicit organization model; the professional bureaucracy corresponds with the "well-oiled machine" model; the full (machine) bureaucracy corresponds with the "pyramid" model; and the simple structure corresponds with the "family" model, while the divisionalized form takes a middle position on both culture dimensions, containing elements of all four models. A typical country near the center of the diagram in Figure 9.2 is the United States, where the divisionalized form has been developed and enjoys much popularity.

Figure 9.2 explains a number of national characteristics known from the professional and anecdotal literature about organizations; these are especially clear in the preferred coordination mechanisms. *Mutual adjustment* fits the market model of organizations and the stress on ad hoc negotiation in the Anglo countries. *Standardization of skills* explains the traditional emphasis in countries such as Germany and Switzerland on the professional qualification of workers and the high status in these countries of apprentice systems. *Standardization of work processes* fits the French concept of bureaucracy.[20] *Direct supervision* corresponds to Chinese organizations, including those outside mainland China, which emphasize coordination through personal intervention of the owner and his relatives. *Standardization of outputs* is very much the preferred philosophy in the United States, even in cases in which outputs are difficult to assess.

Planning, Control, and Accounting

Planning and control processes in organizations are strongly influenced by culture. Planning and control go together: planning tries to reduce uncertainty, and control is a form of power. So, planning and control processes in a country are likely to vary according to the prevailing uncertainty-avoidance and power-distance norms. Planning and control systems are often considered rational tools, but in fact they are partly ritual. It is extremely difficult to know how effective planning and control really are. The ritual elements make an objective evaluation impossible: there will always be believers and nonbelievers.

Therefore, it is difficult to identify effective and ineffective planning and control systems in other cultures. Let us take the case of strategic planning and control by top management. In Chapter 6 we referred to a study (published in 1980 by the Frenchman Jacques Horovitz) of top management in France, Germany, and Great Britain. According to the criteria set by the U.S. designers of planning and control systems, British managers did a better job of strategic planning than their German and French counterparts; the latter two focused on details and short-term feedback. Yet the national economies of France and Germany at that time did at least as well as those of the United Kingdom and the United States. Mintzberg, himself a Canadian, has expressed strong skepticism about the effects of strategic planning.[21] Rituals are effective for those who believe in them.

Following are some of the ways in which national power distance and uncertainty avoidance affect planning and control processes in organizations:[22]

- Higher PDI supports political rather than strategic thinking.
- Higher PDI supports personal planning and control rather than impersonal systems. The higher in the hierarchy, the less formal the planning and control.
- Lower-PDI control systems place more trust in subordinates; in higher-PDI cultures such trust is lacking.
- Higher UAI makes it less likely that strategic planning activities are practiced because these activities may call into question the certainties of today.
- Higher UAI supports a need for more detail in planning and more short-term feedback.
- Higher UAI implies leaving planning to specialists.
- Higher UAI implies a more limited view of what information is relevant.

When companies go international, their planning and control systems continue to be strongly influenced by the national culture specific to the company. European researchers Anne-Wil Harzing and Arndt Sorge collected information on how multinationals controlled their subsidiaries' performance. The decisive influence was the *home country* of the multinational, not the subsidiary. It explained the variations in the use of both impersonal control by systems and personal control by expatriates.[23]

National cultures are also reflected in the role of accountants in organizations. Not only managers and management professors but even accountants are human; moreover, they play a particular role in the culture of a society.[24]

In Chapter 1 culture was shown to be manifested in the form of symbols, heroes, rituals, and values. Accounting is said to be the language of business: this means that accounting is the handling of *symbols* that have meaning only to those initiated in business. At the level of symbols one also finds money. Money has no intrinsic value, nor an intrinsic meaning, other than that which is attributed to it by convention. It also means different things to different people. For example, it means one thing in the culture of accountants and something else in the culture of bankers. There is a national component to the meaning of money: in Chapter 5 the importance of money was associated with masculinity. In more masculine societies, such as the United States and Germany, accounting systems stress the achievement of purely financial targets more than they do in more feminine societies, such as Sweden and the Netherlands. In societies that are shorter-term oriented, such as the United States, the systems' stress is obviously more on short-term results than is the case in societies that are longer-term oriented.

Accountants themselves are unlikely to ever become *heroes* in organizations, but they have an important role in identifying and anointing heroes elsewhere in the organization, because they determine who are the good guys and the bad guys. Their major device for this purpose is *accountability*: holding someone personally responsible for results. As measurable results are more important in masculine societies than in feminine ones, the former's accounting systems are more likely to present results in such a way that a responsible manager is pictured as a hero or as a villain.

From a cultural point of view, accounting systems in organizations are best understood as uncertainty-reducing *rituals*, fulfilling a cultural need for certainty, simplicity, and truth in a confusing world, regardless of whether this truth has any objective base. Trevor Gambling, a professor and former accountant from the United Kingdom, has written that much of accounting information is after-the-fact justification of decisions that were taken for nonlogical reasons in the first place. The main function of accounting information, according to Gambling, is maintaining morale in the face of uncertainty. The accountant "enables a distinctly demoralized modern industrial society to live with itself, by reassuring that its models and data can pass for truth."[25]

This explains the lack of consensus across different countries on what represents proper accounting methods. For the United States these methods are collected in the accountant's holy book of generally accepted accounting principles, the *GAAP Guide*. Being "generally accepted" within a certain population is precisely what makes a ritual a ritual. It does not need any other justification. Once you have agreed on the ritual, a lot of problems become technical again, such as how to perform the ritual most effectively. To a naive observer, accounting practice has a lot in common with religious practice (which also serves to avoid uncertainty). British journalist Graham Cleverley called accountants the "priests" of business.[26] Sometimes we find explicit links between religious and accounting rules, such as in Islam in the Koranic ban on calculating interest.

Geert's doctoral research in the 1960s dealt with the behavioral consequences of budgeting, and it unwittingly supported the ritual nature of budget accounting. This is remarkable, because the budget process is probably one of the most action-oriented parts of the accounting system. In those days Geert worked as a production manager in a Dutch textile mill, and he had been struck by a number of behavioral paradoxes when a budget system was introduced: observable behavior that was the opposite of what the system intended.

The main conclusion of the research was captured in the title of the dissertation: *The Game of Budget Control*.[27] It was based on a field study in five Dutch business companies. It did not refer to rituals or culture, but it found that for budget control to have a positive impact on results, it should be played as a game. Games in all human societies are a very specific form of ritual: they are activities carried out for their own sake. Basically the research showed that the proper ritual use of the system was a prime condition for its impact on results. The technical aspects of the system used—the things the professional literature worried and still worries most about—did not affect the results very much. The way the game was played gave the system its meaning in the minds of the actors, and this determined the impact. This was a cultural interpretation *avant la lettre*.

If accounting systems are rituals rooted in avoiding uncertainty, one can expect that a society's score on uncertainty avoidance will strongly affect its accounting practices: societies that are more strongly uncertainty avoiding will have more precise rules on how to handle different cases; in societies that are less strongly uncertainty avoiding, more will be left to the discretion of the organization or even of the accountant.

Behind the symbols, heroes, and rituals in accounting there are *values*. The less an activity is determined by technical necessity, the more it is ruled by values and thus influenced by cultural differences. Accounting is a field in which the technical imperatives are weak: historically based conventions are more important to it than laws of nature. So, it is logical for accounting systems and the ways they are used to vary along national cultural lines.

In large-power-distance countries, accounting systems will be frequently used to justify the decisions of the top power holder(s): they are seen as the power holder's tool to present the desired image, and figures will be twisted to this end. The accounting scandals in the United States in 2002 (of which the Enron Corporation case was the most infamous example) fit the picture of a shift in U.S. society to larger power distances, signaled at the end of Chapter 3.

Power distance also affects the degree to which people at lower levels in organizations will be asked to participate in setting accounting standards. When three large state enterprises in Thailand tried to introduce a participative costing system designed in the United States, they met with strong resistance, because redistribution of power went against Thai values.[28]

In stronger uncertainty-avoidance countries such as Germany and France, accounting systems not only will be more detailed, as argued previously, but also will to a larger extent be theoretically based—claiming to derive from consistent general economic principles. In weak uncertainty-avoidance countries, systems will be more pragmatic, ad hoc, and folkloristic. We already cited the example of the generally accepted accounting principles (GAAP) in the United States. In Germany and Japan, annual reports to shareholders are supposed to use the same valuation of the company's assets as is used for fiscal purposes; in the Dutch, British, and U.S. systems, reports to the fiscal authorities are a completely different thing from reports to shareholders.

In individualist cultures the information in the accounting system will be taken more seriously and considered more indispensable than in collectivist ones. The latter—being "high-context," according to Edward Hall—possess many other and subtler clues to find out about the well-being of organizations and the performance of people, so they rely less on the explicit information produced by the accountants. The accounting profession in such societies is therefore likely to carry lower status; the work of accountants is a ritual without practical impact on decisions.

Multinationals, when going abroad, have to impose universal accounting rules for consolidation purposes. If, as the research in IBM showed, even in this tightly coordinated corporation employees in different countries hold markedly different personal values, it is likely that interpretations of accounting rules in the subsidiaries of multinationals will often deviate from what headquarters expect.

Differences among occupational value systems play a role in the communication between accountants and other organization members. U.S. students majoring in accounting were found to attribute higher value to being clean and responsible and lower value to being imaginative than other students, which suggests a self-selection on uncertainty-avoiding values.[29] In a Dutch and an international sample, Geert found that accountants stress the *form* of information, where people in operating roles will stress its *content*.[30]

Accountants are also the people who determine the value of the organization's assets. Ways of valuing assets reflect underlying nonrational value systems, such as the fact that machines are considered assets while people are not. Hardware is less uncertain than software.

Corporate Governance and Business Goals

Traditionally, patterns of *corporate governance*, the ownership and control of corporations, differ vastly among countries. A study across twelve European countries, published in 1997,[31] showed that while in Britain sixty-one of the hundred largest companies had dispersed shareholders (no single owner holding more than 20 percent), in Austria and Italy no large companies at all had this ownership type. The percentages of dispersed ownership were significantly correlated with individualism (IDV).[32]

Capitalism is historically linked to individualism. The United Kingdom inherited the ideas formulated by a Scot, Adam Smith (1723–90), about the market as an invisible hand. In the individualist value pattern, the relationship between the individual and the organization is *calculative* both for the owners and for the employees; it is based on enlightened self-interest. In more collectivist societies, in comparison, the link between individuals and their organizations is *moral* by tradition (Chapter 4). A hire-and-fire approach, as with a buy-and-sell approach, is considered immoral or indecent. Sometimes firing employees is even prohibited by law. If it is not, selling companies and firing redundant employees still carry a high cost in terms of loss of public image and of goodwill with authorities.

Differences in power distance also affect corporate governance. Across the same twelve European countries, dominant ownership of the hundred largest companies (one person, family, or company owning between 20 and 50 percent) was positively correlated with power distance.[33] In high-PDI France, banking, the development of large companies, and foreign trade were historically strongly directed and controlled by the state according to the principle of mercantilism; other fairly large companies continue to be family owned.

In the Nordic countries of Denmark, Finland, Norway, and Sweden, but also in Austria, ten or more of the hundred largest corporations were owned by a cooperative; in Britain and Italy, virtually none. The share of cooperatively owned corporations was negatively correlated with masculinity.[34] Cooperatives appeal to the need for cooperation in a feminine society.

A Russian economist, Radislav Semenov, compared (in 2000) the systems of corporate governance in seventeen Western countries and showed that culture scores explained their differences better than any of the economic variables suggested in the literature.[35] By a combination of power distance, uncertainty avoidance, and masculinity, he was able to classify countries in terms of market, bank, or other control; concentration of ownership; mind-sets of politicians, directors, employees, and investors; formation and implementation of economic policy; and industrial relations. In a separate analysis he studied ownership of firms across forty-four countries worldwide; this time he found a significant relationship with uncertainty avoidance only. His study shows the importance of cultural considerations when exporting one country's solutions to another, as was frequently tried in Eastern Europe in the 1990s.

Corporate governance is also related to corporate financial goals. It is a naive assumption that such goals are culture free. In interviews by the Dutch researcher Jeroen Weimer with Dutch, German, and U.S. business executives, besides the subject of making profits, the Dutch talked about assets, the Germans about independence from banks, and the Americans about shareholder value.[36] This diversity reflects the institutional differences among the countries (the strong role of banks in Germany, for example) as well as the prevailing ideologies (the shareholder as a culture hero in the United States).

Personal goals of top business executives are not limited to financial matters, of course, but how to find out what they really are is problematic. Asking the executives themselves will predictably produce self-serving, politically correct answers. Geert resolved this dilemma by asking junior managers and professionals enrolled in part-time M.B.A. courses to rate the goals of successful business leaders in their country. M.B.A. students with work experience are probably among the best-informed judges available. With the help of an international network of colleagues, Geert and three coauthors polled more than 1,800 M.B.A. students—part-timers or others with work experience—at twenty-one local universities in fifteen countries (later extended to seventeen), using a list of fifteen potential goals.[37] These goals and their average attributed order of priority across all seventeen countries are listed in Table 9.1.

TABLE 9.1 Overall Order of Priority of 15 Potential Business Goals Attributed to Their Country's Business Leaders by Part-Time M.B.A. Students from 17 Countries

TOP FIVE:

1. **Growth of the business**
2. **Continuity of the business**
3. **This year's profits**
4. **Personal wealth**
5. **Power**

MIDDLE FIVE:

6. Honor, face, reputation
7. Creating something new
8. Profits ten years from now
9. Staying within the law
10. Responsibility toward employees

BOTTOM FIVE:

11. *Respecting ethical norms*
12. *Responsibility toward society in general*
13. *Game and gambling spirit*
14. *Patriotism, national pride*
15. *Family interests (e.g., jobs for relatives)*

The top five goals focus on immediate interests of the company—growth, continuity, and short-term profits—and on the leader's ego, represented by personal wealth and power. The middle five deal with stakeholder relationships and the future: reputation, creativity, long-term profits, legitimacy, and employee interests. The bottom five deal with spiritual and special interests: individual and societal ethics, game spirit, nation, and family.

Attributions within individual countries, however, differed considerably from this average. Using the ranking in Table 9.1 as a baseline, we computed country profiles, showing for each country the goals on which it deviated most (plus or minus) from this ranking.

Table 9.2 shows the profiles for five important economies: the United States, India, Brazil, China, and Germany. The scores for the United States were produced by M.B.A. students from five universities in different regions of the country; the five produced almost identical goal rankings. Their consensus ranking closely resembled the seventeen-country average from Table 9.1; none of the other sixteen countries came closer. Four of the top five goals—growth, personal wealth, this year's profits, and power—were rated even more important for U.S. business leaders than for their colleagues elsewhere. In the past half century, U.S. business has grown into a model for global business; the master of business administration course is an American invention.

The two most notable differences between the U.S. ranking and the overall average are continuity of the business, which U.S. M.B.A.s rated less important than their colleagues from any other country, and respecting ethical norms, internationally among the bottom five but rated quite important in the United States. As we have shown in previous chapters, what is considered ethical may differ from one country to the next. Across the seventeen countries, ratings for respecting ethical norms tended to correlate with ratings for staying within the law and for honor, face, and reputation.

The countries next most similar to the international average were India and Brazil, also shown in Table 9.2. In India, continuity of the business came out on top. Notable differences from the international average were patriotism, internationally near the bottom but in India much more important than average, and profits ten years from now, which replaced this year's profits among India's top five.

Brazil's profile gave game and gambling spirit and family interests much more importance than the average; creating something new, prof-

TABLE 9.2 Perceived Business Goals Priorities in Five Countries, Compared with the 17-Country Average

International top five in **bold**; international bottom five in *italics*.

UNITED STATES

MORE IMPORTANT	LESS IMPORTANT
Growth of the business	Profits ten years from now
Respecting ethical norms	Responsibility toward employees
Personal wealth	*Family interests*
This year's profits	Creating something new
Power	**Continuity of the business**

INDIA

MORE IMPORTANT	LESS IMPORTANT
Continuity of the business	*Family interests*
Patriotism, national pride	Staying within the law
Power	*Game and gambling spirit*
Growth of the business	**This year's profits**
Profits ten years from now	*Respecting ethical norms*

BRAZIL

MORE IMPORTANT	LESS IMPORTANT
Game and gambling spirit	*Patriotism, national pride*
Power	Creating something new
This year's profits	*Responsibility toward society*
Continuity of the business	Profits ten years from now
Family interests	Responsibility toward employees

CHINA

MORE IMPORTANT	LESS IMPORTANT
Respecting ethical norms	*Family interests*
Patriotism, national pride	*Game and gambling spirit*
Power	**This year's profits**
Honor, face, reputation	**Personal wealth**
Responsibility toward society	Staying within the law

GERMANY

MORE IMPORTANT	LESS IMPORTANT
Responsibility toward society	**Power**
Responsibility toward employees	*Patriotism, national pride*
Creating something new	**Personal wealth**
Profits ten years from now	**Growth of the business**
Respecting ethical norms	**This year's profits**

its ten years from now, and responsibility toward employees were rated equally as unimportant as responsibility toward society in general and patriotism. Our first article about the business goals project described Brazilian business leaders as family entrepreneurs; to a greater degree than their colleagues in most other countries, they focused on their own inner circle, without much concern for other stakeholders, the longer-term future, society, and nation.

The two other countries in Table 9.2, China and Germany, were the most *dissimilar* from the international average. China's profile nevertheless resembled India's in a number of respects. Both China and India put patriotism much higher than average, together with power, and both rated this year's profits and staying within the law less important than average. Notable differences between China and India were that China placed respecting ethical norms even higher than the United States, while India put it at the bottom. China also rated responsibility toward society in general much more important than average, as well as face (the Chinese term for honor and reputation); face surpassed personal wealth, which was rated much less important.

Germany's profile represents almost a reversal of the international ranking in Table 9.1. In Germany four of the five international top goals were rated less important, and responsibility toward society in general was rated even higher than in China. As in India (and China), profits ten years from now were rated more important than this year's profits.

The fifteen goals were, naturally, not entirely independent of each other. Statistically,[38] they split into five clusters, which can be seen as dilemmas: (1) continuity and power versus honor, laws, and ethics; (2) wealth and family versus responsibility toward employees; (3) game and creativity versus patriotism; (4) short-term profits versus long-term profits; and (5) growth versus responsibility toward society.

As could be predicted, cluster 4, the relative importance of this year's profits over profits ten years from now, reflected a country's *long-term orientation* score.[39]

Cluster 5 opposes growth to responsibility toward society in general. Table 9.1 shows that in the average ranking, growth was strongly dominant. In fact, the extent to which responsibility toward society in general was balanced against growth in a country turned out to be the main determinant of how much that country deviated from the overall average.[40] Scores on cluster 5 showed that the United States, Australia, and Hong Kong most strongly focused on growth; the Netherlands, Germany, and Great Britain were strongest on recognizing business's responsibility toward society in general.

Around 2000 many people assumed that globalization and the acquisition of companies across borders would wipe out differences like those in Table 9.2 and that all business leaders would acquire the American profile. The 2008 economic crisis and the fact that national goal profiles reflect national cultures with centuries-old roots make that assumption unlikely. Goal conflicts between leaders from different countries, as well as between expatriate leaders and their local personnel, are predictable.

The 2008 recession started as a financial crisis in the United States. Irresponsible practices had put U.S. banks on a disaster track, and the interdependence of the modern global economy spread the damage worldwide.

Our country-by-country comparison from around 1998 had pictured U.S. business leaders as—even more than their counterparts elsewhere—fascinated by bigness, greedy, short-term oriented, and out for power. They were seen as less interested than their foreign colleagues in the longer-term future, taking less responsibility for their employees, less innovative, and caring less for the continuity of their businesses.

Aspects of the U.S. national culture described in various chapters of this book reinforced this pattern—in particular, strong individualism, masculinity, and short-term orientation. Until the 1980s, checks and balances in U.S. legislation, introduced after the 1929 crisis, had prevented abusive business practices, but successive presidencies released controls, lowered business taxes, and opened the gates for a race to get bigger and wealthier in ways that had been closed before. This process led to giant deficits in the U.S. national budget and to astronomical self-payments by business leaders, plus a number of outright scandals, which also spread to other countries.

In hindsight, the 2008 financial crisis could have been predicted from our 1998 business goals study. Subsequent to the crisis, national governments stepped in, trying at considerable cost to repair the damage by rebalancing the interests of society, wage earners, and clients with those of shareholders. In the present financial reshuffling, top leaders from other parts of the world such as the European Union, China, India, and Brazil play an increasingly important role. Whoever owns the resources sets the goals, so global business objectives will very likely shift in the direction of their values.

This scenario presupposes that economists get rid of the shibboleth of undisputed economic growth. In the goals attributed to business leaders, a fixation on growth opposed a sense of responsibility toward society in general. Nothing can grow forever—management is the art of balancing.

Different national business goals limit the exportability of "agency theory." *Agency* refers to the delegation of discretionary power by a principal to an agent, and since the 1980s the term has in particular been applied to the delegation by owners to managers. Agency theories are based on implicit assumptions about societal order, contractual relationships, and motivation. Such assumptions are bounded by national borders.

Motivation Theories and Practices

Motivation is an assumed force operating inside an individual, inducing him or her to choose one action over another. Culture as collective programming of the mind thus plays an obvious role in motivation. Culture influences not only our behaviors but also the explanations we give for our behaviors. As a result, an American may explain putting in extra effort on the job by the money received, a French person by personal honor, a Chinese person by mutual obligations, and a Dane by collegiality.

Different assumptions about motivation lead to different motivation theories. The founding father of motivation theory was the Austrian Sigmund Freud, but ironically he is rarely quoted in relation to management.[41] The classic motivation theorists in a management context are Americans. We met Abraham Maslow's hierarchy of human needs in Chapters 4 and 6, and in Chapter 6 we also encountered David McClelland's theory of the achievement motive. A third popular theory about work motivation that reflects its U.S. origin is Frederick Herzberg's motivation versus hygiene.

In 1959 Herzberg and two coworkers published a now-classic study,[42] which argued that the work situation contains elements with a positive motivation potential (the real motivators) and elements with a negative potential (the hygiene factors). The motivators are the work itself, achievement, recognition, responsibility, and advancement. These were labeled the *intrinsic* elements of the job. The hygiene factors, which must be present in order to prevent a lack of motivation but cannot motivate by themselves, are company policy and administration, supervision, salary, and working conditions: *extrinsic* elements of the job. Herzberg assumed this distinction to be a universal characteristic of human motivation. He proposed that it is the *job content*, not the job context, that makes people act.

Herzberg's conclusion resembles the quote from his compatriot Mary Parker Follett earlier in this chapter, in which she asserts that people should "take their orders from the situation." Culturally, both fit an environment in which power distances are small and uncertainty avoidance is weak: neither dependence on more powerful superiors nor a need for rules is deemed to be functional or necessary for making people act. The theory fits the cultures of the upper left-hand corner of Figure 9.1.

In countries occupying the lower left-hand corner of Figure 9.1, contrary to Herzberg's theory, rules as part of what Herzberg called "company policy and administration" should not be seen only as hygiene. Enforced by a superego (see Chapter 6; in ordinary language, by a sense of duty), they can be real motivators in these countries.

In a similar way within countries in the right-hand half of Figure 9.1, "supervision" should not be seen as a hygienic factor. When power distances are large, dependence on more powerful people is a basic need that can be a real motivator. In the lower right-hand corner, incorporating most Latin countries, the motivator could be labeled the *boss* in the sense of the formally appointed superior. At INSEAD business school in Fontainebleau (where Stevens did his analysis reported earlier in this chapter), leaderless discussion groups composed entirely of French participants were known to often waste time in internal fights for leadership at the expense of productivity, unlike groups of German or British students and also unlike internationally mixed groups including French participants.

In the upper right-hand corner, where we find Asian and African countries, the motivator should rather be labeled the *master*. The master differs from the boss in that this person's power is based on tradition and charisma more than on formal position.

In summary, Herzberg's theory, as with the other U.S. theories of motivation considered in previous chapters, is valid only in the cultural environment in which it was conceived. It is culturally constrained and reflects the part of the U.S. environment in which its author grew up and did his research.

Another classic U.S. motivation theory is Douglas McGregor's distinction between "Theory X" and "Theory Y." McGregor's work carries a strong humanistic missionary flavor characteristic of the 1950s, when his ideas were formulated. The main thrust of Theory X is that the average human being has an inherent dislike of work and will avoid it if possible; therefore, people must be coerced, punished, and controlled to make them contribute to organizational objectives. The main thrust of Theory Y is that the expenditure of physical and mental effort in work is as natural as play or rest, and that under proper conditions, people will not only accept but even seek responsibility and exercise effort toward achieving organizational objectives. McGregor evidently defended Theory Y.[43]

In the 1980s Geert was invited to speak at a seminar on human resource development in Jakarta, Indonesia. Someone suggested he should address the problem of how to train Indonesian managers to replace Theory X by Theory Y. This suggestion led him to reflect on what basic, unspoken cultural assumptions are present in *both* Theories X *and* Y. He arrived at the following list:

1. Work is good for people. It is God's will that people should work.
2. People's capacities should be maximally utilized. It is God's will that people should use their capacities to the fullest extent.
3. There are "organizational objectives" that exist apart from people.
4. People in organizations behave as unattached individuals.

These assumptions reflect the value positions of an individualist, masculine society, such as the United States, where McGregor grew up. None of them applies in Indonesia or other Southeast Asian cultures. Southeast Asian assumptions would rather be these:

1. Work is a necessity but not a goal in itself.
2. People should find their rightful place, in peace and harmony with their environment.
3. Absolute objectives exist only with God. In the world, persons in authority positions represent God, so their objectives should be followed.
4. People behave as members of a family and/or group. Those who do not are rejected by society.

Because of these different culturally determined assumptions, McGregor's Theory X–Theory Y distinction is irrelevant in Southeast Asia. A distinction more in line with Southeast Asian cultures would not oppose mutually exclusive alternatives that disrupt the norm of harmony. The ideal model would be one in which opposites complement each other and fit harmoniously together. Let us call them Theory T and Theory T+, in which *T* stands for "Tradition."

Theory T could be as follows:

1. There is an order of inequality in this world in which everyone has his or her rightful place. High and low are protected by this order, which is willed by God.
2. Children have to learn to fulfill their duties at the place where they belong by birth. They can improve their place by studying under a good teacher, working with a good patron, and/or marrying a good partner.
3. Tradition is a source of wisdom. Therefore, the average human being has an inherent dislike of change and will rightly avoid it if possible.

Without contradicting Theory T, Theory T+ would affirm these premises:

1. In spite of the wisdom in traditions, the experience of change in life is natural, as natural as work, play, or rest.
2. Commitment to change is a function of the quality of leaders who lead the change, the rewards associated with the change, and the negative consequences of not changing.
3. The capacity to lead people to a new situation is widely, not narrowly, distributed among leaders in the population.
4. The learning capacities of the average family are more than sufficient for modernization.

Thus, a Southeast Asian equivalent of human resource development might be based on something like Theories T and T+, and not on an irrelevant import like the Theory X–Theory Y distinction.

National differences in motivation patterns are reflected in different forms of compensation. Wages and other conditions are established by comparison with others in the same national labor market. A study across twenty-four countries found significant correlations between compensation practices and our culture indexes, as follows:[44]

- Employers in small-power-distance countries more often provided on-site child care for managers and professional and technical staff and stock options for nonmanagers.
- Employers in individualist countries more often paid for individual performance and provided stock options for managers.

■ Employers in masculine countries more often paid commission to nonmanagerial employees; in feminine countries they more often provided flexible benefits and on-site child care and maternity leave to clerical and manual workers.

■ Employers in uncertainty-avoiding countries more often related pay to seniority and skill and less often to performance.

Leadership, Decision Making, and Empowerment

One of the oldest theorists of leadership in the world literature is Niccolò Machiavelli (1469–1527).[45] He was a former statesman, and his book *The Ruler* described the most effective techniques for manipulation and remaining in power, including deceit, bribery, and murder, which has given him a bad reputation in the centuries afterward. In truth, Machiavelli just described what he had observed—today he would be called a sociologist. Machiavelli wrote in and about the Italy of his day, and what he described was clearly a large-power-distance, masculine context. Power distance in Italy in the IBM studies was found to be medium large, and there is no reason to assume this would have been different in the sixteenth century. Italy in the IBM studies still scored highly masculine.

As we argued in Chapter 3, leadership and subordinateship in a country are inseparable. Vertical relations in organizations are based on the common values of superiors *and* subordinates. Beliefs about leadership reflect the dominant culture of a country. Asking people to describe the qualities of a good leader is a way of asking them to describe their culture. The leader is a culture hero, in the sense of being a model for behavior (see Figure 1.2).

Authors from individualist countries tend to treat leadership as an independent characteristic that a person can acquire, without reference to its context. In the management literature from individualist, masculine cultures such as Australia, Britain, and the United States, romanticized descriptions of masculine leaders are popular. They describe what the readers would like to be and to believe. What really happens depends on leaders, on followers, and very much on the situation.

Feminine cultures believe in modest leaders. A prestigious U.S. consulting firm was once asked to analyze decision making in a leading Dutch corporation. The firm's report criticized the corporation's decision-making style for being, among other things, "intuitive" and "consensus-based."[46] The in-depth comparison of a U.S., a Dutch, and a French organization by

Philippe d'Iribarne (see Chapter 3) showed that the consensus principle was precisely the essence of the success of the Dutch plant. The Dutch "polder" consensus model is supposed to have been a keystone of the country's economy. Imposing a foreign leadership model (believed to be universal) in such a situation is a destruction of cultural capital.

Two U.S. researchers, Ellen Jackofsky and John Slocum, analyzed descriptions of chief executives in the management press in five countries. French CEOs were described as taking autocratic initiatives (high PDI); Germans as stressing the training and responsibilities of their managers and workers (low PDI, high UAI); Japanese as practicing patience and letting the organization run itself, aiming at long-term market share (high LTO); Swedes as taking entrepreneurial risks and at the same time caring for their people's quality of working life (low UAI, low MAS); and the one Taiwanese CEO in the sample as stressing hard work and the family (high LTO, low IDV).[47]

Ingrid Tollgerdt-Andersson, from Sweden, compared more than 1,400 job advertisements for executives from eight European countries. She looked for whether the ads mentioned personal and social abilities, such as ability to cooperate. This was the case in 80 percent or more of the ads in Sweden, Denmark, and Norway but only in some 50 percent in Italy and Spain. Weak uncertainty avoidance explains most of the differences. Ability to cooperate is a soft criterion considered more valid in low-UAI countries. Femininity explains nearly all the remaining differences: cooperation is a more important value in feminine than in masculine cultures.[48]

Studies of the satisfaction and productivity of subordinates under different types of leaders show the influence of national cultures. French IBM technicians were most satisfied when they saw their boss as persuasive or paternalistic, unlike their British and German colleagues, who more often liked consultative and democratic bosses. Workers from Peru liked close supervision, unlike similar workers from the United States. Indian assistants showed the highest satisfaction and performance when working under foremen who behaved like elder brothers. What represents appropriate leadership in one setting does not have to be appropriate for a differently programmed group of subordinates.[49]

Leadership behaviors and leadership theories that do not take collective expectations of subordinates into account are basically dysfunctional. Harry Triandis described how the U.S. leadership style was dysfunctional in Greece and vice versa.[50] What usually happens when foreign theories are taught abroad is that they are preached but not practiced. Wise local managers silently adapt the foreign ideas to fit the values of their subordinates. A country in which this has happened a lot is Japan.[51] Not-so-wise managers may try an unfitting approach once, find out it does not work, and fall back into their old routine.

The existence and functioning of *grievance channels*, through which lower-level organization members can complain about those at the top, is obviously very much culturally influenced. Grievance channels in large-power-distance environments are difficult to establish. On the one hand, subordinates will fear retaliation (for good reason); on the other hand, there will be more unrealistic and exaggerated grievances, and the channels may be used for personal revenge against a superior who is not accessible otherwise. Uncertainty avoidance plays a role too: allowing complaints means allowing the unpredictable.

The term *empowerment* became fashionable in the 1990s. It can refer to any kind of formal and informal means of sharing decision-making power and influence between leaders and subordinates. Earlier terms for such processes were *participative management, joint consultation, Mitbestimmung, industrial democracy, worker representation, worker self-management, shop floor consultation,* and *codetermination.* Their feasibility depends on the value systems of the organization members—of the subordinates at least as much as of the leaders. The first cultural dimension involved is again power distance. Distributing influence comes more naturally to low- than to high-PDI cultures.[52] Ideologies may go the other way around; in the IBM surveys, the statement "Employees in industry should participate more in the decisions taken by management" was more strongly endorsed in high- than in low-PDI countries; an ideology can compensate for reality.

Classic mid-twentieth-century U.S. leadership models such as Douglas McGregor's Theory Y (discussed earlier), Rensis Likert's System 4, and Robert Blake and Jane Mouton's Managerial Grid reflected small but not very small power distances (in the IBM studies, the United States ranked moderately low on PDI).[53] They all advocated participative management in the sense of participation by subordinates in the superior's decisions, but *at the initiative of the superior.* In countries with still lower PDI values— including Sweden, Norway, Germany, and Israel—models of management were developed that assumed the initiatives could be taken by the subordinates. In the United States this concept tends to be seen as infringing on management prerogatives, but in the lowest-PDI countries people do not think in those terms. A Scandinavian was cited as remarking to an American lecturer: "You are against participation for the very reason we are in favor of it—one doesn't know where it will stop. We think that is good."[54] On the other hand, U.S. theories of participative management are also unlikely to apply in countries much higher on the power distance scale. Harry Triandis reported the embarrassment of a Greek subordinate when his expatriate U.S. boss asked his opinion on how much time a job should take: "He is the boss. Why doesn't he tell me?"[55] One of the critical notes about the GLOBE research project studying national culture, organizational culture, and leadership (see Chapter 2) is that the questionnaires were designed on the basis of a U.S. concept of leadership.[56]

The choice of informal versus formal empowerment is affected by the country's level of uncertainty avoidance. Thus, both PDI and UAI should be taken into account, and the four quadrants of Figure 9.1 represent four different forms of dividing power. In the upper left-hand corner (Anglo countries, Scandinavia, the Netherlands: PDI and UAI both low), the stress is on informal and spontaneous forms of participation on the shop floor. In the lower left-hand corner (German-speaking countries: PDI low, UAI higher), the stress is on formal, legally determined systems (*Mitbestimmung*). On the right-hand side (high PDI), distributing power is basically a contradiction; it will meet with strong resistance from elites and sometimes even from underdogs, or their representatives, such as labor unions. Where it is tried, it has to be pushed by a powerful leader— by a father type such as an enlightened entrepreneur in the high-PDI, low-UAI countries (higher right-hand corner) or by political leadership using legislative tools in the high-PDI, high-UAI countries (lower right-hand corner). Both mean imposed participation, which, of course, is a paradox. One way of making it function is to limit participation to certain spheres of life and to maintain tight control in others; this is the Chinese solution, in which participative structures in work organizations can be combined with a strictly controlled hierarchy in ideological issues.[57] That this has a long history too is evident from the story with which Chapter 7 opened: eighteenth-century participative management in the *Dream of the Red Chamber* garden.

Performance Appraisal and Management by Objectives

Any organization in any culture depends on the performance of people. Monitoring the performance of subordinates is a theme in most management development programs right from the lowest management level upward. Often there is a formal performance appraisal program requiring periodic written and/or oral evaluations by the superior. Exporting such programs across national borders once more calls for adaptation. In collectivist countries social harmony is an important ingredient for organizational functioning, even more crucial than formal performance, and a program that harms the former eventually damages the latter.[58] Personal criticism may have to be given in an indirect way or through a trusted intermediary, such as an older relative. Geert remembers a case in Pakistan in which the personnel department of a multinational produced all the paperwork of an internationally prescribed appraisal system to the satisfaction of its international head office—but the local managers carefully avoided conducting the expected appraisal interviews.

In the United States, management guru Peter Drucker (1909–2005) developed performance appraisal into *management by objectives.*[59] MBO was probably the most popular management technique of the twentieth century. Based on a cybernetic control-by-feedback philosophy, it is supposed to spread a results orientation throughout the organization. MBO has been considerably more successful where results are objectively measurable than where they are a matter of subjective interpretation. It reflects an American value position in that it presupposes the following:

- That the subordinate is sufficiently independent to have a meaningful dialogue with the boss (not too high PDI)
- That both superior and subordinate are prepared to accept some ambiguity (low UAI)
- That high performance is seen as an important goal by both (high MAS)

Let us now take the case of Germany. This is also a below-average PDI country, so the dialogue element in MBO should present no problem. However, Germany scored considerably higher on UAI; consequently, the acceptance of ambiguity is weaker. MBO in Germany has been strongly formalized and converted into "management by joint goal setting."[60]

In France the concept of MBO was first introduced in the early 1960s; it became extremely popular for a time after the student revolts that shook up the Western world in 1968. People expected that this new technique would lead to the long-overdue democratizing of organizations. DPO (*direction par objectifs*), the French name for MBO, became DPPO (*direction participative par objectifs*). After a few years, however, a French management author wrote, "I think that the career of DPPO is terminated, or rather that it has never started, and it won't ever start as long as we in France continue our tendency to confound ideology and reality." The journal editor added: "French blue- and white-collar workers, lower-level and higher-level managers, and patrons all belong to the same cultural system which maintains dependency relations from level to level. Only the deviants really dislike this system. The hierarchical structure protects against anxiety; DPO, however, generates anxiety."[61]

Management Training and Organization Development

It will be evident from all that has been written in this book and, in particular, in this chapter that there is no single formula for developing successful managers that can be used in all cultures. Not only is success differently defined in different cultures, but systems of initial education in schools and training on the job are also very different.

Developing managers across cultural barriers could thus be seen as an impossible task, but fortunately programs should not be judged exclusively on the basis of their subject matter. They have other important functions too. They bring people from different cultures and subcultures together and thereby broaden their outlook. In many organizations international management development programs have become rites of passage, which signal to the manager-participant as well as to the person's environment that he or she now belongs to the manager caste. They provide a form of socialization for the managerial subculture, either company-specific or in general. They also provide a break from the job routine that stimulates reflection and reorientation.

Management development packages have been developed in the United States since the middle of the twentieth century. Some approaches have used intensive discussion of interpersonal processes, such as sensitivity training and transactional analysis. Culturally, these approaches assumed low PDI, low UAI, medium to high IDV, and medium to low MAS; the latter made them somewhat countercultural in the United States.

In cases in which such programs were used with international participants, dysfunctional behaviors occurred that their trainers rarely understood. With Japanese participants, for example, the giving and receiving of personal feedback appeared virtually impossible and, when tried, resulted in ritualized behavior: the receiver of feedback felt that he must have insulted the sender in some way. Japanese participants in such programs concentrated on tasks rather than interpersonal process issues. Most Germans too did not appreciate talking about process issues, because this was seen as a wasteful deviation from the task.[62]

A parallel trend was *organization development,* in which managers and others tried to learn and resolve actual common problems at the same time. It sometimes also included intensive interpersonal process analysis.

In Latin countries, trainers—themselves Latin—gave a wide range of reasons for the organization development program's cultural incompatibility:

- We Latins (high PDI) lack the equality ethos needed for such programs.
- We Latins don't believe in self-development.
- We Latins tend to interpret interpersonal feedback competitively, unless it comes from a person seen as superior.
- The organization development process creates insecurity, which we Latins cannot tolerate.
- Our Latin languages and discussion styles are more suitable for abstract discussions than for actual problem solving.
- Our Latin organizations are not changed by development but by crisis and revolution.[63]

Conclusion: Nationality Defines Organizational Rationality

In 1980 Geert published an article in the U.S. journal *Organizational Dynamics* entitled "Motivation, Leadership, and Organization: Do American Theories Apply Abroad?" It had a stormy history; after the untimely demise of the editor who had invited and accepted it, it was at first refused and then published hesitatingly by his successor. He asked a U.S. and an Australian colleague to write assuaging comments, which were published in a later volume, along with Geert's reply.[64] The article raised an upheaval far beyond what he had expected. Many reprints were ordered, especially from Canada.

The idea that the validity of a theory is constrained by nationality was more obvious in Europe, with all its borders, than in a huge borderless country such as the United States. In Europe the cultural relativity of the laws that govern human behavior had been recognized as early as the sixteenth century in the skepticism of Michel de Montaigne (1533–92). The quote from Blaise Pascal (1623–62) referred to earlier in this chapter— "There are truths on this side of the Pyrenees which are falsehoods on the other" (the Pyrenees being the border mountains between France and Spain)—was in fact inspired by Montaigne.[65] Since Montaigne and Pascal, the link between nationality and ways of thinking has sometimes been recognized but more often forgotten.

The previous chapters have demonstrated six ways in which national cultures differ; all of these have implications for organization and management processes. Theories, models, and practices are basically culture-specific; they may apply across borders, but this should always be proved. The naive assumption that management ideas are universal is not found only in popular literature: in scholarly journals—even in those explicitly addressing an international readership—the silent assumption of universal validity of culturally restricted findings is frequent. Articles in such journals often do not even mention the country in which the data were collected (which usually is the United States, as can be concluded from the affiliations of the authors). As a matter of scientific etiquette we suggest that articles written for an international public should always mention the country or countries—and the time period—in which the data were collected.

Lack of awareness of national limits causes management and organization ideas and theories to be exported without regard for the values context in which they were developed. Fad-conscious publishers and gullible readers in those other countries encourage such exports. Unfortunately, to rephrase a famous dictum, there is nothing as impractical as a bad theory.[66]

The economic success of the United States in the decades before and after World War II has led some people in other parts of the world to believe that U.S. ideas about management must be superior and therefore should be copied. They forgot to ask about the kind of society in which these ideas were developed and applied—*if* they were really applied as the books and articles claimed. U.S. management researchers Mark Peterson and Jerry Hunt wrote, "A question for many American normative theories is whether they even apply in the United States."[67] U.S. ethnopsychologist Edward Stewart had this to say: "North American decision-makers do not observe rational decision-making in their own work and lives, as a general rule, but they restructure past events according to a decision-making model. . . .Thus, in the United States rational decision-making is a myth."[68] According to U.S. business historian Robert Locke, the successful industrialization of the United States took place in a distinct historical context and owed much more to external circumstances than to the quality of the management principles used.[69]

The belief in the superiority of American theories is reinforced by the fact that most "international" management journals are published in the United States with U.S. editors, and it is notoriously difficult for non–North American authors to get their papers accepted.[70] British professors David Hickson and Derek Pugh in their anthology *Great Writers on Organizations* included seventy-one names, of whom forty-eight were American, fifteen British, and two Canadian; only six were non-Anglo.[71]

U.S. business professor and consultant Michael Porter analyzed why some nations succeeded much better than others in the international competition of the latter part of the twentieth century. His "diamond" of the determinants of national advantage recognized four attributes: (1) factor conditions, by which he meant the availability of necessary production factors such as skilled labor and infrastructure, (2) demand conditions, (3) related and supporting industries, and (4) firm strategy, structure, and rivalry. Porter stopped short of the question of *why* some countries get better diamonds than others. He still assumed universal applicability of the ethnocentric laws of competitive markets.[72]

Just as certain nations excel in certain sports, others are associated with specific disciplines. Psychology, including social psychology, is predominantly a U.S. discipline: individualist and mostly masculine. Sociology is predominantly European,[73] but even European sociologists rarely consider the influence of their nationality on their thinking. The great French sociologist Pierre Bourdieu fiercely rejected critiques explaining his ideas from the standpoint of his being French.[74] In our eyes, far from invalidating Bourdieu's theories, recognizing the fact of their French origin makes them more understandable to others—just as U.S. models become more useful if we realize their American origin.

In organization theories, the nationality of the author reflects implicit assumptions as to where organizations came from, what they are, and what they try to achieve. These national "paradigms" all have the same starting point: "In the beginning was . . ." After God had created men, men made organizations; but what did they have in mind when making them? Here is Geert's list of the paradigms he observed: *In the beginning was* . . .

In the United States	the market
In France	the power
In Germany	order
In Poland and Russia	efficiency
In the Netherlands	consensus
In Scandinavia	equality
In Britain	systems
In China	the family
In Japan	Japan

In Paris in 1994, U.S. economist Oliver Williamson (2009 winner of the Nobel Prize) engaged in a public discussion with two French social scientists, economist Olivier Favereau and sociologist Emmanuel Lazega. Williamson defended an "efficiency approach" for studying organizations, even for the phenomena of power and authority. "I submit that there is less to power than meets the eye," he said. Favereau and Lazega criticized Williamson's concept of "transaction cost" as being too thin to be the basis of a general theory of organization; efficiency as being a weak incentive; and Williamson's conception of power as too limited. The discussion had been announced as dealing with a supposed *con*vergence between economics and sociology, but in fact it dealt with a *di*vergence of national paradigms, opposing United States (market) to France (power). All the sources Williamson cited were American; all the sources Favereau and Lazega cited were French. But neither side seemed to be aware that the other spoke from a different context, not even that there was such a thing as a national context from which theories are written and criticized.[75]

The lack of universal solutions to management and organization problems does not mean that countries cannot learn from each other. On the contrary, looking across the border is one of the most effective ways of getting new ideas for management, organization, or politics. But their export calls for prudence and judgment. Nationality constrains rationality.

The Elephant and the Stork: Organizational Cultures

Heaven's Gate BV (HGBV) is a sixty-year-old production unit in the chemical industry of the Netherlands. Many of its employees are old-timers. Stories about the past abound. Workers tell about how strenuous the jobs used to be, when loading and unloading was done by hand. They tell about the heat and the physical risk. HGBV used to be seen as a rich employer. For several decades the demand for its products exceeded the supply. Products were not sold but were distributed. Customers had to be nice and polite in order to be served. The money was made very easily.

HGBV's management style used to be paternalistic. The old general manager made his daily morning walk through the plant, shaking hands with everyone he met. This, people say, is the root of a tradition that still exists and which they call the "HGBV grip": when one arrives in the morning, one shakes hands with one's colleagues. This greeting ritual would be normal in France, but in the Netherlands it is unusual. Rich and paternalistic, HGBV has long been considered a benefactor, both to its employees in times of need and to the local community. Some of this glory has survived untarnished. Employees still feel HGBV to be a desirable employer, with good pay, benefits, and job security. A job with HGBV is still seen as a job for life. HGBV is a company one would like one's children to join. Outside, HGBV is a regular sponsor of local sports and humanitarian associations. As they say, "No appeal to HGBV has ever been made in vain."

The working atmosphere is good-natured, with a lot of freedom given to employees. The plant has been pictured as a club, a village, a family. Twenty-five-year and forty-year service anniversaries are given lots of attention; the plant's Christmas parties are famous. These celebrations represent rituals with a long history, which people still value. In HGBV's culture—or, as people express it, "the HGBV way"—unwritten rules for social behavior are important. One doesn't live in order to work; one works in order to live. What one does counts less than *how* one does it. One has to fit into the informal network, and this holds for all hierarchical levels. "Fitting" means avoiding conflicts and direct confrontations, covering other people's mistakes, loyalty, friendliness, modesty, and genial cooperation. Nobody should be too conspicuous, either in a positive or in a negative sense.

HGBVers grumble, but never directly about other HGBVers. Also, grumbling is reserved for one's own circle; in relations with superiors or outsiders, one does not soil the nest. This concern for harmony and group solidarity fits well into the regional culture of the geographic area in which HGBV is located. Newcomers are quickly accepted, as long as they adapt. The quality of their work counts less than their social adaptation. Who-ever disrupts the harmony is rejected, however good a worker he or she is. Disturbed relationships may take years to heal. Says one HGBVer, "We prefer to let a work problem continue for another month, even if it costs a lot of money, above resolving it in an unfriendly manner." Company rules are never absolute. The most important rule, an interviewee said, is that rules are flexible. One may break a rule if one does it gently. It is not the rule breaker who is at risk, but rather the one who makes an issue of it.

Leadership in HGBV, in order to be effective, should be in harmony with the social behavior patterns. Managers should be accessible, fair, and good listeners. The present general manager is such a leader. He does not give himself airs. He has an easy manner with people of all levels and is felt by employees to be one of them. Careers in HGBV are made primarily on the basis of social skills. One should not behave too conspicuously; one need not be brilliant, but one does need good contacts; one should know one's way in the informal network, being invited rather than volunteering. One should belong to the tennis club. All in all, one should respect what someone called the strict rules for being a nice person.

This romantic picture, alas, has recently been disturbed by outside influences. First, market conditions have changed, and HGBV finds itself in an unfamiliar competitive situation with other European suppliers. Costs had to be cut, and the workforce reduced. In the HGBV tradition, this problem was resolved without collective layoffs, but instead through early retirement. Still, the old-timers who had to leave prematurely were shocked that the company did not need them anymore.

Second, and even more seriously, HGBV has been attacked by environmentalists because of the pollution it causes, a point of view that has received growing support in political circles. It is not impossible that the licenses necessary for HGBV's operation will one day be withdrawn. HGBV's management has tried to counter this problem with an active lobbying effort, with a press campaign, and with organized public visits to the company, but success is by no means certain. Inside HGBV, this threat is belittled. People are unable to imagine that one day there may be no more HGBV: "Our management has always found a solution. There will be a solution now." In the meantime, attempts are being made to increase HGBV's competitiveness through quality improvement and product diversification. These initiatives also imply the introduction of new people from the outside. These new trends, however, clash head-on with HGBV's traditional culture.[1]

The Organizational Culture Craze

The short case study just presented is a description of an organization's culture. People working for Heaven's Gate BV have a specific way of acting and interacting that sets them apart from people working for other organizations, even within the same region. In the past chapters this book has mainly associated culture with nationality. English-language literature attributing cultures to organizations first appeared in the 1960s: *organizational culture* became a synonym for *organizational climate*. The equivalent *corporate culture*, coined in the 1970s, gained popularity after the book *Corporate Cultures*, by Terrence Deal and Allan Kennedy, appeared in the United States in 1982. The usage became common parlance through the success of a companion volume—like the former, from a McKinsey–Harvard Business School team: Thomas Peters and Robert Waterman's *In Search of Excellence*, which appeared in the same year.[2] After that, an extensive literature in different languages developed on the topic.

Peters and Waterman wrote:

> *Without exception, the dominance and coherence of culture proved to be an essential quality of the excellent companies. Moreover, the stronger the culture and the more it was directed toward the marketplace, the less need was there for policy manuals, organization charts, or detailed procedures and rules. In these companies, people way down the line know what they are supposed to do in most situations because the handful of guiding values is crystal clear.*[3]

Talking about the culture of a company or organization became a fad, among managers, among consultants, and, with somewhat different concerns, among academics. Fads pass, and so did this one, but not without having left its traces. Organizational, or corporate, culture has become as fashionable a topic as organizational structure, strategy, and control. There is no standard definition of the concept, but most people who write about it would probably agree that organizational culture is all of the following:

- **Holistic:** referring to a whole that is more than the sum of its parts
- **Historically determined:** reflecting the history of the organization
- **Related to the things anthropologists study:** such as rituals and symbols
- **Socially constructed:** created and preserved by the group of people who together form the organization
- **Soft:** although Peters and Waterman assured their readers that "soft is hard"
- **Difficult to change:** although authors disagree on *how* difficult

In Chapter 1 culture in general was defined as "the collective programming of the mind that distinguishes the members of one group or category of people from others." Consequently, organizational culture can be defined as "the collective programming of the mind that distinguishes the members of one organization from others." An organization's culture, however, is maintained not only in the mind of its members but also in the minds of its other "stakeholders," everybody who interacts with the organization (such as customers, suppliers, labor organizations, neighbors, authorities, and the press).

Organizations with strong cultures, in the sense of the quote from Peters and Waterman, arouse positive feelings in some people, negative in other people. The universal desirability of having a strong culture from an organizational point of view has frequently been questioned; it could be a source of fatal rigidity.[4] The attitude toward strong organizational cultures is partly affected by national culture elements. The culture of IBM Corporation, one of Peters and Waterman's most excellent companies, was depicted with horror by Max Pagès, a leading French social psychologist, in a 1979 study of IBM France; he called it *"la nouvelle église"* ("the new church").[5] French society as compared with U.S. society is characterized by a greater dependence of the average citizen on hierarchy and on rules (see Chapters 3, 6, and 9). French academics are also children of their society and therefore more likely than American academics to stress intellectual rules—that is, rational elements in organizations. At the same time, French culture according to Chapter 4 is individualistic, so there is a need to defend the individual against the rational system.[6]

Dutch sociologist Joseph Soeters showed the similarity between the descriptions of Peters and Waterman's "excellent companies" and of social movements preaching civil rights, women's liberation, religious conversion, or withdrawal from civilization. In the United States itself, postcards were sold with the slogan "I'd rather be dead than excellent." In a more dispassionate way, Soeters's compatriot Cornelis Lammers showed that the "excellent companies" were simply the latest scion of an entire genealogy within organizational sociology of ideal types of "organic organizations" described already by the German sociologist Joseph Pieper in 1931, if not by others before, and reiterated in the sociological literature on both sides of the Atlantic.[7]

Another type of reaction was found in the Nordic countries Denmark, Sweden, and, to some extent, Norway and Finland. In their case society is *less* built on hierarchy and rules than in the United States. The idea of "organizational cultures" in these feminine, uncertainty-tolerant countries was greeted with approval, because it tended to stress the irrational and the paradoxical. This attribute did not at all prevent a basically positive attitude toward organizations.[8]

In a review of twenty years of organizational culture literature, Swedish sociologist Mats Alvesson distinguishes eight metaphors used by different authors:

- Control mechanism for an informal contract
- Compass, giving direction for priorities
- Social glue for identification with the organization
- Sacred cow to which people are committed
- Affect-regulator for emotions and their expression
- Mixed bag of conflict, ambiguity, and fragmentation
- Taken-for-granted ideas leading to blind spots
- Closed system of ideas and meanings, preventing people from critically exploring new possibilities[9]

Probably the most basic distinction among writers on organizational cultures exists between those who see culture as something an organization *has* and those who see it as something an organization *is*. The former leads to an analytic approach and a concern with change. It predominates among managers and management consultants. The latter supports a synthetic approach and a concern with understanding and is found almost exclusively among academics.[10]

Differences Between Organizational and National Cultures: The IRIC Project

Using the word *culture* for both nations and organizations suggests that the two kinds of culture are identical phenomena. This is incorrect: a nation is not an organization, and the two types of culture are of a different nature.

The difference between national and organizational cultures is based on their different mix of values and practices, as illustrated in Figure 10.1, which is based on Figure 1.3. *National cultures* are part of the mental software we acquired during the first ten years of our lives, in the family, in the living environment, and in school, and they contain most of our basic values. *Organizational cultures* are acquired when we enter a work organization as young or not-so-young adults, with our values firmly in place, and they consist mainly of the organization's practices—they are more superficial.[11]

In Figure 10.1 we also located several other levels of culture: a gender level, even more basic than nationality; a social class level, with some

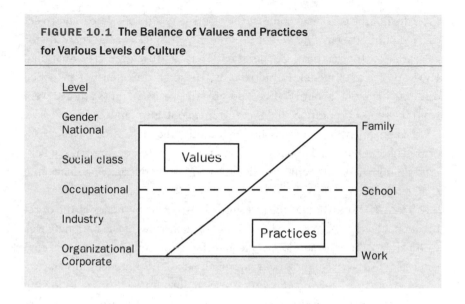

FIGURE 10.1 The Balance of Values and Practices for Various Levels of Culture

possibilities of ascent or descent; an occupational level, linked to the kind of education chosen; and an industry level between occupation and organization. An industry, or line of business, employs specific occupations *and* maintains specific organizational practices, for logical or traditional reasons.

Among national cultures—comparing otherwise similar people—the IBM studies found considerable differences in values, in the sense described in Chapter 1 of broad, nonspecific feelings of good and evil, and so on. This is notwithstanding similarities in practices among IBM employees in similar jobs but in different national subsidiaries.

When people write about national cultures in the modern world becoming more similar, the evidence cited is usually taken from the level of practices: people dress the same, buy the same products, and use the same fashionable words (symbols); they see the same television shows and movies (heroes); they engage in the same sports and leisure activities (rituals). These relatively superficial manifestations of culture are sometimes mistaken for all there is; the deeper, underlying level of the values, which moreover determine the meaning for people of their practices, is overlooked. Studies at the values level continue to show impressive differences among nations; this is true for not only the IBM studies and their various replications (Table 2.1) but also the successive rounds of the World Values Survey based on representative samples of entire populations.[12]

Most of the present chapter is based on the results of a research project carried out between 1985 and 1987 under the auspices of the Institute for Research on Intercultural Cooperation (IRIC). It used the cross-national IBM studies as a model. Paradoxically, these studies had not provided direct information about IBM's corporate culture, as all units studied were from the same corporation, and there were no outside points of comparison. As a complement to the cross-national study, the IRIC study was cross-organizational: instead of one corporation in a number of countries, it covered a number of different organizations in two countries, Denmark and the Netherlands.

The IRIC study found the roles of values versus practices at the organizational level to be exactly the opposite of their roles at the national level. Comparing otherwise similar people in different organizations showed considerable differences in practices but much smaller differences in values.

At that time, the popular literature on corporate cultures, following Peters and Waterman, insisted that shared values represented the core of a corporate culture. The IRIC project showed that *shared perceptions of daily practices* should be considered the core of an organization's culture. Employees' values differed more according to their gender, age, and education (and, of course, their nationality) than according to their membership in the organization per se.

The difference between IRIC's findings and the statements by Peters and Waterman and their followers can be explained by the fact that the U.S. management literature tends to describe the values of corporate heroes (founders and significant leaders), whereas IRIC asked the ordinary members who are supposed to carry the culture. IRIC assessed to what extent leaders' messages had come across to members. Without doubt, the values of founders and key leaders shape organizational cultures, but the way these cultures affect ordinary members is through shared practices. Founders' and leaders' values become members' practices.

Effective shared practices are the reason that multinational corporations can function at all. Employing personnel from a variety of nationalities, they cannot assume common values. They coordinate and control their operations through worldwide practices that are inspired by their national origin (be it U.S., Japanese, German, Dutch, etc.) but that can be learned by employees from a variety of other national origins.[13]

If members' values depend primarily on criteria other than membership in the organization, the way these values enter the organization is through the hiring process: a company hires people of a certain nationality, gender, age, or education. Their subsequent socialization in the organization is a matter of learning the practices: symbols, heroes, and rituals.

Two Dutch researchers, Joseph Soeters and Hein Schreuder, compared employees in Dutch and foreign accounting firms operating in the Netherlands. They found differences in values between the two groups, but they could prove that these differences were based on self-selection by the candidates, not on socialization to the firm's values after entering.[14] Human resources departments that preselect the people to be hired play an important role in maintaining an organization's values (for better or for worse), a role of which HR managers—and their colleagues in other functions—are not always conscious.

Qualitative and Quantitative Approaches in the IRIC Project

The original design of the IRIC project had been to compare only organizations within one country (the Netherlands), but finding sufficient Dutch participants willing to grant access *and* share in the project's cost proved too difficult. Generous help by a Danish consultant resulted in adding a number of Danish units. Thus, the final project was carried out on twenty units representing ten different organizations: five in Denmark, five in the Netherlands. On the IBM national culture dimensions, these two countries scored fairly similar: both belong to the same Nordic-Dutch cluster. Within these national contexts IRIC sought access to a wide range of work organizations. By seeing how different organization cultures can be, one acquires a better insight into how different is different and how similar is similar. Units of study were both entire organizations and parts of organizations that their management assumed to be culturally reasonably homogeneous (the research outcome later allowed for testing of this assumption).

Table 10.1 lists the activities in which the twenty units were engaged. Unit sizes varied from 60 to 2,500 persons. The number of units was small enough to allow studying each unit in depth, qualitatively, as a separate case study. At the same time, it was large enough to permit statistical analysis of comparative quantitative data across all cases.

The first, qualitative phase of the study consisted of in-depth person-to-person interviews of two to three hours duration each with nine informants per unit (thus a total of 180 interviews). These interviews yielded

TABLE 10.1 Organizations Participating in the IRIC Project

Private manufacturing companies (electronics, chemicals, consumer goods)	
Total divisions or production units	6
Head office or marketing units	3
Research and development units	2
Private service companies (banking, transport, trade): units	5
Public institutions (telecommunications, police): units	4
Total number of units studied	**20**

both a qualitative feel for the whole (the gestalt) of the unit's culture and a collection of issues to be included in the questionnaire for the ensuing survey. Informants were handpicked in a discussion with the person who served as the researchers' contact in the unit, on the basis that they would have something interesting and informative to relate about the culture. The group of informants included in all cases the unit top manager and his (never her) secretary; along with these were a selection of people in different jobs from all levels, both old-timers and newcomers, women and men. Sometimes the gatekeeper or doorman was found to be an excellent informant; an employee representative (equivalent to a shop steward) was always included.

The interviewer team consisted of eighteen members (Danish or Dutch), most of them with a social science training but all deliberately naive about the type of activity going on in the unit studied. Each unit's interviews were divided between two interviewers, one woman and one man, as the gender of the interviewer might affect the observations obtained. All interviewers received the same project training beforehand, and all used the same broad checklist of open-ended questions.

The interview checklist contained questions along the following lines:

- **About organizational symbols:** What are special terms here that only insiders understand?
- **About organizational heroes:** What kinds of people are most likely to advance quickly in their careers here? Whom do you consider as particularly meaningful persons for this organization?

- **About organizational rituals:** In what periodic meetings do you participate? How do people behave during these meetings? Which events are celebrated in this organization?
- **About organizational values:** What things do people very much like to see happening here? What is the biggest mistake one can make? What work problems can keep you awake at night?

Interviewers were free to probe for more and other information if they felt it was there. Interviews were taped, and the interviewers wrote a report on each session using a prescribed sequence, quoting as much as possible the respondents' actual words.

The second, quantitative phase of the project consisted of a paper-and-pencil survey with precoded questions; contrary to the first phase, it was administered to a strictly *random* sample from the unit. This sample was composed of about twenty-five managers (or as many as the unit contained), twenty-five college-level nonmanagers ("professionals"), and twenty-five non-college-level nonmanagers. The questions in the survey included those used in the cross-national IBM study plus a number of later additions; most, however, were developed on the basis of the interviews from the first phase. Questions were formulated about all issues that the interviewers suspected to differ substantially between units. These included in particular many perceptions of daily practices, which had been missing in the cross-national studies.

The results of both the interviews and the surveys were discussed with the units' management and were sometimes fed back to larger groups of employees if the management consented.

Results of the In-Depth Interviews: The SAS Case

The twenty units of focus produced twenty case studies, insightful descriptions of each unit's culture composed by the interviewers after the one-on-one sessions and with the survey results as a check on their interpretations. The case of Heaven's Gate BV presented at the beginning of this chapter was taken from the survey results. One more case will now be described: the Scandinavian Airlines System (SAS) Copenhagen passenger terminal.

SAS in the early 1980s went through a spectacular turnaround process. Under the leadership of a new president, Jan Carlzon, it switched from a product-and-technology orientation to a market-and-service orientation. Before, planning and sales had been based on realizing a maximum number of flight hours with the most modern equipment available. Pilots, technicians, and disciplinarian managers were the company's heroes. Deteriorating results forced the reorganization.

Carlzon was convinced that in the highly competitive air transport market, success depended on a superior way of catering to the needs of the present and potential customers. These needs should be best known by the employees who had daily face-to-face customer contact. In the old situation these people had never been asked for their opinions: they were a disciplined set of uniformed soldiers, trained to follow the rules. Now they were considered "the firing line," and the organization was restructured to support them rather than order them around. Superiors were turned into advisers; the firing line received considerable discretion in dealing with customer problems on the spot. They only needed to report their decisions to superiors after the fact—which meant a built-in acceptance of employees' judgment with all risks involved.[15]

One of the units participating in the IRIC study was the SAS passenger terminal at Copenhagen airport. The interviews were conducted three years after the turnaround operation. The employees and managers were uniformed, disciplined, formal, and punctual. They seemed to be the kind of people who *like* to work in a disciplined structure. People worked shift hours with periods of tremendous work pressure alternating with periods of relative inactivity. They showed considerable acceptance of their new role. When talking about the company's history, they tended to start from the time of the turnaround; only some managers referred to the earlier years.

The interviewees were demonstrably proud of the company: their identity seemed to a large extent derived from it. Social relationships outside the work situation frequently involved other SAS people. Carlzon was often mentioned as a company hero. In spite of their being disciplined, relationships between colleagues seemed to be good-natured, and there was a lot of mutual help. Colleagues who met with a crisis in their private lives were supported by others and by the company. Managers of various levels were visible and accessible, although clearly managers had more trouble accepting the new role than nonmanagers. New employees entered via a formal introduction and training program that included simulated encounters with problem clients. This program served also as a screening device, showing whether the newcomer had the values and the skills necessary for this profession. Those who successfully completed the training felt quickly at home in the department. Toward clients the employees demonstrated a problem-solving attitude: they showed considerable excitement about original ways in which to resolve customers' problems, ways in which some rules could be stretched in order to achieve the desired result. Promotion was from the ranks and was felt to go to the most competent and supportive colleagues.

It is not unlikely that this department benefited from a certain "Hawthorne effect"[16] because of the key role it had played in a successful turnaround. At the time of the interviews, the euphoria of the successful turnaround was probably at its peak. Observers inside the company commented that people's values had not really changed but that the turnaround had transformed a discipline of obedience toward superiors into a discipline of service toward customers.

Results of the Survey: Six Dimensions of Organizational Cultures

The IBM studies had resulted in the identification of four dimensions of *national* cultures (power distance, individualism-collectivism, masculinity-femininity, and uncertainty avoidance). These were dimensions of *values*, because the national IBM subsidiaries primarily differed on the cultural values of their employees. The twenty units studied in the IRIC cross-organizational study, however, differed only slightly with respect to the cultural values of their members, but they varied considerably in their practices.

Most questions in the paper-and-pencil survey measured *people's perceptions of the practices in their work unit*. These were presented in a "Where I work . . ." format; for example:

WHERE I WORK:

Meeting times are kept very punctually	1 2 3 4 5	Meeting times are only kept approximately
Quantity prevails over quality	1 2 3 4 5	Quality prevails over quantity

Each item thus consisted of two opposite statements: which statement was put in the right column and which in the left column was decided on a random basis, so that their position could not suggest their desirability.

All sixty-one "Where I work . . ." questions were designed on the basis of the information collected in the open interviews and were subjected to a statistical analysis very similar to the one used in the IBM studies. They produced six entirely new dimensions: of practices, not of values. What was used was a factor analysis of a matrix of sixty-one questions by twenty units; for each unit, a mean score was computed on each question across all respondents (who comprised one-third managers, one-third professionals, and one-third nonprofessionals). This analysis produced six clear factors reflecting dimensions of (perceived) practices distinguishing the twenty organizational units from each other. These six dimensions were mutually independent; that is, they occurred in all possible combinations.

Choosing labels for empirically found dimensions is a subjective process: it represents the step from data to theory. The labels chosen have been changed several times. Their present formulation was discussed at length with people in the units. As much as possible, the labels had to avoid suggesting a "good" and a "bad" pole for a dimension. Whether the score of a unit on a dimension should be interpreted as good or bad depends entirely on where the people responsible for managing the unit wanted it to go. The terms finally arrived at are the following:

1. Process oriented versus results oriented
2. Employee oriented versus job oriented
3. Parochial versus professional
4. Open system versus closed system
5. Loose versus tight control
6. Normative versus pragmatic

The order of the six cross-organizational dimensions (their number) reflects the order in which they appeared in the analysis, but it has no theoretical meaning; number 1 is not more important than number 6. A lower number only shows that the questionnaire contained more questions dealing with dimension 1 than with dimension 2, and so on; this can well be seen as a reflection of the interests of the researchers who designed the questionnaire.

For each of the six dimensions, three key "Where I work . . ." questions were chosen to calculate an index value of each unit on each dimension, very much the same way as index values in the IBM studies were computed for each country on each cross-national dimension. The unit scores of the three questions chosen were strongly correlated with each other.[17] Their content was such that together they would convey the essence of the dimension, as the researchers saw it, to the managers and the employees of the units in the feedback sessions.

Dimension 1 opposes a concern with means (*process oriented*) to a concern with goals (*results oriented*). The three key items show that in the process-oriented cultures, people perceived themselves as avoiding risks and spending only a limited effort in their jobs, while each day was pretty much the same. In the results-oriented cultures, people perceived themselves as comfortable in unfamiliar situations and as putting in a maximal effort, while each day was felt to bring new challenges. On a scale from 0 to 100, in which 0 represents the most process-oriented unit and 100 the most results-oriented unit among the twenty, HGBV, the chemical plant described earlier, scored 2 (very process oriented, little concern for results), while the SAS passenger terminal scored 100: it was the most results-oriented unit of all. For this dimension it is difficult not to attach a "good" label to the results-oriented pole and a "bad" label to the other side. Nevertheless, there are operations for which a single-minded focus on the process is essential. The most process-oriented unit (score 0) was a production unit in a pharmaceutical firm. Drug manufacturing is an example of a risk-avoiding, routine-based environment in which it is doubtful whether one would want its culture to be results oriented. Similar concerns exist in many other organizational units. So, even a results orientation is not always "good" and its opposite not always "bad."

One of the main claims from Peters and Waterman's book *In Search of Excellence* was that "strong" cultures are more effective than "weak" ones. A problem in verifying this proposition was that in the corporate culture literature one would search in vain for a practical (operational) measure of culture strength. As the issue seemed important, the IRIC project developed a method for measuring the strength of a culture. A strong culture was interpreted as a homogeneous culture—that is, one in which all survey respondents gave about the same answers on the key questions, regardless of the content of the questions. A weak culture was a heterogeneous one: this type was evidenced when answers among people in the same unit varied widely. The survey data showed that across the twenty units studied, culture strength (homogeneity) was significantly correlated with results orientation.[18] To the extent that *results oriented* stands for *effective*, Peters and Waterman's proposition about the effectiveness of strong cultures was therefore confirmed.

Dimension 2 opposes a concern for people (*employee oriented*) to a concern for completing the job (*job oriented*). The key items selected show that in the employee-oriented cultures, people felt that their personal problems were taken into account, that the organization took a responsibility for employee welfare, and that important decisions were made by groups or committees. In the job-oriented units, people experienced strong pressure to complete the job; they perceived the organization as interested only in the work employees did, not in their personal and family welfare; and they reported that important decisions were made by individuals. On a scale from 0 to 100, HGBV scored 100 and the SAS passenger terminal 95—both of them extremely employee oriented. Scores on this dimension reflected the philosophy of the unit or company's founder(s), but they reflected as well the possible scars left by past events: units that had recently been in economic trouble, especially if this had been accompanied by collective layoffs, tended to score job oriented, even if according to informants the past had been different. Opinions about the desirability of a strong employee orientation differed among the leaders of the units in the study. In the feedback discussions some top managers wanted their unit to become more employee oriented, but others desired a move in the opposite direction.

The employee-oriented versus job-oriented dimension corresponds to the two axes of a classic U.S. leadership model: Robert Blake and Jane Mouton's *managerial grid*.[19] Blake and Mouton developed an extensive system of leadership training on the basis of their model. In this training, employee orientation and job orientation are treated as two independent dimensions: a person can be high on both, on one, or on neither. This treatment seems to be in conflict with our placing of the two orientations at opposite poles of a single dimension. However, Blake and Mouton's grid applies to individuals, while the IRIC study compared organizational units. What the IRIC study shows is that while individuals may well be both job oriented *and* employee oriented at the same time, organizational cultures tend to favor one or the other.

Dimension 3 opposes units whose employees derive their identity largely from the organization (*parochial*) to units in which people identify with their type of job (*professional*). The key questions show that members of parochial cultures felt that the organization's norms covered their behavior at home as well as on the job; they felt that in hiring employees, the company took their social and family background into account as much as their job competence; and they did not look far into the future (they probably assumed the organization would do this for them). On the other side, members of professional cultures considered their private lives their own business, they felt the organization hired on the basis of job competence only, and they did think far ahead. U.S. sociologist Robert Merton has called this distinction *local versus cosmopolitan*, the contrast between an internal and an external frame of reference.[20] The parochial type of culture is often associated with Japanese companies. Predictably in the IRIC survey, unit scores on this dimension were correlated with the unit members' level of education: parochial units tended to have employees with less formal education. SAS passenger terminal employees scored quite parochial (24); HGBV employees scored about halfway (48).

Dimension 4 opposes *open systems* to *closed systems*. The key items show that in the open system units, members considered both the organization and its people open to newcomers and outsiders; almost anyone would fit into the organization, and new employees needed only a few days to feel at home. In the closed system units, the organization and its people were felt to be closed and secretive, even among insiders; only very special people fitted into the organization, and new employees needed more than a year to feel at home (in the most closed unit, one member of the managing board confessed that he still felt like an outsider after twenty-two years). On this dimension, HGBV again scored halfway (51) and SAS extremely open (9). What this dimension describes is the communication climate. It was the only one of the six "practices" dimensions associated with nationality: it seemed that an open organizational communication climate was a characteristic of Denmark more than of the Netherlands. However, one Danish organization scored very closed.

Dimension 5 refers to the amount of internal structuring in the organization. According to the key questions, people in *loose control* units felt that no one thought of cost, meeting times were only kept approximately, and jokes about the company and the job were frequent. People in *tight control* units described their work environment as cost-conscious, meeting times were kept punctually, and jokes about the company and/or the job were rare. It appears from the data that a tight formal control system is associated, at least statistically, with strict unwritten codes in terms of dress and dignified behavior. On a scale where 0 equals loose and 100 equals tight, SAS with its uniformed personnel scored extremely tight (96), and HGBV scored once more halfway (52); halfway, though, was quite loose for a production unit, as a comparison with other production units showed.

Dimension 6, finally, deals with the popular notion of customer orientation. *Pragmatic* units were market driven; *normative* units perceived their task in relation to the outside world as the implementation of inviolable rules. The key items show that in the normative units, the major emphasis was on correctly following organizational procedures, which were more important than results; in matters of business ethics and honesty, the unit's standards were felt to be high. In the pragmatic units, there was a major emphasis on meeting the customer's needs; results were more important than correct procedures; and in matters of business ethics, a pragmatic rather than a dogmatic attitude prevailed. The SAS passenger terminal was the top-scoring unit on the pragmatic side (100), which shows that Jan Carlzon's message had come across. HGBV scored 68, also on the pragmatic side. In the past as it was described in the HGBV case study, the company might have been more normative toward its customers, but it seemed to have adapted to its new competitive situation.

The Scope for Competitive Advantages in Cultural Matters

Inspection of the scoring profiles of the twenty units on the six dimensions shows that dimensions 1, 3, 5, and 6 (process versus results, parochial versus professional, loose versus tight, and normative versus pragmatic) relate to the type of work the organization does and to the type of market in which it operates. These four dimensions partly reflect the industry (or business) culture according to Figure 10.1. On dimension 1, most manufacturing and large office units scored process oriented; research and development units and service units scored more results oriented. On dimension 3, units with a traditional technology scored parochial; high-tech units scored professional. On dimension 5, units delivering precision or risky products or services (such as pharmaceuticals or money transactions) scored tight; those with innovative or unpredictable activities scored loose. To the researchers' surprise, the two city police forces studied scored on the loose side (16 and 41): the work of a police officer, however, is highly unpredictable, and police personnel have considerable discretion in the way they want to carry out their tasks. On dimension 6, service units and those operating in competitive markets scored pragmatic; units involved in the implementation of laws and those operating under a monopoly scored normative.

While the task and market environment thus affect the dimension scores, the IRIC study, as noted, also produced its share of surprises: production units with an unexpectedly strong results orientation even on the shop floor, along with a unit such as HGBV with a loose control system in relation to its task. These surprises represent the distinctive elements in a unit's culture (as compared with similar units) and the competitive advantages or disadvantages of a particular organizational culture.

The other two dimensions, 2 and 4 (employee versus job and open versus closed), seem to be less constrained by task and market but rather based on historical factors such as the philosophy of the founder(s) and recent crises. In the case of dimension 4, open versus closed system, the national cultural environment was already shown to play a role as well.

Figure 10.1 indicates that although organizational cultures are *mainly* composed of practices, they do have a modest values component. The cross-organizational IRIC survey included the values questions from the cross-national IBM studies. The organizations differed somewhat on three clusters of values. The first resembled the cross-national dimension of uncertainty avoidance, although the differences showed up on other survey questions than those used for computing the country UAI scores. The cross-organizational uncertainty-avoidance measure was correlated with dimension 4 (open versus closed), with weak uncertainty avoidance obviously on the side of an open communication climate. The relationship was reinforced by the fact that the Danish units, with one exception, scored more open than the Dutch ones. Denmark and the Netherlands, though similar on most national culture scores, differed most on their national uncertainty avoidance scores, Denmark scoring much lower.

A second cluster of cross-organizational values bore some resemblance to power distance. It was correlated with dimension 1 (process oriented versus results oriented): larger power distances were associated with process orientation and smaller ones with results orientation.

Clusters of cross-organizational value differences associated with individualism and masculinity were not found in the IRIC study. It is possible that this was because the study was restricted to business organizations and public institutions. If, for example, health and welfare organizations had been included, the study might have shown a wider range of values with regard to helping other people, which would have produced a feminine-masculine dimension.

Questions that in the cross-national study composed the individualism and masculinity dimensions appeared in the cross-organizational study in a different configuration. It was labeled *work centrality* (strong or weak): the importance of work in one's total life pattern. It was correlated with dimension 3: parochial versus professional. Work centrality obviously is stronger in professional organization cultures. In parochial cultures, people do not take their work problems home.

From the six organizational culture dimensions, numbers 1, 3, and 4 were thus to some extent associated with values. For the other three dimensions—2, 5, and 6—no link with values was found at all. These dimensions just described practices to which people had been socialized without their basic values being involved.

Organizational Culture and Other Organizational Characteristics

In the IBM studies, a national culture's antecedents and consequences were proved by correlating the country scores with all kinds of external data. These included such economic indicators as the country's gross national income per capita, political measures such as an index of press freedom, and demographic data such as the population growth rate. Comparisons were also made with the results of other surveys that covered the same countries but used different questions and different respondents. The IRIC cross-organizational study included a similar "validation" of the dimensions against external data. This time, of course, the data used consisted of information about the organizational units obtained in other ways and from other sources.

Besides the interviews and the survey, the IRIC study included the collection of quantifiable data about the units as wholes. Examples of such information (labeled *structural data*) are total employee strength, budget composition, economic results, and the ages of key managers. All structural data were personally collected by Geert. Finding out what meaningful structural data *could* be obtained was a heuristic process that went along with the actual collection of the data. This process was too complicated to be shared across researchers. The informants for the structural data were the top manager, the chief personnel officer, and the chief budget officer.

They were presented with written questionnaires, followed up by personal interviews.

Out of a large number of quantifiable characteristics tried, about forty provided usable data. For these forty characteristics, the scores for each of the twenty units were correlated with the unit scores on the six practices dimensions.[21] In the following paragraphs, for each of the six practice dimensions the most important relationships found are described.

There was a strong correlation between the scores on practice dimension 1, process orientation versus results orientation, and the balance of labor cost versus material cost in the operating budget (the money necessary for daily functioning). An operation can be characterized as labor-intensive, material-intensive, or capital-intensive, depending on which of the three categories of cost takes the largest share of its operating budget. Labor-intensive units (holding number of employees constant) scored more results oriented, while material-intensive units (again holding number of employees constant) scored more process oriented. If an operation is labor-intensive, the effort of people by definition plays an important role in its results. This situation appears more likely to breed a results-oriented culture. The yield of material-intensive and capital-intensive units tends to depend on technical processes, which fact seems to stimulate a process-oriented culture. It is therefore not surprising that one finds research and development units and service units on the results-oriented side; manufacturing and office units, subject to more automation, are more often found on the process-oriented side.

The second-highest correlation of results orientation was with lower absenteeism. This is a nice validation of the fact that, as one of the key questions formulated it, "people put in a maximal effort." Next there were three significant correlations between results orientation and the structure of the organizations. Flatter organizations (larger span of control for the unit top manager) scored more results oriented. This confirms one of Peters and Waterman's maxims: "simple form, lean staff." Three simplified scales were used based on the Aston Studies of organizational structure referred to in Chapter 9,[22] measuring centralization, specialization, and formalization. Both specialization and formalization were negatively correlated with results orientation: more specialized and more formalized units tend to be more process oriented. Centralization was not correlated with this dimension. Results orientation was also correlated with having a top-management team with a lower education level and promoted from the ranks. Finally, in results-oriented units, union membership among employees tended to be lower.

The strongest correlations with dimension 2 (employee orientation versus job orientation) were with the way the unit was controlled by the organization to which it belonged. Where the top manager of the unit stated that his superiors evaluated him on profits and other financial performance measures, the members scored the unit culture as job oriented. Where the top manager of the unit felt that his superiors evaluated him on performance versus a budget, the opposite was the case: members scored the unit culture to be employee oriented. It seems that operating against external standards (profits in a market) breeds a less benevolent culture than operating against internal standards (a budget). Where the top manager stated that he allowed controversial news to be published in the employee newsletter, members felt the unit to be more employee oriented, which validated the top manager's veracity.

The remaining correlations of employee orientation were with the average seniority (years with the company) and age of employees (more senior employees scored a more job-oriented culture), with the education level of the top-management team (less-educated teams correspond with a more job-oriented culture), and with the total invested capital (surprisingly, not with the invested capital per employee). Large organizations with heavy investment tended to be more employee oriented than job oriented.

On dimension 3 (parochial versus professional), units with a traditional technology tended to score parochial and high-tech units professional. The strongest correlations of this dimension were with various measures of size: it was not unexpected that the larger organizations fostered the more professional cultures. Also as could be expected, professional cultures had less labor union membership. Their managers had a higher average education level and age. Their organizational structures showed more specialization. An interesting correlation was with the time budget of the unit top manager, by which is meant the way the unit top manager claimed to spend his time. In the units with a professional culture, the top managers claimed to spend a relatively large share of their time in meetings and person-to-person discussions. Finally, the privately owned units tended to score more professional than the public ones.

Dimension 4 (open versus closed system) was responsible for the single strongest correlation with external data: between the percentage of women among the employees and the openness of the communication climate.[23]

The percentage of women among *managers* and the presence of at least one woman in the top-management team were also correlated with openness. However, this correlation was affected by the binational composition of the research population. Among developed European countries, Denmark at the time of the research had one of the highest participation rates of women in the workforce, while the Netherlands had one of the lowest. Also, as mentioned earlier, Danish units as a group (with one exception) scored more open than Dutch units. This does not necessarily exclude a causal relationship between the participation of women in the workforce and a more open communication climate: it could very well be the explanation as to *why* the Danish units were so much more open.

Also connected with the open versus closed dimension were the associations of formalization with a more closed culture (a nice cross-validation of both measures), of allowing controversial issues in the employee newsletter with an open culture (obviously), and of higher average seniority with a more open culture.

The strongest correlation of dimension 5 (loose versus tight control) was with an item in the self-reported time budget of the unit top manager: where the top manager claimed to spend a relatively large part of his time reading and writing reports and memos from inside the organization, control was found to be tighter. This finding makes perfect sense. We also found that material-intensive units have more tightly controlled cultures. As the results of such units often depend on small margins of material yields, this makes sense too.

Tight control was also correlated with the percentage of female managers and of female employees, in that order. This was most likely a consequence of the simple, repetitive, and clerical activities for which, in the organizations studied, the larger numbers of women tended to be hired. Tighter control was found in units with a lower education level among male and female employees and also among its top managers. This reminds us of the finding in Chapter 3 that employees in lower-educated occupations maintained larger power distances. In units in which the number of employees had recently increased, control was felt to be looser; where the number of employees had been reduced, control was perceived as tighter. Employee layoffs are obviously associated with budget squeezes. Finally, absenteeism among employees was lower where control was perceived to be less tight. Absenteeism is evidently one way of escape from the pressure of a tight control system.

For dimension 6 (normative versus pragmatic), only one meaningful correlation with external data was found. Privately owned units in the sample were more pragmatic, public units (such as the police departments) more normative.

Missing from the list of external data correlated with culture were measures of the organizations' performance. This does not mean that culture is not related to performance; it means only that the research did not find comparable yardsticks for the performance of so varied a set of organizational units.

The relationships described in this section show objective conditions of organizations that were associated with particular culture profiles. They point to the things one has to change in order to modify an organization's culture—for example, certain aspects of its structure, or the priorities of the top manager. We will come back to this theme at the end of the chapter.

Organizational Subcultures

A follow-up study by IRIC investigated organizational subcultures.[24] In 1988 a Danish insurance company commissioned IRIC to study the cultures of all its departments, surveying its total population of 3,400 employees. The study used the same approach as the previous Danish-Dutch project: open-ended interviews leading to the composition of a survey questionnaire.

The total respondent population could be divided into 131 "organic" working groups. These were the smallest building blocks of the organization, whose members had regular face-to-face contact. Managers were not included in the groups they managed but were combined with colleagues at their level of the hierarchy.

On the basis of their survey answers, the 131 groups could be sorted into three clearly distinct subcultures: a *professional*, an *administrative*, and a *customer interface* subculture. The first included all managers and employees in tasks for which a higher education was normally required, the second all the (mostly female) employees in clerical departments, and the third two groups of employees dealing directly with customers: salespeople and claim handlers.

Using the six dimensions from the Danish-Dutch study, the researchers showed various culture gaps among the three subcultures. The professional groups were the most job oriented, professional, open, tightly controlled, and pragmatic; the administrative groups the most parochial and normative; the customer interface groups the most results and employee oriented, closed, and loosely controlled. The customer interface subculture represented a counterculture to the professional culture.

Just before the survey was conducted, the company had gone through two cases of internal rebellion: from the salespeople and from the women. The sales rebellion had been a conflict about working conditions and compensation; a sales strike had only just been prevented. This problem can be understood from the wide gap between the professional and customer interface subcultures. This rift on the culture map of the company proved dangerous. The customer interface people generate the business—without them, an insurance company cannot survive. The managers and professionals who made the key decisions in this company belonged to a notably different subculture: a high-profile, glorified environment in which big money, business trends, and market power were daily concerns—far from the crowd who did the actual work and brought in the daily earnings.

The women's rebellion was about a lack of careers for women, and it happened when the share of female employees had passed the 50 percent mark. The rebellion can be understood by looking at the gap between the professional and the administrative subcultures. Management, from their professional subculture, saw women as belonging to the administrative subculture: employees in routine jobs, not upwardly mobile. But this image was no longer accurate, if it had ever been so. Of the 1,700 women in the company, 700 had a higher education; many worked in professional roles, and even those in administrative roles were nearly as much interested in a career as their male colleagues. The interviews had revealed that managers believed most women to experience conflicts between their work and their private and family lives. The survey, however, showed that whereas 21 percent of the women employees claimed to suffer from such conflicts, 30 percent of the men did. The women's explanation of this result was that if a woman took a job, she had to have her family problems resolved, whereas many men never consciously resolved them.

For an understanding of the culture of this insurance company, the subculture split was essential. Unfortunately, the members of management—caught in their professional culture—did not recognize the alarming aspects of the culture rifts. They took little action as a result of the survey. Soon afterward the company started losing money; a few years later it changed ownership and top management.

Individual Perceptions of Organizational Cultures

Different individuals within the same organizational unit do not necessarily give identical answers to questions about how they see their organization's practices. The IRIC study did not look at differences among individuals: its concern was with differences among organizational cultures. Michael Bond, at the Chinese University of Hong Kong, who was interested in individual differences, offered to reanalyze the IRIC database from this point of view. Chung-Leung Luk, at that time Bond's assistant, performed the necessary computer work. His results show the structure in the variation of individual scores around the means of the organizational units: in what ways individuals' answers differed *after organization culture differences were eliminated.* This extension of the IRIC project has been described in a joint paper by Hofstede, Bond, and Luk.[25]

The individual perceptions study first analyzed the values questions and the practices questions separately. As is natural, individuals within the same unit differed more in their values, which were private, than in their perceptions of the unit's practices, in which they shared. Yet it became clear that for individuals, values and perceptions of practices were related, so in the further analysis they could be combined. This combination produced six dimensions of individuals' answers:

1. **Alienation**, a state of mind in which all perceptions of practices were negative. Alienated respondents were misers: they scored the organization as less professional, felt management to be more distant, trusted colleagues less, saw the organization as less orderly, felt more hostile to it, and perceived less integration between the organization and its employees. Alienation was stronger among employees who were younger, less educated, and nonmanagerial.

2. **Workaholism**, a term chosen by the researchers for a strong commitment to work (for example, the job is more important than leisure time), as opposed to a need for a supportive organization (for example, wanting to work in a well-defined job situation). Workaholism was stronger among employees who were younger, more educated, male, and managerial.

3. **Ambition**, or personal need for achievement (for example, wanting to contribute to the success of the organization and wanting opportunities for advancement).

4. **Machismo**, or personal masculinity (for example, parents should stimulate children to be best in class, and when a man's career demands it, the family should make sacrifices).

5. **Orderliness**; employees who had more orderly minds saw the organization as more orderly.

6. **Authoritarianism** (for example, it is undesirable that management authority can be questioned). Authoritarianism was stronger for employees who were less educated and female.

Systematic individual differences in perceptions of organizational cultures are most likely based on personality. In fact, five of the dimensions listed here resemble the Big Five dimensions of personality described in Chapter 2 (openness to experience, conscientiousness, extroversion, agreeableness, and neuroticism). The individual perceptions dimensions can be associated with Big Five dimensions as follows:[26]

1. Alienation with neuroticism
2. Workaholism with extraversion (which includes *active* and *energetic*)
3. Ambition with openness to experience
4. Machismo negatively with agreeableness
5. Orderliness with conscientiousness

No personality factor was available for an association with authoritarianism, which surprised us. In Chapter 2 we described how Geert and Big Five author Robert R. McCrae found mean personality scores for comparative samples from thirty-three countries to correlate significantly with all four IBM culture dimensions, but not with long-term orientation.[27] Geert wondered whether this could be explained from the fact that both classifications were conceived by Western minds. Could the Big Five model miss out on a personality dimension that across countries might relate to long- versus short-term orientation?

There is research evidence suggesting that the Big Five personality measure, developed in the West, may be incomplete in Asia.[28] Findings from China and the Philippines yielded a sixth personality factor: *interpersonal relatedness*, or *gregariousness*. Our organizational culture study located in Europe, meanwhile, missed a personality factor related to authoritarianism.

Gregariousness and authoritarianism may be interpreted as two facets of a common sixth personality factor, dealing with dependence on others. Across countries, this might very well correlate with long-term orientation. Extending the Big Five to a Big Six may increase its cross-cultural universality.[29]

Gardens, Bouquets, and Flowers of Social Science

The choice of a level of analysis, as discussed in Chapters 1 and 2, has figured prominently in the present chapter. When we compared the same kind of data across countries, across organizational units, and across individuals, we found three different sets of dimensions, belonging to three different social science disciplines: anthropology, sociology, and psychology.

The cross-national study of the IBM data took what were first supposed to be psychological data and aggregated them to the country level. At that level they melted into concepts describing societies, such as collectivism versus individualism, which really belong to anthropology and/or to political science. The database of the IRIC organizational culture study, analyzed at the level of organizational units, produced basic distinctions from organizational sociology, like Merton's local versus cosmopolitan. The same database, analyzed at the level of individual differences from the organizational unit's mean, supported the results of personality research in individual psychology.

Societies, organizations, and individuals represent the gardens, bouquets, and flowers of social science. Our research has shown that the three are related and part of the same social reality. If we want to understand our social environment, we cannot fence ourselves into the confines of one level only: we should be prepared to count with all three.[30]

Occupational Cultures

In Figure 10.1 an occupational culture level was placed halfway between nation and organization, because entering an occupational field means the acquisition of both values and practices; the place of socialization is the school, apprenticeship, or university, and the time is between childhood and entering work.

We know of no broad cross-occupational study that allows identifying dimensions of occupational cultures. Neither the five national culture (values) dimensions nor the six organizational culture (practices) dimensions will automatically apply to the occupational level. From the five cross-national dimensions, only power distance and masculinity-femininity were applicable to occupational differences in IBM. Chapter 4 showed that IBM occupations could not be described in terms of "individualist" or "collectivist," but rather as "intrinsic" or "extrinsic" according to what motivated most of those engaged in the occupation, the work itself or the conditions and the material rewards provided.

From a review of the literature and some guesswork, we predict that in a systematic cross-occupational study the following dimensions of occupational cultures may well be found:[31]

1. Handling people versus handling things (for example, nurse versus engineer)
2. Specialist versus generalist—or, from a different perspective, professional versus amateur (for example, psychologist versus politician)
3. Disciplined versus independent (for example, police officer versus shopkeeper)[32]
4. Structured versus unstructured (for example, systems analyst versus fashion designer)
5. Theoretical versus practical (for example, professor versus sales manager)
6. Normative versus pragmatic (for example, judge versus advertising agent)

These dimensions will have stronger associations with practices than the national culture dimensions and stronger associations with values than the organizational culture dimensions. They may also be used for distinctions *within* professions; for example, medical specialists can be placed on a "handling people versus handling things" continuum, with pediatricians landing far on the handling people side (they often deal with not only the child but the family as well) and surgeons and pathologists, who focus on details of the body, far on the handling things side.

Conclusions from the IRIC Research Project: Dimensions Versus Gestalts

The IRIC research project produced a six-dimensional model of organizational cultures, defined as perceived common practices: symbols, heroes, and rituals. The research data came from twenty organizational units in two northwestern European countries, and one should therefore be careful not to claim that the same model applies to any organization anywhere. Certain important types of organizations, such as those concerned with health and welfare, government, and the military, were not included.[33] We do not know what new practice dimensions may still be found in other countries. Nevertheless, we believe that the fact that organizational cultures can be meaningfully described by a number of practice dimensions is probably universally true. Also, it is likely that such dimensions will generally resemble, and partly overlap, the six described in this chapter.[34]

The geographic and industry limitations of the six-dimensional model imply that our questionnaire is not suitable for blanket replications. Interpreting the results is a matter of comparison. The formulas we used for computing the dimension scores were made for comparing an organization with the twenty units in the IRIC study, but they are meaningless in other environments and at other times. New studies should choose their own units to compare and develop their own standards for comparison. They should again start with interviews across the organizations to be included, in order to get a feel for the organizations' gestalts, and then compose their own questionnaire covering the crucial differences in the practices of these organizations.[35]

The dimensions found describe the culture of an organization, but they are not prescriptive: no position on one of the six dimensions is intrinsically good or bad. In Peters and Waterman's book *In Search of Excellence*, eight conditions for excellence were presented as norms. Their book suggested there is one best way toward excellence. The results of the IRIC study refute this. What is good or bad depends in each case on where one wants the organization to go, and a cultural feature that is an asset for one purpose is unavoidably a liability for another. Labeling positions on the dimension scales as more or less desirable is a matter of strategic choice, and this process will vary from one organization to another. In particular, a stress on customer orientation (becoming more pragmatic on dimension 6) is highly relevant for organizations engaged in services and the manufacturing of custom-made quality products but may be unnecessary or even harmful for, say, the manufacturing of standard products in a competitive price market.

This chapter referred earlier to the controversy about whether an organization *is* or *has* a culture. On the basis of the IRIC research project, we propose that practices are features an organization *has*. Because of the important role of practices in organizational cultures, the latter can be considered *somewhat* manageable. We saw that changing collective values of adult people in an intended direction is extremely difficult, if not impossible. Collective practices, however, depend on organizational characteristics such as structures and systems, and they can be influenced in more or less predictable ways by changing these organizational characteristics. Nevertheless, as argued previously, organization cultures are also in a way integrated wholes, or gestalts, and a gestalt can be considered something the organization *is*. Organizations are sometimes compared to animals; thus, HGBV could be pictured as an elephant (slow, bulky, self-confident) and the SAS passenger terminal as a stork (reliable, caring, transporting). The animal metaphor suggests limits to the changeability of the gestalt; one cannot train an elephant to become a racehorse, let alone to become a stork.

Changes in practices represent the margin of freedom in influencing these wholes, the kinds of things the animals can learn without losing their essence. Because they are wholes, an integrating and inspiring type of leadership is needed to give these structural and systems changes a meaning for the people involved. The outcome should be a new and coherent cultural pattern, as was illustrated by the SAS case.

Managing (with) Organizational Culture

Back in the 1980s, when Geert tried to sell participation in the organizational culture research project to top managers of organizations, he claimed that "organizational culture represents the psychological assets of the organization that predict its material assets in five years' time." As we see it now, the crucial element is not the organizational culture itself, but what (top) management does with it. Four aspects have to be balanced (Figure 10.2).[36]

The performance of an organization should be measured against its objectives, and top management's role is to translate objectives into strategy—even if by default all that emerges is a laissez-faire strategy. *Strategies* are carried out via the existing *structure* and *control* system, and their

FIGURE 10.2 Relationships Among Strategy, Structure, Control, and Culture

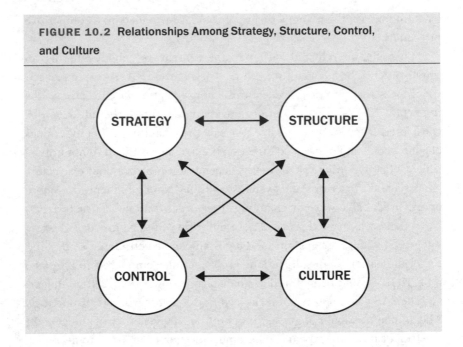

outcome is modified by the organization's *culture*—and all four of these elements influence each other.

The IRIC study has shown that, as long as quantitative studies of organizational cultures are not used as isolated tricks but are integrated into a broader approach, they are both feasible and useful. In a world of hardware and bottom-line figures, the scores make organizational culture differences visible; by becoming visible, they move up on management's priority list.

Practical uses of such a study for managers and members of organizations, as well as for consultants, are listed here:

- Identifying the subcultures in one's own organization. The extension of the IRIC project to the insurance company demonstrated the importance of this application. As Figure 10.3 illustrates, organizations may be culturally divided according to hierarchical levels: top management, middle- and lower-level managers, professional employees, and other employees (office or shop floor). Other potential sources of internal cultural divisions are functional area (such as sales versus production versus research), product/market division, country of operation, and, for organizations having gone through mergers,

FIGURE 10.3 Potential Subdivisions of an Organization's Culture

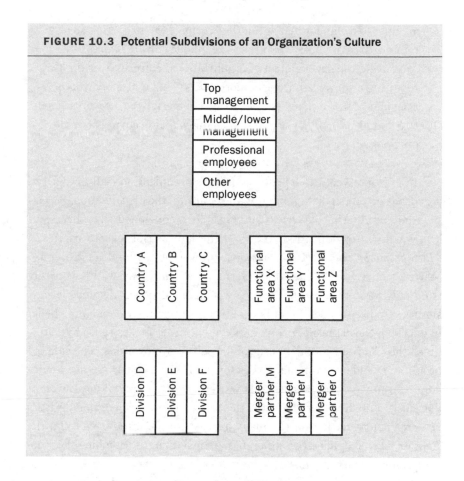

former merger partners. We have met cases in which twenty years after a merger the cultural traces of the merged parts could still be found as slightly different moral circles (see Chapter 1). Not all of these potential divisions will be equally strong, but it is important for the managers and members of a complex organization to know its cultural map—which, as we found, is not always the case.

- Testing whether the culture fits the strategies set out for the future. Cultural constraints determine which strategies are feasible for an organization and which are not. For example, if a culture is strongly normative, a strategy for competing on customer service has little chance of success.
- In the case of mergers and acquisitions, identifying the potential areas of culture conflict between the partners. This can be either an input to the decision on whether to merge, or, if the decision has been made,

an input to a plan for managing the postmerger integration so as to minimize friction losses and preserve unique cultural capital.

■ Measuring the development of organizational cultures over time, by repeating a survey after one of more years. This will show whether attempted culture changes have, indeed, materialized, as well as identify the cultural effects of external changes that occurred after the previous survey.

In practice, what can one do about one's organization's culture? First, it depends on one's position in, or with regard to, the organization. A classic study by Eberhard Witte, from Germany, concluded that successful innovations in organizations required the joint action of two parties: a *Machtpromotor* and a *Fachpromotor* (a power holder and an expert).[37] Witte's model was developed on German data and may well be entirely valid only for countries like Germany with small power distance (accessibility of power holders) and fairly strong uncertainty avoidance (belief in experts). Nevertheless, in any national culture it makes sense to distinguish the two roles. Both are crucial for culture innovations. The support of a power holder—preferably a person with some charisma, not a pure administrator—is indispensable. However, expertise in making the right diagnosis and choosing the right therapy is also indispensable. Witte's research suggests that, in Germany at least, the *Machtpromotor* and the *Fachpromotor* should be two different persons; trying to combine the roles compromises one of them.

The *Fachpromotor* should provide a proper diagnosis of the present state of the organization's culture and subcultures. It is dangerous to assume one knows one's organization's present cultural map and how it should be changed. Organizations can look very different from the top compared with the middle or bottom where the actual work is done. The IRIC researchers, when feeding back the interview and survey results to the units' management members, always asked them to guess where their organization stood on the various dimensions, before showing them how their people had answered the survey questions. Some managers were uncannily insightful and correct in their guesses, but others were way off. In the latter case, wishful thinking and unfounded fears often affected their answers. So, a proper diagnosis is essential.

With sound diagnostic information, the *Machtpromotor* should then make cultural considerations part of the organization's *strategy*. What are the strengths and weaknesses of the present cultural map? Can the strengths be better exploited and the weaknesses circumvented? Can the organization continue to live with its present culture? If management wants it to change, is this feasible? Do the benefits outweigh the costs (which are always higher than expected)? Are the material resources and human skills available that will be needed for changing the culture? And if it has been decided that the culture should change, what steps will be taken to implement the changes? Does the *Machtpromotor* realize his or her own crucial and lasting role in this process? Will he or she be given enough time by superiors, directors, or banks to take the process to its completion (and it always takes longer than one thinks)? Can a sufficient amount of support for the necessary changes be mobilized within the organization? Who will be the supporters? Who will be the resisters? Can the latter be circumvented or put in positions where they can do no harm?

Although culture is a "soft" characteristic, changing it calls for "hard" measures. *Structural changes* may mean closing departments, opening other departments, merging or splitting activities, or moving people and/or groups geographically. The general rule is that when people are moved as individuals, they will adapt to the culture of their new environment; when people are moved as groups, they will bring their group culture along. People in groups have developed, as part of their culture, ways of interacting that are highly stable and difficult to change. Changing them means that all interpersonal relationships have to be renegotiated. If new tasks or a new environment force such a renegotiation, however, there is a good chance that undesirable aspects of the old culture will be cleaned up.

Process changes mean instituting new procedures, eliminating controls or establishing new controls, implementing or discontinuing automation, and short-circuiting communications or introducing new communication links.

A bulk chemicals company wanted to move into the more profitable specialty chemicals market. The company was successful only after managers renounced their usual detailed process figures and replaced them with checks on delivery time and on customer satisfaction.

Processes can be controlled on the basis of their outputs or through their inputs. The former, if possible, is more effective. Especially in the public sector, activities whose outputs can be clearly defined are often controlled only by their inputs, for traditional budget reasons.

Personnel changes mean new hiring and promoting policies. The gatekeeper role of the human resources department should be recognized. HR managers unconsciously maintain hero models for the organization that in a new culture may have to be revised. Could the hero be a heroine? Can a man with an earring be promoted? Training programs, often the first thing managers think of when wanting to change cultures, are functional only after the need for retraining has been established by structural, process, and personnel changes (as in the SAS case). Training programs without the support of hard changes usually remain at the level of lip service and are a waste of money. In general, one should always be suspicious about suggestions to train *someone else*. Training is effective only if the trainee wants to be trained.

In attempted culture changes, new symbols often receive a lot of attention. They are easily visible: new name, logo, uniforms, slogans, and portraits on the wall—all that belongs to the fashionable area of *corporate identity*. But symbols are only the most superficial level of culture. New symbols without the support of more fundamental changes at the deeper levels of heroes, rituals, and the values of key leaders just mean a lot of hoopla, the effects of which wear off quickly.

This includes formulating *corporate values*, which, as of the 1990s, represents a fad in which many international corporations seem to have believed. The word *values* in this case means something entirely different from our definition in Chapter 1. Corporate values are written statements of desirable principles for corporate behavior; they belong to ideology and are not empirically based on people's feelings or preferences. In our opinion, most corporate values statements are no more than pious wishful thinking, corresponding to one or more top executives' hobbies. Corporate cultures are moved not by what top managers say or write, but by who they are and what they do. The corporate values of the infamous U.S.-based Enron Corporation, which went bankrupt in 2001, included *professionalism* and *integrity*. Unless they are confirmed by the corporation's behavioral records, and maintained by sanctions against those not respecting them, corporate values are worth less than the paper they are written on. Hypocrisy is worse than silence.[38]

Culture change in an organization asks for persistence, as well as sustained attention by the *Machtpromotor*. If the process was started by a culture diagnosis, it is evidently useful to repeat this diagnosis after sufficient time has passed for the planned changes to become noticeable. In this way, a process of monitoring is started in which changes actually found are compared with intended changes and further corrections can be applied. If organizational culture is *somewhat* manageable, this is the way to go about it.

In Table 10.2 the main steps in managing (with) culture have been summarized as a practical checklist.

TABLE 10.2 Managing (with) Organizational Culture

- Is a task of top management that cannot be delegated
- Demands both power and expertise
- Should start with a cultural map of the organization
- Demands strategic choices
  - Is present culture matched with strategy?
  - If not, can strategy be adapted?
  - If not, what change of culture is needed?
  - Is this change feasible—do we have the people?
  - What will be the costs in management attention and money?
  - Do the expected benefits outweigh these costs?
  - What is a realistic time span for the changes?
  - If in doubt, better change strategy anyway.
  - Different subcultures may demand different approaches.
- Create a network of change agents in the organization
  - Some key people at all levels.
  - If key people start, others will follow.
  - Can resisters be circumvented?
- Design necessary structural changes
  - Opening or closing departments.
  - Merging or splitting departments or tasks.
  - Should groups or individuals be moved?
  - Are tasks matched with talents?
- Design necessary process changes
  - Eliminating or establishing controls.
  - Automating or eliminating automation.
  - Establishing or cutting communication links.
  - Replace control of inputs by control of outputs?
- Revise personnel policies
  - Reconsider criteria for hiring.
  - Reconsider criteria for promotion.
  - Is human resource management up to its new task?
  - Design timely job rotation.
  - Be suspicious of plans to train others.
  - The need for training has to be felt by trainees themselves.
- Continue monitoring development of organizational culture
  - Persistence, sustained attention.
  - Periodically repeat culture diagnosis.

IMPLICATIONS

Intercultural Encounters

The English Elchi [ambassador] had reached Tehran a few days before we arrived there, and his reception was as brilliant as it was possible for a dog of an unbeliever to expect from our blessed Prophet's own lieutenant. . . . The princes and noblemen were enjoined to send the ambassador presents, and a general command issued that he and his suite were the Shah's guests, and that, on the pain of the royal anger, nothing but what was agreeable should be said to them.

All these attentions, one might suppose, would be more than sufficient to make infidels contented with their lot; but, on the contrary, when the subject of etiquette came to be discussed, interminable difficulties seemed to arise. The Elchi was the most intractable of mortals. First, on the subject of sitting. On the day of his audience of the Shah, he would not sit on the ground, but insisted upon having a chair; then the chair was to be placed so far, and no farther, from the throne. In the second place, of shoes, he insisted upon keeping on his shoes, and not walking barefooted upon the pavement; and he would not even put on our red cloth stockings. Thirdly, with respect to hats: he announced his intention of pulling his off to make his bow to the king, although we assured him that it was an act of great indecorum to uncover the head. And then, on the article of dress, a most violent dispute arose: at first, it was intimated that proper dresses should be sent to him and his suite, which would cover their persons (now too indecently exposed) so effectually that they might be fit to be

seen by the king; but this proposal he rejected with derision. He said that he
would appear before the Shah of Persia in the same dress he wore when before
his own sovereign.

—James Morier, *The Adventures of Hajji Baba of Ispahan*, 1824,
    Chapter LXXVII

James J. Morier (1780–1849) was a European, and *The Adventures of Hajji Baba of Ispahan* is a work of fiction. Morier, however, knew what he wrote about. He was born and raised in Ottoman Turkey as a son of the British consul at Constantinople (now Istanbul). Later on he spent altogether seven years as a British diplomat in Persia (present-day Iran). When *Hajji Baba* was translated into Persian, the readers refused to believe that it had been written by a foreigner. "Morier was by temperament an ideal traveler, reveling in the surprising interests of strange lands and peoples, and gifted with a humorous sympathy that enabled him to appreciate the motives actuating persons entirely dissimilar to himself," to quote the editor of the 1923 version of his book.[1] Morier obviously read and spoke Turkish and Persian. For all practical purposes he had become multicultural.

Intended Versus Unintended Intercultural Conflict

Human history is composed of wars between cultural groups. Joseph Campbell (1904–87), an American author on comparative mythology, found the primitive myths of nonliterate peoples without exception affirming and glorifying war. In the Old Testament, a holy book of both Judaism and Christianity and a source document for the Muslim Koran, there are numerous quotes like the following:

> *But in the cities of these people that the Lord your God gives you for an inheritance, you shall save alive nothing that breathes, but you shall utterly destroy them, the Hittites and the Amorites, the Canaanites and the Perizzites, the Hivites and the Jebusites, as the Lord your God has commanded.*
>
> —Deuteronomy 20:16–18

This is a religiously sanctified call for genocide.[2] The fifth commandment, "Thou shalt not kill," from the same Old Testament obviously applies only to members of the moral circle. Territorial expansion of one's own tribe by killing off others is not only permitted but also supposed to be ordered by God. Not only in the land of the Old Testament but also in many other parts of the world, territorial conflicts involving the killing or expelling of other groups continue to this day. The Arabic name of the modern Palestinians who dispute with the Israelis the rights on the land of Israel is Philistines, the same name by which their ancestors are described in the Old Testament.

Territorial expansion is not the only casus belli (literally, "reason for war"). Human groups have found many other excuses for collectively attacking others. The threat of an external enemy has always been one of the most effective ways to maintain internal cohesion. In Chapter 6 it was shown that a basic belief in many cultures is "What is different is dangerous." Racism assumes the innate superiority of one group over another and uses this assumption to justify resorting to violence for the purpose of maintaining this superiority. Totalitarian ideologies like apartheid imposed definitions of which groups were better and which were inferior—definitions that might be changed from one day to another. Culture pessimists wonder whether human societies can exist without enemies.

Europe, except in parts of the former Yugoslavia, seems to have reached a stage in its development in which countries that within human memory still fought each other have now voluntarily joined a supranational union. Africa, on the other hand, has become the scene of large-scale war and genocide that some have compared to the World Wars of its former colonizers.[3] A functioning supranational African union still seems far away.

While cultural processes have a lot to do with issues of war and peace, war and peace will not be a main issue in this chapter. Wars represent "intended conflict" between human groups, an issue too broad for this book. The purpose of the present chapter is to look at the *unintended conflicts* that often arise during intercultural encounters and that happen although nobody wants them and all suffer from them. They have at times contributed to the outbreak of wars. However, it would be naive to assume that all wars could be avoided by developing intercultural communication skills.

Owing to advances in travel and communication technology, intercultural encounters in the modern world have multiplied at a prodigious rate. Today embarrassments like those between Morier's English Elchi and the courtiers of the shah occur between ordinary tourists and locals, between schoolteachers and the immigrant parents of their students, and between businesspeople trying to sct up international ventures. Subtler misunderstandings than those pictured by Morier but with similar roots still play a prominent role in negotiations between modern diplomats and/or political leaders. Intercultural communication skills can contribute to the success of negotiations, on the results of which depend the solutions to crucial global problems. Avoiding unintended cultural conflicts will be the overall theme of this chapter.

Culture Shock and Acculturation

Intercultural encounters are often accompanied by similar psychological and social processes. The simplest form of intercultural encounter is between one foreign individual and a new cultural environment.

The foreigner usually experiences some form of *culture shock*. As illustrated over and over again in earlier chapters, our mental software contains basic values. These values were acquired early in our lives, and they have become so natural as to be unconscious. They form the basis of our conscious and more superficial manifestations of culture: rituals, heroes, and symbols (see Figure 1.2). The inexperienced foreigner can make an effort to learn some of the symbols and rituals of the new environment (words to use, how to greet people, when to bestow presents), but it is unlikely that he or she can recognize, let alone feel, the underlying values. In a way, the visitor in a foreign culture returns to the mental state of an infant, in which the simplest things must be learned over again. This experience usually leads to feelings of distress, of helplessness, and of hostility toward the new environment. Often one's physical functioning is affected. Expatriates and migrants have more need for medical help shortly after their displacement than before or later.[4]

People residing in a foreign cultural environment have reported shifts of feelings over time that follow more or less the *acculturation curve* pictured in Figure 11.1. Feelings (positive or negative) are plotted on the vertical axis, and time is plotted on the horizontal axis. Phase 1 is a (usually short) period of *euphoria*: the honeymoon, the excitement of traveling and of seeing new lands. Phase 2 is the period of *culture shock* when real life starts in the new environment, as described earlier. Phase 3, *acculturation*, sets in when the visitor has slowly learned to function under the new conditions, has adopted some of the local values, finds increased self-confidence, and

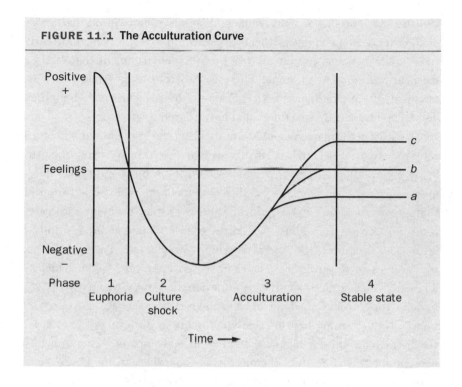

FIGURE 11.1 The Acculturation Curve

becomes integrated into a new social network. Phase 4 is the *stable state* of mind eventually reached. It may remain negative compared with home (4a)—for example, if the visitor continues to feel alienated and discriminated against. It may be just as good as before (4b), in which case the visitor can be considered to be biculturally adapted, or it may even be better (4c). In the last case the visitor has "gone native"—becoming more Roman than the Romans.

The length of the time scale in Figure 11.1 is variable; it seems to adapt to the length of the expatriation period. People on short assignments of up to three months have reported euphoria, culture shock, and acculturation phases within this period, perhaps bolstered by the expectation of being able to go home soon; people on long assignments of several years have reported culture shock phases of a year or more before acculturation set in.

Culture shocks and the corresponding physical symptoms may be so severe that assignments have to be terminated prematurely. Most international business companies have experiences of this kind with some of their expatriates. There have been cases of expatriate employees' suicides.

Culture shock problems of accompanying spouses, more often than those of the expatriated employees themselves, seem to be the reason for early return. The expatriate, after all, has the work environment that offers a cultural continuity with home. There is the story of an American wife, assigned with her husband to Nice, France, a tourist's heaven, who locked herself up inside their apartment and never dared to go out.

Articles in the management literature often cite high premature return rates for expatriates. Dutch-Australian researcher Anne-Wil Harzing critically reviewed more than thirty articles on the subject and found statements such as this: "Empirical studies over a considerable period suggest that expatriate failure is a significant and persistent problem with rates ranging between 25 and 40 percent in the developed countries and as high as 70 percent in the case of developing countries." Trying to check the sources of these figures, Harzing discovered very little evidence. The only reliable multicountry, multinationality study was by Professor Rosalie Tung, from Canada, who had shown that in the late 1970s, before intercultural training became really common, mean levels of premature recall of expatriates for Japanese and European companies were under 10 percent; for U.S. companies the mean was somewhere in the lower teens, with exceptional companies reporting recall rates at the 20 to 40 percent level. And this situation probably improved in the years afterward, if we assume that human resources managers worked on solving their problems. The message of dramatically high expatriate failure rates sounds good to intercultural consultants trying to sell expatriate training and to convince themselves and others of the importance of their work, but it is a myth.[5] A better sales argument for the trainers is that premature return may be low but that it doesn't really measure the problem of expatriation: the damage caused by an incompetent or insensitive expatriate who stays is much more significant.

Among refugees and migrants there is a percentage who fall seriously physically or mentally ill, commit suicide, or remain so homesick that they return, especially within the first year.

Expatriates and migrants who successfully complete their acculturation process and then return home will experience a reverse culture shock in readjusting to their old cultural environment. Migrants who have returned home sometimes find that they do not fit anymore and emigrate again, this time for good. Expatriates who successively move to new foreign environments report that the culture shock process starts all over again. Evidently, culture shocks are environment-specific. For every new cultural environment there is a new shock.

Ethnocentrism and Xenophilia

There are also standard types of reactions within host environments exposed to foreign visitors. The people in the host culture receiving a foreign culture visitor usually go through another psychological reaction cycle. The first phase is *curiosity*—somewhat like the euphoria on the side of the visitor. If the visitor stays and tries to function in the host culture, a second phase sets in: *ethnocentrism*. The hosts will evaluate the visitor by the standards of their culture, and this evaluation tends to be unfavorable. The visitor will show bad manners, as with the English Elchi; he or she will appear rude, naive, and/or stupid. Ethnocentrism is to a people what egocentrism is to an individual: considering one's own little world to be the center of the universe. If foreign visitors arrive only rarely, the hosts will probably stick to their ethnocentrism. If regularly exposed to foreign visitors, the hosts may move into a third phase: *polycentrism*, the recognition that different kinds of people should be measured by different standards. Some will develop the ability to understand foreigners according to these foreigners' own standards. This is the beginning of bi- or multiculturality.[6]

As we saw in Chapter 6, cultures that are uncertainty avoiding will resist polycentrism more than cultures that are uncertainty accepting. However, individuals within a culture vary around the cultural average, so in intolerant cultures one may meet tolerant hosts, and vice versa. The tendency to apply different standards to different kinds of people may also turn into *xenophilia*, the belief that in the foreigner's culture, everything is better. Some foreigners will be pleased to confirm this belief. There is a tendency among expatriates to idealize what one remembers from home. Neither ethnocentrism nor xenophilia is a healthy basis for intercultural cooperation, of course.

Group Encounters: Auto- and Heterostereotypes

Intercultural encounters among groups rather than with single foreign visitors provoke group feelings. Contrary to popular belief, intercultural contact among groups does *not* automatically breed mutual understanding. It usually confirms each group in its own identity. Members of the other group are perceived not as individuals but rather in a stereotyped fashion: all Chinese look alike; all Scots are stingy. As compared with the *heterostereotypes* about members of the other group, *autostereotypes* are fostered about members of one's own group. Such stereotypes will even affect the perception of actual events: if a member of one's own group attacks a member of the other group, one may be convinced ("I saw it with my own eyes") that it was the other way around.

As we saw in Chapter 4, the majority of people in the world live in collectivist societies, in which, throughout their lives, people remain members of tight in-groups that provide them with protection in exchange for loyalty. In such a society, groups with different cultural backgrounds are out-groups to an even greater extent than out-groups from their own culture. Integration across cultural dividing lines in collectivist societies is even more difficult to obtain than in individualist societies. This is the major problem of many decolonized nations, such as those of Africa in which national borders inherited from the colonial period in no way respect ethnic and cultural dividing lines.

Establishing true integration among members of culturally different groups requires environments in which these people can meet and mix as equals. Sports clubs, universities, work organizations, and armies can assume this role. Some ethnic group cultures produce people with specific skills, such as sailors or traders, and such skills can become the basis for their integration in a larger society.

Language and Humor

In most intercultural encounters the parties also speak different native languages. Throughout history this problem has been resolved by the use of trade languages such as Malay, Swahili or, more and more, derivations from English. *Trade languages* are pidgin forms of original languages, and the trade language of the modern world can be considered a form of business pidgin English. Language differences contribute to cultural misperceptions. In an international training program within IBM, trainers used to rate participants' future career potential. A follow-up study of actual careers during a period of up to eight years afterward showed that the trainers had consistently overestimated participants whose native language was English (the course language) and underestimated those whose languages were French or Italian, with native German speakers taking a middle position.[7]

Communication in trade languages or pidgin limits exchanges to the issues for which these simplified languages have words. To establish a more fundamental intercultural understanding, the foreign partner must acquire the host culture language. Having to express oneself in another language means learning to adopt someone else's frame of reference. It is doubtful whether one can be bicultural without also being bilingual.[8] Although the words of which a language consists are symbols in terms of the onion diagram (Figure 1.2), which means that they belong to the surface level of a culture, they are also the vehicles of culture transfer. Moreover, words are obstinate vehicles: our thinking is affected by the categories for which words are available in our language.[9] Many words have migrated from their language of origin into others because they express something unique: *algebra, management, computer, apartheid, machismo, perestroika, geisha, sauna, weltanschauung, weltschmerz, karaoke, mafia, savoir vivre.*

The skill of expressing oneself in more than one language is unevenly distributed across countries. People from smaller, affluent countries, such as the Swiss, Belgians, Scandinavians, Singaporeans, and Dutch, benefit from both frequent contact with foreigners and good educational systems, and therefore they tend to be polyglot. Their organizations possess a strategic advantage in intercultural contacts in that they nearly always have people available who speak several foreign languages, and whoever speaks more than one language will more easily pick up additional ones.

Paradoxically, having English, the world trade language, as one's native tongue is a liability, not an asset, for truly communicating with other cultures. Native English speakers do not always realize this. They are like the proverbial American farmer from Kansas who is alleged to have said, "If English was good enough for Jesus Christ, it is good enough for me."[10] Geert once met an Englishman working near the Welsh border who said he turned down an offer of a beautiful home across the border, in Wales, because there his young son would have had to learn Welsh as a second language at school. In our view, he missed a unique contribution to his son's education as a world citizen.

Language and culture are not so closely linked that sharing a language implies sharing a culture, nor should a difference in language always impose a difference in cultural values. In Belgium, where Dutch and French are the two dominant national languages (there is a small German-speaking area too), the scores of the Dutch-speaking and French-speaking regions on the four dimensions of the IBM studies were fairly similar, and both regions scored rather like France and different from the Netherlands. This finding reflects Belgian history: the middle and upper classes used to speak French, whatever the language of their ancestors, and tended to adopt the French culture; the lower classes in the Flemish part spoke Dutch, whatever the language of their ancestors, but when they moved up in status, they conformed to the culture of the middle classes. The IBM studies included a similar comparison between the German- and French-speaking regions of Switzerland. In this case the picture was different: the German-speaking part scored similar to Germany, and the French-speaking part scored similar to France. Switzerland's historical development was different from Belgium's: in Switzerland the language distribution followed the cantons (independent provinces) rather than the social class structure. This also helps to explain why language is a hot political issue in Belgium but not in Switzerland.[11]

Without knowing the language, one will miss a lot of the subtleties of a culture and be forced to remain a relative outsider. One of these subtleties is humor. What is considered funny is highly culture-specific. Many Europeans are convinced that Germans have no sense of humor, but this simply means they have a different sense of humor. In intercultural encounters the experienced traveler knows that jokes and irony are taboo until one is absolutely sure of the other culture's conception of what represents humor.

Raden Mas Hadjiwibowo, the Indonesian business executive whose description of Javanese family visits was quoted in Chapter 4, has written an insightful analysis of the difference between the Indonesian and the Dutch senses of humor. One of his case studies runs as follows:

> It was an ordinary morning with a routine informal office meeting. They all sat around the meeting table, and found themselves short of one chair. Markus, one of the Indonesian managers, looked in the connecting office next door for a spare chair.
>
> The next door office belonged to a Dutch manager, Frans. He was out, but he would not mind lending a chair; all furniture belonged to the firm anyway. Markus was just moving one of Frans's chairs through the connecting door when Frans came in from the other side.
>
> Frans was in a cheerful mood. He walked over to his desk to pick up some papers, and prepared for leaving the room again. In the process he

threw Markus a friendly grin and as an afterthought he called over his shoulder: "You're on a nice stealing spree, Markus?" Then he left, awaiting no answer.

When Frans returned to his office after lunch, Markus was waiting for him. Frans noticed Markus had put on a tie, which was unusual. "Markus, my good friend, what can I do for you?" Frans asked. Markus watched him gloomily, sat straight in his chair and said firmly and solemnly: "Frans, I hereby declare that I am not a thief."

Dumbfounded, Frans asked what the hell he was talking about. It took them another forty-five minutes to resolve the misunderstanding.[12]

In the Dutch culture, in which the maintenance of face and status is not a big issue, the "friendly insult" is a common way of joking among friends. "You scoundrel" or "you fool," if pronounced with the right intonation, expresses warm sympathy. In Indonesia, where status is sacred and maintaining face is imperative, an insult is always taken literally. Frans should have known this.

The Influence of Communication Technologies

Popular media often suggest that communication technologies, including television, e-mail, the Internet, mobile telephones, and social software, will bring people around the world together in a global village where cultural differences cease to matter. This dominance of technology over culture is an illusion. The software of the machines may be globalized, but the software of the minds that use them is not.

Electronic communication enormously increases the amount of information accessible to its users, but it does not increase their capacity to absorb this information, nor does it change their value systems. As users, we select information according to our values. Following the model of our parents, we read newspapers and watch TV programs that we expect to present our preferred points of view, and confronted with the almost unlimited offer of electronic information, we again pick whatever reinforces our preexisting ideas. The experience with the Internet has shown that people use it to do mostly things they would have done anyway, only maybe now they do these things more and faster.

Communication technologies increase our consciousness of differences between and within countries. Some disadvantaged groups, watching TV programs showing how people live elsewhere in the world, will want their share of the world's wealth. Some privileged groups, informed about suffering and strife elsewhere, will want to close their borders. Many authoritarian governments actively block foreign sources of information. Even Google, supposed champion of free information, has closed down access to certain sites in certain countries depending on local taboos.

In summary, communication technologies will not by themselves reduce the need for intercultural understanding. The Internet, in particular, makes it easy for extremist groups to create their own moral circle, removed from mainstream society and often exceedingly hostile toward it. On the other hand, when wisely used, communication technologies may be among the tools for intercultural learning.

Intercultural Encounters in Tourism

Tourism represents the most superficial form of intercultural encounter. Tourists traveling in mass may spend two weeks in Morocco, Bali, or Cancun without gleaning anything about the local culture at all. Personnel in the host country who work in the tourism industry will learn something about the culture of the tourists, but their picture of the way the tourists live at home will be highly distorted. What one group picks up from the other group is on the level of symbols (see Figure 1.2): words, fashion articles, music, and the like.

The economic effects of mass tourism on the host countries may or may not be favorable. Traditional sources of income are often destroyed, and the revenues of tourism go to governments and foreign investors, with the consequence that the local population may suffer more than it benefits. The environmental effects can be disastrous. Tourism is, from many points of view, a mixed blessing.

Tourism can nevertheless be the starting point for more fundamental intercultural encounters. It breaks the isolation of cultural groups and creates an awareness that there exist other people who have other ways. The seeds planted in some minds may take root later. Some tourists start learning the language and history of the country they have visited and to which they want to return. Hosts start learning the tourists' languages to promote their businesses. Personal friendships develop between the most unlikely people in the most unlikely ways. On the basis of intercultural encounters, the possibilities of tourism probably outweigh the disadvantages.

Intercultural Encounters in Schools

An American teacher at a foreign-language institute in Beijing exclaimed in class, "You lovely girls, I love you." Her students, according to a Chinese observer, were terrified. An Italian professor teaching in the United States complained bitterly about the fact that students were asked to formally evaluate his course. He did not think that students should be the judges of the quality of a professor. An Indian lecturer at an African university had a student who arrived six weeks late for the curriculum, but he had to admit him because he was from the same village as the dean. Intercultural encounters in schools can lead to much perplexity.[13]

Most intercultural encounters in schools are of one of two types: between local teachers and foreign, migrant, or refugee students or between expatriate teachers, hired as foreign experts or sent as missionaries, and local students. Different value patterns in the cultures from which the teacher and the student have come are one source of problems. Chapters 3 through 7 described consequences for the school situation of differences in values related to power distance, individualism, masculinity, uncertainty avoidance, and long- or short-term orientation. These differences often affect the relationships between teacher and students, among students, and between teacher and parents.

Because language is the vehicle of teaching, what was mentioned earlier about the role of language in intercultural encounters applies in its entirety to the teaching situation. The chances for successful cultural adaptation are better if the teacher teaches in the students' language than if the student has to learn in the teacher's language, because the teacher has more power over the learning situation than any single student.

The course language affects the learning process. At INSEAD international business school, in France, Geert taught the same executive course in French to one group and in English to another; both groups were composed of people from several nationalities. Discussing a case study in French led to highly stimulating intellectual discussions but few practical conclusions. When the same case was discussed in English, it would not be long before someone asked, "So what?" and the class tried to become pragmatic. Both groups used the same readings, partly from French authors translated into English, partly vice versa. Both groups liked the readings originally written in the class language and condemned the translated ones as "unnecessarily verbose, with a rather meager message which could have been expressed on one or two pages." The comments of the French-language class on the readings translated from English therefore were identical to the comments of the English-language class on the readings translated from French. What is felt to be a message in one language does not necessarily survive the translation process. Information is more than words: it is words that fit into a cultural framework. Culturally adequate translation is an undervalued art.

Beyond differences in language, students and teachers in intercultural encounters run into differences in cognitive abilities. "Our African engineers do not think like engineers; they tend to tackle symptoms, rather than view the equipment as a system," said a British training manager, unconscious of his own ethnocentrism. Fundamental studies by development psychologists have shown that the things we have learned are determined by the demands of the environment in which we grew up. People will become good at doing the things that are important to them and that they have occasion to do often. Being from a generation that predates the introduction of pocket calculators in schools, Geert will perform calculations in his head for which his grandchildren prefer to use a machine. Learning abilities, including the development of memory, are rooted in the total pattern of a society. In China the nature of the script (for a moderately literate person, at least three thousand complex characters)[14] develops children's ability at pattern recognition, but it also imposes a need for rote learning.

Intercultural problems arise also because expatriate teachers bring irrelevant materials with them. A Congolese friend, studying in Brussels, recalled that at primary school in Lubumbashi her teacher, a Belgian nun, made the children recite in her history lesson *"Nos ancêtres, les Gaulois"* ("Our ancestors, the Gauls"). During a visiting teaching assignment to China, a British lecturer repeated word for word his British organizational behavior course. Much of what students from poor countries learn at universities in wealthy countries is hardly relevant in their home country situation. What interest does a future manager in an Indian company have in mathematical modeling of the U.S. stock market? The know-how supposed to make a person succeed in an industrial country is not necessarily the same as what will help the development of a country that is currently poor.

Finally, intercultural problems can be based on institutional differences in the societies from which the teachers and students have come, differences that generate different expectations as to the educational process and the role of various parties in it. From what types of families are students and teachers recruited? Are educational systems elitist or antielitist? Visiting U.S. professors in a Latin American country may think they contribute to the economic development of the country, while in actual fact they contribute only to the continuation of elite privileges. What role do employers play in the educational system? In Switzerland and Germany, traineeships in industry or business are a respected alternative to a university education, allowing people to reach the highest positions, but this is not the case in most other countries. What role do the state and/or religious bodies play? In some countries (France, Russia) the government prescribes the curriculum in painstaking detail; in others the teachers are free to define their own. In countries in which both private and public schools exist, the private sector may be for the elites (United States) or for the dropouts (the Netherlands, Switzerland). Where does the money for the schools come from? How well are teachers paid, and what is their social status? In China teachers are traditionally highly respected but poorly paid. In Britain the status of teachers has traditionally been low; in Germany and Japan, high.

Minorities, Migrants, and Refugees

What are considered minorities in a country is a matter of definition. It depends on hard facts, including the distribution of the population, the economic situation of population groups, and the intensity of the interrelations among groups. It also depends on cultural values (especially uncertainty avoidance and collectivism, which facilitate labeling groups as outsiders) and on cultural practices (languages, felt and attributed identities, interpretations of history). These factors affect the ideology of the majority and sometimes also of the minority, as well as their level of mutual prejudice and discrimination. Minority problems are always also, and often primarily, majority problems.

Minorities in the world include a wide variety of groups, of widely varying status, from underclass to entrepreneurial and/or academic elite:

- Original populations overrun by immigrants (for example, native Americans and Australian aborigines)
- Descendants of economical, political, or ethnic migrants or refugees (now the majorities in the United States and Australia, among other countries)

- Descendants of imported labor (examples are American blacks, Turks, and Mediterraneans in northwestern Europe)
- Natives of former colonies (for example, Indians and Pakistanis in Britain and northern Africans in France)
- International nomads (Sinti and Roma people—Gypsies—in most of Europe and partly even overseas)

In many countries the minority picture is highly volatile because of ongoing migration. The number of people in the second half of the twentieth century who left their native countries and moved to a completely different environment is larger than ever before in human history. The effect in all cases is that persons and entire families are parachuted into cultural environments vastly different from the ones in which they were mentally programmed, often without any preparation. They have to learn a new language, but a much larger problem is that they have to function in a new culture. Hassan Bel Ghazi, a Moroccan immigrant to the Netherlands, wrote:

> *Imagine: One day you get up, you look around but you can't believe your eyes. . . . Everything is upside down, inside as well as outside. . . . You try to put things back in their old place but alas—they are upside down forever. You take your time, you look again and then you have an idea: "I'll put myself upside down too, just like everything else, to be able to handle things." It doesn't work. . . . And the world doesn't understand why you stand right.*[15]

Political ideologies about majority-minority relations vary immensely. Racists and ultrarightists want to close borders and expel present minorities—or worse. The policies of civilized governments aim somewhere between two poles on a continuum. One pole is *assimilation,* which means that minority citizens should become like everybody else and lose their distinctiveness as fast as possible. The other pole is *integration,* which implies that minority citizens, while accepted as full members of the host society, are at the same time encouraged to retain a link with their roots and their collective identity. Paradoxically, policies aiming at integration have led to better and faster adaptation of minorities than policies enforcing assimilation.

Migrants and refugees often came in as presumed temporary expatriates but turned out to be stayers. In nearly all cases they moved from a more traditional, collectivist society to a more individualist society. For their adaptation it is essential that they find support in a community of compatriots in the country of migration, especially if they are single, but even when they come with their families, which anyway represent a much narrower group than they were accustomed to in their home country. Maintaining migrant communities fits into an integration philosophy as previously described. Unfortunately, host country politicians, responding from their individualist value position, often fear the forming of migrant ghettos and try to disperse the foreigners, falsely assuming that this action will accelerate their adaptation.

Migrants and refugees usually also experience differences in power distance. Host societies tend to be more egalitarian than the places the migrants have left. Migrants experience this difference both negatively and positively—lack of respect for elders but better accessibility of authorities and teachers, although they tend to distrust authorities at first. Differences on masculinity-femininity, on uncertainty avoidance, and on indulgence between migrants and hosts may go either way, and the corresponding adaptation problems are specific to the pairs of cultures involved.

First-generation migrant families experience standard dilemmas. At work, in shops and public offices, and usually also at school, they interact with locals, learn some local practices, and are confronted with local values. At home, meanwhile, they try to maintain the practices, values, and relationship patterns from their country of origin. They are marginal people between two worlds, and they alternate daily between one and the other.

The effect of this marginality is different for the different generations and genders. The immigrating adults are unlikely to trade their home country values for those of the host country; at best they make small adaptations. The *father* tries to maintain his traditional authority in the home, but at work his status is often low. Migrants start in jobs nobody else wants. The family knows this, and he loses face toward his relatives. If he is unemployed, this makes him lose face even more. He frequently has problems with the local language, which makes him feel foolish. Sometimes the father is illiterate even in his own language. He has to seek the help of his children or of social workers in filling out forms and dealing with the authorities. He is often discriminated against by employers, police, authorities, and neighbors.

The *mother* in some migrant cultures is virtually a prisoner in the home, not expected to leave it when the father has gone to work. In these cases she has no contact with the host society, does not learn the language, and remains completely dependent on her husband and children. In other cases the mother has a job too. She may be the main breadwinner of the family, a severe blow to the father's self-respect. She meets other men, and her husband may suspect her of unfaithfulness. The marriage sometimes breaks up. Yet there is no way back. As noted earlier, migrants who have returned home often find that they do not fit anymore and remigrate.

The second generation, children born in or brought early to the new country, acquires conflicting mental programs from the family side and from the local school and community side. Their values reflect partly their parents' culture, partly their new country's, with wide variations among individuals, groups, and host countries.[16] The *sons* suffer most from their marginality. Some succeed miraculously well, and benefiting from the better educational opportunities, they enter skilled and professional occupations. Others, escaping parental authority at home, drop out of school and find collectivist protection in street gangs; they risk becoming a new underclass in the host society. The *daughters* often adapt better, although their parents worry more about them. At school they are exposed to an equality between the genders unknown in the society from which they have come. Sometimes parents hurry them into the safety of an arranged marriage with a compatriot.[17]

On the upside, however, many of these problems are transitional; third-generation migrants are mostly absorbed into the population of the host country, exhibiting concomitant values, and are distinguishable only by a foreign family name and maybe by specific religious and family traditions. This three-generation adaptation process has also operated in past generations; an increasing share of the population of modern societies descends partly from foreign migrants.

Whether migrant groups are thus integrated or fail to adapt and turn into permanent minorities depends as much on the majority as on the migrants themselves. Agents of the host society who interact frequently with minorities, migrants, and refugees can do a lot to facilitate their integration. They are the police, social workers, doctors, nurses, personnel officers, counter clerks in government offices, and teachers. Migrants coming from large-power-distance, collectivist cultures may distrust such authorities more than locals do, for cultural reasons. In contrast, teachers, for example, can benefit from the respect their status earns them from the parents of their migrant students. They will have to *invite* those parents (especially fathers) for discussion; the social distance perceived by the migrant parents is much larger than most teachers are accustomed to. Unfortunately, in any host society a share of the locals (politicians, police, journalists, teachers, neighbors) fall victim to ethnocentric and racist philosophies, compounding the migrants' adaptation problems through primitive manifestations of uncertainty avoidance: "What is different is dangerous."

Particular expertise is demanded from mental health professionals dealing with migrants and refugees. Ways of dealing with health concerns and disability differ considerably between collectivist and individualist societies. The high level of acculturative stress in migrants puts them at risk for mental health disorders, and methods of psychiatric treatment developed for host country patients may not work with migrants, again for cultural reasons. Most countries with a large migrant population such as Australia recognize transcultural psychiatry (and transcultural clinical psychology) as a special field. Some psychiatrists and psychologists specialize in the treatment of political refugees suffering from the aftereffects of war or torture.

Not just host country citizens can be blamed for racism and ethnocentrism; migrants themselves sometimes behave in racist and ethnocentric ways, toward other migrants and toward hosts. Living as they do in an unfamiliar and often hostile environment, the migrants can be said to have a better excuse. Some resort to religious fundamentalisms although at home they were hardly religious at all. Fundamentalism is often found among marginal groups in society, and these migrants are the new marginals.

Intercultural Negotiations

Negotiations, whether in politics or in business and whether international or not, share some universal characteristics:

- Two or more parties with (partly) conflicting interests
- A common need for agreement because of an expected gain from such agreement
- An initially undefined outcome
- A means of communication between parties
- A control and decision-making structure on either side by which negotiators are linked to their superiors or their constituency

Books have been published on the art of negotiation; it is a popular theme for training courses. Negotiations have even been simulated on computers. However, the theories and computer models tend to use assumptions about the values and objectives of the negotiators taken from Western societies, in particular from the United States. In international negotiations, different players may hold different values and objectives.[18]

National cultures will affect negotiation processes in several ways:

- Power distance will affect the degree of centralization of the control and decision-making structure and the importance of the status of the negotiators.
- Collectivism will affect the need for stable relationships between (opposing) negotiators. In a collectivist culture replacement of a person means that a new relationship will have to be built, which takes time. Mediators (go-betweens) are key in maintaining a viable pattern of relationships that allows progress.
- Masculinity will affect the need for ego-boosting behavior and the sympathy for the strong on the part of negotiators and their superiors, as well as the tendency to resolve conflicts by a show of force. Feminine cultures are more likely to resolve conflicts by compromise and to strive for consensus.
- Uncertainty avoidance will affect the (in)tolerance of ambiguity and (dis)trust in opponents who show unfamiliar behaviors, as well as the need for structure and ritual in the negotiation procedures.
- Long-term orientation will affect the perseverance to achieve desired ends even at the cost of sacrifices.
- Indulgence will affect the atmosphere of the negotiations and the strictness of protocols.

Effective intercultural negotiations demand an insight into the range of cultural values to be expected among partners from other countries, in comparison with the negotiator's own culturally determined values. They also demand language and communication skills to guarantee that the messages sent to the other party or parties will be understood in the way they were meant by the sender. They finally demand organization skills for planning and arranging meetings and facilities, involving mediators and interpreters, and handling external communications.

Experienced diplomats have usually acquired a professional savoir faire that enables them to negotiate successfully with other diplomats regarding issues on which they are empowered to decide themselves. The problem, however, is that in issues of real importance diplomats are usually directed by politicians who have the power but not the diplomatic savoir faire. Politicians often make statements intended for domestic use, which the diplomats are obliged to explain to foreign negotiation partners. The amount of discretion left to diplomats is in itself a cultural characteristic that varies from one society and political system to another. Modern communication possibilities contribute to limiting the discretion of diplomats; Morier's English Elchi had a lot of discretionary power by virtue of the simple fact that communicating with England in those days took at least three months.

Notwithstanding, there is no doubt that the quality of intercultural encounters in international negotiations can contribute to avoiding unintended conflict, *if* the actors are of the proper hierarchical level for the decisions at stake. This is why summit conferences are so important—here are the people who do have the power to negotiate. The hitch is that they usually rose to their present position because they hold strong convictions in harmony with the national values of their country, and for this same reason they have difficulty recognizing that others function according to different mental programs. A trusted foreign minister or ambassador who has both the ear of the top leader *and* diplomatic sensitivity is an invaluable asset to a country.

Permanent international organizations, such as the various United Nations agencies, the European Commission, and the North Atlantic Treaty Organization, have developed their own organizational cultures, which affect their internal international negotiations. Even more than in the case of the diplomats' occupational culture, these organizational cultures reside at the more superficial level of practices, common symbols, and rituals, rather than of shared values. Exceptions are "missionary" international nongovernmental organizations (NGOs), such as the International Red Cross, Amnesty International, and Greenpeace.

Thus, the behavior of international negotiators is influenced by culture at three levels: national, occupational, and organizational.

Business negotiations differ from political negotiations in that the actors are more often amateurs in the negotiation field. Specialists can prepare negotiations, but especially if one partner is from a large-power-distance culture, persons with appropriate power and status have to be brought in for the formal agreement. International negotiations have become a special topic in business education, so it is hoped that future generations of businesspersons will be better prepared. The following discussion will argue for the need for corporate diplomats in multinationals.

Multinational Business Organizations

If intercultural encounters are as old as humanity, multinational business is as old as organized states. Business professor Karl Moore and historian David Lewis have described four cases of multinational business in the Mediterranean area between 1900 and 100 B.C., run by Assyrians, Phoenicians, Greeks, and Romans. History does not justify claims that one particular type of capitalism is inevitably and forever superior to everything else.[19]

The functioning of multinational business organizations hinges on intercultural communication and cooperation. Chapters 9 and 10 related shared values to *national* cultures and shared practices to *organizational* (corporate) cultures. Multinationals abroad meet alien value patterns, but their shared practices (symbols, heroes, and rituals) keep the organization together.

The basic values of a multinational business organization are determined by the nationality and personality of its founder(s) and later significant leaders. Multinationals with a dominant home culture have a clearer set of basic values and therefore are easier to run than international organizations that lack such a common frame of reference. In multinational business organizations the values and beliefs of the home culture are taken for granted and serve as a frame of reference at the head office. Persons in linchpin roles between foreign subsidiaries and the head office need to be bicultural, because they need a double trust relationship, on the one side with their home culture superiors and colleagues and on the other side with their host culture subordinates. Two roles are particularly crucial:

- **The country business unit manager:** this person reports to an international head office.
- **The corporate diplomat:** this person is a home country or other national impregnated with the corporate culture, whose occupational background may vary but who is experienced in living and functioning in various foreign cultures. Corporate diplomats are essential to make multinational structures work, as liaison persons in international, regional, or national head offices or as temporary managers for new ventures.[20]

Other managers and members of foreign national subsidiaries do not have to be bicultural. Even if the foreign subsidiaries formally adopt home culture ideas and policies, they will internally function according to the value systems and beliefs of the host culture.

As mentioned before, biculturality implies bilingualism. There is a difference in coordination strategy between most U.S. and most non-U.S. multinational organizations. Most American multinationals put the burden of biculturality on the foreign nationals. It is the latter who are bi- or multilingual (most American executives in multinationals are monolingual). This goes together with a relatively short stay of American executives abroad; two to five years per foreign country is fairly typical. These executives often live in ghettos. The main tool of coordination consists of unified worldwide policies that can be maintained with a regularly changing composition of the international staff because they are highly formalized. Most non-American multinationals put the burden of biculturality on their own home country nationals. They are almost always multilingual (with the possible exception of the British, although even they are usually more skilled in other languages than the Americans). The typical period of stay in another country tends to be longer, between five and fifteen years or more, so that expatriate executives of non-American multinationals may "go native" in the host country; they mix more with the local population, enroll their children in local schools, and live less frequently in ghettos. The main tool of coordination is these expatriate home country nationals, rather than formal procedures.[21]

Biculturality is difficult to acquire after childhood, and the number of failures would be larger were it not that what is necessary for the proper functioning of multinational organizations is only *task-related biculturality*. With regard to other aspects of life—tastes, hobbies, religious feelings, and private relations—expatriate multinational executives can afford to, and usually do, remain monocultural.

Chapter 9 argued that implicit models of organizations in people's minds depend primarily on the combination of power distance and uncertainty avoidance. Differences in power distance are more manageable than differences in uncertainty avoidance. In particular, organizations headquartered in smaller-power-distance cultures usually adapt successfully in larger-power-distance countries. Local managers in high-PDI subsidiaries can use an authoritative style even if their international bosses behave in a more participative fashion.

Chapter 3 opened with the story of the French general Bernadotte's culture shock after he became king of Sweden. A Frenchman sent to Copenhagen by a French cosmetics company as a regional sales manager told Geert about his first day in the Copenhagen office. He called his secretary and gave her an order in the same way as he would do in Paris. But instead of saying, "Oui, Monsieur," as he expected her to do, the Danish woman looked at him, smiled, and said, "Why do you want this to be done?"

Countries with large-power-distance cultures have rarely produced large multinationals; multinational operations demand a higher level of trust than is normal in these countries, and they do not permit the centralization of authority that managers at headquarters in these countries need in order to feel comfortable.

Differences in uncertainty avoidance represent a serious problem for the functioning of multinationals, whichever way they go. This is because if rules mean different things in different countries, it is difficult to keep the organization together. In cultures manifesting weak uncertainty avoidance such as the United States and even more in Britain and, for example, Sweden, managers and nonmanagers alike feel definitely uncomfortable with systems of rigid rules, especially if it is evident that many of these rules are never followed. In cultures with strong uncertainty avoidance such as most of the Latin world, people feel equally uncomfortable without the structure of a system of rules, even if many of these dictates are impractical and impracticable. At either pole of the uncertainty-avoidance dimension, people's feelings are fed by deep psychological needs, related to the control of aggression and to basic security in the face of the unknown (see Chapter 6).

Organizations moving to unfamiliar cultural environments are often sorely unprepared for negative *reactions of the public or the authorities* to what they do or want to do. Perhaps the effect of the collective values of a society is nowhere as clear as in such cases. These values have been institutionalized partly in the form of legislation (and in the way in which legislation is applied, which may differ considerably from what is actually written in the law); in labor union structures, programs, and power positions; and in the existence of organizations of stakeholders such as consumers or environmentalists. The values are partly invisible to the newcomer, but they become all too visible in press reactions, government decisions, or organized actions by uninvited interest groups. A few inferences from the value differences exposed in Chapters 3 through 7 with regard to the reactions of the local environment are listed here:

- Civic action groups are more likely to be formed in low-PDI, low-UAI cultures than elsewhere.
- Business corporations will have to be more concerned with informing the public in low-PDI, low-UAI cultures than elsewhere.

- Public sympathy and legislation on behalf of economically and socially weak members of society are more likely in low-MAS countries.
- Public sympathy and both government and private funding for aid to economically weak countries and for disaster relief anywhere in the world will be stronger in affluent low-MAS countries than in affluent high-MAS countries.
- Public sympathy and legislation on behalf of environmental conservation and maintaining the quality of life are more likely in low-PDI, low-MAS countries.

In world business there is a growing tendency for tariff and technological advantages to wear off, which automatically shifts competition, besides toward economic factors, toward cultural advantages or disadvantages. On at least the first five dimensions of national culture, any position of a country offers potential competitive advantages as well as disadvantages; these are summarized in Table 11.1.

Table 11.1 serves to show that no country can be good at everything; cultural strengths imply cultural weaknesses. Chapter 10 arrived at a simi-

TABLE 11.1 Competitive Advantages of Different Cultural Profiles in International Competition

Power Distance (small)	Power Distance (large)
Acceptance of responsibility	Discipline

Uncertainty Avoidance (weak)	Uncertainty Avoidance (strong)
Basic innovations	Precision

Collectivism	Individualism
Employee commitment	Management mobility

Femininity	Masculinity
Personal service	Mass production
Custom-made products	Efficiency
Agriculture	Heavy industry
Food	Chemistry
Biochemistry	Bulk chemistry

Short-Term Orientation	Long-Term Orientation
Fast adaptation	Developing new markets

lar conclusion with regard to organizational cultures. This is a strong argument for making cultural considerations part of strategic planning and locating activities in countries, in regions, and in organizational units that possess the cultural characteristics necessary for competing in these activities.

Coordinating Multinationals: Structure Should Follow Culture

Most multinational corporations cover a range of businesses and/or product or market divisions, in a range of countries. They have to bridge both national and business cultures.

The purpose of any organizational structure is the coordination of activities. These activities are carried out in business units, each involved in one type of business in one country. The design of a corporate structure is based on three choices, whether explicit or implicit, for each business unit:

- Which of the unit's inputs and outputs should be coordinated from elsewhere in the corporation?
- Where should the coordination take place?
- How tight or loose should the coordination be?

Multinational, multibusiness corporations face the choice between coordination along type-of-business lines or along geographic lines. The key question is whether business know-how or cultural know-how is more crucial for the success of the operation. The classic solution is a *matrix* structure. This means that every manager of a business unit has two bosses, one who coordinates the particular type of business across all countries, along with one who coordinates all business units in the particular country. Matrix structures are costly, often requiring a doubling of the management ranks, and their functioning may raise more problems than it resolves. That said, a single structural principle is unlikely to fit for an entire corporation. In some cases the business structure should dominate; in others geographic coordination should have priority. The result is a patchwork structure that may lack beauty but that does follow the needs of markets and business unit cultures. Its justification is that variety within the environment in which a company operates should be matched with appropriate internal variety. The diversity in structural solutions advocated is one not only of place but also of time: optimal solutions will very likely change over time, so that periodic reshufflings make sense.

Expanding Multinationals: International Mergers and Other Ventures

Mergers, acquisitions, joint ventures, and alliances across national borders have become frequent,[22] but they remain a regular source of cross cultural clashes. Cross-national ventures have often turned out to be dramatic failures. Leyland-Innocenti, Vereinigte Flugzeugwerke–Fokker and later DASA-Fokker, Hoogovens-Hoesch and later Hoogovens–British Steel, Citroen-Fiat, Renault-Volvo, Daimler-Chrysler, and Alitalia-KLM are just a few of the more notorious ones. There is little doubt that the list will continue growing as long as management decisions about international ventures are based solely on financial considerations. They are part of a big money and power game and are seen as a defense against (real or imaginary) threats by competitors. Those making the decision rarely imagine the operating problems that can and do arise inside the newly formed hybrid organizations. Even within countries, such ventures have a dubious success record, but across borders they are all the less likely to succeed. If cultural conditions do look favorable, the cultural integration of the new cooperative structure should still be managed; it does not happen by itself. Cultural integration takes lots of time, energy, and money unforeseen by the financial experts who designed the venture.

Five ways of international expansion can be distinguished, in increasing order of cultural risk: (1) the greenfield start, (2) the international strategic alliance, (3) the joint venture with a foreign partner, (4) the foreign acquisition, and (5) the cross-national merger.

The *greenfield start* means that the corporation sets up a foreign subsidiary from scratch, usually sending over one expatriate or a small team, who will hire locals and gradually build a local branch. Greenfield starts are by their very nature slow, but their cultural risk is limited. The founders of the subsidiary can carefully select employees from the host country who fit the corporation's culture. The culture of the subsidiary becomes a combination of national elements (mainly values; see Chapter 9) and corporate elements (mainly practices; see Chapter 10). Greenfield starts have a high success rate. IBM, many other older multinationals, and international accounting firms until the 1980s almost exclusively grew through greenfield starts.

The *international strategic alliance* is a prudent means of cooperation between existing partners. Without creating a new venture, the partners agree to collaborate on specific products and/or markets for mutual benefit. Given that the risks are limited to the project at hand, this is a safe way of learning to know each other; neither party's existence is at stake. The acquaintance could develop into a joint venture or merger, but in this case the partners can be expected to know each other's culture sufficiently to recognize the cultural pitfalls.

The *joint venture with a foreign partner* creates a new business by pooling resources from two or more founding parties. The venture can be started greenfield, or the local partner can transfer part of its people wholesale to the venture. In the latter case, of course, it transfers part of its culture as well. The cultural risk of joint ventures can be controlled by clear agreements about which partner supplies which resources, including what part of management. Joint ventures in which one partner provides the entire management have a higher success rate than those in which management responsibility is shared. Foreign joint ventures can develop new and creative cultural characteristics, based on synergy of elements from the founding partners. They are a limited-risk way of entering an unknown country and market. Not infrequently, eventually one of the partners buys the other(s) out.

In the *foreign acquisition* a local company is purchased wholesale by a foreign buyer. The acquired company has its own history and its own organizational culture; on top of this it represents a national culture differing from the acquiring corporation's national culture. Foreign acquisitions are a fast way of expanding, but their cultural risk is considerable. To use an analogy from family life (such analogies are popular for describing the relationships among parts of corporations), foreign acquisitions are to greenfield starts as the bringing up of a foster child, adopted in puberty, is to the bringing up of one's own child. In regard to the problems of integrating the new member, one solution is to keep it at arm's length—that is, not to integrate it but to treat it as a portfolio investment. Usually, though, this is not why the foreign company has been purchased. When integration is imperative, the cultural clashes are often resolved by brute power: key people are replaced by the corporation's own men and women. In other cases key people have not waited for this to happen and have left on their own account. Foreign acquisitions often lead to a destruction of human capital, which is eventually a destruction of financial capital as well.

The same applies for acquisitions in the home country, but abroad the cultural risk is even larger. It is advisable for potential foreign (and domestic) acquisitions to be preceded by an analysis of the cultures of the corporation and of the acquisition candidate. If the decision is still to go ahead, such a match analysis can be used as the basis for a culture management plan.

The *cross-national merger* poses all the problems of the foreign acquisition, plus the complication that power has to be shared. Cultural problems can no longer be resolved by unilateral decisions. Cross-national mergers are therefore extremely risky.[23] Even more than in the case of the foreign acquisition, an analysis of the corporate and national cultures of the potential partners should be part of the process of deciding to merge. If the merger is concluded, this analysis can again be the basis of a culture integration plan that needs the active and permanent support of a *Machtpromotor* (see Chapter 10), probably the chief executive.

Two classic cases of successful cross-national mergers are Royal Dutch Shell (dating from 1907) and Unilever (dating from 1930), both Dutch–British. They show a few common characteristics: the smaller country holds the majority of shares; *two* head offices have been maintained so as to avoid the impression that the corporation is run from one of the two countries only;[24] there has been strong and charismatic leadership during the integration phase; there has been an external threat that kept the partners together for survival; and governments have kept out of the business.

A highly visible international project that is a combination of a strategic alliance and a joint venture is the Airbus consortium in Toulouse, France. Airbus has become one of the two largest aircraft manufacturers in the world. Parts of the planes are manufactured by the participating companies in Britain, Germany, and Spain and then flown over to Toulouse, where the planes are assembled.

International Marketing, Advertising, and Consumer Behavior

Culture is present in the design and quality of many products and in the presentation of many services. An example is the difference in the design of the cockpit in passenger aircraft between Airbus (European, primarily French or German) and Boeing (U.S.). The Airbus has been designed to fly itself with minimum interference from the pilot, while the Boeing design expects more discretion from and interaction with the pilot.[25] The Airbus is the product of an uncertainty-avoiding design culture; the Boeing version respects the pilot's supposed need to feel in command.

In 1983 Harvard University professor Theodore Levitt published an article, "The Globalization of Markets," in which he predicted that technology and modernity would lead to a worldwide convergence of consumers' needs and desires. This presumed convergence should enable global companies to develop standard brands with universal marketing and advertising programs. In the 1990s more and more voices in the marketing literature expressed doubts about this convergence and referred to Geert's culture indexes to explain persistent cultural differences.[26] Chapters 4 through 8 provided ample evidence of significant correlations of consumer behavior data with culture dimension indexes, mainly based on research by Marieke de Mooij. Analyzing national consumer behavior data over time, de Mooij showed that contrary to Levitt's prediction, buying and consumption patterns in affluent countries in the 1980s and '90s diverged as much as they converged. Affluence implies more possibilities to choose among products and services, and consumers' choices reflected psychological and social influences. De Mooij wrote:

> *Consumption decisions can be driven by functional or social needs. Clothes satisfy a functional need, fashion satisfies a social need. Some personal care products serve functional needs, others serve social needs. A house serves a functional, a home a social need. Culture influences in what type of house people live, how they relate to their homes and how they tend to their homes. A car may satisfy a functional need, but the type of car for most people satisfies a social need. Social needs are culture-bound.*[27]

De Mooij's analysis of the development of the market for private cars across fifteen European countries shows that the number of cars per one thousand inhabitants depended less and less on income: it was strongly related to national wealth in 1969 but no longer in 1994. This finding could be read as a sign of *convergence.* However, the preference for new over secondhand cars in both periods depended not on wealth but only on uncertainty avoidance: cultures that were uncertainty tolerant continued buying more used cars, without any convergence between countries. Owning two cars in one family in 1970 related to national wealth, but in 1997 it related only to masculinity. In masculine cultures husband and wife each wanted an individual car; in equally wealthy feminine cultures they more often shared a car. In this respect there has been a *divergence* between countries.[28]

From the cultural indexes, UAI and MAS resist convergence most: UAI is mostly, and MAS entirely, independent of wealth and therefore unaffected by it. Uncertainty avoidance stands for differences in the need for purity and for expert knowledge; masculinity versus femininity "explains differences in the need for success as a component of status, resulting in a varying appeal of status products across countries. It also explains the roles of males and females in buying and in family decision making."[29] Such differences are often overlooked by globally oriented marketeers who assume their own cultural choices on these dimensions to be universal.

The literature on *advertising* in the 1990s has increasingly stressed the need for cultural differentiation. On the basis of more than 3,400 TV commercials from eleven countries, de Mooij identified specific advertising styles for countries, linked to cultural themes. For example, single-person pictures are rare in collectivist cultures (if nobody wants to join this person, the product must be bad!). Discussions between mothers and daughters are a theme in TV spots in both large- and small-power-distance cultures, but where PDI is high, mothers advise daughters, and where it is low, daughters advise mothers.[30]

The same global brand may appeal to different cultural themes in different countries. Advertising, and television advertising in particular, is directed at the inner motivation of prospective buyers. TV commercials can be seen as modern equivalents of the myths and fairy tales of previous generations, told and retold because they harmonize with the software in people's minds—and in spite of Professor Levitt's prediction, these minds have not been and will not be globalized.[31]

Migrant communities have created their own markets across the world, notably in the food industry. Food has strong symbolic links with traditions and with group identity, and migrants—especially those from collectivistic, uncertainty-avoiding cultures—like to retain these links.

Further cultural differentiation, even in firms with globalized marketing approaches, is provided by the intermediate role of local sales forces who translate (sometimes literally) the marketing message to the local customers.[32] For example, the degree of directness a salesperson can use is highly culturally dependent. Ways of management and compensation of sales forces should be based on cultural values (theirs and the customers') and on characteristics of the industry. Conceptions of business ethics for salespersons vary strongly from one culture to another; they are a direct operationalization of some of the values involved in the culture indexes.

Markets for services support globalization even less than the markets for goods. Services are by their nature personalized toward the customer. International companies in the service field tend to leave considerable marketing discretion to local management.

Any traveler in a new country can attest to the insecurity about how to relate to personal service personnel: when to give tips, in what way, and how much. Tipping customs differ by country; they reflect the mutual roles of client and service person. The giving of tips stresses their inequality (power distance) and conflicts with their independence (collectivism).[33]

Chances for globalization are relatively better for *industrial marketing*, the business-to-business arena where international purchasers and international salespersons meet. Technical standards are crucial, and participation in their establishment is a major industrial marketing instrument, in which negotiation processes, as described previously, become paramount.

International Politics and International Organizations

Glen Fisher, a retired U.S. foreign service officer, has written a perceptive book called *Mindsets* on the role of culture in international relations. In the introduction to the chapter titled "The Cultural Lens," he states:

> *Working in international relations is a special endeavor because one has to deal with entirely new patterns of mindsets. To the extent that they can be identified and anticipated for particular groups or even nations, some of the mystery inherent in the conduct of "foreign" affairs will diminish.*[34]

Different mind-sets must have played a role in the history of nations as long as there have been nations. Dutch sociologist Cornelis Lammers (1928–2009) demonstrated this fact in a case study from the early eighteenth century in the Spanish Netherlands (present-day Belgium). After the departure of the Spanish overlords, during a period of some ten years (1706–16) the territory was occupied partly by French troops, partly by British, and partly by Dutch. From the available records, Lammers compared the different regimes established by the three different occupying nations. The French tried to reform obsolete institutions and to establish a French style of centralized, rationalized authority. The English and

Dutch kept the old order intact, but the Dutch tried to persuade the local authorities to modernize in the name of efficiency, while the English kept at arm's length and tried to get as little involved in civil affairs as possible.[35] We recognize stronger power distance plus uncertainty avoidance in the French approach as opposed to both the English and the Dutch, and from the latter two the Dutch showed their femininity in attempts at governing by consensus.

Each of Chapters 3 through 8 has related a cultural values dimension to national political *processes* and/or political *issues*. The former are the ways the political game is played; the latter are the problems to which country politicians attach priority, and which they tend to defend on the international scene. These chapters showed that relationships between values and politics should always be seen against the backdrop of a country's national wealth or poverty; the implication of values is moderated by the level of economic prosperity.

Differences in power distance and uncertainty avoidance affect primarily the political processes. Larger power distance implies political centralization, lack of cooperation between citizens and authorities, and more political violence. Stronger uncertainty avoidance implies more rules and laws, more government intervention in the economy, and perceived incompetence of citizens versus authorities; stronger uncertainty avoidance implies more perceived corruption, after elimination of the effect of national poverty.

Individualism-collectivism and masculinity-femininity affect primarily the issues that countries will defend. Individualism implies concern with human rights, political democracy, and market capitalism; collectivism implies concern with group interests. Masculinity implies a focus on economic growth and competition and a belief in technology; femininity implies a focus on supporting needy people in the country (welfare) and in the world (development cooperation) and on preservation of the global environment. Masculinity versus femininity relates to political processes in that in masculine cultures the political discourse is more adversarial, in feminine cultures more consensus oriented.

Long- versus short-term orientation relates to pragmatism in politics versus fundamentalism: the latter means a focus on principles, even ineffective ones, and vested rights.

Indulgence versus restraint shows the conflict between a need for freedom of speech versus a need for order.

The influences of values and of economic prosperity imply that a number of Western political axioms cannot be applied to non-Western countries and are not very helpful as global guidelines:

- The solution of pressing global problems does not presuppose worldwide democracy. The rest of the world is not going Western. Authoritarian governments will continue to prevail in most of the world. The rise of China and India will affect hierarchy in corporations and in international collaboration worldwide. Elections are not a universal solution to political problems. In poor, collectivist, high-PDI and strong UAI cultures, elections may generate more problems than they resolve. One example is Algeria, where the first general elections in 1990 were won by fundamentalists committed to end political freedoms, after which the military declared the results invalid, and a wave of terrorism set in, which lasted for eight years and made tens of thousands of victims. Another example is Russia, where the disappearance of communism and of the Soviet Union in 1991 left a power vacuum; institutions necessary to execute democratically taken decisions were missing, and the local mafia established a kleptocracy (government by thieves). An authoritarian government again took hold.
- Free market capitalism cannot be universal; it presumes an individualist mentality that is missing in most of the world. Chapter 4 showed a statistical relationship between individualism and national wealth, but with the arrow of causality pointing from wealth to individualism: countries became more individualist after they increased in wealth, not wealthier by becoming more individualist. Free market capitalism suits countries already wealthy and is unlikely to turn poor countries into wealthy ones. The "dragon" economies of East Asia that grew very fast in the mid-1960s to mid-1990s had a variety of economic systems with often strong involvement of government.
- Economic development has ecological costs, which economists tend to ignore. The Western democracies' standard of living implies a degree of environmental pollution and depletion of resources that precludes extending this standard of living to the entire world population. Whoever seeks development for everybody should find a new way of handling our ecosystem: sustaining the rich countries' quality of life but drastically reducing its ecological cost. The concept of economic growth may in this respect already be obsolete; another measure for

the quality and survival power of economic and ecological systems will have to be found.

- Concepts of human rights cannot be universal. The Universal Declaration of Human Rights adopted in 1948 was based on individualist Western values that were and are not shared by the political leaders nor by the populations of the collectivist majority of the world population. Without losing the benefits of the present declaration, which in an imperfect way presents at least a norm used to appeal against gross violations, the international community should revise the declaration to include, for example, the rights of groups and minorities. On the basis of such a revised declaration, victims of political and religious fundamentalisms can be protected; this protection should prevail over national sovereignty.

Public and nongovernmental organizations that span national boundaries depend, for their functioning, entirely on intercultural communication and cooperation. Most international organizations are not supposed to have a home national culture; key decision makers usually have to come from different countries. Examples are the United Nations with its subsidiaries such as UNESCO and UNIDO, the European Union, the International Labour Organization, and the World Council of Churches. Others have an implicit home culture related to their past: religious organizations, such as the Roman Catholic Church (Italian) and the Mormon Church (American), and humanitarian organizations, such as the Red Cross (Swiss) and Amnesty International (British).

Confederations such as the United Nations and the European Union by definition should not have a dominant national culture. This mandate is less a problem for the political part of such organizations, in which people are supposed to act as representatives of their own countries and to settle their differences by negotiation. It is, however, a considerable problem in daily operations in which people are supposed to represent not their countries but the organization as such. Organizations can function only if their members share some kind of culture—if together they can take certain things for granted. In the daily operations of the UN and the EU, few things can be taken for granted. Personnel selection, nomination, and promotion procedures have to take into account arguments other than suitability for the job. Key persons may be moved before they have learned their jobs; often objectives are unclear, and where they are clear, means-ends relations are nebulous. Such organizations can escape from ineffectiveness and waste only by the development of a strong organizational culture at the level of shared practices (see Chapter 10). A viable system of performance evaluation is critical. Differences in nationality within these organizations again affect both the *process* and the *content* of the organization's work: the way the organization's bureaucracy functions and the projects the organization decides to undertake. As in the case of national politics, process is primarily linked with power distance and uncertainty avoidance, and content relates to individualism and masculinity.

Ad hoc international actions such as joint military interventions and peacekeeping missions are fraught with cultural conflict potential, not only between foreign military personnel and local populations but also between nationalities within the foreign forces. The success of such actions calls for expert culture management skills.[36]

Economic Development, Nondevelopment, and Development Cooperation

The nineteenth century and the first half of the twentieth century was the age of Europe; Europeans and their offspring overseas were the "lords of humankind,"[37] who colonized most of the outside world while wealth flowed from outside to inside. World War II was the breaking point that completely changed the relationships between continents and between rich and poor countries. In the thirty years after the war, nearly all former colonies became independent. Freedom from want became recognized as a fundamental human right, and around 1950 programs of development aid were gradually started, financed by the rich countries and with the poor ones as receivers. Between 1950 and 2000 the equivalent of more than a trillion U.S. dollars of public money from the rich countries was spent on the development of the poor ones.

In Chapter 5 it was shown that the percentage of their gross national income that governments of rich countries have allocated to development cooperation varies considerably (in 2005 the United States spent 0.22 percent of its GNI, while Denmark, Luxembourg, the Netherlands, Norway, and Sweden each spent more than 0.7 percent) and that this percentage was strongly correlated with the rich countries' femininity scores. Development assistance money is allocated according to the (psychological) needs of the donor countries more than according to the material needs of the receivers.

Looking back to half a century of development assistance, most observers agree that the effectiveness of much of the spending has been dismal. A number of countries did cross the line from poor to rich, especially in East Asia, but this progress was due to their populations' own values and efforts, not to the amount of aid money received. In spite of the aid money flow, the income gap between rich and poor countries has not been reduced. Development of poor countries is an uphill struggle because population growth often swallows any increase in resources. Cultural and religious traditions (in poor and in rich countries) that resist population control, besides threatening regional and global peace, are development's worst enemies.

Nobody can develop a country but its own population. Development is in the minds, not in the goods. Foreign money and foreign expertise are effective only to the extent that they can be integrated into local knowledge. Success stories in the development literature always stress the emancipation of the locals from foreign expertise. The World Bank in 1992 launched a research program on "best practices" in Africa that in a number of case studies shows how quickly results could be obtained by building on indigenous institutions that had a strong hold on people's commitment, dedication, and sense of identity, while at the same time implementing essential modernizations such as strengthening the rule of law.[38]

The dominant philosophy of development cooperation has too rarely recognized this need for local integration. Economic models dictated policies. Developing a country has for decades been considered primarily an economic and technical problem, a matter of transferring money and technology. Decisions about spending were made by politicians advised by technocrats at the giving end and often also at the receiving end. The existence of cultural mental programs on either side received lip service at best, and the only mental programs used in development planning were those of the donors. The very real fact of corruption, for example, was hardly ever addressed in the literature.[39] Very little money was spent on studying the mutual relationship between culture and technological change, although anthropologists for decades had shown culture's crucial impact on results.

Intercultural encounters in the context of development cooperation have an institutional side and an interpersonal side. On the institutional level many receiving countries, but also many donor countries, lack the organizational framework to make the cooperation a success. Usually, the primitive institutional structures in the receiving countries are blamed. On the donor side, however, the situation is not always better. Many development agencies have grown out of the foreign service, the main objective of which is the promotion of the donor country's interests abroad. Diplomats lack both the skills and the organizational culture to act as successful entrepreneurs for development consulting activities. Development aid money often has political strings attached to it: it has to be spent in a way that satisfies the values, if not the interests, of the donor country citizens and politicians, whether or not such values are shared by citizens and politicians at the receiving end. Projects funded by *international* agencies such as the World Bank in theory do not have this constraint, but they have to satisfy the agency's objectives, which often also conflict with the receivers' objectives.[40]

The institutional problem at the receiving end is the most serious for countries in which traditional institutional frameworks did not survive colonization and decolonization. Most of these lie in sub-Saharan Africa. Even when local wars do not destroy the products of peaceful development, forces in society make development difficult to attain. Without institutional traditions, personal interests can prevail unchecked. Politicians are out to enrich themselves and their families without being controlled by traditional norms. Institutions cannot be created from scratch: they are living arrangements, rooted in values and history, which have to grow. The economic success of certain countries of East Asia owes much to the fact that centuries-old institutional frameworks existed that were adapted to modern times.

Development cooperation has suffered from various implicit models of how organizations should function (see Chapter 9) between donor and host country technicians.

Take the story of a German engineering firm installing an irrigation system in an African country. Overcoming serious technical difficulties, the engineers constructed an effective and easy-to-operate system. They provided all the necessary documentation for later use and repairs, translated into English and Swahili. Then they left. Four months later the system broke down, and it was never repaired. The local authority structure had not had an opportunity to adopt the project as its family property; the project had no local "master."[41]

A classic study sponsored by the Canadian International Development Agency looked at factors determining the effectiveness of donor country personnel overseas. It covered 250 Canadian expatriates in six host countries, as well as 90 of their host country counterparts. It identified three components:

1. Intercultural interaction and training, related to involvement with the local culture and people and with transfer of skills
2. Professional effectiveness, related to the performance of daily tasks, duties, and responsibilities on the job
3. Personal and family adjustment and satisfaction, related to the capacity for basic satisfaction while living abroad, as an individual and as a family unit

From these three, the expatriates were found to be generally competent on components 2 and 3 but lacking on component 1. Local counterparts stressed the transfer of job skills through intercultural interaction and training as the most crucial dimension of expatriate success.[42]

A study by the development cooperation agencies of the Nordic countries Denmark, Finland, Norway, and Sweden focused on the effectiveness of Nordic technical assistance personnel in eastern Africa. It criticized the priorities set by the donors: from nine hundred Nordic expatriates, two-thirds were implementers (carrying out projects themselves) while only one-fifth were trainers of local personnel or consultants in local institution building. According to the researchers, the ratio between the two categories should have been reversed. This format would have sharply reduced the number of expatriates needed and changed the profile of skills required from them.[43]

In summary, assuming sufficient institutional support, intercultural encounters in the context of development cooperation will be productive if there is a two-way flow of know-how: technical know-how from the donor to the receiver, and cultural know-how about the context in which the technical know-how should be applied, from the receiver to the donor. A technical expert meets a cultural expert, and their mutual expertise is the basis for their mutual respect.

Learning Intercultural Communication

The acquisition of intercultural communication abilities passes through three phases: awareness, knowledge, and skills. *Awareness* is where it all starts: the recognition that I carry a particular mental software because of the way I was brought up and that others brought up in a different environment carry a different mental software for equally good reasons. Max Pagès, a French social psychologist who went to the United States in the 1950s to study group training, described a situation in which such awareness was lacking:

> *It became very clear to me that it was I, Max, but not my culture which was accepted. I was treated as just another American who had this exotic peculiarity of being a Frenchman, which was something like, say, a particular style of shirt. In general no curiosity existed about the intellectual world I was living in, the kinds of books I had written or read, the differences between what is being done in France or Europe and in the United States.*[44]

Strong cultural awareness was ascribed to the author James Morier. The quote about him at the beginning of this chapter characterized him as "gifted with a humorous sympathy that enabled him to appreciate the motives actuating persons entirely dissimilar to himself."

Knowledge should follow. If we have to interact with particular other cultures, we have to learn about these cultures. We should learn about their symbols, their heroes, and their rituals; while we may never share their values, we may at least get an intellectual grasp of where their values differ from ours.

Skills are based on awareness and knowledge, plus practice. We have to recognize and apply the symbols of the other culture: recognize their heroes, practice their rituals, and experience the satisfaction of getting along in the new environment, being able to resolve first the simpler and later on some of the more complicated problems of life among the others.

Intercultural communication can be taught. Some students are more gifted at learning it than others. Persons with unduly inflated egos, a low personal tolerance for uncertainty, a history of emotional instability, or known racist or extreme left- or right-wing political sympathies should be considered bad risks for a training program that, at its core, assumes people's ability to distance themselves from their own cherished beliefs. Such persons are probably unfit for expatriation anyway; if a family will be expatriated, it is wise to make sure that the spouse and children, too, have the necessary emotional stability.

There are two types of intercultural communication training courses. The more traditional ones focus on specific knowledge of the other culture; they are sometimes called *expatriate briefings*. They inform the future expatriates, and preferably their spouses too, as well as sometimes their children, about the new country, including its geography, some history, customs, hygiene, dos and don'ts, what to bring—in short, how to live. They do not provide much introspection into the expatriates' own culture. They are extremely useful, but the strongly motivated expatriate-to-be can also get this information from books, videos, and Web resources. In fact, the institutes offering this type of training usually maintain good book and video libraries or websites for urgent individual preparation.

An even better preparation for a specific assignment is, of course, learning the local language. There is a plethora of crash courses available, but unless the learner is exceptionally gifted, learning a new language at the business level will take several months full-time—a bit less if the course takes place in the foreign country so that the learner is fully immersed. Most employers do not plan far enough ahead to allow their expatriates such an amount of time for language learning, to their own detriment. If a male expatriate gets this chance, it is highly beneficial to involve his spouse as well. Women, on average, are faster learners of languages than men. They are also better at picking up nonverbal cultural clues.

The other type of intercultural communication course focuses on awareness of and general knowledge about cultural differences. *Awareness training* focuses on one's own mental software and where it may differ from others. It is not specific to any given country of expatriation; the knowledge and skills taught apply in any foreign cultural environment. They deal not so much with the question of how to live in the other culture as with how to work: how to get a job done. Along with the (future) expatriate, the course may be attended by the spouse, too, because an understanding spouse is a major asset during the culture shock period.[45] It should, in any case, definitely be attended by the expatriate's boss at the head office and by staff specialists who communicate with the expatriates. Experience has taught that a chief problem of expatriates is getting the understanding and support of the staff who act as their contacts in the home country organization. The home front should acquire the same cultural sensitivity demanded of the expatriate. Conditions for success of this type of course are the commitment of top management, the investment of a sufficient share of the trainees' time, and the participation in the same type of program of a critical mass of company personnel.

In the design of intercultural competence courses, *process* is as important as *content*. The learning process itself is culturally constrained, and trainers who are not aware of this constraint communicate something other than what they try to teach. Writing from extensive experience in Hong Kong, Michael Bond has warned against using Western procedures with Asian audiences.[46] The occupational culture of the emerging profession of intercultural trainers and consultants is built on the use of Western, mainly U.S., practices.

Using ideas from U.S. counseling expert Paul Pedersen and from Geert's five-dimensional model, Gert Jan has developed a method of group training in exploring cultural variety that can be used with a wide variety of participants and for an equally wide variety of practical applications. It asks participants to identify with a choice of ten *synthetic cultures*, "pure" culture types derived from the extremes of the dimensions described in this book (except indulgence versus restraint, which had not yet been introduced). Participants then play their culture in a simulated problem-solving situation. They learn from their experience and develop intercultural skills in a "safe" environment.[47]

Self-instruction is also possible. A classic instrument for this purpose is the *Culture Assimilator*. This is a programmed learning tool consisting of a number of short case descriptions, each featuring an intercultural encounter in which a person from the foreign culture behaves in a particular way. Usually four explanations are offered of this behavior. One of these is the insider explanation by informants from the foreign culture. The three others are naive choices by outsiders. The student picks one answer and receives a comment explaining why the answer chosen was correct (corresponding to the insiders' view) or incorrect (naive). Early culture assimilators were culture-specific toward both the home and the host cultures. They therefore were costly to make and had relatively limited distribution, but an evaluation study showed their long-term effects to be quite positive. Later on, a General Culture Assimilator was published, incorporating the main common themes from the earlier specific ones.[48]

Cultural sensitivity is subtle, and bias is always looming around the corner. When children of Vietnamese refugees began attending regular schools in small towns in the United States in 1976, the U.S. Office of Education issued an instruction for teachers, *On Teaching the Vietnamese*:

> *Student participation was discouraged in Vietnamese schools by liberal doses*
> *of corporal punishment, and students were conditioned to sit rigidly and to*

speak only when spoken to. This background . . . makes speaking freely in
class hard for a Vietnamese. Therefore, don't mistake shyness for apathy.[49]

To most western European and North American readers, this instruction
looks OK at first. However, it becomes more problematic when we delve
for all the clues about U.S. culture that the quote supplies, all of which
reflect sources of bias. In fact, the U.S. Office of Education ascribes to the
Vietnamese all the motivations of young Americans—such as a supposed
desire to participate—and explains their submission by corporal punishment, rather than, for example, respect. At a doctoral seminar Geert taught
in Sweden, one of the participants[50] opened the eyes of the others by reversing the statement—supposing American students would have to attend
Vietnamese schools:

Students' proper respect for teachers was discouraged by a loose order
and students were conditioned to behave disorderly and to chat all the
time. This background makes proper and respectful behavior in class hard
for an American student. Therefore, don't mistake rudeness for lack of
reverence.

Educating for Intercultural Understanding: Suggestions for Parents

For if one were to offer men to choose out of all the customs in the world
such as seemed to them the best, they would examine the whole number, and
end by preferring their own; so convinced are they that their own usages
far surpass those of all others.

   —Herodotus, *The Histories*, 420 B.C.[51]

The English, of any people in the universe, have the least of a national
character; unless this very singularity may pass for such.

   —David Hume, Essay XXI, 1742[52]

The Germans live in Germany, the Romans live in Rome,
the Turkeys live in Turkey; but the English live at home.

   —A nursery rhyme by J. H. Goring, 1909[53]

In terms of the foregoing quotes, the message of this book so far has been that everybody is like Herodotus's experimental subjects and Hume's or Goring's English. Everybody looks at the world from behind the windows of a cultural home, and everybody prefers to act as if people from other countries have something special about them (a national character), but home is normal. Unfortunately, there is no normal position in cultural matters. This is an uncomfortable message, as uncomfortable as Galileo Galilei's claim in the seventeenth century that Earth is not the center of the universe.

The basic skill for surviving in a multicultural world, as has been argued, is understanding first one's own cultural values and next the cultural values of the others with whom one has to cooperate. As parents, we have more influence on creating multicultural understanding in future world citizens than in any other role. Values are mainly acquired during the first ten years of a child's life. They are absorbed by observation and imitation of adults and older children rather than by indoctrination. The way parents live their own culture provides the child with his or her cultural identity. The way parents talk about and behave toward persons and groups from other cultures determines the degree to which the child's mind will be opened or closed for cross-cultural understanding.

Growing up in a bicultural environment can be an asset to a child. This environment can take the form of having parents from different nationalities, living abroad during childhood, or attending a foreign school. Whether such biculturality really is an asset or instead becomes a liability depends on the parents' ability to cope with the bicultural situation themselves. Having foreign friends, hearing different languages spoken, and traveling with parents who awaken the children's interests in things foreign are definite assets. Learning at least one other language is a unique ingredient of education for multicultural understanding. This supposes, of course, that the teaching of the other language is effective: a lot of language classes in schools are a waste of time. The stress should be on full immersion, whereby using the foreign language becomes indispensable for practical purposes. Becoming truly bi- or multilingual is one of the advantages available to children belonging to a minority group or to a small nation. It is more difficult for those belonging to a large nation, unless of course that nation is itself multilingual, as for example in the case of India.

Spreading Multicultural Understanding: The Role of the Media

Media representatives—journalists, reporters, and radio and TV producers—play a uniquely important role in creating multicultural understanding (or misunderstanding). The battle for survival in a multicultural world will, to a large extent, be fought in the media. Media representatives are human, which means they have cultural values of their own. With regard to other cultures, their position is ambiguous: on the one hand, they cater to a public, and their success depends on the extent to which they write or speak what the public wants to read or hear; on the other hand, they are in a position to direct people's attention—to create an image of reality that to many people becomes reality itself. A member of the public has to be pretty sophisticated to critically scrutinize the beliefs about other cultures reflected in television shows, radio programs, and newspapers.

The consciousness that people in other parts of one's society (not to mention people in other societies entirely) think, feel, and act on the basis of other but not necessarily evil value assumptions may or may not be recognized by media representatives and reflected in their productions. The simple act of informing the public about such cultural divides can help to avoid serious misunderstandings. Doubtless, there exist reporters who want only simple, black-and-white messages, as well as those with a vested interest in showing who are the good guys and who the bad ones. For those with higher ambitions, however, there still is considerable untapped potential for spreading understanding about differences in cultural values and practices. For example, using the television eye to compare similar aspects of daily behavior in different countries can be extremely powerful and is too seldom done.[54]

A problem particular to small countries such as the Netherlands is that both TV and newspapers buy content from larger countries and disseminate it locally without stressing the different cultural contexts in which these materials were produced. An example is the use of newspaper articles reporting on survey research about trends in society. The material in question is most frequently from the United States, and the implicit assumption of the editor responsible is that the conclusions are valid for the Netherlands as well. If one realizes the large distance between the two societies on the masculinity-femininity dimension (Chapter 5), which affects many

societal phenomena, Dutch readers should at least be cautioned when interpreting U.S. data. Surprisingly, few Dutch journalists would dream of producing Japanese or German statistics with the tacit assumption that their
conclusions apply in the Netherlands.

Global Challenges Call for Intercultural Cooperation

Humankind today is threatened by a number of disasters that have all been
man-made: they are disasters of culture rather than the disasters of nature
to which our ancestors were regularly exposed.

Their common cause is that people have become both too numerous
and too clever for the limited size of our globe. While we are clever about
technology and are getting more so each day, we are still naive about ourselves. Our mental software is not adapted to the environment we created
in recent centuries. The only way toward survival is getting to understand
ourselves better as social beings, so that we may control our technological
cleverness and not use it in destructive ways. This goal demands concerted
action on issues for which, unfortunately, different cultural values lead
people to disagree rather than agree. In these circumstances intercultural
cooperation has become a prime condition for the survival of humankind.

A number of value-laden world problems have been signaled in this
book. There are the economic problems: international economic cooperation versus competition; the distribution of wealth and poverty across and
within countries. There are the technology-induced problems. In the past,
whenever a new technology was invented, it could also be applied. This is
no longer the situation, and decisions have to be made regarding whether
some of the things people can produce should be produced, and if so, subject to what precautions. Such decisions should be agreed upon on a world
scale, and if countries, groups, or persons do not respect the decisions or
the precautions, they should be forced to do so. Examples are certain uses
of nuclear energy both for peaceful and for aggressive purposes, certain
chemical processes and products, certain applications of information science, and certain applications of genetic manipulation. An example of the
latter is influencing whether a baby to be born will be a boy or a girl. In
some cultures the desirability of having boys over girls is inordinately
strong (see Chapter 5). In view of both ethical and demographic consid-

erations, should this technology be allowed to spread? If so, to where and under what conditions? If not, can one stop it?

The combination of world population growth, economic development, and technological developments affects the world ecosystem in ways that are known only in small part. Uncontrolled tree-cutting in many parts of the world destroys forests. Long-term climate changes due to the green-house effect of increased emission of carbon dioxide and other gases are evident; they have a built-in delay of decades, so that even if we were to stop emitting now, the greenhouse effect will increase for a long time. Coping with these problems requires worldwide research and political decision making in areas in which both perceived national interests and cultural values are in conflict. Decisions about sacrifices undertaken today for ben-efits to be reaped by the next generation have to be made by politicians whose main concern is with being reelected next year or surviving a power struggle tomorrow. In addition, the sacrifices may lie in other parts of the world than the region occupied by the main benefactors. The greenhouse effect can be reduced if the tropical countries preserve their rain forests. These countries are mainly poor, and their governments want the revenue of selling their hardwoods. Can they be compensated for leaving intact what remains of their rain forests?

The trends outlined are threats to humanity as a whole. They repre-sent the common enemy of the future. Confronting a common enemy has always been the most effective way of making leaders and groups with con-flicting values and interests cooperate. Maybe these threats will become so imminent as to force us to achieve a level of global intercultural coopera-tion that has never existed.

Much will depend on the acquisition of intercultural cooperation skills as part of the mental software of politicians. Former U.S. diplomat Glen Fisher, in his book *Mindsets*, stated the following about the relationship among economics, culture, and politics:

> *An interdisciplinary approach to international economic processes hardly exists. Most important, routine applications of conventional economic analysis cannot tolerate "irrational" behavior. But, from a cross-national and cross-cultural perspective, there is a real question as to what is rational and what irrational; both are very relative terms and very much culture bound; one person's irrationality might turn out to be another's orderly and*

predictable behavior. . . . Despite the frequent assertion that sentimentality and the pursuit of economic interests don't mix, economic systems are in fact ethical systems. Whether by law and regulation or by custom, some economic activities are sanctioned while others are not. And what is sanctioned differs from culture to culture.[55]

Both what is "rational" and what is "ethical" depend on cultural value positions. In politics, value positions are further confounded by perceived interests. There is a strong tendency in international politics to use different ethical standards toward other countries versus one's own.

A case study that should encourage modesty about ethics in politics is the international drug trade. Western countries for decades have been involved in a virtual war to prevent the importation of drugs. Not so long ago, from 1839 to 1842, a Western country (Britain) fought an "Opium War" with Imperial China. The Chinese emperor took the same position that Western governments are taking now: trying to keep drugs out of his country. The British, however, had strong economic interests in a Chinese market for the opium they imported from India, and through an active sales promotion they got large numbers of Chinese addicted. The British won the war, and in the peace treaty they not only got the right to continue importing opium but also acquired Hong Kong Island as a permanent foothold on the Chinese coast. The returning of Hong Kong to China in 1997 in a way was a belated victory for the Chinese in their war against drugs.[56]

From a values point of view, it is difficult to defend the position that the trade in arms is less unethical than the trade in drugs. One difference is that in the drug traffic, the poor countries tend to be the sellers; in the arms traffic, it's the rich countries. The latter have made more money on selling arms to third-world countries than they spent on development assistance to these countries. Of course, in this case the buyers and the sellers are both to blame, but the rich countries are in a better position to break the vicious circle.

Reducing the trade in arms would reduce civil wars, terrorism, and murder. It would improve the chances of respect for human rights in the world: these arms are often used to crush human rights. While it is unrealistic to expect all countries of the world to become Western-style democracies, a more feasible goal is to strive for more respect for human rights even in autocratically led states.

As argued earlier in this chapter, the Universal Declaration of Human Rights adopted in 1948 is based on universalist, individualist Western values that clearly are not shared by the political leaders nor by the populations of all other parts of the world. On the other hand, the declaration is a fact, and international organizations as well as individuals will no doubt continue to signal infringements, regardless of the country in which these infringements take place. No government is powerful enough to silence, for example, Amnesty International. All but the most ruthless governments try to maintain an appearance of international respectability. The fact that the world has become one scene leads to the public's being informed about more suffering than ever before; it also offers more opportunities to act against this suffering.

If we inhabit a global village,[51] it consists only of a theater and a marketplace. We need houses, sanctuaries, and places to meet and talk. In London, in the fall of 2003, Gert Jan sat in a pub with four students from four continents. A man from India and a man from Ghana were arguing about whether and how they could help their respective countries. The Indian pressed the other to admit that if he could spare just one pound a day for educating children in his home country, that would make a difference. But the Ghanean said that giving money only made things worse and that, for the time being, educating himself was the only thing he could do. They got pretty heated and did not agree, but they did listen to one another, and they parted as friends. In the global village we need many meetings like that one.

The Evolution of Cultures

It must not be forgotten that although a high standard of morality gives but a slight or no advantage to each individual man and his children over the other men of the same tribe, yet that an increase in the number of well-endowed men and an advancement in the standard of morality will certainly give an immense advantage to one tribe over another. A tribe including many members who, from possessing in a high degree the spirit of patriotism, fidelity, obedience, courage, and sympathy, were always ready to aid one another, and to sacrifice themselves for the common good, would be victorious over most other tribes; and this would be natural selection.

—Charles Darwin, *The Descent of Man*, 1874

The recent discovery on the Indonesian island of Flores of *Homo floresiensis* fossils, nicknamed "hobbits," has caused quite a stir. *Homo erectus*, to whose lineage the fossils belong, was believed to have been extinct for a million years, but these fossils are about eighteen thousand years old, and today's inhabitants of Flores still recount legends of "forest people." Our prehistory is not far away. Many of us may not want to know it, but we carry apes and early hominins[1] in our genes and in our behaviors. How, throughout the centuries, did we become the beings that we are today, with our mix of old-fashioned mammalian and newfangled symbolic properties?

We need not assume a historical discontinuity. There is no magical point in time at which we changed into ourselves, although our in-group—out-group logic strongly prompts us to believe that a divine spark separates us humans from theose apes. Instead, a gradual process of coevolution has changed both our nature and our cultures. Primatologists have documented the fact that different chimpanzee populations have different cultures when it comes to tool use and hunting practices. The same has held for our ancestors. Our cultural psychology is shaped by our history as a species. Over the last millions of years (yes, millions), we have gone through an accelerating process of cultural evolution that has been gaining in importance alongside good old genetic evolution. The capacity for culture has by now become an essential element in our biology. In the last tens of thousands of years, human cultures have diversified in a way similar to groups of species in the natural world, only much faster. Culture has become a vehicle that helps people build civilizations. We can now live reasonably peacefully in huge, anonymous groups. Where is this leading us? As a final concern, this twelfth chapter glances into the present and future of cultural evolution. Understanding how we acquired our cultures raises issues about how to shape our future.

So, in short, this chapter deals with questions that are usually thought of as philosophical: who are we, where are we from, and where are we going? The discussion takes a perspective that involves biological evolution, of which, in our view, cultural evolution is an integral part. This is an approach of *consilience*: uniting viewpoints that are usually not considered together.[2] This angle reconciles the biological, the philosophical, the historical, the social scientific, and indeed the practical. The price is that this grand perspective cannot yet be underpinned by the kind of empirical proof that underlies most of this book. The evidence is scattered across time and across disciplines. For interested readers the notes give some pointers to further reading on some of the topics on which the chapter touches.

A Time-Machine Journey Through History

What follows is a time-machine view of human evolution. The time machine will start five million years ago. It will slow down as it approaches the present, but as it does, the speed of change will pick up, so that the view keeps changing fast. Over the last million years, survival of fit *tribes* or *societies* has gained importance compared with survival of fit individuals. This is what Charles Darwin, the nineteenth-century English pioneer of evolution by means of natural selection, expresses in the quote with which this chapter opened. Humans have become nicer to one another, and to more others too. American evolutionist David Sloan Wilson puts it as follows:

> *When between-group selection dominates within-group selection, a major evolutionary transition occurs and the group becomes a new, higher-level organism with elaborate specialization and immensely complex interdependencies.*[3]

This transition is now happening to humans, and it is causing the extraordinary acceleration of evolution of which we are a part. Chimps, bonobos, and orangutans can learn to use symbols if exposed to them, and they are surprisingly clever. But they cannot organize in massive anonymous societies. Humanity's biggest evolutionary leap since our days as just another ape has been social.

During the time-machine ride, the history of the moral circle will be a point of concern. Until very recently, the chief threats to survival were natural. Cold, heat, and predators had to be kept at bay through clever, coordinated action and often through migration. Scarcity was another enemy to survival, to be countered by finding food and drink, which again required intelligence and collaboration. Reproductive units that were too small were dangerous, because they would lead to genetic inbreeding and loss of resilience. This threat, no doubt, has been a strong driver for enlargement of human reproductive units, since those who isolated themselves tended to die out. Quite recently, as the earth became more densely populated with humans, the danger took on a different form: contagious disease, depletion of resources, and economic or military warfare are now our main human-caused threats. In conclusion, the main challenges to human groups have provided survival value to good collaboration skills. This in turn has driven the evolution of culture as a mechanism for building and maintaining the moral circle.

Five Million to One Million Years Ago: Lonely Planet

For millions of years our ancestors lived in groups of a few dozen as hunters, gatherers, or both. About five million years ago the lineage of our ancestors split from that of chimpanzees, bonobos, and gorillas, and these ancestral hominins began leaving forests for savanna habitats. This transition made walking on two legs a good idea, because it affords a better view of prey and predators in high grass. Once on two legs, our ancestors could use their hands to carry things, which was an advantageous evolutionary step that they did not retrace when ice ages began to occur around 2.6 million years ago. The comparatively stable, well-watered, warm climates during the earlier part of this period had made it advantageous also for them to gradually lose their body hair and acquire the capacity for sweating. Evidence for loss of body hair comes from parasites: humans have head lice and body lice that are closely related but pubic lice that are thought to have split around 3.3 million years ago from gorilla lice—so, this may have been a time at which our ancestors started to kill gorillas, and it must have been a time at which they had separate head and pubic hair.[4]

During this period the total hominin population was always modest in number, perhaps in the tens of thousands, and everybody lived in Africa, surrounded by animals that hunted them or that they hunted. Whether any hunting was done by populations older than *Homo erectus* 1.8 million years ago is still being debated, but the fact that today's chimpanzees can hunt in groups suggests that early hominins might have done it too. Whatever the case, all African animals either died out or coevolved with their hunters— to become hard to catch. Based on analogies with apes and with recent hunter-gatherer populations, it is thought that our hominin ancestors lived in territorial bands of no more than a few dozen individuals, because there never was more food in one place that could have sustained a larger population. These groups in all probability exchanged young females, as do gorillas, chimpanzees, and bonobos today.[5] Indeed, in most human societies of today the wives are "given away," move to the home of their in-laws, and take on a new name—not the husbands.

Most of these ancestral bands probably also engaged in skirmishes along territorial boundaries initiated by groups of males. Physical strength, resilience to disease, and capacity for coordinated collaborative action were factors that jointly determined the success in these actions. Larger bands would have assimilated smaller ones, sometimes by killing adult males and infants and adopting females. Successful groups would have split up when an aspiring leader left the mother group, followed by part of the group members.[6]

So, fission and fusion of groups has been a mechanism for combining genetic and cultural evolution for millions of years. The normal course of evolution among apes has been that separation of subpopulations gradually led to the formation of new races and, after millions of years, new species—a process called *speciation*. In contrast, the splitting and merging and the exchange of females among our ancestors would have tended to promote genetic similarity but cultural variation between groups, instead of genetic divergence and speciation as is usual in the animal kingdom. Fossil evidence is sketchy and still growing, which means that naming is still controversial and subject to revision. So far, the evidence suggests that a few million years ago, several isolated populations of hominins existed in what is now Africa. They created diversity in genetic materials and developed into very different forms—for example, the recently announced "Ardi" (*Ardipithecus ramidus*), who lived 4.4 million years ago in what is now Ethiopia, or the well known "Lucy" (*Australopithecus afarensis*), who lived in the same area a million years later. Many lineages have died out since then. No traces of anything but the crudest tool use were found.

From around 1.8 million years ago, brain size started to grow rapidly. This development was probably associated with refinements in communication skills and in what evolutionary psychologists call "theory of mind." Theory of mind is the level of understanding of the beliefs, desires, and intentions of others. Today's humans can understand utterances five levels of mind deep—for example, "I believe that you think that he hoped that she would rejoice at his distress." Theory of mind is crucial for maintaining moral circles in a socially complex world, and it has gradually developed during our history.

There are still many guesses concerning this period, such as about how soon and how often hominins left Africa. The forebears of *Homo erectus* may have left Africa 1.8 million years ago, giving rise over several hundred thousand years to *Homo heidelbergensis*, which later evolved into *Homo neanderthaliensis* in Europe, while keeping the name *Homo erectus* in Asia. During most periods the Sahara was inhospitable, so that with the sea, it prevented human colonization of other continents. Our own ancestors left Africa just recently, and we will meet them again in the next section.

Of all the species and subspecies of apes that populated the world five million years ago, only ours has thrived, and few have survived. Culture, though, is not uniquely human. Even the apes that did not make it into world conquerors—today's great apes (bonobo, chimpanzee, gorilla, orangutan, gibbon)—have developed cultural differences among their populations. Dutch-American primatologist Frans de Waal has shown that various species of apes have different sets of behaviors for maintaining moral circles.[7] In-group solidarity is always matched with out-group violence, although the balance is widely different for different species: chimpanzee males form bands that raid neighboring tribes, while bonobo males tend to go no further than to be somewhat stiff during otherwise peaceful between-tribe encounters. Actually, experiences in zoos have shown that chimps and bonobos are perfectly mutually fertile. As with other related species, the genetic differences are small enough to allow for cross-fertilization. They have just developed distinctly different cultures, probably after a small settling population of bonobos diverged from mainstream chimp culture, perhaps after crossing the Congo River less than a million years ago.[8]

It is thus likely that along with the genetic variation, a wide variety of human cultures has existed throughout ancient times. Fossil findings of early hominins show huge differences in skeleton robustness and in size ratio between the sexes. Our early ancestors showed marked variability and adaptability to circumstances.

One Million to Forty Thousand Years Ago: Ice and Fire

Ice ages intensified about one million years ago; the last ice age set in about a hundred thousand years ago, and we may still be in it today, enjoying a warmer interlude. Even on smaller time scales of hundreds of years, climates were fluctuating a lot, and they still do. To what extent the African continent partook of icy conditions is not certain, but the climate obviously fluctuated there as well. Our migrating ancestors had been using simple tools for at least a million years, and they may well have mastered fire, although we cannot be sure because fossil evidence for fire is far more difficult to find than for stone tools. Fire must in turn have allowed them the freedom to spend time socializing and communicating in relative safety from predators. Cooking food also allows for extraction of more nutrients, and this benefit helped larger bands survive. While gathered around the fire, they may have invented and gradually perfected skills for laughing, singing, and dancing as ways of increasing group harmony. Finally, mastering fire is eminently handy when climates change erratically and cold winters set in every other century. Besides fire, animal skins probably started being used as elementary clothing during cold spells. Our body lice are related to our head lice, not to our pubic lice—body lice must have thrived on animal skins with fine hairs worn inside out, not on coarse body hair.[9]

Actually, not just humans but all mammals that lived through the ice ages developed larger brains, according to fossil finds.[10] Apparently, they had to become clever to avoid dying out. Anatomically modern human skeletons occur in the fossil record from about that time. The people of those times buried their dead but were not conspicuous for creative skills. Simple hand axes and scrapers are the most advanced technologies recovered from them. They nevertheless managed to survive in various habitats, some of them under ice age conditions—so, they must have been respectably clever and good at collaborating.

Although evidence is scant, paleoanthropologists tend to agree that during this period our ancestors lived in small primary groups of dozens of individuals who gathered periodically in larger secondary groups of a few hundred or, in times of plenty, a few thousand.[11] These secondary groups were the cultural and reproductive unit. The primary groups were small enough to find food throughout the year, while the secondary groups were large enough to allow for maintenance of genetic variation and to buffer fluctuations in birthrate between boys and girls. The secondary group might also fight other cultural groups or might exchange genetic material with them, as can happen through voluntary migration, rape, theft of females and children, or tolerance of a lone youngster from another band. As with genes, inventions could travel in this way. Still, such travel would have been slow, and favorable genetic mutations would have been rare, since their occurrence is proportional to the total population—and that total number was in the order of hundreds of thousands.

Modern humans throughout the world have descended from migrations out of Africa that started around seventy thousand years ago and intensified about forty thousand years ago, and since then all species died out but *Homo sapiens*. Today human genetic variation is largest on the African continent, testifying to the small size of the early human groups that founded non-African populations.

Forty Thousand to Ten Thousand Years Ago: Creative Spark, Extermination

Our ancestors start to show signs of much richer art and technology from around eighty thousand years ago in southern Africa and around thirty-two thousand years ago in Europe. This latter period is called the Aurignacien, for the site of artistic cave paintings of many species of animals found in what is now Aurignac, France. The oldest statuettes of voluptuous female figures, such as the recently uncovered "Venus of Hohle Fels," likewise date from this period. People also started to hunt dangerous animals. Whether they also actively fought their close relatives is not certain as yet. However that may be, *Homo neanderthaliensis* and the descendants of *Homo erectus* both died out less than some thirty thousand years ago, the first group in what is now Spain, the second on the Indonesian island of Flores.

According to geneticists Gregory Cochran and Henry Harpending,[12] Neanderthals and modern humans may well have mixed their genes. Their lineages split half a million years earlier, diverging enough to create genetic differences but not enough to create infertility. When modern humans followed Neanderthal-style humans out of Africa, the groups met. The Neanderthals had specialized in hunting big game and may have had collaborative skills that benefited the moderns. The moderns outcompeted the Neanderthals, probably because of better technology, enhanced language capacities, or more trade with distant others, or perhaps because of resistance to diseases. Trade and disease could be related. The moderns already traded over long distances, which the Neanderthals never did,[13] and trade leads first to contagion and subsequently to the spread of resistance to diseases.

Many non-African larger animals were exterminated by humans. Humans now became much more numerous and migrated to all the continents, leaving only some isolated islands not colonized. Waves of migration were associated with extermination of other species. In Eurasia mammoths died out where human fossils appeared. Whether hunting or other factors—for instance, small genetic diversity and climate change—caused the demise of the mammoth is still controversial. For other species the picture is clearer. In the Americas the immigrating humans soon exterminated local large mammals, such as the placid giant sloths. *Homo sapiens* had begun to appropriate the earth.

During this period world population grew markedly. The growth of population meant a proportional rise in the chance of favorable mutations. As a consequence, genetic evolution could speed up. No doubt this was an enabler of social and intellectual development, as it had always been, but the standard of development in our social and intellectual capacities had now become so high that cultural evolution could begin to take wing. The takeoff of cultural innovation was spectacular: art, technology, and hunting techniques started to change at an increasing pace. Culture became a more and more prominent mechanism of evolution. With people living in small, egalitarian bands that had mutual exchanges while still being limited to modest world populations, there was no experience of inaccessible, awe-inspiring leaders. With abundant natural resources and good, protein-rich diets, and with discoveries being made regularly, this was probably a rather satisfying period for our ancestors. The statuettes of female figurines with plentiful breasts and genitals may have indicated admiration of Mother Earth. They certainly indicate a relaxed attitude toward the human body.

What culture would these hunter-gatherer bands have had? Or better, what range of cultures—because there is no reason to suppose that they were all alike. Cultural values leave no fossils, making speculation unavoidable. A band of, say, thirty hunter-gatherers had to be on the move, and everybody had to walk and to help carry things. It had to be democratic too; the group was not large enough to have dictators with armies or secret police. There were hardly any possessions: most of the world consisted of common goods of which the group had little control. Everybody's contribution was needed in order to provide food. The human digestive system needs a varied diet, and gathering probably supplied most of the nutrients to most populations at most times. Gathering fruits, leaves, seeds, roots, grubs, or eggs required memory of the topology of places. Pursuing animals that weren't dangerous—for example, fishing with nets—was akin to gathering but might require group collaboration. Smart hunting techniques, such as driving prey off cliffs or into ambushes using fire, could sharply reduce the risk involved. Risky types of hunting for large, dangerous animals may have been more useful as a bonding ritual, or as defense, than for providing nutrition. Hunting large prey required careful collaborative planning, mutual support, and quick opportunistic reaction to unexpected events.

Gender roles could be flexible, depending on the hazards of life. Some bands at some time must have been short on males and required female assistance for hunting, and that form of inclusion could then become a tradition. Success at the hunt, particularly since it required hard work and did not occur all the time, would provide an opportunity to socialize and feel good. It would yield both plenty of food and a need for further hard work by the entire group in preparing the meat and curing the skins. Given that it was not possible to store food, sharing would be evident. Only life-threatening activities such as fighting other bands or engaging in risky types of hunting would be reserved to males, since females could not afford to put their lives in jeopardy for fear of endangering the band's future. Imagine a tribe in which all females died valorously in battle—that tribe would be doomed to extinction.

Under conditions of plenty, competition from other bands of humans could occur, and in that case collective fighting would be important, while under conditions of scarcity and hardship, internal cohesion and tolerance would be vital, because infighting could weaken the group's resistance. More aggressive bands might push more peaceful bands to less rich habitats. However, as we can see in the lifestyles of hunter-gatherers today, there will have been many variations on this theme. This is a case of *path dependency*: the fact that evolution is constrained by its own history. As a consequence, from every next evolutionary step there is no way back. It follows, then, that a tradition of between-group aggression, if it turned to within-group violence, could quickly invalidate a tribe.

Improvising was always necessary. Uncertainty about the weather, the movements of prey, and the occurrence of predators would be the norm in daily life. If the climate changed, which it did all the time, people would either move on or adapt. They might live outdoors, in caves, or in self-built huts, as circumstances required. A variety of tools and weapons in different styles from this period have been found, testifying to a creative spirit. People made clever boats and probably increased the variety in their diet. They probably created a rich variety of languages, songs, stories, and ritual, as well. There are also traces of trade between groups, and we can be pretty sure that trade was accompanied by genetic contact. In this way, genetic variety in a group would be enhanced while genetic divergence in the species would remain small, as groups differentiated themselves from others by their art and rituals.

So, it can be speculated that hunter-gatherer societies tended to be merit-based, egalitarian, opportunistic, flexible, and relaxed. In terms of the cultural dimensions described in this book, their cultures had a small power distance, and they were rather individualistic, uncertainty tolerant, and indulgent.

What about the other dimensions of culture: masculinity versus femininity and long- versus short-term orientation? Although this is of course no more than an educated guess, a comparison with present-day hunter-gatherers may help. English family members and jacks-of-all-trades Michael, Henry, and Kathryn Davies spent the best time of their lives trying to draw a coherent picture of our prehistoric social evolution. Using as their basis the work of various anthropologists, they show evidence of the Mbuti tribe from central Africa, whose members until very recently lived as hunter-gatherers.[14] They paint a picture that fits the suggestion presented in the preceding discussion. For instance, the roles of the sexes were deemed to some extent to be interchangeable and undifferentiated. Discipline was exerted not through heavy punishment but through ridicule. Mixed marriages from different primary groups were tolerated, and in the case of noncompatibilities of temper, people could migrate to another group. Sexual infidelity by either husband or wife was not a contentious issue. So, society was permissive, but this liberty did not include permission to boast. The most able group members were expected to disguise their adroitness, so as to avoid creating jealousy. In conclusion, among the Mbuti the moral circle was every group member's responsibility, and it was live and let live. To summarize, their description seems to show what this book has introduced as a feminine, flexhumble (long-term oriented) culture.

The Davieses present the Mbuti as an example of what they call an "abundant-scale" hunter-gatherer society, one in which extreme climate and food scarcity are not a major threat. For "scarce-scale" hunter-gatherers, such as the aborigines who live in the arid regions of Australia, the picture is different and more complicated. Scarce food leads to low population densities, which poses a threat to genetic fitness. Splitting of groups or migration of couples away from the group would thus be hazardous, since it lowers population size even further. As a result, there is little leeway for interpersonal conflict. In aboriginal regions traditional society was characterized by strict land rights, game rights, and marriage prescriptions. Elder men held sway. They allocated marriage partners. Girls were married at puberty, while men normally married at around the age of thirty, after spending many years in a life of male rituals, some of them quite painful, which created solidarity. Status had to be achieved through individual merit. Rituals and, in general, all activities that support the spiritual life of the community are described as "dreamtime"; we might also speak of religion. An intense, rewarding dreamtime could compensate for harshness of circumstances, and its bonding rituals could keep a secondary group united. Among males, dreamtime performance was essential. Dreamtime secrets were divulged by older men only to those younger ones who had proved their worth.

Extramarital sex would occur, some of it in communal ritual. A way to avoid the allocation of partners was elopement, if violent passion was involved. Women were disempowered early in life by having to move to another group and live with an older man at puberty. Then again, older men frequently died first, and their widows could remarry with younger men and achieve status by guiding the younger wives of those men. Yet they remained the subservient gender and would occasionally be beaten into compliance. All in all, this society is like the Mbuti in that it is egalitarian and individualistic, but leeway for social role performance is limited, and severity of punishments is harsh. The moral circle is under permanent threat, and this peril is reflected in a value system that strongly penalizes misconduct. In terms of dimensions of culture, this seems to indicate a more masculine, uncertainty-avoiding, monumentalist (short-term-oriented), restrained value system.[15]

These are just two examples, and no doubt numerous types of cultures have existed among hunter-gatherers, even in central Africa and in Australia, and certainly in other parts of the world. When the level of plenty changed through climate changes, culture probably followed, but slowly due to the self-maintaining characteristics of culture-bound habits. More hardship would induce the creation of a more intense dreamtime. An intensive dreamtime, in return, possesses strong rituals that help it perpetuate itself even when the circumstances under which it came to be have changed. These dynamics would have pushed humanity toward increasing amounts of spiritual feeling and ritual over time.

Twelve Thousand to Seven Thousand Five Hundred Years Ago: Villages and Agriculture

The last ice age was at its coldest twenty thousand years ago. It took another eight millennia to fade away—at least temporarily—and by twelve thousand years ago the warm Holocene began. This was a time of plenty for plant and animal life, allowing humans to stay in one place for longer periods. In the beginning, they were still hunter-gatherers living in small bands, as they had done for millions of years, but they had an asset that their predecessors lacked: a superior creative intelligence and powers of organization. Holocene humans did things that were hitherto unheard of. Their sense of a moral circle had become more flexible, and they started to draw animals and plants into it. In other words, they started to domesticate plants and animals. Over a few thousand years, they domesticated various species of both, and in so doing they started a drastic process of genetic selection.

Historian Steven Mithen describes the daily life of the Natufians, who lived in the Levant from 12,300 years ago to 10,800 years ago and who, during this period, developed into horticulturalists.[16] Mithen hypothesizes that in the beginning of this period they collected wild cereals with sickles, and this method of collecting must have selected in favor of those grains that stuck to the ear longer. Some of the grains germinated near the villages, either by accident or as was intended. Soon, human-selected strands of grain with nonbrittle ears grew near the villages. In addition, archaeological finds show that each of these villages had its own style of jewels. These villagers apparently used their finery as a means of developing symbolic group identity, much as do present-day societies and subgroups.

Agriculture was invented simultaneously in various places on the planet. Biologist Jared Diamond mentions that food production was invented between six and eleven times in various continents.[17] Animals were domesticated in various places as well, including sheep and goats in the Mediterranean, cattle in Europe, and horses in central Asia. The availability of species that could be domesticated varied widely across continents, at least partly due to the different moments at which they had come into contact with humans. In Africa mammals had coevolved with humans for millions of years, and placid characteristics were selected against, because at that time humans were not yet smart enough to domesticate, but they could certainly kill. In Eurasia wolves, cattle, horses, and sheep were available for domestication by humans who had migrated out of Africa at a time when they were smart enough to domesticate them but unable or prudent enough not to exterminate them. The size of Eurasia compared with the modest numbers of human immigrants probably helped save the gentle grazing species in the region from extinction.

Agriculture and technology both enabled and facilitated trade. The addition of domesticated animals such as horses and camels could help people travel far. Human population now increased to millions, and people from different parts of the world met ever more frequently. As a result, they maintained a well-mixed genome—albeit certain continents were still isolated. Genes that could spread quickly would be those that provided an advantage in food tolerance or disease resistance or that were actively selected for sexually. One example of genetic mixing is the spread of blue eyes. All blue eyes in the world are thought to have arisen from a mutation in a single gene somewhere around what is now Lithuania some ten thousand to six thousand years ago.[18] Today they have spread as far as the Sahara and Afghanistan. Blue-eyed people must have been desirable partners in many cultures. One can speculate as to why this has been so. Blue eyes, or other light-colored irises, may have relational advantages. They show the size of the pupil, and pupil size is connected with emotional state. Experiments have shown that people who gaze at a face adapt the size of their pupils to that of the face at which they are looking.[19] This response may help in creating mutual sympathy. Of course, one who falls in love with a blue-eyed person does not consciously realize this phenomenon, but it could have facilitated the falling in love.

Agriculture changed the outlook of life dramatically. For the first time, humans had possessions: they could create storable food, in the form of live cattle or plant harvests. Possessions could pass from one person to another in a way that enabled two innovations: inheritance and large-scale theft. Social organization responded. Moral systems evolved, backed by religious injunctions. Inheritable possessions could lead to differences in wealth and status much larger than those among hunter-gatherers.

A recent study by U.S. anthropologist Monique Borgerhoff Mulder and her author team among twenty-one historical and contemporary small-scale societies confirmed this hypothesis.[20] It concludes that indeed, hunter-gatherers and horticulturalists had societies that were as egalitarian as the most egalitarian of modern societies, while agriculture (agricultural societies and pastoralists) was associated with a strong hierarchy in society, exceeding the most unequal modern industrial economies. Theft required guards, who were fed from the surpluses in return for keeping out thieves. As long as social groups were no larger than villages in which everyone knew everyone else, the scale of stealing within the group and the necessity for violence to keep it in check were probably modest. Raids by neighboring villages or by wandering groups were probably a bigger threat and a justified cause for anxiety.

The most fertile areas could sustain sedentary agriculturalists. Once people had mastered the art of domesticating animals, they could start to exploit less favored areas by herding stock while moving around. The pressures on herders were different from those on sedentary farmers. Herds could easily be stolen. The cattle could walk away with the thief to his home territory and be kept alive for later use. One would expect that in order to avoid widespread theft, herders had to be both entirely trustworthy within their own groups—involving heavy sanctions against offenders—and considerably less trusting toward outsiders than hunters. Here again, path dependency is crucial: there are large variations among groups. Trust or distrust in a group is very much a self-fulfilling prophecy. A cycle of stealing and revenge, once begun, is hard to interrupt. Children learn basic patterns of whom to trust and who can be stolen from when they are quite young. So, uncertainty-avoiding cultures would be likely among herders. Regular theft between or among tribes would be accompanied by strong prohibitions against misbehaving within the in-group and by a culture of armed vigilance. Herders guard; they do not sweat and toil to the degree that farmers do. Guarding could be associated with a proud, monumentalist culture. Today, in pastoralist areas of Africa, mutual cattle raids and violence between tribes are still endemic. They are an understandable response to resource scarcity in a world of strong in-group loyalty and out-group suspicion.[21]

Agriculture also had genetic influences. Early herders only ate their cattle. Eventually, they found out how to feed themselves by drawing blood from the cattle without killing them, which was more effective because the cattle could go on converting grass into blood. Around 8,500 years ago they started to drink milk. This practice enabled them to get still more energy from their animals. At first very few adults tolerated milk. This is because lactose intolerance has evolved among almost all mammals, probably as a way to ensure that older offspring do not compete with new babies for milk. By now, though, genetic variants for lactose tolerance have become common, an example of how behavioral and genetic evolution can go hand in hand. Small genetic differences in only a few alleles (an allele is a variant of a gene) can have large influences. Mutations in the gene that allows us to produce lactase, the enzyme that digests milk, have been selected for since about 8,500 years ago, when our ancestors started to keep cattle, as just explained. Apparently, milk-tolerant individuals have produced more offspring, thus spreading the trait. Today close to 100 percent of northern Europeans are lactose tolerant, which testifies to a long history of drinking cattle milk.

The cultivation of plants created different selective pressures. Farmers had reasons to worry. Things could go wrong in many ways for them: everybody knew where they lived, the farm could be raided, and stores could be stolen. Even in the absence of human enemies, farmers had to work hard. Plants needed care, or weeds might overgrow them, animals could eat them, thunderstorms might wreck them, or they might dry out and die. Agricultural crops led to attendant evolution among plague animals and disease organisms. Population concentration along the Nile was an ideal condition for pollution and diseases to evolve fast and to concentrate. Crops might be hit by any of the ten biblical plagues that beset the Egyptian empire: water poisoning, frogs, gnats, flies, livestock diseases, hail, fire, locusts, darkness, and child death. Many more plagues must have occurred as well, or perhaps caused some of the biblical ones: animal-borne human diseases, mice, rats, fungi, viruses, bacterial diseases, and others. Agriculture caused the level of health and average age to drop for the common person, because of the less nutritious diets that plants provided. Certainly at first, before human populations had begun to adopt genetic ways to cope with their new numbers and diets, agriculture was a curse in disguise.

In terms of culture, then, uncertainty avoidance seems to be a good adaptation to the hazards of farming life. Besides, farmers had to collaborate in monotonous, season-bound work, and they lived in much greater numbers than hunter-gatherers or herders. This situation requires a certain meekness, associated perhaps with larger collectivism and power distance. Culture would also coevolve with production systems. The labor-intensive rice terraces in Southeast Asia fit with a long-term-oriented (flexhumble) culture: diligent, self-effacing care is needed to sustain the system. If raids were endemic, a division of labor between agricultural women and fighting men could ensue, with a correspondingly more masculine value system.

All in all, in terms of culture, it would seem that compared with the days of hunting and gathering, the advent of the various forms of agriculture expanded the spectrum of values that would be adaptive for human groups. Possessions introduced an inherited hierarchy in agricultural society. Pastoralism with its strong temptation of stealing in arid environments would lead to particularly strong needs for protecting the moral circle. Individualism would be lower, masculinity would be higher, and uncertainty avoidance and short-term orientation (monumentalism) would be notably high.

Seven Thousand Five Hundred Years Ago Until Now: Large-Scale Civilizations

By around 7,500 years ago, agriculture and its surpluses led to societies that were so populous that villages slowly but surely grew into towns and then into cities, and cities expanded into states and empires. The earliest clusters of cities arose about 3,500 years ago along the fertile banks of large rivers: in particular, the Tigris and Euphrates delta (Mesopotamia in today's Iraq), the Indus, and the Nile.[22] The oldest empire still in existence is China. Although it has not always been unified, the Chinese Empire possesses a continuous history of about four thousand years. Other empires disintegrated. In the eastern Mediterranean and southwestern part of Asia, empires grew, flourished, and fell, only to be succeeded by others: the Sumerian, Babylonian, Assyrian, Egyptian, Persian, Greek, Roman, and Ottoman empires, to mention only a few. The South Asian subcontinent and the Indonesian archipelago had their empires, including the Maurya, the Gupta, and later the Mughal in India and the Majapahit on Java. In Central and South America the Aztec, Maya, and Inca empires have left their monuments. And in Africa, Benin, Ethiopia, and Mali are examples of ancient states.

Historians John Robert McNeill and his father, William H. McNeill, describe how city-level civilization led to two major social innovations.[23] Sumerian cities were first held together mainly by religious rites and beliefs. A pantheon of seven great gods both male and female (symbolizing sun, moon, earth, sky, fresh water, salt water, and storm) presided over the cosmos and inspired the deities of many later Indo-European civilizations. As the Sumerians' wealth attracted raiding bands of horsemen from the steppes, a military force was created. Besides fighting the horsemen, this force started to compete with the religious force. Through the centuries, as population sizes increased further, military protection became more and more important for the survival of communities, and centralization increased. Deities tended to mirror the changes, becoming fewer in number and masculine. Stories of ancient civilizations are full of power conflicts between worldly and religious powers.

Still, the survival value of war was usually inferior to that of trade. Multinational companies existed as early as 2000 B.C.; the Assyrians, Phoenicians, Greeks, and Romans all had their own versions of globalized business.[24] Trade gradually replaced war as the prevailing mechanism of transferring wealth, although wars for wealth still occur today.

Plants and animal herds enable concentration of harvests in one place, along with increase in the scale of society. This advance made theft even more rewarding than it was in villages. As people became more skilled agriculturalists, population sizes increased. Scale increases opened possibilities for specialization. Armed forces could be kept to protect stores of food. Once established, though, they could be under temptation to seize power. For instance, armed factions could rise in competition for succeeding a deceased emperor or for contesting taxes. An escalation in violence was probable unless people grew even more meek, to the point of virtual slavery, or else accepted arbitration, impersonal justice, and separation of powers. Once states started to appear, the complexity of behavioral and symbolic evolution soared, while still being highly path dependent.

People are still learning how to live in large-scale anonymous societies; after all, such societies started to occur only some four hundred generations ago. To help explain some of the societal innovations that our ancestors have evolved during this period, the work of American sociologist Talcott Parsons (1902–79) will be referenced here. Parsons was revolutionary in that he thought of social inventions as evolutionary. Once they have been hit upon, he said, these innovations will not go away. He made the analogy to biological evolutionary innovations such as vision— vision provides such crucial advantages that selection will preserve it and improve it once it has begun. Only, in this case the evolution takes place at the group level. Large-scale societies both enabled and necessitated social evolution.

Thinking about the growth of civilizations, Parsons proposed a number of such pivotal, irreversible innovations. These he termed "evolutionary universals in society." In a 1964 article he mentioned the following list: social stratification, alongside cultural legitimation, bureaucratic organization, money and markets, generalized universalistic norms, and the democratic association.[25] In the discussion that follows, each of these six evolutionary universals will be the subject of a section. The order is not necessarily historic; these innovations have occurred gradually, in interdependence, and elements of them have been present in preagricultural communities. Nevertheless, agriculture and the attendant population increase immensely favored their development.

Social Stratification

Stratum is the Latin word for "layer." Stratification is the process of creating different classes in society, usually two at first. In growing villages, there will have been an increasing need for coordination, along with simple social stratification of the kind that one observes in other apes, based on a combination of physical force and personal liking. Cities needed to create ascribed authority for their leaders based on their role, or the social organization would collapse and another city, or bands of plunderers, might destroy the city. This need must have driven the growth of acceptance of ascribed authority among the majority of the population.

City-states fought and acquired prisoners, who could be put to use. From the beginning of life in states, slavery has been an obvious form of two-class social stratification. One might say that the ruling classes were keeping people in the same way that they were keeping cattle and crops. There is actually biological evidence to support the idea that the ruling few had domesticated the numerous masses: average brain size in humans has fallen since the arrival of agriculture, as it has done in domesticated animals.[26] So, life in large-scale agricultural societies not only enabled our ancestors to extract a much larger part of the earth's energy to fulfill their needs but also induced vast cultural changes. Feelings of awe for leaders who were distant figures, residing in a different sphere of life and with immense power, were new in our evolution. Large power distance is one of the adaptations to life in a large, anonymous society that was made possible by agriculture. This was more so in the temperate climates in which cities and states came to bloom than in colder areas; in the latter, climatic conditions would not allow agriculture to be quite so successful, and population levels would remain much lower for many centuries, with the result that the common fight against the forces of nature would be the primary concern. So, society would remain egalitarian in those areas.

Cultural Legitimation

Cultural legitimation of acts was not a new phenomenon when societies expanded, but it took on new forms because anonymity had to be coped with. Cultural legitimation of the group was never difficult as long as groups were limited to a few hundred people. To distinguish group members from others, human beings had counted on individual recognition for millennia. A state-level society with so many citizens that they could not possibly know one another personally required new mechanisms for legitimizing group identity. A strong symbolic identity that transcended blood relationships was a precondition for continued existence of a state. The ancient states along the Indus, Nile, and Tigris-Euphrates all evolved systems of legitimation in which their leaders were directly related to their deities. They also tended to develop male-centered, monotheistic religions. A single god is a strong asset to provide continuity of existence for a numerous people surrounded by enemy peoples: a dangerous power vacuum that could lead to civil war need not occur when consecutive rulers pledge alliance to the same god, and religious rulers can be active in transferring leadership when a monarch dies. So, worldly leaders of states and empires have always tended to seek support of religion, even in secular countries.

A state-level identity can still be problematic if there are divided loyalties within the state, even if religion is not involved. This, as discussed in Chapter 7, is the case in many parts of Africa, where tribal ties prevail. As the extreme example of a failed state, we mentioned Somalia, where only the clan loyalties typical of a pastoral society survived.

The phenomenon of cultural legitimation occurs in all walks of life. When the first slave ship visited the port of Vlissingen in the Netherlands in the seventeenth century, the local inhabitants were shocked to see the inhuman conditions in which the slaves were kept, and they proceeded to set the slaves free. Soon afterward, though, priests were convincing the people of the Netherlands that slavery was in the best interest of these lesser creatures, and it took generations before it was finally abolished.[27] All peoples that go to war believe that God is with them. We justify what we do, rather than doing that which is a priori justifiable. All the while, few of us are aware of this dynamic; apparently, being aware that our beliefs serve the continuation of the existence of the groups to which we belong has not been advantageous for group survival.

Bureaucratic Organization

The Greek philosopher Plato (427–347 B.C.), to whose ideas we referred in Chapters 3 and 5, wrote his principles of organization of the State in the treatise *Politeia*.[28] This is the root of the words *politics*, *polity* (political unit), and, in the communist world, *politburo* for the highest body of government. The latter term leads us to *bureaucracy*, which we described in Chapter 9 as Max Weber's ideal of an impersonal organization, combining small power distance and strong uncertainty avoidance.

Bureaucracy is not necessarily popular with those who undergo its effects. It is thought of as a huge machinery, grinding slowly, with no feelings and no regard for the concerns of individuals—but this is precisely its strength. Parsons holds that a personalistic governance system can never control a large polity in a satisfactory way if its citizens are enfranchised. These citizens will want fair treatment. Bureaucracy detaches people who are employed in them from the interests that their organizations serve. A functionary is supposed to treat all customers equally. Of course, the reality is that in most societies some customers are more equal than others; Venezuela's Hugo Chávez can fill hour after hour on national TV with his program *"Aló Presidente,"* and be admired for it, in a way that Britain's Gordon Brown could only dream of. It is clear that in some societies citizens want more enfranchisement than in others. The culture dimension of power distance explains a lot of the variation. Nevertheless, bureaucratic organization is still a powerful device for organizing states fairly, in particular with regard to the provision of public goods.

Money and Markets

Exchange of goods for one another as the main mechanism of trade becomes impractical in a large state or between states. The use of seashells as currency probably predates city-states, and money was used in all of them. Money can travel easily and is not perishable. It provides a mechanism to assess the utility of very different goods and services. It can buy food, slaves, or military service. It cannot talk or negotiate, though; for this purpose, fairs were held regularly in the ancient world, and markets for common goods emerged.

Money represented a big evolutionary step because it made societies more adaptive: money can always wait and be used at a propitious moment for buying the assets that turn out to be most wanted. Traders, farmers, and states could profit from the flexibility of money. Money, however, has no memory. It was trade and the need for bookkeeping that prompted the Sumerians to invent the first written script.[29] Though not mentioned by Parsons, written script certainly qualifies as an evolutionary universal.

Generalized Universalistic Norms

Bureaucracy, money and markets, and written script all point in the direction of universalism, of comparability among all people in the case of bureaucracy, among all things in the case of money and markets, and among all times and places in the case of written script. We met the distinction between universalism and exclusionism in Chapter 4 as one of Misho's WVS-based dimensions of national culture; it correlated strongly with individualism versus collectivism. The absence of universalistic norms can limit the quality of bureaucratic functioning if some of its customers are out-group, and it can limit the use of money if currency cannot be changed into currency of other groups. The idea that all humans are comparable and should be part of the same moral circle is relatively recent.[30] The Universal Declaration of Human Rights (see also Chapter 4) is a manifesto of universalism. Nevertheless, societies around the world still feel that they are somehow better, and more human, than others. This situation strongly suggests that exclusionism had survival value for groups in past centuries. Those people who did not believe that their group was somehow better than others would be tempted to affiliate with another, "better" group, instead of starting to believe that all people were equal. Universalism is still a contested area; according to some observers, it is the most prominent variable of societal cultures.

The Democratic Association

By the democratic association, Parsons meant elective leadership and fully enfranchised membership. He was writing in the United States in the 1960s, when many people assumed that this model would spread rapidly across the world. Other U.S. thinkers have echoed his thoughts—for instance, Francis Fukuyama, who in 1989, after the fall of the Berlin Wall, announced "the end of history." Fukuyama meant that liberal democracy is simply the only acceptable form of governance of polities. Both Parsons and Fukuyama, of course, gave a culturally colored picture. In Chapter 11 we discussed at length the limitations to Western political axioms. The Chinese state had been very wealthy for hundreds of years before the nineteenth century and is in the process of becoming so once more, yet it has never been a model of what Parsons calls a democratic association. The Chinese are much more willing than are Anglo-Saxon people to accept that authority is there and that dutifulness and obedience are necessary. Whether the democratic association will turn out to be an evolutionary universal remains to be seen. Even if our future proves it to be so, the styles of democracies around the world will be adapted to the cultures of their citizens, as they are today.

Sources of Cultural Diversity and Change

The time-machine trip might have made it look as if there is one royal evolutionary road for humankind, with but a few variations. This is not so. Today's peoples differ vastly in their historical experience with these various innovations. Next to and often within the territory of larger empires, smaller units survived in the form of independent small "kingdoms" or tribes. Even now, in New Guinea most of the population lives in small and relatively isolated tribes, each with its own language and hardly integrated into the larger society. In the same vein, Australia's aborigines have always been hunter-gatherers. Ancient herding cultures in the Old World developed traditions of fights between clans. Societies with a long-standing agricultural tradition tend to be hierarchical and collectivistic. Northwestern European societies and the Anglo spin-offs are all individualistic and egalitarian, and there is no trace of a collectivistic, large-power-distance past for these parts of the world. The picture is complex, path dependency is important, and no simple causal link can be made.

The exposure of different peoples to different means of subsistence varies widely. So do their climates, flora, fauna, and geographic contextual factors. Moreover, if selective pressures differ in different places, evolution tends to diverge. Selection mechanisms at the group level tend to keep values and some practices stable within the group and to maintain symbolic boundaries between groups. As a result, the present world shows an amazing variety of cultures, both in terms of values and in terms of practices. Most cultures have ancient roots, despite major changes. Culture changes have been brought about, and will continue to be brought about, by major impacts of forces of nature and forces of humans. The first reason for cultural diversity has been adaptation to new natural environments. As humankind gradually populated almost the entire world, the need for survival led to different cultural solutions. Collective migrations to different environments were often forced by famines, owing to climate changes (such as desertification), to overpopulation, or to political mismanagement (as by the British rulers of Ireland in the nineteenth century). Natural disasters, such as earthquakes and floods, have sometimes wiped out entire societies and created new opportunities for others.

In recent centuries humans have rapidly become better at what biologists call *niche construction*. Through fire, clothing, housing, and all kinds of technology, we have appropriated almost all of the biosphere. Yet climate is still a major factor, as shown by Dutch social psychologist Evert van de Vliert.[31] Van de Vliert looks at the effects of climate during the last ten thousand years when our civilizations developed. He labels climates as *demanding* to the extent that mean daily temperatures deviate from an ideal twenty-two degrees centigrade (seventy-two degrees Fahrenheit). His meta-analysis of country-level data includes both cold winters and hot summers. Demanding climates cause a split between affluent societies that have the resources to actively cope and societies that are poor and can only endure. In the former, cultures allow self-expression; in the latter, they are constrained by survival needs. Cultures in countries with a bearable climate throughout the year do not show this dependence on affluence: people in them can manifest self-expression even if they are poor. What remains is the question of causality: why some societies became affluent while others remained poor.

During these last ten thousand years, world populations have risen dramatically, and today the world is entirely populated with competing polities. So, in recent times there has been a rapid shift in evolutionary pressure. Where natural forces used to be the most important drivers of culture, forces of other humans have rapidly become more important. Military conquest has drastically changed cultures by killing, moving, and mixing populations and imposing new lords and new rules. Symbolic evolution in the form of missionary zeal converting people to new religions has also changed cultures. If we trace the religious history of countries, however, what religion a population has embraced and which version of that religion seem to have been a *result* of previously existing cultural value patterns more than a *cause* of cultural differences. The major religions of the world, at some time in their history, have all undergone profound schisms: among Roman Catholic, Eastern Orthodox, and various Protestant groups in Christianity; between Sunni and Shia in Islam; between liberals and various fundamentalist groups in Jewry; between Hinayana and Mahayana in Buddhism. Preexisting cultural differences among groups of believers figured prominently in these schisms. For example, the Reformation movement within the Roman Catholic Church in the sixteenth century initially affected all of Europe. However, in countries that more than a thousand years earlier had belonged to the Roman Empire, a Counter-Reformation reinstated the authority of the Roman church. In the end, the Reformation succeeded only in countries without a Roman tradition. Although today most of northern Europe is Protestant and most of southern Europe is Roman Catholic, what is at the origin of the cultural differences is not this religious split but the inheritance of the Roman Empire. Religious affiliation by itself is therefore less culturally relevant than is often assumed.[32] Notwithstanding, once a religion has settled, it reinforces the culture patterns on the basis of which it was adopted, by making these patterns into core elements in its teachings.

Scientific discoveries and innovations, whether native or imported from outside, as previously argued, tend to affect the practices more than the underlying values. They also tend to operate worldwide. When cultures change together because of a common cause, the differences between them often remain intact. This is why common cultural origins can often be traced many centuries back.

The End of History? No!

The time-machine trip showed that there has not been a mysterious break between our times as primitive social mammals, our early human days, and our centuries of living in civilizations. Nor is there any reason to believe that evolution has come to a halt. Rather, there is ample reason to believe that human evolution is accelerating. So, it is time to get familiar with evolutionary thinking. Making sense of our history in the light of evolution will allow for better-informed guesses about what to do now in order to improve our future. Cultural evolution is all around us. Far from having ended, history is speeding up. It has recently seen the spectacular increase in scale of societies in a few hundred generations. This process has not ended yet. Some seven hundred generations ago, in 15,000 B.C., there may have been 600,000 polities on Earth, each consisting of tens or hundreds of individuals. Today there are 200, each consisting of millions of people. We are in a rapid process of conquering nature, as a result of which our *human* environment is becoming relatively more important. More and more, threats as well as opportunities come from other people. In response, we have embarked on a process of massive merging and expansion of our moral circles. This process is probably the most conspicuous evolutionary trend of the last few hundred generations. At the same time, we retain many of the adaptations to life in small tribes that characterized our ancestors for millions of years. Regardless, because we are so immensely numerous and have created such a rich social life, innovations are happening in a frenzy of change all around us.

The paradox is that practices and technologies can change so fast only because, and as long as, societies function in stable ways. A society requires cultural homogeneity at the level of implicit values in order to have capacity for collective action, which is a condition for a group to be adaptive to its environment. And cultural homogeneity does not allow for rapid change in values, because values are acquired, for the most part, in infancy and for life. Value system changes require generations. So, while groups with common cultural values will be good at collectively responding to circumstances, they will be slow to shift their shared value system even if changes in circumstances would give such value shifts survival advantages. Note that a slow change in value systems is still very fast compared with a situation without culture, in which genetic change is the only mechanism.

People are in the thick of history, and a complex, interwoven web of competition and collaboration between cohesive groups is the game. Some elite groups in some societies would wish to expand the moral circle to include every living thing, creating a brave new world in which all humans and other inhabitants of that world live in peace. It is a beautiful ideal worth striving for, but for now this is as realistic as biblical ideas of paradise on earth. Yet this tendency to expand the moral circle has brought us to where we are today, and it will take us further. We are; therefore, we evolve.

The Essence of Evolution

If the rapid changes that humans and their societies are undergoing are really evolutionary, and the previous account has shown this clearly to be so, then it follows that a firm understanding of evolution is important to managing human affairs. Unfortunately, *evolution* is a word with an undeserved bad reputation. Because poorly understood evolutionary ideas have been used in political ideologies,[33] and because of antihistoric, absolutist thinking in some religious doctrines, there is a lot of trepidation and taboo around it. Evolution really is a simple and uncontroversial phenomenon. It need not interfere with any ideology or religion. All you need is generations that produce *surplus* descendants that *inherit* from parent generations, but with *variation,* and *selection* that weeds out less successful variants in each generation. To put it more formally, for evolution to happen, one needs the following conditions:

- Something that can be copied, the so-called *replicator*: a gene, an organism, a rumor, a ritual, an ideology, a form of government, a culture, and so forth
- A copying mechanism that is good but not perfect, so that the next generation looks like the previous one but is not quite identical to it
- Production of more copies than can survive
- Preservation of some of the copies based on some kind of selective pressure

Here are five simple but crucial points about evolution:

1. **Evolution is unavoidable.** In a universe in which time proceeds in only one direction, things that are not permanent and do not reproduce will die out. By implication, anything nonpermanent that exists today must have evolved. This holds for all living things. It holds for viruses, DNA molecules, cells, bodies, and groups. Any instance of any of these things must have either evolved or been permanent. Since evolution across the generations is plainly happening for humans, pets, and diseases, the likely conclusion is that it is happening to human cultures as well. Note that depending on cycle length, genetic evolution is very, very slow. New strands of viruses—if not new species—evolve each year, but it may take millions of years for a new species of mammal to evolve.

2. **Evolution does not look ahead.** Selection, the mechanism that steers evolution, can work only on the current situation. In fact, this word *selection* is misleading, because it suggests that the best variants are being somehow picked out in a goal-directed way. This can happen, as in selection for lactose-tolerant variants among peoples who keep cattle for milk, but the converse is that variants that are unfit are removed, simply because they are less successful at reproducing. In addition, *drift* occurs. Drift is the process through which variants die out randomly, and it is stronger to the extent that populations are smaller. In small populations it is likely that even favorable genetic variants die out because nobody happens to be born who carries them or because those who carry them happen to die childless. So, to sum-

marize, selection takes place at the bottom of the fitness scale, at the top, and randomly. Given a large enough population, natural selection will preserve any variants that are not harmful to reproductive capacity. In a large population this means that many variants will occur that have no obvious effects but that constitute a potential for adaptation to possible new circumstances.

3. **Evolution is path dependent.** It might seem that evolution could do anything, but this is a mistaken point of view. Evolution is always limited by circumstances, notably by its own history. And there is no turning back. Human evolution shows this clearly. People frequently suffer from aches in their lower vertebrae, hips, and knees because these joints have become more heavily taxed since our ancestors started to walk upright, perhaps as an adaptation to moving in tall grass. Once upright, humans have continued to walk on two legs even in forest habitats, because of the side benefits of freeing the hands.[34]

4. **Evolution uses many replicators.** Darwin knew nothing about genes, but he was very insightful about evolution. The discovery of DNA molecules as the carriers of genes a century later proved him to be in the right. Though genes are an eminently successful replicator for evolution on our planet, they are by no means the only one, and there is no sense in which nongenetic evolution is less evolutionary than genetic evolution. The evolution of human civilizations is only loosely coupled to genes. Many kinds of knowledge reproduce themselves through the transmission of skills through teaching, and as we have seen, cultural values are also transmitted to new generations. So, the society, as a unit of transmission of knowledge and of culture, has also become a powerful replicator among humans. The idea that evolution can simultaneously take place using different replicators—for instance, using genes at the level of the individual and using knowledge and values at the level of society—is called *multilevel selection*. We are now about as much in the dark about society-level evolution as Darwin was about genes when he wrote *On the Origin of Species*: observation has provided us with credible arguments in favor of cultural evolution of societies, but we do not know just how it happens. In other words, we have no sound idea about the precise nature of the replicators, what is called the *proximate mechanisms* of evolution. The discussion about how culture replicates itself, and how it is selected, is still open.[35] Further, while the delimitation of an individual is clear, it

is not easy to know the delineation of groups. Humans can at any point in time be part of many groups with sometimes ambiguous boundaries. It is to be hoped that the coming century will see a strong growth in knowledge about the dynamics of cultural evolution. Fortunately, the *evolutionary mechanism* is always the same in essence, whatever the mix of replicators. If there is reproduction with modification, and selection, then evolution will occur.

5. **Evolution evolves.** Over the five billion years of the earth's history, evolution has increased in complexity. Evolution does not involve only genes. It occurred in protein soups before genes existed, and it has stumbled on more than just genes as well. From mixes of proteins to DNA molecules to simple cells without nuclei to complex cells containing symbiotic microorganisms (organelles) to colonies of cells to organisms to social groups,[36] it keeps stumbling on new inventions. We humans are now trying to use our evolved brains to anticipate the future and to influence that future. So, although selection pressures still operate on the current situation, this current situation has come to include predictions of the future. Humans have refined a few tricks, notably cultural values and practices, but we still have a poor understanding of our current evolutionary setting. In particular, we tend to underestimate the importance of the society as an evolutionary replicator.

Evolution: More than Genes

This meant that symbolic evolution among human communities largely supplanted genetic evolution as the driving force of biological change on earth, and what may properly be called the human era of ecological history began about 40,000 years ago.

—McNeill and McNeill, *The Human Web*, 2003

Have you ever fallen in love? If so, did you worry about the anti-immune system of your beloved? Probably not; yet research has shown that we tend to fall in love with people whose anti-immune systems are complementary to our own.[37] From an evolutionary viewpoint, this tendency is not surprising; contagious diseases have been our most deadly enemy, and selection must have favored people with a mixed immune system, because they are resistant to more diseases.[38] Yet none of us has ever consciously noticed it. To us, these prospective partners simply look, feel, or smell better. We may not even notice a given quality much: we simply love them. Thus, one of the proximate mechanisms of determining with whom to fall in love serves the evolutionary aim of making our progeny healthy. Also in this matter, many more proximate mechanisms for survival-boosting partner selection related to genes are likely to be discovered in the years to come. In addition, all people are familiar with cultural mechanisms for partner selection: the incest taboo, in more or less strict form, exists in all societies, and many elaborate rules affect partner selection based on symbolic information, such as religious affiliation. These rules vary across societies and tend to be more strict in more collectivist, masculine, uncertainty-avoiding, short-term-oriented, restrained cultures.

This example of partner selection shows that father and son McNeill may be overstating their point a bit. Yes, symbolic evolution is becoming more and more important, and yes, it can operate at tremendous speed—but no, people have not got rid of good old genetic evolution. The claim also disregards cultural evolution as an enabler of technological and symbolic evolution. This absence is explainable by the fact that cultural values do not leave fossils, while practices often do.

So, people evolve at various levels, using various replicators. To further complicate the picture, the various levels at which they evolve are themselves cooperating and sometimes competing. What are these levels? The following sections offer a summary.[39]

Genetic Selection

Genes were discovered by Gregor Mendel in the late nineteenth century, and the double helix of DNA molecules was discovered in 1953 by James Watson and Francis Crick. Genetic evolution rests on the following mechanism: Each cell in a human body carries our entire *genome*, with all the genes located on two homologous sets of twenty-three chromosomes, one half-genome set inherited from our mother and one from our father. Our eggs and semen are formed by a reductive division (*meiosis*) of the chromosomes, so that each egg or sperm cell contains only one of the two sets of twenty-three chromosomes. During meiosis, errors and recombination between the pair of homologous chromosomes can occur, so that neither the eggs nor the sperm cells are quite identical to their parent's set or to one another. Then at fertilization time, the half-genomes of an egg and a sperm cell recombine, again with some possible errors, to form a new complete genome. The errors are usually called *mutations*. Any human being is likely to carry a number of them. They tend to be either neutral or harmful, but one in many carries an advantage. Hence, the frequency of favorable mutations is directly proportional to total population.

Favorable mutations in the human genome that have occurred in the last ten thousand years, and that are still in the process of spreading, lie in the areas of metabolism, defenses against infectious diseases, reproduction, and the central nervous system.[40] It seems that our genetic evolution is still adapting to agriculture and to our vastly increased population size.

The phrase *the selfish gene* was introduced by Richard Dawkins as the title of a book in 1976, and it caught the imagination of many people. The basic idea is that our bodies are merely the carriers of our genes, and according to the laws of chance, evolution will favor any mutation that makes a gene increase in frequency in subsequent generations. This idea is supported by a lot of evidence, but it is not the whole picture.

Epigenetic Selection

Our body cells are genetically identical, but they still somehow know how to differentiate into various tissues. Apparently, there is a complex machinery of evolution on top of (in Greek: *epi-*) the genetic mechanism. In recent years evidence has been accumulating for variation among genetically identical individuals and cells. There are ways in which genes can be switched on and off. Proteins, not DNA, are the proximate mechanism of epigenetic variation. The coming years will see new discoveries in this area that will add nuance to our ideas regarding "a gene for property X." Groups of genes, fine-tuned by epigenetic mechanisms, are complex engines for coping with environmental circumstances to yield adaptive responses, and it is rare to find one gene responsible for one trait, as was suggested for the occurrence of blue eyes.

Sexual Selection

Why do teenagers spend so much time getting rid of their acne, applying cosmetics, working out, or writing love messages? Why do peacocks have magnificent, impractical tails? Why do songbirds announce their presence to potential predators by singing? Why do male deer risk severe injury in fights with other males? In all these cases the answer is the same: to gain access to reproduction with more or better partners. However, sexual selection is asymmetric. In a system with two genders of which the female gender is limited in the number of offspring that it can produce, while the male gender is virtually unlimited, reproduction requires fewer males than females. Females can thus afford to be picky, and males in many species compete for females. This situation will usually result in larger body size for the males. Human males and females have had varying body size ratios during deep history; currently the difference is about 10 percent. The average human group has twice as many ancestors in the female line as in the male line. This is because whereas most women have children, many males do not beget any offspring, while others beget hundreds[41]—or, in the case of Mongol emperor Genghis Khan, thousands.

Sexual selection is a vehicle of genetic selection between individuals, but in humans it is strongly related to symbolic group boundaries. In collectivist societies partner selection is a crucial event, not only for the partners but also for both their families (Chapter 4). Marriages between royal families have frequently been used to reconcile or to join empires. Sexual attraction between Romeo and Juliet caused major fights because they belonged to competing families. Many religions penalize marriages with nonadherents. People are still being killed every day because of sexual relations with out-group members. The working of the moral circle can be very explicit when it comes to sexual rules. Sexual selection is a special case of *behavioral selection*, the next category.

Behavioral Selection

When Gert Jan was a child, almost everybody around him smoked. It was the chic, social thing to do. Refined people had a smoke after dinner. Today in individualistic parts of the world, smoking is confined to certain subgroups, and smokers are widely considered losers who endanger their own health. For someone who is looking for a partner or a friend, or for a club to join, smoking could be a sensitive issue. So it goes for all kinds of behaviors. Within a group, some individuals will be more liked and more imitated than others, with the result that their behaviors spread. Among groups, some groups develop more viable patterns of interaction, so that they win out against other groups. This form of selection is not directly genetic, although of course we cannot behave beyond our biological means.

Behavioral selection can also proceed through the intermediary of the environment. Groups may burn vegetation to create habitats for large grazing animals, and these or other groups may hunt those animals. Groups may migrate to an island and learn to fish out of necessity. They may pollute the environment and destroy their sources of food or water. They may find new ways to extract nutrients or energy from plants and thereby extend the carrying capacity of their habitats. The range of human behaviors is endless, but it is not unbounded.

Symbolic Selection

During World War II, looking remotely as if one might be Jewish and not possessing a non-Jew declaration while being in a European country was tantamount to a condemnation. In other recent wars and acts of terrorism, a typical trend has been for fighters to kill one another off for symbolic reasons. Being of the wrong religion is probably the most important of these reasons, although ethnic appearance also scores high, and being a supporter of the wrong soccer team has proved lethal in occasional cases as well. These are extreme examples of symbolic selection: selection based not on what one does but on what symbolic identity is attributed to one. Such selection is, beyond doubt, an evolutionary force.

Groups that are being persecuted for symbolic reasons usually create strong responses, as argued by biologist-historian Peter Turchin.[42] Basing his work on extensive analyses of historical data, and citing many examples of historical empires, Turchin demonstrates that the life history of empires shows three nested cyclic patterns. The largest of these, one that operates on a time scale of several centuries, involves the decay of the *capacity for concerted collective action* among the people at the center of an empire, while at the same time, some of the oppressed groups at its periphery gain in this capacity. For his explanation, Turchin borrows the term *asabiya* from Ibn Khaldun, the great fourteenth-century Tunisian thinker. Ibn Khaldun discussed the conflicts between city dwellers and nomads, and his analysis was that the capacity for collective action, which he called *asabiya*, was the decisive factor. Asabiya, then, is a variable that directly captures the degree to which a people can act cohesively like a superorganism, instead of being plagued by intragroup competition. From an evolutionary point of view, this means that a people with high asabiya will best be able to replicate its values and its practices, and probably its genes as well.

All Levels Interact

Whereas genetic and epigenetic selection operate at the replicator level of individuals, behavioral and symbolic selection are group-level forces. Sexual selection can operate at both levels, because it is modified by symbolic clues at the group level. So, competition between individuals and competition between groups do not exclude one another but rather happen simultaneously. Competition between individuals in a group could be advantageous or detrimental to the survival of the group to which the individuals belong, depending on contingencies. Throughout evolutionary history, new replicators have been added while the old ones continue to function. For instance, sexual selection uses genetic evolution to spread attractive characteristics through the population, but it is itself constrained by behavioral and symbolic evolution in the form of societal rules about who do and do not qualify as acceptable partners for reproduction. In this sense, we are both children and creators of evolution, in an increasingly complex mix of proximate mechanisms. Also remember that all of evolution, whatever the replicator, is subject to chance in the form of drift. If a certain replicator level has few instances, drift will be more prominent. The current merging of societies to only a few hundred, associated with loss of religions and languages, would seem to enhance drift. On the other hand, within-society variation among subgroups of many kinds may well be on the rise and can lead to new variety.

Evolution Beyond Selfishness: Groups over Individuals

Behavioral and symbolic selection operate between groups, as was argued. Culture operates at the group level, as this book maintains. In evolutionary terms, culture is a proximate mechanism of behavioral and symbolic selection at the group level. Even more proximate are the psychological mechanisms on which culture builds. In particular, all people except sociopaths strive to be good group members. "Good" is a culture-relative notion: what is considered good depends on the cultural rules of the group, the conditions, and one's personal characteristics. Nevertheless, the tendency to wish to be a good, upstanding member of the community is ubiquitous, and human emotions associated with that tendency such as pride, awe, shame, and guilt can be violent. These emotions cause people to devote their lives to their group or even to risk their lives for it. On the other hand, tendencies to compete for dominance or affiliation within one's group, along with emotions such as envy and jealousy, are also violent. Between-individual competition is just as alive as is between-group competition.

These two replicators, groups and individuals, are themselves in competition, but groups are winning. In Chapter 1 we used the example of thirty people, strangers to one another, who find themselves stranded on a plentiful desert island. These thirty shipwrecked people will survive only if all thirty are good to each other. Besides not being sociopaths, they must consider one another to be part of the same moral circle and avoid individual-level competition. Otherwise (keeping things simple for the sake of the example), they would start to compete for resources, fight, and eventually kill one another. Now suppose there is an archipelago of similar islands, on each of which a random mix of people gets stranded. What will happen now? Easy: only the people on islands where all manage to build a common moral circle will survive. On islands where fights break out, the population will be decimated and survival chances will be reduced. This example seems trivial, but it is profound. Natural selection among groups will benefit peaceful, tolerant, moral-circle-building individuals, because groups that tolerate infighting will not thrive.

While human symbolic intelligence seems to be unmatched by other species on Earth, humans' social skills are shared with others. Researchers of animal behavior have pointed out that all social species of animals, such as ants, bees, blind mole rats, dolphins, jackdaws, and wolves, to name a few, have intricate patterns of communication and clever ways of understanding complex messages. This trait is in fact a prerequisite for any social species. Bees, for instance, though having minimal brain capacity, are nonetheless able to indicate very accurately to one another where they should go to collect honey. There are ants that build colonies made up of their own bodies, and others keep lice as we keep cattle, including raising the lice larvae. Over geologic time, groups have done well in evolution: today half the biomass of insects in the world is estimated to be from the few insect taxa (ants, bees, termites, wasps) that developed eusociality. *Eusociality (eu* is Greek for "good") refers to the condition in which groups, possibly numbering thousands or more individuals, have integrated so well that they live as a superorganism capable of doing things that none of its members could achieve individually.

In fact, the irreversible success of groups is a constant in the evolution of life on Earth.

The bodies of humans and other multicellular organisms are made of *eukaryotic* cells. These cells contain small subcellular bodies (organelles, such as mitochondria) that have DNA of their own. Such eukaryotic cells started billions of years ago as groups of simpler, *prokaryotic* cells that gobbled one another up without killing one another, and they took to reproducing as one unit. Their grouping in eukaryotic cells constituted a change from competition to collaboration, and it proved a highly successful innovation. Many millions of years later, multicellular organisms were the next great leap. Today many species of organisms have developed eusocial groups of organisms as a new level of selection; in terms of biomass, humans are the most successful of all, excepting perhaps eusocial ants, which were estimated in 1990 to constitute more biomass than humans.[43]

The success of groups at all levels, even the almost brainless social insects, shows that big brains are not needed to form a complex, well-communicating society. From an evolutionary point of view, brains are just the latest invention, but excellent communication is always needed for group success. Insects rely on visual and chemical clues as proximate mechanisms for their communication. Through time, evolution has found many proximate mechanisms for achieving a leap to a higher level of sociality. A common element among these mechanisms, a truly evolutionary one, is the existence of "good" and "bad" in an evolutionary sense. Being good implies serving one's group according to the categorical imperative of German philosopher Immanuel Kant (1724–1804): "do to others as you would be done unto," while being bad implies serving one's own interests at the expense of the group. For instance, a cancer cell is good to itself by replicating faster than other cells, but it kills the organism to which it belongs by stepping out of role, so it is bad for the group to which it belongs, its organism. This means that there is strong selection against cancer in young people: if a young person gets cancer, he or she will not reproduce, so the sensitivity to cancer cannot be reproduced in other bodies. By analogy, thieves are good to themselves but bad to their society, whose things get stolen. Thus, what is good at a certain replicator level in evolution could be bad one level up.

Once the next level of sociality is reached, as long as there is between-group competition, there is no turning back unless major catastrophes occur. There is no chance that humans will revert to solitary lifestyles. On the contrary, the evolved tendency to include others in a common moral circle seems to be pushing humans to ever more collaboration in ever greater numbers.

Individuals and Institutions in the Stream of Life

If groups are so important, then what is the proper level of analysis to study human behavior? Is it the individual or the group, and if it's the latter, which level of grouping? This is like asking which is more important: the sea, the rivers, or brooks—all are important, and they complement one another. Figure 12.1 presents two primary levels, the individual and society, the latter being the unit that carries deep cultural values. It shows how analyses at the level of the individual (top) and at the level of society (bottom) complement one another because they both contribute to understanding what happens in the arena of everyday life. Available roles meet willing candidates there, and the stream of social life flows on, ritual by ritual. Given a sufficiently large pool of individuals from which to choose, the variation in individuals and their adaptive capacities allows for filling every available role with different individuals over time. This process gives substantial continuity to the social life of a society. Rituals tend to persist in their essence even if, across generations, they are overloaded with new symbolic meanings, change names, or are performed with new technologies.

The figure draws attention to the fact that individuals come to the rituals of social life with their unique personalities and find roles available to them depending on the nature of the institutions that exist in society. Other levels of grouping have been ignored in the figure; in reality,

FIGURE 12.1 Mutual Homeostasis System of Individual and Society Levels

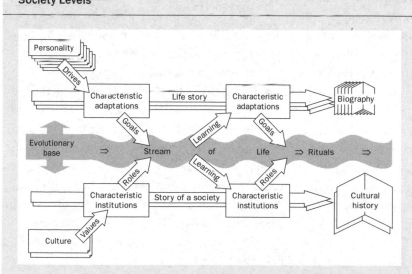

Time runs from left to right. The top tier (inspired by McCrae and Costa, 2003) shows how individuals live; the bottom tier shows how societies have similar life stories but at an aggregated level.

the level of societies is itself complex, featuring all kinds of subgroups. In individualistic societies it is common for individuals to operate in various disconnected groups, while in collectivistic ones there is less freedom of choice but more cohesion. In the course of time, both individuals and institutions learn, and selection operates on both. However, at both levels there are *homeostatic* ("sameness-preserving") forces at work. While people can learn to adopt new behaviors, one's personality remains stable during life, unless catastrophic accidents or diseases cause disruption. The same tends to hold for societies. They can learn new practices, but they have a hard time changing their basic values.

This book has jumped from one level to the other throughout. It had to, because social life occurs through the interaction of individuals and institutions.

Evolution at Work Today

So, what good can it do politicians, leaders, researchers, and citizens to view human affairs as taking place in the framework of evolution? A lot. A brief eclectic tour of contemporary issues will provide confirmation.

Business

Companies are replicators, and good companies also function as moral circles, albeit not necessarily at the level of values, as shown in this book. They are continually being created, bought, and sold, and they go bankrupt. On a time scale of years, new businesses are being created. These entities are not necessarily better than their predecessors, but they are mutations, some of which may be better adapted to current evolutionary pressures. The selective mechanism is based on many factors, including the ability to make friends in high places, to remain within the law, to use new communication technologies, to create an acceptable public image, to limit cost, to produce quality, and to innovate. The time scale is months or years. The whole landscape of business evolution is being governed by nations and international organizations—at least, these bodies attempt to administer favorable selective pressure that enhances good practice and curbs practices deemed detrimental to society.

Sprouting or cutting off subsidiaries (Chapter 11) is a subfield of organizational evolution. This process is an effective means of causing mutations. A new company, initiated by new leaders or by leaders who try a new formula, can be the start of a new type of company. A multinational startup company is a bit like our thirty people finding themselves stranded on a desert island. Their first job is to create working rules for everyday life, an organization culture.

Organization theory and business economics study business evolution, though they do not usually call it by that name just yet. Understanding the tribal roots of our social instincts and the dynamic properties of cultural evolution should lead to a better understanding of the success and failure of organizations.[44] Managing is, in essence, mentoring evolutionary pressure on the organization, its stakeholders, and its employees. Marketing, in this light, is the study of attempts to change selective pressure imposed by consumer behavior in favor of one's products.

Government

Polities are replicators at the moral circle level. Politicians are continually negotiating and changing the rules of our most obvious moral circles of today: our states. Numerous forms of government coexist that carry elements of dictatorships, one-party systems, theocracies, military governments, pluralistic democracies, populist democracies, and so on. Governments adopt ideas from another and try to collaborate. There is a worldwide tendency to find more common ground now that markets and trade streams, as well as problems of many kinds and their solutions, are obviously global. The time scale is years, decades, or centuries. The outcome is uncertain, because our innate group fission-fusion tendencies are often stronger than our conscious decisions. At some pivotal moments the presence of one person or one new idea can change the world, but most of the time, we are led by the current. Once the tide of a people's collective feeling is released, there is no swimming against it.

Technology

The effect of evolutionary hazards holds for technologies too. Technologies are replicators that are invented and then improved. There is considerable flexibility when a new evolutionary track starts, and a degree of freezing sets in after that. Consider road transportation. The Romans were the first to build a road network across their empire. They set the standard by using wheel carts with at most two horses side by side, not three. Road tracks across Europe and its colonies inherit their template from the Roman two-horse carts. Train rails and car tire span have adopted this width for practical reasons. The first cars looked like horse carriages, and car shapes gradually developed from that point. Today's drop-shaped aerodynamic car bodies have resulted from recent pressure to lower air resistance so as to enhance fuel efficiency at higher speeds.

Language

Evolution can also be purely symbolic, as in the case of language. Symbolic language probably arose gradually out of song and simpler vocalizations around one million to forty thousand years ago. It has enabled spectacular changes and has itself recently been the object of ultrarapid symbolic evolution. Storytelling is a central element of all human cultures that evolved based on language, and it is one of the major inventions in our evolution.[45] Besides being born storytellers, we are uncannily good at creating new languages. Since around 10,000 B.C., because of increases of scale and of networking, the total number of polities and of peoplewide languages in the world has decreased sharply. At the same time, though, neologisms for new discoveries, cryptographic languages, computer languages, group-based jargon, and poetry are being invented. Dictionaries notwithstanding, language is now evolving at a time scale of months to decades. As a set of replicators, language is complex: words, phrases, stories, idioms—all could be meaningfully considered units of language evolution.

These were just a few examples. As social scientists, we authors would also like to make a few remarks about our own profession in the light of evolutionary thought. Although it is not always perceived as such, any study of human behavior, any discipline of the social sciences and humanities, is involved in looking at an aspect of behavioral or symbolic evolution. The scope of these disciplines varies from the individual to the small group to the society to international affairs. To further complicate matters, time scales of most of these disciplines are in the order of years at most, or they might even be ahistorical. As a result, they do not usually link to human evolutionary history. This specialization has created a scattered landscape of disciplines that misunderstand or neglect one another and that have limited predictive value in real social life. This situation itself is understandable given that the object of study is so complex and is so much a moving target. As an upshot, it has created the "ivory archipelago,"[46] divorced from society, leaving a void to be filled by ill-informed ideologies that tend to self-serve the groups that adopt them. Such systems of thought become popular because they afford the holistic view that is not being covered by the sciences. A more historic and integrated approach that acknowledges human nature to the full will do the social sciences and humanities a lot of good.

This is the direction in which meaningful innovations can be expected in the coming decades. Social sciences themselves need to evolve. Current "publish or perish" incentives are not helping, since they promote more specialization and less integration. New incentives for integrative work that places the social sciences within a larger evolutionary framework are needed.

Evolutionary insights tend to be fairly straightforward, as these examples have shown. Readers are encouraged to try to figure out evolutionary pressures and trends for themselves. The preceding sections sketched brief thoughts on business, governance, technology, and language from an evolutionary perspective. What about music, football, school curricula, movies . . . ? Or what about mobile technologies and the Web? This is a much-debated current development that merits a closer look.

The Web and Group Agency

Will the Web and mobile communication networks lead to one worldwide culture? Will humanity adopt the so-called hyve mind, as predicted by Kevin Kelly in 1994? As of 2009, "I hyve, I am" (sic) is the Cartesian slogan with which Gert Jan's university attracts students in communication science. Does that imply "you don't hyve, you are not"?

Mobile communication certainly appeared on the scene like a comet, and it constitutes a real change. On March 23, 1997, Dutch Ajax supporter Carlo Picornie became a soccer martyr. Groups of hooligan supporters of soccer clubs Ajax and Feyenoord had used mobile phones to search one another out without police interference and then staged a fight in a meadow near the city of Beverwijk. Carlo inadvertently got killed with sticks, knives, and a hammer. Fighting and vandalism for fun around soccer matches by rival groups of young males is not just a Dutch phenomenon, and mobile phone contact to coordinate actions is now routine among businesspeople, children, criminals, and police alike.

Since 1997 computerized systems for socializing have offered a fascinating arena of symbolic evolution. Children in many countries are routinely logged in on social network software whenever possible. This practice allows them to keep in touch with their friends almost all of the time that they are not in school, engaged in physical activity, or in bed. Even during those times they may have their mobile phones switched on. From an evolutionary viewpoint, the speed of adoption of social network software is staggering. Social network software such as Facebook, Hyves,

LinkedIn, Plaxo, Twitter, Xing, and others have spread with speeds that exceed flu epidemics, and we are just getting started.

In 2009 a Dutch vaccination program targeting a uterine cancer–producing virus directed to teenage girls had to be repeated because rumors had spread on social network software that the vaccination was hazardous. Authoritative information was disregarded, and the rumors induced some 15 percent of the target group to stay at home. Refusing vaccination has a long history in the Netherlands, but it used to be confined to stable religious communities and not a function of ephemeral Internetworks.

The newness of the accounts just described is on the surface only. They involve ancient human dynamics—groups of males staging a fight, groups of girls gossiping—yet the use of new technologies of communication is a change that constitutes an evolution. What is the replicator in these two examples, as well as in the millions of other instances of rapid adoption of social software? Group agency. Intergroup competition is facilitated in the hooligan case, and group cohesion is enhanced in the vaccination-refusal case. Any new tool that allows for improvement of these two forces will be rapidly adopted, because it gives a selective advantage to the groups that use it. Major catastrophes aside, there is no turning back from these bits of evolution.

Which of the levels of selection (genetic, epigenetic, sexual, behavioral, symbolic) are affected by these examples? Well, all of them. People who are genetically or epigenetically less fit to use the new communication tools will suffer a social cost and be less likely to find partners. People who cannot learn to master them or whose language capacities are insufficient will also be at a disadvantage. The larger selective effect will, however, be at the level of the group: groups that use the new technologies to good purposes will perform better. That is, they will do better in terms of cohesion. Whether they intrinsically perform better depends. So, social software is another tool to facilitate group-level selection. We can expect fast advances in social software, software that supports relationship building and reputation maintenance, and in other appliances that help maintain the moral circle. In cultures in which education is important, new technologies are used for education, and in groups in which socializing is important, they will be used for that.[47] To summarize, these advances in communication technologies will not eliminate group boundaries, but they will enable existing groups to organize more effectively, building on existing culture.

Cultural Convergence and Divergence

Research about the development of cultural values has shown repeatedly that there is little evidence of international convergence over time, except an increase of individualism for countries having become wealthier. Value differences among nations described by authors centuries ago are still present today, in spite of continued close contacts. For the next few hundred years at least, and probably for millennia afterward, countries will remain culturally diverse.

Not only will cultural diversity among countries remain with us, but also it looks as if differences within countries are increasing. Ethnic groups arrive at a new consciousness of their identity and ask for a political recognition of this fact. Of course, these ethnic differences have been there for generations. What has changed is the intensity of contact among groups, which has confirmed group members in their own identities. Also, the spread of information (by international media) regarding how people live elsewhere in the world has affected minorities, who compare their situations with the lives of others whom they suppose to be better off. World news media also spread information about suffering and strife much wider than ever before. "Ethnic cleansing," uprisings, and violent repression are not new inventions, but in the past relatively few people beyond those directly involved would know about them; now they are visible on TV screens around the world. This broad dissemination has the effect of increasing anxiety, particularly in uncertainty-avoiding cultures. Our sense of morality is awakened to the fate of other groups than our own. It is not a call for becoming culturally alike, but it is a call for collaboration. Humans urgently need to become better able to collaborate across different moral circles while tolerating symbolic differences among them. For the longer term, evolutionary thinking provides hope in this respect. Since technology is continually lowering the costs of collaboration and increasing those of conflict, there is selective pressure toward peaceful coexistence of moral circles. The way ahead, however, is difficult, and the potential cost of conflict requires responsible behavior by us all.

The Future of Culture

The combination "cultural evolution" is so little used that a popular text processor underlines the second word and suggests "cultural *revolution*" as an alternative. This example, ironic as it is, flashes on the urgent need for humans to acquire a better understanding of how the incentives that we create affect the cultural evolution that we undergo. Culture accelerates our *material* evolution, but can we control our *cultural* evolution?

Culture adapts to ecological circumstances, and our ecological circumstances are rapidly changing, both in a physical and in a social sense and by our own doing. The six dimensions of culture that this book has described are a snapshot showing on which issues our history in the last millennia, in particular the invention of agriculture and large-scale societies, has created variation among societies in various parts of the world. If investigators could travel back in time twenty thousand years and investigate culture in a world populated only by hunter-gatherers, they would find different dimensions. For instance, all societies being egalitarian bands, they would be unlikely to find a marked dimension similar to power distance.

At this stage in our discussion, it is useful to revisit the five "simple but crucial points" made about evolution and consider what they mean for the future of culture.

Evolution Is Unavoidable

Those who hold a worldview based on strongly monumentalist values are likely to adopt religious or ideological views that are based on perceived immutability of nature, people, and moral rules. Such attitudes will come into violent conflict with factual reality, and such conflict may lead to a vicious circle of further strengthening the counterfactual beliefs. We humans need to emancipate into accepting that our own evolution is happening all around us and that it must be faced.

Evolution Does Not Look Ahead

Evolution lives by the day, but it stumbled on human societies, and we humans *can* look ahead. As a consequence, we face a duty, for both moral and pragmatic reasons, to learn from history and to prepare a sustainable world for the creatures who come after us. This duty also entails a need to understand our own evolution as best we can. Specifically, a focus on individual-level selection while disregarding group-level selection leads to the glorification of self-interest and is therefore potentially dangerous to society.

Evolution Is Path Dependent

Any genes, creatures, or cultures that become extinct are lost forever. The threat of extinction is not always a reason for preservation; since evolution is unavoidable, there is no way that the earth can be turned into a huge museum. It does, though, pose ethical problems of preservation of species, cultures, languages, and artifacts. If nothing else, self-interest can motivate preservation, such as of genetic diversity.

Evolution Uses Many Replicators

Genes, societal subgroups, and societies are some of today's main replicators that evolve. The laws of chance suggest that the more numerous we are, the faster genetic evolution proceeds. Cultural evolution may have lost us a lot of variety as polities have merged on a massive scale, but in compensation it is becoming more varied as societies become more complex internally.

Evolution Evolves

Currently we have limited understanding of cultural evolution as a recent addition. The knowledge we do have is mainly from biologists and has only just begun to influence the social sciences and humanities, let alone the public domain. Social scientists from various disciplines are now beginning to publish findings about cultural evolution using techniques that model the behavior of individuals or smaller units and to study the behavior of the larger social system.[48] There is a lot of work to do in these areas if humanity wishes to surf the current high waves of its evolution successfully.

Can we humans meet these challenges? For the moment, our propensity as group animals is to bend our mental powers to our own, or our group's, interests. We tend to believe anything that makes our group look good, such as being God's special favorites, rather than to be impartial about who we are. Philosophy and religion are still pretty much divorced from the material, biological world. These circumstances stand in the way of a sober assessment and of the joint taking of responsibility for our world.

Our societies are deeply influenced by recent events in our evolution. Each of us is likely to be involved in activities that have characteristics of hunting, gathering, herding, and agriculture. Some activities have a lot in common with hunting. Consultants, salespeople, and creative professionals, for instance, move from one successful contract or creation to the next; they experience the thrill of a success and the need for hunting the next one. Other activities are alike to herding. Investors, politicians, and researchers are busy accumulating companies, voters, and publications, respectively, and have to be anxious about theft and deceit. Many everyday activities such as shopping and browsing are similar to gathering. Factory workers, teachers, and functionaries can be likened to farmers who toil in predictable lives, using social ritual besides their work to make their lives bearable. One can also apply this kind of thinking to social organization. In big multinationals, for instance, the top of the organization leads a lifestyle closer to hunting or herding, while the employees lead an agriculturalist life. These descriptions are of course prototypical and no doubt wrong in many cases, but they are useful for showing how the social organization of our past could affect our present.

Human groups today live in a split. We have more or less global marketplaces, but as was argued in Chapter 11, we do not live in a global village. Among groups there is connection of inventions but separation of loyalties. Today we are so well connected that humanity as a whole can progress by adopting any innovation in technology provided it is invented just once on the planet. In this newly gained ease of communication, our environment resembles the ocean in which marine cetaceans (dolphins and whales) live. Some of the larger species have been found to use sound to communicate with one another across vast distances. To them, the ocean is indeed akin to a global village; they are all in the same bath, so to speak. Has this fact been important during their evolution? Cetaceans are remarkably peaceful and socially intelligent. They are descendents of land mammals that returned to the sea more than twenty million years ago. It is likely that their preexisting brain capacity and social structure, combined with environmental factors and with the potential for long-distance communication in the ocean, have led to evolutionary pressures to increase their powers of peaceful coexistence. Sperm whales, for instance, are the largest hunting animals in the world, with the largest brains of any animal. They make the loudest clicking noises of all animals—and they need them: for instance, for echolocating the giant squid that they hunt at a depth of several kilometers. Sperm whales have been found to have at least four nested levels of social organization, which include up to thousands of individuals across a thousand kilometers.[49] Their social organization may even be wider in scope, but for obvious reasons that is hard to assess.

For us humans, at least for many of us, the world has become even smaller than the ocean is for whales. News and innovations can travel the world in days, if not seconds. We can pity victims of calamities at the other side of the globe and try to help, but feelings of group loyalty still hold sway. Culture evolved to enable group coordination, and keeping group boundaries intact is one of the prerequisites for that. The motor of cultural evolution is fission-fusion dynamics. People perceive these dynamics in moral terms: "we" are good, while "they" are bad. Yet we urgently need to get rid of the split between the global connectedness of our trade and armies on the one hand and the parochial loyalties of our peoples on the other. In recent millennia, evolution has pressed toward enlargement of the moral circle, but we are not done yet. We have no choice but to pursue the direction of expansion of the moral circle to all people in the world. And to do this, we need to manage selective pressures at all levels of sociality, from neighborhoods to the "global village community." Depriving any group of moral rights or moral duties must be denounced.

The message of this chapter is an encouraging one: *you* are an integral part of human evolution, the future is ours to create, and you can make a contribution, if ever so small. In contrast, the message of the rest of the book was sobering: although moral circles can be expanded, cultures resist change. It is therefore not realistic to expect that all world citizens should become alike. Nor is it desirable or necessary that they should do so. Peoples will differ, but they have to learn to coexist without wanting others to become just like them. Any other road is a dead end.

Notes

Chapter 1

1. British sociologist Anthony Giddens (born 1938) defines sociology as "the study of human life, groups and societies" (Giddens, 2001, p. 2), which would incorporate social anthropology. The practical division of labor between sociologists and anthropologists is for the former to focus on social processes within societies and for the latter to focus on societies as wholes.

2. A *group* means a number of people in contact with each other. A *category* consists of people who, without necessarily having any contact, have something in common (e.g., all women managers, or all people born before 1940).

3. Culture as "collective programming of the mind" resembles the concept of habitus proposed by the French sociologist Pierre Bourdieu (1930–2002): "Certain conditions of existence produce a *habitus*, a system of permanent and transferable dispositions. A habitus . . . functions as the basis for practices and images . . . which can be collectively orchestrated without an actual conductor" (Bourdieu, 1980, pp. 88–89; translation by GH).

4. Results obtained with the same personality test (the NEO-PI-R, measuring the Big Five personality dimensions) in different countries show that average or "normal" personality varies with culture (Hofstede & McCrae, 2004). See Chapter 2; relationships between culture and personality will be discussed in Chapters 4 through 6.

5. For a critical discussion of this genetic inferiority thesis, see Neisser et al., 1996.

6. Discourse is an area of study uniting linguists, psychologists, and other social scientists. For a broad introduction, see van Dijk, 1997a, 1997b.

7. This example is inspired by William Golding's novel *Lord of the Flies*, in which a group of children who have hardly met before find themselves on an island together.

8. destentor.nl/regio/veluwewest/4803075.

9. The concept of a moral circle was developed in the nineteenth century by the Irish historian William Lecky and popularized by the Australian philosopher Peter Singer, who teaches bioethics at Princeton University, in the United States.

10. See Chapter 7 on the teachings of Confucius and Socrates. The issue occupies a central role in the work of the German philosopher Immanuel Kant (1724–1804).

11. Adopted by the General Assembly of the United Nations on December 10, 1948.

12. Even eminent geneticist Luigi Luca Cavalli-Sforza, despite giving strong evidence from his human genome project on the structured variation of human genes across continents, argues in his 2000 book, *Genes, Peoples and Languages*, that we should be called one race. However, the basis of such arguments is moral, not genetic.

13. Brown, Bradley, & Lang, 2006.

14. Navarrete et al., 2009.

15. In an Australian experiment by Platow et al. (2006), science students who had been set a painful task were comforted by a passerby who was a confederate of the experimenter. They felt less pain when the passerby pretended to be another science student than when she claimed to be an arts student.

16. Tocqueville, 1956 [1835], p. 155.

17. Some nations are less culturally integrated than others. Examples are some of the former colonies and multilingual, multiethnic countries such as Belgium, Malaysia, and the former Yugoslavia. Still, even in these cases ethnic and/or linguistic groups that consider themselves to be very different from each other may have common traits in comparison with the populations of other countries. We have shown this to be the case for Belgium and the former Yugoslavia (*Culture's Consequences*, 2001, p. 501).

18. Montesquieu, 1979 [1742], p. 461.

19. Harris, 1981, p. 8.

20. Translation by GH from Lévi-Strauss & Éribon, 1988, p. 229.

Chapter 2

1. In popular parlance, the words *norm* and *value* are often used indiscriminately, or the twin expression *values and norms* is handled as an inseparable pair, like Laurel and Hardy. In this latter case one of the two words is redundant.

2. *Culture's Consequences*, 2001, p. 91.

3. Inkeles & Levinson, 1969 [1954], pp. 447ff.

4. This analysis is extensively described in *Culture's Consequences*, 2001, Chapter 2.

5. *Culture's Consequences*, 2001, p. 64.

6. *Culture's Consequences* uses both *product moment* (Pearson) correlation coefficients and *rank order* (Spearman) correlation coefficients; the first are based on the absolute values of measurements, the second on their relative ranks.

7. Codes used for correlations in this book follow general social science conventions. The lowercase letter r stands for the product moment (zero-order) correlation coefficient. The Greek letter rho (ρ) stands for the Spearman rank correlation coefficient. An uppercase R stands for a multiple correlation coefficient based on two or more variables. Significance levels are indicated by asterisks: * beyond the 0.05 level, ** beyond the 0.01 level, and *** beyond the 0.001 level. Other significance levels are specified by the letter p. The letter n stands for the number of cases in the correlation.

8. IMEDE (now IMD), Lausanne, see *Culture's Consequences*, 2001, pp. 91 and 219.

9. The VSM is a standard set of questions available to researchers who wish to include a replication of the Hofstede national culture research in their projects. The 2008 version is the VSM08. It is accessible via geerthofstede.nl. Earlier versions were issued in 1982 and 1994.

10. Søndergaard, 1994.

11. Ng et al., 1982.

12. Hofstede & Bond, 1984.

13. Published in a 1987 article authored by the Chinese Culture Connection, the name chosen by Michael Bond for his team of twenty-four researchers. See Chapters 3 through 7 and Hofstede & Bond, 1988.

14. *Culture's Consequences*, 2001, pp. 503–20. The summary table on p. 520 counts 355 significant zero-order correlations, 62 significant second-order correlations, and 9 significant third-order correlations.

15. Margaret Mead in her preface to the 1959 edition of Benedict's book *Patterns of Culture*.

16. The highest correlation was 0.64*** between extraversion and individualism (Hofstede & McCrae, 2004). See Chapter 4.

17. The words "in your life" suggest that what is asked for is the desired, but "a guiding principle" turns it into an abstract statement about the desirable.

18. Both the number of value items and the number of countries have grown over time. A version of Schwartz's survey on the Internet in 2009 lists seventy-nine values. Schwartz & Bardi, 2001, report student samples from fifty-four countries and teacher samples from fifty-six countries.

19. See Schwartz, 1994; Sagiv & Schwartz, 2000; *Culture's Consequences*, 2001, p. 265. Smith, Peterson, & Schwartz, 2002, show correlations of our indexes with three summary dimensions computed from Schwartz's data; all three are most strongly correlated with individualism-collectivism.

20. House, Hanges, Javidan, Dorfman, & Gupta, 2004.

21. Hofstede, 2006.

22. An illustration is an item in the latest wave of the World Values Survey that asks respondents how much "democraticness" there is in their country. According to the answers provided by the nationally representative samples, there is more democraticness in Ghana, Vietnam, and Jordan than in any Western country, such as Switzerland, Germany, the United States, Sweden, or Finland.

23. This was empirically shown by personality psychologists McCrae, Terracciano, Realo, & Allik, 2008.

24. Trompenaars, 1993.

25. The first five from Parsons & Shils, 1951; the latter two from Kluckhohn & Strodtbeck, 1961.

26. Among others, Stouffer & Toby, 1951.

27. Smith, Trompenaars, & Dugan, 1995; Smith, Dugan, & Trompenaars, 1996; Smith, Peterson, & Schwartz, 2002. As far as we know, these are the only academic publications about Trompenaars's database. The numbers and categories of respondents reported differ from those claimed by Trompenaars (1993). See *Culture's Consequences*, 2001, p. 274, notes 26 and 27.

28. worldvaluessurvey.com. A printed summary of then available WVS data has been published in Inglehart, Basañez, & Moreno, 1998.

29. Minkov (2007) used the spelling "flexumility"; we added the letter *h* to be able to use the adjective *flexhumble*.

30. Our cooperation had earlier resulted in a new, 2008 version of the Values Survey Module (VSM08). In addition to the five established Hofstede dimensions, the VSM08 includes two Minkov dimensions; the VSM Manual already predicted that "monumentalism versus flex(h)umility" might turn out to be a variant of short-term orientation.

31. Russell, 1979 [1927], pp. 23–24.

32. See note 9.

Chapter 3

1. Mulder, 1976, 1977.

2. The matrix on which the factor analysis was carried out consisted of thirty-two questions (variables) and forty countries (cases). Handbooks on factor analysis do not recommend using the technique for matrices with few cases, because the factors become unstable: they can be too much affected by a single deviant case. This limitation does not apply, however, for *ecological* factor analyses, in which the score for each case is the mean of a large number of independent observations. In this situation the stability of the factor structure is determined by the number of individuals whose answers went into the mean scores. Therefore, ecological factor analyses give stable results even with fewer cases than variables.

3. In statistical terms: items with high loadings on the factor.

4. The labels *autocratic, paternalistic, consultative,* and *majority* for the four styles were attached by Geert in the analysis. For the descriptions in the questionnaire, see *Culture's Consequences*, 2001, p. 470.

5. For details, see *Culture's Consequences*, 2001, pp. 501–2; Kolman, Noorderhaven, Hofstede, & Dienes, 2003; Huettinger, 2006.

6. Pierre Bourdieu (see Chapter 1, note 3) sees this as one of the key characteristics of a *habitus*. It represents necessity turned into virtue (*nécessité faite vertu*). See Bourdieu, 1980, p. 90.

7. Sadler & Hofstede, 1976.

8. The correlation coefficients *r* with PDI measured for the populations listed in Table 2.1 were 0.67*** for the elites (0.80*** with the newer VSM formulas), 0.59***

for the employees of six other organizations, 0.76*** for the airline pilots, 0.71*** for the heads of municipal organizations, and 0.59** for the bank employees.

9. The correlations between the various replications were weaker than the correlations of each of them with the original IBM set (e.g., in van Nimwegen, 2002, p. 153).

10. de Mooij, 2004.

11. Chinese Culture Connection, 1987. Across the twenty countries in both studies, moral discipline correlated with $r = 0.55**$ with power distance and $-0.54**$ with individualism.

12. Across forty-eight common countries, PDI and in-group collectivism "as is" were correlated 0.73***. PDI and power distance "as is" correlated 0.33*. PDI and power distance "should be" correlated -0.12. Across these countries, power distance "as is" and "should be" between them were strongly negatively correlated: $r = -0.52***$. House, Hanges, Javidan, Dorfman, & Gupta (2004, p. 543) reported across forty-seven countries a correlation with PDI for their power distance "as is" of 0.57*** and for their power distance "should be" of 0.03.

13. UAI and power distance "as is" correlated 0.50***. UAI and power distance "should be" correlated $-0.31*$.

14. The term *working class* is, of course, curiously archaic. If anything, in many countries it covers more people who are *out of* work than the middle class.

15. The reason is that the country PDI scores measure social inequality. Differences in social status are also a prime criterion for distinguishing occupations.

16. *Culture's Consequences*, 2001, p. 89.

17. The samples of IBM employees on which the cross-national comparison was based included all the categories in Table 3.2 except unskilled workers. The mean score of the cross-national samples for Great Britain, France, and Germany was 46.

18. Kohn, 1969.

19. The classic motion picture *Four Families*, produced by the National Film Board of Canada in 1959, with expert advice from anthropologist Margaret Mead, shows the relationships between parents and small children in more or less matched farmer families in India, France, Japan, and Canada. Audiences to whom we showed the film, before giving them the PDI scores, were able to rank the four countries correctly on this dimension just on the basis of the parent-child relationships pictured.

20. Flash Eurobarometer 247, 2008. Across eighteen countries with a 2007 GNI per capita over 19,000 euros, high PDI explained 40 percent of the differences in percentages of families with both parents working full-time; low PDI explained 49 percent of the differences in percentages of families with one parent working part-time. (Calculations courtesy of Marieke de Mooij.)

21. *Transcultural psychiatry* has become a special subdiscipline for mental health professionals dealing with immigrants.

22. Meeuwesen, van den Brink-Muinen, & Hofstede, 2009. The study used videotaped interactions between 307 general practitioners and 5,820 patients in ten European countries (Belgium, Estonia, Germany, Great Britain, the Netherlands, Poland, Romania, Spain, Sweden, and Switzerland).

23. Deschepper, Grigoryan, Lundborg, Hofstede, Cohen, Van der Kelen, Deliens, & Haaijer-Ruskamp, 2008. The study summarizes the results of three studies across European countries: a survey of patients in nineteen countries about prescribed medication and self-medication, a study of distribution or reimbursement of antibiotics in twenty-four countries, and Eurobarometer data about medication use from representative samples of the population in fifteen countries.

24. de Kort, Wagenmans, van Dongen, Slotboom, Hofstede, & Veldhuizen, 2010. Across the twenty-five countries, PDI correlated with donors per one hundred inhabitants with $r = -0.54$**, with blood collections per one thousand inhabitants with -0.77***, and with blood supplied to hospitals with -0.65***.

25. d'Iribarne, 1989, p. 77. Translation by GH.

26. Management by objectives is a system of periodic meetings between superior and subordinate in which the latter commits him- or herself to the achievement of certain objectives. In the next meeting this achievement is assessed and new objectives for the coming period are agreed on.

27. Smith, Peterson, & Schwartz, 2002. The correlation of the verticality index with PDI across forty overlapping countries was 0.60***. It was the strongest correlation with external data found in the event management research project.

28. *Culture's Consequences*, 2001, p. 93. The correlation coefficient between traditional authority and PDI across twenty-seven overlapping countries was 0.56**.

29. According to Eurobarometer 69.1, 2008, across the nineteen wealthier countries (2007 GNI per capita over 19,000 euros), high PDI explained 50 percent of the differences in percentages not trusting the police. In the Eurobarometer survey among young Europeans, 2007, for the same nineteen wealthier countries, low PDI explained 41 percent of the differences in percentages joining a political party and 39 percent in having participated in debates with policy makers. (Calculations courtesy of Marieke de Mooij.)

30. More about Confucianism will be discussed in Chapter 7.

31. "Store up no treasures for yourselves on earth, where moth and rust corrode, where thieves break in and steal: store up treasures for yourself in heaven, where neither moth nor rust corrode, where thieves do not break in and steal. For where your treasure lies, your heart will lie there too" (St. Matthew 6:19–21, Moffatt translation).

32. Machiavelli, 1955 [1517], p. 91.

33. Triandis, 1973, pp. 55–68. See also Chapter 9.

34. *Culture's Consequences*, 2001, pp. 115–17.

35. *Culture's Consequences*, 2001, p. 118.

36. van de Vliert, 2009.

37. The IBM research project allowed a comparison between data for 1968 and 1972. During this four-year term the *desire for* independence among IBM employees increased worldwide, no doubt under the influence of the international communication of ideas. However, this desire was matched by a shift in the direction of more equality in *perceived* power only in countries in which power distances had already been small. In fact, countries at opposite ends of the scale grew wider apart (*Culture's Consequences*, 2001, p. 136).

38. Translated by GH from the Dutch newspaper *NRC Handelsblad*, December 23, 1988.

Chapter 4

1. See the scoring guides for the VSM94 and the VSM08 at geerthofstede.nl.

2. Both factors were also strongly correlated with GNI per capita. In a regression analysis on the four IBM dimensions, IDV explained 54 percent of the variance in well-being versus survival, IDV plus MAS (negatively) 74 percent, and these two plus PDI (also negatively) 82 percent. See Chapter 5; Inglehart, 1997, p 93; *Culture's Consequences*, 2001, pp. 222–23 and 266.

3. Minkov, 2007. His latest scores are based on average values from the 1995–2004 and 2005–08 waves of the WVS.

4. The correlation between IDV and exclusionism was $r = -0.77^{***}$ ($n = 41$). In a regression analysis of exclusionism on the four IBM dimensions, IDV (negatively) explained 59 percent of the variance, adding MAS explained 65 percent, and adding PDI explained 69 percent.

5. Eurobarometer 69.1, 2008. The values were democracy, equality, human rights, individual freedom, peace, religion, respect for human life, respect for other cultures, rule of law, solidarity, self-fulfillment, and tolerance. Of country differences in the frequency of people choosing "respect for other cultures," IDV explained 30 percent, and (low) MAS explained an additional 23 percent. (Calculations courtesy of Marieke de Mooij.)

6. The correlation coefficients with IDV measured for the populations listed in Table 2.1 were 0.69^{***} for the elites, 0.63^{***} for the employees of six other organizations, 0.70^{***} for the airline pilots, 0.60^{**} for the consumers, and 0.61^{***} for the bank employees.

7. Chinese Culture Connection, 1987. Across the twenty countries in both studies, integration correlated 0.65^{***} with IDV and -0.58^{**} with PDI. Across seventeen common countries, it correlated -0.70^{**} with Minkov's exclusionism.

8. On the basis of data from teachers in twenty-three countries: Schwartz, 1994, pp. 112–15, and *Culture's Consequences*, 2001, pp. 220–21 and 265. Three of Schwartz's categories that correlated with IDV were even more strongly correlated with GNI per capita. The remaining two were "hierarchy," which was negatively correlated with IDV, and "egalitarian commitment," which was positively correlated.

9. Smith, Peterson, & Schwartz, 2002. Across thirty-nine countries, autonomy versus embeddedness correlated with IDV with $r = 0.64^{***}$ and egalitarianism versus mastery with $r = 0.50^{***}$.

10. See our introduction to the GLOBE study in Chapter 2. Across forty-eight common countries, IDV and in-group collectivism "as is" correlated with -0.77^{***}. In a stepwise regression analysis of all eighteen GLOBE dimensions against IDV, only in-group collectivism "as is" remained, explaining the 58 percent common variance mentioned.

11. Institutional collectivism "should be" correlated -0.46^{**} with UAI and -0.40^{**} with IDV. In a stepwise regression, UAI explained 15 percent of the variance in institutional collectivism "as is"; UAI and IDV together explained 22 percent. In-group collectivism "should be" correlated −0.63** with LTO–CVS and −0.49*** with LTO–WVS, and institutional collectivism "as is" correlated 0.41** with UAI.

12. Smith, Peterson, & Schwartz, 2002. They called one dimension *egalitarian commitment versus conservatism*, and across thirty-five countries it correlated with IDV with $r = 0.61***$. Their second dimension was labeled *loyal involvement versus utilitarian involvement*; it correlated with PDI with $r = 0.74***$ and with IDV with −0.59**.

13. Smith, 2004. Acquiescence in questions dealing not with values, but with descriptions of the actual situation, was correlated with uncertainty avoidance; see Chapter 6.

14. An extensive review of measurements of individualism and collectivism at the individual level was published by Oyserman, Coon, & Kemmelmeier, 2002.

15. The correlation between PDI and IDV across the seventy-six cultures from Tables 3.1 and 4.1 is $r = −0.55***$; across the fifty-three cultures in the IBM database, it is −0.68***.

16. Crozier, 1964, p. 222.

17. d'Iribarne, 1989, p. 59. Translation by GH.

18. Harrison, 1985, pp. 55–56.

19. Keeping national wealth (GNI per capita) constant, the correlation between PDI and IDV across sixty-nine countries from Tables 3.1 and 4.1 was −0.36***; across fifty countries from the IBM database, it was −0.32***.

20. Triandis (1995, pp. 44–52) has introduced a distinction between *horizontal* and *vertical* individualism and collectivism. He applies this distinction mostly at the level of individuals. At the level of societies, the horizontal versus vertical distinction is identical to small versus large power distance.

21. A distinction between occupations in which some demand more individual initiative and some demand more group loyalty is conceivable, but the questions in the IBM database were not suitable for measuring it.

22. Herzberg, Mausner, & Snyderman, 1959.

23. St. Matthew 21:28–31, Moffatt translation.

24. Eurobarometer survey among young Europeans, 2007, across nineteen countries with a 2007 GNI per capita over 19,500 euros. Low IDV explains 24 percent of the country differences on choosing the answer "can't afford to move out" from their parents' home. (Calculations courtesy of Marieke de Mooij.)

25. From a speech by R. M. Hadjiwibowo to Semafor Senior Management College, the Netherlands, September 1983. Translation from the Dutch by GH with suggestions from the author.

26. Flash Eurobarometer 241, 2008. Across nineteen European countries with GNI per capita over 19,500 euros, 72 percent of the differences in answering this question are explained by low IDV. (Calculations courtesy of Marieke de Mooij.)

27. Hall, 1976.

28. Ho, 1976, p. 867.

29. Triandis, 1972, p. 38.

30. Buss, 1989; Buss et al., 1990; *Culture's Consequences*, 2001, pp. 230–31.

31. Yelsma & Athappilly, 1988; Dion & Dion, 1993; *Culture's Consequences*, 2001, p. 230.

32. Levine, Sato, Hashimoto, & Verma, 1995; *Culture's Consequences*, 2001, p. 230.

33. Based on Etcoff, Orbach, Scott, & Agostino, 2006. The categories from which to choose were girlfriends, mother, romantic partner or spouse, media, siblings, girls in general, celebrities, boys in general, and father. Correlation of IDV with the choice "girlfriends" $r = -0.87***$; with "boys in general" $r = 0.74**$ ($n = 10$). (Calculations courtesy of Marieke de Mooij.) See also Chapters 5 and 7.

34. The correlations were $r = -0.75***$ across sixty countries and $-0.64***$ across thirty languages. From Kashima & Kashima, 1998; *Culture's Consequences*, 2001, p. 233. In a follow-up study, Kashima & Kashima, 2003, showed that for countries with pronoun drop, the relationship of IDV with wealth was weaker, but the relationship of IDV with geographic latitude (climate) was stronger.

35. Habib, 1995, p. 102.

36. Hsu, 1971, pp. 23–44. In the title of his article, the concept was labeled *jen*, which is an older transcription of the same Chinese sound.

37. Markus & Kitayama, 1991.

38. R. Bond & Smith, 1996; *Culture's Consequences*, 2001, p. 232. R. Bond & Smith also did a longitudinal analysis of the U.S. data, which showed that conformity declined since the 1950s.

39. The correlation was $r = 0.64***$. The relationship between personality scores and culture dimensions is analyzed in Hofstede & McCrae, 2004.

40. Matsumoto, 1989; *Culture's Consequences*, 2001, p. 232.

41. Levine & Norenzayan, 1999; *Culture's Consequences*, 2001, p. 233.

42. de Mooij, 2004; *Culture's Consequences*, 2001, pp. 241–42.

43. Humana, 1992; OECD, 1995; *Culture's Consequences*, 2001, pp. 242–43.

44. Westbrook & Legge, 1993; Westbrook, Legge, & Pennay, 1993.

45. *Culture's Consequences*, 2001, p. 240.

46. Earley, 1989, pp. 565–81.

47. See Chapter 3, note 26.

48. Flash Eurobarometer 241, 2008. *Information society as seen by EU citizens*, twenty-six countries. Percentage of those who (almost) never access the Internet for personal use, neither at work nor at home: low IDV explains 20 percent of the differences; high MAS (see Chapter 5) explains an additional 15 percent. Differences among countries in use of the following ICT applications are primarily explained by high IDV: buying products or services 38 percent, filling out forms for public administration 36 percent, banking 31 percent, personal e-mail 31 percent. (Calculations courtesy of Marieke de Mooij.)

49. Flash Eurobarometer 241, 2008. *Information society as seen by EU citizens*, twenty-six countries. Percentage of those who strongly agree that people who do not use the Internet have more time for themselves, family, and friends: low IDV explains 27 percent of the country differences. (Calculations courtesy of Marieke de Mooij.)

50. From a paper by Alfred J. Kraemer, "Cultural Aspects of Intercultural Training," presented at the International Congress of Applied Psychology, Munich, August 1978.

51. This was shown empirically by Pedersen & Thomsen, 1997.

52. *Culture's Consequences*, 2001, p. 247.

53. Humana, 1992; *Culture's Consequences*, 2001, pp. 247–48.

54. English version of the text from Harding & Phillips, 1986, p. 86.

55. Stoetzel, 1983, p. 78; *Culture's Consequences*, 2001, p. 275, note 31. The rank correlation ρ between the freedom/equality ratio and IDV was 0.84**; between the freedom/equality ratio and PDI it was about zero.

56. Maslow, 1970.

57. Anchored to the level of the IBM scores for the white Australians, the aboriginals' scores were PDI = 80, IDV = 89, MAS = 22, and UAI = 128. Their anchored score for LTO = CVS was −10. See *Culture's Consequences*, 2001, p. 501.

58. For the countries from the IBM sample, the correlation of IDV with GNI per capita was $r = 0.85^{***}$ in 1970, 0.79*** in 1980, 0.74*** in 1990, and 0.72*** in 2000. For the total set of countries in Table 4.1, it was 0.59*** in 2000.

59. Across ninety-one countries, GNI per capita in 1970 correlated 0.93*** with GNI per capita in 1980, 0.89*** in 1990, and 0.80*** in 2000 and correlated 0.76*** with GNI per capita at PPP in 2007.

60. The IBM data bank allowed measuring shifts in individualism during the four-year period from 1968 to 1972. Out of twenty countries that had been surveyed in both years, nineteen had become richer, and all of these had shifted toward greater individualism. The only country in the set that had become poorer, Pakistan, shifted slightly toward the collectivist side.

Chapter 5

1. For example, Mead, 1962 [1950].

2. Costa, Terraciano, & McCrae (2001) compared mean scores on the NEO-PI-R Big Five personality test for women and men in twenty-six cultures. They found consistent gender differences across cultures. Women scored themselves higher on all facets of N (neuroticism) and A (agreeableness), and from the other dimensions of personality women scored higher on some facets: warmth, gregariousness, positive emotions, and openness to aesthetics. Men scored themselves higher on the facets assertiveness, excitement seeking, and openness to ideas.

3. *Culture's Consequences*, 2001, p. 280, following Broverman, Vogel, Broverman, Clarkson, & Rosenkrantz, 1972.

4. Hofstede et al., 1998.

5. According to the Sign Test, this provides significant support for the dimension at the 0.05 level (one-tailed).

6. *Culture's Consequences*, 2001, p. 265. The correlation across twenty-three countries was $r = 0.53^{**}$.

7. Bond's Chinese Value Survey across twenty-three countries produced a "human-heartedness" dimension correlated with MAS. Students in countries scoring high on

masculinity stressed patience, courtesy, and kindness; those in feminine countries stressed patriotism and righteousness. These associations are surprising; one would have expected the poles to be reversed. Geert has always retained a suspicion that in the data processing a minus sign was lost. If the analysis was right, we have to interpret this result as an example of the difference between the desired and the desirable, described in Chapter 2.

8. Across forty-eight common countries, MAS correlated with $r = 0.30^*$ with assertiveness "as is" and with a multiple $R = 0.43^{***}$ with assertiveness "as is" plus assertiveness "should be," both taken positively. This is remarkable, because assertiveness "as is" and "should be" between themselves were significantly negatively correlated: -0.33^*.

9. In a comparison with other GLOBE dimensions, humane orientation "as is" correlated strongly with a combination of small assertiveness and small power distance "as is." It was not an independent dimension. Humane orientation "should be" was not an independent dimension either: it correlated strongly with low uncertainty avoidance, small institutional collectivism, and small power distance, all of them "should be."

10. *Culture's Consequences*, 2001, p. 266. The multiple correlation with IDV and MAS was $R = 0.86^{***}$.

11. Bem, 1975, p. 636.

12. The percentage of women in the IBM survey population varied from 4.0 in Pakistan to 16.2 in Finland. In *Culture's Consequences*, 2001, p. 286, the MAS scores have been recalculated, keeping the percentage of women constant for all countries. The effect on the scores was minimal, as the percentages of women in themselves were correlated with femininity.

13. Gray, 1993. We owe this observation to Marieke de Mooij.

14. Lynn, 1991; van de Vliert, 1998, Table 7.2; *Culture's Consequences*, 2001, p. 308.

15. Based on *Culture's Consequences*, 2001, pp. 289–91.

16. Stevens, 1973; Gonzalez, 1982; *Culture's Consequences*, 2001, p. 309.

17. Based on Etcoff, Orbach, Scott, & Agostino, 2006. The correlation of MAS with the choice "father" was $r = -0.79^{**}$; with "mother" it was $r = -0.75^{**}$ $(n = 10)$. In a stepwise regression, MAS explained 57 percent of the variance for "mother"; MAS plus PDI explained 76 percent. The correlation of MAS with the choice "media" was $r = 0.88^{***}$; with "celebrities" it was $r = -0.62^*$ $(n = 10)$. (Calculations courtesy of Marieke de Mooij.) See also Chapters 4 and 7.

18. Flash Eurobarometer 247, 2008. Across eighteen countries with a 2007 GNI per capita over 19,000 euros, high MAS explained 24 percent of the differences in percentages of families with one parent working and one parent caring for the household full-time. (Calculations courtesy of Marieke de Mooij.)

19. van Rossum, 1998; *Culture's Consequences*, 2001, p. 300.

20. *Culture's Consequences*, 2001, p. 302.

21. Hofstede, 1996b; *Culture's Consequences*, 2001, p. 302.

22. Mead, 1962 [1950], pp. 271ff.

23. *Culture's Consequences*, 2001, p. 309.

24. From a description in a KLM in-flight magazine on a transatlantic flight during which the film was shown. *Lucas* was a 1986 film aimed at U.S. teenagers, directed by David Seltzer.

25. This section draws heavily on Hofstede et al., 1998, Chapter 10 ("Comparative Studies of Sexual Behavior").

26. Hofstede, Neuijen, Ohayv, & Sanders, 1990. See also Chapter 8.

27. Pryor, DeSouza, Fitness, Hutz, Kumpf, Lubbert, Pesonen, & Erber, 1997, p. 526.

28. *Culture's Consequences*, 2001, p. 325; Ross, 1989.

29. Dr. Jan A. C. de Kock van Leeuwen, personal communication.

30. As in the onetime U.S. bestseller *In Search of Excellence* (Peters & Waterman, 1982).

31. The difference between the two types of ethos is not a recent phenomenon. Lord Robert Baden-Powell (1857–1941), the founder of the international Boy Scouts movement, wrote a book for Rover Scouts (boys over age sixteen) called *Rovering to Success*. Its translation into Dutch, dating from the 1920s, is called *Zwervend op de weg naar levensgeluk* (*Roving on the Road to Happiness*). To the Dutch translators, *success* was not a goal likely to appeal to young men. The word in Dutch has a flavor of superficiality. No youth leader would defend it as a prime purpose in life.

32. Sandemose, 1938. Translation by GH with thanks to Denise Daval Ohayv.

33. Cohen, 1973.

34. Lasch, 1980, p. 117, attributed this dictum to George Allen; others claim that it came from Vince Lombardi.

35. Hastings & Hastings, 1980; *Culture's Consequences*, 2001, p. 303. The samples were quite large: about 1,500 per country. Hastings & Hastings provided no information about the gender distribution of the respondents, but we assume fifty-fifty for all five countries. In the picture of the fighters, the actors were clearly boys.

36. Correlation was $r = 0.97**$.

37. Ryback, Sanders, Lorentz, & Koestenblatt, 1980; *Culture's Consequences*, 2001, p. 301.

38. Cooper & Cooper, 1982, p. 80.

39. Verhulst, Achenbach, Ferdinand, & Kasius, 1993; *Culture's Consequences*, 2001, pp. 303–4.

40. U.S. author Christopher Lasch (1980) called this *The Culture of Narcissism*.

41. OECD, 1995; Hofstede et al., 1998, Table 5.2; *Culture's Consequences*, 2001, p. 304. Across seven countries and language groups, the percentages of those rating themselves "excellent" were rank correlated with MAS with $\rho = 0.71*$.

42. *Culture's Consequences*, 2001, p. 304.

43. Witkin, 1977, p. 85; Witkin & Goodenough, 1977, p. 682.

44. A study comparing two masculine and two less masculine countries is Kühnen, Hannover, Roeder, Shah, Schubert, Upmeyer, & Zakaria, 2001. The authors erroneously attribute the differences found to individualism versus collectivism.

45. *Culture's Consequences*, 2001, pp. 310–11; de Mooij & Hofstede, 2002; de Mooij, 2004.

46. Tannen, 1992.

47. Flash Eurobarometer 241, 2008. *Information society as seen by EU citizens.* Percentages of those who access the Internet for personal use several times a day (in past three months): across twenty-six countries, low MAS explains 20 percent of the differences, and high IDV explains an additional 17 percent. Across the nineteen wealthier countries, only low MAS is significant, explaining 36 percent of the country differences. (Calculations courtesy of Marieke de Mooij.)

48. Fleishman, Harris, & Burtt, 1955; Blake & Mouton, 1964.

49. Philippe d'Iribarne considers the need for consensus the key characteristic of management in the Dutch manufacturing plant he studied. See d'Iribarne, 1989, pp. 234ff.

50. D'Iribarne (1989, p. 144) describes these contracts as a unique feature of the U.S. industrial relations scene.

51. About this sense of moderation in France, see d'Iribarne, 1989, pp. 31 and 60–61.

52. *Culture's Consequences*, 2001, pp. 290 and 317.

53. Quoted by William F. Whyte in Webber (ed.), 1969, p. 31.

54. *Culture's Consequences*, 2001, p. 317.

55. Statham, 1987.

56. *Culture's Consequences*, 2001, pp. 307–8.

57. Herzberg, 1966.

58. *Culture's Consequences*, 2001, pp. 315–16.

59. *Human Development Report 2006*, Table 4.

60. The correlations were $r = 0.93$*** for the percentages of functional illiterates, 0.72** for the percentages of people who are poor, and 0.64** for the percentages of people earning less than half the median income.

61. Diderot, 1982 [1780], pp. 124–25. Translation by GH.

62. Eurobarometer, 1990; *Culture's Consequences*, 2001, pp. 318–19. The correlation with MAS across eleven countries (excluding Luxembourg) was −0.63*.

63. European Values Study: Stoetzel, 1983, p. 37. The rank correlation coefficient between permissiveness index and MAS was −0.83**.

64. Eurobarometer, 1997. *Racism and xenophobia in Europe*. The correlation with MAS was −0.72**.

65. Eurobarometer 69.1, 2008. The values were democracy, equality, human rights, individual freedom, peace, religion, respect for human life, respect for other cultures, rule of law, solidarity, self-fulfillment, and tolerance. Of country differences in the frequency of people choosing "respect for other cultures," IDV explained 30 percent, and (low) MAS explained an additional 23 percent. (Calculations courtesy of Marieke de Mooij.)

66. UNDP website. In 2000 the U.S. contribution was 0.10 percent. Part of the increase was due to projects in Iraq and Afghanistan.

67. Across twenty donor countries, the correlation between MAS and aid in 2000 in percentage of GNI was −0.75***.

68. Across twenty-one donor countries, the correlation between MAS and CDI was −0.46*. Data from *Foreign Policy*, 2003.

69. *Culture's Consequences*, 2001, p. 271.

70. An eloquent defense of the need to limit growth is Schumacher, 1973.

71. *Culture's Consequences*, 2001, p. 321. Rank correlations across twenty-six countries of MAS were with "center," 0.59**, and with "left," −0.36*.

72. Lammers, 1989, p. 43.

73. *Human Development Report 2006*, Tables 25 and 29.

74. The first correlation of the Catholic/Protestant ratio is with uncertainty avoidance; see Chapter 5 and *Culture's Consequences*, 2001, p. 200.

75. Cooper & Cooper, 1982, p. 97.

76. Verweij, 1998; Verweij, Ester, & Nauta, 1997; *Culture's Consequences*, 2001, p. 327.

77. St. Matthew 22:37–40, Moffatt translation.

78. Stoetzel, 1983, pp. 98–101.

79. Halman & Petterson, 1996.

80. Reported in *The Economist*, June 22, 1996. The correlation with MAS was −0.60**. Low MAS explains 36 percent of the variance; low MAS plus low PDI together explain 57 percent.

81. Levine, Norenzayan, & Philbrick, 2001; Hofstede, 2001b. The rank correlation with MAS was −0.36*.

82. Walter, 1990, p. 87.

83. Stoetzel, 1983, p. 92.

84. The quotations are from the Authorized Version of the British and Foreign Bible Society (1954).

85. From H. Samsonowicz, "Die Bedeutung des Grosshandels für die Entwicklung der polnischen Kultur bis zum Beginn des 16. Jahrhunderts," in *Studia Historiae Economica* 5 (1970), 92ff., cited in Schildhauer, 1985, p. 107.

86. Erasmus, 2001 [1524], pp. 174–81.

87. Haley, 1988, pp. 39 and 110–11.

88. Schama, 1987, pp. 404, 541, and 240.

89. A French reader on collective identities edited by Michaud (1978, p. 75) referred to the "feminine image of France."

90. *Culture's Consequences*, 2001, p. 331.

91. Levinson, 1977, p. 763.

92. From 2004 to 2015 the population of the high-income countries in the world is expected to grow by an average of 0.5 percent per year; of the low-income countries by 1.7 percent per year (*Human Development Report 2006*, Table 5).

93. Among wealthy countries, fertility rates in the period 1995–2000 rank correlate significantly negatively with uncertainty avoidance; in the period 2000–2005 primarily with individualism (*Human Development Report 2002* and *2006*).

94. Hudson & den Boer, 2004.

Chapter 6

1. Personal communication.

2. Lawrence, 1980, p. 133.

3. The term first appeared in Cyert & March, 1963, pp. 118ff.

4. *Webster's New World Dictionary of the American Language*, College Edition, 1964.

5. The rank correlation was $\rho = 0.73$***. Lynn, 1971; *Culture's Consequences*, 2001, pp. 155–56 and 188.

6. Wikipedia, 2008.

7. Costa & McCrae's NEO-PI-R. Correlation coefficients were UAI with "neuroticism" $r = 0.58$**; UAI plus MAS multiple $R = 0.74$***; UAI with "agreeableness" $r = -0.55$**. Source: Hofstede & McCrae, 2004.

8. *Culture's Consequences*, 2001, p. 199.

9. Across the forty-eight countries, UAI and GLOBE's uncertainty avoidance "as is" correlated with $r = -0.61$***; UAI and GLOBE's uncertainty avoidance "should be" correlated $+ 0.37$*; while GLOBE's uncertainty avoidance "as is" and "should be" between them correlated -0.70***.

10. In a stepwise regression across the forty-eight countries, GLOBE's uncertainty avoidance "as is" explains 36 percent of our UAI, adding humane orientation "as is" increases this to 48 percent, and subsequently adding assertiveness "should be" lifts it to 51 percent.

11. GLOBE's uncertainty avoidance "should be" and our PDI were correlated with $r = +0.702$***, GLOBE's uncertainty avoidance "should be" and our IDV were correlated -0.698***, while GLOBE's uncertainty avoidance "should be" and our UAI were correlated only $+0.37$**. Our UAI and GLOBE's power distance "as is" correlated 0.50***; our UAI and GLOBE's power distance "should be" correlated -0.31*.

12. In a stepwise regression across the forty-eight countries, 48 percent of GLOBE's uncertainty avoidance "as is" was explained by our PDI, adding IDV increased this to 56 percent, and subsequently adding our UAI lifted it to 59 percent.

13. A check was done in which UAI scores per country were computed *controlling for age*. It showed that assuming a constant average age, the country differences remained very similar to those in Table 6.1. See *Culture's Consequences*, 2001, pp. 184–85.

14. Personal communication.

15. Douglas, 1966.

16. Kashima & Kashima, 1998. Across fifty-two countries, the correlation between UAI and having more than one second-person pronoun was $r = 0.43$**.

17. *Culture's Consequences*, 2001, pp. 157 and 191. Rank correlation across nineteen wealthier countries was -0.71***.

18. Standard Eurobarometer 69, 2008. *Very satisfied with the life you lead*. Across twenty-six countries, GNI per capita explained 44 percent of the differences. Across nineteen affluent countries, low UAI explained 43 percent, low MAS an additional 24 percent, and high GNI per capita an additional 9 percent. Flash Eurobarometer 247, 2008. *Very satisfied with family life*. Across twenty-five countries, GNI per cap-

ita explained 64 percent. Across eighteen affluent countries, high GNI per capita explained 59 percent, and low UAI an additional 14 percent. (Calculations courtesy of Marieke de Mooij.)

19. Flash Eurobarometer 247, 2008. *Facing difficulty with the cost of raising children.* Across twenty-five countries, correlation with GNI per capita was $r = 0.66$***. Across eighteen affluent countries, correlation with GNI per capita was $r = -0.54$*; with UAI it was $r = 0.52$*. (Calculations courtesy of Marieke de Mooij.)

20. World Values Survey, 1995–2004. Across forty-seven countries, the correlation between UAI and percentages feeling "very healthy" was $r = 0.60$***.

21. Payer, 1989.

22. Meeuwesen, van den Brink-Muinen, & Hofstede, 2009. The study used video-taped interactions between 307 general practitioners and 5,820 patients in Belgium, Estonia, Germany, Great Britain, the Netherlands, Poland, Romania, Spain, Sweden, and Switzerland.

23. *Human Development Report 1999*, Table 9. Rank correlation of nurses per doctor with UAI was -0.54***.

24. Based on Veenhoven, 1993. See *Culture's Consequences*, 2001, p. 158. Correlation across twenty-one countries was $r = -0.64$**.

25. Correlation of UAI with dispersion of happiness across twenty-six countries was 0.50**. *Culture's Consequences*, 2001, on p.158, erroneously refers to a negative correlation but interprets it correctly.

26. World Values Survey, 1995–2004. Across fifty countries, UAI and percentages "not very happy" correlate with $r = 0.47$***. UAI and percentages "very happy" correlate with $r = -0.30$*.

27. Smith, 2004. The data were from the "As is" section of the GLOBE study. The correlation between overall level of scores and UAI was $r = -0.68$**.

28. Stroebe, 1976, pp. 509–11.

29. For example, the works of Pierre Bourdieu cited in previous chapters.

30. *Culture's Consequences*, 2001, p. 163. The studies were done by Chandler, Shama, Wolf, & Planchard (1981) and by Yan & Gaier (1994) and used an American scale, the Multidimensional-Multiattributional Causality Scale (MMCS). Attributions could be made to ability and effort (internal locus of control), to context (or task), and to luck (external). In spite of the small numbers of countries, the relative tendency to attribute achievement to ability was significantly negatively correlated with UAI (with Chandler et al.'s data $r = -0.87$*, with Yan & Gaier's data -0.91*).

31. de Mooij, 2004, 2010; *Culture's Consequences*, 2001, p. 170; de Mooij & Hofstede, 2002.

32. Special Eurobarometer 298, 2008. *Consumer protection in the Internet market.* Across nineteen prosperous countries, UAI explained 48 percent of differences. (Calculations courtesy of Marieke de Mooij.)

33. Gert Jan Hofstede (2001) analyzed World Bank data for the years when mobile phones came on the market and found a strong relationship with uncertainty avoidance that decreased over time as mobile phones became common in all countries.

34. Flash Eurobarometer 241, 2008. *Information society as seen by EU citizens.* Percentages without access to the Internet across nineteen prosperous EU countries: 61 percent of country differences were explained by UAI. (Calculations courtesy of Marieke de Mooij.)

35. Flash Eurobarometer 243, 2009. *Consumers' view on switching service providers.* Differences among nineteen prosperous EU countries: low UAI explains 46 percent, low MAS an additional 10 percent, and high IDV an additional 10 percent—together 75 percent. (Calculations courtesy of Marieke de Mooij.)

36. Special Eurobarometer 298, 2008. *Consumer protection in the Internet market.* Across nineteen prosperous countries, UAI explained 36 percent of differences, IDV an additional 22 percent. (Calculations courtesy of Marieke de Mooij.)

37. de Mooij, 2004, p. 154.

38. Flash Eurobarometer 247, 2008. Percentages finding it very or fairly "difficult to find the right work-life balance": across twenty-five countries, high UAI explained 42 percent of differences; accross eighteen affluent countries, high UAI explained 53 percent. Converging wealth made culture as an explaining variable more important! (Calculations courtesy of Marieke de Mooij.)

39. d'Iribarne, 1989, pp. 26 and 76.

40. *Culture's Consequences*, 2001, pp. 190 and 192.

41. Horovitz, 1980.

42. *Culture's Consequences*, 2001, p. 167; Shane, 1993.

43. *Culture's Consequences*, 2001, p. 166; Shane, Venkataraman, & Macmillan, 1995.

44. d'Iribarne, 1998.

45. Wildeman, Hofstede, Noorderhaven, Thurik, Verhoeven, & Wennekers, 1999; *Culture's Consequences*, 2001, p. 165. For one country, Great Britain, a longitudinal study proved that people who started businesses for themselves did become more satisfied with their lives than similar people employed by others. For these people at least, the flight from dissatisfaction into self-employment paid off (Blanchflower & Oswald, 1998).

46. *Culture's Consequences*, 2001, pp. 163–65 and 192. The rank correlation coefficient between UAI and McClelland's "need for achievement" scores for 1925 was −0.64***; the multiple correlation coefficient of "need for achievement" with UAI and MAS was $R = 0.73$***. The 1950 ranking of countries does not show any correlation with any of the IBM indexes *nor* with the 1925 ranking of the same countries. A plausible explanation is that only the 1925 stories were like the anthropologists' folktales that McClelland sought to match. In 1950 (after World War II) international communication had increased dramatically, and children's books from this period were more likely to reveal the ideas of innovative educators and less the old traditions.

47. McClelland's "need for affiliation" scores for 1925 were rank correlated positively with IDV ($r = 0.48$**), showing that affiliation is more important if relationships are not predetermined by the social structure. "Need for power" scores for 1925 and scores for all three needs for 1950 did not produce any significant correlations with either IBM indexes or GNI per capita. See *Culture's Consequences*, 2001, p. 192.

48. The data are from Djankov, La Porta, Lopez-de-Silanes, & Shleifer, 2003, and were obtained with the kind help of Professor Erhard Blankenburg, of the Free University of Amsterdam. We found across the sixty-seven countries a Spearman rank correlation of 0.42 for the duration of check collection, 0.40 for tenant eviction, and 0.47 for the mean duration of the two procedures (all beyond the 0.001 level).

49. Almond & Verba, 1963.

50. In Hofstede, 1994a, Chapter 11, Geert published a real-life case study, "Confrontation in the Cathedral," based on an event in 1972 in a secondary school in Lausanne, Switzerland, in which Gert Jan was involved as a student. Another student, a brilliant prize-winner, during a solemn ceremony uses his speaking time to criticize the educational system. The local establishment is profoundly shocked, and the case dramatically escalates.

51. *Culture's Consequences*, 2001, p. 172.

52. Eurobarometer Young Europeans 2007. *Have you done any of the following?* Across nineteen countries, correlation of UAI with "signed a petition" was $r = -0.54**$; with "took part in a public demonstration" it was $r = 0.41*$. (Calculations courtesy of Marieke de Mooij.)

53. Aberbach & Putnam, 1977; *Culture's Consequences*, 2001, p. 173.

54. Based on data from the 1990–93 World Values Survey and the 1994 Eurobarometer; see *Culture's Consequences*, 2001, pp. 171 and 174.

55. Personal communication.

56. Levine, Norenzayan, & Philbrick, 2001; Hofstede, 2001b. Rank correlation with UAI was $0.59**$.

57. *Culture's Consequences*, 2001, p. 172, and *NRC Handelsblad*, September 28, 2001. Contrary to what was mentioned in *Culture's Consequences*, there is no identity card obligation in Austria; in the Netherlands it was reintroduced in 2005. This lowers the correlation to $0.75**$.

58. *Culture's Consequences*, 2001, p. 129.

59. Georges Brassens: *La mauvaise réputation*; Pierre Chastellain: *La recherche infinie*; Catherine Leforestier: *Normal*; Henri Tachan: *Serpents à sornettes*.

60. The correlation between wealth and CPI was $r = 0.85***$. Wealthier countries were those with a PPP (purchasing power parity) per capita in 2005 above 13,300 U.S. dollars; cleaner countries were those with a 2008 CPI of 5.0 or higher. Poorer but rated cleaner than average were Chile, Uruguay, Malaysia, and Costa Rica. Wealthier but rated more corrupt than average were Italy, Greece, Lithuania, Poland, and Argentina.

61. Countries with a 2005 PPP per capita of more than 18,000 U.S. dollars. The correlation coefficient was $r = 0.73***$.

62. Because of the wide gaps in wealth between rich and poor exporters, we used rank correlations. Across the twenty-two countries, the rank correlation coefficients (Spearman) of BPI 2008 with 2005 PPP per capita is $\rho = 0.79***$; with PDI, $\rho = -0.72***$. Wealth explains 64 percent of BPI differences; wealth plus PDI explains 76 percent.

63. Personal communication from "Anneke" and her parents.

64. One of the exceptions was Bruno Kreisky, the leader of the socialist majority party who for many years was the chancellor (prime minister). Paradoxically, Kreisky was enormously popular among large groups of the Austrian population.

65. *Culture's Consequences*, 2001, pp. 175 and 196.

66. *Culture's Consequences*, 2001, p. 200.

67. Paul Schnabel in *NRC Handelsblad*, December 23, 1989.

68. According to the U.S. author on mythology Joseph Campbell, religion is rooted in science. The present world religions reflect the state of science at the time they were founded, thousands of years ago. Campbell, 1988 [1972], p. 90.

69. *Deduction*: reasoning from a known principle to a logical conclusion. *Induction*: reaching a general conclusion by inference from particular facts.

70. Observations from Marieke de Mooij in an unpublished conference paper, "The Reflection of Values of National Culture in Literature," September 2000.

71. *Culture's Consequences*, 2001, p. 201.

72. Lynn, 1975; *Culture's Consequences*, 2001, p. 182. Lynn computed scores for 1935, 1950, 1955, 1960, 1965, and 1970; data for 1940 and 1945 were missing because of World War II.

Chapter 7

1. Cao, 1980 [1760], vol. 3, p. 69.

2. Chinese Culture Connection, 1987.

3. Across all twenty-three countries, the new dimension correlated with economic growth during 1965–85 with $r = 0.64$**; with economic growth during 1985–95 with $r = 0.70$***. See Hofstede & Bond, 1988; *Culture's Consequences*, 2001, p. 367.

4. This refutes a criticism by Fang (2003), who, as an insider of Chinese culture, argues that our combining these values into a dimension does not make Chinese sense. As Geert argued in *Culture's Consequences*, 2001, p.17, eco-logic differs from individual logic: "One point that anthropologists have always made is that aspects of social life which do not seem to be related to each other, actually are related" (Harris, 1981, p. 8).

5. Michael Bond had earlier described the positive pole as "Confucian work dynamism." In Hofstede & Bond, 1988, the dimension was called "Confucian Dynamism." As country scores on the dimension were collected from all inhabited continents, mostly from respondents who never heard of Confucius, Geert in his ensuing book chose a label referring to the nature of the values involved, rather than to the origin of the questionnaire.

6. In the 1980s communication between Chinese universities and Western researchers was still laborious, and the Chinese data came in only after the scores for the other countries had already been put into a 0–100 scale. This explains the score value 118 for China.

7. The Values Survey Module 1994 included four LTO items, but in replications only two produced answers consistent with those of the CVS respondents. We also used an index correlated with LTO, Read's (1993) marginal propensity to save, for extrapolating to a number of countries not in the CVS.

8. Elias, 1969, pp. 336–41.

9. Schneider & Lysgaard (1953) in a survey of U.S. high school students showed that deferment of gratification increased with the occupational class of the parents.

10. Levine, Sato, Hashimoto, & Verma, 1995; *Culture's Consequences*, 2001, p. 360.

11. *Culture's Consequences*, 2001, pp. 360–61.

12. Best & Williams, 1996; *Culture's Consequences*, 2001, p. 361.

13. *Culture's Consequences*, 2001, p. 359; Hill & Romm, 1996. Their study also included mothers from Israel, whose answers were somewhere in between those from the two Australian groups.

14. Bond & Wang, 1983, p. 60.

15. Chew-Lim, 1997, p. 98.

16. From the *Li Chi*, a collection of writings of the disciples of Confucius codified around 100 B.C.; in Watts, 1979, p. 83.

17. Wirthlin Worldwide, 1996.

18. *Culture's Consequences*, 2001, p. 356. The correlation with 1993 WVS data across eleven countries was −0.51*. Leisure time was rated very important by 68 percent of respondents in Nigeria and by 14 percent in China.

19. Mamman & Saffu, 1998.

20. See Chapter 9 and Hofstede, van Deusen, Mueller, Charles, & the Business Goals Network, 2002, p. 800. The multiple correlation across twelve overlapping countries was $R = 0.62*$.

21. Redding, 1990, p. 209.

22. Hastings & Hastings, 1981. The correlation across eleven countries was 0.69**.

23. Yeung & Tung, 1996.

24. Across the nineteen countries for which 2002 data were available, BPI and LTO were correlated with −0.67**, high-LTO countries more often paying bribes.

25. Herman Vuijsje, "Twee koffie, twee koekjes," in *NRC Handelsblad*, April 16, 1988. Quotes translated by GH.

26. *Culture's Consequences*, 2001, p. 363.

27. Data from an article by Rob Schoof in *NRC Handelsblad*, January 18, 2003, based on information from the International Center for Prison Studies, King's College, London.

28. Campbell, 1988 [1972], pp. 71–75.

29. Hastings & Hastings, 1981; *Culture's Consequences*, 2001, p. 361.

30. Worm, 1997, p. 52, citing the 1936 book *My Country and My People*, by the Chinese author Lin Yutang.

31. Carr, Munro, & Bishop, 1996.

32. Gao, Ting-Toomey, & Gudykunst, 1996, p. 293.

33. Kim, 1995, p. 663.

34. Yukawa Hideki, in Moore, 1967, p. 290.

35. Minkov (2007) uses the spelling "flexumility"; we reintroduced the *h* to allow use of the adjective *flexhumble*.

36. Correlation $r = -0.65**$ across twenty-two of the twenty-three CVS countries (all except Thailand, for which the necessary WVS data were not available).

37. In the new, 2008 version of the Values Survey Module (VSM08), we included both monumentalism and long-term orientation items, expecting they might merge into one dimension.

38. Heine, 2003; Minkov, 2007, pp. 164ff.

39. "Service to others" appeared only in the WVS prior to 2005. For the sake of consistency, Misho excluded the 2005–08 wave for all three items. From the 1995–2004 period, he used the latest data for each item.

40. We followed Misho's method, which he borrowed from Inglehart: using percentages of people who selected a particular position on the item scale, not national averages. In accordance with that method, we used the positive extremes: percentages of people who selected options such as "very important," "very proud," or "very much like me." The reason for adopting this method is that when it is used with nationally representative samples, it appears to yield results having the highest predictive powers with respect to many external variables.

41. The correlations between these items and LTO-CVS were as follows: thrift $r = 0.53$ ($p = 0.013$, $n = 21$); national pride $r = -0.64$ ($p = 0.002$, $n = 21$); service to others $r = -0.70$ ($p = 0.008$, $n = 13$).

42. Factor-analyzed, the three items yielded a single factor with an eigenvalue of 2.10, explaining 70 percent of the variance. The item loadings were as follows: service to others 0.94; national pride 0.86; thrift for children -0.70. Because service to others had quite a few missing values, we used linear regression on the two other variables to predict the missing factor scores. Both items were significant predictors in stepwise regression with a highly reliable cumulative R^2 of 0.97. After adding the predicted scores to those obtained from the factor analysis, we transferred the scores to a 0–100 scale, reversing the sign.

43. As mentioned in note 39, Misho excluded the 2005–08 wave. For nine countries for which one or more scores from 1994–2004 were missing but 2005–08 data were available, we used the latter anyway. In Table 7.4 these countries are marked with an asterisk (*).

44. Across twenty-one common cases, $r = 0.72***$ (excluding Hong Kong and Thailand, for which missing data in the 1995–2004 period had been replaced by data from 2005–08).

45. Importance of tradition was measured in the 2005–08 wave of the WVS with item v89, which—as with the other items in the same section—is based on the work of Shalom Schwartz. Item v89 is worded as follows: "Using this card, would you please indicate for each description whether that person is very much like you, like you, somewhat like you, not like you, or not at all like you? (Code one answer for each description): Tradition is important to this person: to follow the customs handed down by one's religion or family." Our new measure of LTO correlates with the percentages of respondents who chose "very much like me" at $r = -0.56***$ ($n = 37$). Importance of perseverance is measured in the WVS as a desirable trait for children, just like "thrift" in our new LTO score. The item is coded as A039 prior to 2005 and v18 afterward.

LTO-WVS correlates at $r = 0.49$*** with A039 ($n = 83$) and at $r = 0.49$** with v18 ($n = 41$).

46. Across the fifty-seven countries for which Minkov (2007) provides monumentalism scores, these are correlated with LTO-WVS with $r = -0.85$***.

47. Across sixty-three common countries, the correlations between LTO-WVS and the IBM dimensions were as follows: with PDI $r = 0.05$, with IDV 0.08, with MAS 0.03, with UAI -0.04.

48. Across eighty-eight common countries, the correlation between LTO-WVS and 2005 national wealth at PPP was $r = 0.28$** ($p = 0.009$).

49. Rank correlation (Spearman) $\rho = 0.85$*** ($n = 17$).

50. LTO-CVS correlated with performance orientation "should be" with $r = -0.73$***. In a stepwise regression, only this dimension remained.

51. LTO-WVS correlated with performance orientation "should be" with $r = -0.46$** and with group collectivism "should be" with -0.49***. A stepwise regression produced a confusing pattern: group collectivism "should be" negative 22 percent, adding institutional collectivism "as is" positive 35 percent, humane orientation "as is" negative 47 percent, and power distance "as is" positive 51 percent (based on adjusted R^2).

52. Future orientation "as is" correlated with UAI with $r = -0.60$*** and with PDI with -0.38**. In a stepwise regression, UAI explained 34 percent of the variance, and UAI plus (low) PDI together explained 40 percent (based on adjusted R^2).

53. Future orientation "should be" correlated with PDI with $r = 0.47$** and with LTO-WVS with -0.33*. In a stepwise regression, PDI explained 17 percent of the variance, and PDI plus (low) LTO-CVS together explained 23 percent (based on adjusted R^2). Across fifty-three countries, future orientation "as is" and "should be" were negatively correlated: $r = -0.47$***.

54. Based on Etcoff, Orbach, Scott, & Agostino, 2006. Correlation of LTO-WVS with "My mother has positively influenced my feelings about myself and beauty" $r = -0.80$**; with "My mother's ideas of beauty have shaped my own" $r = -0.57$* ($n = 10$). (Calculations courtesy of Marieke de Mooij.)

55. *Culture's Consequences*, 2001, p. 365.

56. Minkov, 2007, 2008.

57. Yan & Gaier, 1994; Stevenson & Lee, 1996, p. 136.

58. Correlations of LTO-CVS were $r = 0.82$** ($n = 11$, $p = 0.002$) with fourth-grade math and 0.57 ($n = 11$, $p = 0.065$) with fourth-grade science; 0.65* ($n = 10$, $p = 0.043$) with eighth-grade math and 0.42 ($n = 10$, $p = 0.230$) with eighth-grade science. Controlling for 2005 GNI per capita at PPP made the contrast even stronger. And this while the correlations between math and science performance were 0.93*** for both age groups!

59. Correlations of LTO-WVS were $r = 0.70$*** with fourth-grade math ($n = 30$) and 0.66*** ($n = 30$) with fourth-grade science; $r = 0.73$*** ($n = 36$) with eighth-grade math and 0.68*** ($n = 36$) with eighth-grade science.

60. After controlling for 2005 GNI per capita at PPP, the correlations of LTO-WVS with math and science performance of fourth-grade students became insignificant.

Only the correlations for eighth-grade students remained significant, with the effect on math still stronger than on science.

61. Hofstede, 1986; Biggs, 1996.

62. G. J. Hofstede, 1995.

63. Redding, 1980, pp. 196–97.

64. Chenery & Strout, 1966.

65. Colombia's GNI per capita was \$340 in 1970 and \$2,080 in 2000. In South Korea the figures were \$250 in 1970 and \$8,910 in 2000 (World Bank, 1972; World Development Report, 2002).

66. Kahn, 1979.

67. See note 3. Across all twenty-three CVS countries, the new dimension correlated with growth in GNI per capita from 1965 to 1985 with $r = 0.64**$; with growth from 1985 to 1995 with $r = 0.70***$.

68. Across seventy countries for which data were available, LTO-WVS correlated with growth in GNI per capita from 1970 to 1995 with $r = 0.52***$. The rank correlation coefficient that reduces the effect of extreme scores was $\rho = 0.34**$. We combined 1970 data for the Soviet Union with 1995 Russia, 1970 Yugoslavia with 1995 Serbia and Montenegro, and 1979 Czechoslovakia with 1995 Czech Republic.

69. Across eighty-four countries, LTO-WVS correlated with growth in GNI per capita from 1995 to 2000 with $r = 0.10$; the rank correlation ρ was 0.12.

70. Ranked by 1995 GNI per capita, the list of eighty-four countries showed a gap in the middle that formed a natural split between fifty-four poor countries, from Tanzania with \$120 to Uruguay with \$5,170, and thirty wealthy countries, from Argentina with \$8,030 to Luxembourg with \$41,210.

71. The wealthy countries were Argentina, Australia, Austria, Belgium, Canada, Denmark, Finland, France, Germany, Great Britain, Greece, Hong Kong, Iceland, Ireland, Israel, Italy, Japan, Korea, Luxembourg, the Netherlands, New Zealand, Norway, Portugal, Singapore, Slovenia, Spain, Sweden, Switzerland, Taiwan, and the United States. Figure 7.1 contains separate regression lines for these thirty countries and for the fifty-four poor countries, which demonstrate the reversal of correlation. The difference in correlation coefficients is strongest if we use the Spearman rank correlation coefficient ρ, which reduces the influence of extreme cases of the GNI per capita ratio. Across the rich countries, $\rho = -0.46*$ ($p = 0.011$). Across the poor countries, $\rho = 0.32*$ ($p = 0.018$).

72. Minkov & Blagoev, 2009. Their article inspired the present section.

73. Read, 1993. The correlation between LTO and MPS across the twenty-three CVS countries was $r = 0.58**$.

74. de Mooij, 2004. The rank correlations across fifteen countries were 0.43 for real estate (nearly significant, 0.054 level) and $-0.66**$ for mutual funds.

75. Ben Knapen in *NRC Handelsblad*, February 9, 1989. Back-translated from the Dutch by GH.

76. World Development Reports 1977 and 2009.

77. Hofstede & Bond, 1988, p. 19.

78. McDonald & Robinson, 2009.

79. Russell, 1976 [1952], p. 101.

80. Lewis, 1982, pp. 297, 229, 224, 168, and 302.

81. Adapted from Hofstede, 1994b.

82. http://aneki.com/countries.

83. van der Veen, 2002, pp. 171–75.

84. Active from 1980 to 2004, most recently in Tilburg.

85. Noorderhaven & Tidjani, 2001.

86. The article by Noorderhaven & Tidjani refers to eight factors, but they split the first and strongest factor again into three subfactors. Our interpretation of factors 3 through 6 differs slightly from Noorderhaven & Tidjani, but it is based on the same data.

87. *Culture's Consequences*, 2001, pp. 369–70. The correlation across the ten countries for which LTO-CVS scores were available was −0.95***.

88. Stiglitz, 2002.

89. Research by Ray Simonsen. See *Culture's Consequences*, 2001, p. 501.

90. Kelen, 1983 [1971], p. 44.

91. Helgesen & Kim, 2002, pp. 28–29.

92. Helgesen & Kim, 2002, pp. 8–9.

Chapter 8

1. *The Economist*, December 22, 2001.

2. Rice & Steele, 2004.

3. Diener & Diener, 1995. The two aspects of SWB are often called "cognitive" and "hedonic."

4. Veenhoven, 1993.

5. Minkov, 2009.

6. For a fairly exhaustive list, see Minkov, 2009.

7. Inglehart & Baker, 2000. More precisely, Inglehart used the percentage of respondents who stated they were *not* very happy. Instead of "well-being," Inglehart's later publications use "self-expression."

8. Extreme response style—the tendency of some nations to systematically prefer the extreme positive position, regardless of the content of the question, when presented with a number of choices (such as "very happy, quite happy, not very happy, not at all happy")—does not seem to play a role in this case. Minkov (2009) shows that precisely the extreme position of the happiness item in the WVS yields the highest correlations with many external variables. Therefore, it is the most meaningful, rather than the least.

9. Minkov, 2009. Results of factor analysis always depend on the particular variables included. Because there is no single right way to choose items for analysis, the process inevitably involves some subjectivity.

10. The average scores are statistically the same as the percentage choosing 6 or higher on the scale.

11. In the WVS studies between 1995 and 2004, these items were coded as follows: happiness was A008, life control was A173, and importance of leisure was A003. In

the 2005–08 study, happiness was v10, life control was v46, and importance of leisure was v6.

12. Minkov, 2007.

13. The scores were calculated after averaging each country's score from 1995–2004 and 2005–08. For countries that were studied only once, we used their single scores for each item. Then, the average country scores for the three items were factor-analyzed. They yielded a single factor with the following loadings: very happy 0.87, average life control 0.84, leisure very important 0.84. Finally, the factor scores were converted into scores on a 0–100 scale.

14. Pelto, 1968; Earley, 1997, p. 53; Triandis, 2002.

15. *Culture's Consequences*, 2001, pp. 176 and 207.

16. Across sixty-two overlapping countries, the correlation of IVR with PDI was $r = -0.30*$. The correlations between IVR and the other three Hofstede dimensions were not significant: with IDV 0.16, with MAS 0.07, with UAI -0.06. Across the twenty-three countries in the Chinese Value Survey, IVR and LTO-CVS correlated with $r = -0.30$ ($p = 0.17$).

17. The correlation of IVR with LTO-WVS was $r = -0.45***$, both across all ninety-one common countries and, excluding the extrapolated values of LTO-WVS, across eighty-two countries.

18. Across eighty-seven countries, the correlation of IVR with 2005 GNI per capita at PPP was $r = 0.32**$ ($p = 0.002$).

19. Kuppens, Ceulemans, Timmerman, Diener, & Kim-Prieto, 2006.

20. Across forty-five common countries, $r = 0.65***$.

21. Data from Schimmack, Oishi, & Diener, 2002, Table 1, p. 709. Correlation across thirty-six common countries, $r = 0.49*$.

22. Chinese Culture Connection, 1987, p. 151.

23. See Chapter 3, note 11. Because of the larger number of common countries (twenty-two), the correlation of moral discipline with IVR is stronger than with PDI and IDV: $r = -0.54***$.

24. Bond et al., 2004.

25. Across thirty-nine common countries, $r = -0.49**$.

26. Across thirty-four countries, the indulgence scores correlate with extraversion (McCrae, 2002) at $r = 0.42*$ and with neuroticism at $-0.46**$.

27. Across seventy-nine countries, the correlation between indulgence and the percentages of respondents who described their health as "very good" (1995–2004) is $r = 0.67***$. Across twenty-two wealthy countries, this correlation is $r = 0.78***$.

28. Data are from Pew Research Center, 2007, q4. Correlation across thirty-nine common countries, $r = 0.54***$.

29. Across the twenty-eight wealthy countries, the zero-order correlation between indulgence and total fertility rates between 2005 and 2010 (data from UN Statistics Division, 2009) is $0.63***$. In stepwise regression, indulgence explains 42 percent of variance in fertility rates, and differences in education (UNDP education index in UNDP, 2006) explain an additional 21 percent, whereas differences in wealth do not explain anything.

30. The correlation between indulgence and age-standardized mortality rate for cardiovascular diseases per 100,000 population in 2002 (data from World Health Organization, 2008) is −0.60*** ($n = 88$). After controlling for GNI per capita in 1999, a significant correlation of −0.41 remains.

31. Flash Eurobarometer 247, 2008. *Family life*, twenty-five EU countries (all except Cyprus and Luxembourg). Percentage of those who are very satisfied with family life, $r = 0.91$***. Difficulties in daily life faced by families: percentage of those choosing unequal sharing of household tasks between partners, $r = 0.45$*.

32. Flash Eurobarometer 241, 2008. *Information society as seen by EU citizens*, twenty-five EU countries. Percentage of those who participate in sports every day plus percentage of those who participate at least once a week, $r = 0.82$***.

33. Eurobarometer 278, 2007. *European cultural values*, twenty-five EU countries. Percentage of those who exchange e-mails with family, friends, and colleagues, $r = 0.53$** ; percentage who conduct e-mail or Internet communications with foreigners, $r = 0.69$***.

34. Euromonitor 1997. *Consumption of various food and drink products in 1996*, fourteen European countries plus twenty-four other countries worldwide. IVR correlates negatively with consumption of fish ($r = -0.48$***) and positively with consumption of carbonated drinks ($r = 0.62$***); it appears in a stepwise regression for consumption of beer (after low PDI) and all soft drinks (after GNI per capita and MAS).

35. The zero-order correlation between indulgence and obesity in these twenty-six rich countries (average national rates calculated on the bases of data for men and women in World Health Organization, 2005) is 0.39*. Controlling for GNI per capita at PPP in 1999 raises this correlation to 0.48*.

36. Across forty-nine countries, the correlation of IVR with gender egalitarianism "should be" was $r = 0.49$***.

37. Correlation of IVR with in-group collectivism "as is" $r = -0.46$** and with in-group collectivism "should be" $r = 0.42$**.

38. Correlation of IVR with performance orientation "should be" $r = 0.35$* and with assertiveness "should be" $r = -0.29$*.

39. Schmitt, 2005, p. 247.

40. Sociosexuality scores from Schmitt, 2005. The correlation is 0.45* for men's mean national scores and 0.54** for women's.

41. Item F131, correlation across thirty-four countries, $r = 0.52$**.

42. Myasoedov, 2003.

43. The smile norm dates from the amateur photography era. Before that, exposure times were too long for smiles to look natural.

44. Item E003.

45. Across eighty-three countries, $r = -0.46$***.

46. Across eighty-three countries, $r = 0.62$***. The freedom-of-speech item is also positively correlated with power distance and individualism. However, in stepwise linear-regression analysis, the only significant predictors of freedom of speech as a first national goal are power distance and indulgence.

47. Standard Eurobarometer 69, 2008. *European values*, twenty-five EU member states plus Turkey. Correlation of IVR with percentage who chose "freedom of speech" among goals to be pursued for the future, $r = 0.75***$. Correlation with percentage who chose "democracy" as most important in connection with their idea of happiness, $r = 0.59***$. (Calculations courtesy of Marieke de Mooij.)

48. Data from UN Office on Drugs and Crime, 2004. The correlation between indulgence and police officers per 100,000 inhabitants is $-0.42***$. None of the other dimensions discussed in this book yields a higher correlation with this variable.

49. Minkov, 2007, 2009.

50. Diener & Tov, 2007.

Chapter 9

1. Pugh & Hickson, 1976.

2. Negandhi & Prasad, 1971, p. 128.

3. van Oudenhoven, 2001. The countries were Belgium, Canada, Denmark, France, Germany, Greece, the Netherlands, Spain, the United Kingdom, and the United States.

4. *Culture's Consequences*, 2001, p. 378. The correlations were bureaucracy with PDI $r = 0.66*$ and with UAI $0.63*$; individual work with IDV 0.47; hostile work ambience with MAS 0.49, both $p < 0.10$.

5. In 2005 the Dutch parliament voted in favor of a system change that involved replacing the appointed mayor by an elected mayor, but the proposal was stranded in the senate.

6. Mouritzen & Svara, 2002, pp. 55–56 and 75.

7. Fayol, 1970 [1916], p. 21. Translation by GH.

8. Weber, 1976 [1930], p. 224.

9. Weber, 1970 [1948], p. 196. Translated from *Wirtschaft und Gesellschaft*, 1921, Part III, Chapter 6, p. 650.

10. Fayol, 1970 [1916], p. 85.

11. Laurent, 1981, pp. 101–14.

12. From a paper presented in 1925, in Metcalf & Urwick, 1940, pp. 58–59.

13. Confucian values were also evident in Sun Yat-sen's extension of the *trias politica*: the examination and control branches had to guarantee the virtue of the civil servants.

14. Williamson, 1975.

15. Ouchi, 1980, pp. 129–41.

16. Kieser & Kubicek, 1983.

17. Crozier & Friedberg, 1977; Pagès, Bonetti, de Gaulejac, & Descendre, 1979.

18. Mintzberg, 1983. Later on (Mintzberg, 1989), the author added a "missionary configuration" with "standardization of norms." To us, this is an aspect of the other types rather than a type by itself. It deals with the "strength" of an organization's culture, which will be discussed in Chapter 10.

19. Mintzberg, 1983, pp. 34–35.

20. As described in a French classic: organization sociologist Michel Crozier's *The Bureaucratic Phenomenon* (Crozier, 1964).

21. Mintzberg, 1993.

22. *Culture's Consequences*, 2001, p. 382.

23. Harzing & Sorge, 2003, based on nearly three hundred foreign subsidiaries in twenty-two countries, from more than one hundred multinationals originating from nine countries in eight industries. Their article does not describe in what way the home cultures affect the control process, but an obvious hypothesis is that home-country uncertainty avoidance affects impersonal control by systems, while home-country power distance affects personal control by expatriates.

24. Hypotheses for research on the subject have been formulated by Gray, 1988, pp. 1–15.

25. Gambling, 1977, pp. 141–51.

26. Cleverley, 1971.

27. Hofstede, 1967.

28. Morakul & Wu, 2001.

29. Baker, 1976, pp. 886–93.

30. Hofstede, 1978.

31. Pedersen & Thomsen, 1997. The countries were Austria, Belgium, Denmark, Finland, France, Germany, Italy, the Netherlands, Norway, Spain, Sweden, and the United Kingdom.

32. The correlation was $r = 0.65^*$.

33. The correlation was $r = 0.52^*$. See *Culture's Consequences*, 2001, p. 384.

34. In spite of the Austrian score, the correlation was $r = -0.77^{**}$.

35. Semenov, 2000. The countries were the same as in the study by Pedersen & Thomsen plus Australia, Canada, Ireland, New Zealand, and the United States.

36. Weimer, 1995, p. 336; *Culture's Consequences*, 2001, p. 385.

37. Hofstede, van Deusen, Mueller, Charles, & the Business Goals Network, 2002. Data about China were supplied by Chinese students with work experience in their country but who were studying in Australia and the United States; data from Denmark (Århus, $n = 62$) were added in 2002 (see Hofstede, 2007b).

38. Through a factor analysis of the fifteen goals × seventeen countries matrix: five almost equally strong factors explained 78 percent of the variance.

39. LTO-CVS, $r = -0.59^*$, $n = 13$.

40. The countries' factor scores on cluster 5 correlated with their order of similarity to the average ranking with $r = 0.73^{***}$.

41. An exception is the Dutch scholar Manfred Kets de Vries, who analyzed the behavior of managers in Freudian terms (e.g., Kets de Vries, 2001).

42. Herzberg, Mausner, & Snyderman, 1959.

43. McGregor, 1960. The following part is based on Hofstede, 1988, and *Culture's Consequences*, 2001, p. 387.

44. Schuler & Rogovsky, 1998; *Culture's Consequences*, 2001, pp. 387–88.

45. *The Ruler*, Machiavelli, 1955 [1517].

46. *Culture's Consequences*, 2001, p. 388.

47. Jackofsky & Slocum, 1988; *Culture's Consequences,* 2001, p. 388.

48. Tollgerdt-Andersson, 1996. The countries were Denmark, France, Germany, Italy, Norway, Spain, Sweden, and the United Kingdom. The percentages were correlated with UAI: -0.86** and with UAI plus MAS: -0.95***.

49. *Culture's Consequences,* 2001, pp. 388–89.

50. Triandis, 1973, p. 165.

51. *Culture's Consequences,* 2001, p. 389.

52. Klidas, 2001.

53. McGregor, 1960; Blake & Mouton, 1964; Likert, 1967.

54. Jenkins, 1973, p. 258; the lecturer was Frederick Herzberg.

55. Triandis, 1973, pp. 55–68.

56. Hoppe & Bhagat, 2007.

57. Laaksonen, 1977.

58. *Culture's Consequences,* 2001, p. 391.

59. Drucker, 1955, Chapter 11.

60. *Führung durch Zielvereinbarung;* Ferguson, 1973, p. 15.

61. Franck, 1973. Translation by GH.

62. *Culture's Consequences,* 2001, p. 390.

63. Inspired by Magalhaes, 1984, and by discussions with Anne-Marie Bouvy and Giorgio Inzerilli.

64. Hofstede, 1980b; comments by Goodstein, 1981, and by Hunt, 1981, and a reply by Hofstede, 1981a. An amusing detail is that in the final version of the article a number of changes had been made at the request of the editor, but by an administrative error the original, unchanged version got published.

65. Pascal, *Pensées,* 60, 294: "Vérité en-deça des Pyrenées, erreur au-delà." Montaigne, *Essais* II, XII, 34: "Quelle vérité que ces montagnes bornent, qui est mensonge au monde qui se tient au delà?" ("What kind of a truth is this that is bounded by a chain of mountains and is falsehood to the people living on the other side?" Translation by GH.)

66. "There is nothing as practical as a good theory," attributed to Kurt Lewin.

67. Peterson & Hunt, 1997, p. 214.

68. Stewart, 1985, p. 209.

69. Locke, 1996.

70. Generally felt in Europe but proved by Baruch, 2001, based on an analysis of the location of almost two thousand authors in more than one thousand articles in seven top management journals.

71. Pugh & Hickson, 1993; Hickson & Pugh, 2001, p. 8.

72. Porter, 1990. For critiques of Porter's ethnocentrism, see van den Bosch & van Prooijen, 1992, with an answer by Porter, 1992; Davies & Ellis, 2000; Barney, 2002, p. 54.

73. In the Social Science Citation Index the most cited psychologists are all Americans; the most cited sociologists are nearly all Europeans, in spite of the fact that the SSCI is mainly based on U.S. journals.

74. Bourdieu & Wacquant, 1992, pp. 45 and 115.

75. Hofstede, 1996a; *Culture's Consequences,* 2001, p. 381. In an article published in 2000, Williamson committed himself to the New Institutional Economics, which does have a place for culture but not necessarily for national constraints on theories.

Chapter 10

1. This case is derived from Hofstede, Neuijen, Ohayv, & Sanders, 1990. The remainder of this chapter also draws heavily on this paper.

2. Deal & Kennedy, 1982; Peters & Waterman, 1982.

3. Peters & Waterman, 1982, pp. 75–76.

4. See, for example, the critiques of Wilkins & Ouchi, 1983, p. 477; Schein, 1985, p. 315; Weick, 1985, p. 385; and Saffold, 1988.

5. Pagès, Bonetti, de Gaulejac, & Descendre, 1979.

6. This is also noticeable in French organization sociology, such as in the work of Crozier, 1964, and Crozier & Friedberg, 1977.

7. Soeters, 1986; Lammers, 1988.

8. For example, in Westerlund & Sjöstrand, 1975; March & Olsen, 1976; Broms & Gahmberg, 1983; Brunsson, 1985.

9. Alvesson, 2002, pp. 38–39.

10. Smircich, 1983.

11. What we call *practices* can also be labeled *conventions, customs, habits, mores, traditions,* or *usages.* They were recognized as part of culture already by the British pioneer anthropologist Edward Tylor (1924 [1871]): "Culture is that complex whole which includes knowledge, beliefs, art, morals, law, customs and any other capabilities and habits acquired by man as a member of society."

12. Inglehart, Basañez, & Moreno, 1998; Halman, 2001; worldvaluessurvey.org.

13. Harzing & Sorge, 2003.

14. Soeters & Schreuder, 1986.

15. Carlzon, 1987.

16. A *Hawthorne effect* means that employees selected for an experiment are so motivated by their being selected that this alone guarantees the experiment's success. It is named after the Hawthorne plant of Western Electric Co., in the United States, where Professor Elton Mayo in the 1920s and 1930s conducted a series of classic experiments in work organization.

17. In a factor analysis of only these $6 \times 3 = 18$ questions for the twenty units, they accounted for 86 percent of the variance in mean scores among units.

18. Culture strength was statistically operationalized as the mean standard deviation, across the individuals within a unit, of scores on the eighteen key practices questions (three per dimension): a low standard deviation meaning a strong culture. Actual mean standard deviations varied from 0.87 to 1.08, and the Spearman rank order correlation between these mean standard deviations and the twenty units' scores on results orientation was $\rho = -0.71$***.

19. Blake & Mouton, 1964.

20. Merton, 1968 [1949].

21. Crossing forty characteristics with six dimensions, one can expect by chance two or three correlations significant at the 0.01 level and twelve at the 0.05 level. In fact, there were fifteen correlations at the 0.01 level and beyond and twenty-eight at the 0.05 level. Chance, therefore, could account for only a minor part of the relationships found.

22. Pugh & Hickson, 1976.

23. Correlated $r = 0.78***$.

24. *Culture's Consequences*, 2001, pp. 405–8.

25. Hofstede, Bond, & Luk, 1993; *Culture's Consequences*, 2001, pp. 411–13.

26. McCrae & John, 1992.

27. Hofstede & McCrae, 2004. Across the thirty-three countries, all five culture dimensions were significantly associated with at least one personality factor. However, in multiple regressions of the personality scores against the five culture dimensions, only the original four IBM dimensions remained; the correlations of personality with long-term orientation disappeared after the first four culture dimensions were controlled for.

28. *Culture's Consequences*, 2001, p. 210.

29. Hofstede, 2007a.

30. *Culture's Consequences*, 2001, pp. 413–14; Hofstede, 1995, p. 216.

31. *Culture's Consequences*, 2001, pp. 414–15.

32. Soeters, 2000, pp. 465–66, found common occupational cultures in uniformed occupations: police, armed forces, and fire brigade, all of whom are relatively isolated from their societies.

33. Sanders & van der Veen, 1998, reported on the reuse of the IRIC questionnaire in intensive care units in hospitals in twelve countries. Unit cultures varied along four dimensions: the numbers 1, 2, and 4 from the IRIC study, plus a dimension of high versus low need for security. A custom-designed questionnaire, based on interviews within the units, might have produced additional, maybe new, dimensions.

34. Swiss management consultant Cuno Pümpin has described a model with seven dimensions, of which five are similar to those found in the IRIC project (results orientation, employee orientation, company orientation, cost orientation, and customer orientation); his publications do not explain how these dimensions were found (Pümpin, 1984; Pümpin, Kobi, & Wüthrich, 1985). In India, Professor Pradip Khandwalla, 1985, in a study of managers across seventy-five organizations, using five-point survey questions similar to our "Where I work . . ." questions, found a first factor closely resembling our process versus results orientation.

35. The article by Hofstede, Neuijen, Ohayv, & Sanders, 1990, lists the content of the questions used to compute the indexes in the IRIC study.

36. This is simpler than McKinsey consultants' "7-S" framework: Structure, Strategy, Systems, Shared values, Skills, Style, and Staff (Peters & Waterman, 1982, p. 10).

37. Witte, 1973. A summary in English appeared in Witte, 1977.

38. Doctoral research by van Nimwegen (2002) analyzed the differences in interpretation and implications of the corporate values of an international bank in nineteen

country subsidiaries; his is one of the major replications of the IBM survey cited in Chapter 2.

Chapter 11

1. Morier, 1923 [1824]. The quote from the text is from pp. 434–35; the quote from the editor is from p. vi.

2. This paragraph was inspired by Campbell, 1988 [1972], pp. 174–206.

3. van der Veen, 2002.

4. For a review of studies with regard to culture shock, see Ward, Bochner, & Furnham, 2001.

5. Harzing, 1995, 2001; Tung, 1982, pp. 57–71.

6. U.S. Professor Howard V. Perlmutter developed the sequence *ethnocentric, polycentric, geocentric* as three phases in the development of a multinational business corporation. In the case of a host population, it is unlikely that they will ever become "geocentric"—abolishing all nation-specific standards.

7. Hofstede, 1994a, Chapter 15.

8. Peterson & Pike, 2002.

9. In cultural anthropology the phenomenon that our thinking is influenced by our language is known as the Sapir-Whorf theorem, after Edward Sapir and Benjamin Lee Whorf, who formulated it.

10. Attributed to Henry Louis Mencken (1880–1956), U.S. critic and satirist.

11. *Culture's Consequences*, 2001, pp. 63–65.

12. From a speech by R. M. Hadjiwibowo, September 1983. Translation from the Dutch by GH with suggestions by the author.

13. This section uses extracts from Hofstede, 1986.

14. Taiwan, Hong Kong, and Macau use the traditional script, in which a character may contain up to twenty-three strokes. Mainland China and Singapore use a simplified version, which to a non-Chinese person is still highly complex.

15. Bel Ghazi, 1982, p. 82. Translation from the Dutch by GH.

16. For a review of relevant research, see *Culture's Consequences*, 2001, pp. 430–31 and notes.

17. Many Muslim cultures are endogamous (they allow marriage between first cousins), and girls are conveniently married to relatives back home.

18. For some examples, see Sebenius, 2002.

19. Moore & Lewis, 1999, p. 278.

20. Saner & Yiu, 2000.

21. This leads to different criteria in the selection of candidates for expatriation. See Caligiuri, 2000, and Franke & Nicholson, 2002.

22. World Investment Report, 2000.

23. Schenk, 2001; Apfelthaler, Muller, & Rehder, 2002.

24. In 2007 Shell concentrated its head office operations in The Hague, the Netherlands, while functioning under the laws of Britain.

25. Sherman, Helmreich, & Merritt, 1997.

26. For example, Lord & Ranft, 2000; Lynch & Beck, 2001; for a review, see *Culture's Consequences*, 2001, p. 448 and notes.

27. de Mooij, 1998, pp. 58–59.

28. de Mooij, 2004, p. 256.

29. de Mooij, 1998, p. 57.

30. de Mooij, 2010, Chapter 9.

31. Another area of sustained and sometimes increasing cultural differentiation is packaging design. The same products, in order to be sold in different cultures, need different packaging (van den Berg-Weitzel & van de Laar, 2000).

32. The rest of this section is a summary of research reported in *Culture's Consequences*, 2001, pp. 450–51 and notes.

33. Lynn, 2000, reported on a tipping study; Misho obtained country data from Lynn in 2006. Tip giving correlated with PDI with $r = 0.49^{**}$ and with IDV with $r = -0.41^*$ $(n = 27)$.

34. Fisher, 1988, p. 41. Without being aware of Geert's work, Fisher used a very similar approach to culture. For example, he also used the computer analogy for the human mind.

35. Lammers, 2003.

36. Groterath, 2000; Soeters & Recht, 2001.

37. This is the title of a book by Kiernan (1969) about the British imperial age.

38. Dia, 1996.

39. For example, Michael Porter's 1990 book *The Competitive Advantage of Nations* does not mention corruption.

40. The World Bank is perceived by many parties as serving U.S. interests (Stiglitz, 2002).

41. A group of authors committed to the development of Africa stresses fulfilling social rather than individual achievement needs (Afro-Centric Alliance, 2001). See also d'Iribarne, 2002.

42. Hawes & Kealey, 1979.

43. Forss, Carlsen, Frøyland, Sitari, & Vilby, 1988. This study continued a pilot study by the Institute for Research on Intercultural Cooperation in the Netherlands. IRIC's design had been to combine development agencies *and* multinationals in the same study about factors leading to the effectiveness of expatriates. See Andersson & Hofstede, 1984. After the proposed public and private cooperation fell through, the Nordic development agencies went ahead on their own.

44. Pagès, 1971, p. 281.

45. Professor Nancy Adler, from Canada, has focused on the role of the executive spouse and produced videos of interviews with spouses. See also Adler, 1991.

46. Bond, 1992.

47. Hofstede, Pedersen, & Hofstede, 2002.

48. Cushner & Brislin, 1996. The differences it covers are mainly those between the United States and third-world cultures: most deal with individualism-collectivism and power distance.

49. Taken from an unpublished conference paper by Alfred J. Kraemer, Munich, 1978.

50. Åke Phillips.

51. Herodotus, *The Histories*, 1997 ed., book 3 ("Thalia"), entry 38, p. 243.

52. Hume, 1882 [1742], p. 252.

53. "The Ballad of Lale Laloo and Other Rhymes," quoted by Renier, 1931.

54. A classic example is Margaret Mead's film *Four Families*, showing the relationship between parents and small children in India, France, Japan, and Canada, produced in 1959 by the National Film Board of Canada. Another example is a video produced along with a book by Tobin, Wu, & Danielson (1989) about classroom behavior of four-year-old preschool children in Japan, China, and Hawaii.

55. Fisher, 1988, pp. 144 and 153.

56. The war of 1839–42 was only the First Opium War. After the Second Opium War, in 1860, the British also got Kowloon (or Jiulong) on the Chinese mainland opposite Hong Kong Island, and in 1898 they leased the New Territories adjacent to Kowloon. This lease was concluded for ninety-nine years and expired in 1997, at which point the entire colony was returned to China.

57. The term *global village* was coined by the Canadian media philosopher Marshall McLuhan. See de Mooij, 2004, p. 1.

Chapter 12

1. *Hominins* is the new name that systematists give to what was formerly called *hominids*. Hominins include the genera *Ardipithecus*, *Australopithecus*, *Paranthropus*, and *Homo*.

2. *Consilience: The Unity of Knowledge* is the title of a visionary book by biologist Edward O. Wilson (1998), who pleads for the practice of looking across disciplinary boundaries in research.

3. Wilson, Van Vugt, & O'Gorman, 2008.

4. Weiss, 2009, provides a very readable account and interpretation of recent research on human parasites.

5. Even today, people are instinctively scared of faces of outsiders but can learn to overcome these fears better if the outsiders are female. See Navarrete et al., 2009. The authors did a study on black and white U.S. citizens. They expected to find neurophysiological markers of anxiety and xenophobia.

6. This behavior has been documented in today's mountain gorillas. A BBC documentary, *The Gorilla King*, shows how Titus, the old alpha male of a large group in which one of his sons aspires to leadership, takes his group to the cold, barren top of a mountain and stays there until, two days later, the young male just leaves, followed by nearly half the group. Then the old leader also leaves, going the other way with the remainder of the group.

7. de Waal, 1982, 1997.

8. In *Chimpanzee Politics* (1982), Frans de Waal describes the chimp population of the Arnhem zoo in the early 1980s. One female, Mama, was the head of the group and remained so even after three adult males were introduced. Only after Mama was

kept away from the group for a few weeks did the males assume leadership roles, not to relinquish leadership after she finally returned. The settlement history of bonobos may have led to the female dominance that characterizes their societies.

9. Weiss, 2009.

10. Richerson & Boyd, 2005.

11. Davies, Davies, & Davies, 1992.

12. Cochran & Harpending, 2009.

13. Cochran & Harpending, 2009.

14. Davies, Davies, & Davies, 1992.

15. This suggestion receives some confirmation from data collected by Dr. Ray Simonsen, of Victoria University, in Darwin, Australia, and communicated orally to Geert in 1998 (see Chapter 5). For aborigines, Simonsen found PDI 80, IDV 90, MAS 22, UAI 128, and LTO −10.

16. Mithen, 2003.

17. Diamond, 1997.

18. Cochran & Harpending, 2009, p. 150. These authors expect more discoveries about eye color and its evolutionary advantages in coming years.

19. Harrison et al., 2006.

20. Borgerhoff Mulder et al., 2009.

21. Kuznar & Sedlmeyer, 2005, with numerous references to anthropological articles.

22. In Peru a cluster of ancient cities along the Rio Supe was found rather unexpectedly in recent years. They date from about five thousand years ago, long before the Inca. The city of Caral is the best known. See, for example, http://en.wikipedia.org/wiki/norte_chico_civilization.

23. McNeill & McNeill, 2003.

24. Moore & Lewis, 1999.

25. Parsons, 1964.

26. Cochran & Harpending, 2009.

27. English historian Simon Schama wrote about this in his 1987 book on the Dutch Golden Age, *The Embarrassment of Riches*.

28. "The State," translated as "The Republic." See Plato, 1974 [375 B.C.]).

29. McNeill & McNeill, 2003.

30. According to historian Felipe Fernández-Armesto, 2004.

31. van de Vliert, 2009. Van de Vliert's analysis is based on WVS data.

32. This means we disagree with Huntington's (1998) *Clash of Civilizations*.

33. Nazi ideology trampled tenuous moral circles between ethnic or pseudoethnic symbolically defined groups. This ideology appeals to older feelings of racial loyalty, but it goes against the direction of the history of morality in recent centuries, in which moral circles keep merging and expanding.

34. In biology the phenomenon that the behavior of a system changes suddenly while an input variable changes but little, and does not change back when conditions change back, is called *hysteresis*.

35. Richard Dawkins (1976) proposed the concept of *meme* as the symbolic equivalent of the gene; while it caught the imagination, it does not seem adequate to cope with the complexity of social evolution.

36. It would not be feasible to cover the whole evolution of life on Earth in this chapter. David Sloan Wilson's *Evolution for Everyone* (2007) would be a good place to start reading about it, but many other sources exist.

37. Garver-Apgar et al., 2006. This article reports a subsequent finding that women with immune system genes similar to those of their mates are more likely to be sexually attracted to other males.

38. For a glimpse of the coevolution between our diseases and our immune systems, see Nesse & Williams, 1995.

39. Inspired by Jablonka & Lamb, 2005.

40. Cochran & Harpending, 2009. The authors illustrate their point with a genetic explanation of the superior academic performance of Ashkenazi Jews in recent centuries.

41. Baumeister, 2007.

42. Turchin, 2006.

43. Holldobler & Wilson, 1990.

44. Richerson, Collins, & Genet, 2006.

45. About the evolution of storytelling, see Boyd, 2009.

46. A term coined by David Sloan Wilson in *Evolution for Everyone*, previously cited, to denote the isolation and fragmentation of science.

47. G. J. Hofstede, 2001. In a study of World Bank data, Gert Jan found that both the spread of new communication technologies and the specific uses to which they were put were culture-dependent.

48. See, for example, work by economists and game theorists Robert Axtell and Joshua M. Epstein, game theorist Robert Axelrod, and sociologist Nigel Gilbert, among many others. So-called agent-based models are a thriving modeling technique for studying the emergent behavior of societies using the behavior of individuals as input. Gert Jan contributes to this stream of research through agent-based models that include culture in agents.

49. Mann, Connor, Tyack, & Whitehead (ed.), 2000.

Glossary

For terms not mentioned in this Glossary see the Subject Index.

AGENCY: the way in which persons empowered to act on behalf of an organization fulfill this task. See also **group agency**.

ANTHROPOLOGY: the science of humans in their physical, social, and cultural variations. In this book the term always stands for social or cultural anthropology, which is the integrated study of human societies, in particular (although not only) traditional or preliterate ones.

ANXIETY: a diffuse state of being uneasy or worried about what may happen.

BUREAUCRACY: a form of organization based on strict rules and responsibilities attached to positions, not persons.

COLLECTIVISM: the opposite of *individualism*; together, they form one of the dimensions of national cultures. *Collectivism* stands for a society in which people from birth onward are integrated into strong, cohesive in-groups, which throughout people's lives continue to protect them in exchange for unquestioning loyalty.

CONFUCIAN DYNAMISM: a dimension of national cultures found through research among student samples using the Chinese Value Survey. Rebaptized in this book *long-term versus short-term orientation* (see under these catchwords).

CORPORATE CULTURE: organizational culture at the level of a corporation. See **organizational culture**.

CORPORATE IDENTITY: common symbols (such as logos) for subsidiaries belonging to the same corporation.

CORPORATE VALUES: a list of descriptions of desirable traits and behaviors for employees and managers of a corporation.

CORRELATION: in statistics, the degree of common variation of two sets of numbers. The coefficient of correlation can vary from a maximum of 1.00 (perfect agreement) via the value 0 (no relationship) to a minimum of -1.00 (perfect disagreement).

CULTURAL IDENTITY: see **Identity**. Identity is conscious and not to be confused with culture, which is usually unconscious.

CULTURAL LEGITIMATION: finding symbolic justification for practices so that they become morally acceptable. It is usually driven unconsciously by interests and always by cultural values.

CULTURE: (1) the training or refining of the mind; civilization; (2) the unwritten rules of the social game, or more formally the collective programming of the mind that distinguishes the members of one group or category of people from another—this meaning corresponds to the use of the term *culture* in anthropology and is likewise used throughout this book.

CULTURE ASSIMILATOR: a programmed-learning tool for developing intercultural communication skills.

CULTURE SHOCK: a state of distress following the transfer of a person to an unfamiliar cultural environment. It may be accompanied by physical illness symptoms.

DIMENSION: an aspect of a phenomenon that can be measured (expressed in a number) independently of other aspects.

DIMENSIONAL MODEL: a set of dimensions used in combination to describe a phenomenon.

EMPOWERMENT: the process of increasing employees' influence on their work situation.

ETHNOCENTRISM: applying the standards of one's own society to people outside that society.

EVOLUTION: a process in which generations of a replicator (e.g., gene, individual, or group) produce surplus descendants with small variations, and some of these produce more offspring than others; in other words, less successful variants are weeded out by natural selection.

EXCLUSIONISM: the cultural tendency to treat people on the basis of their group affiliation and to reserve favors for groups with which one identifies, while excluding outsiders. Together with its opposite pole, *universalism*, this is one of Misho Minkov's WVS-based dimensions of national cultures.

EXTENDED FAMILY: a family group including relatives in the second and third degree (or beyond), such as grandparents, uncles, aunts, and cousins.

FACE: in collectivist societies, a quality attributed to someone who meets the essential requirements related to his or her social position. To "give face" means to show due respect for that position.

FACE VALIDITY: a property of a research item in a questionnaire that seems to measure exactly what the wording of the item suggests, rather than something hidden and that can be revealed only after an analysis of the research results.

FACTOR ANALYSIS: a statistical technique designed to assist the researcher in explaining the variety in a set of observed phenomena by a minimum number of underlying common factors. The phenomena that are combined in a factor will be strongly correlated.

FEMININITY: the opposite of *masculinity*; together, they form one of the dimensions of national cultures. *Femininity* stands for a society in which emotional gender roles overlap: both men and women are supposed to be modest, tender, and concerned with the quality of life.

FLEXHUMILITY (ALSO SPELLED "FLEXUMILITY"): a coined term for the characteristic of societies whose cultures promote humility, flexibility, and adaptability to changing circumstances. Together with its opposite pole, *monumentalism*, this is one of Misho Minkov's WVS-based dimensions of national cultures.

FUNDAMENTALISM: the belief that there is only one unchanging Truth and that one's own group is in possession of this Truth, which is usually defined in great detail.

GESTALT: an integrated whole that should be studied as such and that loses its meaning when divided into parts; from a German word meaning "form."

GROSS NATIONAL INCOME (GNI): a measure of the total flow of goods and services produced by the economy of a country over a year, including income from foreign investments by domestic residents, but excluding income from domestic investments by foreign residents.

GROUP AGENCY: the capacity for concerted collective action of a group.

GROUP IDENTITY: see **identity**.

HEROES: persons, alive or dead, real or imaginary, assumed to possess characteristics highly prized in a culture and thus serving as models for behavior.

HOMEOSTASIS: the tendency of an organism or social system to maintain internal stability by compensating for external changes.

HOMININ: an ancestor of modern humans. Used to be called "hominid" in previous classification systems.

HUMAN NATURE: the set of traits that are shared by all of today's human beings.

IDENTITY: a person's self-affiliation as a member of a group or category. Often rooted in national or regional origin, language, and/or religious affiliation, it is conscious and visible both to the holders of the identity and to the environment that does not share it. See also **corporate identity**.

IDEOLOGY: a coherent set of ideas that serves to give a purpose to life and to set moral standards.

INDIVIDUALISM: the opposite of *collectivism*; together, they form one of the dimensions of national cultures. *Individualism* stands for a society in which the ties between individuals are loose: everyone is expected to look after him- or herself and his or her immediate family only.

INDIVIDUALISM INDEX (IDV): a measure for the degree of *individualism* in a country's culture, originally based on the IBM research project.

INDULGENCE: the opposite of *restraint*; together, they form one of the dimensions of national cultures. *Indulgence* stands for a society that allows relatively free gratification of basic and natural human desires related to enjoying life and having fun.

IN-GROUP: a cohesive group that offers protection in exchange for loyalty and provides its members with a sense of identity.

INSTITUTION: an organized set of activities to which the people in a group attribute a symbolic function. Institutions can be purely symbolic (marriage) or have a physical form (a school).

LONG-TERM ORIENTATION: the opposite of *short-term orientation*; together, they form a dimension of national cultures. *Long-term orientation* stands for the fostering of pragmatic virtues oriented toward future rewards, in particular perseverance, thrift, and adapting to changing circumstances.

LONG-TERM ORIENTATION INDEX (LTO): a measure for the degree of *long-term orientation* in a country's culture. LTO-CVS scores are based on the Chinese Value Survey among student samples; LTO-WVS scores are based on the World Values Survey of representative samples of national populations.

MASCULINITY: the opposite of *femininity*; together, they form one of the dimensions of national cultures. *Masculinity* stands for a society in which emotional gender roles are clearly distinct: men are supposed to be assertive, tough, and focused on material success; women are supposed to be more modest, tender, and concerned with the quality of life.

MASCULINITY INDEX (MAS): a measure for the degree of *masculinity* in a country's culture, originally based on the IBM research project.

MATRIX ORGANIZATION: an organization structure in which a person can report to two or three superiors for different work aspects—for example, one for the task and one for the professional side, or one for the business line and one for the country.

MONUMENTALISM: a characteristic of societies that reflect the state in which the human self is like a proud and stable monolithic monument. Together with its opposite pole, *flexhumility*, this is one of Misho Minkov's WVS-based dimensions of national cultures.

MORAL CIRCLE: the group of all people to whom full moral rights and obligations are granted, usually unconsciously. A moral circle requires a culture. People can belong to several moral circles with different degrees of reach—for example, nationality, religion, organization, family.

MOTIVATION: an assumed force operating internally that induces an individual to choose one action over another.

NATIONAL CHARACTER: a term used in the past to describe what is called in this book *national culture*. A disadvantage of the term *character* is that it stresses the individual aspects at the expense of the social system.

NATIONAL CULTURE: the collective programming of the mind acquired by growing up in a particular country.

NATURAL SELECTION: differential survival of descendants of the same parent form, leading to evolution of that form (the *replicator*).

NUCLEAR FAMILY: a family group including only relatives in the first degree (parents and children).

ORGANIZATIONAL CULTURE: the collective programming of the mind that distinguishes the members of one organization from another.

PARADIGM: a set of common assumptions that dominate a scientific field and constrain the thinking of the scientists in that field.

PARTICULARISM: a way of thinking prevailing in collectivist societies, in which the standards for the way a person should be treated depend on the group to which the person belongs.

PATH DEPENDENCY: the fact that evolution (or any other process) is constrained by its own history. As a consequence, from every next evolutionary step there is no way back.

POWER DISTANCE: the extent to which the less powerful members of institutions and organizations within a country expect and accept that power is distributed unequally. One of the dimensions of national cultures (from small to large).

POWER DISTANCE INDEX (PDI): a measure for the degree of *power distance* in a country's culture, originally based on the IBM research project.

PRACTICES: the scope of what people do, including the symbols to which they respond, the heroes they venerate, and the rituals in which they take part, but not their values.

PURCHASING POWER PARITY (PPP): a basis for comparing gross national income that takes the local purchasing power of money into account.

PROXIMATE MECHANISM OF EVOLUTION: the actual process of replication and selection that leads to evolution of the units that undergo it. For instance, stories evolve through retelling with modifications, orally or in writing; individuals evolve through sexual reproduction with mutation.

RELATIVISM: a willingness to consider other persons' or groups' theories and values to be as reasonable as one's own.

REPLICATOR: a unit of selection in an evolutionary process. A replicator can be a gene, an individual, a group, or a cultural value or practice—anything that reproduces with variation, whether biologically or otherwise.

RESTRAINT: the opposite of *indulgence*; together, they form one of the dimensions of national cultures. *Restraint* stands for a society that suppresses gratification of needs and regulates it by means of strict social norms.

RISK: the chance that an action will have an undesirable but known outcome.

RITUALS: collective activities that are technically superfluous to reach desired ends but that, within a culture, are considered to be socially essential; they are therefore carried out for their own sake.

SHORT-TERM ORIENTATION: the opposite of *long-term orientation*; together, they form a dimension of national cultures. *Short-term orientation* stands for the fostering of virtues related to the past and present, such as national pride, respect for tradition, preservation of *face*, and fulfilling social obligations.

SIGNIFICANT: see **statistically significant**.

SOCIALIZATION: the acquisition of the values and practices belonging to a culture, by participating in that culture.

SOCIAL STRATIFICATION: the existence of two or more classes in a society that have markedly different status and prerogatives.

STATISTICALLY SIGNIFICANT: the state in which the relationship between two measures for which only a sample of the entire population has been investigated is sufficiently strong to rule out the possibility that this relationship is due to pure chance. The "significance level," usually 0.05, 0.01, or 0.001, indicates the extent to which the relationship could still be accidental.

STEREOTYPING: a form of reasoning in which similar characteristics are ascribed to all members of a collective (group, category, or culture).

SUBJECTIVE WELL-BEING: a person's evaluative reaction to his or her life, in terms of either life satisfaction (cognitive evaluations) or affect (ongoing emotional reactions).

SYMBOLS: words, pictures, gestures, or objects that carry a particular meaning recognized as such only by those who share a culture.

TYPOLOGY: a set of ideal types used to describe a phenomenon.

UNCERTAINTY AVOIDANCE: the extent to which the members of a culture feel threatened by ambiguous or unknown situations. One of the dimensions of national cultures (from weak to strong).

UNCERTAINTY AVOIDANCE INDEX (UAI): a measure for the degree of *uncertainty avoidance* in a country's culture, originally based on the IBM research project.

UNIVERSALISM: a way of thinking prevailing in individualist societies, in which the standards for the way a person should be treated are the same for everybody. Together with its opposite pole, *exclusionism*, this is one of Misho Minkov's WVS-based dimensions of national cultures.

VALIDATION: testing the conclusions from one piece of research against data from independent other sources.

VALUES: broad tendencies to prefer certain states of affairs over others, largely unconscious. To be distinguished from *practices*. See also **corporate values**, in which the word *values* means something entirely different.

XENOPHILIA: the feeling that persons and things from abroad must be superior.

XENOPHOBIA: the feeling that foreign persons or things are dangerous.

Bibliography

Newspaper items and unpublished documents other than theses have not been listed.

Aberbach, J. D., and R. D. Putnam (1977). *Paths to the Top: The Origins and Careers of Political and Administrative Elites*. Ann Arbor: University of Michigan Press.

Adebayo, A. (1988). "The masculine side of planned parenthood: An explanatory analysis." *Journal of Comparative Family Studies* 19: 55–67.

Adler, N. J. (1991). *International Dimensions of Organizational Behavior*. 2nd ed. Boston: Kent Publishing Company.

Afro-Centric Alliance (2001). "Indigenising organisational change: Localisation in Tanzania and Malawi." *Journal of Managerial Psychology* 16: 59–78.

Almond, G. A., and S. Verba (1963). *The Civic Culture: Political Attitudes and Democracy in Five Nations*. Princeton, NJ: Princeton University Press.

Alvesson, M. (2002). *Understanding Organizational Culture*. London: Sage.

Andersson, L., and G. Hofstede (1984). *The Effectiveness of Expatriates: Report on a Feasibility Study*. Tilburg, Neth.: IRIC.

Apfelthaler, G., H. J. Muller, and R. R. Rehder (2002). "Corporate global culture as competitive advantage: Learning from Germany and Japan in Alabama and Austria?" *Journal of World Business* 37: 108–18.

Argyle, M., M. Henderson, M. Bond, Y. Iizuka, and A. Contarello (1986). "Cross-cultural variations in relationship rules." *International Journal of Psychology* 21: 287–315.

Baker, C. R. (1976). "An investigation of differences in values: Accounting majors versus non-accounting majors." *The Accounting Review* 51 (4): 886–93.

Barney, J. B. (2002). "Strategic management: From informed conversation to academic discipline." *Academy of Management Executive* 16: 53–57.

Baruch, J. (2001). "Global or North American? A geographical based comparative analysis of publications in top management journals." *International Journal of Cross-Cultural Management* 1: 109–26.

Baumeister, R. F. (2007). "Is There Anything Good About Men?" Invited address, American Psychological Association annual convention, San Francisco.

Bel Ghazi, H. (1982). *Over twee culturen: Uitbuiting en opportunisme*. Rotterdam: Futile.

Bem, S. L. (1975). "Sex role adaptability: One consequence of psychological androgyny." *Journal of Personality and Social Psychology* 31: 634–43.

Benedict, R. (1959 [1934]). *Patterns of Culture (with a Preface by Margaret Mead)*. Boston: Houghton Mifflin.

Best, D. L., and J. E. Williams (1996). "Anticipation of aging: A cross-cultural examination of young adults' views of growing old." In *Asian Contributions to Cross-Cultural Psychology*, ed. J. Pandey, D. Sinha, and D. P .S. Bhawuk, 274–88. New Delhi: Sage.

Biggs, J. B. (1996). "Approaches to learning of Asian students: A multiple paradox." In *Asian Contributions to Cross-Cultural Psychology*, ed. J. Pandey, D. Sinha, and D. P. S. Bhawuk, 180–99. New Delhi: Sage.

Blake, R. R., and J. S. Mouton (1964). *The Managerial Grid*. Houston: Gulf Publishing Co.

Blanchflower, D. G., and A. J. Oswald (1998). "What makes an entrepreneur?" *Journal of Labour Economics* 16 (1): 26–60.

Bond, M. H. (1992). "The process of enhancing cross-cultural competence in Hong-Kong organizations." *International Journal of Intercultural Relations* 16: 395–412.

Bond, M. H., and S. H. Wang (1983). "Aggressive behavior and the problem of maintaining order and harmony." In *Global Perspectives on Aggression*, ed. A. P. Goldstein and M. H. Segall, 58–73. New York: Pergamon.

Bond, M. H., et al. (2004). "Culture-level dimensions of social axioms and their correlates across 41 cultures." *Journal of Cross-Cultural Psychology* 35: 548–70.

Bond, R., and P. B. Smith (1996). "Culture and conformity: A meta-analysis of studies using Asch's (1952, 1956) line judgment task." *Psychological Bulletin* 119: 111–37.

Borgerhoff Mulder, M., et al. (2009). "Intergenerational wealth transmission and the dynamics of inequality in small-scale societies." *Science* 326: 682–88.

Bourdieu, P. (1980). *Le sens pratique*. Paris: Editions de Minuit.

Bourdieu, P., and L. J. D. Wacquant (1992). *Réponses: Pour une anthropologie réflexive*. Paris: Seuil.

Boyd, B. (2009). *On the Origin of Stories*. Cambridge, MA: Harvard University Press.

Broms, H., and H. Gahmberg (1983). "Communication to self in organizations and cultures." *Administrative Science Quarterly* 28: 482–95.

Broverman, I. K., S. R. Vogel, D. M. Broverman, F. E. Clarkson, and P. S. Rosenkrantz (1972). "Sex-role stereotypes: A current appraisal." *Journal of Social Issues* 28 (2): 59–78.

Brown, L. M., M. M. Bradley, and P. J. Lang (2006). "Affective reactions to pictures of ingroup and outgroup members." *Biological Psychology* 71: 303–11.

Brunsson, N. (1985). *The Irrational Organization.* Chichester, UK: Wiley.

Buss, D. M. (1989). "Sex differences in human mate preferences: Evolutionary hypotheses tested in 37 cultures." *Behavioral and Brain Sciences* 12: 1–49.

Buss, D. M., et al. (1990). "International preferences in selecting mates." *Journal of Cross-Cultural Psychology* 21: 5 47.

Caligiuri, P. M. (2000). "The Big Five personality characteristics as predictors of expatriate's desire to terminate the assignment and supervisor rated performance." *Personnel Psychology* 53: 67–88.

Campbell, J. (1988). *Myths to Live By.* New York: Bantam Books. [Original work published 1972.]

Cao Xueqin (1980). *The Story of the Stone, also known as The Dream of the Red Chamber.* Vol. 3: *The Warning Voice.* Translated by David Hawkes. Harmondsworth, Mddx., UK: Penguin Books. [Original Chinese version published c. 1760.]

Carlzon, J. (1987). *Moments of Truth.* Cambridge, MA: Ballinger Publishing Company.

Carr, S. C., D. Munro, and G. D. Bishop (1996). "Attitude assessment in non-Western countries: Critical modifications to Likert scaling." *Psychologia* 39: 55–59.

Castells, M. (2001). *The Internet Galaxy.* Oxford: Oxford University Press.

Cavalli-Sforza, L. L. (2000). *Genes, Peoples and Languages.* Berkeley: University of California Press.

Chandler, T. A., D. D. Shama, F. M. Wolf, and S. K. Planchard (1981). "Multiattributional causality: A five cross-national samples study." *Journal of Cross-Cultural Psychology* 12: 207–21.

Chenery, H. B., and A. M. Strout (1966). "Foreign assistance and economic development." *American Economic Review* 56 (4): 679–733.

Chew-Lim, F. Y. (1997). "Evolution of Organisational Culture: A Singaporean Experience." Ph.D. dissertation, University of Hong Kong, School of Business.

Chinese Culture Connection (1987). "Chinese values and the search for culture-free dimensions of culture." *Journal of Cross-Cultural Psychology* 18 (2): 143–64.

Cleverley, G. (1971). *Managers and Magic.* London: Longman.

Cochran, G., and H. Harpending (2009). *The 10,000 Years Explosion: How Civilization Accelerated Human Evolution.* New York: Basic Books.

Cohen, P. (1973). *The Gospel According to the Harvard Business School: The Education of America's Managerial Elite.* Garden City, NY: Doubleday.

Cooper, R., and N. Cooper (1982). *Culture Shock! Thailand . . . , and How to Survive It.* Singapore: Times Books International.

Costa, P. T. Jr., A. Terraciano, and R. R. McCrae (2001). "Gender differences in personality traits across cultures: Robust and surprising findings." *Journal of Personality and Social Psychology* 81: 322–31.

Crozier, M. (1964). *The Bureaucratic Phenomenon*. Chicago: University of Chicago Press.

Crozier, M., and E. Friedberg (1977). *L'acteur et le système: Les contraintes de l'action collective*. Paris: Seuil.

Cushner, K., and R. W. Brislin (1996). *Intercultural Interactions: A Practical Guide*. 2nd ed. Thousand Oaks, CA: Sage.

Cyert, R. M., and J. G. March (1963). *A Behavioral Theory of the Firm*. Englewood Cliffs, NJ: Prentice-Hall.

Darwin, C. (2004 [1874]). *The Descent of Man*. Harmondsworth, Mddx., UK: Penguin.

Davies, H., and P. Ellis (2000). "Porter's competitive advantage of nations: Time for the final judgement?" *Journal of Management Studies* 37 (December 8): 1189–1213.

Davies, M., H. Davies, and K. Davies (1992). *Humankind the Gatherer-Hunter: From Earliest Times to Industry*. Swanley, Kent, UK: Myddle-Brockton.

Dawkins, R. (1976). *The Selfish Gene*. Oxford: Oxford University Press.

Deal, T. E., and A. A. Kennedy (1982). *Corporate Cultures: The Rites and Rituals of Corporate Life*. Reading, MA: Addison-Wesley.

de Kort, W., E. Wagenmans, A. van Dongen, Y. Slotboom, G. Hofstede, and I. Veldhuizen (2010). "Blood product collection and supply: Just a matter of money?" *Vox Sanguinis*, 98.

de Mooij, M. (1998). "Masculinity/femininity and consumer behavior." In G. Hofstede et al., *Masculinity and Femininity: The Taboo Dimension of National Cultures*, 55–73. Thousand Oaks, CA: Sage.

de Mooij, M. (2004). *Consumer Behavior and Culture: Consequences for Global Marketing and Advertising*. Thousand Oaks, CA: Sage.

de Mooij, M. (2010). *Global Marketing and Advertising: Understanding Cultural Paradoxes*. 3rd ed. Thousand Oaks, CA: Sage.

de Mooij, M., and G. Hofstede (2002). "Convergence and divergence in consumer behavior: Implications for international retailing." *Journal of Retailing* 78: 61–69.

Deschepper, R., L. Grigoryan, C. Stålsby Lundborg, G. Hofstede, J. Cohen, G. Van der Kelen, L. Deliens, and F. M. Haaijer-Ruskamp (2008). "Are cultural dimensions relevant for explaining cross-national differences in antibiotic use in Europe?" *BMC Health Services Research* 8. London: BioMed Central.

de Waal, F. (1982). *Chimpanzee Politics: Power and Sex Among Apes*. New York: Harper & Row.

de Waal, F. (1997). *Good Natured: The Origins of Right and Wrong in Humans and Other Animals*. Cambridge, MA: Harvard University Press.

de Waal, F. (2001). *The Ape and the Sushi Master: Cultural Reflections of a Primatologist*. New York: Basic Books.

Dia, M. (1996). *Africa's Management in the 1990s and Beyond: Reconciling Indigenous and Transplanted Institutions*. Washington, DC: World Bank.

Diamond, J. (1997). *Guns, Germs, and Steel: The Fates of Human Societies*. New York: W. W. Norton.

Diderot, D. (1982). *Voyage en Hollande*. Paris: François Maspéro. [Original work published 1780.]

Diener, E., and M. Diener (1995). "Cross-cultural correlates of life-satisfaction and self-esteem." *Journal of Personality and Social Psychology* 68: 653–63.

Diener, E., and W. Tov (2007). "Culture and subjective well-being." In *Handbook of Cultural Psychology*, ed. S. Kitayama and D. Cohen, 691–713. New York: Guilford.

Dion, K. K., and K. L. Dion (1993). "Individualistic and collectivistic perspectives on gender and the cultural context of love and intimacy." *Journal of Social Issues* 49 (3): 53–69.

d'Iribarne, P. (1989). *La logique de l'honneur: Gestion des entreprises et traditions nationales*. Paris: Seuil.

d'Iribarne, P. (1998). "Comment s'accorder: Une rencontre franco-suédoise." In *Cultures et mondialisation: Gérer par-delà des frontières*, ed. P. d'Iribarne, A. Henry, J. P. Segal, S. Chevrier, and T. Globokar, 89–115. Paris: Seuil.

d'Iribarne, P. (2002). "Motivating workers in emerging countries: Universal tools and local adaptations." *Journal of Organizational Behavior* 23 (3): 243–56.

Djankov, S., R. La Porta, F. Lopez-de-Silanes, and A. Shleifer (2003). *The Practice of Justice*. Report by the World Bank. worldbank.org/publicsector/legal/index.cfm.

Douglas, M. (1966). *Purity and Danger*. London: Routledge and Kegan Paul.

Drucker, P. F. (1955). *The Practice of Management*. London: Mercury.

Earley, P. C. (1989). "Social loafing and collectivism: A comparison of the United States and the People's Republic of China." *Administrative Science Quarterly* 34: 565–81.

Early, P. C. (1997). *Face, Harmony and Social Structure: An Analysis of Organization Behavior Across Cultures*. New York: Oxford University Press.

The Economist (2001). "An Anthropology of Happiness." In *Christmas Special*, December 22, p. 70.

Elias, N. (1969). *Ueber den Prozess der Zivilisation*. Frankfurt (Main): Suhrkamp.

Erasmus, D. (2001). *Gesprekken (Colloquia)*. Amsterdam: Athenaeum–Polak & van Gennep. [Original Latin text 1524.]

Etcoff, N., S. Orbach, J. Scott, and H. Agostino (2006). *Beyond Stereotypes: Rebuilding the Foundation of Beauty Beliefs*. campaignforrealbeauty.com/dovebeyondstereotypeswhitepaper.pdf.

Eurobarometer (various issues and years). Brussels: European Commission.

Euromonitor (various issues and years). London: Euromonitor International.

Fang, T. (2003). "A critique of Hofstede's fifth national culture dimension." *International Journal of Cross-Cultural Management* 3 (3): 347–68.

Fayol, H. (1970). *Administration industrielle et générale*. Paris: Dunod. [Original work published 1916.]

Ferguson, I. R. G. (1973). *Management by Objectives in Deutschland*. Frankfurt: Herder und Herder.

Fernández-Armesto, F. (2004). *So You Think You're Human? A Brief History of Humankind*. Oxford: Oxford University Press.

Fisher, G. (1988). *Mindsets: The Role of Culture and Perception in International Relations*. Yarmouth, ME: Intercultural Press.

Fleishman, E. A., E. F. Harris, and H. E. Burtt (1955). *Leadership and Supervision in Industry.* Columbus: Ohio State University, Bureau of Educational Research.

Foreign Policy magazine and the Center for Global Development (2003). "Ranking the Rich: Which Country Really Helps the Poor?" foreignpolicy.com, May 9.

Forss, K., J. Carlsen, E. Frøyland, T., Sitari, and K. Vilby (1988). *Evaluation of the Effectiveness of Technical Assistance Personnel Financed by the Nordic Countries.* Stockholm: Swedish International Development Authority.

Franck, G. (1973). "Ëpitaphe pour la D.P.O." *Le Management* 3: 8–14.

Franke, J., and N. Nicholson (2002). "Who shall we send? Cultural and other influences on the rating of selection criteria for expatriate assignments." *International Journal of Cross-Cultural Management* 1: 21–36.

Gambling, T. (1977). "Magic, accounting and morale." *Accounting, Organizations and Society* 2: 141–51.

Gao, G., S. Ting-Toomey, and W. B. Gudykunst (1996). "Chinese communication processes." In *The Handbook of Chinese Psychology,* ed. M. H. Bond, 280–93. Hong Kong: Oxford University Press.

Garver-Apgar, C. E., S. W. Gangestad, R. Thornhill, R. D. Miller, and J. J. Olp (2006). "MHC alleles, sexual responsivity, and unfaithfulness in romantic couples." *Psychological Science* 17: 830–35.

Giddens, A. (2001). *Sociology.* 4th ed. Cambridge, UK: Polity Press.

Golding, W. (1978 [1954]). *Lord of the Flies.* Brighton: Guild Books.

Gonzalez, A. (1982). "Sex roles of the traditional Mexican family: A comparison of Chicano and Anglo students' attitudes." *Journal of Cross-Cultural Psychology* 13: 330–39.

Goodstein, L. D. (1981). "Commentary: Do American theories apply abroad?" *Organizational Dynamics* 10 (1): 49–54.

Gould, S. J. (1996). *The Mismeasure of Man.* New York: Norton & Company.

Gray, J. (1993). *Men Are from Mars, Women Are from Venus.* London: HarperCollins.

Gray, S. J. (1988). "Towards a theory of cultural influence on the development of accounting systems internationally." *Abacus* 24 (1): 1–15.

Groterath, A. (2000). *Operatione Babele: La comunicazione interculturale nelle missioni di pace.* Thesis Peacekeeping and Security Course, Rome University.

Habib, S. (1995). "Concepts fondamentaux et fragments de psychosociologie dans l'oeuvre d'Ibn-Khaldoun: Al-Muqaddima (1375–1377)." *Les Cahiers Internationaux de Psychologie Sociale* 27: 101–21.

Haley, K. H. D. (1988). *The British and the Dutch: Political and Cultural Relations Through the Ages.* London: George Philip.

Hall, E. T. (1976). *Beyond Culture.* Garden City, NY: Doubleday Anchor Books.

Halman, L. (2001). *The European Values Study: A Third Wave.* Tilburg, Neth.: ESC, WORC, Tilburg University.

Halman, L., and T. Petterson (1996). "The shifting sources of morality: From religion to post-materialism?" In *Political Value Change in Western Democracies: Integration, Values, Identification, and Participation,* ed. L. Halman and N. Nevitte, 261–84. Tilburg, Neth.: Tilburg University Press.

Harding, S., and D. Phillips, with M. Fogarty (1986). *Contrasting Values in Western Europe.* London: Macmillan.

Harris, M. (1981). *America Now: The Anthropology of a Changing Culture.* New York: Simon & Schuster.

Harrison, L. E. (1985). *Underdevelopment Is a State of Mind.* Lanham, MD: Madison Books.

Harrison, N. A., T. Singer, P. Rothstein, R. J. Dolan, and H. D. Critchley (2006). "Pupillary contagion: Central mechanisms engaged in sadness processing." *Social, Cognitive and Affective Neuroscience* 1 (1): 5–17.

Harzing, A. W. (1995). "The persistent myth of high expatriate failure rates." *International Journal of Human Resource Management* 6: 457–74.

Harzing, A. W. (2001). "Are our referencing errors undermining our scholarship and credibility? The case of expatriate failure rates." *Journal of Organizational Behavior* 23: 127–48.

Harzing, A. W., and A. Sorge (2003). "The relative impact of country of origin and universal contingencies on internationalization strategies and corporate control in multinational enterprises: Worldwide and European perspectives." *Organization Studies* 24 (2): 187–214.

Hastings, H. E., and P. K. Hastings (1980). *Index to International Public Opinion 1979–1980.* Oxford: Clio.

Hastings, H. E., and P. K. Hastings (1981). *Index to International Public Opinion 1980–1981.* Oxford: Clio.

Hawes, F., and D. J. Kealey (1979). *Canadians in Development: An Empirical Study of Adaptation and Effectiveness on Overseas Assignment.* Ottawa: Canadian International Development Agency.

Heine, S. J. (2003). "An exploration of cultural variation in self-enhancing and self-improving motivations." In *Cross-Cultural Differences in Perspectives of the Self,* ed. V. Murphy-Berman and J. J. Berman, 101–28. Nebraska Symposium on Motivation, vol. 49. Lincoln: University of Nebraska Press.

Helgesen, G., and U. Kim (2002). *Good Government: Nordic and East Indian Perspectives.* Copenhagen: NIAS Press in collaboration with DUPI (Dansk Udenrigspolitisk Institut–Danish Institute of International Affairs).

Helmreich, R. L., and A. C. Merritt (1998). *Culture at Work in Aviation and Medicine: National, Organizational and Professional Influences.* Aldershot, Hants., UK: Ashgate.

Herodotus (1997 [420 B.C.]). *The Histories.* Translated by Rosalind Thomas. New York: Everyman's Library.

Herzberg, F. (1966). *Work and the Nature of Man.* Boston: World Publishing Co.

Herzberg, F., B. Mausner, and B. B. Snyderman (1959). *The Motivation to Work.* New York: John Wiley & Sons.

Hickson, D. J., and D. S. Pugh (2001). *Management Worldwide: Distinctive Styles amid Globalization.* New enhanced ed. Harmondsworth, Mddx., UK: Penguin Books.

Hill, C., and C. T. Romm (1996). "The role of mothers as gift givers: A comparison across 3 cultures." *Advances in Consumer Research* 23: 21–27.

Ho, D. Y. F. (1976). "On the concept of face." *American Journal of Sociology* 81: 867–84.

Hofstede, G. (1967). *The Game of Budget Control: How to Live with Budgetary Standards and Yet Be Motivated by Them.* Assen, Neth.: Van Gorcum.

Hofstede, G. (1978). "The poverty of management control philosophy." *Academy of Management Review* 3: 450–61.

Hofstede, G. (1980a). *Culture's Consequences: International Differences in Work-Related Values.* Beverly Hills, CA: Sage.

Hofstede, G. (1980b). "Motivation, leadership, and organization: Do American theories apply abroad?" *Organizational Dynamics* 9 (1): 42–63.

Hofstede, G. (1981a). "Do American theories apply abroad? A reply to Goodstein and Hunt." *Organizational Dynamics* 10 (1): 63–68.

Hofstede, G. (1981b). "Management control of public and not-for-profit activities." *Accounting, Organizations and Society* 6 (3): 193–221.

Hofstede, G. (1984). *Culture's Consequences: International Differences in Work-Related Values.* Abridged ed. Beverly Hills, CA: Sage.

Hofstede, G. (1986). "Cultural differences in teaching and learning." *International Journal of Intercultural Relations* 10 (3): 301–20.

Hofstede, G. (1988). "McGregor in Southeast Asia?" In *Social Values and Development: Asian Perspectives*, ed. D. Sinha and H. S. R. Kao, 304–14. New Delhi: Sage.

Hofstede, G. (1991). *Cultures and Organizations: Software of the Mind.* London: McGraw-Hill UK.

Hofstede, G. (1994a). *Uncommon Sense About Organizations: Cases, Studies, and Field Observations.* Thousand Oaks, CA: Sage.

Hofstede, G. (1994b). "Cultural and other differences in teaching and learning." In *The Principles of Multicultural Tertiary Education*, ed. A. van der Walt, 71–79. Selected papers delivered at an international conference. Vaal Triangle Technikon, Vanderbijlpark, South Africa.

Hofstede, G. (1995). "Multilevel research of human systems: Flowers, bouquets, and gardens." *Human Systems Research* 14: 207–17.

Hofstede, G. (1996a). "An American in Paris: The influence of nationality on organization theories." *Organization Studies* 17: 525–37.

Hofstede, G. (1996b). "Gender stereotypes and partner preferences of Asian women in masculine and feminine cultures." *Journal of Cross-Cultural Psychology* 27: 533–46.

Hofstede, G. (2001a). *Culture's Consequences: Comparing Values, Behaviors, Institutions, and Organizations Across Nations.* Thousand Oaks, CA: Sage.

Hofstede, G. (2001b). "Comparing behaviors across nations: Some suggestions to Levine and Norenzayan." *Cross Cultural Psychology Bulletin* 35 (3): 27–29.

Hofstede, G. (2006). "What did GLOBE really measure? Researchers' minds versus respondents' minds." *Journal of International Business Studies* 37: 882–96.

Hofstede, G. (2007a). "A European in Asia." *Asian Journal of Social Psychology* 10: 16–21.

Hofstede, G. (2007b). "Asian management in the 21st century." *Asia Pacific Journal of Management* 24: 411–20.

Hofstede, G., and M. H. Bond (1984). "Hofstede's culture dimensions: An independent validation using Rokeach's Value Survey." *Journal of Cross-Cultural Psychology* 15 (4): 417–33.

Hofstede, G., and M. H. Bond (1988). "The Confucius connection: From cultural roots to economic growth." *Organizational Dynamics* 16 (4): 4–21.

Hofstede, G., M. H. Bond, and C. L. Luk (1993). "Individual perceptions of organizational cultures: A methodological treatise on levels of analysis." *Organizational Studies* 14: 483–503.

Hofstede, G., and R. R. McCrae (2004). "Personality and culture revisited: Linking traits and dimensions of culture." *Cross-Cultural Research* 38 (1): 52–88.

Hofstede, G., B. Neuijen, D. D. Ohayv, and G. Sanders (1990). "Measuring organizational cultures." *Administrative Science Quarterly* 35: 286–316.

Hofstede, G., C. A. van Deusen, C. B. Mueller, T. A. Charles, and the Business Goals Network (2002). "What goals do business leaders pursue? A study in fifteen countries." *Journal of International Business Studies* 33 (4): 785–803.

Hofstede, G., et al. (1998). *Masculinity and Femininity: The Taboo Dimension of National Cultures*. Thousand Oaks, CA: Sage.

Hofstede, G. J. (1995). "Open problems, formal problems." *Revue des Systèmes de Décision* 4 (2): 155–65.

Hofstede, G. J. (2001). "Adoption of communication technologies and national culture." *Systèmes d'Information et Management* 3 (6): 55–74.

Hofstede, G. J., P. B. Pedersen, and G. Hofstede (2002). *Exploring Culture: Exercises, Stories and Synthetic Cultures*. Yarmouth, ME: Intercultural Press.

Holldobler, B., and E. O. Wilson (1990). *The Ants*. Cambridge, MA: Harvard University Press.

Hoppe, M. H. (1990). "A Comparative Study of Country Elites: International Differences in Work-Related Values and Learning and Their Implications for Management Training and Development." Ph.D. dissertation, University of North Carolina at Chapel Hill.

Hoppe, M. H. (1998). "Validating the masculinity/femininity dimensions on elites from nineteen countries." In G. Hofstede et al., *Masculinity and Femininity: The Taboo Dimension of National Cultures*, 29–43. Thousand Oaks, CA: Sage.

Hoppe, M. H., and R. S. Bhagat (2007). "Leadership in the United States: The leader as a cultural hero." In *Culture and Leadership Across the World: The GLOBE Book of In-Depth Studies of 25 Societies*, ed. J. S. Chhokar, F. C. Brodbeck, and R. J. House, 475–535. Thousand Oaks, CA: Sage.

Horovitz, J. H. (1980). *Top Management Control in Europe*. London: Macmillan.

House, R. J., P. Hanges, M. Javidan, P. W. Dorfman, and V. Gupta, ed. (2004). *Culture, Leadership, and Organizations: The GLOBE Study of 62 Societies*. Thousand Oaks, CA: Sage.

Hsu, F. L. K. (1971). "Psychological homeostasis and jen: Conceptual tools for advancing psychological anthropology." *American Anthropologist* 73: 23–44.

Hudson, V. M., and A. den Boer (2004). *Bare Branches: The Security Implications of Asia's Surplus Male Population*. Cambridge, MA: MIT Press.

Huettinger, M. (2006). "Cultural dimensions in business life: Hofstede's indices for Latvia and Lithuania." *Baltic Journal of Management* 3: 359–67.

Humana, C. (1992). *World Human Rights Guide.* 3rd ed. New York: Oxford University Press.

Human Development Report, 1999. New York: Oxford University Press.

Human Development Report, 2002. New York: Oxford University Press.

Human Development Report, 2006. New York: Oxford University Press.

Hume, D. (1882). *The Philosophical Works,* 3 vol. Edited by T. H. Green and T. H. Grose. London; reprinted in facsimile, 1964, by Scientia Verlag, Aalen, Ger. FRG. [Original text published 1742.]

Hunt, J. W. (1981). "Commentary: Do American theories apply abroad?" *Organizational Dynamics* 10 (1): 55–62.

Huntington, S. P. (1998). *The Clash of Civilizations and the Remaking of the World Order.* New York: Simon & Schuster.

Inglehart, R. (1997). *Modernization and Postmodernization: Cultural, Economic, and Political Change in 43 Societies.* Princeton, NJ: Princeton University Press.

Inglehart, R., and W. E. Baker (2000). "Modernization, cultural change, and the persistence of traditional values." *American Sociological Review* 65: 19–51.

Inglehart, R., M. Basañez, and A. Moreno (1998). *Human Values and Beliefs: A Cross-Cultural Sourcebook.* Ann Arbor: University of Michigan Press.

Inkeles, A., and D. J. Levinson (1969). "National character: The study of modal personality and sociocultural systems." In *The Handbook of Social Psychology,* ed. G. Lindzey and E. Aronson. 2nd ed., vol 4. Reading, MA: Addison-Wesley. [Original work published 1954.]

Jablonka, E., and M. J. Lamb (2005). *Evolution in Four Dimensions: Genetic, Epigenetic, Behavioral, and Symbolic Variation in the History of Life.* Cambridge, MA: MIT Press.

Jackofsky, E. F., and J. W. Slocum (1988). "CEO roles across cultures." In *The Executive Effect: Concepts and Methods for Studying Top Managers,* ed. D. C. Hambrick, 76–99. Greenwich, CT: JAI.

Jenkins, D. (1973). *Blue and White Collar Democracy.* Garden City, NY: Doubleday.

Kahn, H. (1979). *World Economic Development: 1979 and Beyond.* London: Croom Helm.

Kashima, E. S., and Y. Kashima (1998). "Culture and language: The case of cultural dimensions and personal pronoun use." *Journal of Cross-Cultural Psychology* 29: 461–86.

Kashima, Y., and E. S. Kashima (2003). "Individualism, GNP, climate, and pronoun drop: Is individualism determined by affluence and climate, or does language use play a role?" *Journal of Cross-Cultural Psychology* 34 (1): 125–34.

Kelen, B. (1983). *Confucius in Life and Legend.* Singapore: Graham Brash (Pte.) Ltd. [Original work published 1971.]

Kelly, K. (1994). *Out of Control: The New Biology of Machines, Social Systems, and the Economic World.* Reading, MA: Addison-Wesley.

Kets de Vries, M. F. R. (2001). *The Leadership Mystique: A User's Manual for the Human Enterprise.* London: Financial Times/Prentice-Hall.

Khandwalla, P. N. (1985). "Pioneering innovative management: An Indian excellence." *Organization Studies* 6: 161–83.

Kiernan, V. G. (1969). *The Lords of Humankind: European Attitudes Towards the Outside World in the Imperial Age.* Harmondsworth, Mddx., UK: Pelican.

Kieser, A., and H. Kubicek (1983). *Organisation.* Berlin: Walter de Gruyter.

Kim, U. (1995) "Psychology, science, and culture: Cross-cultural analysis of national psychologies." *International Journal of Psychology* 30: 663–79.

Klidas, A. K. (2001). "Employee Empowerment in the European Hotel Industry: Meaning, Process and Cultural Relativity." Ph.D. dissertation, University of Tilburg. Amsterdam: Thela Thesis.

Kluckhohn, F. R., and F. L. Strodtbeck (1961). *Variations in Value Orientations.* Westport, CT: Greenwood.

Kohn, M. L. (1969). *Class and Conformity: A Study in Values.* Homewood, IL: Dorsey Press.

Kolman, L., N. G. Noorderhaven, G. Hofstede, and E. Dienes (2003). "Cross-cultural differences in Central Europe." *Journal of Managerial Psychology* 18: 76–88.

Kuhn, T. S. (1970). *The Structure of Scientific Revolutions.* 2nd enlarged ed. Chicago: University of Chicago Press.

Kühnen, U., B. Hannover, U. Roeder, A. A. Shah, B. Schubert, A. Upmeyer, and S. Zakaria (2001). "Cross-cultural variations in identifying embedded figures: Comparisons from the United States, Germany, Russia, and Malaysia." *Journal of Cross-Cultural Psychology* 32 (3): 365–71.

Kuppens, P., E. Ceulemans, M. E. Timmerman, E. Diener, and C. Kim-Prieto (2006). "Universal intracultural and intercultural dimensions of the recalled frequency of emotional experience." *Journal of Cross-Cultural Psychology* 37: 491–515.

Kuznar, L., and R. Sedlmeyer (2005). "Collective violence in Darfur: An agent-based model of pastoral nomad/sedentary peasant interaction." *Mathematical Anthropology and Cultural Theory: An International Journal* 1 (4): 1–22.

Laaksonen, O. J. (1977). "The power of Chinese enterprises." *International Studies of Management and Organization* 7 (1): 71–90.

Lammers, A. (1989). *Uncle Sam en Jan Salie: Hoe Nederland Amerika ontdekte.* Amsterdam: Balans.

Lammers, C. J. (1988). "Transience and persistence of ideal types in organization theory." *Research in the Sociology of Organizations* 6: 203–24.

Lammers, C. J. (2003). "Occupational regimes alike and unlike." *Organization Studies* 9: 1379–1403.

Lasch, C. (1980). *The Culture of Narcissism: American Life in an Age of Diminishing Expectations.* New York: Warner.

Laurent, A. (1981). "Matrix organizations and Latin culture." *International Studies of Management and Organization* 10 (4): 101–14.

Lawrence, P. (1980). *Managers and Management in West Germany.* London: Croom Helm.

Leung, K., and F. J. R. van de Vijver (2008). "Strategies for strengthening causal inferences in cross-cultural research: The consilience approach." *International Journal of Cross-Cultural Management* 8: 145–69.

Levine, R., S. Sato, T. Hashimoto, and J. Verma (1995). "Love and marriage in 11 cultures." *Journal of Cross-Cultural Psychology* 30: 178–205.

Levine, R. V., and A. Norenzayan (1999). "The pace of life in 31 countries." *Journal of Cross-Cultural Psychology* 30: 178–205.

Levine, R. V., A. Norenzayan, and K. Philbrick (2001). "Cross-cultural differences in helping strangers." *Journal of Cross-Cultural Psychology* 32 (5): 543–60.

Levinson, D. (1977). "What have we learned from cross-cultural surveys?" *American Behavioral Scientist* 20: 757–92.

Lévi-Strauss, C., and D. Eribon (1988). *De près et de loin.* Paris: Editions Odile Jacob.

Lewis, B. (1982). *The Muslim Discovery of Europe.* London: Weidenfield & Nicholson.

Likert, R. (1961). *New Patterns of Management.* New York: McGraw-Hill.

Locke, R. R. (1996). *The Collapse of the American Management Mystique.* Oxford: Oxford University Press.

Lord, M. D., and A. L. Ranft (2000). "Organizational learning about new international markets: Exploring the internal transfer of local market knowledge." *Journal of International Business Studies* 31 (4): 573–89.

Lynch, P. D., and J. C. Beck (2001). "Profiles of Internet buyers in 20 countries: Evidence for region-specific strategies." *Journal of International Business Studies* 32 (4): 725–48.

Lynn, M. (2000). "National character and tipping customs: The needs for achievement, affiliation and power as predictors of the prevalence of tipping." *International Journal of Hospitality Management* 19 (2): 205–10.

Lynn, R. (1971). *Personality and National Character.* Oxford: Pergamon Press.

Lynn, R. (1975). "National differences in anxiety 1935–65." In *Stress and Anxiety,* Part 2, ed. I. G. Sarason and C. D. Spielberger, 257–74. Washington, DC: Hemisphere.

Lynn, R. (1991). *The Secret of the Miracle Economy: Different National Attitudes to Competitiveness and Money.* London: Social Affairs Unit.

Machiavelli, N. (1955). *The Ruler.* Translated by P. Rodd. Los Angeles: Gateway Editions. [Originally published in Italian, 1517.]

Magalhaes, R. (1984). "Organisation development in Latin countries: Fact or fiction." *Leadership and Organization Development Journal* 5 (5): 17–21.

Mamman, A., and K. Saffu (1998). "Short-termism, control, quick-fix and bottom line." *Journal of Managerial Psychology* 13: 291–308.

Mann, J., R. C. Connor, P. L. Tyack, and H. Whitehead, ed. (2000). *Cetacean Societies: Field Studies of Dolphins and Whales.* Chicago: University of Chicago Press.

March, J. G., and J. P. Olsen (1976). *Ambiguity and Choice in Organizations.* Bergen, Norway: Universitetsforlaget.

Markus, H. R., and S. Kitayama (1991). "Culture and the self: Implications for cognition, emotion, and motivation." *Psychological Review* 98: 224–53.

Maslow, A. H. (1970). *Motivation and Personality.* 2nd ed. New York: Harper & Row.

Matsumoto, D. (1989). "Cultural influences on the perception of emotion." *Journal of Cross-Cultural Psychology* 20: 92–105.

McClelland, D. (1961). *The Achieving Society*. Princeton, NJ: Van Nostrand.

McCrae, R. R. (2002). "NEO-PI-R data from 36 cultures: Further intercultural comparisons." In *The Five-Factor Model of Personality Across Cultures*, ed. R. R. McCrae and J. Allik. New York: Kluwer Academic/Plenum Publishers.

McCrae, R. R., and P. T. Costa (2003). *Personality in Adulthood: A Five-Factor Theory Perspective*. New York: Guilford Press.

McCrae, R. R., and O. P. John (1992). "An introduction to the five-factor model and its applications." *Journal of Personality and Social Psychology* 60: 175–215.

McCrae, R. R., A. Terracciano, A. Realo, and J. Allik (2008). "Interpreting GLOBE societal practices scales." *Journal of Cross-Cultural Psychology* 39: 805–10.

McDonald, L. G., and P. Robinson (2009). *A Colossal Failure of Common Sense: The Inside Story of the Collapse of Lehman Brothers*. New York: Crown Business.

McGregor, D. (1960). *The Human Side of Enterprise*. New York: McGraw-Hill.

McNeill, J. R., and W. H. McNeill (2003). *The Human Web: A Bird's-Eye View of World History*. New York: W. W. Norton.

Mead, M. (1962). *Male and Female*. London: Penguin Books. [Original work published 1950]

Meeuwesen, L., E. van den Brink-Muinen, and G. Hofstede (2009). "Can dimensions of national culture predict cross-national differences in medical communication?" *Patient Education and Counseling* 75: 58–66.

Merritt, A. (2000). "Culture in the cockpit: Do Hofstede's dimensions replicate?" *Journal of Cross-Cultural Psychology* 31 (3): 283–301.

Merton, R. K. (1968). *Social Theory and Social Structure*. Enlarged ed. New York: Free Press. [Original work published 1949]

Metcalf, H. C., and L. Urwick (1940). *Dynamic Administration: The Collected Papers of Mary Parker Follett*. New York: Harper & Row.

Michaud, G., ed. (1978). *Identités collectives et relations inter culturelles*. Paris: Presses Universitaires de France.

Minkov, M. (2007). *What Makes Us Different and Similar: A New Interpretation of the World Values Survey and Other Cross-Cultural Data*. Sofia, Bulgaria: Klasika i Stil.

Minkov, M. (2008). "Self-enhancement and self-stability predict school achievement at the national level." *Cross-Cultural Research* 42: 172–96.

Minkov, M. (2009). "Predictors of differences in subjective well-being across 97 nations." *Cross-Cultural Research* 43: 152–79.

Minkov, M., and V. Blagoev (2009). "Cultural values predict subsequent economic growth." *International Journal of Cross-Cultural Management* 9 (1): 5–24.

Mintzberg, H. (1983). *Structure in Fives: Designing Effective Organizations*. Englewood Cliffs, NJ: Prentice-Hall.

Mintzberg, H. (1989). *Mintzberg on Management: Inside Our Strange World of Organizations*. New York: The Free Press.

Mintzberg, H. (1993). "The pitfalls of strategic planning." *California Management Review* 36 (1): 32–47.

Mithen, S. (2003). *After the Ice: A Global Human History 20,000–5,000 B.C.* London: Weidenfeld & Nicolson.

Montesquieu, C.-L. de (1979). *De l'esprit des lois*, vol.1. Paris: GF-Flammarion. [Original work published 1742.]

Moore, C. A. (1967). Editor's supplement: "The enigmatic Japanese mind." In *The Japanese Mind: Essentials of Japanese Philosophy and Culture*, ed. C. A. Moore, 288–313. Tokyo: C. E. Tuttle.

Moore, K., and D. Lewis (1999). *Birth of the Multinational: Two Thousand Years of Ancient Business History, from Ashur to Augustus.* Copenhagen: Copenhagen Business School Press.

Morakul, S., and F. H. Wu (2001). "Cultural influences on the ABC implementation in Thailand's environment." *Journal of Managerial Psychology* 16: 142–58.

Morier, J. J. (1923). *The Adventures of Hajji Baba of Ispahan.* Edited with an introduction and notes by C. W. Stewart. London: Oxford University Press. [Original work published 1824.]

Mouritzen, P. E., and J. H. Svara (2002). *Leadership at the Apex: Politicians and Administrators in Western Local Governments.* Pittsburgh, PA: University of Pittsburgh Press.

Mulder, M. (1976). "Reduction of power differences in practice: The power distance reduction theory and its applications." In *European Contributions to Organization Theory*, ed. G. Hofstede and M. S. Kassem, 79–94. Assen, Neth.: Van Gorcum.

Mulder, M. (1977). *The Daily Power Game.* Leiden, Neth.: Martinus Nijhoff.

Myasoedov, S. (2003). "Chairperson's introduction." In *Business Cooperation and Business Schools Cooperation: New Opportunities Within CEEMAN*, ed. M. Minkov and B. Vilfan, 17. 11th CEEMAN Annual Conference, Sofia, Bulgaria. Ljubljana, Slovenia: CEEMAN.

National Center for Education Statistics (1999). *TIMSS (Third International Mathematics and Science Study).* http://nces.ed.gov/timss.

Navarrete, C. D., A. Olsson, A. K. Ho, W. B. Mendes, L. Thomsen, and J. Sidanius (2009). "Fear extinction to an out-group face: The role of target gender." *Psychological Science* 20 (2): 155–58.

Negandhi, A. R., and S. B. Prasad (1971). *Comparative Management.* New York: Appleton-Century-Crofts.

Neisser, U., G. Boodoo, T. J. Bouchard, A.W. Boykin, N. Brody, S. J. Ceci, D. F. Halpern, J. C. Loehlin, R. Perloff, R. J. Sternberg, and S. Urbina (1996). "Intelligence: Knowns and unknowns." *American Psychologist* 51 (2): 77–101.

Nesse, R. M., and G. C. Wiliams (1995). *Why We Get Sick: The New Science of Darwinian Medicine.* New York: Times Books.

Ng, S. H., et al. (1982). "Human Values in Nine Countries." In *Diversity and Unity in Cross-Cultural Psychology*, ed. R. Rath et al., 196–205. Lisse, Neth.: Swets & Zeitlinger.

Noorderhaven, N. G., and B. Tidjani (2001). "Culture, governance, and economic performance: An explorative study with a special focus on Africa." *International Journal of Cross-Cultural Management* 1: 31–52.

OECD (Organization for Economic Cooperation and Development) (1995). *Literacy, Economy and Society: Results of the First International Adult Literacy Survey.* Paris: OECD and Development Statistics Canada.

Ouchi, W. G. (1980). "Markets, bureaucracies and clans." *Administrative Science Quarterly* 25: 129–41.

Oyserman, D., H. M. Coon, and M. Kemmelmeier (2002). "Rethinking individualism and collectivism: Evaluations of theoretical assumptions and meta-analyses." *Psychological Bulletin* 128: 3–72.

Page, M. (1972). *The Company Savage: Life in the Corporate Jungle.* London: Coronet.

Pagès, M. (1971). "Bethel culture, 1969: Impressions of an immigrant." *Journal of Applied Behavioral Science* 7: 267–84.

Pagès, M., M. Bonetti, V. de Gaulejac, and D. Descendre (1979). *l'Emprise de l'organisation.* Paris: Presses Universitaires de France.

Parsons, T. (1964). "Evolutionary universals in society." *American Sociological Review* 29 (3): 339–57.

Parsons, T., and E. A. Shils (1951). *Toward a General Theory of Action.* Cambridge, MA: Harvard University Press.

Pascal, B. (1972). *Pensées.* Preface and introduction by Léon Brunschvicg. Paris: Le Livre de Poche. [Original publication 1667.]

Payer, L. (1989). *Medicine and Culture: Notions of Health and Sickness in Britain, the U.S., France and West Germany.* London: Victor Gollancz.

Pedersen, T., and S. Thomsen (1997). "European patterns of corporate ownership: A twelve-country study." *Journal of International Business Studies* 28: 759–78.

Pelto, P. J. (1968). "The difference between 'tight' and 'loose' societies." *TransAction* (April): 37–40.

Peters, T. J, and R. H. Waterman (1982). *In Search of Excellence: Lessons from America's Best-Run Companies.* New York: Harper & Row.

Peterson, M. F., and J. G. Hunt (1997). "International perspectives on international leadership." *Leadership Quarterly* 8 (3): 203–31

Peterson, M. F., and K. L. Pike (2002). "Emics and ethics for organizational studies: A lesson in contrast from linguistics." *International Journal of Cross-Cultural Management* 2: 5–19.

Pew Research Center (2007). *Global Opinion Trends 2002–2007.* Internet publication. Retrieved February 20, 2008, from http://pewglobal.org/reports/pdf/257.pdf and http://pewglobal.org/reports/pdf/257topline-trend.pdf.

Plato (1974 [375 B.C.]). *The Republic.* Translated by Desmond Lee. Harmondsworth, Mddx., UK: Penguin Classics.

Platow, M. J., N. J. Voudouris, M. Coulson, N. Gilford, R. Jamieson, L. Najdovski, N. Papaleo, C. Pollard, and L. Terry (2006). "In-group reassurance in a pain setting produces lower level of physiological arousal: Direct support for a self-categorization analysis of social influence." *European Journal of Social Psychology* 37: 649–60.

Porter, M. E. (1990). *The Competitive Advantage of Nations.* London: Macmillan.

Porter, M. E. (1992). "A note on culture and competitive advantage: Response to van den Bosch and van Prooijen." *European Management Journal* 10: 178.

Pryor, J. B., E. R. DeSouza, J. Fitness, C. Hutz, M. Kumpf, K. Lubbert, O. Pesonen, and M. W. Erber (1997). "Gender differences in the interpretation of social-sexual behavior: A cross-cultural perspective on sexual harassment." *Journal of Cross-Cultural Psychology* 28: 509–34.

Pugh, D. S., and D. J. Hickson (1976). *Organizational Structure in Its Context: The Aston Programme I*. Westmead, Farnborough, Hants., UK: Saxon House.

Pugh, D. S., and D. J. Hickson (1993). *Great Writers on Organizations*. Omnibus ed. Aldershot: Dartmouth.

Pümpin, C. (1984). "Unternehmenskultur, Unternehmensstrategie und Unternehmenserfolg." *GDI Impuls* 2: 19–30, Bern, Switz.: Gottlieb Duttweiler Institut.

Pümpin, C., J. M. Kobi, and H. A. Wüthrich (1985). *La culture de l'entreprise: Le profil stratégique qui conduit au succès*. Bern, Switz.: Banque Populaire Suisse.

Read, R. (1993). "Politics and Policies of National Economic Growth." Ph.D. dissertation, Stanford University.

Redding, S. G. (1980). "Management education for Orientals." In *Breaking Down Barriers: Practice and Priorities for International Management Education*, ed. B. Garratt and J. Stopford, 193–214. Westmead, Farnborough, Hants.: Gower.

Redding, S. G. (1990). *The Spirit of Chinese Capitalism*. Berlin: Walter de Gruyter.

Rendell, L., and H. Whitehead (2001). "Culture in whales and dolphins." *Behavioral and Brain Sciences* 24 (2): 309–30.

Renier, G. J. (1931). *The English: Are They Human?* London: William & Norgate.

Rice, T. W., and B. J. Steele (2004). "Subjective well-being and culture across time and space." *Journal of Cross-Cultural Psychology* 35: 633–47.

Richerson, P. J., and R. Boyd (2005). *Not by Genes Alone: How Culture Transformed Human Evolution*. Chicago: University of Chicago Press.

Richerson, P. J., D. Collins, and R. M. Genet (2006). "Why managers need evolutionary theory of organizations." *Strategic Organization* 4 (2): 201–11.

Rose, R. (1955). *Twelve Angry Men: A Play in Two Acts*. London: Samuel French.

Ross, M. W. (1989). "Gay youth in four cultures: A comparative study." *Journal of Homosexuality* 17: 299–314.

Russell, B. (1976). *The Impact of Science on Society*. London: Unwin Paperbacks. [Original work published 1952.]

Russell, B. (1979). *An Outline of Philosophy*. London: Unwin Paperbacks. [Original work published 1927.]

Ryback, D., A. L. Sanders, J. Lorentz, and M. Koestenblatt (1980). "Child-rearing practices reported by students in six cultures." *Journal of Psychology* 110: 153–62.

Sadler, P. J., and G. Hofstede (1976). "Leadership styles: Preferences and perceptions of employees of an international company in different countries." *International Studies of Management and Organization* 6 (3): 87–113.

Saffold, G. S. (1988). "Culture traits, strength, and organizational performance: Moving beyond 'strong' culture." *Academy of Management Review* 13: 546–58.

Sagiv, L., and S. H. Schwartz (2000). "A new look at national culture: Illustrative applications to role stress and managerial behavior." In *Handbook of Organizational*

Culture and Climate, ed. N. M. Ashkanasy, C. P. M. Wilderom, and M. F. Peterson, 417–35. Thousand Oaks, CA: Sage.

Sandemose, A. (1938). *En flygtling krydser sit spor* [A Fugitive Crosses His Own Track]. Copenhagen: Gyldendals Bogklub. [Danish translation. Originally published in Norwegian, 1933.]

Sanders, G., and J. van der Veen (1998). "Culture in ICUs." In *Organisation and Management of Intensive Care*, ed. D. Reis Miranda, D. W. Ryan, W. B. Schaufeli, and V. Fidler, 208–19. Berlin: Springer-Verlag.

Saner, R., and L. Yiu (2000). "Developing sustainable trans-border regions: The need for business diplomats, entrepreneurial politicians and cultural ambassadors." *Social Strategies* 23 (October): 411–28.

Schama, S. (1987). *The Embarrassment of Riches: An Interpretation of Dutch Culture in the Golden Age*. New York: Alfred A. Knopf.

Schein, E. H. (1985). *Organizational Culture and Leadership: A Dynamic View*. San Francisco: Jossey-Bass.

Schenk, E. J. J. (2001). *Economie en strategie van de megafusie*. The Hague: Elsevier Wetenschappelijke Publicaties.

Schildhauer, J. (1985). *The Hansa: History and Culture*. Leipzig, Ger.: Edition Leipzig.

Schimmack, U., S. Oishi, and E. Diener (2002). "Cultural influences on the relation between pleasant emotions and unpleasant emotions: Asian dialectic philosophies or individualism-collectivism?" *Cognition and Emotion* 16 (6): 705–19.

Schmitt, D. P. (2005). "Sociosexuality from Argentina to Zimbabwe: A 48-nation study of sex, culture, and strategies of human mating." *Behavioral and Brain Sciences* 28: 247–311.

Schneider, L., and S. Lysgaard (1953). "The deferred gratification pattern: A preliminary study." *American Sociological Review* 18: 142–49.

Schramm-Nielsen, J. (2001). "Cultural dimensions of decision making: Denmark and France compared." *Journal of Managerial Psychology* 16: 404–23.

Schuler, R. S., and N. Rogovsky (1998). "Understanding compensation practice variation across firms: The impact of national cultures." *Journal of International Business Studies* 29: 159–77.

Schumacher, E. F. (1973). *Small Is Beautiful: A Study of Economics as if People Mattered*. London: Sphere.

Schwartz, S. H. (1994). "Beyond individualism/collectivism—new cultural dimensions of values." In *Individualism and Collectivism: Theory, Method and Applications*, ed. U. Kim, H. C. Triandis, Ç. Kagitçibasi, S. C. Choi, and G. Yoon, 85–119. Thousand Oaks, CA: Sage.

Schwartz, S. H., and A. Bardi (2001). "Value hierarchies across cultures: Taking a similarities perspective." *Journal of Cross-Cultural Psychology* 32 (3): 268–90.

Sebenius, J. K. (2002). "The hidden challenge of cross-border negotiations." *Harvard Business Review* (March): 76–85.

Semenov, R. (2000). *Cross-Country Differences in Economic Governance: Culture as a Major Explanatory Factor*. Ph.D. dissertation, Tilburg, Neth.: Tilburg University.

Shane, S. A. (1993). "Cultural influences on national rates of innovation." *Journal of Business Venturing* 8: 59–73.

Shane, S. A. (1995). "Uncertainty avoidance and the preference for innovation championing roles." *Journal of International Business Studies* 26: 47–68.

Shane, S. A., and S. Venkataraman (1996). "Renegade and rational championing strategies." *Organization Studies* 17: 751–72.

Shane, S. A., S. Venkataraman, and I. C. Macmillan (1995). "Cultural differences in innovation championing strategies." *Journal of Management* 21: 931–52.

Sherman, P. J., R. L. Helmreich, and A. C. Merritt (1997). "National culture and flight deck automation: Results of a multination survey." *International Journal of Aviation Psychology* 7 (4): 311–29.

Smircich, L. (1983). "Concepts of culture and organizational analysis." *Administrative Science Quarterly* 28: 339–58.

Smith, P. B. (2004). "Acquiescent response bias as an aspect of cultural communication style." *Journal of Cross-Cultural Psychology* 35: 50–61.

Smith, P. B., S. Dugan, and F. Trompenaars (1996). "National culture and the values of organizational employees: A dimensional analysis across 43 nations." *Journal of Cross-Cultural Psychology* 27: 231–64.

Smith, P. B., M. F. Peterson, and S. H. Schwartz (2002). "Cultural values, sources of guidance, and their relevance to managerial behavior: A 47-nation study." *Journal of Cross-Cultural Psychology* 33 (2): 188–208.

Smith, P. B., F. Trompenaars, and S. Dugan (1995). "The Rotter Locus of Control Scale in 43 countries: A test of cultural relativity." *International Journal of Psychology* 30: 377–400.

Soeters, J. (1986). "Excellent companies as social movements." *Journal of Management Studies* 23: 299–313.

Soeters, J. (2000). "Culture in uniformed organizations." In *Handbook of Organizational Culture and Climate*, ed. N. M. Ashkanasy, C. P. M. Wilderom, and M. F. Peterson, 465–81. Thousand Oaks, CA: Sage.

Soeters, J., and R. Recht (2001). "Convergence or divergence in the multinational classroom? Experiences from the military." *International Journal of Intercultural Relations* 25: 423–40.

Soeters, J., and H. Schreuder (1986). "Nationale en organisatieculturen in accountantskantoren." *Sociologische Gids* 33 (2): 100–21.

Søndergaard, M. (1994). "Hofstede's consequences: A study of reviews, citations and replications." *Organization Studies* 15: 447–56.

Søndergaard, M. (2002). "Values of local government CEOs in job motivation: How do CEOs see the ideal job?" In *Social Bonds to City Hall*, ed. P. Dahler-Larsen, 57–75. Odense, Den.: Odense University Press.

Statham, A. (1987). "The gender model revisited: Differences in the management styles of men and women." *Sex Roles* 16: 409–29.

Stevens, E. P. (1973). "Marianismo: The other face of machismo in Latin America." In *Female and Male in Latin America*, ed. A. Pescatello, 90–101. Pittsburgh, PA: University of Pittsburgh Press.

Stevenson, H. W., and S. Y. Lee (1996). "The academic achievement of Chinese students." In *The Handbook of Chinese Psychology*, ed. M. H. Bond. Hong Kong: Oxford University Press.

Stewart, E. C. (1985). "Culture and decision-making." In *Communication, Culture, and Organizational Processes*, ed. W. B. Gudykunst, L. P. Stewart, and S. Ting-Toomey, 177–211. Beverly Hills, CA: Sage.

Stiglitz, J. E. (2002). *Globalization and Its Discontents*. New York: W. W. Norton & Company.

Stoetzel, J. (1983). *Les valeurs du temps présent*. Paris: Presses Universitaires de France.

Stouffer, S. A., and J. Toby (1951). "Role conflict and personality." *American Journal of Sociology* 56 (5): 395–406.

Stroebe, W. (1976). "Is social psychology really that complicated? A review of Martin Irle's Lehrbuch der Sozialpsychologie." *European Journal of Social Psychology* 6 (4): 509–11.

Tannen, D. (1992). *You Just Don't Understand: Women and Men in Conversation*. London: Virago.

Tobin, J. J., D. Y. H. Wu, and D. H. Danielson (1989). *Pre-school in Three Cultures: Japan, China, and the United States*. New Haven, CT: Yale University Press.

Tocqueville, A. de (1956). *Democracy in America*. Edited and abridged by R. D. Heffner. New York: Mentor Books. [Original work published 1835.]

Tollgerdt-Andersson, I. (1996). "Attitudes, values and demands on leadership: A cultural comparison among some European countries." In *Managing Across Cultures: Issues and Perspectives*, ed. P. Joynt and M. Warner, 166–78. London: Thomson.

Triandis, H. C. (1972). *The Analysis of Subjective Culture*. New York: Wiley-Interscience.

Triandis, H. C. (1973). "Culture training, cognitive complexity and interpersonal attitudes." In *Readings in Intercultural Communication*, ed. D. S. Hoopes, 55–68. Pittsburgh, PA: Regional Council for International Education.

Triandis, H. C. (1995). *Individualism and Collectivism*. Boulder, CO: Westmore.

Triandis, H. C. (2002). "Odysseus wandered for 10, I wondered for 50 years." In *Online Readings in Psychology and Culture*, ed. W. J. Lonner, D. L. Dinnel, S. A. Hayes, and D. N. Sattler. Internet publication. Retrieved July 21, 2005, from wwu.edu/~culture.

Trompenaars, F. (1993). *Riding the Waves of Culture: Understanding Cultural Diversity in Business*. London: Economist Books.

Tung, R. L. (1982). "Selection and training procedures of U.S., European and Japanese multinationals." *California Management Review* 25 (1): 57–71.

Turchin, P. (2006). *War and Peace and War: The Rise and Fall of Empires*. New York: Plume.

Tylor, E. B. (1924). *Primitive Culture*. Gloucester, MA: Smith. [Original work published 1871.]

UNICEF (1995). *The State of the World's Children 1995*. New York: UNICEF/Oxford University Press.

UN Office on Drugs and Crime (2004). *Seventh United Nations Survey of Crime Trends and Operations of Criminal Justice Systems, Covering the Period 1998–2000.* Internet publication. Retrieved January 20, 2006, from unodc.org/pdf/crime/seventh_ survey/7sv.pdf.

UN Statistics Division (2009). *Statistics and Indicators on Women and Men. Social Indicators. Total Fertility Rates.* Internet publication. Retrieved September 28, 2009, from http://unstats.un.org/unsd/demographic/products/indwm/tab2c.htm.

van den Berg-Weitzel, L., and G. van de Laar (2000). "Relation between culture and communication in packaging design." *Brand Management* 8 (3): 171–84.

van den Bosch, F. A. J., and A. A. van Prooijen (1992). "The competitive advantage of European nations: The impact of national culture, a missing element in Porter's analysis." *European Management Journal* 10: 173–78.

van der Veen, R. (2002). *Afrika: Van de Koude Oorlog naar de 21e Eeuw.* Amsterdam: KIT Publishers.

van de Vliert, E. (1998). "Gender role gaps, competitiveness, and masculinity." In G. Hofstede et al., *Masculinity and Femininity: The Taboo Dimension of National Cultures,* 117–29. Thousand Oaks, CA: Sage.

van de Vliert, E. (2009). *Climate, Affluence, and Culture.* New York: Cambridge University Press.

van Dijk, T., ed. (1997a). *Discourse as Structure and Process.* London: Sage.

van Dijk, T., ed. (1997b). *Discourse as Social Interaction.* London: Sage.

van Haaf, J., M. C. C. Vonk, and F. J. R. van de Vijver (2002). "Structural equivalence of the social norms scale of the world values survey." In *New Directions in Cross-Cultural Psychology,* ed. P. Boski, F. J. R. van de Vijver, and A. M. Chodynicka, 165–82. Warsaw: Wydawnictwo Instytutu Psychologii PAN.

van Nimwegen, T. (2002). "Global Banking, Global Values: The In-House Reception of the Corporate Values of ABN AMRO." Ph.D. dissertation, Nyenrode University, Delft: Eburon.

van Oudenhoven, J. P. (2001). "Do organizations reflect national cultures? A 10-nation study." *International Journal of Intercultural Relations* 25: 89–107.

van Rossum, J. H. A. (1998). "Why children play: American versus Dutch boys and girls." In G. Hofstede et al., *Masculinity and Femininity: The Taboo Dimension of National Cultures,* 130–38. Thousand Oaks, CA: Sage.

Veenhoven, R. (1993). *Happiness in Nations: Subjective Appreciation of Life in 56 Nations, 1946–1992.* Rotterdam: Erasmus University, Department of Social Sciences.

Verhulst, F. C., T. M. Achenbach, R. F. Ferdinand, and M. C. Kasius (1993). "Epidemiological comparisons of American and Dutch adolescents' self-reports." *Journal of the American Academy of Child and Adolescent Psychiatry* 32: 1135–44.

Verweij, J. (1998). "The importance of femininity in explaining cross-national differences in secularization." In G. Hofstede et al., *Masculinity and Femininity: The Taboo Dimension of National Cultures,* 179–91. Thousand Oaks, CA: Sage.

Verweij, J., P. Ester, and R. Nauta (1997). "Secularization as an economic and cultural phenomenon: A cross-national analysis." *Journal for the Scientific Study of Religion* 36: 309–24.

Walter, T. (1990). "Why are most churchgoers women?" In *Vox Angelica XX: Biblical and Other Essays from London Bible College*, ed. H. Rowdon. London: Paternoster.

Ward, C., S. Bochner, and A. Furnham (2001). *The Psychology of Culture Shock*. 2nd ed. London: Routledge.

Watts, A. (1979). *Tao: The Watercourse Way*. Harmondsworth, Mddx., UK: Pelican.

Webber, R. A., ed. (1969). *Culture and Management*. Homewood, IL: Irwin.

Weber, M. (1970). *Essays in Sociology*. Edited by H. H. Gerth and C. W. Mills. London: Routledge & Kegan Paul. [Original work published 1948.]

Weber, M. (1976). *The Protestant Ethic and the Spirit of Capitalism*. London: George Allen & Unwin. [Original work published 1930.]

Weick, K. E. (1985). "The significance of corporate culture." In *Organizational Culture*, ed. P. J. Frost, L. F. Moore, M. R. Louis, C. C. Lundberg, and J. Martin, 381–89. Beverly Hills, CA: Sage.

Weimer, J. (1995). *Corporate Financial Goals: A Multiple Constituency Approach to a Comparative Study of Dutch, U.S., and German Firms*. Ph.D. dissertation. Enschede, Neth.: Twente University.

Weiss, R. A. (2009). "Apes, lice and prehistory." *Journal of Biology* 8: 20.

Westbrook, M. T., and V. Legge (1993). "Health practitioners' perceptions of family attitudes towards children with disabilities: A comparison of six communities in a multicultural society." *Rehabilitation Psychology* 38 (3): 177–85.

Westbrook, M. T., V. Legge, and M. Pennay (1993). "Men's reactions to becoming disabled: A comparison of six communities in a multicultural society." *Journal of Applied Rehabilitation Counseling* 24 (3): 35–41.

Westerlund, G., and S. E. Sjöstrand (1975). *Organizational Myths*. London: Harper & Row.

Wildeman, R. E., G. Hofstede, N. G. Noorderhaven, A. R. Thurik, W. H. J. Verhoeven, and A. R. M. Wennekers (1999). *Culture's Role in Entrepreneurship: Self-Employment out of Dissatisfaction*. Rotterdam: Rotterdam Institute for Business Economic Studies.

Wilkins, A. L., and W. G. Ouchi (1983). "Efficient cultures: Exploring the relationship between culture and organizational performance." *Administrative Science Quarterly* 28: 468–81.

Williamson, O. E. (1975). *Markets and Hierarchies: Analysis and Antitrust Implications*. New York: Free Press.

Williamson, O. E. (2000). "The New Institutional Economics: Taking stock, looking ahead." *Journal of Economic Literature* 38: 595–613.

Wilson, D. S. (2007). *Evolution for Everyone: How Darwin's Theory Can Change the Way We Think About Our Lives*. New York: Bantam Dell.

Wilson, D. S., M. Van Vugt, and R. O'Gorman (2008). "Multilevel selection theory and major evolutionary transitions: Implications for psychological science." *Current Directions in Psychological Science* 17 (1): 6–9.

Wilson, E. O. (1998). *Consilience: The Unity of Knowledge*. London: Abacus.

Wirthlin Worldwide (1996). *Asian Values and Commercial Success*. decima.com/pub-liens/report/wr9603.htm.

Witkin, H. A. (1977). "Theory in cross-cultural research: Its uses and risks." In *Basic Problems in Cross-Cultural Psychology*, ed. Y. H. Poortinga, 82–91. Amsterdam: Swets & Zeitlinger.

Witkin, H. A., and D. R. Goodenough (1977). "Field dependence and interpersonal behavior." *Psychological Bulletin* 84: 661–89.

Witte, E. (1973). *Organisation für Innovationsentscheidungen: Das Promotoren-Modell*. Göttingen FRG: Verlag Otto Schwarz & Co.

Witte, E. (1977). "Power and innovation: A two-center theory." *International Studies of Management and Organization* 7 (1): 47–70.

World Bank. (1972). *World Bank Atlas*. Washington, DC: World Bank.

World Development Report (2009). *Building Institutions for Markets*. New York: Oxford University Press.

World Health Organization (2005). *WHO Global InfoBase Online. BMI/Overweight/Obesity*. Internet publication. Retrieved December 7, 2006, from who.int/ncd_surveillance/infobase/web/infobasecommon.

World Health Organization (2008). *World Health Statistics 2008*. Geneva: WHO Press.

World Investment Report (2000). *Cross-Border Mergers and Acquisitions and Development*. New York: United Nations.

World Values Survey (current). worldvaluessurvey.org.

Worm, V. (1997). *Vikings and Mandarins: Sino-Scandanavian Business Cooperation in Cross-Cultural Settings*. Copenhagen: Handelshøjskolens Forlag.

Wu, T. Y. (1980). *Roots of Chinese Culture*. Singapore: Federal Publications.

Yan, W. F., and E. L. Gaier (1994). "Causal attributions for college success and failure: An Asian-American comparison." *Journal of Cross-Cultural Psychology* 25: 146–58.

Yelsma, P., and K. Athappilly (1988). "Marital satisfaction and communication practices: Comparisons among Indian and American couples." *Journal of Comparative Family Studies* 19: 37–54.

Yeung, I. Y. M., and R. L. Tung (1996). *Achieving Business Success in Confucian Societies: The Importance of Guanxi (Connections)*. New York: American Management Association.

Zürcher, E. (1993). "Confucianism for Development?" Valedictory lecture, Leiden University.

Name Index

Subject Index

(Page numbers in **bold** refer to definitions.)

About the Authors

Geert Hofstede (born 1928) graduated from Delft Technical University as a mechanical engineer and spent ten years in Dutch industry in technical and management jobs. Studying part-time, he completed a doctorate in social psychology at Groningen University; his thesis was called "The Game of Budget Control." He subsequently joined IBM Europe, where he founded and managed the Personnel Research department. His academic career started at IMD (Lausanne) and continued at INSEAD (Fontainebleau), the European Institute for Advanced Studies in Management (Brussels), IIASA (Laxenburg Castle, Austria), and the University of Maastricht, where he taught organizational anthropology and international management until his retirement in 1993. From 1980 to 1983 he made a brief return to industry as a director of human resources for Fasson Europe at Leiden. He was the cofounder and first director of the Institute for Research on Intercultural Cooperation (IRIC), which moved with him to Maastricht and after his retirement shifted to the University of Tilburg; it was closed in 2004. As an emeritus, Geert has been an honorary professor and a regular visitor at Hong Kong University and an Extra-Mural Fellow of the CentER for Economic Research at the University of Tilburg. He also taught in Hawaii, Australia, and New Zealand.

Geert's books have appeared in twenty languages, and his articles have been published in social science and management journals around the world. He is a Fellow of the Academy of Management in the United States, an Eminent Scholar of the Academy of International Business, and an Honorary Fellow of the International Association for Cross-Cultural Psychology. He holds honorary doctorates from universities in seven European countries. In 2006, in his honor, the University of Maastricht founded the Geert Hofstede Chair in cultural diversity management. In 2009 a group of six European schools jointly teaching international communication named itself the Geert Hofstede Consortium. Geert is a polyglot, having lectured at universities, training institutes, and in-company programs in Dutch, English, French, and German. He has served as a consultant or guest speaker for national and international business and government organizations. A *Wall Street Journal* article on May 5, 2008, listed him among the top twenty most influential management thinkers, as the only continental European.

 Gert Jan Hofstede (born 1956), eldest of four sons of Geert, attended school in the Netherlands and Switzerland and acquired French as his second language. He holds a degree in population biology from Wageningen University, in the Netherlands. In 1984 he became a computer programmer. Since 1986 he has taught at Wageningen University. In 1992 he completed a Ph.D. in production planning from the same university; his thesis was called "Modesty in Modelling." Currently he is an associate professor of information management in the Social Sciences Group of Wageningen University.

In the eighties and nineties Gert Jan mainly taught, wrote, and consulted in the area of data modeling. As the Web brought society closer to computer users, and ideas of the virtual "international office of the future" circulated in his profession, he started using Geert's work for creating simulation games about cross-cultural communication. This work resulted in the book *Exploring Culture: Exercises, Stories and Synthetic Cultures* (2002).

Gert Jan's interest is in the interplay of the contrasting forces of societal change and cultural stability. He is a prolific author of journal articles and book chapters. Recently he has published on trust and transparency in organizational networks and the consequences for adoption of e-business. In 2008 he coedited the book *Why Do Games Work?*, a practical investigation of the secret of simulation games. A focus for the coming years is social simulation, including modeling culture in software agents. His wider ambition is to further investigate the biological basis of culture for human behavior and its consequences for contemporary societies. This endeavor requires crossing boundaries between disciplines.

Michael Minkov (born 1959), or Misho, is a lecturer on cross-cultural awareness and organizational behavior, teaching as part of the University of Portsmouth (UK) management programs delivered through International University College, in Sofia, Bulgaria. He also teaches these subjects as in-company seminars for international organizations.

Misho graduated from University of Sofia "St. Kliment Ohridski" in 1987 with a master's degree in linguistics, culture, and literature and is currently finishing his Ph.D. at the Department of Scandinavian Studies of the same university. He has studied anthropology at New Bulgarian University and management at the International Executive Development Center in Slovenia. In addition to his theoretical knowledge, he has gained practical cross-cultural competence during his ten years of living, studying, and working in Iceland, the Faroe Islands, Norway, Slovenia, Tunisia, the United Kingdom, and the United States. During the 1990s Misho was secretary general of the Central and East European Management Development Association (CEEMAN), based in Slovenia— an organization of some 170 management schools and corporations from more than forty countries.

In his early academic career, Misho specialized in early Old English and Old Norse and did translations from those languages into French and Bulgarian, published in Belgium and Bulgaria. Later, he authored four books on cultural differences as well as a number of academic articles published in Sage journals. He is a disciple and follower of Geert Hofstede and an enthusiastic advocate of his paradigm of cross-cultural analysis. This association has enabled Misho to discover some new dimensions of culture, one of which is presented in this book as an enrichment of the now classic Hofstede cultural model.